IFIP Advances in Information and Communication Technology 662

Editor-in-Chief

Kai Rannenberg, Goethe University Frankfurt, Germany

Editorial Board Members

IFIP – The International Federation for Information Processing

IFIP was founded in 1960 under the auspices of UNESCO, following the first World Computer Congress held in Paris the previous year. A federation for societies working in information processing, IFIP's aim is two-fold: to support information processing in the countries of its members and to encourage technology transfer to developing nations. As its mission statement clearly states:

> IFIP is the global non-profit federation of societies of ICT professionals that aims at achieving a worldwide professional and socially responsible development and application of information and communication technologies.

IFIP is a non-profit-making organization, run almost solely by 2500 volunteers. It operates through a number of technical committees and working groups, which organize events and publications. IFIP's events range from large international open conferences to working conferences and local seminars.

The flagship event is the IFIP World Computer Congress, at which both invited and contributed papers are presented. Contributed papers are rigorously refereed and the rejection rate is high.

As with the Congress, participation in the open conferences is open to all and papers may be invited or submitted. Again, submitted papers are stringently refereed.

The working conferences are structured differently. They are usually run by a working group and attendance is generally smaller and occasionally by invitation only. Their purpose is to create an atmosphere conducive to innovation and development. Refereeing is also rigorous and papers are subjected to extensive group discussion.

Publications arising from IFIP events vary. The papers presented at the IFIP World Computer Congress and at open conferences are published as conference proceedings, while the results of the working conferences are often published as collections of selected and edited papers.

IFIP distinguishes three types of institutional membership: Country Representative Members, Members at Large, and Associate Members. The type of organization that can apply for membership is a wide variety and includes national or international societies of individual computer scientists/ICT professionals, associations or federations of such societies, government institutions/government related organizations, national or international research institutes or consortia, universities, academies of sciences, companies, national or international associations or federations of companies.

More information about this series at https://link.springer.com/bookseries/6102

Luis M. Camarinha-Matos ·
Angel Ortiz · Xavier Boucher ·
A. Luís Osório (Eds.)

Collaborative Networks in Digitalization and Society 5.0

23rd IFIP WG 5.5 Working Conference on
Virtual Enterprises, PRO-VE 2022
Lisbon, Portugal, September 19–21, 2022
Proceedings

 Springer

Editors
Luis M. Camarinha-Matos (iD)
Universidade Nova de Lisboa
Monte da Caparica, Portugal

Angel Ortiz (iD)
Polytechnic University of Valencia
Valencia, Spain

Xavier Boucher (iD)
École des Mines de Saint-Étienne
Saint-Étienne Cedex, France

A. Luís Osório (iD)
Instituto Politécnico de Lisboa
Lisbon, Portugal

ISSN 1868-4238   ISSN 1868-422X   (electronic)
IFIP Advances in Information and Communication Technology
ISBN 978-3-031-14846-0   ISBN 978-3-031-14844-6   (eBook)
https://doi.org/10.1007/978-3-031-14844-6

This Springer imprint is published by the registered company Springer Nature Switzerland AG
The registered company address is: Gewerbestrasse 11, 6330 Cham, Switzerland

Preface

The widespread digital transformation in industry and services is strongly enabled by the results achieved through more than two decades of research and development in the inter-disciplinary collaborative networks (CNs) area. The paradigm of Society 5.0, recently established, is rapidly gaining importance and awareness as a disruptive concept for most economic sectors. This 5.0 paradigm is having a direct impact on organizations, affecting their journey towards digital transformation, innovative working environments, and new organizational modes.

The term "digitalization" still represents a major ongoing transformation in industry and services. The adoption and integration of a large variety of novel information and communication technologies leads to more efficient, flexible, agile, and sustainable systems. Digitalization became one of the key aspects of Industry 4.0. Current trends towards Industry 5.0 introduce a complementary view, targeting a sustainable, human-centric, and resilient industry. Of course, the notion of resilience, notably based on agile capabilities of processes, organizational structures, and business models has seen increasing growth over the three last years due the strong disruptive crisis the world has faced. However, even for the industrial sector, increasing the resilience capacity of our modern societies cannot be addressed solely with an economy-centered vision. Social and human factors are strongly questioning the capacity to maintain the right level of skills and competencies required for a global industrial resilience; most industrial sectors are being affected by unforeseen factors of an ecological, political, or energy- or climate-related nature. The nature of Industry 5.0 is necessarily multi-dimensional, with the need to collaborate at a large scale, and goes beyond the potential contradiction between resilience, human factors, and sustainability. Current crises have highlighted the need for collaboration as a crucial success factor at all granularity levels (country, ecosystem, company, human actor, and even human-machine cooperation levels).

Beyond Industry 5.0, this multi-dimensional complexity affects many other activity sectors. In all these fields, the integration of resilience, human factors, and sustainability represents the key challenge, leading to the development of Health 5.0, Agriculture 5.0, Cities 5.0, Logistics 5.0, Education 5.0, or even Tourism 5.0. The notion of Society 5.0 represents a comprehensive strategy on science, technology, and innovation aiming at a people-centric super-smart society. With an eye on these diverse application fields, PRO-VE 2022 provided a forum for sharing experiences, discussing trends, and identifying new opportunities together with innovative solutions to cope with challenges ahead towards a collaborative Society 5.0. The conference contributions came from both the engineering/computer science and the managerial/socio-human communities, including industrial and electrical engineering, computer science, manufacturing, organization science, logistics, managerial, and social sciences. These multiple points of view fuel both the interdisciplinary nature of the research and development of collaborative networks, as well as the multidisciplinary networking spirit of the PRO-VE working conferences.

PRO-VE 2022, the 23rd IFIP Working Conference on Virtual Enterprises, was held in Lisbon, Portugal, during September 19–21, 2022. The event was the latest in the series of successful conferences which began in 1999 and have been held at various locations throughout Europe and in Brazil.

These proceedings include selected papers from the PRO-VE 2022 conference submissions. They provide a comprehensive overview of major challenges of the Society 5.0 transition journey, covering the following topics:

- AI and digital transformation for collaborative systems
- Distributed cognition in collaborative systems
- Collaborative, resilient, and sustainable business models and production systems
- Collaborative business ecosystems
- Cyber-physical systems and their applications in CNs
- Value creation and impact of CNs
- Smart collaborative logistics and transportation networks
- Human-machine collaboration
- Hybridization of collaboration – organizations, people, machines, systems
- Agility, resilience, and sustainability of networked organizations
- Human-centric and resilient collaborative systems
- Industry 5.0, Agriculture 5.0, Healthcare 5.0, and Society 5.0
- Ethics, security, and trust
- Collaborative digital innovation hubs
- Applications and case studies in multiple fields

A total of 55 papers were accepted from 119 papers submitted for peer review, which is an acceptance rate of 46.2%. The review process was double blind, with 3.5 average reviews per submission and 4 papers on average per reviewer.

We would like to express our thanks to all authors for their contributions, originating in academia, research institutions, and industry. Continuing with the tradition of the PRO-VE conferences, we hope this collection of papers will represent both a valuable tool for those interested in research advances and emerging applications in collaborative networks, and in identifying future open challenges for research and development in this area. Finally, we would also like to show our extreme appreciation for the time, efforts, and dedication shared by the members of the PRO-VE International Program Committee, who provided their support in the selection of articles for this conference and provided valuable and constructive comments to help authors to improve the quality of their papers.

July 2022   Luis M. Camarinha-Matos
                                                                          Angel Ortiz
                                                                          Xavier Boucher
                                                                          A. Luís Osório

Organization

Conference Chair

A. Luís Osório   Polytechnic Institute of Lisbon, Portugal

Program Committee Chair

Luis M. Camarinha-Matos NOVA University of Lisbon, Portugal

Program Committee Co-chairs

Angel Ortiz   Polytechnic University of Valencia, Spain
Xavier Boucher   Ecole des Mines de Saint Etienne, France

International Program Committee

Antonio Abreu	Polytechnic Institute of Lisbon, Portugal
Hamideh Afsarmanesh	University of Amsterdam, The Netherlands
Maria del Mar Alemany	Polytechnic University of Valencia, Spain
Thecle Alix	Institut de Mécanique et d'Ingénierie de Bordeaux, France
Dario Antonelli	Politecnico di Torino, Italy
Vincent Augusto	Ecole des Mines de Saint-Etienne, France
Américo Azevedo	University of Porto, Portugal
Thomas Beach	Cardiff University, UK
Frédérick Bénaben	Ecole des Mines d'Albi-Carmaux, France
Peter Bernus	Griffith University, Australia
Valérie Botta-Genoulaz	INSA Lyon, France
Xavier Boucher	Ecole des Mines de Saint-Etienne, France
Jeremy Bryans	Coventry University, UK
João Calado	Polytechnic Institute of Lisbon, Portugal
Luis M. Camarinha-Matos	NOVA University of Lisbon, Portugal
Wojciech Cellary	Poznan University of Economics and Business, Poland
Nicolas Daclin	Ecole des Mines d'Alès, France
Rob Dekkers	University of Glasgow, UK
Xavier Delorme	Ecole des Mines de Saint-Etienne, France
Filipa Ferrada	NOVA University of Lisbon, Portugal
Adriano Fiorese	Santa Catarina State University, Brazil
Adrian Florea	'Lucian Blaga' University of Sibiu, Romania
Rosanna Fornasiero	CNR, Italy
Gary Fragidis	International Hellenic University, Greece
Cesar Garita	ITCR, Costa Rica

Chrysostomos Stylios	University of Ioannina, Greece
Thomas Suesse	Bielefeld University of Applied Science, Germany
Lorna Uden	Staffordshire University, UK
Paula Urze	NOVA University of Lisbon, Portugal
Katri Valkokari	VTT, Finland
Rolando Vallejos	Universidad de Ingeniería y Tecnologia, Peru
Elise Vareilles	ISAE SUPAERO, France
Agostino Villa	Politecnico di Torino, Italy
Bernd-Friedrich Voigt	South Westphalia University of Applied Sciences, Germany
Shaun West	Lucerne University of Applied Sciences and Arts, Switzerland
Stefan Wiesner	Bremer Institut für Produktion und Logistik, Germany
Lai Xu	Bournemouth University, UK
Peter Weiß	Pforzheim University, Germany
Greg Zacharewicz	Ecole des Mines d'Albi-Carmaux, France
Andrea Zangiacomi	CNR, Italy

Special Session Organizers

Special Session on AI and Digital Tools for Collaborative Healthcare Networks 5.0

Elena Pessot	National Research Council, Italy
Daniele Spoladore	National Research Council, Italy
Julia Fleck	Ecole des Mines Saint-Etienne, France
Laurent Navarro	Ecole des Mines Saint-Etienne, France

Special Session on Dynamic Interplay of Humans and AI in Collaborative Networks

Thomas Süße	Bielefeld University of Applied Sciences, Germany
Bernd-Friedrich Voigt	South Westphalia University of Applied Sciences, Germany

Special Session on Contribution of Digital Transformation to Sustainable Supply Chains

Ricardo Zimmermann	INESC TEC, Portugal
Luis M. D. Ferreira	University of Coimbra, Portugal
Gustavo Dalmarco	INESC TEC, Portugal
Ana Correia Simões	INESC TEC, Portugal

Special Session on Digital Transformation Through the Lens of Sociotechnical Systems

António Lucas Soares	University of Porto, Portugal
Ricardo Zimmermann	INESC TEC, Portugal
Donna H. Rhodes	MIT, USA

Eric Rebentisch   MIT, USA
Joana L. F. P. Cardoso   MIT, USA

Special Session on Architectures for Collaborative Enterprise Integration

Arturo Molina   Tecnologico de Monterrey, Mexico
Guy Doumeingts   IMS, University of Bordeaux, France
James Brown   NUI Galway, Ireland
Peter Bernus   Griffith University, Australia
Ricardo Rabelo   Federal University of Santa Catarina, Brazil

Special Session on Value Co-creation in Ecosystems

Shaun West   Hochschule Luzern, Switzerland
Tobias Larsson   Blekinge Institute of Technology, Sweden
Xavier Boucher   Ecole des Mines de Saint-Etienne, France

Special Session on Shaping Values Through Collaborative Work

Christian Zinke-Wehlmann   Institute of Applied Informatics, Germany
Julia Friedrich   University of Leipzig, Germany

Special Session on Service Design for Society 5.0 and Industry 5.0

Gary Fragidis   International Hellenic University, Greece

Technical Sponsors

IFIP WG 5.5 COVE
Cooperation Infrastructure for Virtual Enterprises
and Electronic Business

Society of Collaborative Networks

Organizational Co-sponsors

Contents

Contribution of Digital Transformation to Sustainable Supply Chains

Agile and Responsive Supply Chains

Risk and Resilience in Collaborative Networks

Sociotechnical Strategies in Collaborative Systems

Digitalization in Collaborative Networks

Influence of Collaboration in Sustainable Manufacturing Networks

Paula Graça[1,2(✉)] and Luis M. Camarinha-Matos[1(✉)]

[1] School of Science and Technology, Uninova-CTS, NOVA University of Lisbon, Campus de Caparica, 2829-516 Caparica, Portugal
paula.graca@isel.pt, cam@uninova.pt
[2] Instituto Superior de Engenharia de Lisboa, Instituto Politécnico de Lisboa, Rua Conselheiro Emídio Navarro 1, 1959-007 Lisbon, Portugal

Abstract. Recent trends towards Industry 5.0 focus on a sustainable and resilient industry, aiming to make technology and innovation more focused on humans and today's societal concerns. Consequently, this trend also leads to more sustainable and resilient manufacturing, for which collaborative networks play a main role due to the needed involvement of multiple players, being important to consider a perspective of co-responsibility. Establishing adequate performance indicators to assess how collaborative manufacturing ecosystems can support sustainability is thus relevant. Furthermore, this work also analyses how such performance indicators can be used as an influencing factor contributing to improving the players' behaviour, representing the idea of co-responsibility for a more sustainable manufacturing network. This article proposes a set of performance indicators and a related simulation model to set up several scenarios to analyse how collaboration can influence sustainability in horizontal manufacturing networks. Results from simulation scenarios are included and discussed.

Keywords: Collaborative networks · Sustainable manufacturing · Performance indicators

1 Introduction

Recent trends towards Industry 5.0 aiming at a more sustainable and resilient industry are pushing the manufacturing sector engaged in the digital transformation to focus more on human and societal concerns. As a result, the notion of sustainable manufacturing is becoming more relevant in recent years [1]. To this end, the discipline of Collaborative Networks (CNs) plays an essential role in the collaborative perspective of the multiple stakeholders involved, which need to share co-responsibility in the achievement of such sustainability and resilience [2]. This evidence is agreed by various authors arguing that to address the challenges of sustainability: (i) there must be new strategies for organisations to collaborate with suppliers, customers and other stakeholders to fulfil not only their economic, social and environmental responsibilities but also to gain competitive

© IFIP International Federation for Information Processing 2022
Published by Springer Nature Switzerland AG 2022
L. M. Camarinha-Matos et al. (Eds.): PRO-VE 2022, IFIP AICT 662, pp. 3–17, 2022.
https://doi.org/10.1007/978-3-031-14844-6_1

advantages [3]; (ii) there is a need for the development of structures and processes for collaboration to achieve individually and collectively business sustainability [4]; and (iii) broader collaboration is needed, as the changes required to go beyond the capacity and capability of individual actors [2].

Sustainability is defined at the intersection of financial, social, and environmental "health" [4], and thus sustainable manufacturing encompasses these three dimensions. For its effective implementation, CNs and, more specifically, business communities (or business ecosystems) can offer important insights due to the interactions, interdependencies and co-responsibility of the actors involved regarding the underlying challenges [1]. As such, we propose that the establishment of adequate performance indicators to assess how collaborative manufacturing ecosystems (CMEs) can support sustainability in horizontal manufacturing networks is a critical issue. Furthermore, a simulation model to analyse how such performance indicators can influence the ecosystem's players in contributing to improving their behaviour is also proposed. This influence relates to the idea of co-responsibility for a more sustainable manufacturing network. Various simulation scenarios are then characterised, established, and discussed.

The remaining sections of this article are organised as follows: Sect. 2 presents the research approach, identifying the research question and hypothesis; Sect. 3 explains the structure of the simulation model to represent a CME, including the embedded performance assessment and the influence mechanism; Sect. 4, presents several simulation scenarios discussing the results; the last section concludes identifying limitations of the study, and ongoing and future work.

2 Research Approach

This research work focuses on assessing the players' collaboration in horizontal manufacturing networks and influencing their behaviour, expecting to improve the network's sustainability. We do this by means of an Information System (IS) design artefact in the form of a simulation model, which positions our research in the design science research (DSR) paradigm [5]. DSR tries to focus human creativity on designing and building artefacts that have utility in application environments [6].

Design science was conceptualised by Simon [7] as a research paradigm that pointed to the need to create artefacts to solve real-world problems as a means for the production of scientific knowledge from an epistemological point of view. Adapting this thinking as well as the design research of other fields to the unique context of IS design research [6], the authors [5] came out with a conceptual framework for understanding IS research and a set of guidelines for conducting and evaluating good DSR. DSR seeks to develop prescriptive design expertise by building and evaluating innovative information technologies (IT) artefacts aimed at solving a class of identified problems [5] or shown to have utility [8]. DSR thus deals with a wide range of *"socio-technical"* artefacts, such as decision support systems, modelling tools, governance strategies, and IS evaluation methods [6].

To conduct this research, we adopted the methods and guidelines of Hevner et al. [5] that support researchers in bringing a rigorous scientific design research process [6] in which the three DSR cycles (Fig. 1) must be present and clearly identifiable [9]. Based on the identified research gaps, we developed an artefact, the Performance Assessment and Adjustment Model (PAAM), to evaluate a CME through simulation, to understand how the assessment of collaboration using a set of adopted performance indicators (with a given associated importance, i.e., a weight that can vary), can influence the behaviour of the players, contributing to improving the sustainability of the ecosystem.

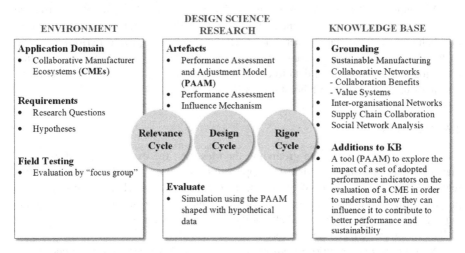

Fig. 1. DSR cycles of the research approach. Adapted from Hevner and Chatterjee [6, 9].

2.1 Relevance Cycle

DSR starts with the Relevance Cycle, i.e. "the opportunity/problem to be addressed in the application domain as input and the acceptance criteria for evaluating the research results" [9]. The application domain of this work is in the area of horizontal manufacturing networks, referred to in this article as CMEs, and the problem is identified and expressed by the following research question:

"How can performance assessment methods based on economic and social values promote sustainability in a CME?"

The following corresponding hypothesis guides the research:

"Performance indicators are a helpful mechanism for assessing a CME if they can contribute as a factor of influence for the stakeholders to evolve by self-adjusting their behaviour, thereby improving the ecosystem's performance and sustainability."

The primary grounding theories that underlie this research are the benefits of collaboration, the methods and mechanisms to evaluate that collaboration and sustainability. Collaboration thrives on divergent thinking for innovation, solving problems, developing new understandings, designing new products [10], and reducing or eliminating conflicts [11].

2.2 Design Cycle

The Design Cycle is the core of a DSR project, consisting of an iteration between the construction of the designed artefacts to find practical solutions for the identified opportunity/problem and their evaluation [5]. As such, to address the research question, we propose a novel artefact in the form of a simulation model designated by PAAM. The PAAM includes a Performance Assessment element composed of a set of performance indicators and an Influence Mechanism hoping to assess and influence the collaboration behaviour of the stakeholders in a CME, leading to improved performance and sustainability. The artefact evaluation process includes establishing several simulation scenarios using hypothetical data to characterize the organisations' profile and human resources used to handle collaboration opportunities.

2.3 Rigor Cycle

The Rigor Cycle provides the grounding theories, i.e., the experiences and expertise that represents the state-of-art in the application domain, connecting DSR activities with the "knowledge base" of the scientific foundations [5]. Thus, according to the purpose of this work, the main areas of research considered are Sustainable Manufacturing, CNs (including studies of collaboration benefits and value systems), Supply Chain Collaboration (SCC), and Social Network Analysis (SNA).

"*Sustainable manufacturing is no longer just nice-to-have, but a business imperative*" [12]. As manufacturing faces challenges of global resource depletion, climate change and pollution [13], many organisations have started to move to green growth, ensuring economically and environmentally sustainable development [12]. To address these concerns, the "Organisation for Economic Co-operation and Development" (OECD), in the assumption that performance measurement "*is a vital first step to improvement*", initiated the project OECD Sustainable Manufacturing Toolkit to provide a set of indicators internationally applicable to measure the environmental performance of manufacturing facilities [12].

On the other hand, the potential benefits of collaboration have extensive evidence in the literature, notably in the research area of CNs [14], in which the work on benefits analysis for CNs, value systems to promote sustainability in CNs, and a proposal of performance indicators for CNs [15–17] are examples, and whose concepts, methods and tools can strengthen the relationships of the multiple stakeholders who are the influential players in sustainability efforts [2].

The area of Inter-organisational Networks, a sub-area of collaborative networks, studies networks of organisations (linked to facilitate the achievement of a common objective) at the network level, emphasizing the whole network [18]. Moreover, collaboration through an inter-organisational network corresponds to an approach increasingly used to improve competitiveness and disaster preparedness, among other benefits [18].

The area of SCC, in which several works highlight collaboration as a means to improve performance in traditional supply chains [19, 20], provides a rich set of performance measures and metrics [21–23] and suggests that the success of collaboration leads to long-term future collaboration contributing for sustainable businesses [24].

Inspired by the motivations for sustainable manufacturing [12], combining the views of the above research areas with the social capital metaphor of a network structure [25] and concepts and measures of SNA [26, 27], complemented by the concepts of social and economic networks [28], we gathered the needed foundations to design the PAAM.

3 Performance Assessment and Adjustment Model

Networked structures arise in several contexts, such as the example of collaborative networks in the social context. Their topological structures show great heterogeneity in the connections' intensity, which can be represented in a graph by a weight proportional to such intensity [29]. Moreover, the analysis of the weights and the correlation between weights and the network topology gives complementary insights to understanding the architecture of real weighted networks [29]. Following this rationale, a CME can be modelled as a network of organisations or players (the nodes) connected by relationships (the links) that mean the market opportunities in which they participate, called collaboration opportunities (*CoOps*). The links are weighted by the number of collaboration opportunities (*#CoOps*) they participated in during a period. Figure 2 shows the conceptual view of the CME simulation model designated for PAAM.

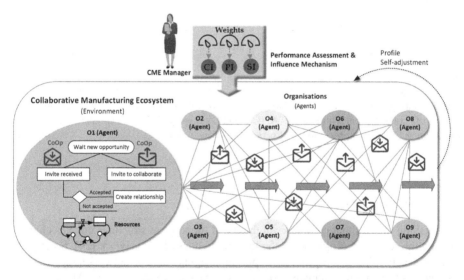

Fig. 2. Conceptual view of the PAAM.

A zoom-in of the agent shown in Fig. 2 shows the conceptual behaviour of an agent: when a new opportunity arises in the CME, the receiver can decide to invite a partner to collaborate. When the receiving partner receives the invitation, he may decide to accept it if he has available resources, creating a new relationship called *CoOp*.

3.1 Profile of the Organisations

Organisations have different profiles corresponding to a diversity of levels of collaboration willingness, which characterise their collaborative behaviour to be involved in relationships with the other players. As implicit in Virtual organisations Breeding Environments, the notion of business ecosystem facilitates the organisations' preparedness for being involved in collaboration in potential VOs and induces a perception of co-responsibility of all actors involved [2] regarding the sustainability challenges [1].

In the CME model, each profile consists of a set of attributes, e.g. *contact rate*, *accept rate*, and *sustainability index*, whose values (decimals between 0 and 1) represent a collaboration intensity factor, i.e., the "propensity to collaborate" by inviting other partners within the CME, the tendency to accept the invitations, and an intensity of sustainability according to the main facets: environmental, economic, and social [12]. Figure 3 illustrates four different hypothetical profiles displayed in the form of radar charts.

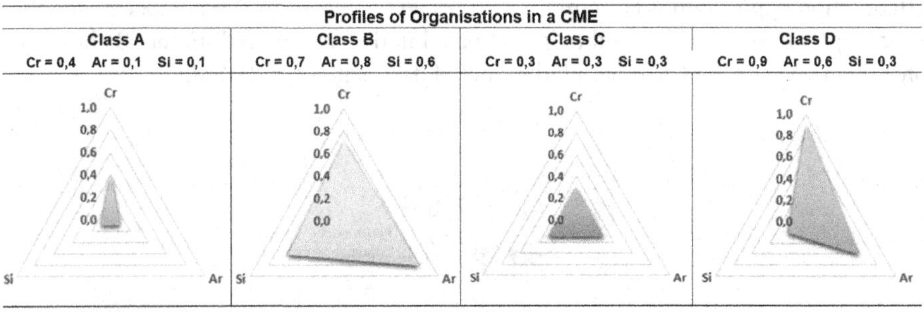

Fig. 3. Example profiles of the organisations involved in the CME, which are classified into four classes of "collaboration willingness" (A, B, C and D), displayed using radar charts showing the *contact rate* (Cr), *accept rate* (Ar), and *sustainability index* (Si).

3.2 Performance Assessment

Establishing metrics that combine weighted and topological structures enables characterising the statistical properties of the links and nodes of the network [29]. Social and economic network analysis provides important insights based on network structure [26–28] and has been applied in many research areas such as CNs [15–17, 30, 31] and, more specifically, on Inter-organisational Networks [18, 25, 32–34]. In particular, measures of centrality and density allow the comparison of nodes providing information about how a given node relates to the whole network and describing the general characteristics of a network [26–28]. Several authors defined prestige and power of the nodes in a social network based on centrality measures [28].

On the other hand, some authors have interpreted network structures as social capital: identifying structural holes (absence of connections between groups, measured as a structural hole centrality [35]) as a competitive advantage for those who fill the holes by offering connections between separated or sparsely inter-connected groups [25], network closure (related to dense networks) as a mean to facilitate access to information to improve communication [25], denser organisational networks likely to have more frequent innovations [33]. The strength of the ties (strength of social relationships) is seen as a measure of the frequency of the interactions during a period of time [36], also calculated by the frequency of the interactions among organisations [33].

Finally, doing business by adopting good environmental practices is increasingly critical in the eyes of all ecosystem players, bringing reputation, attracting investment, stimulating innovation, and securing loyal customers [12]. Well established indicators contribute to measuring, tracking, and improving performance [12]. Table 1 shows an example adapted from [12] of quantitative metrics to measure environmental performance in the three stages of manufacturing: raw materials, operations and products. Organisations can adopt the most relevant metrics according to the environmental and business impact and normalise the values using other peers' same normalisation factors (NFs). The CME manager can provide standard factors.

Table 1. Example of environmental sustainability metrics for sustainable manufacturing (adapted from [12]).

Environmental sustainability metrics					
Raw materials		Operations		Products	
R_1	Non-renewable materials intensity	O_1	Water intensity	P_1	Recycled/reused content
R_2	Restricted substance intensity	O_2	Energy intensity	P_2	Recyclability of products
R_3	Recycled/reused materials	O_3	Residuals intensity	P_3	Renewable materials content
		O_4	Air releases intensity	P_4	Greenhouse gas emission intensity
		O_5	Water releases intensity		

The metrics to evaluate the organisations, i.e., the players in a CME, as described in Table 2, were defined assuming the above assumptions, thus relying mainly on measures of density, centrality, and links' strength. Based on the metrics defined in Table 2, we propose a set of performance indicators that allow the individual evaluation of CME's organisations (players) in terms of collaboration and the CME globally.

Table 3 describes the indicators and respective calculation formulas of the individual organisations (players), and Table 4 shows the same information but considering the CME as a whole. In short, the indicators here used are the Contribution Indicator (CI), to account for the organisations that create the most opportunities for collaboration in the CME; the Prestige Indicator (PI), to account for the organisations that stand out as being involved in "collaboration opportunities" in the CME; and the Sustainability Indicator (SI), to measure the sustainability commitment and practices in the CME. The values of these indicators are normalised in the scale [0..1].

Table 2. Metrics to evaluate the organisations (players) in a CME, individually and as a whole.

Metrics of the organisations (players) in a CME	
Metric	Description
$O_1..O_n$	Organisations in the CME
#CoOp$_i$ in	Number of collaboration opportunities O_i caught from the CME
#CoOp$_i$ out	Number of collaboration opportunities O_i brought to the CME
#CoOp$_i$	Number of collaboration opportunities in which O_i had relationships in the CME
#CoOp$_{kj}$	No. of collaboration opportunities between O_k and O_j in the CME
$C_D(O_i)$ in/out	Weighted indegree/outdegree centrality (C_D) of O_i in the CME, meaning the sum of direct connections in/out of O_i to the others O_j, with weight #CoOp$_{ij}$
$C_B(O_i)$ in/out	Weighted betweenness centrality (C_B) of O_i in the CME, meaning the sum of overall partial betweenness of O_i relative to all pairs O_{kj}, assuming that connections between O_k and O_j weight #CoOp$_{kj}$
$Rsl_i = \sum rk \frac{R_{rk}}{NF}$	Raw materials sustainability level of Oi (rk = nr. of raw materials adopted metrics)
$Osl_i = \sum ok \frac{O_{ok}}{NF}$	Operations sustainability level of Oi (ok = nr. of adopted operations metrics)
$Psl_i = \sum pk \frac{P_{pk}}{NF}$	Products sustainability level of Oi (pk = nr. of adopted products metrics)
Metrics related to all organisations (players) in a CME	
Metric	Description
#O	Total number of organisations in the CME
$\sum_i$ #CoOp$_i$	Total number of collaboration opportunities generated in the CME
$C_D(O^*)$ in/out	Maximum indegree/outdegree centrality of all $O_1..O_n$
$C_B(O^*)$	Maximum betweenness centrality of all $O_1..O_n$
$\sum_i Rsl_i$	Raw materials sustainability level of all $O_1..O_n$
$\sum_i Osl_i$	Operations sustainability level of all $O_1..O_n$
$\sum_i Psl_i$	Products sustainability level of all $O_1..O_n$

Table 3. Individual performance Indicators of the organisations (players) in a CME.

Performance Indicators of the organisations (players) in a CME	
Performance Indicator	Description
$CI_i in = \frac{C_D(O_i)in}{C_D(O^*)in} = \frac{\sum_j O_{ij}\#CoOp_{ij}in}{\max \sum_j O_{ij}\#CoOp_{ij}in}$	Evaluates the contribution of O_i related to the number of accepted CoOps ($\#CoOp_{in}$)
$CI_i out = \frac{C_D(O_i)out}{C_D(O^*)out} =$ $\frac{\sum_j O_{ij}\#CoOp_{ij}out}{\max \sum_j O_{ij}\#CoOp_{ij}out}$	Evaluates the contribution of O_i related to the number of created CoOps ($\#CoOp_{out}$)
$PI_i = \frac{C_B(O_i)}{C_B(O^*)} = \frac{\sum_k \sum_j O_{kj}(O_i)}{\max \sum_k \sum_j O_{kj}(O_i)}$	Evaluates the prominence/influence of O_i related to the number of CoOps ($\#CoOp$)
$SI_i =$ $\frac{w_r \sum_{k=1}^{rk} Rsl_k + w_o \sum_{k=1}^{ok} Osl_k + w_p \sum_{k=1}^{pk} Psl_k}{w_r+w_o+w_p}$	Evaluates the sustainability of O_i considering different weights (w_r, w_o and w_p) of the raw material, operations and products

Table 4. Performance Indicators to evaluate the collaboration in a CME as a whole.

Performance Indicators related to all organisations (players) in the CME	
Performance Indicator	Description
$CI_{CBE}in = \frac{\sum_i [C_D(O^*)in - C_D(O_i)in]}{C_D(O^*)in*(\#O-1)}$	Evaluates the degree to which the most popular organisation $[C_D(O^*)in]$ exceeds the contribution of the others
$CI_{CBE}out = \frac{\sum_i [C_D(O^*)out - C_D(O_i)out]}{C_D(O^*)out*(\#O-1)}$	Evaluates the degree to which the most active organisation $[C_D(O^*)out]$ exceeds the contribution of the others
$CI_{CBE}t = \frac{\sum_i \#CoOp_i}{\#O}$	Ratio of the $\#CoOp$ created/accepted in the CME by $\#O$
$PI_{CBE} = \frac{\sum_i [C_B(O^*) - C_B(O_i)]}{C_B(O^*)*(\#O-1)}$	Evaluates the degree to which the most prominent/influent organisation $[C_B(O^*)]$ exceeds the contribution of the others
$SI_{CBE} = \frac{\sum_i SI_i}{\#O}$	Ratio of the total value of sustainability of all $O_1..O_n$ by $\#O$

3.3 Influence Mechanism

Considering the organisations (players) of a CME featured by a profile as described in Fig. 3, the CME Manager can use the Performance Assessment to assign a certain weight to each adopted performance indicator (wCI, wPI, wSI) and vary these weights, hoping to influence the players so that they change their behaviour towards improved performance and sustainability of the CME. This process of influencing, assuming a reaction of the CME players similar to that of individuals when they are evaluated, consists of the proposed **Influence Mechanism.** The inferred influence on the organisations is calculated by adding a percentage of a given factor of influence ($0 < FI < 1$) to their collaborative profile, as described in Table 5. The CI weight (wCI) influences the *contact rate*, the PI weight (wPI) influences the *accept rate*, and the SI weight (wSI) influences the *sustainability index*.

Table 5. Calculation method of the Influence Mechanism used in the PAAM

P. Indicator (weight)	Influence	Influence FI
CI (wCI)	Contact rate	$contact_{rate} \mathrel{+}= FI_{wCI}$
PI (wPI)	Accept rate	$accept_{rate} \mathrel{+}= FI_{wPI}$
SI (wSI)	Sustainability index	$sustainab_{index} \mathrel{+}= FI_{wSI}$

The formulas to calculate the respective factors of influence are listed in (1), (2) and (3). An additional factor ($\pm F_e$) is also considered to allow introducing a random positive or negative influence due to exogenous causes. This factor can be used in the simulation model, for example, to induce collaboration in a player that did not ever accept or invite others, or it can be used to decrease collaboration in cases where it deteriorates and fails.

$$contact_{rate}(O_i) \mathrel{+}= contact_{rate}(O_i) * wCI * \frac{FI}{wCI + wPI + wSI} + F_e \tag{1}$$

$$accept_{rate}(O_i) \mathrel{+}= accept_{rate}(O_i) * wPI * \frac{FI}{wCI + wPI + wSI} + F_e \tag{2}$$

$$sustainability_{index}(O_i) \mathrel{+}= sustainability_{index}(O_i) * wSI * \frac{FI}{wCI + wPI + wSI} + F_e \tag{3}$$

4   Experimental Evaluation

The experimental evaluation uses hypothetical data (although inspired on real cases) to instantiate some simulation scenarios of the artefact PAAM. The PAAM was designed using the AnyLogic tool [37] and comprises agent-based modelling to simulate the autonomous organisations (players), and system dynamics to keep and manage human resources (expressed in person-day). The classes of willingness that characterise the collaboration behaviour of the agents use distribution functions; in this case, the Bernoulli distribution [37], parametrised by the *contact rate*, *accept rate* and *sustainability index*, meaning that the higher the parameter, the higher the probability of resulting in an answer "*yes*".

Figure 4 shows a snapshot of a simulation scenario using PAAM, instantiated with six organisations (players) from each profile as defined in Fig. 3. A Poisson distribution [37] is used to generate the incoming market opportunities. After running for a year (virtual time), the connections are established due to the collaboration, allowing the use of the adopted performance indicators to assess the organisations and the CME.

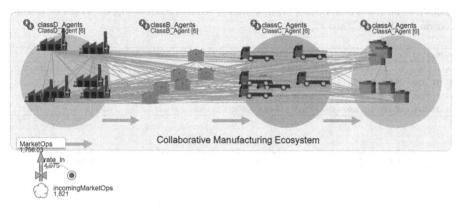

Fig. 4. A snapshot of the PAAM artefact for a CME instantiated with 6 organisations (CME players) from each profile defined by the classes of willingness (A, B, C and D).

For the performance assessment and use of the influence mechanism, the following scenarios were established:

(1) The CI, PI and were adopted considering the weights $wCI = 2$, $wPI = 2$ and $wSI = 2$. No factor of influence was used;
(2) The CI, PI and were adopted considering the weights $wCI = 2$, $wPI = 2$ and $wSI = 2$. A factor of influence FI = 20% was used;
(3) The CI, PI and SI were adopted, increasing the weight $wSI = 4$. The factor of influence was maintained.

After running PAAM for one year (virtual time) for each scenario, we have achieved the results of Table 6, a measure of density $CI_{CBE}t$ - the ratio of the number of $CoOp$ generated in the CME by the total number of organisations, a measure of centrality PI_{CBE} - the degree to which the most prominent/influent organisation in the CME exceeds the contribution of the others, and a measure of sustainability SI_{CBE} – the ratio of the value of sustainability of all the organisations in the CME by the total number of organisations.

Table 7 details the results of PI_i of individual organisations for each simulation scenario, whose graphical view is shown in Fig. 5. The node sizes are related to the PI_i value, i.e., the larger the nodes, the larger the measures; the links strength represents the number of shared $CoOps$. The strengths of connections are weighted by the number of exchanged $CoOps$.

Table 6. CI, PI and SI measures of the CME globally.

Perf. Indicators	$CI_{CBE}t$	PI_{CBE}	SI_{CBE}
Scenario (1)	21,417	0,750	0,325
Scenario (2)	23,917	0,782	0,325
Scenario (3)	24,250	0,808	0,325

Table 7. PI measures of individual organisations (CME players) resulting from each simulation scenario PI_i (1), PI_i (2) and PI_i (3).

Profile	Class A						Class B						Class C						Class D					
O_i	0	1	2	3	4	5	6	7	8	9	10	11	12	13	14	15	16	17	18	19	20	21	22	23
PI_i (1)	0,00	0,00	0,02	0,00	0,00	0,00	0,76	0,57	0,34	0,11	0,25	0,19	0,02	0,00	0,00	0,05	0,03	0,00	1,00	0,84	0,39	0,59	0,26	0,55
PI_i (2)	0,01	0,00	0,00	0,01	0,00	0,03	0,16	0,10	0,38	0,29	0,28	0,18	0,08	0,03	0,13	0,03	0,05	0,05	1,00	0,68	0,80	0,38	0,14	0,44
PI_i (3)	0,00	0,00	0,00	0,00	0,00	0,00	0,30	0,07	0,60	0,18	0,08	0,13	0,01	0,06	0,04	0,08	0,02	0,11	1,00	0,38	0,64	0,32	0,12	0,47

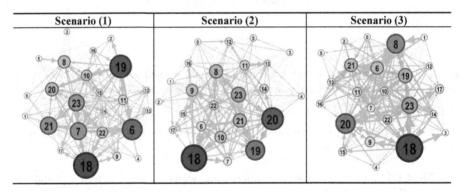

Fig. 5. Graphical view of the PI measures of individual organisations (CME players).

After analysing the results related to $CI_{CBE}t$ in Table 6 (collaboration activity in the CME) in the three simulation scenarios, we can note that after influencing the CME by introducing a FI = 20%, considering $wCI = 2$, $wPI = 2$ and $wSI = 2$ (scenario 2), the organisations in response, tried to be more active, creating more collaboration in the CME: $CI_{CBE}t$ increased from 21,417 to 23,917. The influence also increased the value of PI_{CBE} from 0,75 to 0,782, meaning a more prominence/influence of some organisations with higher collaboration rates.

The increment of the wSI from 2 to 4 (scenario 3) resulted in even more collaboration: $CI_{CBE}t$ increased to 24,250. The greater weight of sustainability induced in organisations with a high collaboration rate, an even greater collaboration with the partners with a higher index of sustainability. As a result, once again, the PI_{CBE} increased to 0,808, meaning the reinforcement of organisations with more influence in the CME.

5 Conclusions

The contribution of this work is a design artefact, the PAAM, consisting of a simulation model that includes a "Performance Assessment and an Influence Mechanism" that allows the exploration by the CME Manager of simulation scenarios, considering diverse CME players with different profiles, seeking benefits due to collaboration [15] and more sustainability [10–12].

We can conclude that we have partially answered the research question. A set of performance indicators can be adopted to measure and influence the collaborative behaviour of organisations, varying the weights of the indicators to induce changes in the desired direction of more sustainability. However, this work has some limitations. Due to the difficulty of getting actual collaboration information, we used hypothetical data considering the same number of organisations of each profile, which can differ from a real context of a CME.

For future work, we aim to gather some actual data from manufacturing cases to deduce and analyse simulation scenarios more consistent with reality, add the social and economic facets to the SI metrics and use different combinations of the set of performance indicators adopted by the CME.

Furthermore, considering that the area of manufacturing is vast, including not only different manufacturing processes but also different collaborative manufacturing processes, future work should consider the specificities of the different sectors. A framework and methodology of collaborative performance management [38] can be established to guide how a set of performance indicators can be applied to different collaborative manufacturing processes.

Acknowledgement. This work was supported in part by the Portuguese FCT program UIDB/00066/2020 (Center of Technology and Systems – CTS).

References

1. Camarinha-Matos, L.M., Rocha, A.D., Graça, P.: Brief overview of collaborative approaches in sustainable manufacturing. In: Camarinha-Matos, L.M., Boucher, X., Afsarmanesh, H. (eds.) PRO-VE 2021. IAICT, vol. 629, pp. 3–18. Springer, Cham (2021). https://doi.org/10.1007/978-3-030-85969-5_1
2. Camarinha-Matos, L.M., Afsarmanesh, H., Boucher, X.: The role of collaborative networks in sustainability. In: Camarinha-Matos, L.M., Boucher, X., Afsarmanesh, H. (eds.) PRO-VE 2010. IFIP AICT, vol. 336, pp. 1–16. Springer, Heidelberg (2010). https://doi.org/10.1007/978-3-642-15961-9_1
3. Elkington, J.: Towards the sustainable corporation: Win-win-win business strategies for sustainable development. Calif. Manage. Rev. **36**(2), 90–100 (1994)
4. Bradbury-Huang, H.: Sustainability by collaboration: the seer case. Organ. Dyn. **39**(4), 335–344 (2010)
5. Hevner, A., March, S.T., Park, J., Ram, S.: Design science research in information systems. MIS Q. **28**(1), 75–105 (2004)
6. Hevner, A., Chatterjee, S.: Design science research in information systems. In: Hevner, A., Chatterjee, S. (eds.) Design Research in Information Systems, pp. 9–22. Springer, Boston (2010). https://doi.org/10.1007/978-1-4419-5653-8_2

7. Simon, H.A.: The Sciences of the Artificial, 3rd edn. MIT Press, Cambridge (1996)
8. Baskerville, R., Pries-Heje, J., Venable, J.: Soft design science methodology. In: Proceedings of the 4th International Conference on Design Science Research in Information Systems and Technology, DESRIST 2009. Association for Computing Machinery, New York (2009)
9. Hevner, A.R.: A three cycle view of design science research. Scand. J. Inf. Syst. **19**(2), 4 (2007)
10. Denise, L.: Collaboration vs. c-three (cooperation, coordination, and communication). Innovating **7**(3), 1–6 (1999)
11. Lozano, R.: Collaboration as a pathway for sustainability. Sustain. Dev. **15**(6), 370–381 (2007)
12. OECD: The OECD sustainable manufacturing toolkit. https://www.oecd.org/innovation/green/toolkit/48704993.pdf. Accessed 5 May 2022
13. Joung, C.B., Carrell, J., Sarkar, P., Feng, S.C.: Categorization of indicators for sustainable manufacturing. Ecol. Ind. **24**, 148–157 (2013)
14. Camarinha-Matos, L.M., Afsarmanesh, H.: Collaborative Networks: Reference Modeling. Springer, Boston (2008). https://doi.org/10.1007/978-0-387-79426-6
15. Abreu, A., Camarinha-Matos, L.M.: A benefit analysis model for collaborative networks. In: Camarinha-Matos, L.M., Afsarmanesh, H. (eds.) Collaborative networks: Reference modeling, pp. 253–276. Springer, Boston (2008). https://doi.org/10.1007/978-0-387-79426-6_18
16. Abreu, A., Camarinha-Matos, L.M.: On the role of value systems to promote the sustainability of collaborative environments. Int. J. Prod. Res. **46**(5), 1207–1229 (2008)
17. Camarinha-Matos, L.M., Abreu, A.: Performance indicators for collaborative networks based on collaboration benefits. Prod. Plan. Control **18**(7), 592–609 (2007)
18. Provan, K.G., Fish, A., Sydow, J.: Interorganizational networks at the network level: a review of the empirical literature on whole networks. J. Manag. **33**(3), 479–516 (2007)
19. Ramanathan, U.: Performance of supply chain collaboration - a simulation study. Expert Syst. Appl. **41**(1), 210–220 (2014)
20. Singh, H., Garg, R., Sachdeva, A.: Supply chain collaboration: a state-of-the-art literature review. Uncertain Supply Chain Manag. **6**(2), 149–180 (2018)
21. Ramanathan, U., Gunasekaran, A., Subramanian, N.: Supply chain collaboration performance metrics: a conceptual framework. Benchmarking Int. J. **18**(6), 856–872 (2011)
22. Gopal, P.R.C., Thakkar, J.: A review on supply chain performance measures and metrics: 2000–2011. Int. J. Prod. Perform. Manag. **61**(5), 518–547 (2012)
23. Mishra, D., Gunasekaran, A., Papadopoulos, T., Dubey, R.: Supply chain performance measures and metrics: a bibliometric study. Benchmarking Int. J. **25**(3), 932–967 (2018)
24. Ramanathan, U., Gunasekaran, A.: Supply chain collaboration: impact of success in long-term partnerships. Int. J. Prod. Econ. **147**, 252–259 (2014)
25. Burt, R.S.: The network structure of social capital. Res. Organ. Behav. **22**, 345–423 (2000)
26. Freeman, L.C.: A set of measures of centrality based on betweenness. Sociometry **40**(1), 35–41 (1977)
27. Freeman, L.C.: Centrality in social networks conceptual clarification. Soc. Netw. **1**(3), 215–239 (1978)
28. Jackson, M.O.: Social and Economic Networks, vol. 3. Princeton University Press, Princeton (2008)
29. Barrat, A., Barthélemy, M., Pastor-Satorras, R., Vespignani, A.: The architecture of complex weighted networks. Proc. Natl. Acad. Sci. **101**(11), 3747–3752 (2004)
30. Abreu, A., Camarinha-Matos, L.M.: On the role of value systems and reciprocity in collaborative environments. In: Camarinha-Matos, L.M., Afsarmanesh, H., Ollus, M. (eds.) PRO-VE 2006. IFIP, vol. 224, pp. 273–284. Springer, Boston (2006). https://doi.org/10.1007/978-0-387-38269-2_29

31. Abreu, A., Camarinha-Matos, L.M.: An approach to measure social capital in collaborative networks. In: Camarinha-Matos, L.M., Pereira-Klen, A., Afsarmanesh, H. (eds.) PRO-VE 2011. IFIP AICT, vol. 362, pp. 29–40. Springer, Heidelberg (2011). https://doi.org/10.1007/978-3-642-23330-2_4

32. Zaheer, A., Gözübüyük, R., Milanov, H.: It's the connections: the network perspective in interorganizational research. Acad. Manag. Perspect. **24**(1), 62–77 (2010)

33. Manuel Portugal Ferreira and Sungu Armagan: Using social networks theory as a complementary perspective to the study of organizational change. BAR Braz. Adm. Rev. **8**, 168–184 (2011)

34. Ahuja, G., Soda, G., Zaheer, A.: The genesis and dynamics of organizational networks. Organ. Sci. **23**(2), 434–448 (2012)

35. Ghaffar, F., Hurley, N.: Structural hole centrality: evaluating social capital through strategic network formation. Comput. Soc. Netw. **7**(1), 1–27 (2020). https://doi.org/10.1186/s40649-020-00079-4

36. Granovetter, M.S.: The strength of weak ties. Ame. J. Sociol. **78**(6), 1360–1380 (1973)

37. Borshchev, A.: The Big Book of Simulation Modeling: Multimethod Modeling with AnyLogic 6. AnyLogic North America, Oakbrook Terrace (2013)

38. Jung, J.-Y., Lee, J.S., Jung, J., Kim, S., Shin, D.: A methodology of collaborative performance measurement for manufacturing collaboration. Int. J. Ind. Eng. Theory Appl. Pract. **19**(3), 149–160 (2012)

Knowledge-Driven Data Provision to Enhance Smart Manufacturing – A Case Study in Swedish Manufacturing SME

Wei Min Wang[1], Helena Ebel[1(✉)], Steffen Kohler[2], and Rainer Stark[1]

[1] Department of Industrial Information Technology, Technische Universität Berlin,
Pascalstrasse 8-9, 10587 Berlin, Germany
{w.wang,helena.ebel,rainer.stark}@tu-berlin.de
[2] Nytt AG, Östermalmstorg 1, 114 42 Stockholm, Sweden

Abstract. Various novel and data-driven business concepts have emerged during the fourth industrial revolution. Smart manufacturing, for example, utilizes data from manufacturing equipment, human operators, and organizational IT systems to enable dynamic adaptions in production systems. Nowadays, these data are often distributed among multiple partners in collaborative value creation networks. Hence, to identify and collect relevant data for given business cases has become an important, but complex issue. To support the process of establishing comprehensive data provision in industrial practice, a reference model for knowledge-driven data provision processes was developed. It describes a systematic approach to drive operationalization of data provision from knowledge requirements to identify, extract and provide raw data until the application of such data sets. To evaluate the applicability of the reference model, a case study was conducted in which it was used to guide the implementation of an IoT Solution in four Swedish manufacturing companies.

Keywords: Knowledge · Data provision process · Smart manufacturing

1 Introduction

During the fourth industrial revolution, also known as industry 4.0, data has become the essential resource to drive innovations in the industry. Smart manufacturing (SM), as one of these novel data-driven concepts, utilizes data from manufacturing equipment, human operators, and organizational IT systems to enable integrated production systems to adapt to changes in external demands (e.g., supply networks or customer needs) in real-time [1]. Nowadays, companies often engaged in collaborative networks comprising partners with complementary expertise to provide competitive and innovative products and services. These partners, in turn, are characterized by their processes, equipment, and IT systems. In order to make data usable in such networks, the relevant data and data sources must be identified, and their transfer, processing, and subsequent application must also be carefully planned.

© IFIP International Federation for Information Processing 2022
Published by Springer Nature Switzerland AG 2022
L. M. Camarinha-Matos et al. (Eds.): PRO-VE 2022, IFIP AICT 662, pp. 18–30, 2022.
https://doi.org/10.1007/978-3-031-14844-6_2

To implement data-driven approaches such as SM, data provision processes must therefore be considered continuous processes and regarded in the context of the strategic structuring of business processes. Respectively, the goals of implementation projects have to be defined at the very beginning starting from the intended target state after a successful implementation. From there, the required knowledge for reaching this state must be derived, and subsequently, the information required to create that knowledge. At last, the necessary data on which the information is built can be identified and collected. Various models in Knowledge Discovery and Data Mining (KDDM), such as CRISP-DM, SEMMA, and KDD, describe detailed steps to elaborate data requirements for business cases. However, all these models focus on single data mining endeavors and do not support the strategic planning and integration of continuous data provision processes as part of the organization processes.

Hence, Wang et al. proposed a reference model for knowledge-driven data provision processes (referred to as the "reference model" in the further content of this article) covering this approach [2]. By establishing a continuous data provision process, companies can apply advanced analytics and Artificial Intelligence (AI) capabilities to improve data sets' identification, preparation, and delivery. According to the reference model (see Fig. 1), the process is initiated by business problems emerging from the companies' value creation process. These problems lead to knowledge that needs to be fulfilled to resolve them. The satisfaction of these needs demands raw data acquired through a streamlined and automated data provision process. After the data extraction, the raw data must be transformed and applied within exploration models to obtain the information needed to satisfy the required knowledge [2].

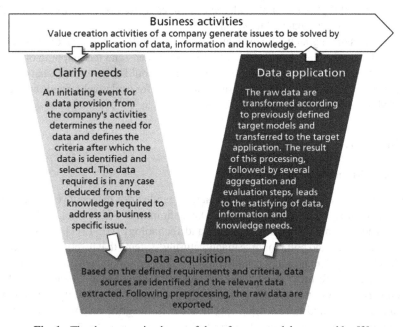

Fig. 1. The three generic phases of the reference model proposed by [2]

However, the reference model in its current state can only deliver a detailed theoretical concept for integrating knowledge-driven data provision processes. It must be examined in practical use cases to evaluate its applicability in industrial practice and identify potential improvements. Therefore, the reference model was applied in a use case that aimed to introduce SM solutions in small manufacturing companies in Sweden. Integrating a continuous data supply process is essential as SM relies on constant supply and analysis of field data. Also, to exploit optimization potentials, in-depth knowledge of the manufacturing and organizational processes is necessary to determine the relevant data obtained, suitable analysis methods, and proper ways to deliver results. The SM solution applied in the use case was provided by the Swedish company Nytt which uses IoT (internet of things) devices to monitor manufacturing processes. The gathered data are aggregated, processed, and displayed in customizable dashboards, which provide managers and machine operators with general information about their production lines (e.g., load, downtimes, outages). This information is the baseline for more advanced use cases and can be used to optimize the manufacturing processes or reduce downtime.

In the case study presented in this paper, the reference model was applied during the introduction of Nytt's solution in four Swedish SMEs. In this study, the focus was put on the "Clarify needs" phase of the model. In this phase, the knowledge objectives to be achieved are defined, determining the required information and data. Hence, in-depth interviews were carried out to examine the knowledge needs of managers and machine operators from the manufacturing companies beforehand to identify the required data and prepare to introduce the SM solution. The steps from the "data acquisition" and the "data application" phase were only regarded theoretically as Nytt's solution already included standard procedures for both. Still, the standard repertoire of data collected in the data tables of Nytt's solution could be used to evaluate if the identified knowledge needs can be explicitly mapped to actual data types.

The study's main goal was to evaluate to what extent the application of the reference model could support the identification of knowledge needs and the mapping of those to information carriers and factual data. Furthermore, it should be examined what obstacles can emerge while establishing a data provision process for a relatively simple application of the SM approach.

2 State of the Art

2.1 Smart Manufacturing

SM has attracted the attention of the manufacturing industries in recent years. Still, there are various definitions in the literature [3]. One definition of SM is given by Kang et al., based on The National Institute of Standards and Technology (NIST) [1]. It describes SM as "fully-integrated and collaborative manufacturing systems that respond in real-time to meet the changing demands and conditions in the factory, supply network, and customer needs." Kang et al. further extend this definition and explain SM as "manufacture-based technologies and systems that can respond to complicated and diversified situations of the manufacturing field in real-time." [1] In order to integrate responsive manufacturing systems, the manufacturing assets must be connected by technological devices like sensors, communication technology, computing platforms, and others. Monitoring the manufacturing assets in real-time improves the factory's productivity, quality, delivery, and flexibility [1]. The application of the SM concept leads toward the connectivity of the physical manufacturing equipment layer with a cyber layer [3]. The connection is ensured by devices and sensors that acquire data from the manufacturing process [4].

The cyber-layer contains the intelligence of the smart system. It receives data from every connected machine [5] via the devices and sensors in the interface layer. Information is extracted from gathered data by applying data analytics at the cyber-layer. This information enables machines to monitor, compare performances, and predict future behavior [5]. The cyber-layer transmits decisions to the physical equipment to adjust the manufacturing process based on the gathered data. According to [3], each manufacturing equipment has intelligence [3]. This contributes to the ability of the manufacturing equipment "to cope with a complex environment and customized products" [6]. New digital concepts and technologies such as digital twins, IoT, and cloud are being established alongside data-driven models to ensure that the required intelligence is technically implemented in SM [7].

2.2 Knowledge Discovery and Data Mining

The required data and information flow must be clarified to enable a proper level of automation in manufacturing systems. Different approaches can be found to describe the flow of information in the literature. Forza and Salvador [8] classify the information flow within companies into three groups regarding their direction: vertical, horizontal, and external information flow. The international standard IEC 62264-1 [9] itself presents a functional data flow model, including the interactions between the activities at the manufacturing operations management level and business planning and logistics level. This functional model varies from the vertical structure of a company and leads to a complex outline of the vertical data flow between the above two levels. Lower levels as the actual production process are not included in the model. Tao et al. [10] present a manufacturing data life cycle involving seven components for transforming data into understandable information. The increasing application of sensors and connected machines leads to the creation of high-volume data (big data) [5]. This results in difficulty extracting relevant information and knowledge hidden within those data sets [10]. By obtaining the knowledge, industrial practitioners hope to reveal potential improvements in their organizational processes [2].

Hence, collecting and analyzing of high quantities of data has become crucial. Approaches to extract information and knowledge from large amounts of data cover Knowledge Discovery (KD), Data Mining (DM), Knowledge Discovery in Databases (KDD), or KDDM. The terms are frequently reviewed in various academic papers in the past years, and various opinions have emerged regarding the differentiation of the concepts. Some academic papers define DM only as part of KDD's overall knowledge discovery process [11]. Others describe DM as a synonym for the KDD process [12, 13]. Lately, the term KDDM was suggested as an overall name for the process [14]. Despite differences in understanding, all approaches aim at revealing hidden information and knowledge from large amounts of data. The increasing attention for KDDM is related to techniques and methods from machine learning and AI to exploit hidden knowledge from huge data sets [15]. Still, the existing KDDM models mainly focus on single data mining projects and do not support establishing continuous data provision processes.

Another well-known procedure for the application of DM is CRISP-DM, which is based on KDD approaches [16]. CRISP-DM is a methodology to discover the knowledge of a business use case with DM [17]. Although this methodology primarily focuses on business understanding and identifying business goals for the use case, it has a gap in business processes, where several activities are done to achieve a business goal. In addition, CRISP-DM assumed that all data is known and already available [18], which is not necessarily the case with new business models and resulting business processes.

Data requirements for novel data-driven products and business models lead to continuous data provision processes that are indispensable base on the organizations' strategic orientation and enable constant data acquisition and knowledge discovery. Furthermore, a continuous knowledge-driven data provision process enables AI capabilities and advanced data analytics to exploit the collected data and improve the organizational processes [2].

3 Case Study

3.1 Case Setting

The foundation for SM is connected manufacturing systems and respective means to collect machine and process-related data. Nytt has developed a production monitoring solution based on smartphones that can be added to various types of manufacturing machines. The product is integrated into the physical production process and extracts data directly from the manufacturing operations. The primary function of the solution is to monitor the current manufacturing process and continuously collect real-time data from the ongoing operations. It enables the exchange between the physical production assets and computer-based systems through wireless networks. The product involves a system consisting of three main components: the *SetApp*, the *OpApp*, and the *dashboard* to create this connectivity. Data gathered by the *SetApp* (process data) and the *OpApp* (operator and machine data) are processed and displayed via standardized graphs within the *dashboard* to overview the manufacturing assets. These graphs display predefined production metrics, e.g., productivity or production volume, and can be customized by the user through different filters, e.g., time. However, the available data were limited to the given capabilities of Nytt's solution at that time. They included captured machine state, time of the capture, input from machine operators, and additional sensor data, i.e., input-output measuring, acceleration, brightness, and volume level.

3.2 Evaluation Goals and Methods

The goal of the use case was to evaluate two main research questions (RQ) that can shed light on the applicability of the reference model proposed by [2]:

- RQ1: Can knowledge emerging from the current business situation of the hosting companies be explicitly mapped to data that is collectible from the manufacturing process?
- RQ2: What challenges emerge from integrating a continuous data provision process in a realistic environment?

To answer RQ1, two kinds of data had to be collected: firstly, the knowledge needs of the interviewees, and secondly, the operational data from the manufacturing processes.

According to [2], the definition of the knowledge needs is the foundation for target-oriented data provision processes as they allow for identifying the relevant information and data to be collected. In the current case study, the knowledge needs of the interviewees were used to identify concrete data needs and map them to available data in the data tables of Nytt's solution. If the required data was available in the data tables, the according to visualization graph was selected and presented to the interviewees asking them to determine whether their knowledge needs could be satisfied with the given data and their visualization.

As an evaluation method for the knowledge needs and their fulfillment by the presented visualization, semi-structured interviews were chosen as they promised a balanced approach to collect comparable results while allowing the interviews to be led in conversational manners to explore the thoughts and desires of the interviewees [19, 20]. In total, interviews with seven employees at five Swedish manufacturing companies (A–E) were arranged, and Nytt's product was introduced. All companies were small-sized companies. Managers (n = 5) and machine operators (n = 2) were interviewed to obtain insights from different perspectives.

All interviews lasted between 26 and 35 min and were conducted through video calls. The interviews were all held in English. Following [20], all interviews were recorded and transcribed after they were conducted. These transcripts were the basis for the interview analysis. The interview results were analyzed using qualitative content analysis, namely the ordinal deductive category assignment method [21].

4 Results

4.1 Results Regarding RQ1

During the interviews, a total of 21 knowledge needs could be identified in the four companies (see Table 1). 13 of these knowledge needs could be directly mapped to concrete data collected by Nytt's solution. The required data could be identified for the eight remaining knowledge needs, but they were unavailable as they were not or only partially collected by Nytt's solution at that time.

Table 1. Identified knowledge needs and availability of concrete data

Nr	Knowledge need	Company	Could be mapped to available data? (yes/no)
KN1	How are the machines currently performing, especially how much output do they currently generate?	A	Yes
KN2	When did the performance in the past not meet the expectations, and why?	A	Yes

(continued)

Table 1. (*continued*)

Nr	Knowledge need	Company	Could be mapped to available data? (yes/no)
KN3	How much time is necessary to prepare the machines?	A	Yes
KN4	What is the exact time the single manufacturing jobs require, and how much interference is necessary?	A	No
KN5	How can I obtain the output of the production process at any requested time without performing a manual data collection process	B	Yes
KN6	What number of production cycles have the machines been running with each worn-out tool?	B	Yes
KN7	How much of the production time was the equipment not producing?	B	Yes
KN8	How are the machines on the shop floor currently performing, and what is the current uptime of the machines?	B	Yes
KN9	How much time do we spent on reworking defective parts?	B	No
KN10	How can I overview the key metrics and stops of my manufacturing equipment at all times without performing a manual data collection process?	C	Yes
KN11	Does the performance of the current production operations meets the re-quired level? Did it exceed this level, or did it fall behind?	C	Yes
KN12	What is the status of the assigned maintenance tasks at any time?	C	Yes
KN13	How can I overview the performance and stops of my manufacturing machines at any time?	D	Yes
KN14	How much time do the employees need to assemble a product?	D	Yes
KN15	What is the necessary information a new employee needs, to be able to operate the machines after a shorter teach-in phase?	D	No
KN16	What is the output of parts of the production process at any requested time?	D	No
KN17	What kind of maintenance service do the manufacturing equipment require and when?	D	No
KN18	How can I collect data from the older machines to monitor their performance without a costly and complex installation process of sensors?	E	Yes

(*continued*)

Table 1. (*continued*)

Nr	Knowledge need	Company	Could be mapped to available data? (yes/no)
KN19	How high is the strength of the Wi-Fi signal, the brightness, or sound volume in the factory at all time?	E	No
KN20	What is the filling level of the pallets in the production's lines, and how can I receive automated notifications if the filling level is low?	E	No
KN21	How can I locate AGVs, employees on the shop floor, and products in real-time?	E	No

Eleven graphs from the portfolio currently provided by Nytt's solution could be identified that would satisfy these needs (see Table 2). The following section describes how these graphs were used to satisfy the knowledge needs.

Table 2. Graph types that supports the satisfaction of knowledge need

Nr	Graph type
1	Productivity and the "production", "setup", and "no production" time
2	Daily Overview
3	Production Volume
4	Throughput Rate
5	Total number of Stops (categorised in four classes according to length of the stops)
6	Scatter plot of Stop distribution with complementary display of reasons for stops (as bar chart)
7	Maintenance tasks
8	Assembly activities
9	Development production metrics over time
10	Production cycles
11	Comparing Production Volume

KN1 - "How are the machines currently performing, especially how much output do they currently generate?" This knowledge need is answered by illustrating the metrics used in company A to measure manufacturing performance. These metrics are "Productivity", "Production Volume", and "Production Time". To evaluate the current performance, real-time data from the manufacturing processes are transformed into these metrics. Thus, the metrics continuously reflect the current manufacturing performance. The knowledge need can be satisfied with graphs 1, 2, and 3. Satisfying the knowledge need also significantly improved the manufacturing performance of a specific machine with an automized loading mechanism and produced almost independently. The autonomous loading mechanism and the machine's good condition result in higher productivity than 90 percent. Due to the high productivity, the managers/production managers could not increase the output during the regular shift. By evaluating the visualized production data over several weeks, the most significant potential to increase the output was the exploitation of the production time between midnight and 7 am. The production output increased by almost 15 percent by satisfying the urge for higher transparency. The satisfaction of a knowledge need did unlock potential improvement of the organizational processes at the use case. It proves that business problems can be solved and value creation improved, as suggested by [2].

KN2 - "When did the performance in the past not meet the expectations, and why?" Fulfilling this knowledge need leads to capturing the performance over time and displaying it in a manner that the user has the chance to compare past performances. Graph type 9 illustrates the development of the metrics over time, can consequently satisfy the knowledge need, and allows company A to conclude past performances.

KN3 - "How much time is necessary for preparing the machines?" This question can be satisfied by displaying the machine's overall "setup" time, which is presented daily, weekly, monthly, or yearly in graph 1.

KN5 - "What is the output of the production process at any requested time without performing a manual data collection process?" KN5 can be answered by graph type 3 as it provides the production volume in real-time. Furthermore, applying filters enables examining the production volume of past days, weeks, months, and years. The satisfaction of this knowledge needs to lead to an increased production volume by 6 percent of company B. However, unlike company A, not the graph enabled the improvement, but the "Raw Data."

KN6 - "What number of production cycles have the machines been running with each worn-out tool?" The knowledge need is satisfied by graph type 10. It contains the number of production cycles that the machines conduct. Additionally, by selecting a specific time, company B can look up the number of production cycles before every tool change.

KN7 - "How much of the production time was the equipment not producing?" The illustration of the "no production" time and "setup" time in graph type 1 satisfies the required knowledge. The two figures can be displayed daily, weekly, monthly, or yearly.

KN8 - "How are the machines on the shop floor currently performing, and what is the current uptime of the machines?" Similar to company A, company B measures its performance with manufacturing metrics. These metrics are "Production Volume", "Production Time", and "Equipment Downtime". The information about these metrics is displayed in graphs 1, 2, and 3. The real-time visualization creates the desired overview of the performance. The machine uptimes can be displayed in a time unit (hours) or as a percentage share of the overall "production" time.

KN10 - "How can I overview the key metrics and stops of my manufacturing equipment at all times without performing a manual data collection process?" Company C measures its performance with the metrics "Productivity", "Production Volume", and "Production Time". Graph types 1, 2, and 3 provide real-time information reflecting these metrics to satisfy the knowledge need. Furthermore, the graph types 5, and 6 illustrate each machine stop alongside the metrics.

KN11 - "Does the performance of the current production operations meets the required level? Did it exceed this level, or did it fall behind?" The knowledge need is answered by comparing the current performance metrics to values the metrics should reach by the end of the preferred period. The interviewee named the production output as a key metric for measuring the performance level. Graph type 11 provides the information required to satisfy the knowledge need.

KN12 - "What is the status of the assigned maintenance tasks at any time?" Graph type 7 and the detailed table are essential to answer this knowledge need. The information shows which and how many tasks are completed.

KN13 - "How can I overview the performance and stops of my manufacturing machines at any time?" This knowledge need is equivalent to KN10 of company C. Thus, it can be satisfied similarly. The relevant metrics to measure the manufacturing performance at company D are "Production Volume" and "Throughput Rate". This information is illustrated by the graph types 3, 4, 5, and 6.

KN14 - "How much time do the employees need to assemble a product?" This knowledge need is closely related to the production metric "Through-put Rate". The interviewee from company D wished to understand the duration of the assembly activities better. Graph type 8 shows the duration of the single assembly activities and the preparation time of these activities. This graph satisfies the knowledge need.

KN18 - "How can I collect data from the older machines to monitor their performance without a costly and complex installation process of sensors?" Company E is not applying NYTT's product in their production processes but as a tool for proof of concept. Therefore, the interviewee from company E did not request any specific production metrics or figures. The currently available graphs in the dashboard were sufficient to conduct a limited amount of tests. The information is available in graphs types 1, 2, and 3.

4.2   Results Regarding RQ2

Interviewing employees from two different groups at the five companies did not only lead to further insights into the use cases themselves but also revealed different perceptions of the benefits provided by the continuous data provision process. At company A and company D, two employees from different positions participated in the interviews. The answers included significant variations in the expressed knowledge needs and acceptance of the continuous data provision process. While the two interviewees from the manager/production manager position are relatively positive toward the data provision process, the two machine operators agree that the process does not benefit their daily tasks. The two managers/production managers seem more curious about the possible benefits the product can provide them. They were expressed several knowledge needs that could be satisfied applying of the continuous data provision process.

Furthermore, the two managers/production managers are the managing directors of their respective companies, and they initiated the use of the data provision process. That indicates that the use of the product aligns with the organizational goals they are following. The answers given by the two managers/production managers can be reflected in the statements from the other interviewed managers/production managers. The managers/production managers demanded data from their manufacturing processes and expressed similar knowledge needs. That confirms the favorable position of the managers/production managers towards applying a continuous data provision process. The opinions of the two machine operators from different companies showed the same analogy, but they did not see the benefits of the data provision process.

5   Discussion

The analysis of the interview results showed that all interviewees could conclude the detailed data needed for the knowledge they stated before. This shows that the knowledge needs can be captured explicit enough through a semi-structured interview to be mapped to collectible data, as suggested by [2]. The information provided by the graphs enabled the identification of improvement potentials in all companies. In two cases, the identified potentials led to direct actions. This supports the hypothesis by [2] that the reference model can support establishing data provision processes that improve a company's value creation process. Consequently, RQ1 could be answered positively.

This evaluation showed that the company size significantly influenced continuous data provision processes in realistic environments. It was observed that the integration of data provision processes was easier in smaller companies due to less complex value creation processes, short and direct communications, and more significant influences of single employees. Moreover, in smaller companies, the effort to involve the entirety of the employees was lower, leading to a higher level of staff commitment. For RQ2, it can be stated that – at least in this sample – the challenges did not emerge from data-related aspects (e.g., availability, accessibility, quality) but from organizational aspects, mainly company size and the commitment of the personnel.

6   Conclusion and Outlook

The current case study showed that the reference model proposed by [2] could be applied in an industrial context. As the results show, the process of integrating Nytt's IoT solution for smart manufacturing could be supported by the model, independently of the size of the company, their process complexity, or the level of digitization. The data collected could be mapped to the identified knowledge needs in most cases. Thus, the data could be integrated into a continuous process to supply specialized graphs in the dashboards.

Using these dashboards, all companies in the study sample could identify improvement potentials or even take direct actions.

However, the case study revealed some significant limitations to the reference model. One limitation relates to the strong foundation of the reference model on the knowledge needs of the individuals applying the model. Individuals usually try to solve problems based on their experiences and routines, but the knowledge that needs to be derived is limited to the individuals' imagination of the solution. That can lead to a lack in exploiting the full use of a continuous data provision process, especially for companies with a low level of digitalization, as problems are solved without exploiting modern tools. The second limitation is based on the different perceptions of the usefulness continuous data provision process during this study. Some interviewees shared a prevail of manual work over the benefits of the process. They questioned the value of a data provision process as they were worried about getting additional work without immediate benefits. That applies especially to the individuals responsible for maintaining the continuous data provision process through manual work. For a successful application of the reference model in realistic environments, the benefits and efforts of every individual involved should be considered and communicated transparently.

Furthermore, the results of this case study are also limited by its setting. As this case study only included small-sized companies, the reference model will need further evaluations in the context of bigger companies with more complex organizational structures. Also, the "data collection" and "data application" phase of the reference model could only be considered in a theoretical manner as Nytts solution already included standardized procedures for both phases. Consequently, both aspects must be further investigated in academic research or industrial use cases.

References

1. Kang, H.S., et al.: Smart manufacturing: past research, present findings, and future directions. Int. J. Precis. Eng. Manuf. Green Technol. **3**(1), 111–128 (2016). https://doi.org/10.1007/s40 684-016-0015-5
2. Wang, W.M., Preidel, M., Fachbach, B., Stark, R.: Towards a reference model for knowledge driven data provision processes. In: Camarinha-Matos, L.M., Afsarmanesh, H., Ortiz, A. (eds.) PRO-VE 2020. IAICT, vol. 598, pp. 123–132. Springer, Cham (2020). https://doi.org/10.1007/978-3-030-62412-5_10
3. Kusiak, A.: Smart manufacturing. Int. J. Prod. Res. **56**, 508–517 (2018)
4. Jiang, J.-R.: An improved cyber-physical systems architecture for Industry 4.0 smart factories. Adv. Mech. Eng. **10**, 15 (2018)
5. Lee, J., Bagheri, B., Kao, H.-A.: A Cyber-Physical Systems architecture for Industry 4.0-based manufacturing systems. Manuf. Lett. **3**, 18–23 (2015). https://doi.org/10.1016/j.mfg let.2014.12.001
6. Brettel, M., Friederichsen, N., Keller, M., Rosenberg, M.: How virtualization, decentralization and network building change the manufacturing landscape: an Industry 4.0 perspective. Int. J. Mech. Aerosp. Ind. Mechatron. Manuf. Eng. **8**, 37–44 (2014)
7. Stark, R.: Virtual Product Creation in Industry. Springer, Heidelberg (2022). https://doi.org/10.1007/978-3-662-64301-3
8. Forza, C., Salvador, F.: Information flows for high-performance manufacturing. Int. J. Prod. Econ. **70**, 21–36 (2001)

9. ISO: IEC 62264-1: 2013: Enterprise-control system integration—Part 1: models and terminology
10. Tao, F., Qi, Q., Liu, A., Kusiak, A.: Data-driven smart manufacturing. J. Manuf. Syst. **48**, 157–169 (2018)
11. Fayyad, U., Piatetsky-Shapiro, G., Smyth, P.: From data mining to knowledge discovery in databases. AI Mag. **17**, 37–54 (1996)
12. Cios, K.J., Kurgan, L.A.: Trends in data mining and knowledge discovery. In: Pal, N.R., Jain, L. (eds.) Advanced Techniques in Knowledge Discovery and Data Mining, pp. 1–26. Springer, London (2005). https://doi.org/10.1007/1-84628-183-0_1
13. Han, J., Kamber, M., Pei, J.: Data Mining. Concepts and Techniques. Morgan Kaufmann/Elsevier, Waltham (2012)
14. Mariscal, G., Marbán, Ó., Fernández, C.: A survey of data mining and knowledge discovery process models and methodologies. Knowl. Eng. Rev. **25**, 137–166 (2010)
15. Smyth, P.: Data mining: data analysis on a grand scale? Stat. Methods Med. Res. **9**, 309–327 (2000)
16. Azevedo, A., Santos, M.F.: KDD, SEMMA and CRISP-DM: a parallel overview. In: IADIS European Conference on Data Mining, Amsterdam, The Netherlands (2008)
17. Wirth, R., Hipp, J.: CRISP-DM: towards a standard process model for data mining. In: Proceedings of the 4th International Conference on the Practical Applications of Knowledge Discovery and Data Mining, vol. 1, pp. 29–40 (2000)
18. Wiemer, H., Drowatzky, L., Ihlenfeldt, S.: Data mining methodology for engineering applications (DMME)—a holistic extension to the CRISP-DM model. Appl. Sci. **9**, 2407 (2019). https://doi.org/10.3390/app9122407
19. Loosen, W.: Das Leitfadeninterview – eine unterschätzte Methode. In: Averbeck-Lietz, S., Meyen, M. (eds.) Handbuch nicht standardisierte Methoden in der Kommunikationswissenschaft. SN, pp. 139–155. Springer, Wiesbaden (2016). https://doi.org/10.1007/978-3-658-01656-2_9
20. Longhurst, R.: Semi-structured interviews and focus groups. In: Key Methods in Geography, vol. 3, pp. 143–156 (2003)
21. Mayring, P.: Qualitative content analysis: theoretical foundation, basic procedures and software solution (2014)

Toward a Collaborative Sensor Network Integration for SMEs' Zero-Defect Manufacturing

Badreddine Tanane[1,3(✉)] , Baudouin Dafflon[2] , Mohand Lounes Bentaha[1] ,
Nejib Moalla[1] , and Vincent Ferreiro[3]

[1] Univ Lyon, Université Lumière Lyon 2, INSA Lyon, Université Claude Bernard Lyon 1, DISP, EA4570, 69676 Bron, France
{badreddine.tanane,mohand.bentaha,nejib.moalla}@univ-lyon2.fr
[2] Univ Lyon, Université Claude Bernard Lyon 1, INSA Lyon, Université Lumière Lyon 2, DISP, EA4570, 69621 Villeurbanne, France
baudouin.dafflon@univ-lyon1.fr
[3] TARDY SAS, La Grand-Croix, France

Abstract. The increasing challenges in industry paved the way towards the next generation factory model or namely "Industry 4.0" through the availability and development of recent technologies in ICT such as industrial internet of things (IIoT) and cyber-physical production systems (CPPS). One of the main pillars of this paradigm is Zero defect manufacturing (ZDM), which aims to get workpieces "right the first time". However, this technological uplift can prove itself to be very challenging in an industrial environment especially when it comes to the choice of available sensors, the motivation behind that choice, and the insurance that they comply with different guidelines for further exploitation in decision support. This is even more relevant when addressing low-volume high-variety industrial entities such as make-to-order (MTO) SMEs, inherently characterized by limited resources and highly variable business processes collaborating to respond to the demands of an increasingly cutting-edged market. This paper presents a collaborative approach to devise a suitable sensor network in an industrial machining environment generally and in an MTO SME context specifically, based on a joint analysis of all business process data related to quality control issues. Furthermore, the paper showcases the benefits of the approach in a real-world case study involving a 3-axis universal machining center as early validation.

Keywords: Sensor network · IIoT · Machining process · Industry 4.0 · Zero-defect manufacturing · Collective manufacturing

1 Introduction

The cost of poor quality, including the tolls of repair, rework, scrap, service calls, and so on, is estimated to range between 5 and 30% of a manufacturing company's total income with most of them ranging in the 10–20% area [14].

L. M. Camarinha-Matos et al. (Eds.): PRO-VE 2022, IFIP AICT 662, pp. 31–43, 2022.
https://doi.org/10.1007/978-3-031-14844-6_3

Industry 4.0, first introduced in Germany [7], has managed to make a breakthrough in manufacturing quality control (QC) through concepts such as Industrial Internet of Things (IIoT) and Cyber-Physical Systems (CPS) through data-based defect detection.

ZDM is generally defined as a strategy to get rid of defects in production. As such, it has always been considered the next level of quality control and consequently was seen from a "quality" lens mainly through quality management strategies. The framework (Fig. 1) depicts this tendency from a high-level schematic perspective by only pointing sensors toward products on the CNC machine. Nevertheless, this approach has been increasingly questioned and deemed limited in literature as per recent reviews [12] asking for a more holistic approach by taking into consideration other production-related aspects.

Most SMEs trying to undergo an early lift towards an industry 4.0 approach face the hurdle of a high initial expenditure with no result certainties [9]. While bigger companies can afford certain strategies such as extensively equipping the shop floor with the necessary technologies to implement a smart-factory approach [2], small manufacturing factories can find it difficult to strategically statue between the early acquisition and development cost and the inaction toll on their business and hence justify a similar approach. This situation begs the question of how to ensure that the required expenditure is in sync with the company's needs and typology of issues.

Contrary to the widespread data-driven approach which starts from gathering data as much as possible through shop-floor sensor coverage, uncorrelated to the business processes and quality issues, and then diagnoses what problems can arise and how to treat them, our work strives for a more end-to-end and holistic and collaborative approach by analyzing business processes and linking them to non-compliance (NC) history to determine the problems which can typically arise in the shop-floor to negatively impact the end-product. Starting from this all-processes collaborative NC analysis, we determine the needs in terms of data coverage, and hence the typology and characteristics of the sensors to be used to bridge the data-flow gap based upon a grid of attributes, leading to an SN minimizing the needed sensing resources while maximizing detection to provide the necessary informative capacity for sensing the defects, which is the necessary first foothold for a ZDM initiative. This paper presents an answer to "how to appropriately design a sensor network for zero defect manufacturing in a high-variety manufacturing environment" by taking into account SMEs' characteristics when aiming toward I4.0.

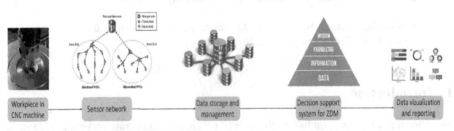

Fig. 1. ZDM overview in industry 4.0

While the approach is thought to be global and can be applied to any type of industry where raw material transformation is at stake to conceive the final product, our paper scope will focus on subtractive manufacturing with the case study being implemented in a metallurgical industry machining SME which production is heavily oriented towards an MTO business model.

The paper will be structured as follows: Sect. 2 will discuss literature work related to the topic at hand, Sect. 3 will present the proposed framework of our approach, Sect. 4 will be dedicated to its implementation steps, and Sect. 5 will describe a real-world case study based on the implementation while Sect. 6 will conclude this paper and introduce future research perspectives.

2 Related Works

Many papers regarding the use of SN, in the manufacturing industry in general and in QC in particular, provide solutions for a specific industry and type of machines or the application of a specific solution. As such, Zheng et al. [15] give a conceptual framework for smart manufacturing and some implementation showcases for industry 4.0 but don't delve into the devising of the sensing strategy if not being globally depending on the typology of considered machines.

Kulinska et al. [6] present a study to reduce non-conformity and improve quality control through a Poka-Yoke sensor-enabled approach. And while the study considers NCs as an input it offers no link between the choice of the solution and the problems at hand and is rather specific to the hydraulic industry. A generic situation stated by the study of Silva et al. [13] regarding the lack of general methodology for AI and machine vision systems in industrial QC.

Additionally, Marques et al. [8], while dealing with IoT-based automatic NC detection in the scope of a metalworking SME use case similar to our work, focuses on architecture and interoperability of the data collection and communication, not covering the initial part regarding the choice of sensors and its link with business-oriented data or NC history.

Govindarajan et al. [4] present an approach to dealing with legacy systems in the manufacturing industry, but the scope of the paper encases the data acquisition phase and how to integrate it into a particular architecture and project. Preuveneers et al. [10] in its overview of I4.0 and the smart factory confirm the lack of context-aware decision making and how it can influence the cost of automation in general and sensors in particular as one of the main pillars of data acquisition. Psarommatis et al. [11] propose a generic methodology to provide a tool for designing a manufacturing system that can enable a ZDM approach using digital twin models that were based on simulations.

Eleftheriadis et al. [1] emphasized the difficulty of implementing ZDM when the manufacturing processes involve complex operations or a large number of components, such products often have a high probability of detective output and hence documentation of best practices has been gathered on the process management side.

On a wider scope, Psarommatis et al. [12] presented a literature review on zero defect manufacturing summarizing the state-of-the-art, highlighting shortcomings and further directions in research regarding ZDM in which they concluded that cost-benefit comparative analysis is not evident when it came to implementing it, especially for the early technological expenditure. The paper also stated that certain industries are under-researched in the literature, among which we find the metal industry and complex 3D parts since collecting defect data and training algorithms on well-defined NCs can be challenging.

Similarly, Galetto et al. [3] show the difficulty of predicting defects and costs for quality inspection in low-volume productions due to multi-level uncertainty and developed an approach targeting the inspection level to accurately analyze and compare different inspection strategies.

Compared to the cited papers, our work suggests an approach in which we aim to address the choice of a sensor network for ZDM by starting from shopfloor NCs, paving the way for a cost-effective and reliable early industry 4.0 uplift regarding the IoT-based monitoring choice.

3 Proposed Framework

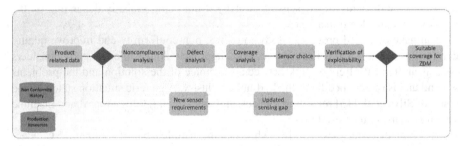

Fig. 2. The approach's general framework

3.1 Overview

An overview of our approach can be seen in (Fig. 2) as a framework in which the input will be all the data related to defects. From in-process product control by machine operators on the shopfloor to process monitoring by the quality inspector through final control checks reports with laser precision machines. The expected output will be an accurately designed sensor network to help optimize machine behavior, ultimately leading to iterative reduction of defects towards a zero-defect manufacturing policy. This overview can be decomposed into several building blocks as follows:

3.2 Non-compliances

A non-compliance [5] is the absence or the inability to meet a planned requirement. It encompasses all the breaches in specifications for a manufactured product. Requirements which can be fixed either by the client or by internal standards such as customer requirements, quality requirements, quality management requirements, Regulatory requirements ...

NCs can be classified by tiers from minor to critical depending on many criteria such as occurrence or impact. Each NC is reported with many other attributes such as the problem, the detection time, the impacted product, details on why/how it happened, in which machine, the cost, and the decision (salvaged/scrapped ...), and so on.

In industry, and especially for manufacturing actors which are bound by demanding and challenging norms such as ISO-9001 and EN-9001 (aerospace and armament sectors), these non-compliances or nonconformities are to be closely monitored from the beginning of the process (client's request for quotation) until the products end of manufacturing life (EOML).

3.3 Defects Analysis

As stated by ISO-9001 [5], a defect is a type of NC where a product (for the manufacturing scope) will fail to meet intended use requirements. This specific type of nonconformity needs to be filtered out from the different quality data sources (ERP, quality reports, quality reviews). This will on one hand ensure that the SN will be able to "sense" the defect through physical measurements and on another hand will be the input specifying the type and specifications of these measurements, which will be the stepping stone for the sensor network choice.

The defect analysis can be tricky to perform and even trickier to link to specific processes or operations in an MTO industrial environment. Notably, the high variety tag implies that there are multiple types of products, specifications, clients, and so on. Each workpiece can be conceptually considered to be virtually a new one, which will introduce several complexity layers in the root-cause analysis.

Another difficulty comes from the low-volume aspect which gives little to no historical data to extract knowledge from in order to build the defect classification.

3.4 Sensor Choice

For the main manufacturing-related data sources that can be monitored in-process, we find the following when thinking of suitable industrial monitoring for SMEs:

- Temperature: can be used to detect surface condition issues, tool-wear, tool chatter, and also inappropriate machining parameters such as speed or advance for cutting (milling, drilling, turning ...). Thermocouples are inserted into cutting material through holes or welding and are unsuited for out-of-lab research since tools are changed hundreds of times a day in the industry, making the monitoring unpractical and costly as well as dangerous for the tool integrity (compliance with ISO/client norms). Contact-less pyrometers with suitable metal wavelengths compatibility and measuring range (150 to 1000 °C) should be privileged, as close as possible to the cutting field.
- Force: it can be used to detect excessive clamping, plastic deformations, collisions, spindle head condition, coaxial misalignment, and tool wear. Laboratory dynamometric table dimensions aren't suited for industrial purposes due to dimension and measuring range, and customized spindle-head force/torque acquirers are costly and

raise the same issue of interchangeability and tool integrity as the one raised by embedded thermocouples. If necessary, can be indirectly measured through spindle electric current.

- Acoustic emissions: can detect surface condition issues, tool chatter, and elastic stress. The sensor placement can however be tricky since it needs to be close to the machining field while also keeping a distance in order to not be flooded by ambient noise and the clogged environment. They can add another layer of redundancy and variability with the vibration sensors since they both convey energy-related data from the material (tool and/or workpiece).
- Vibration: industrial metal-removal machining involves operations (milling, drilling, turning …) where a lot of rotation movements are entangled, from the engine to the bearings to the spindle until the cutting tool, vibration is one of the most important data sources for process and machine monitoring and can detect surface condition issues, poor clamping, bearings condition, imbalances, and tool chatter. Since the physical phenomenon is related to the rotation oscillations, the sensor needs to be positioned as close as possible to the operation field to capture a high ratio of signal to noise.

For vibration, one of the main choice criteria is the measuring range. The sensor's frequency needs to be adapted to the transformation operation speed. At the very least, to be able to capture the fundamental frequency of the operation the sensor has to have a maximum frequency range of:

$$f_{sensor} = \frac{R_{spindle} * n_{teeth}}{60}$$

With f_{sensor} being the maximum frequency the sensor can acquire in Hz, $R_{spindle}$ the maximum spindle rotation speed in rpm, and n_{teeth} being the maximum number of teeth of the machining used tools (1 for drills, generally 3–4 for mills but can go as far as 12 or more).

In general, one preferably needs to have at least 3 or 4 times the maximum calculated frequency in order to be able to also capture the frequency spectrum harmonics which also conveys crucial information about vibratory energy.

4   Implementation

4.1   Overview

The proposed approach in this paper was implemented in Tardy SAS, a subtractive metallurgy industry SME that offers a wide range of services from conceiving to realizing metal workpieces and special purpose machines. As an MTO rank 1 subtractor for different critical sectors such as armament and aerospace, Tardy is faced with growing demand over technically challenging low-volume/high-variety requests. As such, implementing an approach toward zero-defect strategies is of the utmost importance to keep client satisfaction and company reputation in an increasingly competitive market.

In order to do so Tardy needs an efficient uplift towards this I4.0 concept to enhance the reactivity, security, and control over the highly variable production processes while keeping in mind the inherent conditions and resources (old legacy machine, technological investments limitations …).

4.2 Defect Classification

A thorough analysis was conducted to come up with a classification of the main manufacturing deviation causes, both on a quantitative level with QC data, NCs reports,
business process bottlenecks, cost prices, and customers feedback as on a qualitative
level with field surveys of different process stakeholders. As a result, we achieved the
following classification:

- Tool issues: Accounted for roughly 49% of the critical deviations. Using the right
  tool for the right operation can be very challenging for make-to-order production in
  which every workpiece is unique in terms of specifications, machining parameters
  used materials, and so on. This results in a lack of visibility and control of tools
  functioning and lifetime management, leading to cutting tool issues such as wear,
  breakage, heating, and deviation.
- Material deformation: Accounted for 27% of the critical deviations. Since The transformation process involves material removal from raw parts, depending on the draw-
  ings, production process, and operations sequence, the raw will need to be locked
  down at different angles/positions/intensity.

If the clamping is too tight a raw deformation can occur during the cutting with risks
of tool breakage or making the produced piece outside of tolerance limits, which can be
very precise (up to 2×10^{-5} m). If the clamping is not tight enough slight movements
or vibrations throughout the removal process can occur, leading to bad surface quality
such as roughness or altered material coating and deviation in the tool path.

The make-to-order nature results in a lack of control over the clamping dispositions,
which not only can cause tool issues but is also related to machine safety in terms of
spindle, clamping table, and claws.

4.3 Target Data Sources

From the critical deviations classification stated above as well, it was decided to deploy
a sensor network that will be able to monitor vibration in order to tend to the deviations.

The SN must also be able to differentiate between different sets of machine-cutting
parameters, i.e. {tool feed rate, cutting depth, rotation speed} in addition to differentiating
between other parameters such as tool type (shape, material, geometry), angle, and so
on. While there are general guidelines for those parameters such as tool feed rate cutting
advance and rotation speed depending on the material couple workpiece/tool suggested
by raw/tool suppliers, precisely and accurately defining them remains a difficult task in
an MTO paradigm considering the variety and complexity of the processes. It is often
decided by rule of thumb and left for the machine operator to customize on the go
depending on how the machining unfolds.

This lack of fine-tuning leads to many issues by reducing cutting efficiency, the
quality of the final product (finish, roughness …) and its compliance with requirements,
the safety of the machine (especially the spindle head), the consumption rate of new
cutting tools and so on. Optimizing it can lead to greater customer satisfaction, machine
up-time, and fabrication costs.

5 Experimentation

5.1 Overview

From the implementation of the approach that was devised above and the deviations classification that collaboratively resulted from it, an initial SN was deployed and real-world experimental steps were devised to validate it.

5.2 Setup

The used machine was a 3-axis portal-type universal machining CINCINNATI Dart 500 (Fig. 3), with a maximum rotation speed of 6000 rpm.

The global setup of the SN was comprised of 2 piezoelectric ICP 603C01 industrial stainless-steel accelerometers (Fig. 4) with a measurement range of 0–10000 Hz, a sensitivity of 100 mV/g, a temperature working range of −54 to +124 °C and an IP protection index: IP68. The sensors were linked through 2 × 3 m Heavily reinforced waterproof data cables to an industrial data acquisition module (DAQ) (Fig. 5).

Fig. 3. CNC machine   **Fig. 4.** ICP 603C01   **Fig. 5.** KRYPTON DAQ

The data source, i.e., vibration, was chosen for its compatibility with the monitoring of material deformation and tool issues. The sensors were chosen for their cost-effectiveness and characteristics (measuring range, sensitivity, working temperature, and waterproofing).

The DAQ is an industrial Dewesoft KRYPTON with a certified robustness an IP68 index, and a maximum sampling rate of 250 kHz.

In terms of placement, the first sensor was fixed as close to the spindle head as possible (left in Fig. 6) while the second was placed on the table clamping claw (right in Fig. 6). Both positions were secured using a magnetic mounting base and accurately placed to not hinder machining operations while also having minimal distance from the cutting operation area.

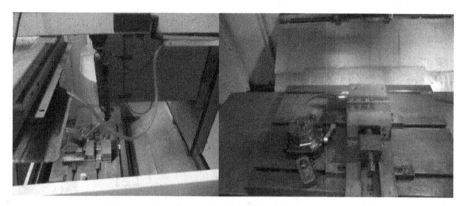

Fig. 6. Sensors placement

5.3 Experiment Protocol

An experimental protocol was devised to validate the sensor characteristics as well as their exploitability. The protocol consisted of different variations of milling and drilling. The varying parameters were feed rate, rotation speed, usage of lubricant or not, and used material.

Milling. The milling operations used two mills. A 16 mm 2-teeth carbide inserts mill (nominal feed of 800 mm/min and a nominal rotation of 3200 rpm). A second 63 mm 3-teeth carbide inserts mill (nominal feed of 390 mm/min and a nominal rotation speed of 1200 rpm).

The chosen variations were combinations of feed rate (140%, 120%, 100%, 75%, 50%), rotation (120%, 100%, 75%, 50%), lubricant (with/without), and material (mild steel/aluminum).

The milling was done on 120 × 90 × 41 mm (X-Y-Z axis) cuboids in two sequences for each raw. The first sequence using the first mill milled 2 grooves in X-axis in respectively 18 and 9 runs of 0.5 and 1 mm depth each until −9 mm, then 3 grooves in Y-axis in respectively 18–9–6 runs each with 0.5–1–1.5 mm depth until −9 mm. The second sequence used the second mill for a first surfacing until −4.5 mm depth in two runs and a second until −9 mm in two runs also.

Drilling. The drilling was made in two sequences using two drills. An 8 mm steel point drill with a nominal feed rate of 150 mm/min and a nominal rotation speed of 1000 rpm. A second 8 mm steel drill with a nominal feed rate of 150 mm/min and a nominal rotation speed of 1250 rpm with the same variations in parameters.

The drilling was made on the milled raws in two sequences. A first sequence of 6 × 4 holes of −1.5 mm each for guiding. Then a second sequence of 6 × 4 holes, each drilled in 10 runs with a logarithmically decreasing depth until reaching the maximum depth of −15 mm.

5.4 Data Pipeline

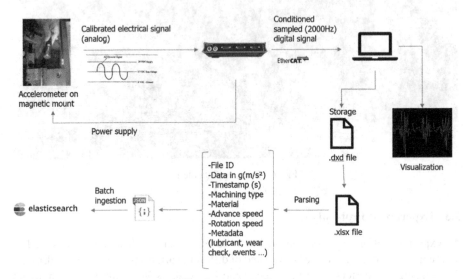

Fig. 7. Data pipeline

As per Fig. 7, the DAQ powers the accelerometers. It receives analog signals, and calibers and converts them (2 kHz sample rate) to a numerical signal. The signal can be visualized on *Dewesoft X* and stored in compressed files in near real-time. After conversion into regular data files (text, CSV, HDF5, JSON, S3 …), parsing will extract suitable data/metadata which is then sent to Elasticsearch (ES) for batch ingestion. Each data point is stored as a JSON document (Fig. 8) in a 3 nodes distributed (1 master, 2 slaves) ES cluster for a total load of 30 Gb storage representing around 220 million ES documents.

```
{
    "_index": "poc1",
    "_type": "_doc",
    "_id": "70H6DnA8FVtNmcp0c_-I",
    "_version": 1,
    "_seq_no": 238111,
    "_primary_term": 1,
    "found": true,
    "_source": {
        "sensor": {
            "name": "acc_table",
            "unit": "g"
        },
        "Date": "2022-02-20T14:15:37.548000",
        "Data": -0.99936405,
        "seq": 110057,
        "meta": {
            "number": "13",
            "fileName": "C:\\Users\\Badreddine\\Desktop\\POC\\Experimentations\\Fraisage\\Acier\\Avec lubrifiant\\13_2022_01_10_135525_1",
            "start": 0,
            "end": 882.8075,
            "date": "2022-01-10T13:55:25",
            "rate": "2000",
            "usinage": "fraisage",
            "matiere": "acier",
            "lubrifiant": "avec lubrifiant",
            "avance": "120%",
            "rotation": "100%",
            "control d'usure": "non"
        }
    }
}]
```

Fig. 8. JSON data-scheme

5.5 Exploitation

An analysis of the time series data indicates that the end-to-end proposed solution offers the ability to sense and monitor the machining operations in terms of precision (up to 10^{-6} g) and variability of data. The SN meets the different requirements in terms of targeted phenomenon by being able to finely represent the different machining sequences (Fig. 9). It also accurately captures the variation in machine parameters (Fig. 10), tool wear impact as well as tool breakage (Fig. 11).

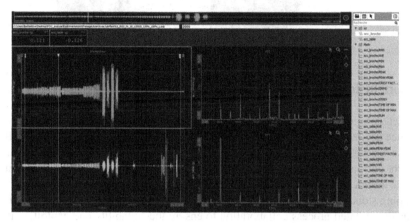

Fig. 9. Table/spindle milling time series

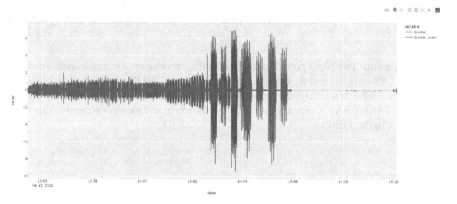

Fig. 10. Milling variations time series

The designed SN also offers good scalability perspectives since more sensors can be added to the DAQ (vertical) and DAQs can be synced to monitor several machines (horizontal). The data pipeline can also be turned from a batch-oriented strategy to a stream-oriented one for near real-time monitoring and reactivity.

Fig. 11. Second mill (left) insert breakage

6 Conclusion

Zero defect manufacturing as an I4.0 concept that aims to provide a holistic approach to reduce deviations presents a lot of challenges to adopting for industrial actors, all the more so for MTO SMEs with high-volume/low-variety aspects and limited resources. As such, our paper offers an approach to tackle this issue through the angle of sensor network design, an essential building block for the IIoT and CPPS systems aiming to be a stepping stone towards ZDM. The methodology presents a design of the SN through all business-related process collaboration to ensure the suitability and exploitability of the acquired data. The different steps of the approach were validated in a real-world case study from both architectural and data angles. For future work, we aim to increase the scope of machines and sensor types to tackle more NC as well as integrate this work into a more holistic approach by including an AI-centered decision support system for ZDM.

Acknowledgment. This paper presents some results that are developed in collaboration between the TARDY SAS company and the University Lumiere Lyon 2, DISP Lab. This research is established under a CIFRE contract (2020/1663). The content of this paper reflects an R&D initiative promoted by TARDY SAS. Responsibility for the information and views expressed in this paper lies entirely with the authors.

References

1. Eleftheriadis, R., Myklebust, O.: A guideline of quality steps towards zero defect manufacturing in industry, September 2016
2. Frank, A.G., Dalenogare, L.S., Ayala, N.F.: Industry 4.0 technologies: Implementation patterns in manufacturing companies. Int. J. Prod. Econ. **210**, 15–26 (2019). https://doi.org/10.1016/j.ijpe.2019.01.004
3. Galetto, M., Verna, E., Genta, G., Franceschini, F.: Uncertainty evaluation in the prediction of defects and costs for quality inspection planning in low-volume productions. Int. J. Adv. Manuf. Technol. **108**(11–12), 3793–3805 (2020). https://doi.org/10.1007/s00170-020-05356-0

4. Govindarajan, N., Ferrer, B.R., Xu, X., Nieto, A., Martinez Lastra, J.L.: An approach for integrating legacy systems in the manufacturing industry. In: 2016 IEEE 14th International Conference on Industrial Informatics (INDIN) (2016). https://doi.org/10.1109/indin.2016.7819247

5. ISO-standard: ISO 9001:2015(en) Quality management systems—requirements (2015). https://www.iso.org/obp/ui/#iso:std:iso:9001:ed-5:v1:en

6. Kulinska, E., Maslowski, D., Dendera-Gruszka, M., Zbyrad, A.: Analysis of solutions dedicated to non-conformity prevention. Eur. Res. Stud. J. **XXIII**(3), 434–445 (2020). https://doi.org/10.35808/ersj/1648

7. Lasi, H., Fettke, P., Kemper, H.-G., Feld, T., Hoffmann, M.: Industry 4.0. Bus. Inf. Syst. Eng. **6**(4), 239–242 (2014). https://doi.org/10.1007/s12599-014-0334-4

8. Marques, M., Cunha, A., Mohammed, W.M., Jardim-Gonçalves, R., Agostinho, C.: IoT-based automatic non-conformity detection: a metalworking SME use case. In: Popplewell, K., Thoben, K.-D., Knothe, T., Poler, R. (eds.) Enterprise Interoperability VIII. PIC, vol. 9, pp. 155–165. Springer, Cham (2019). https://doi.org/10.1007/978-3-030-13693-2_13

9. Masood, T., Sonntag, P.: Industry 4.0: adoption challenges and benefits for SMEs. Comput. Ind. **121**, 103261 (2020). https://doi.org/10.1016/j.compind.2020.103261

10. Preuveneers, D., Ilie-Zudor, E.: The intelligent industry of the future: a survey on emerging trends, research challenges and opportunities in Industry 4.0. J. Amb. Intell. Smart Environ. **9**(3), 287–298 (2017). https://doi.org/10.3233/ais-170432

11. Psarommatis, F.: A generic methodology and a digital twin for zero defect manufacturing (ZDM) performance mapping towards design for ZDM. J. Manuf. Syst. **59**, 507–521 (2021). https://doi.org/10.1016/j.jmsy.2021.03.021

12. Psarommatis, F., May, G., Dreyfus, P.A., Kiritsis, D.: Zero defect manufacturing: state-of-the-art review, shortcomings and future directions in research. Int. J. Prod. Res. **58**(1), 1–17 (2019). https://doi.org/10.1080/00207543.2019.1605228

13. Silva, R.L., Rudek, M., Szejka, A.L., Junior, O.C.: Machine vision systems for industrial quality control inspections. In: Chiabert, P., Bouras, A., Noël, F., Ríos, J. (eds.) PLM 2018. IFIP AICT, vol. 540, pp. 631–641. Springer, Cham (2018). https://doi.org/10.1007/978-3-030-01614-2_58

14. Sundblad, W.: What's at Stake in the Race to Industry 4.0? August 2018. https://www.forbes.com/sites/willemsundbladeurope/2018/07/30/whats-at-stake-in-the-race-to-industry-4-0/

15. Zheng, P., et al.: Smart manufacturing systems for Industry 4.0: conceptual framework, scenarios, and future perspectives. Front. Mech. Eng. **13**(2), 137–150 (2018). https://doi.org/10.1007/s11465-018-0499-5

A Multi-supplier Collaborative Monitoring Framework for Informatics System of Systems

Carlos Gonçalves[1(✉)], Tiago Dias[1,2(✉)], A. Luís Osório[1(✉)],
and Luis M. Camarinha-Matos[3(✉)]

[1] ISEL – Instituto Superior de Engenharia de Lisboa, IPL – Instituto Politécnico de Lisboa, and POLITEC&ID, Lisbon, Portugal
{carlos.goncalves,tiago.dias}@isel.pt, lo@isel.ipl.pt
[2] INESC-ID – Instituto de Engenharia de Sistemas e Computadores - Investigação e Desenvolvimento, Lisbon, Portugal
[3] School of Science and Technology, UNINOVA-CTS, NOVA University of Lisbon, Caparica, Portugal
cam@uninova.pt

Abstract. Managing interdependent cooperating informatics systems from multiple suppliers is a complex and challenging endeavor. Due to the lack of complete open standards, informatics systems from different suppliers are developed using incompatible protocols and programmatic interfaces (API). Often, incompatibilities also exist for informatics systems developed by the same supplier. Nevertheless, organizations must be able to monitor the systems that compose their Information Technology (IT) landscape transparently and independently of each system's supplier. This paper discusses a collaborative networks strategy associated with adopting the Informatics System of Systems (ISoS) framework for coordinated monitoring and support afforded by different supplying responsibilities. We argue that the adopted model simplifies the integration required by the digital, and makes efficient the collaboration among technology and service suppliers in supporting products' life cycle maintenance and evolution. Accordingly, we discuss the implementation of the proposed model in the HORUS project, which is motivated by the need to rethink a fuelling post-payment model of a petroleum company.

Keywords: Distributed monitorization · Systems integration · Collaborative networks · Distributed systems

1 Introduction

Organizations adopting informatics systems from different suppliers face several difficulties when managing integrated solutions. Although contemporary Information Technology (IT) systems are expected to incorporate informatics systems from multiple suppliers, each system exhibits its protocols and programming interfaces (API), often proprietary. Moreover, empirical evidence shows practices where tight collaboration

L. M. Camarinha-Matos et al. (Eds.): PRO-VE 2022, IFIP AICT 662, pp. 44–53, 2022.
https://doi.org/10.1007/978-3-031-14844-6_4

with suppliers leads to tailored solutions with fuzzy responsibility borders. The statement of a representative executive officer of Hitachi [17] - "... *rather than delivering systems ..., what is needed is to hone solutions in partnership with customers ...*" - is a paradigmatic offering of a tailored approach. Such customized diversity of systems makes it very difficult and expensive to replace existing monolithic and proprietary solutions with new or evolved systems showing equivalent capabilities from a competing supplier.

Furthermore, many of those monolithic proprietary systems are accountable for critical business processes that depend on computation services that rely on heterogeneous and interdependent complex systems. System elements need to be smarter and more cooperative in coping with the required reliability and resilience of the underlying technology. Approaches may range from a simple verification if a sub-system is available, e.g., reachable by a ping command, or a more complex inspection to infer performance metrics to check if technology elements are within a predefined set or ranges of values. Therefore, monitoring the health of specific technology elements that compose an organization's informatics systems landscape is challenging and of utmost importance for the reliability of the implemented services.

This paper presents and discusses a collaborative strategy for monitoring elements of informatics systems in a gas-fueling service area. The research problem relies on coordinating partial responsibilities when supplied by organizations with different processes and technology cultures. Our approach considers a collaborative strategy, challenging the participation of competing stakeholders collaboratively managing service failures and interdependencies. The proposed model also challenges the participation of the IT of the supporting stakeholder, since different systems on the provider's IT landscape need to interact with service elements of the informatics landscape of the fueling area. A simple example is the failure of a video camera on the responsibility of the Closed-Circuit Television (CCTV) maintainer company that compromises the vehicle identification service of the HORUS informatics system under the responsability of another company.

We validate the adoption of the Informatics System of Systems (ISoS) framework [11] as a strategy to move towards a Model-Driven Open Systems Engineering (MDEOS) vision and contribute to an open competitive technology market philosophy. The collaborative monitoring framework monitors services under the responsibility of different suppliers in the context of the HORUS research project [13]. The suggested strategy aims to support technology independence for the solution's owner and offers a basis for the recent trends on technology sovereignty [2] since the proposed approach reduces technology dependencies [11].

The remaining paper is organized as follows. Section 2 briefly presents the most prominent related research, the ISoS framework, and the HORUS project. Section 3 discusses the adoption of the ISoS framework to support the collaborative monitoring of the systems composing the HORUS project. Finally, Sect. 4 presents the conclusions and discusses future work.

2 Background

Monitoring is a long-discussed topic with contributions from complementary research perspectives ranging from technology to business. When observed from the computer distributed systems area, the research is more concerned with development issues, *"Monitoring supports the debugging, testing, and performance evaluation of computer programs"* [16]. Conversely, the communication networks have for long contributed centered on networks reliability based on Simple Network Management Protocol (SNMP) and Network Management Stations (NMS) systems *"...the SNMP has two types of entities: managers and agents. Managers work in Network Management Stations and receive messages and traps from SNMP agents..."* [19]. Regardless of the approach, monitoring is gaining added attention with the evolving digital transition and the risks associated with the increasing diversity of technology artifacts that participate in the complex growth of the web of interdependencies. Moreover, the technology artifacts, being them communication infrastructure elements, cyber-physical systems, or software entities running on a cloud-based execution environment, public, private or hybrid, are critical for the proper support of people and businesses. This section briefly reviews the research work background, with Sect. 2.1 addressing the ISoS framework concepts and Sect. 2.2 revisiting the HORUS project.

2.1 The ISoS Framework

The ISoS framework [11] proposes a nonintrusive integration model to establish a multi-supplier or multi-vendor technology landscape to reduce the vendor lock-in risks, and ultimately be an enabler for technology sovereignty. The ISoS framework is based on three core modeling elements: ISystem, CES, and Service. The ISoS abstraction models the informatics landscape of an organization as a composite of one or more ISystems. An ISystem comprises one or more CES, whereas a CES consists of one or more Services. ISoS elements model the technology artifacts through a set of properties, e.g., name, version, supplier, or description. In the case of a Service, the modeling element instance has associated the metadata required for a peer *Service* to access the implemented functionalities. Figure 1 depicts the primary elements that make an organization ISoS enabled, using the SysML block syntax [6].

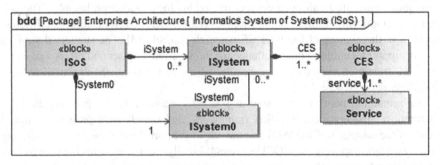

Fig. 1. The simplified SysML block definition diagram of the ISoS model

The ISoS model considers a meta-*element* with management or coordination roles at the ISoS, ISystem, and CES levels, respectively, $ISystem_0$, CES_0, and $Service_0$.

The initial reference implementation of the ISoS framework is based on the Java ecosystem. The proof-of-concept implementation further relies on the open-source Apache Zookeeper [7] to ensure that the ISoS metadata stored by $ISystem_0$ shows higher availability to the systems and services that compose the informatics landscape of an organization. A primary role of the $ISystem_0$ is to act as a directory service managing the metadata of the ISoS elements that exist within an organization, which we refer to as the Organization's computing-related technology artifacts (or Organization's information system). Accordingly, to be ISoS-enabled, an organization needs to instantiate, at least, the meta-$ISystem$, i.e., needs to hold running an instance of the $ISystem_0$, which has the unique role of managing the ISoS technology landscape. The ISoS framework model details are provided in [5].

2.2 The HORUS Project

The HORUS project was motivated by a real industry problem: how to improve the user experience in refueling vehicles by removing the (manual) pre-payment authorization procedure. Before HORUS, authorization had to be granted by the operator of the refueling area before a user could start to refuel the vehicle. This authorization typically involved manually checking an event list of vehicles with pending payments. Such lists used to be paper-based and very difficult to maintain and update with the aggregated information from all the refueling areas. Thus, the refueling areas without an automatic control of payments typically chose to operate in a pre-payment operation mode, demanding that the user had to pay before refueling.

The payment control with HORUS has simplified the refueling process. When a vehicle enters a refueling area, an image of the vehicle license plate is obtained and identified to produce a hash of its license plate. When the user removes the nozzle to fill the vehicle's tank, the payment console system presents a message to the operator to warn him about any pending payments for that vehicle. If there are pending payments, the operator may choose not authorize the refueling. Suppose a vehicle leaves the refueling area without paying. In that case, the hash of its license number is inserted in an events list stored by a persistence service available to all the refueling areas. The next time such a vehicle with a pending payment tries to refuel, the operator is shown a message to warn him about the faulty situation. In that case, the driver has to follow the pre-payment procedure until the payment issue is solved.

Although the rationale of the HORUS project is quite simple, its implementation involves heterogeneous systems implemented by different suppliers. Thus, the HORUS is an informatics system that uses other informatics systems, like the Point of Sale (POS) or the Closed-Circuit Television (CCTV) system responsible for the video cameras used by the License Plate Recognition (LPR) service used to identify the vehicles. The fact that the fueling network has its CCTV system under the responsibility of different companies introduces an added complexity to the management of monitoring events.

The above scenario clearly shows that the informatics systems landscape of a fuelling forecourt can be viewed as a network of different informatics and cyberphysical systems, each one with diverse responsibilities and that need to cooperate. Thus, it is imperative to provide a monitoring strategy based on anticipating reactions to any problem that might affect the several components of the HORUS that each service provider is responsible for.

The strategic goal is to manage interdependent monitoring and maintenance responsibilities in a collaborative network context. By collaborative monitoring and maintenance, we mean each participating stakeholder shall be aware of another participating stakeholder's failure and maintenance actions. In other words, from our previous research, it means that any informatics system has a tandem system we suffix by '-M' specialized to make effective monitoring and support maintenance processes [12].

3   The HORUS Project Case Study

Figure 2 shows the different elements composing the informatics landscape of a forecourt gas station modeled by adopting the ISoS framework. Besides the $ISystem_0$, we can see the "HORUS" and the "CCTV" informatics systems, as well as the corresponding monitoring sub-systems, denoted by the labels "HORUS-M" and "CCTC-M", the tandem informatics system as discussed above.

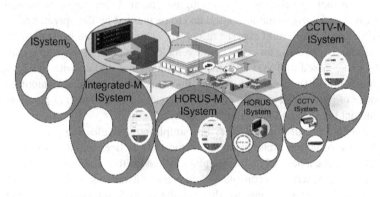

Fig. 2. Elements involved in the HORUS project for a gas station forecourt

Different suppliers support the maintenance and evolution of the HORUS and the CCTV systems. Following the adopted model, monitoring and maintenance management must coordinate with supplier's informatics infrastructure. Thus, the integrated monitoring view of the forecourt gas station, denoted by the "Integrated-M" system, must work collaboratively with all the internal informatics and also with those of the suppliers. The remaining sections discuss how the ISoS framework is adopted to support the collaboration among the diverse technology elements, focusing on monitoring the participating related informatics systems. Section 3.1 discusses alternatives for supporting the monitoring systems, and Sect. 3.2 details the usage of the ISoS framework to support the collaboration between the elements of a forecourt and the collaborative network of support and maintenance providers.

3.1   Monitoring Systems

Monitoring plays a crucial role in an organization's multi-provider informatics technology landscape. Because an informatics technology landscape holds different types of systems and system elements, one may consider choosing alternative monitoring systems, each one better fitting a class of available parts. For example, we might consider a monitoring system to handle the IoT devices and another for monitoring the health of existing servers. However, this approach can quickly become infeasible if the Organization's amount and type of elements increase.

Monitoring solutions like ICinga [10], Nagios [1], and, more recently, OpenNMS [4], are systems aimed at monitoring the health of network elements such as routers and switches. The main idea behind these systems is that every network equipment has associated a Management Information Base (MIB), which can be seen as a modeling element representing the properties of the technology elements within a network of computers. The concept of a MIB is often associated with the Simple Network Management Protocol (SNMP) used by the monitoring systems to obtain the status/properties of the elements under monitoring. Other solutions like Zabbix [9] and Prometheus [18] target the monitoring of informatics systems, e.g., to verify if a system is responding or if some system metrics are within predefined values.

An hypothesis is to generalize SNMP-based monitoring to informatics systems, such as the case of applying it to a campus infrastructure [19] or enterprise servers [8]. If adopting SNMP, the selection of OpenNMS to monitor the state of any element (hardware or software) that composes the informatics landscape of an organization requires that any computational service implements an SNMP agent and the corresponding MIB interface. The approach taken in the HORUS project is to develop agents for the elements that initially were not SNMP enabled and use the OpenNMS solution to monitor both computational and cyberphysical elements involved in a forecourt gas station. For example, in the case of the cameras shared with the CCTV system, one agent was developed to read the state of the cameras using the Open Network Video Interface Forum (ONVIF) [14] and export that state information using a custom MIB. The adopted approach makes it possible to monitor legacy network of new informatics systems elements following a unified approach based on the SNMP protocol. While latencies introduced by the monitoring are not critical in the HORUS system, other application domains may require further validations, e.g., performance dimension as discussed in [8].

3.2   Collaborative Monitoring Using the ISoS Framework

A characteristic feature of the ISoS framework is its independence from any specific technological solution. ISoS framework offers simple mechanisms for service elements within an organization, hardware or software, to publish their associated metadata to the $ISystem_0$. The metadata supports the discovery of Service elements through the path $ISystem/CES/Service$ elements. Thus, when a service S_A from system A needs to use the service S_B from system B, it just needs to contact the $ISystem_0$ and issue a lookup operation to obtain the metadata of service S_B.

The metadata registered in the $ISystem_0$ is composed of a set of XML documents, where there is an XML document associated to each $ISystem$, CES, and $Service$. Using the ISoS framework metadata is possible to have different services from distinct suppliers with additional responsibilities working together in a collaborative network.

The collaboration is possible because services from collaborative organizations or suppliers can mutually find each other and interoperate based on the $ISystem_0$ canonical entry point and ISoS metadata facilities.

Additionally, the metadata can support a user interface capable of browsing organization elements and providing a unified view and introspection mechanisms. An example is the Service SerUI included in the ISoS $ISystem_0$ [5], which allows an administrator to browse all the System, CES, and Service elements that exist in the informatics system of an ISoS enabled Organization. The above mentioned Service SerUI is a simple service that collects and shows an organization's existing elements (System, CES, and Service). However, using the same logic, it is possible to implement a new system responsible for monitoring virtually all the elements within the Organization.

Since in an ISoS-enabled organization, informatics systems publish their metadata, it is possible to offer a dashboard showing the status of informatics systems. Figure 3 illustrates an interface view of a Synoptic of Things (SoT) framework [15, 16] showing the global state of the informatics systems in a forecourt gas station adopting the HORUS informatics system. The SoT framework uses the concept of widgets to support the interaction with the end-user. We call Widgets-IoT to such widgets, which are abstractions of hardware or software elements, e.g., a video camera device or a license plate recognition software. A Widget-IoT comprises common properties such as size, color or image. Also, specializations of Widget-IoT might contain properties for accessing a cyber-physical device. A Widget-IoT is a standard Web Component [3] making it possible to use Widgets-IoT in other contexts than the SoT framework.

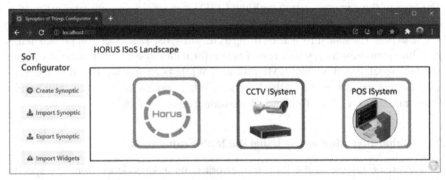

Fig. 3. Synoptic of Things for a gas station forecourt that is using the HORUS project (Color figure online)

Building the dashboard presented in Fig. 3 is a quite straightforward procedure: i) Access the ISoS framework of the Organization through the well-known access point at the default port 2058; ii) Issue a lookup request to find the metadata of the existing monitoring systems; iii) For each monitoring system, display the corresponding icon and a colored frame denoting the state of the system, for example, green, yellow, and red, respectively, corresponding to the states OK, Warning, or Problem. For example, using this syntax, the analysis of Fig. 3 reveals that the HORUS and POS systems are operational, but there is a problem with the CCTV system. Then, by inspecting the metadata associated with the CCTV system and the corresponding monitoring system, denoted as "CCTC-M" in Fig. 2, it is possible to access a second-level synoptic for the elements that compose the CCTV system. From the analysis of this second synoptic, presented in Fig. 4, and once more using the same syntax for the color of the frames, we can see a problem with a particular camera. In this case, the camera with the label "AXIS P137" is the problematic element. Once resolved the problem, the states of the camera and the system CCTV will become OK.

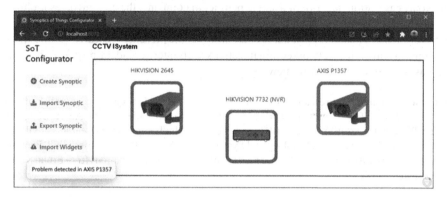

Fig. 4. Synoptic for the CCTV system

Internally, each monitoring system on our research uses OpenNMS to collect data from the elements under monitoring using the SNMP protocol. The SoT framework uses the OpenNMS API to obtain the status of the service elements under monitoring. Also, using the OpenNMS API it is possible to send notifications to the users. For example, send an email to a system administrator when the state of a given element is critical. Another advantage of using the OpenNMS API, or the API of another monitoring system, is that a synoptic does not need to understand the protocols of the different elements under monitoring. It just needs to understand the API of the various monitoring systems. This approach makes possible a distributed monitoring, collaborative and scalable from the point of view of an organization. It can be further extended to monitor the state of elements in different organizations using a single synoptic if all the organizations adopt the ISoS framework (i.e., are ISoS enabled).

4   Conclusions and Further Research

This paper discusses the collaborative monitoring of informatics systems supported by the ISoS framework, which models an open organization's integrated computing technology landscape. The Java ecosystem adopting the Apache Zookeeper and other opensource projects supports validating the ISoS framework, and the approach followed in the HORUS project. Beyond the $ISystem_0$ as a core technological element for any ISoS enabled organizations, we present and discuss the usage of the metadata stored within the ISoS framework to make possible the cooperation between monitoring systems that may exist within the informatics landscape of organizations participating in a collaborative network.

We further discuss the feasibility and advantages of using the ISoS metadata to feed a Synoptic of Things, extending the traditional concept of industrial synoptics of SCADA systems to show the status of the elements that exist in an organization's informatics technology landscape.

Although the case study presented in this work focused on the elements that exist in a forecourt gas station network of a single petroleum company, the case involves multiple supplying companies, each with interdependent responsibilities concerning their supported systems. Thus, it is reasonable to assume that the presented research results apply to scenarios involving networked organizations with interdependent responsibilities as long as they adopt the ISoS framework.

Acknowledgments. The research conducted by GIATSI/ISEL/IPL develops in collaboration with the SOCOLNET scientific network and its ARCON-ACM initiative. The ANSR/SINCRO, BP/HORUS, and FORDESI/SITL-IoT-PT-2020 projects partially support the research. Partial support also from the Center of Technology and Systems – UNINOVA, the Portuguese FCT Foundation (project UIDB/00066/2020). We also recognize the excellent contributions from Bruno Serras as a research fellow.

References

1. Barth, W.: Nagios: System and Network Monitoring, 2nd edn. No Starch Press, San Francisco (2008). ISBN 1593271794
2. Crespi, F., Caravella, S., Menghini, M., Salvatori, C.: European technological sovereignty: an emerging framework for policy strategy. Intereconomics **56**(6), 348–354 (2021). https://doi.org/10.1007/s10272-021-1013-6
3. Farrell, B.: Web Components in Action. Manning Publications, Shelter Island (2019). ISBN 9781617295775
4. Furman, L., Zufelde, K.: Network management: open source solutions to proprietary problems (2000). https://www.semanticscholar.org/paper/Network-Management-%3A-Open-Source-Solutions-to-Furman-Zufelde/7c9f70e43dfbf4f829a5ad96fec7108172e6b98d
5. Gonçalves, C., Osório, A.L., Camarinha-Matos, L.M., Dias, T., Tavares, J.: A collaborative cyber-physical microservices platform – the SITL-IoT case. In: Camarinha-Matos, L.M., Boucher, X., Afsarmanesh, H. (eds.) PRO-VE 2021. IAICT, vol. 629, pp. 411–420. Springer, Cham (2021). https://doi.org/10.1007/978-3-030-85969-5_38
6. Hause, M., et al.: The SysML modelling language. In: Fifteenth European Systems Engineering Conference, vol. 9, pp. 1–12 (2006)
7. Hunt, P., Konar, M., Junqueira, F.P., Reed, B.: ZooKeeper: wait-free coordination for internet-scale systems. In: Proceedings of the 2010 USENIX Conference on USENIX Annual Technical Conference. USENIX Association (2010)
8. Kaushik, A.: Use of open source technologies for enterprise server monitoring using SNMP. Int. J. Comput. Sci. Eng. **2**, 10 (2010)
9. Macura, L., Rozhon, J., Lin, J.C.-W.: Employing monitoring system to analyze incidents in computer network. In: Gottvald, J., Praus, P. (eds.) Proceedings of the 3rd Czech-China Scientific Conference 2017, Chap. 7. IntechOpen, Rijeka (2017). https://doi.org/10.5772/intechopen.71102

10. Maulana, H., Al-Khowarizmi: Analyze and designing low-cost network monitoring system using ICinga and Raspberry Pi. IOP Conf. Ser. Earth Environ. Sci. **704**(1), 012038 (2021). https://doi.org/10.1088/1755-1315/704/1/012038
11. Osório, A.L., Belloum, A., Afsarmanesh, H., Camarinha-Matos, L.M.: Agnostic informatics system of systems: the open ISoS services framework. In: Camarinha-Matos, L.M., Afsarmanesh, H., Fornasiero, R. (eds.) PRO-VE 2017. IAICT, vol. 506, pp. 407–420. Springer, Cham (2017). https://doi.org/10.1007/978-3-319-65151-4_37
12. Osório, A.L., Camarinha-Matos, L.M., Afsarmanesh, H., Belloum, A.: Liability in collaborative maintenance of critical system of systems. In: Camarinha-Matos, L.M., Afsarmanesh, H., Ortiz, A. (eds.) PRO-VE 2020. IAICT, vol. 598, pp. 191–202. Springer, Cham (2020). https://doi.org/10.1007/978-3-030-62412-5_16
13. Osório, A.L.F.G.: Collaborative networks as open Informatics System of Systems (ISoS). Ph.D. thesis, Faculty of Science, Informatics Institute, University of Amsterdam, December 2020. https://hdl.handle.net/11245.1/233a4628-282e-4650-9ffb-b3d7b3187e2a
14. Senst, T., Patzold, M., Evangelio, R.H., Eiselein, V., Keller, I., Sikora, T.: On building decentralized wide-area surveillance networks based on ONVIF. In: 2011 8th IEEE International Conference on Advanced Video and Signal Based Surveillance (AVSS). IEEE, August 2011. https://doi.org/10.1109/avss.2011.6027365
15. Serras, B., Gonçalves, C., Dias, T., Osório, A.L.: Synoptics of Things (SoT): an open framework for the supervision of IoT devices. In: 5th International Young Engineers Forum on Electrical and Computer Engineering. IEEE Xplore Digital Library (2021). https://doi.org/10.1109/YEF-ECE52297.2021.9505145
16. Serras, B., Gonçalves, C., Dias, T., Osório, A.L.: Extending the Synoptics of Things (SoT) framework to manage ISoS technology landscapes. In: 6th International Young Engineers Forum on Electrical and Computer Engineering. IEEE Xplore Digital Library (2022, to appear)
17. Shiotsuka, K.: Combining ot, it, and products to help realize Society 5.0, May 2022. https://www.hitachi.com/rev/archive/2018/r2018_05/message/index.html
18. Sukhija, N., Bautista, E.: Towards a framework for monitoring and analyzing high performance computing environments using kubernetes and prometheus. In: 2019 IEEE Smart-World, Ubiquitous Intelligence & Computing, Advanced & Trusted Computing, Scalable Computing & Communications, Cloud & Big Data Computing, Internet of People and Smart City Innovation (SmartWorld/SCALCOM/UIC/ATC/CBDCom/IOP/SCI). IEEE, August 2019. https://doi.org/10.1109/smartworld-uic-atc-scalcom-iop-sci.2019.00087
19. Villalobos, R.I.E., Triana, E.A., Ceballos, H.Z., Triviño, J.E.O.: Design and implementation of network monitoring system for campus infrastructure using software agents. Ingenierá e Investigación **42**(1), e87564 (2021). https://doi.org/10.15446/ing.investig.v42n1.87564

Digital Twins in Industry

A Photorealistic Digital Twin for a Tank Truck Washing Robotic System

Luís Vicente[1], Pedro Lomelino[1], Fernando Carreira[1,3], Francisco M. Campos[1], Mário J. G. C. Mendes[1,2(✉)], and J. M. F. Calado[1,3]

[1] ISEL – Instituto Superior de Engenharia de Lisboa, Instituto Politécnico de Lisboa, 1959-007 Lisbon, Portugal
{a42292,a43640}@alunos.isel.pt, {fernando.carreira, francisco.campos,mario.mendes,joao.calado}@isel.pt
[2] CENTEC – Centre for Marine Technology and Ocean Engineering, Lisbon, Portugal
[3] LAETA/IDMEC – Instituto de Engenharia Mecânica, Lisbon, Portugal

Abstract. In the current industrial context, the adoption of a digital twin (DT) has proven to be an appropriate tool to optimize the entire lifecycle of a system. This vision includes the adoption of a DT, in the collaborative network of organizations from the virtual modeling of a system, through its control, operation, namely simulation, implementation, and monitoring/supervision. To take full advantage of DTs, it is essential that they are as photorealistic as possible, allowing all kinds of simulations to be carried out, for example testing vision algorithms. In this context, this paper presents the development of a DT that is integrated as a collaborative system to monitor all phases of the life cycle of a robot destined to wash tank truck. The Unreal Engine 4 software was used to develop a DT and the communication architecture was designed, using the standard OPC UA protocol.

Keywords: Digital twin · Robotic simulation · Factories of the future · Unreal Engine 4 · Tank truck washing

1 Introduction

The fourth industrial revolution (Industry 4.0) introduced several changes in manufacturing processes and service provision, driven by the need for their digitalization. Today's business competitiveness requires manufacturers and service providers to be able to respond and adapt to the increasingly diverse requirements of customers in ever shorter periods of time, demanding the adoption of collaborative networks [1]. One way to achieve this goal is to implement the smart factory concept, introduced by Industry 4.0 [2]. Cyber-physical systems (CPS) and digital twins (DT) are two important technologies for the digital transformation in organizations. Both concepts seek to connect the physical with the cybernetic world. However, while CPSs focus on the interaction between the two worlds, DTs provide a complete digital description of the physical world/process. A DT can be considered a digital representation of a physical system [3].

L. M. Camarinha-Matos et al. (Eds.): PRO-VE 2022, IFIP AICT 662, pp. 57–66, 2022.
https://doi.org/10.1007/978-3-031-14844-6_5

With the recent advances in computing technologies, the DT concept has evolved into a safe virtual space for simulation, testing and validation [4]. From this perspective, a solution for the creation of simulation models is to construct a DT that mirrors and observes the behavior of the real world, allowing to achieve a virtual commissioning (VC) scenario [5, 6]. VC is typically viewed as a hardware-in-the-loop (HiL) configuration that is used before the actual (physical) commissioning of an industrial device, for the purpose of testing and verifying the control logic. In HiL simulation, the real controller is connected to a DT that replicates the physical system [7].

In recent years, the DT concept has evolved quickly and been widely used. The authentic representation of physical systems, has advantages in several areas such as: manufacturing [5], health care [8], smart cities [9] and robotics [10, 11]. DT in robotics are embedded throughout their lifecycle, taking a key role in VC in order to test their design and improve control algorithms for robots at the development stage [10]. With DTs it is possible to test different scenarios to improve performance related to cost and time. In [11], the authors proposed a DT to monitor the collaborative work of various robots.

The implementation of a DT in an organization's communication network allows achieving a digital transformation towards collaborative manufacturing [6, 12]. In the development of a new system, the use of a DT facilitates the simulation of several scenarios previously related to being physically implemented, allowing the identification of bugs in efficiency systems, i.e. reducing costs related with tests of new processes in physical systems [6, 8, 9].

This paper addresses the DT implementation applied to a tank truck washing process automation, contributing with an effective solution for testing vision algorithms in a photorealistic virtual environment. Currently, tank washing is carried out through rotary jet heads which are manually inserted into the tanks. Motivated by the need to build collaborative, resilient and sustainable systems and meet the concept of factories of the future, this paper focuses on a robotic system to automatically perform the washing task. Specifically, this paper describes the development of a DT to support the entire lifecycle of the robotic system and promote its integration into the organization's collaborative network. One of the features of this system is the use of computer vision to detect the loading port. Given the need to validate computer vision algorithms, we propose a DT based on the Unreal Engine 4 (UE4), which allows rendering photorealistic images captured by virtual cameras.

To guarantee the smart factory concept, it is intended to develop a DT interoperable with the different systems present in organizations. The DTs must have the ability to simulate the changes that may occur in the production/service delivery processes. Several research works have been developed to implement a Service Oriented Architecture (SOA) in which all control, automation and supervision systems are designed as a combination of different services. These architectures allow the functions performed by the robot to be quickly improved and adapted to changes in the industry [10]. For that matter, the Informatics System of Systems (ISoS) architecture was adopted, where the developed DT constitutes a service. The implementation of this architecture allows the DT to communicate with the other services that are part of an organization, ensuring interoperability between all systems [13].

This paper is organized into the following sections: Sect. 2 describes the various stages of the DT development for the robotic system for tank truck washing; Sect. 3 presents the architecture developed for the communication between the DT and the system controller; Sect. 4 presents the tests performed to verify the functioning of the proposed communication architecture, and finally, Sect. 5 presents the work conclusions.

2 Development of a Digital Twin

This work addresses the development of a DT for an automated tank truck washing system. The use of a DT has advantages in the development of the robotic system and in its monitoring during operation. For example, a DT enables testing of control algorithms in parallel with the mechanical design, production and installation phases. Once implemented, the DT may be used to complement the existing supervision system, by providing a realistic visualization of the system in real time.

The choice of the supporting software is an important step in the development of a DT. In the present work, this choice is influenced by the requirement of detecting the loading port through an image processing system. Since image processing is essential for the robotic system operation, special emphasis was placed on the photorealism of the DT. For this reason, it was chosen the Unreal Engine 4 (UE4) software, from Epic Games®, for the virtual environment development, due to the sophisticated methods that it provides for rendering realistic images. The use of a game engine allows testing the system under varying lighting, by changing weather settings or artificial lighting, which is essential for validating a computer vision system. This software, which was initially developed for the creation of first-person shooter (FPS) games, has been successfully used in a wide variety of applications, including robotics [14, 15]. Additionally, UE4 is free to use, therefore it does not increase the robotic system cost.

According to Lei, et al. [16], the development of a DT can be divided into the construction of three models: 3D model, kinematic model and rules model. In the first stage, a three-dimensional model of the environment is built, including the robotic system and the tank truck. Next, a kinematic model of the system is defined, by establishing the mechanism constraints. The final stage defines the rules for interaction with the DT and the data exchanged between the controller and the DT. Next, the application of these stages in the DT development on the proposed robotic system is detailed.

The first stage in DT development is 3D modeling. To obtain a realistic DT, the 3D shapes, colors and textures used in the model must closely resemble those of the real world. Such models can be created with a computer aided design (CAD) software or by digitizing the physical system with 3D scanners. Since the proposed robotic system is still under development, the second approach was not viable and, thus, the 3D model was developed in the CAD software Solidworks®.

The DT model essentially includes a gantry robot, a jet head, and a tank truck, whose models were obtained from various sources. The gantry robot design was carried out through a specialized software from LUCAS [17], which also provided 3D models of that equipment (Fig. 1a). The jet head was selected from the catalogue of the Alfa Laval® manufacturer [18], which also provides corresponding 3D models (gantry robot end effector depicted in Fig. 1a). The tank truck model (Fig. 1b) was selected from the GRABCAD® repository [19].

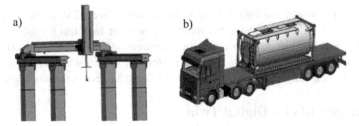

Fig. 1. 3D model: a) tank truck washing robotic system; b) tank truck.

Fig. 2. DT realistic environment developed in UE4.

Besides the aforementioned items, the virtual environment was enriched with a realistic model of the scenario where the washing operation takes place, by resorting to objects from the UE4 marketplace [20]. The complete virtual environment is shown in Fig. 2.

The 3D model described above represents the appearance of a static system. However, to develop a DT it is essential to set the kinematic properties that are relevant to the simulation. In the present work, the robot is described by a cartesian kinematic configuration, which yields linear relations. In this case, to impose the kinematic constraints on the objects of the system, it is necessary to: i) establish the rigid coupling among objects that are fixed together, ii) allow the translation movement of the x, y, and z axis and iii) establish the hierarchy between the axes. For this purpose, the objects in UE4 were organized in a hierarchical tree that defines the kinematic order, as usual in 3D modeling programs.

The purpose of the rules model is to define the interaction protocol with the DT and to identify the data exchanged between the virtual world and the controller. Within this interaction, the role of the controller is to send action commands in the form of x (longitudinal movement), y (transverse movement) and z (vertical movement) values that describe the movement of each robot axis.

The action commands should depend on visual feedback from the virtual world. For this purpose, a "Fusion Camera Actor" element was also added to the model (element

A depicted in Fig. 3a). This element simulates a virtual camera and enables capturing images in the DT, as illustrated in Fig. 3b. The data sent from the virtual model to the controller consists of image data, which is later processed by image processing algorithms that compute the position targets for the gantry.

 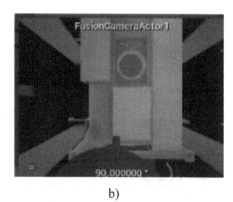

a)   b)

Fig. 3. Virtual camera in UE4: a) camera position and orientation; b) captured image.

3   System Architecture

The proposed robotic system for tank truck washing is controlled by a programmable logical controller (PLC) connected to a computer, running a software platform for supervision, control and a data acquisition (SCADA).

In the present work, an HiL architecture is configured with the DT controlled by the same PLC that control the real system. This aims to validate the logical control developed and the SCADA system functionalities. Furthermore, this architecture allows to use the DT in a hybrid commissioning, with the PLC connection to the real system, simultaneously.

As mentioned earlier, the robotic system DT was created with UE4. However, this software is not geared towards automation and the communication with a PLC is not provided as standard. For this reason, a custom designed communication architecture was required. Matlab® was used in the communication between the PLC and the DT due to need of its image processing capabilities, required by the current task, and to achieve future project goals that build on artificial intelligence (AI) algorithms. Taking this into account, Matlab® was selected to develop image processing algorithms. This allowed greater flexibility in choosing the most appropriate techniques from a wide range of classic and advanced tools available in the Matlab® computer vision toolboxes. From the communication architecture point of view, this choice implies that images recorded in the DT must be sent to Matlab® and that targets found by the detection algorithm must be sent back to the DT. To support this communication a custom library, Matlab_Unreal Interface, was developed, building on the existing UnrealCV library [21]. UnrealCV is a set of python functions developed to support computer vision research by providing an interface to UE4 synthetic worlds. Matlab_Unreal Interface extends this library with Matlab® functions that port the same functionalities to the Matlab® environment. In addition to exchanging image data, the library features include reading and setting the position of objects in the virtual environment.

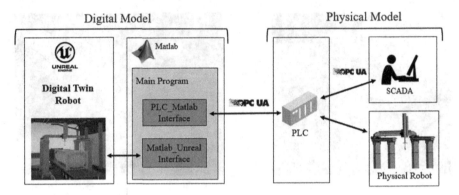

Fig. 4. Communication architecture

Once a communication interface has been established between Matlab® and UE4, it can be used to mediate communication between the PLC and UE4. The OPC UA is the preferred PLC communication protocol, due to its high reliability, cross communication and uniformity of access [16]. This protocol is based on a client/server model, where the OPC UA server defines the address space and provides an access interface, and the OPC UA client implements the data acquisition that references that interface [11]. In the proposed communication architecture, shown in Fig. 4, the PLC performs the role of the OPC UA server while the other OPC UA nodes are clients. This is the case of Matlab®, which mediates the communication between the PLC and UE4. To achieve this functionality, another library was created, called PLC_Matlab interface. This library, based on the python library freeopcua [22], is a set of functions that enables Matlab® to perform the OPC UA client role. In the proposed architecture, Matlab® is responsible for both the image processing task and communication dispatch. All the operations underlying these tasks are integrated in a Matlab® program, *Main Program* (see Fig. 4), which is executed in parallel with the other agents of the system.

4 Communication Architecture Verification

The developed system was tested according with the control real system specifications. It is considered a controller performed by the PLC CPX-E+CMMT, supplied by FESTO® and programed by the Codesys® software. Notice that the PLC has a server OPC UA, which specification is required in the developed architecture. The robotic tanks washing process was programmed in the PLC, according to the flowchart depicted in Fig. 5. The axes movements allow the validation of the developed DTs models and proposed architecture. The robot moves a virtual camera, coupled to the y axis, to detect the loading

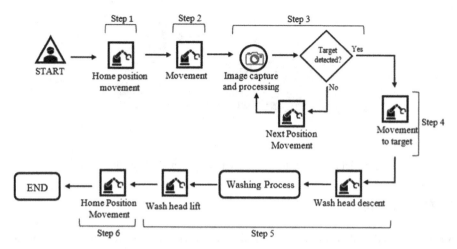

Fig. 5. Flowchart of the robotic system for road tank washing.

port position through the image processing algorithms of captured images. The loading port position is estimated from the relative position to the virtual camera.

According with the flowchart depicted in Fig. 5, after the operator press the "START" bottom in the HMI, the washing cycle begins the following steps:

1. the robot moves to the home position, defining the cycle start position.
2. the y axis moves the jet head and the camera to the vehicle longitudinal axis.
3. the x axis moves the terminal element along the tank until the loading port is detected, through image processing algorithms.
4. both x and y axes are moved to ensure that the terminal element is over the loading port, resorting to image processing.
5. The jet head is introduced inside the tank, carried out the tank washing process for a predefined time and is removed again.
6. The axes are moved to the Home Position, finishing the washing cycle.

The process was executed, and the DT jet head positions were obtained by the Matlab® software.

Figure 6 shows the DT jet head positions throughout the washing cycle, where it is possible to observe the steps executed by the implemented algorithm. Notice that the path does not show step 1, since the robot was already in the home position when the washing cycle was started. Observing the results, the proposed architecture was successfully validated.

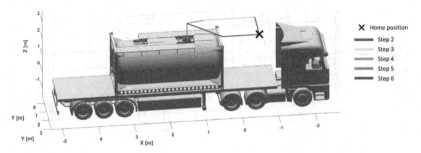

Fig. 6. Jet head trajectory described throughout the operating cycle.

5 Conclusion

A DT is one of the pillars of a digital transformation. This allows to create virtual replicas of physical systems, providing a simulation and supervision environment. The use of a DT makes it possible to configure and test a collaborative system before physical commissioning, to be integrated into the factory concept of the future. This work presented the DT development of a tank truck washing robotic system. The DT was implemented in UE4 in order to achieve a high level of realism. The use of this software allows the development of control algorithms based on image processing. For that purpose, the DT components were modeled in UE4, including a virtual camera to capture images from the environment. It was implemented an architecture to ensure the communication between devices and platforms: DT, PLC, SCADA software and Matlab®, resorting to OPC UA communication protocol. The results have shown that the architecture was successfully implemented, allowing the DT development in many real frameworks that requires a high-level photorealism and advanced computation. The DT will be tested for supervision of a laboratory gantry and is intended to be tested on a gantry in an industrial environment.

Acknowledgments. This work was supported by the project POCI-01-0247-FEDER-039764 under the Program PORTUGAL2020.

References

1. Camarinha-Matos, L.M., Rocha, A.D., Graça, P.: Brief overview of collaborative approaches in sustainable manufacturing. In: Camarinha-Matos, L.M., Boucher, X., Afsarmanesh, H. (eds.) PRO-VE 2021. IFIP AICT, vol. 629, pp. 3–18. Springer, Cham (2021). https://doi.org/10.1007/978-3-030-85969-5_1
2. Karagiannis, D., et al.: OMiLAB: a smart innovation environment for digital engineers. In: Camarinha-Matos, L.M., Afsarmanesh, H., Ortiz, A. (eds.) PRO-VE 2020. IFIP AICT, vol. 598, pp. 273–282. Springer, Cham (2020). https://doi.org/10.1007/978-3-030-62412-5_23
3. Ward, R., Soulatiantork, P., Finneran, S., Hughes, R., Tiwari, A.: Real-time vision-based multiple object tracking of a production process: Industrial digital twin case study. Proc. Inst. Mech. Eng. Part B J. Eng. Manuf. **235**, 1861–1872 (2021). https://doi.org/10.1177/09544054211002464

4. Bilberg, A., Malik, A.A.: Digital twin driven human–robot collaborative assembly. CIRP Ann. **68**, 499–502 (2019). https://doi.org/10.1016/j.cirp.2019.04.011
5. Leng, J., Wang, D., Shen, W., Li, X., Liu, Q., Chen, X.: Digital twins-based smart manufacturing system design in Industry 4.0: a review. J. Manuf. Syst. **60**, 119–137 (2021). https://doi.org/10.1016/j.jmsy.2021.05.011
6. Gavin, C.: Digital Twins Calibrated with Operational Data Drive Efficiency. InTech Magazine (2021)
7. Martins, A., Costelha, H., Neves, C.: Supporting the design, commissioning and supervision of smart factory components through their digital twin. In: 2020 IEEE International Conference on Autonomous Robot Systems and Competitions, ICARSC 2020, pp. 114–119 (2020). https://doi.org/10.1109/ICARSC49921.2020.9096072
8. Rasheed, A., San, O., Kvamsdal, T.: Digital twin: values, challenges and enablers from a modeling perspective. IEEE Access **8**, 21980–22012 (2020). https://doi.org/10.1109/ACCESS.2020.2970143
9. Qi, Q., Tao, F., Zuo, Y., Zhao, D.: Digital twin service towards smart manufacturing. Procedia CIRP. **72**, 237–242 (2018). https://doi.org/10.1016/j.procir.2018.03.103
10. Jhunjhunwala, P., Atmojo, U.D., Vyatkin, V.: Applying Skill-based engineering using OPC-UA in production system with a digital twin. In: 2021 IEEE International Symposium on Industrial Electronics, June 2021. https://doi.org/10.1109/ISIE45552.2021.9576342
11. Zong, X., Luan, Y., Wang, H., Li, S.: A multi-robot monitoring system based on digital twin. Procedia Comput. Sci. **183**, 94–99 (2021). https://doi.org/10.1016/j.procs.2021.02.035
12. Mrabti, N., Gargouri, M.A., Hamani, N., Kermad, L.: Towards a sustainable collaborative distribution Network 4.0 with blockchain involvement. In: Camarinha-Matos, L.M., Boucher, X., Afsarmanesh, H. (eds.) PRO-VE 2021. IFIP AICT, vol. 629, pp. 41–52. Springer, Cham (2021). https://doi.org/10.1007/978-3-030-85969-5_4
13. Vicente, L., et al.: Industrial collaborative robotics platform. In: Camarinha-Matos, L.M., Boucher, X., Afsarmanesh, H. (eds.) PRO-VE 2021. IFIP AICT, vol. 629, pp. 567–576. Springer, Cham (2021). https://doi.org/10.1007/978-3-030-85969-5_53
14. Alvey, B., Anderson, D.T., Buck, A., Deardorff, M., Scott, G., Keller, J.M.: Simulated photorealistic deep learning framework and workflows to accelerate computer vision and unmanned aerial vehicle research. In: 2021 IEEE/CVF International Conference on Computer Vision Workshops (ICCVW), pp. 3882–3891. Institute of Electrical and Electronics Engineers (IEEE) (2021). https://doi.org/10.1109/iccvw54120.2021.00435
15. Müller, M., Casser, V., Lahoud, J., Smith, N., Ghanem, B.: Sim4CV: a photo-realistic simulator for computer vision applications. Int. J. Comput. Vision **126**(9), 902–919 (2018). https://doi.org/10.1007/s11263-018-1073-7
16. Lei, Z., Zhou, H., Hu, W., Liu, G.-P., Guan, S., Feng, X.: Toward a web-based digital twin thermal power plant. IEEE Trans. Ind. Inf. **18**(3), 1716–1725 (2022). https://doi.org/10.1109/TII.2021.3086149
17. RC3 - 1 ROBOT - 3-AXES GANTRY ROBOT - LUCAS FRANCE. https://lucas-robotic-embedded.partcommunity.com/3d-cad-models/rc3-1-robot-3-axes-gantry-robot-lucas-france?info=lucas%2Frobot_cartesien_3_axes%2Frc3_1_robot.prj&cwid=3603. Accessed 14 Jan 2022
18. Alfa Laval: Alfa Laval TJ MultiJet 25 Rotary Jet Head - Product leaflet (2021)
19. grand - Recent models I 3D CAD Model Collection I GrabCAD Community Library. https://grabcad.com/library/tag/grand?page=1&time=all_time&sort=recent. Accessed 14 Jan 2022
20. Content Search - UE Marketplace. https://www.unrealengine.com/marketplace/en-US/assets?count=20&sortBy=effectiveDate&sortDir=DESC&start=0&tag=19467. Accessed 24 Feb 2022

21. Qiu, W., Yuille, A.: UnrealCV: connecting computer vision to unreal engine. In: Hua, G., Jégou, H. (eds.) ECCV 2016. LNCS, vol. 9915, pp. 909–916. Springer, Cham (2016). https://doi.org/10.1007/978-3-319-49409-8_75
22. GitHub - FreeOpcUa/python-opcua: LGPL Pure Python OPC-UA Client and Server. https://github.com/FreeOpcUa/python-opcua. Accessed 25 Feb 2022

Incorporating a Prediction Engine to a Digital Twin Simulation for Effective Decision Support in Context of Industry 4.0

Rushan Arshad$^{(\boxtimes)}$, Paul de Vrieze, and Lai Xu

Department of Computing and Informatics, Faculty of Science and Technology,
Bournemouth University, Talbot Campus, Bournemouth BH12 5BB, UK
{arshadr,pdvrieze,lxu}@bournemouth.ac.uk

Abstract. Simulation has been widely used as a tool to enhance the manufacturing processes by effectively detecting the errors and performance gaps at an early stage. However, in context of industry 4.0, which involves increased complexity, decisions need to be made more quickly to maintain higher efficiency. In this paper, we use a prediction engine along with a Digital Twin simulation to enhance the decision-making process. We show how, based upon a simulation of a process, a prediction model can be used to determine process parameters based upon desired process outcomes that enhance the manufacturing process. To evaluate our architecture, an industrial case study based on Inventory, Storage and Distribution will be used.

Keywords: Digital twins · Industry 4.0 · Simulation · Federated simulation · Machine learning

1 Introduction

Simulation of complex processes is used to enhance the understanding of the working of the overall system as well as enhancing the processes through comprehensive analysis of simulation data. In context of modern manufacturing systems and industrial phase shift towards industry 4.0, the processes have become more complex and difficult to simulate. In a collaborative context, the requirement of independence presents an additional challenge for simulation of the overall process. Traditional simulation approaches (like Discrete Event, Agent Based) and industrial tools (like Simio, AnyLogic) are not capable of simulating these processes in an isolated way.

In making decisions to generate maximum business value there is value in decision support, using analysis techniques especially related to data. A key technique of decision support is through simulation of What-if scenarios which provides the data that can then be used to make decisions related to error detection, process enhancement, system improvements among other things. To generate maximum benefits, accuracy of decisions is significant because inaccurate decisions can lead to severe financial consequences for the business.

L. M. Camarinha-Matos et al. (Eds.): PRO-VE 2022, IFIP AICT 662, pp. 67–76, 2022.
https://doi.org/10.1007/978-3-031-14844-6_6

When simulating complex processes the simulation involves simulation of multiple parts. Digital twins, as digital representations of physical entities, provide such partial simulation capability. The data from the physical system is shared with the Digital Twin for updated results [8]. Using predictive modelling and Artificial Intelligence, these updated simulations can be transformed into meaningful data that can help in enhancing the decision-making process. However, in the context of collaborative processes (with different types of stakeholders and needs of confidentiality), it is not realistic to expect all digital twin simulation models to be shared with all partners, or even for the simulation models to be based on the same simulation platform.

In this paper, we present an architecture based on the Digital Twin concept which can be used for predictive analysis of processes to enhance decision making. This architecture can simulate a collaborative process involving multiple organizations and then it extracts the relevant and meaningful data. This data is then fed into a prediction engine for predictive analysis and efficient decision making. A secondary manufacturing process is used to evaluate the architecture and depict basic understanding of the working of the proposed architecture.

It is worth noting here that the optimization of simulation or predictive parameters is not the primary objective at this point for the proposed architecture. The goal is to show the working of a Digital Twin based simulation of collaborative processes and how predictive engine can be used to process that simulation data into meaningful decisions. For the remainder of this paper, Sect. 2 provides related work for digital twins and decision support, Sect. 3 introduces the architecture and the core working elements whereas Sect. 4 depicts the evaluation and implementation of the architecture using an industrial case study. Section 5 concludes the paper.

2   Related Work

Simulation has been widely used in manufacturing industry as a tool to analyse, monitor and in some cases, to predict the behaviour of a system or a process in a particular scenario. Simulation has been used in each part of the manufacturing, from design, machining. production to scheduling, planning and supply chain. As the manufacturing industry is evolving, the simulation practices are also improving with the proactive usage of Virtual Reality and Augmented reality to simulate different parts of the manufacturing process [11].

The manufacturing industry have seen a significant improvement due to the integration with information technology. The complexity of modern manufacturing systems has increased many folds during the last decade with the advancements in technologies like Internet of Things (IoTs), Robotics and due to the varying (dynamic) demands of the consumers. COVID-19 pandemic led to a shift in the manufacturing industry when many industries had to make drastic changes to their supply chain and production mechanisms. For example, some cosmetics and chemical production industries started manufacturing sanitizers and related products due to a high increase in demand by making changes to their production lines. This caused companies to make highly informed decisions to remain competitive in a highly uncertain environment. This is where the importance of decision support becomes extremely relevant.

Decision Support Systems (DSS) corresponds to systems which are designed to enhance the decision-making process with the help of integrated and updated data. Simulation has been used to enhance the decision-making process in many ways. For example, simulation is used to design dispatching rules for dynamic scheduling [18], defect prevention in production systems [13], in measuring the time constraints in a semiconductor manufacturing plant [1] to name a few. However, in context of collaborative manufacturing and industry 4.0, traditional simulation approaches in isolation are generally monolithic in nature and hence have inherent limitations.

2.1 Simulation Using Digital Twins

In a complex, heterogeneous process and its simulation, digital twins are a key enabler. This is enabled through providing continuously updated simulation models representing the physical entities. A Digital Twin is essentially an updated simulation of a system and utilizes technologies like Artificial Intelligence to help detect errors at an early stage and provide predictive behavior of the system in a particular scenario. The most widely talked about concept in simulation when it comes to industry 4.0 and collaborative processes is of Digital Twins because of its usage under varying complex simulation scenarios.

Digital Twins based models and simulations present a significantly improved alternative to traditional simulations when it comes to decision support. These models provide enhanced simulations as well as analytical support for business managers to gather useful insights for better decision making. Such an architecture is capable of modelling shop floor assets, data storage and analytical support [17]. The real-time simulations and the data insights extracted from it help enhance the decision-making process.

Predictive and Preventive maintenance provide the solution to the maintenance issues that can lead to serious financial consequences. Predicting the possible errors or anomalies can help in making decisions that can save a lot of problems that otherwise can hinder the execution of time-sensitive and processes of higher priorities. A Digital Twin architecture is used to build dynamic models to implement preventive maintenance operations using updated simulations [12]. The scope, however, is limited to the scheduling and considers only a few indicators like downtime and machine idleness for preventive maintenance.

Supply chain twins [3] are also introduced to monitor the challenges of supply chain during the aftermath of COVID-19 pandemic. The data from customer behavior, online ordering, irregular shipments, and inventory is used to simulate the overall supply chain process. Disruptions such as increased demand, problems in transportation, supplier shutdown problems are introduced to analyze the response and resilience of supply chain twin. However, predictive analytics can be introduced to enhance the decision making for future supply chain disruptions.

Digital Twins are used for decision support in various applications, developed from different perspectives for example in urban agriculture and urban farming production [6], enhancing production systems [16], order management [9] etc. The accuracy of the Digital Twins based simulation remains a challenge because of the lack of approaches to determine the faults and performance of a Digital Twin and in some cases lack of sufficient data that reduces the quality of predictions.

2.2 Predictive Analytics and Digital Twins

Predictive analytics is one of the key areas which can help in realizing true potential of Digital Twins. The data from the twin of physical device or process can help in predicting key parameters that can enhance the overall manufacturing system. One solution is to use hybrid and cognitive twins along with predictive algorithms to improve the production performance and to reduce the manufacturing overheads such as over-heating of machines causing downtime. COGNITWIN [19] is a toolbox consisting of tools for simulation, data acquisition from sensors, predictive analytics and provides a modular approach for integrating hybrid and cognitive twins for process enhancement. The quality of data, computing power required, and the lack of support for collaborative processes are some of the challenges of this approach.

Predictive analytics is also utilized in Maintenance, Repair and Overhaul (MRO) operations of aircraft industry by utilizing data fusion with other operations of Digital Twin ecosystem such as sensors, physical models etc. [10]. Assumptions like achieving high Signal to Noise Ratio (SNR) for better data collection and over-reliance on sensory data for predictive decision making deem this approach less reliable in context of collaborative processes.

Machine Learning and data analytic techniques are utilized for error correction [20], scheduling maintenance of production machines, transport systems [15] and preventive, corrective, and predictive maintenance of manufacturing systems [4]. There are approaches where AutomationML is used to create efficient data models to be used as a Digital Twin for enhancement of the production systems. However, challenges such as communication between twins, making efficient decisions based on integrated data of all collaborators still need to be addressed to achieve maximum benefits.

Most of the approaches based on Digital Twins use monolithic simulations and try to address a problem within a part of an organization. However, in context of collaborative processes and industry 4.0, the capabilities of such approaches are limited. Hence, to address this issue, we propose an architecture based on Digital Twins concept in the next section which is capable of simulating collaborative process which can involve multiple stakeholders.

3 Digital Twins Simulation System Architecture

Simulation of complex collaborative processes requires an architecture that not only supports effective simulation, but also allows for the diversity of components and limits to sharing of information. To meet these needs, a federated simulation architecture, as presented in Fig. 1, is needed. This architecture, based on the digital twin concept, allows component simulations to be independent. The architecture consists of four main parts: Input, Simulation, Results and Data Processing and Prediction Engine.

The inputs consist of initial configurations that are provided to start the simulation. This can be initialization of parameters, a random seed etc. This provides a starting point to the simulation. Then, we have a Digital Twin of a process or a system. As it can be seen in Fig. 1, there are multiple simulators within this Digital Twin. This simulation concept is derived from our federated simulation framework [2].

The multiple simulators are part of a federated environment. Each simulator represents a collaborator and is responsible for simulating a part of a collaborative process. The rationale behind using this framework is to make sure maximum confidentiality of each collaborator is ensure while sharing necessary data between the simulators as required and through simulation coordinator. The details of working of each component can be found in our previous work [2].

The simulation coordinator governs the data exchanges between the collaborating simulators. The synchronization of simulators to ensure simulation accuracy and to minimize redundancy is also a responsibility of the simulation coordinator. This collaborative (and federated) environment enables the collaborative partners to use existing simulators while simulating their own designated part of the process efficiently.

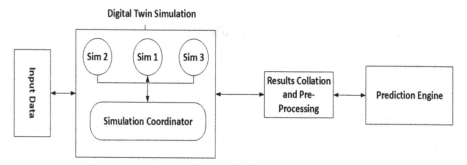

Fig. 1. Digital twins architecture

Data sharing is an important part of this Digital Twin simulation. There are two mechanisms that are used for the communication between the simulators: 1) messaging and 2) buffer queues. All messages are communicated through the simulation coordinator between the simulators. For data sharing, a buffer queue is created. Concept of producer and consumer is used as depicted in Fig. 3. The implementation details are briefly discussed in Sect. 4.

The data during the simulation process is being generated by multiple simulators. It is important to collate them in way that redundancy is avoided, and the integrity of data is also maintained. The results collation module combines the data from the simulators as it is being generated. After data is collated (on the cloud or stored locally in logs and CSV files), it is pre-processed for prediction. Pre-processing involves gathering the data that is necessary and helpful for predictions. For example, the features that are used to predict a certain type of outcome.

The prediction engine deals with the prediction based on the input features and target variables that are selected. The prediction is used to predict the required parameter (output variable). It can be any variable from the simulation. Simulation can provide the data for certain variables in a particular scenario but prediction using Machine Learning for example can predict the value of a variable based on the inputs provided with reasonable accuracy. Hence, prediction is more suitable in this case.

Machine Learning and Deep Learning algorithms can be used according to the requirements of the simulation data. There are certain criteria that can be followed to select appropriate algorithms for example classification, forecasting etc. The data from the prediction can then be fed back for comparisons with the simulated data for further decision making. In terms of accuracy of the prediction model, various parameters can be used for example Means Squared Error or accuracy score etc. Again, this depends on the type of Algorithms that are used and the machine learning approach that is being implemented. The architecture provides flexibility in this.

The proposed architecture provides a process which can result in improvement of decision-making through comprehensive simulation, effective prediction and using a reliable data. The simulation in the architecture is also scalable to accommodate collaborative processes which is essential in context of industry 4.0.

4 Evaluation of the Proposed Architecture

To evaluate the proposed architecture, an industrial case study from the literature [5] is used (see Fig. 2). There are some minor changes made to the implementation of the case study, for example instead of a monolithic simulation, different parts of secondary manufacturing are federated into multiple simulators.

The secondary manufacturing (storage, packaging, and distribution) process of medicinal products is simulated. There are three main phases of the process, simulated using 3 different simulators depicting the collaboration. The first phase is *Receipt and Inventory*, then comes *Storage and Monitoring* and finally *Distribution* is done in the last phase. There are 3 types of staff resources, including 18 technicians (G1), 2 service (G2) and 12 Quality Control (G3). In the first phase, different types of materials like cryoproducts and shippers (containers to store products) arrive and are received by the service staff.

Some of shippers are returned due to the bad quality. The remaining shippers are then stored in the pre-storage in phase 2. The shippers are the documented and their data loggers are created. After the documentation phase is completed, the inventory is updated at the last step of Storage and Monitoring phase. In the final phase, the orders that are placed are then sorted out in the order planning and then after the quality check, they are ready to be dispatched.

We applied our digital twins based architecture (Fig. 1) to the manufacturing case. The implementation is done in Python programming language using a Discrete Event based simulation. Three simulators were implemented, simulating 3 phases as part of a federation concept adopted from our previous work [2]. The data sharing mechanism between the simulators is implemented using buffer queues as shown in Fig. 3.

Producer is one simulator, and the consumer is another simulator which want to use the data that can be accessed from the queue. The buffer queue is implemented using the concept of First In First Out (FIFO). At the quality check process, we implemented a soft check to simulate some failures and some successes of the quality checking processes based on the quality control staff performance (quantifiable from 1–5 with 1 being lowest and 5 being the best). The simulation was run 50,000 times to generate enough data for the predictions and to expose the variation in the performance.

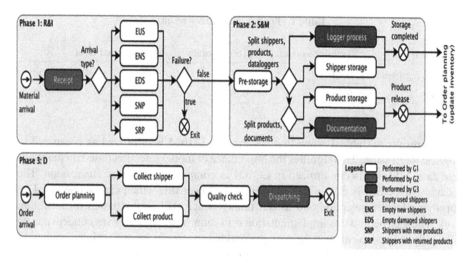

Fig. 2. Secondary manufacturing case study [5]

After gathering data from the simulation runs in form of log files (step by step execution and messaging between the simulators) and organized feature extraction in CSV files, a prediction engine is prepared. The prediction is developed to predict the number of orders that pass the quality check. Firstly, feature extraction process is done and the input features that are selected include Arrival Rate, Number of Orders Processed, Performance of the Quality Control Staff.

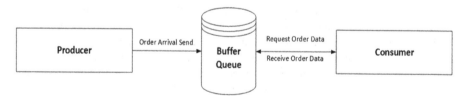

Fig. 3. Data sharing between simulators

The output or predicted feature is the number of orders that pass the quality check. Two different models (Logistic Regression [7] and Light Gradient Boosting Machine (LGBM) [14]) are used to predict the outcome. The data is divided into training (80%) and testing (20%). After applying the models on training and testing data, the accuracy of models is evaluated using Root Mean Square Error (RMSE) and R^2 (which means how well the regression model is fit to the data). The results of the evaluation are shown in Table 1:

Table 1. Prediction accuracy results

Algorithm	Training accuracy	Test accuracy	Mean squared error	R^2
Logistic regression	0.49	0.50	0.67	0.50
LGBM	0.66	0.67	0.45	0.66

The results in Table 1 show that accuracy in LGBM is improved as compared to Logistic Regression. This signifies the importance of model selection based on the available data. MSE is also minimized in LGBM as compared to Logistic Regression. The accuracy in LGBM is 67% which is also on the lower side which can be enhanced by improving feature selection and model tuning which will be continued in the future work. The idea behind this implementation is to show how Digital Twins concept can be efficiently utilized to enhance the decision-making process by incorporating a prediction engine. This experimentation shows that the prediction is feasible but there is a room for improvement as this is a preliminary attempt.

The predictions gathered from the above implementation can be used to make decisions like how many products pass through the quality check and what are the other features of the product that could be responsible for failing a quality check. This implementation is preliminary but provides a basis for enhancement and core working of the proposed architecture.

5   Conclusion and Future Challenges

Simulation is an important ingredient that can help enhance the decision-making process in manufacturing industry. In context of industry 4.0 and collaborative processes, simulation can play a vital role in generating insights regarding performance of each part of the process. In this paper, we proposed a Digital Twins based architecture to enhance the decision support in context of industry 4.0 and collaborative processes. We provided a blueprint to use simulation along with machine learning to predict certain parameters based on the required objectives to enhance the decision making for improved manufacturing processes.

We used Digital Twins based simulation in a federated environment to simulate a secondary manufacturing process for the evaluation of proposed architecture. Using machine learning prediction algorithms and simulation data as input, the desired parameters were predicted. The accuracy of the models, however, can be enhanced by utilizing more correlated features and better parameters tuning. More complex case studies will be utilized to further enhance the working of the proposed architecture.

Acknowledgments. This research is partially funded by the State Key Research and Development Program of China (2017YFE0118700) and it is part of the FIRST project which has received funding from the European Union's Horizon 2020 research and innovation programme under the Marie Skłodowska-Curie grant agreement No. 734599.

References

1. Anthouard, B., Borodin, V., Dauzere-Peres, S., Christ, Q., Roussel, R.: Management of time constraints tunnels in semiconductor manufacturing: A decision support system. In: Proceedings of the 23ème congrès annuel de la Société Française de Recherche Opérationnelle et d'Aide à la Décision (2022)
2. Arshad, R., de Vrieze, P.T., Xu, L.: A federated simulation framework for cross-organisational processes. In: Camarinha-Matos, L.M., Boucher, X., Afsarmanesh, H. (eds.) PRO-VE 2021. IAICT, vol. 629, pp. 267–279. Springer, Cham (2021). https://doi.org/10.1007/978-3-030-85969-5_24
3. Burgos, D., Ivanov, D.: Food retail supply chain resilience and the covid-19 pandemic: A digital twin-based impact analysis and improvement directions. Transp. Res. Part E Logistics Transp. Rev. **152**, 102412 (2021)
4. Eirinakis, P., et al.: Enhancing cognition for digital twins. In: Proceedings of the 2020 IEEE International Conference on Engineering Technology and Innovation (ICE/ITMC), pp. 1–7. IEEE (2020)
5. Erkoyuncu, J.A., Farsi, M., Ariansyah, D., et al.: An intelligent agent-based architecture for resilient digital twins in manufacturing. CIRP Ann. **70**(1), 349–352 (2021)
6. Ghandar, A., Ahmed, A., Zulfiqar, S., Hua, Z., Hanai, M., Theodoropoulos, G.: A decision support system for urban agriculture using digital twin: A case study with aquaponics. IEEE Access **9**, 35691–35708 (2021)
7. Gladence, L.M., Karthi, M., Anu, V.M.: A statistical comparison of logistic regression and different bayes classification methods for machine learning. ARPN J. Eng. Appl. Sci. **10**(14), 5947–5953 (2015)
8. Hou, L., Wu, S., Zhang, G., Tan, Y., Wang, X.: Literature review of digital twins applications in construction workforce safety. Appl. Sci. **11**(1), 339 (2020)
9. Kunath, M., Winkler, H.: Integrating the digital twin of the manufacturing system into a decision support system for improving the order management process. Procedia Cirp **72**, 225–231 (2018)
10. Liu, Z., Meyendorf, N., Mrad, N.: The role of data fusion in predictive maintenance using digital twin. In: Proceedings of the AIP Conference Proceedings, vol. 1949, p. 020023. AIP Publishing LLC (2018)
11. Mourtzis, D.: Simulation in the design and operation of manufacturing systems: State of the art and new trends. Int. J. Prod. Res. **58**(7), 1927–1949 (2020)
12. Neto, A.A., Carrijo, B.S., Brock, J.G.R., Deschamps, F., de Lima, E.P.: Digital twin-driven decision support system for opportunistic preventive maintenance scheduling in manufacturing. Procedia Manuf. **55**, 439–446 (2021)
13. Psarommatis, F., Kiritsis, D.: A hybrid decision support system for automating decision making in the event of defects in the era of zero defect manufacturing. J. Ind. Inf. Integr. **26**, 100263 (2022)
14. Rai, M., Mandoria, H.L.: Network intrusion detection: A comparative study using state-of-the-art machine learning methods. In: Proceedings of the 2019 International Conference on Issues and Challenge in Intelligent Computing Techniques (ICICT), vol. 1, pp. 1–5. IEEE (2019)
15. Rudskoy, A., Ilin, I., Prokhorov, A.: Digital twins in the intelligent transport systems. Transportatio Research Procedia **54**, 927–935 (2021)
16. dos Santos, C.H., Montevechi, J.A.B., de Queiroz, J.A., de Carvalho Miranda, R., Leal, F.: Decision support in productive processes through des and abs in the digital twin era: A systematic literature review. Int. J. Prod. Res., 1–20 (2021)

17. Tao, F., Zhang, M.: Digital twin shop-floor: A new shop-floor paradigm towards smart manufacturing. IEEE Access **5**, 20418–20427 (2017)
18. Turker, A.K., Aktepe, A., Inal, A.F., Ersoz, O.O., Das, G.S., Birgoren, B.: A decision support system for dynamic job-shop scheduling using real-time data with simulation. Mathematics **7**(3), 278 (2019)
19. Unal, P., Albayrak, Ö., Jomâa, M., Berre, A.J.: Data-driven artificial intelligence and predictive analytics for the maintenance of industrial machinery with hybrid and cognitive digital twins. In: Curry, E., Auer, S., Berre, A.J., Metzger, A., Perez, M.S., Zillner, S. (eds.) Technologies and Applications for Big Data Value, pp. 299–319. Springer International Publishing, Cham (2022). https://doi.org/10.1007/978-3-030-78307-5_14
20. Vathoopan, M., Johny, M., Zoitl, A., Knoll, A.: Modular fault ascription and corrective maintenance using a digital twin. IFAC-PapersOnLine **51**(11), 1041–1046 (2018)

Cognitive Digital Twin Enabling Smart Product-Services Systems: A Literature Review

Daisy Valle Enrique[1]([✉]) and António Lucas Soares[1,2]

[1] INESC TEC - Institute for Systems and Computer Engineering, Technology and Science,
Porto, Portugal
{daisy.v.enrique,antonio.l.soares}@inesctec.pt
[2] Faculty of Engineering, Department of Informatic Engineering, University of Porto, Porto,
Portugal

Abstract. Cognitive Digital Twin (CDT) has been taking considerable attention in several recent studies. CDT is considered as a promising evolution of Digital Twin bringing new smart and cognitive capabilities. Therefore, it is important to understand how companies can exploit this new technology and create new data-driven business models. Considering that context this article aims to identify Smart PSS business model based on Cognitive Digital Twin platforms. To reach this goal a literature review was conducted. As a principal contribution this study brings a set of new business models to offer Smart PSS based on cognitive digital twins. Moreover, the study presents several real cases of companies that are currently using the cognitive capabilities supplied by edge companies of the digital twin technologies.

Keywords: Cognitive Digital Twin · Business model · Digital services · Product-services systems

1 Introduction

Digital Twin is recognized as a key enabling technology of Industry 4.0 [1, 2]. DT creates a virtual model of the physical entity of the production system, allowing the interaction and integration of physical world and information world, and collecting a big amount of data [3, 4]. The DT have several manufacturing applications, such as product design, machine status monitoring, simulation, and visualization [5, 6]. However, according to [5], the use of digital twins is frequently limited to be an exact replica of the physical assets, without any cognitive capability that could be bring new opportunities to the company.

Semantic technologies allows augmented cognitive capabilities to a DT [7]. According to [8], cognition requires modeling of, not only the physical characteristics, but also the behavior of production elements and processes. For this, it is necessary to develop data-oriented models through Data Analytics and Machine Learning techniques [8]. The growth of combination of DT with semantic models and data analytics tools emerged the concept of Cognitive Digital Twin (CDT) [1, 9].

L. M. Camarinha-Matos et al. (Eds.): PRO-VE 2022, IFIP AICT 662, pp. 77–89, 2022.
https://doi.org/10.1007/978-3-031-14844-6_7

Several authors (e.g., 1, 9, 10) state that CDT provide a more intelligent, compre-hensive, and full lifecycle representation of complex systems, enabling to find data, and predict system behavior. The CDT can also enable the creation of higher service layers, which provide products with new intelligent behaviors and capabilities of communica-tion. In that sense, companies can develop smart digital product-services systems that could transform customer-supplier relationships and introduce new value propositions [11]. The Smart PSS business model comprises packages of products and services with smart digital capabilities, which can create, deliver, and capture value in real time [12]. These business models can focus on complementary digital services that support the most advanced servitized products or solutions that provide digital product personalization or the offer of Smart PSS of payment for use or payment for results [13].

In this sense, it is necessary to investigate how CDTs can be exploited to enable new Smart PSS business models, find new ways to (co)create value, as well as generate knowledge from data, improve the company's operational and environmental perfor-mance and get a competitive advantage [14]. Considering the context described above this study aims to propose new business models based on digital services enabled by Cognitive Digital Twin. To reach these aims a literature review was conducted.

The remaining sections are organized as follows. First, we start with the methodology section, where we present the methodological phases followed in the study. In Sect. 3 we describe and discuss the results. Finally, in Sect. 4 theoretical implications and managerial insights and future research suggestions directions based on the analysis and results presented.

2 Methodology

We follow three stages to conduct a literature based on the study of [15]: (i) research planning, (ii) research execution, and (iii) summary of results.

In the first phase, the research objective and data sources were defined. The goal defined in this stage was to identify the relation between CDT and PSS. For this, two databases were chosen to search: Scopus and ScienceDirect. Magazines and webpages that present practical application were also analyzed. The research questions that guided the study was: *How the cognitive capabilities provided by cognitive digital twins can be used to innovate in new Smart PSS business models?*

In the execution phase, the keywords were defined, and the definition of criteria for inclusion and exclusion of articles. The keywords defined for the search were: (cognitive digital twin OR Cognitive Twin) AND (services OR product-service system OR digital services OR servitization). The search was filtered by articles writing in English. Also, aiming to include relevant articles in the sample, the "Snowballing" technique was applied. Finally in the Summary of Results phase, was carried out on the content analysis of the articles and the main information was summarized according to the aim of the study.

3 Results

As a result of the literature research, were obtained a total of 19 articles in Science Direct and Scopus. These articles are focused mainly on the concept or architecture of CDT, and on the use of CDT for manufacturing. Therefore, were incorporate other 5 articles about PSS business models. The number of articles found and the year of publication, all in the last two years, shows that it is still an emerging topic, but with growing interest.

3.1 Cognitive Digital Twin Supporting Smart PSS

Cognitive Digital Twin is considering the next generation Digital Twins, which has a strong data-orientation [9, 16]. The CDT, unlike the DT, offers new cognitive abilities [17]. Thus, a CDT can understand, detect early and predict the impact of different types of behavior observed [5]. According to [1] the CDT can be defined, as a digital representation of a physical system that includes a set of semantically interconnected digital models related to the different phases of the life cycle of the physical system, providing cognitive capabilities and supporting to perform autonomous activities.

CDT has applications during all phases of the product life cycle [18]. However, the majority of studies focus on the manufacturing phase [3, 8, 10] and had little explored the use of CDT to innovate in new services models. The addition of services in the after-sale phase can bring new competitive advantages for companies and extend the life cycle of the product [17]. A product/service system (PSS) is the incorporation of services into a product tangible traditionally offered by a manufacturing company, seeking to offer the customer a "complete package" combining goods, support services, self-service and knowledge [18–21].

One of the most used categories is the [19], who proposed three PSS categories: Base Services, Intermediate Services and Advanced Services. Table 1 presents the description of each PSS category.

Table 1. PSS categories [21, 23]

PSS category	Description	Extent of risk
Base	Focus on product provision. Services that facilitate the product sale or usage without significantly altering the product functionality	Low: The customer will take the major risk regarding the product
Intermediate	Services that expand the product functionality. Or services that help the customer to adapt to new products	Medium: increased expose to the consequences of equipment faults
Advanced	Services that replace the purchase of a product, challenging the view that services are always complements to products	High: The company assume the major of product failures risks

PSS business models can be classified in two categories. A product-oriented PSS, mainly focused on to improve or boost product utilization, e.g. maintenance, spare parts, upgrades, project engineering. In other hand, the customer-oriented PSS, where the changes are more radical, and the PSS is mainly concerned with customer needs, and where the product is substituted by the services as a principal offer component [23, 24]. The Base and Intermediate Services are services that support the product selling. Companies that offer this kind of PSS have a business model oriented to a product. Instead, companies that offer advanced services have a business model oriented to a customer [13, 25].

According to [26, 27] the advance of digital technologies such as Internet of Things (IoT), smart connected products (SCPs), artificial intelligence, among others, emerged a new concept of Smart Product Service System. The Smart PSS can be conceptualized as the development of new services and/or the improvement of existing ones using digital technologies [28]. These new Smart PSS transform customer-supplier relationships and introduce new value propositions [11]. In that way companies could take competitive advantage from these solutions, by (co)creating value with customers, and also by the generation of new knowledge from data, improving the firm's operational and environmental performance. In that sense, the cognitive digital twin can offer new opportunities to develop Smart PSS [29]. Companies can collect data by the implementation of CDT and develop machine learning models to monitor the health of a product, perform diagnosis and prognosis that can be offered as services [6]. The CDT allows collecting data from different products and generates information about product usages and product conditions. Using artificial intelligence, it is possible to analyze the data collected from the digital twin for diagnostics and preventive maintenance. Using AI methods, it is possible to identify under and over utilized products performance, identify patterns of anomalies, common faults, and insights in reducing operational costs. Besides, the company can generate detailed condition reports and share them by apps or digital platforms. Considering that context the following conceptual framework (Fig. 1) was constructed.

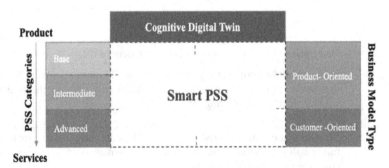

Fig. 1. Conceptual model

In the case of base services, the capabilities supplied by the CDT will be focused on monitoring product conditions to provide the necessary replacement parts at the right time, to avoid warranty issues. In the case of intermediary services, the CDT can be used to support services to guarantee the state and condition of equipment. Finally for advanced services, the CDT allows firms to offer services focused on the result, bringing to the manufacturing company the major responsibility for the product [28,

29]. Furthermore, these solutions can be integrated into a Cognitive Digital Twin platform. Platform approach enable the implementation of advanced service in a easier way [14, 30].

In the market, there are a few DT platforms which have been evolving with the inclusion of applications for data analysis, however some companies refer to these solutions as Cognitive Digital Twin. Some of the most representative companies in the sector of CDT technologies are IBM, Siemens, Bosch, Ansys and General Electric. Next, several case studies of companies that offer products-services based on CDT platforms are presented. These cases were identified through the success stories reported by the suppliers of the CDT platforms.

3.2 Digital Cognitive Twin Platform for Product-Services Systems: Use Cases

IBM has a group of applications related to cognitive digital twins. For example, IBM Watson™ IoT Platform is a cloud-hosted service that makes it simple to derive value from Internet of Things (IoT) devices, through several artificial intelligence applications. In addition, the Maximo Asset Health Insights application, monitoring of asset health and optimize preventive maintenance by combining asset record information and sensor data so that businesses are better able to plan capital improvement. The company also launched the IBM Digital Twin Exchange, which is a marketplace that connects organizations that are looking to buy digital twins with members of IBM's partner ecosystem, who can sell them fault codes, maintenance plans, 3D models, and other data related to physical assets. After buying the digital twin using IBM Digital Twin Exchange, companies could use AI and IoT solutions to fully capitalize on the value of digital twins, using IBM Watson or IBM Maximo enterprise asset management. A success case reported is KONE, a leading manufacturer of elevators delivering a "'people flow' system for small and large buildings with full risk contractual services". For this it uses the IBM Watson IoT platform and its cognitive capabilities in many ways e.g., KONE E-Link™, a facility management tool that allows asset monitoring, provides elevator performance, traffic analysis, and helps to predict the condition of the elevator [30]. This Smart PSS can be classified as *advanced services* because the company guarantees the availability of the system through full risk contracts.

Siemens is one of the most advanced companies in the field of digital twins. The company developed several technologies to implement digital twins such as: MindSphere, and Siemens Digital Enterprise Suite, that include Siemens Product Life Cycles System (PLM), Manufacturing Operation Management System (MOM), among others. A reported example of a company using Siemens digital twin technologies is Saildrone. This company designs, manufactures and operates a fleet of unmanned surface vehicles (USVs) for maritime security, ocean mapping and ocean data collection. The company uses Siemens Digital Twin technologies, such as the Mindsphere IoT platform, which allows the collection of data on sea conditions. The company moved from a business model based on selling the product to a business model based on selling data collected by the USVs. Business customers can rent a drone a day to collect ocean data about specific oceans or regions. Then Saildrone provides customers with the requested data and handles the entire collection process. The USVs utilize machine learning models that run onboard GPU compute processors to provide real-time visual detection of targets that are otherwise not broadcasting their position. Since the company has completely changed its value offering, replacing products with drone rental, data collection and processing services, it can be classified as *advanced services* [32].

Another platform is Bosch IoT hub, which offers tools for digital twin management. The platform is constituted by three modules: (i) IoT device management that manage, update, control, and service your IoT devices throughout their entire life cycle, (ii) IoT data management & analytics that allows to collect, process, store, assess, and use your IoT data to the maximum and (iii) IoT edge and analytics Empower the intelligent edge and enable your devices for AIoT [33]. As a success case, Bosch reports the company HOLMER which has developed a remote diagnostics and maintenance package for its machines called EasyHelp 4.0 using the Bosch IoT hub. Service technicians use it to extract IoT data and learn more about the condition of farm equipment. In this way, the customer benefits from the possibility of remote diagnosis and maintenance and faster service. EasyHelp 4.0 is also connected to the *agrorouter*, the universal data exchange platform for farmers and contractors. This is claimed to allow relevant data to be conveniently transmitted online from the vehicle to a wide variety of endpoints. We consider that this solution can be classified as *intermediary services*, as the company's value proposition is focused not only on offering products and spare parts, but also offering remote maintenance services [33]. Another case reported by Bosch is the company Mann + Hummel. This company uses the Bosh platform to offer device fleet management services. By connecting an entire fleet of devices, fleet managers can remotely check the status of devices or compare the performance of individual devices and machines. It also allows for easy benchmarking across the entire fleet to identify best practices and machines with good/poor performance [33]. This service can be classified as *basic services* because it focuses on device connectivity and information sharing.

Ansys also developed a Twin Builder, which is a digital twin platform that incorporates machine learning capabilities. Ansys reports the company Electronic Cooling Solutions using the Twin Builder for thermal management of lithium batteries for electric cars. With this solution, Electronic Cooling Solutions optimized the product design and increased and shortened the product launch time. In addition, the company began to provide its customers with preventive maintenance services, and recommendations for a high-performance product designed. This service can be classified as a *basic service* because it aims to promote the sale of the product and the major risk is in the customer side [34].

General Electric Company also developed a Digital Twin that integrates analytic models that measure asset health, wear and performance. This company in partnership with Teledyne Controls, create a strategic to transform aircraft engine health monitoring by using the Predix platform and Teledyne's GroundLink® technology to apply data and analytics on continuous flight data to provide customers with more effective engine maintenance operations. Teledyne has three types of service packages: (i) Flight data analysis for maintenance and engineering, (ii) Flight data analysis for flight safety and risk management. Each of these services includes remote monitoring, trouble alarm message, report sharing. The company also provides access to thousands of data points owned by airlines collected every minute by onboard wireless fast access recorders (QARs), such as Teledyne's GroundLink Comm+, which can help equipment manufacturers improve analytics. and processes. In addition, the service enables the export of Fullflight data to third-party services [35]. This Smart PSS can be classified as *intermediate service* because the company offer condition monitoring services and advance data analysis.

Table 2 summarizes the examples discussed earlier according to PSS types and business models.

Table 2. Example of PSS

Smart PSS category	Examples	Business model
Base	- Thermal management solution using Asys Digital Twin technologies - Mann + Hummel- Fleet Management Service	Product-oriented
Intermediate	- HOLMER remote diagnosis and maintenance package using Bosch IoT hub - Teledyne Controls uses GE digital twin to collect data and provided information	
Advanced	- Saildrone used Siemens Digital Twin Technologies to change its business model from product center to data provider - Kone uses IBM digital technologies to supply a flow people management system	Customer-oriented

Summarizing the principal PSS identify through the cases are: (i) Asset Remote monitoring (trouble alarm message, report sharing), (ii) Remote diagnosis and maintenance package, (iii) Risk Management (Failure Causes Analysis), (iv) Predict the product condition, (v) Fleet Management (remotely check the status of devices (eg location, health, usage) or compare the performance of individual devices and machines, (vi) Spare Parts Management, (vii) Provides access to external data, (viii) Allow connection to an universal data exchange platform that include data of different actors of the ecosystem.

3.3 Business Model Canvas for Smart PSS

To understand how companies transit from a product center business model to a services center business model an overview of its changes to different aspects of its business dimensions is needed. In that sense, Business Canvas Model (BMC) allows to simplify and systematize the business dimensions that explains how firms create, deliver and capture value [36].

Several authors have proposed the design of a business model to implement PSS, using BMC [37–41, 42]. Based on these studies and the examples described above were identified changes associated to each of the business models dimensions for each type of Smart PSS BM (Table 3).

To implement product-oriented business model, the company would have to make changes in three principal dimensions of the business model: key resources, key activities, and customer relationships (Fig. 2) [37].

Table 3. Business model configuration for smart PSS.

Business model dimensions	Product-oriented	Customer-oriented
Value proposition	Product Performance information sharing The customer continues being the main product responsible Lower cost of product maintenance	Product Performance Guarantee Lower responsibility of product Lower cost of product maintenance
Customer segment	B2C or B2B	B2C or B2B New customer segments
Key activities	Human Resource training focus on services and digital technologies Some data processing capacity Definition of new process and reasonability for services area Improve of sharing information and customer support area	Human Resource training focus on services and digital technologies Organizational culture manage change Higher understanding of the customer behavior Higher data processing capacity Definition of new process and responsibilities
Key Resources	IoT infrastructure Cloud services CDT platform Human Resources with digital and analytics skills	IoT infrastructure Cloud services CDT platform Human Resources with digital and analytics skills AI technologies investment
Customer Relationship	Long-term relationships Sharing information and knowledge Value co-creation Interaction improvement	Risk Sharing Contracts Sharing information, knowledge Value co-creation Closer relationship with customers
Distribution Channels	Marketing campaigns Retail and sales training (service oriented) Non-physical channels (Remote Support, digital platform)	Marketing campaigns Retail and sales training (service oriented) Non-physical channels (Remote Support, digital platform)

(continued)

Table 3. (*continued*)

Business model dimensions	Product-oriented	Customer-oriented
Partern Network	IT-partern for infrastructure IT-parter for development Finantial Partners	IT-partern for infrastructure IT-parter for development Services provider (data analysis) Finantial Partners
Revenue Stream	Payment is based on a monthly or yearly fixed rate	Pay per use, pay per result, pay per service unit, pay per performance, availability, subscription
Cost Structure	Initial investment on digital technologies and human resources Operational and Maintenance Cost	Higher initial investment Operational and Maintenance Cost

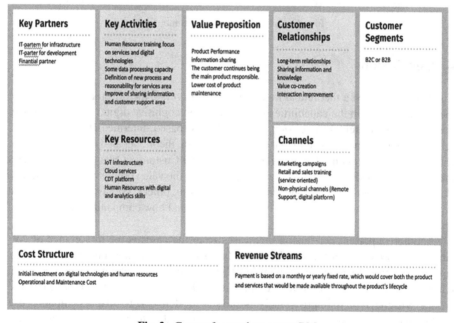

Fig. 2. Canvas for product-center BM

Moreover, in the case of Customer Business Model (Fig. 3), companies will need to do major changes, principally in the dimensions of key activities, key resources, value preposition, cost structure, revenue streams and customer relationships [37].

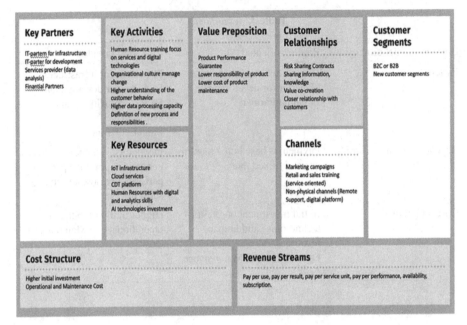

Fig. 3. Canvas for customer-center BM

4   Conclusions

The study proposed a theoretical model that aims to relate the different dimensions of the Smart PSS, with the capabilities provided by the cognitive digital twin. The model considers three different dimensions of Smart PSS (based, intermediate and advanced services) that will be enabled by the CDT. In addition, the model also contemplates two categories of business models, Product-Oriented and Customer Oriented. The business model orientation depends on several aspects such as the value proposition, the relationship with customers and the payment methods, among others. We also presented some digital twin platforms that are already in the market, and how companies are using these platforms to offer Smart PSS.

Another important conclusion that arises from the cases is the importance of collaborating with other partners to develop solutions., with several examples in this study considering more than one technology supplier to reach the company goal. In addition, it is possible to observe how several companies collect external data to integrate into the product's digital twin to improve analysis and service delivery. To do that companies use digital platforms where several ecosystem actors share data to improve their analysis.

Finally, in future research will be important to conduct qualitative studies to understand the mechanism that companies use to develop smart PSS based on CDT, focusing on the business model dimensions. Also, exploratory research could be developed to study the transformation path for companies to move from a product-center business model to a data-driven service-focused business model.

Acknowledgments. The project TRF4p0 - Transformer 4.0 leading to this work is co-financed by the ERDF, through COMPETE-POCI and by the Foundation for Science and Technology under the MIT Portugal Program under POCI-01-0247-FEDER-045926.

References

1. Zheng, X., Lu, J., Kiritsis, D.: The emergence of cognitive digital twin: Vision, challenges and opportunities. Int. J. Prod. Res., 1–23 (2021)
2. Hyre, A., Harris, G., Osho, J., Pantelidakis, M., Mykoniatis, K., Liu, J.: Digital twins: Representation, replication, reality, and relational (4Rs). Manuf. Lett. **31**, 20–23 (2022)
3. Al Faruque, M.A., Muthirayan, D., Yu, S.Y., Khargonekar, P.P.: Cognitive digital twin for manufacturing systems. In: Proceedings of the 2021 Design, Automation & Test in Europe Conference & Exhibition, pp. 440–445 (2021)
4. Li, H., Wang, G., Lu, J., Kiritsis, D.: Cognitive twin construction for system of systems operation based on semantic integration and high-level architecture. Integr. Comput.-Aided Eng. (Preprint), 1–19 (2022)
5. Ali, M.I., Patel, P., Breslin, J.G., Harik, R., Sheth, A.: Cognitive digital twins for smart manufacturing. IEEE Intell. Syst. **36**(2), 96–100 (2021)
6. Semeraro, C., Lezoche, M., Panetto, H., Dassisti, M.: Digital twin paradigm: A systematic literature review. Comput. Ind. **130**, 103469 (2021)
7. Zhou, G., Zhang, C., Li, Z., Ding, K., Wang, C.: Knowledge-driven digital twin manufacturing cell towards intelligent manufacturing. Int. J. Prod. Res. **58**(4), 1034–1051 (2020)
8. Eirinakis, P., et al.: Cognitive digital twins for resilience in production: A conceptual framework. Information **13**(1), 33 (2022)
9. Rožanec, J.M., et al.: Actionable cognitive twins for decision making in manufacturing. Int. J. Prod. Res. **60**(2), 452–478 (2022)
10. Abburu, S., Berre, A.J., Jacoby, M., Roman, D., Stojanovic, L., Stojanovic, N.: COGNITWIN– Hybrid and cognitive digital twins for the process industry. In: Proceedings of the 2020 IEEE International Conference on Engineering, Technology and Innovation (ICE/ITMC). IEEE (2020)
11. Pagoropoulos, A., Maier, A., McAloone, T.C.: Assessing transformational change from institutionalising digital capabilities on implementation and development of product-service systems: Learnings from the maritime industry. J. Clean. Prod. **166**, 369–380 (2017)
12. Dalenogare, L.S., Benitez, G.B., Ayala, N.F., Frank, A.G.: The expected contribution of industry 4.0 technologies for industrial performance. Int. J. Prod. Econ. **204**, 383–394 (2018)
13. Frank, A.G., Mendes, G.H., Ayala, N.F., Ghezzi, A.: Servitization and industry 4.0 convergence in the digital transformation of product firms: A business model innovation perspective. Technol. Forecast. Soc. Chang. **141**, 341–351 (2019)
14. Silva, H., Soares, A.L.: Digital platforms as enablers of smart product-service systems. In: Camarinha-Matos, L.M., Boucher, X., Afsarmanesh, H. (eds.) PRO-VE 2021. IAICT, vol. 629, pp. 506–513. Springer, Cham (2021). https://doi.org/10.1007/978-3-030-85969-5_47
15. Tranfield, D., Denyer, D., Smart, P.: Towards a methodology for developing evidence-informed management knowledge by means of systematic review. Br. J. Manag. **14**(3), 207–222 (2003)
16. Yitmen, I., Alizadehsalehi, S., Akıner, İ, Akıner, M.E.: An adapted model of cognitive digital twins for building lifecycle management. Appl. Sci. **11**(9), 4276 (2021)
17. Lu, J., Zheng, X., Schweiger, L., Kiritsis, D.: A cognitive approach to manage the complexity of digital twin systems. In: West, S., Meierhofer, J., Ganz, C. (eds.) Smart Services Summit. PI, pp. 105–115. Springer, Cham (2021). https://doi.org/10.1007/978-3-030-72090-2_10
18. Vandermerwe, S., Rada, J.: Servitization of business: Adding value by adding services. Eur. Manag. J. **6**, 314–324 (1988)

19. Tukker, A.: Eight types of product–service system: eight ways to sustainability? Experiences from SusProNet. Bus. Strateg. Environ. **13**, 246–260 (2004)
20. Baines, T., Lightfoot, H., Smart, P., Fletcher, S.: Servitization of manufacture: Exploring the deployment and skills of people critical to the delivery of advanced services. J. Manuf. Technol. Manage. (2013)
21. Cusumano, M.A., Kahl, S.J., Suarez, F.F.: Services, industry evolution, and the competitive strategies of product firms. Strateg. Manag. J. **36**(4), 559–575 (2015)
22. Matthyssens, P., Vandenbempt, K.: Service addition as business market strategy: Identification of transition trajectories. J. Serv. Manage. **21**, 693–714 (2010)
23. Ayala, N.F., Paslauski, C.A., Ghezzi, A., Frank, A.G.: Knowledge sharing dynamics in service suppliers' involvement for servitization of manufacturing companies. Int. J. Prod. Econ. **193**, 538–553 (2017)
24. Lerch, C., Gotsch, M.: Digitalized product-service systems in manufacturing firms: A case study analysis. Res. Technol. Manag. **58**(5), 45–52 (2015)
25. Abdel-Basst, M., Mohamed, R., Elhoseny, M.: A novel framework to evaluate innovation value proposition for smart product–service systems. Environ. Technol. Innov. **20**, 101036 (2020)
26. Zinke-Wehlmann, C., Frericks, S., Kluge, A.: Simulating impact of smart product-service systems. In: Camarinha-Matos, L.M., Boucher, X., Afsarmanesh, H. (eds.) PRO-VE 2021. IAICT, vol. 629, pp. 289–297. Springer, Cham (2021). https://doi.org/10.1007/978-3-030-85969-5_26
27. Paschou, T., Rapaccini, M., Adrodegari, F., Saccani, N.: Digital servitization in manufacturing: A systematic literature review and research agenda. Ind. Mark. Manage. **89**, 278–292 (2020)
28. Marcon, É., et al.: Capabilities supporting digital servitization: A multi-actor perspective. Ind. Mark. Manage. **103**, 97–116 (2022)
29. Cenamor, J., Sjödin, D.R., Parida, V.: Adopting a platform approach in servitization: Leveraging the value of digitalization. Int. J. Prod. Econ. **192**, 54–65 (2017)
30. Ardolino, M., Rapaccini, M., Saccani, N., Gaiardelli, P., Crespi, G., Ruggeri, C.: The role of digital technologies for the service transformation of industrial companies. Int. J. Prod. Res. **56**(6), 2116–2132 (2018)
31. Greenfield, D.: Digital Twin Applications by Small Companies. Automation World (2022). https://www.automationworld.com/factory/iiot/article/22171994/siemens-cloudbased-dig ital-twin-used-by-saildrone-and-nemos-garden
32. Jung, S., Ferber, S., Cramer, I., Bronner, W., Wortmann, F.: Bosch IoT suite: Exploiting the potential of smart connected products. In: Gassmann, O., Ferrandina, F. (eds.) Connected Business, pp. 267–282. Springer, Cham (2021). https://doi.org/10.1007/978-3-030-76897-3_15
33. https://www.ansys.com/products/digital-twin
34. General Electric: GE Expands Predix Platform to Advance Industrial Internet Opportunities for Customers (2016)
35. Osterwalder, A., Pigneur, Y.: Business Model Generation: A Handbook for Visionaries, Game Changers, and Challengers. John Wiley & Sons, Hoboken, New Jersey (2010)
36. Barquet, A.P.B., de Oliveira, M.G., Amigo, C.R., Cunha, V.P., Rozenfeld, H.: Employing the business model concept to support the adoption of product–service systems (PSS). Ind. Mark. Manage. **42**(5), 693–704 (2013)
37. Orellano, M., Neubert, G., Gzara, L., Le-Dain, M.A.: Business model configuration for PSS: An explorative study. Procedia CIRP **64**, 97–102 (2017)
38. Poeppelbuss, J., Durst, C.: Smart Service Canvas–A tool for analyzing and designing smart product-service systems. Procedia CIRP **83**, 324–329 (2019)

39. Khan, M.A., Wuest, T.: Upgradable product-service systems: Implications for business model components. Procedia CIRP **80**, 768–773 (2019)
40. Michalik, A., Möller, F., Henke, M., Otto, B.: Towards utilizing customer data for business model innovation: The case of a German manufacturer. Procedia CIRP **73**, 310–316 (2018)
41. Johansson, C., et al.: Urban mining as a case for PSS. Procedia CIRP **47**, 460–465 (2016)

Digital Transformation Through the Lens of Sociotechnical Systems

Exploiting User-Generated Content for Service Improvement: Case Airport Twitter Data

Lili Aunimo[1][(✉)] and Luis Martin-Domingo[2]

[1] Haaga-Helia University of Applied Sciences, Helsinki, Finland
lili.aunimo@haaga-helia.fi
[2] Özyegin University, Istanbul, Turkey
luis.martin@ozyegin.edu.tr

Abstract. The study illustrates how airport collaborative networks can profit from the richness of data, now available due to digitalization. Using a co-creation process, where the passenger generated content is leveraged to identify possible service improvement areas. A Twitter dataset of 949497 tweets is analyzed from the four years period 2018–2021 – with the second half falling under COVID period - for 100 airports. The Latent Dirichlet Allocation (LDA) method was used for topic discovery and the lexicon-based method for sentiment analysis of the tweets. The COVID-19 related tweets reported a lower sentiment by passengers, which can be an indication of lower service level perceived. The research successfully created and tested a methodology for leveraging user-generated content for identifying possible service improvement areas in an ecosystem of services. One of the outputs of the methodology is a list of COVID-19 terms in the airport context.

Keywords: Social media data mining · Topic modelling · Sentiment analysis · Term extraction · Airport services · Collaborative networks · Content analysis · User-generated content

1 Introduction

Due to digitalization, more and more communication between individuals and organizations is happening in digital channels such as social media. One part of the customer service of many organizations is specifically focusing on such digital collaborative networks, since many people tend to post their feelings about service quality into these environments. The user-generated content available in these social media channels, such as Twitter, may be used to mine a wealth of information concerning a selected service and the entities related to it. This information complements the data obtained through traditional customer surveys and stakeholder analysis. In addition, user-generated contents may provide completely new information as new topics of discussion or new stakeholders, and relations between them, may be discovered – be it customer segments or organizations.

Collaborative networks consist of autonomous and heterogeneous entities that collaborate to achieve common or compatible goals through interaction that is made possible

L. M. Camarinha-Matos et al. (Eds.): PRO-VE 2022, IFIP AICT 662, pp. 93–105, 2022.
https://doi.org/10.1007/978-3-031-14844-6_8

through computer networks [1]. Airports can be a good example, they have existed for around 100 years now and have evolved from a simple infrastructure, similar to today's bus station, to a complex set of infrastructures with a large number of stakeholders involved and where computer networks play a vital role in the operation. Airport stakeholders are autonomous an heterogeneous and collaborate with one common aim which is to allow passengers to change transport modes and flying to another destination in an smooth and efficient way. The airport stakeholders shown in Fig. 1 fall under the category of virtual organization, which is one of the categories of collaborative networks.

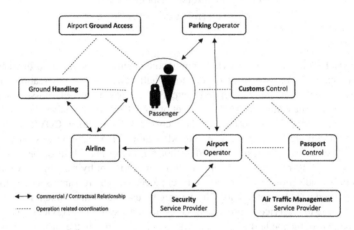

Fig. 1. Collaborative network in the airport environment. Authors, adapted from [2].

Social media platforms offer airports novel and efficient ways of communicating and interacting with customers and other service providers. The interaction often deals with topics related to announcements on current issues, customer service, marketing and recruiting, among others [3]. The communication on social media between the passenger and the airport can lead to co-creation activities that produce new value to all participants of the network. Many platforms with user-generated contents are available for such co-creation activities. Some of them are social media platforms (e.g. Twitter, Facebook, Instagram, LinkedIn) and some other are specialized blogs and interactive digital services that enable the collection of customer feedback, such as TripAdvisor or Skytrax (https://www.airlinequality.com/).

User-generated content can be an important source for customer insight creation and for service development [4]. The data is unstructured and in large quantities, which in social media sites typically refers to natural language data that may be ungrammatical, noisy and very concise.

The airport business was chosen as it represents a complex environment, with many different service providers (airport management companies, airlines, luggage handling companies, food & beverage, shops, etc.), for which although measuring passenger perceptions of service quality is difficult [5], it is important as it correlates to the levels of airport reuse and destination revisit [6]. Data from Twitter microblogging service was selected because it has been found to be better than data from some other platforms, such as Skytrax, for collecting information about air passenger experiences [7]. Twitter was also chosen because it is widely used in a professional setting and in the countries under study [1, 8]. Indeed, social media platforms, including Twitter, enable the creation of virtual customer environments where online communities are formed around specific airports and where airport services are discussed. The four years period of the analyzed data (January 2018 – December 2021) was preferred as it allowed studying changes during the COVID-19 pandemic, as it occurred during the last two years of the period under study.

The goal of this research is to define and test a methodology for analyzing user-generated contents to gain insight into the services provided by airport stakeholders forming a collaborative network, from the topics and sentiments mined from the content. The methodology is tested on COVID-19 related tweets concerning 100 airports. It consists of an automatic language detection of tweets, followed by automatic sentiment analysis and topic discovery. Thereafter, tweets are mined to discover novel topic related terms. Finally, the results are evaluated from the point of view of their value for the airport service providers.

With this approach, the study contributes to the data mining and text analytics debate where social media data is leveraged to enhance managerial decision making, for improving airport services and data engineering methods. The study also contributes to the study of airport services, provided by many stakeholders forming a collaborative network, by developing a model for a co-creation process where user-generated contents is leveraged to identify service potential improvements. To the best of our knowledge, this body of research is the first one to apply the theory of collaborative networks to the airport sector.

The rest of the paper is organized as follows. After the introduction, there is a section covering the related literature, followed by the description of the data and methods used. Section 4 presents the main results obtained in the study and Sect. 5 contains an analysis of the results. The last section concludes the study and presents new avenues for future research.

2 Literature Study

Literature covering collaborative networks and the airport sector, to the best of our knowledge, is scant. However, Viri et al., [9] use the model of a collaborative network of multimodal transport services and big data to improve the services provided to drivers and passengers in the Finnish city of Tampere.

Spring et al. (2016) [2] refers to airports as network of interdependent service providers. In the recent pass, they have been promoting structured information sharing among various members of the network through a project that involves a set of practices called 'Collaborative Decision-Making' (CDM). For example, at Helsinki's Vantaa Airport and Warsaw Airport, partners are required to share freely operational information like the estimated landing time and actual taxi-in time for each flight.

Graça & Camarinha-Matos (2020) [10] indicate that the sustainability of collaboration is not a given and requires continuous performance improvements. While evaluating a collaborative business ecosystem in IT organizations, they highlighted that well-defined performance indicators can be used to both assess the collaboration level and act as a mechanism to induce an improvement in the collaborative behavior of the participating organizations. This is relevant also in the airport environment.

Social media data is being used more and more in the airport service quality field, which aims to measure air passenger perceptions from different service areas of the airport terminal building. It was originally identified as an important component for the planning and design of the land side of a terminal building [11]. This field of research, accordingly to Barakat et al., [12] can be divided into two dimensions: a) identifying service attributes that represent customer satisfaction by referring to surveys that target aviation experts and/or passengers; and b) measuring service quality based on customer feedback, normally through a questionnaire given to passengers.

The use of questionnaires can be costly [13], time consuming [12] and include a delay, since observations are taken until airport managers are able to implement correcting service measures. User-generated content and text mining has been used more often in service management research [14] and started to be used as an alternative to passenger surveys to measure airport service quality: Bae & Chi [15] as well as Gitto & Mancuso [16] used Skytrax, an airport review website which provides independent reviews by passengers; Lee & Yu [17] used Google reviews; Barakat et al., [12] and Martin-Domingo et al. [4] used Twitter as source of data to measure airport service quality. Lu et al. [7] found that Twitter is a better predictor of service quality than Skytrax.

Twitter data, as one of the user-generated content types, can be useful in identifying new service attributes, relevant to airport passengers. For example, Barakat et al., [12] identified that "prayer rooms" were relevant for passengers at King Khaled airport in South Arabia. Thus, Twitter data provides an opportunity to evaluate service attributes which were not included in surveys. User-generated content has also been used to identify which airport services -related topics are relevant at a given airport and at a given time.

The COVID-19 pandemic has provoked substantial changes to the air transport industry as it resulted in a 66 percent decrease in passengers and an estimated loss of €118 billion 2020 [18]. Thus, airports have been dealing with new situations and a new terminology has appeared when communicating with passengers. Within the healthcare sector, Ma et al. (2021) [19] identified 887 English COVID terms that allow medical professionals to retrieve and exchange information. The present research, as part of the value creation of user-generated contents, aims to contribute with coronavirus terminology in the airport environment. This is needed, because words of a natural language evolve over time. Vocabularies have to be kept up-to-date as new words appear and/or words gain new meanings. For example, the Merriam-Webster Dictionary added 455 new words only in October 2021. Four of these words were COVID related words: breakthrough (medical), super-spreader, long COVID and vaccine passport [20]. Our aim was to explore what COVID related terms are used in the airport context by passengers.

Topic modeling is a research method that has been used to discover topics and to group and identify terms in user-generated content where the topics are not known beforehand. Some of the topic modeling techniques used in the service quality literature of the travel and tourism industry include: Structured Topic Analysis (STA) in tourism destination marketing [21], non-negative matrix factorization (NMF) in airlines and Latent Dirichlet Allocation (LDA) in hotels [22] and in airports [23]. This research employs the Latent

Dirichlet Allocation (LDA) [24]. It is a probabilistic model that considers a tweet as a mixture of topics. Topics in turn are modelled as a distribution of words.

3 Data and Methods

3.1 Data

The Twitter airport dataset used in this research was collected from airport users' tweets from a list of 100 airports around the world. The list of airports corresponds to airports' official Twitter accounts with the largest number of followers in 2016. All of the tweets retrieved, using the Twitter Archive (ctrlq.org), included the Twitter account name (Twitter screen name) of each of the 100 airports. For example, for London Heathrow Airport (LHR), the official Twitter account @HeathrowAirport was used.

A total number of 949497 tweets was collected during the period between July 2016 and March 2022. Using the language recognition software Apache TIKA [25], a total of 592131 tweets were filtered as to handle only tweets in English, which is used as the international language of aviation. The World Health Organization (WHO) declared a Public Health Emergency of International concern on 30 January 2020 [26] and pandemic on 11 March 2020. The dataset was divided into two periods: One before the pandemic (2018–2019) with 202061 tweets and the other during the pandemic (2020 – 2021) with 110023 tweets. The number of tweets was considerably smaller during the later period under study because passenger traffic in the airports was very much decreased because of the pandemics [18]. The process of filtering the original Twitter data set to obtain the two data sets under study is illustrated in Fig. 2.

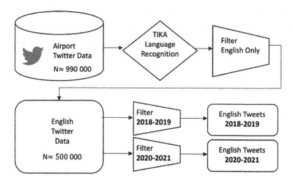

Fig. 2. The process of filtering the original Twitter data to obtain the data sets under study.

3.2 Methods

The data sets were processed using the KNIME software [27]. For the sentiment analysis, a lexicon-based method was used. The lexicon applied is derived from the MPQA Opinion Corpus by Maas et al. [28]. The lexicon-based approach assigns sentiment tags to words in a text based on dictionaries of positive and negative words. A sentiment score is calculated for each tweet as defined in Eq. (1).

$$Sentiment\ score = \frac{(number\ of\ positive\ words) - (number\ of\ negative\ words)}{total\ number\ of\ words} \quad (1)$$

The topic detection was performed using the LDA (Latent Didrichlet Allocation) method. We used the implementation in KNIME by Newman et al. [29], based on SparseLDA sampling scheme and data structure by Yao et al. [30]. The KNIME node used in our experiments uses the MALLET: A Machine learning for language toolkit [31]. The number of topics is automatically determined using the elbow method. The elbow method estimates the optimal number of clusters (or topics), by running k-means clustering on the data set for different values of k (i.e., different numbers of clusters), and then calculating the within-cluster sum of squared errors (SSE), which is the sum of the distances of all data points to their respective cluster centers as depicted in Eq. 2.

$$SSE = \sum\nolimits_{i=1}^{n} (x_i - \bar{x})^2, \quad (2)$$

where n is the number of observations, x_i is the value of the ith observation and $\bar{x}$ is the mean of all observations.

Subsequently, the SSE value for each k is plotted in a scatter chart. The best number of clusters is the number at which there is a drop in the SSE value, giving an angle in the plot. The entire process of topic modelling is illustrated in Fig. 3. Only the topics of the tweets of the latter period were modelled because the term discovery was aimed at discovering terms for a newly emerged topic, which in this case was COVID-related services at the airport. Prior to determining the number of topics, the data was processed. In this phase the tweets were run through a part-of-speech tagger and only nouns were selected. In addition, very low frequency terms were filtered out. After the preprocessing, the dimensionality of the feature space was further reduced using principal component analysis (PCA).

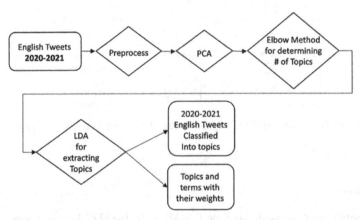

Fig. 3. The topic modeling process using principal component analysis (PCA), the elbow method and the LDA method. As output, all tweets are categorized to the most probable topic. In addition, a list of terms and their weights is produced for each topic.

The process of discovering new COVID-related terms is illustrated in Fig. 4. The input consists of the English tweets of the latter period under study and of a list of COVID terms. The idea is that a list of terms is given as a seed for the system and the system then extracts from the tweets terms that could belong to the same topic. The process of term extraction is as follows: first the COVID-related tweets are filtered from the entire body of tweets. Then they are preprocessed using the same methods as in the topic modeling that was described above (see Fig. 2). After this each term and its frequency is calculated and a list of terms sorted according to term frequency (TF) is produced. This list is one output of the method. The other output is obtained when from the list of frequency-sorted terms those terms that occur in the previous period are filtered out. These terms are called COVID Terms in Fig. 4.

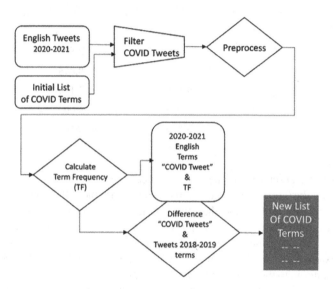

Fig. 4. Discovery of new COVID terms from the tweets.

The initial list of COVID terms used in this study is given in Table 3 below. As can be seen from the table, this list is very short and contains terms that an average native speaker of the language could produce without great effort. Thus, taking this method into use does not require an investment in terms of human resources, which shows that the proposed method has attained one of its goals, namely that of partly automating the process of finding new terms related to an emerging topic. However, there is one requirement that the creator of the initial list of terms should respect: The terms in the initial list should not be polysemous (i.e., words with more than one meaning) in the airport context. Rather, they should only bear a coronavirus-related meaning in the context of airport services.

4 Results

The sentiment analysis of the tweets supports results from previous studies where the overall sentiment concerning the airport services is slightly positive, see e.g., Martin-Domingo [4]. The results of the sentiment analysis may be observed in Table 1. The mean sentiment in the period 2018–2019 is 0.136 and in the period 2020–2021 it is slightly more positive with a mean value of 0.150. However, the mean sentiment value for the COVID-related tweets is lower: 0.095. The COVID-related tweets are those tweets that contain at least one initial COVID term listed in Table 3.

Table 1. The descriptive statistics for the sentiment scores of the three data sets.

Statistic	2018 and 2019	2020 and 2021	COVID-related tweets
Min	−0.800	−1.000	−0.667
Max	1.000	1.000	0.625
Mean	0.136	0.150	**0.095**
SD	0.170	0.181	0.134
Quartile 1	0.000	0.077	0.000
Quartile 3	0.250	0.250	0.167

The topic detection was applied to the tweets from 2020–2021. The number of topics found by the elbow method was three and they are the following: topic 1 is about miscellaneous topics such as spending time at the airport and greetings. Tweets mainly classified into topic 2 are about COVID-related services and issues. Topic 3 contains tweets about spending time at the airport, especially spending the night there. Table 2 lists some examples of the tweets in each topic. The score indicates the probability of the tweet belonging to the topic. After manual inspection of the most probable topics, it was discovered that each topic also contains tweets that are not related to the identified topics. The terms characterizing the topics are surprisingly generic and common to all topics. However, there are some topic specific terms, and the weights of the terms differ in the topics.

Table 2. Examples of tweets in each topic with the score indicating the probability for belonging to the topic.

Score	Topic	Example tweet
0.981	1	Can I get a pint at the bar in your airport
0.980	1	Happy New Year, thanks for sticking by us this year - You had a fairly tough year yourself but took the time to make us smile. Here's hoping we meet again very soon. Until then, stay safe my friend!

(continued)

Table 2. (*continued*)

Score	Topic	Example tweet
0.980	2	After the government's update on the PCR tests here: https://t.co/giipldyjTH, are there any new restrictions on domestic travel within Canada?
0.980	2	Bruh are you guys not testing domestic passengers
0.990	3	Hello again! My flight arrives at 20:15 and my connecting one leaves at 12:05 the next day. Is terminal 5 open 24h and is it ok to spend the night there? Thank you!
0.990	3	Can people spend a night to the airport s hotel waiting for the connecting flight due the day after?

The new list of COVID terms discovered by the proposed method is included in Table 3. Terms not related to coronavirus or terms that are related to it only in some specific contexts (such as the terms arrival and center) have been filtered out from the above list. The accuracy of the system is 50% at 20 and 22% at 100, meaning that among the top 20 terms retrieved by the system, the proportion of coronavirus-related terms is 50%, whereas among the top 100 terms, their proportion is 22%.

Table 3. The initial list of COVID terms given as a seed to the system and the list of coronavirus related terms discovered by the proposed method.

Initial list of COVID terms	New list of COVID terms	
alfa variant	certificate	quarantine
British variant	check	result
corona	crowd	risk
COVID	distance	rule
delta variant	dog	safety
delta virus	fear	sanitizer
Indian variant	force	screening
mask	health	spread
omicron	lockdown	test
pandemics	measure	testing
physical distance	pandemic	vaccine
safe distance	pcr	virus
safety distance		
social distance		

5 Analysis

The study attempted to define and test a methodology for analyzing user-generated contents that allows to gain insight into the services in the airport collaborative network, especially into the sentiment of the passengers and the topics under discussion. The methodology for discovering new terms on an emerging topic was tested on COVID-19 related tweets, but it was designed to be generic enough to enable the discovery of terms and contents related to other emergent topics, such as Brexit consequences or lack of personnel at the airports. Furthermore, the methodology could be applied also to other collaborative networks consisting of various services with abundant user-generated contents, such as a shopping mall or a railway station.

The study used lexicon-based sentiment analysis. The results support previous research by showing that the overall sentiment of the tweets in the airports is slightly positive. When studying the sentiment related to COVID-19 topics, a drop in the sentiment was found. Previous research on sentiment analysis of user-generated content shows a drop in sentiment concerning airport service quality during the COVID period [29]. However, research on the sentiment perceived in relation to services related to COVID-19 (such as control of vaccination certificates or instructions for the usage of masks), is scarce. Thus, the present research results provide new knowledge on this as it conducted sentiment analysis on COVID-19 related tweets where each tweet was somehow related to both COVID-19 and an ecosystem of airport services.

The LDA method was used to discover topics in the tweets. This was successful and three topics were discovered. The terms related to the topics did not very well describe them. Therefore, an inspection of the tweets classified into each topic was used to describe the topics discovered. The terms describing the topics found by the LDA method were the same to a great extent, only some terms were different, and the weights were different. This is probably due to the small number of coronavirus-related tweets and especially due to the small number of terms in the tweets. The small number of terms is partly due to the methodology used. The method used did a considerable dimensionality reduction for the terms as first PCA was performed. After that, in the preprocessing phase, part-of-speech tagging was conducted and all other words except nouns were filtered out. At the end, words with a low term frequency were filtered out. All these three phases contributed to the small number of terms that were passed on first to the elbow method and subsequently to the LDA method.

When evaluating the results of the term discovery method that came up with new COVID-related terms, it was noticed that it is not at all easy to define the borderline between a COVID term and a non-COVID term. The context of use is the ultimate source that tells whether a term in question is a COVID-related term or not. However, in the classification of documents or in libraries, topical terms are commonly used without any context. These terms are used to describe the contents of documents or customer reviews and users use them for search.

In this study, when determining whether a word is a COVID term or not, human expertise in the field of airport service quality and the context of the word were used. The task was not at all easy. Thus, it is probable that it is not at all easy for an automated methodology, either. Words like dog, screening and result were classified as COVID terms even though they are very often also used in the sense of a non-COVID term. However, the dogs that are trained to detect COVID, the testing or screening of COVID certificates upon arrival and the result of a COVID test are common contexts where these words may be regarded as COVID-related terms.

One limitation of the study is that it used lexicon-based sentiment analysis and word-based representations for topic discovery. However, Twitter messages also contain non-textual and rich contents as well as metadata that could be very important to the analysis [32]. Examples of such non-textual or rich contents are emojis, images, and hyperlinks. A future study could process the rich contents in the tweets along with the textual contents and probably reach even more accurate results than the present study. Another limitation of the present study is that it did not leverage the network structure of the Twitter data. It is regarded an important source of additional information. It consists of retweets, likes, mentions of tweets and of twitter accounts, among others. There are methods for discovering communities of Twitter users that are centered around a topic, such as airports [33]. It might be worth investigating if leveraging this network structure would bring additional information for the process of co-creation and help in identifying novel improvement areas in airport services. A third limitation of the study is that it used representations based only on one word. A future study using collocations consisting of several words may bring more insight into the topic.

6 Conclusions

This paper described an attempt to define and test a methodology for analyzing user-generated contents to gain insight into the services provided by an ecosystem of actors forming a collaborative network, from the topics and sentiments mined from the user-generated content. The methodology was tested on COVID-19 related tweets concerning 100 airports.

Twitter data concerning the 100 most followed airports from 2018 and 2022 was used as the data set that was mined. As a result, it was observed that the sentiment of the tweets varied across topics. A difference in mean sentiment was also found when comparing COVID-19 services related tweets (lower sentiment), with the overall sentiment. The study, using automated methods, generated a novel list of COVID-related terms to measure service quality provided by the airport collaborative network. However, the results of the LDA method were a bit surprising as the number of discovered topics was smaller than expected and the terms describing the topics were not as topical as expected. The reason for this was probably the small amount of data and the powerful dimensionality reduction in the preprocessing phase. In a future study, dimensionality reduction before the actual topic modelling phase could be modified to keep more dimensions.

The study contributes to the user-generated data mining and text analytics debate where social media data is leveraged to enhance managerial decision making, for improving airport services and data engineering methods. The study illustrated how airports may leverage the richness of data that is now days available to them as they have become a part of a data-rich collaborative network due to digitalization. The study illustrates how airport collaborative networks can profit from the richness of data using a co-creation process, where passenger generated content is leveraged to identify possible service improvement areas.

Acknowledgments. This research was partly funded by the Ministry of Education and Culture in Finland through the Future Expertise in Sales and Services (FESS) Research Project.

References

1. Camarinha-Matos, L.M., Afsarmanesh, H.: Collaborative networks: A new scientific discipline. J. Intell. Manuf. **16**(4), 439–452 (2005). https://doi.org/10.1007/s10845-005-1656-3
2. Spring, M., Selviaridis, K., Zografos, K.: Coordination in service supply networks: Insights from 'Airport Collaborative Decision Making' (2016)
3. Hallikainen, H., Aunimo, L.: Adoption of digital collaborative networking platforms in companies: A study of twitter usage in Finland. In: Camarinha-Matos, L.M., Afsarmanesh, H., Ortiz, A. (eds.) PRO-VE 2020. IAICT, vol. 598, pp. 98–110. Springer, Cham (2020). https://doi.org/10.1007/978-3-030-62412-5_8
4. Martin-Domingo, L., Martín, J.C., Mandsberg, G.: Social media as a resource for sentiment analysis of Airport Service Quality (ASQ). J. Air Transp. Manag. **78**, 106–115 (2019). https://doi.org/10.1016/j.jairtraman.2019.01.004
5. Bezerra, G.C.L., Gomes, C.F.: Measuring airport service quality: A multidimensional approach. J. Air Transp. Manag. **53**, 85–93 (2016). https://doi.org/10.1016/j.jairtraman.2016.02.001
6. Prentice, C., Kadan, M.: The role of airport service quality in airport and destination choice. J. Retail. Consum. Serv. **47**, 40–48 (2019). https://doi.org/10.1016/j.jretconser.2018.10.006
7. Lu, L., Mitra, A., Wang, Y.-Y., Wang, Y., Xu, P.: Use of electronic word of mouth as quality metrics: A comparison of airline reviews on twitter and skytrax (2022). https://doi.org/10.24251/HICSS.2022.165
8. Statista: Leading countries based on number of Twitter users as of January (2022). https://www.statista.com/statistics/242606/number-of-active-twitter-users-in-selected-countries/
9. Viri, R., Aunimo, L., Aramo-Immonen, H.: Connected and multimodal passenger transport through big data analytics: Case Tampere City Region, Finland. In: Camarinha-Matos, L.M., Afsarmanesh, H., Antonelli, D. (eds.) PRO-VE 2019. IAICT, vol. 568, pp. 527–538. Springer, Cham (2019). https://doi.org/10.1007/978-3-030-28464-0_46
10. Graça, P., Camarinha-Matos, L.M.: Evaluating and influencing the performance of a collaborative business ecosystem – A simulation study. In: Camarinha-Matos, L.M., Afsarmanesh, H., Ortiz, A. (eds.) PRO-VE 2020. IAICT, vol. 598, pp. 3–18. Springer, Cham (2020). https://doi.org/10.1007/978-3-030-62412-5_1
11. Müller, C., Gosling, G.D.: A framework for evaluating level of service for airport terminals. Transp. Plan. Technol. **16**(1), 45–61 (1991). https://doi.org/10.1080/03081069108717470
12. Barakat, H., Yeniterzi, R., Martín-Domingo, L.: Applying deep learning models to twitter data to detect airport service quality. J. Air Transp. Manag. **91**, 102003 (2021). https://doi.org/10.1016/j.jairtraman.2020.102003
13. Greaves, F., Ramirez-Cano, D., Millett, C., Darzi, A., Donaldson, L.: Harnessing the cloud of patient experience: Using social media to detect poor quality healthcare. BMJ Qual. Saf. **22**(3), 251–255 (2013). https://doi.org/10.1136/bmjqs-2012-001527
14. Kumar, S., Kar, A.K., Ilavarasan, P.V.: Applications of text mining in services management: A systematic literature review. Int. J. Inf. Manage. Data Insights **1**(1), 100008 (2021). https://doi.org/10.1016/j.jjimei.2021.100008
15. Bae, W., Chi, J.: Content analysis of passengers' perceptions of airport service quality: The case of Honolulu International Airport. J. Risk Fin. Manage. **15**(1), 5 (2021). https://doi.org/10.3390/jrfm15010005
16. Gitto, S., Mancuso, P.: Improving airport services using sentiment analysis of the websites. Tourism Manage. Perspect. **22**, 132–136 (2017). https://doi.org/10.1016/j.tmp.2017.03.008
17. Lee, K., Yu, C.: Assessment of airport service quality: A complementary approach to measure perceived service quality based on Google reviews. J. Air Transp. Manag. **71**, 28–44 (2018). https://doi.org/10.1016/j.jairtraman.2018.05.004

18. Martín-Domingo, L., Martín, J.C.: The effect of COVID-related EU state aid on the level playing field for airlines. Sustainability **14**(4), 2368 (2022). https://doi.org/10.3390/su1404 2368

19. Ma, H., et al.: COVID term: A bilingual terminology for COVID-19. BMC Med. Inform. Decis. Mak. **21**(1), 231 (2021). https://doi.org/10.1186/s12911-021-01593-9

20. Merriam-Webster: We Added 455 New Words to the Dictionary for October 2021 (2022). https://www.merriam-webster.com/words-at-play/new-words-in-the-dictionary. Accessed 04 May 2022

21. Christodoulou, E., Gregoriades, A., Pampaka, M., Herodotou, H.: Combination of topic modelling and decision tree classification for tourist destination marketing. In: Dupuy-Chessa, S., Proper, H.A. (eds.) CAiSE 2020. LNBIP, vol. 382, pp. 95–108. Springer, Cham (2020). https://doi.org/10.1007/978-3-030-49165-9_9

22. Kaveski Peres, C., Pacheco Paladini, E.: Exploring the attributes of hotel service quality in Florianópolis-SC, Brazil: An analysis of tripAdvisor reviews. Cogent Business & Management **8**(1), 1926211 (2021). https://doi.org/10.1080/23311975.2021.1926211

23. Kiliç, S., Çadirci, T.O.: An evaluation of airport service experience: An identification of service improvement opportunities based on topic modeling and sentiment analysis. Res. Transp. Bus. Manage. **43**, 100744 (2021). https://doi.org/10.1016/j.rtbm.2021.100744

24. Blei, D.M., Ng, A.Y., Jordan, M.I.: Latent dirichlet allocation. J. Mach. Learn. Res. **3**, 993–1022 (2003)

25. Mattmann, C.A., Zitting, J.L.: Tika in action. Manning (2012)

26. WHO: Statement on the Second Meeting of the International Health Regulations (2005) Emergency Committee Regarding the Outbreak of Novel Coronavirus (2019-nCoV) (2020). https://web.archive.org/web/20210815071616/https://www.who.int/news/item/30-01-2020-statement-on-the-second-meeting-of-the-international-health-regulations-%282005%29-emergency-committee-regarding-the-outbreak-of-novel-coronavirus-%282019-ncov%29

27. Berthold, M.R., et al.: KNIME - the Konstanz information miner. ACM SIGKDD Explorations Newsl. **11**(1), 26–31 (2009). https://doi.org/10.1145/1656274.1656280

28. Maas, A., Daly, R.E., Pham, P.T., Huang, D., Ng, A.Y., Potts, C.: Learning word vectors for sentiment analysis. In: Proceedings of the 49th Annual Meeting of the Association for Computational Linguistics: Human Language Technologies, pp. 142–150 (2011)

29. Newman, D., Asuncion, A., Smyth, P., Welling, M.: Distributed algorithms for topic models. J. Mach. Learn. Res. **10**, 1801–1828 (2009)

30. Yao, L., Mimno, D., McCallum, A.: Efficient methods for topic model inference on streaming document collections. In: Proceedings of the 15th ACM SIGKDD International Conference on Knowledge Discovery and Data Mining, pp. 937–946 (2009). https://doi.org/10.1145/155 7019.1557121

31. McCallum, A.K.: Mallet: A machine learning for language toolkit (2002). http://mallet.cs.umass.edu. Accessed 19 Jun 2022

32. Chinnov, A., Kerschke, P., Meske, C., Stieglitz, S., Trautmann, H.: An Overview of Topic Discovery in Twitter Communication through Social Media Analytics (2005)

33. Punel, A., Ermagun, A.: Using Twitter network to detect market segments in the airline industry. J. Air Transp. Manag. **73**, 67–76 (2018). https://doi.org/10.1016/j.jairtraman.2018.08.004

Understanding the Organizational Impact of Robotic Process Automation: A Socio-Technical Perspective

Rafael Götzen[✉], John von Stamm, Ruben Conrad, and Volker Stich

FIR Institute for Industrial Management, RWTH Aachen University, Campus-Boulevard 55, 52074 Aachen, Germany
{Rafael.Goetzen,John.vonStamm,Ruben.Conrad, Volker.Stich}@fir.rwth-aachen.de

Abstract. Interest in AI-driven automation software is growing constantly across all industries, as these technologies enable companies to almost automate administrative processes completely and significantly increase operational efficiency. However, many implementation attempts fail due to a lack of understanding of how these technologies affect the various socio-technical aspects that are intertwined in an organisation. This leads to a widening gap between value propositions of automation software and the ability of companies to exploit them. For long-term success, collaboration between humans and software robots in the organization must be optimised. Therefore, the social, technical, and organizational impact of Robotic Process Automation was investigated. Following a socio-technical systems approach, a model was developed and validated in a use case of a company in the mechanical engineering sector. Knowing the influencing factors before launching large-scale automation initiatives will help practitioners to better exploit efficiency potentials and increase the long-term success.

Keywords: Socio-technical systems · Human-machine collaboration · Robotic Process Automation · Administration

1 Introduction

The future of interaction within organizations is characterized by a tightly interwoven collaboration network of humans and machines. Technological progress is constantly creating new opportunities to achieve operational excellence. One area of application that has gained increasing interest in the last years is administrative processes. Today, organizations optimize their informational processes by using advanced automation technologies [1, 2]. One of these technologies has triggered a real hype recently: Robotic Process Automation (RPA). RPA is used as a collective term for tools that interact on the user interface of computer systems, analogous to the way human actors do [3–5]. Deployment is often seen as a quick win because the conveniently designed interfaces and drag-and-drop functions mean that basically no programming skills are required,

© IFIP International Federation for Information Processing 2022
Published by Springer Nature Switzerland AG 2022
L. M. Camarinha-Matos et al. (Eds.): PRO-VE 2022, IFIP AICT 662, pp. 106–114, 2022.
https://doi.org/10.1007/978-3-031-14844-6_9

making implementation seem trivial from a technological point of view [3, 6]. Nevertheless, many implementation projects fail in practice. It becomes clear that it is not technical functionality that is the biggest obstacle, but organizational adaptation [1, 6]. Change management issues must therefore be taken seriously to reach efficiency targets and leverage cost potentials. However, we currently experience a lack of understanding on how RPA affects the overall organizational system.

According to the socio-technical systems design, integrating technologies which automate administrative processes into the working world is a major challenge [1]. There is a growing gap between the value proposition of RPA and the ability of companies to exploit it. Many companies lack the necessary adaptability, which is essential to tap the full potential of RPA [6]. In this context, orchestrating the interplay of human employees, technology, and organizational structures is pivotal, according to Strohm and Ulich [7, 8].

With this paper we aim to understand the organizational impact of RPA from a socio-technical perspective. It is dedicated to validating the applicability of a previously developed socio-technical system architecture using a real case study in the field of mechanical engineering. In this way, we transfer our research into operational practice to solve the practitioners' dilemma outlined above.

2 Theoretical Background

2.1 Robotic Process Automation

Lacity and Willcocks characterize RPA as the configuration of software to perform administrative tasks previously executed by human employees [2]. Picking up on this idea, Aguirre and Rodriguez emphasize that despite the often-misunderstood term "robotic", RPA is in no way related to electromechanical machines, but is a software-based system [9]. Van der Aalst et al. additionally refer to RPA as a collective term for tools that interact on the user interface of computer systems, analogous to the way a human actor does [4]. Allweyer adds that software robots can support human employees as personal assistants or replace them completely in the execution of various tasks [5].

To use RPA, software robots are installed and operated on a company's server [10]. These software robots are integrated front-end and operate via the user interface [9, 10]. This means that software robots imitate humans when interacting with the user interfaces, but do not require deep intervention in existing IT applications [4, 11].

Due to the high relevance of AI for the development of automation technologies, future RPA applications will increasingly rely on a combination of "conventional RPA" and embedded AI [12]. This leads to an evolution towards intelligent systems. Technologies such as natural language processing, image and pattern recognition, or context analysis will be increasingly used to enable more intuitive perceptions and judgments in daily office and information activities.

2.2 Socio-Technical Systems

The term *socio-technical system* was first used in 1951, when British researchers Trist and Bamforth at London's Tavistock Institute used studies in coal mining to find that the use of the same technologies in different work groups varied greatly in terms of efficiency and effectiveness [13, 14]. They figured that the use of new technologies under conventional conditions brought about enormous changes in the social quality of the work environment [14]. Following their observations, they addressed the interaction of social and technological factors in industrial production systems in their studies. The resulting socio-technical systems approach postulates that each production unit must be viewed as a combined system of social and technical subsystems [8, 13].

The first to transfer socio-technical thinking to the field of computer science was Enid Mumford. She investigated how socio-technical design can be used for successful information systems in the working world [15]. Since then, the socio-technical systems approach for information technology is gaining increasing importance in the literature. With the beginning of the 21st century, the number of publications increased rapidly, especially in the areas of 'computer science' and 'information and communication technologies' [16].

3 Related Research and Innovation Contribution

Since the focus of this paper is to understand the organizational impact of RPA from a socio-technical perspective to promote collaborative work between humans and software robots, an overview of existing socio-technical approaches in this context must first be provided. Following a systematic literature review, Götzen et al. found that socio-technical approaches in the context of RPA are massively underrepresented in the research community [16]. For this reason, we developed a socio-technical framework [16] using the findings from the literature review as well as applying Eisenhardt's case study research [17, 18].

The framework comprises thirteen relevant socio-technical elements that need to be considered when implementing RPA. These elements are assigned to three socio-technical dimensions: Organization, Technical System, and Social System. Collaborative human-machine interaction necessary for task completion is at the center of the socio-technical framework and acts as a link between the three subsystems. In addition, we derived relationships between the individual dimensions to specify these interactions. While the organizational dimension focuses on the orchestration of employees in a company, i.e., the creation of general conditions for collaboration and the design of tasks and processes, the social subsystem considers the individual characteristics and interpersonal relationships that influence action. In addition, RPA implementation requires a technological component to provide functionality which is represented by the technical subsystem. Figure 1 shows how the individual elements relate to each other within the complex socio-technical system architecture.

To address the practitioners' dilemma of not sufficiently considering socio-technical aspects before implementing RPA, our framework will be applied in a real use case. We aim at making a significant innovation contribution by transferring scientific endeavor into practice validating the applicability of research findings. To this end, we address the following central research question:

To what extent can socio-technical research approaches be applied to a real-world RPA implementation scenario?

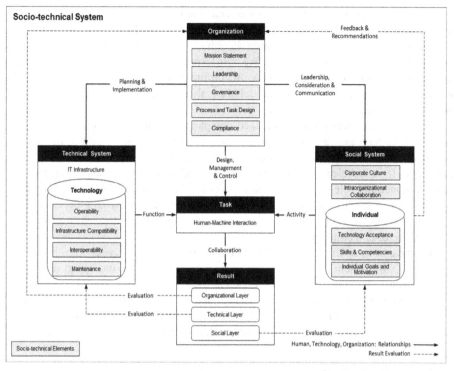

Fig. 1. Socio-technical system architecture for RPA implementation [16]

4   Research Design

The research process follows Ulrich's strategy of applied research. He states that the problems of applied science result from practical challenges. Research findings therefore aim at testing developed design models in an application context [19]. Figure 2 illustrates the research process, including the previous development of the socio-technical system architecture by Götzen et al.

Fig. 2. Research process - strategy of applied research [18]

Götzen et al. postulated that socio-technical challenges encountered in RPA implementation should be a key aspect of future research activities [16]. By using systematic literature review and case study research according to Eisenhardt, problem-relevant theories and approaches were identified. We transferred our findings into a socio-technical system architecture for the use of RPA. According to the strategy of applied research, the last step is to test the developed model in a real-world scenario. The paper will focus on exactly this step.

We selected a German medium-sized company from the mechanical engineering sector, for the RPA use case. This industry was deliberately chosen, as it was not considered in the model development of Götzen et al. The model development focused on large enterprises from the telecommunications, finance, and insurance industries, as these have taken a pioneering role in the implementation of RPA. A successful application of the framework to a medium-sized mechanical engineering business would therefore show that the framework can be used as a supporting management instrument regardless of industry sector and company size.

We have accompanied the implementation process over one year from beginning to end and will present the findings, based on own observations and expert interviews with the Managing Director, who functioned as the project sponsor. Simultaneously, the relationship between the practical experiences and the socio-technical system elements presented earlier (see Fig. 1) will be illustrated. The goal is to verify that all elements are valid in practice and sufficiently represent the complexity of RPA implementations.

5   Case Study Results

5.1   Introduction of the Company and Motivation for RPA

The company, which we accompanied is a medium-sized German company for conveyor, elastomer, and plastics technology. The company currently employs 80 people. The decisive factor for starting the RPA journey was a desire to relieve employees of repetitive and monotonous tasks that can be processed by a software robot. According to the Managing Director, the mere execution of rule-based processes is not viable under today's labor market conditions and the prevalent lack of skilled personnel. Therefore, staff must be deployed in areas of activity that create added value for the company. He stated that in the past, the company employed a certain number of full-time equivalents (FTE) to perform invoice checks. The administrative employee was responsible for checking invoices and matching them with purchase order data. If the information was identical, manual approval was given or in case of discrepancy a ticket was forwarded to the responsible product manager. However, the case study partner preferred to use staff capacity for customer service rather than for administrative tasks. These activities require human competencies, which cannot be covered by software robots. The motivation to introduce RPA arose to free up human resources and use them for cognitively demanding tasks. The motivation is clearly not to rationalize jobs.

The automation team responsible for the implementation process comprised three employees from different departments. The first employee was a process owner with extensive operational knowledge. The second team member has been responsible for the introduction of a Management Execution System (MES) and was therefore assigned as the project manager. In addition, a third employee was released from daily business for six months to exclusively work on the RPA implementation. Moreover, the project received support from an IT employee who took responsibility for the management of hardware and software, e. g. the server installation. The Managing Director emphasized that the small task force was very effective due to efficient communication and result-oriented actions.

5.2   Case Application of the Socio-Technical System Architecture

In the following, we describe all elements of the socio-technical system architecture according to Götzen et al. based on experiences of the case study partner as well as own observations made throughout the implementation process.

Organization

The Managing Director did not envision a **mission statement** for the initial pilot, as it was only an initial proof-of-concept. However, it was emphasized that successful implementation would lead to the creation of an automation strategy for the entire company. During the case study, the need for **leadership** to drive the RPA implementation was rated as high by all participating employees. It is emphasized that a top-down sponsorship is required, which provides the employees with time and budget needed. In the present use case, this role was taken on by the Managing Director. As documented in numerous literature articles and confirmed by various experts, **governance** is a supporting pillar of RPA implementation. Also, the case study partner defined responsibilities within the team constellation. After the pilot phase, the central IT department will keep the automation solutions permanently in operation. The establishment of a Centre of Excellence (CoE) was not pursued, as there are insufficient personnel capacities due to the company size. When introducing RPA, we recommend that the company carries out an analysis for **process and task design** before the automation goes into effect. In the use case, the process analysis was conducted in the form of interviews with the responsible staff. This helped the company to eliminate inconsistencies and design efficient and robust processes before automating. Taking **compliance** requirements into account, the company first examined which data is processed where and by which accounts. The bots used were then stored as digital resources or as external employees in the human resource system to provide access authorizations for the target applications.

Technical System

As part of the rollout, an application partner was brought in to provide the software and ensure **operability**. This partner was also responsible for error and exception handling and guaranteed that each bot went live with a defined status. In this context, the company's own IT department was also trained, as operational performance is closely interrelated with IT skills and competencies. The RPA application acts on the user interface of the in-house systems. Therefore, no complications regarding **infrastructure compatibility** are expected. To prevent the scenario of automating in systems for which the employee has no authorization, the case study company had to develop a technical access and rights concept. Together with the automation team, it was ensured that the RPA application had clear boundaries in form of reading and writing rights for each system served. This ensured **interoperability**. **Maintenance** becomes necessary whenever changes occur in the target system. However, since the company's applications are in-house, changes are predictable and not dependent on external releases. The maintenance effort is thus calculable and controlled by the process management.

Social System

All team members confirmed the need for a digital-savvy and open **corporate culture** for integrating extensive automation. Concerns were mainly expressed due to trust issues. Transparent communication is crucial to reduce uncertainty, as automation is often associated with job loss. However, the company was able to prevent conflicts by effectively redeploying human resources from administrative to cognitive tasks and transparently communicating the results from the start. Despite a dedicated automation team, implementation required a great deal of coordination and, above all, explanation. **Intraorganizational collaboration** is necessary but required extensive coordination to be successful due to the large number of stakeholders involved. This was ensured through regular coordination meetings. At first, the possibilities of RPA were incredibly overestimated by the employees. As the pilot did not produce the desired results from the start, initial **technology acceptance** dropped sharply as expectations could not be met from the get-go. With the help of further system tests, deficiencies were corrected, and acceptance ensured in the further course. There were no social fears of job loss due to transparent communication. While IT staff received extensive training on necessary **skills and competencies** also the IT affinity of employees in administration had to increase. The training was provided by the software provider and contributed immensely to an effective intraorganizational collaboration. For the successful RPA deployment, **individual goals and motivation** of employees were addressed and included in the process. The relief from repetitive tasks contributed significantly to the individual goals of each actor, as they saw a greater sense of purpose in their new field of activity.

The case study makes clear that all the socio-technical system elements shown are relevant for the implementation process. However, due to the individuality of each use case, the relevance varies greatly. Individual elements must therefore be addressed with varying intensity.

6   Managerial Implications and Conclusion

During our research activities, we applied the socio-technical system architecture of Götzen et al. in a real case study. Our investigation contributes to a deeper understanding of the organizational impact of RPA. The case application made it possible to confirm the relevance of the research contribution in the operational context and thus validate the presented framework.

Due to the size of the company, the relatively low software penetration within the respective industry, and limited financial and human resources, the use case company took a different approach to RPA implementation than the highly digitalized companies used for the model development. For this use case three critical success factors stood out:

1. **Project Sponsorship:** For small and medium sized companies it proved to be successful to have the Managing Director sponsor the RPA project. Besides ensuring resource availability, having the direct support of the Managing Director increased the project credibility and the commitment of the employees.
2. **Dedicated Task Force:** In contrast to enterprises with large IT-departments and an extensive range of administrative processes, establishing a discrete automation department is not feasible for smaller companies. Instead of creating a CoE, a small interdisciplinary taskforce for the automation project has shown to be very effective.
3. **Communication:** Addressing potential fears and uncertainties of employees from the beginning was crucial. To maintain trust, project results were communicated openly. In retrospect, the expectations of the employees could have been assessed earlier to minimize deviation between the expected and the actual scope of the software during the pilot phase.

The case study confirmed the high importance of all socio-technical elements and the industry-independence of the system architecture. Nevertheless, we identified a need for further research. To obtain more robust results, firstly, the framework needs to be applied in more cross-industry use cases. Secondly, this paper focused only on testing the relevance of the socio-technical system elements during an RPA implementation. Conversely, we think it would be interesting to investigate to which extent applying this framework before implementation can help to make RPA introductions even more efficient. At last, we consider testing the applicability of the model for the implementation of intelligent systems that consider the use of RPA and AI highly relevant for future research. This would show the extent to which the sociotechnical model hold validity in the context of higher levels of automation development.

Acknowledgments. The presented results are part of the research project "RPAcceptance". The IGF project 21512 N of the Research Association FIR e. V. at RWTH Aachen University, Campus-Boulevard 55, 52074 Aachen, is funded via the AiF within the cooperative industrial research fund (IGF) by the Federal Ministry of Economic Affairs and Climate Action (BMWK) based on a resolution of the German Bundestag. The responsibility for the content of this publication lies with the authors. We would like to thank the AiF for the kind support throughout this research project.

References

1. Syed, R., et al.: Robotic process automation: Contemporary themes and challenges. Comput. Ind. **115**, 1–55 (2020). https://doi.org/10.1016/j.compind.2019.103162
2. Lacity, M.C., Willcocks, L.P.: Robotic process automation at telefónica O2. MIS Q. Exec. **15**, 21–35 (2016)
3. Burnett, S., Aggarwal, M., Modi, A., Bhadola, S.: Studie: Defining Enterprise RPA (2018). https://www.uipath.com/reports/everest-defining-enterprise-rpa
4. van der Aalst, W.M.P., Bichler, M., Heinzl, A.: Robotic process automation. Bus. Inf. Syst. Eng. **60**(4), 269–272 (2018). https://doi.org/10.1007/s12599-018-0542-4
5. Allweyer, T.: Neue Perspektiven durch Robotic Process Automation. Hochschule Kaiserslautern, Kaiserslautern (2016)

6. Beers, A., Heijnsdijk, R., van Dalen, C.: Understanding the challenge of implementing your virtual workforce. Robotic Process Automation as part of a new social-technological paradigm (2018). https://www2.deloitte.com/content/dam/Deloitte/nl/Documents/strategy/deloitte-nl-so-understanding-challange-of-implementing-rpa.pdf
7. Strohm, O., Ulich, E. (eds.): Unternehmen arbeitspsychologisch bewerten: ein Mehr-Ebenen-Ansatz unter besonderer Berücksichtigung von Mensch, Technik und Organisation. MTO Schriftenreihe herausgegeben von Eberhard Ulich, Institut für Arbeitspsychologie der ETH Zürich, vdf, Hochschulverl. an der ETH Zürich (1997)
8. Strohm, O.: Die ganzheitliche MTO-analyse: Konzept und vorgehen. In: Strohm, O., Ulich, E. (eds.) Unternehmen arbeitspsychologisch bewerten: ein Mehr-Ebenen-Ansatz unter besonderer Berücksichtigung von Mensch, Technik und Organisation. MTO Schriftenreihe herausgegeben von Eberhard Ulich, Institut für Arbeitspsychologie der ETH Zürich, pp. 21–38. vdf, Hochschulverl. an der ETH Zürich (1997)
9. Aguirre, S., Rodriguez, A.: Automation of a business process using robotic process automation (RPA): A case study. In: Figueroa-García, J.C., López-Santana, E.R., Villa-Ramírez, J.L., Ferro-Escobar, R. (eds.) WEA 2017. CCIS, vol. 742, pp. 65–71. Springer, Cham (2017). https://doi.org/10.1007/978-3-319-66963-2_7
10. Willcocks, L.P., Lacity, M., Craig, A.: The IT function and robotic process automation. The Outsourcing Unit Working Research Paper Series, pp. 1–39 (2015)
11. Smeets, M., Erhard, R., Kaußler, T.: Robotic Process Automation (RPA) in der Finanzwirtschaft. Springer Fachmedien Wiesbaden, Wiesbaden (2019). https://doi.org/10.1007/978-3-658-26564-9
12. Ng, K.K.H., Chen, C.-H., Lee, C.K.M., Jiao, J., Yang, Z.-X.: A systematic literature review on intelligent automation: Aligning concepts from theory, practice, and future perspectives. Adv. Eng. Inform. **47**, 1–36 (2021)
13. Trist, E.L., Higgin, G.W., Murray, H., Pollock, A.B.: Organizational Choice. Capabilities of Groups at the Coal Face under Changing Technologies. Tavistock Publications, London (1963)
14. Trist, E.L., Bamforth, K.W.: Some social and psychological consequences of the longwall method of coal-getting. Human Relations **4**, 3–38 (1951). https://doi.org/10.1177/001872675100400101
15. Mumford, E.: Sociotechnical systems design: Evolving theory and practice. Working Paper - Manchester Business School, no. 100, Manchester (1985)
16. Götzen, R., Schuh, G., von Stamm, J., Conrad, R.: Soziotechnische Systemarchitektur für den Einsatz von Robotic Process Automation. HMD - Praxis der Wirtschaftsinformatik (2022)
17. Eisenhardt, K.M., Graebner, M.E.: Theory building from cases: Opportunities and challenges. Acad. Manag. J. **50**, 25–32 (2007). https://doi.org/10.5465/amj.2007.24160888
18. Eisenhardt, K.M.: Building theories from case study research. Acad. Manag. Rev. **14**, 532–550 (1989). https://doi.org/10.2307/258557
19. Ulrich, H.: Die Betriebswirtschaftslehre als anwendungsorientierte Sozialwissenschaft. In: Geist, M., Köhler, R. (eds.) Die Führung des Betriebes, pp. 1–25. C. E. Poeschel, Stuttgart (1981)

Impact Maximisation of Collaborative Projects Through Informal Leadership

Tiina Leino[1]([✉]) [ID], Omar Veledar[2] [ID], Georg Macher[3] [ID], Margherita Volpe[4],
Eric Armengaud[5] [ID], and Niina Koivunen[1] [ID]

[1] University of Vaasa, Wolffintie 34, 65200 Vaasa, Finland
{tiina.leino,niina.koivunen}@uwasa.fi
[2] AVL List GmbH, Hans-List-Platz 1, 8020 Graz, Austria
omar.veledar@avl.com
[3] Graz University of Technology, Inffeldgasse 16, 8010 Graz, Austria
georg.macher@tugraz.at
[4] Zabala Innovation, Rue Belliard 20, 1040 Brussels, Belgium
mvolpe@zabala.eu
[5] Armengaud Innovate, Haselsdorfbergstraße 8, 80144 Haselsdorf-Tobelbad, Austria
eric@armengaud.at

Abstract. The practice of collaborative innovation promises added benefits for the concerned stakeholders based on the capacity that the product of the knowledge, experience, and skills shared by the collaborating parties outweighs the sum of all the inputs. However, collaborations also carry the challenge associated with leadership, which is often established through informal influence. The paper presents the best practices for impactful informal leadership in collaborative innovation networks in project execution. The research is based on expert interviews with European start-ups, SMEs, large enterprises, and universities. The findings and recommendations focus on enhancing the impact of the innovative solutions once they are institutionalised in the organisations. The impact generally leverages the consequence of informal leadership, a naturally occurring phenomenon, emphasising the variability and reciprocity of leading, the meaning of strategic goals, and investing in human relations, and deeply contributing to the transition towards Industry 5.0 and Society 5.0.

Keywords: Collaborative · Informal · Leadership · Network

The work is supported by The Foundation for Economic Education, Huittinen Savings Bank Foundation, and Nissi Foundation, Finland. This research has received funding from the Horizon 2020 Programme of the European Union within the OpenInnoTrain project under grant agreement no. 823971. The content of this publication does not reflect the official opinion of the European Union. Responsibility for the information and views expressed in the publication lies entirely with the author(s).

L. M. Camarinha-Matos et al. (Eds.): PRO-VE 2022, IFIP AICT 662, pp. 115–123, 2022.
https://doi.org/10.1007/978-3-031-14844-6_10

1 Collaborative Networks and Informal Leadership

Collaborative working and leading are essential in the complex, contemporary organisational setting, and are also essential components of the transition towards Industry 5.0 and Society 5.0 where the economic advancement is balanced with the resolution of social problems [1]. Through collaboration, simultaneous projects are managed through people networks. The emphasis of this work is on the process, change, and emergence, which implies that these ongoing activities can be prioritised over stable entities [2]. Thus, engagement in collaborative project networks can enhance value creation for the organisation through the generation of innovative ideas.

In these networks, leadership is no longer associated only with individuals. Leadership is a collective behaviour, which results from several interdependent entities interacting with one another [3]. Leadership can also be understood as a network of influence relationships [4]. In collective leadership, the leadership roles and responsibilities change depending on the expertise required [5]. In these transitions of leadership, no formal leadership relations exist and informal leadership is utilised. Informal leadership is manifested in exerted influence over other people and the collective work without a formal leadership position [6] and is continuously re-negotiated based on the group's complex socially constructed interaction process [7]. Informal leadership influence in groups is characterised by competence, warmth [8], motivation to lead, and emotional intelligence [9]. These qualities contribute to creating a collaborating force that is willing to collectively contribute to a common purpose. As relationships and collaborative groups mature over time, leadership evolves and becomes more distributed, which contributes to group efficacy [8–10]. Eventually, the flow of informal leadership is affected by the ties in the network and the purpose of the group [11]. The changes in efficacy and the influence on a group's performance are bound to influence the acceptance of informal and collective leadership in collaborative networks. On one hand, this highlights the importance of informal leadership on a path to a common purpose from the organisational perspective, while, on the other hand, it raises the significance of informal leadership for individual performance and the development of people networks.

Informal leadership is intertwined with advanced knowledge [12]. This can be seen as expertise, which means having a good practical and theoretical knowledge of a subject, understanding own expertise, and being able to put the expert interpretations into practice towards an intended goal [13]. When collaborative problem-solving in complex scenarios is done, it is enhanced by the expertise [14], simultaneously creating space for the knowledge of all. In fact, collective decision-making is a form of collective leadership, and the quality of these collective decisions is enhanced through collective intelligence [15]. Also, considering multinational teams targeting cooperative innovation, they are more effective, if they oscillate between assertive and cooperative knowledge exchange processes [16] and their leadership is emphasised by the leader's competencies in knowledge management and transfer [17]. So, being open to the knowledge of others and collaborative working, enhances the leadership and quality of decisions in the group. The value is seen in the people who understand entities and their relations, and are willing to take part in collective and informal leading. That topic is especially relevant in the context of innovation for SMEs [18].

This research seeks answers to the question, of how informal and collective leadership function in collaborative networks. We also aim to suggest the best practices. The findings are based on conclusions drawn from interviews with multinational project experts in nine European countries. The experts operate in organisations of varying sizes and types i.e., start-ups, SMEs, large enterprises, and universities. Some of those are part of European cascade-funded projects that heavily rely on cooperation and informal leadership [19]. These projects are heavily reliant on cooperation, which speeds up access to the markets and improves project assets to generate sustainable impact [20].

2 Method

Eighteen semi-structured expert interviews were completed in March and April 2022. The interviewees were handpicked by the researchers based on the understanding that they have the essential knowledge of the question at hand [21] due to the perception of their experience.

Ten respondents are female and eight are male, representing nine nations: Austria (5), Spain (3), Ireland (2), Italy (2), Slovenia (2), Czech Republic (1), France (1), Portugal (1), and the UK (1). Two-thirds of the respondents are focused on operations in the technology sector. Thirteen of the respondents represented SMEs, three are from large enterprises, and two respondents are university employees. Seven interviewees hold top management positions, eight are operating in middle management, and three are employees with no formal management powers. The common theme for the interviewees is their active involvement in diverse multinational collaborative project environments and networks.

The interviewees are asked to review their actions regarding informal leadership and to unambiguously differentiate it from any formal leadership power which they might be granted in their organisation i.e., the focus is placed on collective work with those over whom no formal leadership position is existing. When evaluating the degree of understanding and utilisation of informal leadership, the characteristics defining the phenomenon, as described earlier, were taken into account. For example, it is evaluated if the interviewees are responding from the perspective of someone who is using their ties in the network to achieve their purpose, or if they try to exercise their hierarchical position. Also, the depth of engagement in the discussion regarding informal leadership, recognising it being separate from formal leadership, was evaluated. That includes evaluating if interviewees differentiate in terms of which approaches they apply when dealing with situations of different formality levels. In this process, fourteen respondents are categorised as having a clear understanding of informal leadership, while two have a clear recognition of the phenomenon, and two are not fully aware of it. The data is analysed using content analysis [22], and NVivo is used to manage and code the data [23]. In order to provide a solid foundation for comprehensive analysis and interpretation, the data acquired is approached from several angles.

3 Findings

Three approaches to informal leadership emerged: 1. Leading and being led, 2. Clear targets, and 3. Human relations, complemented by experienced positive and negative aspects regarding it. Approach Leading and being led emphasises collective leading, understanding leadership, leading, and being led. Clear targets emphasise strategic vision and values connecting. Human relations emphasise knowing people and trustworthiness. The themes are depicted in Fig. 1. They are further detailed in the following paragraphs.

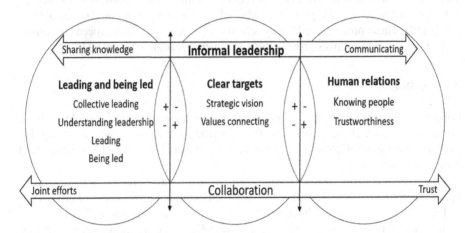

Fig. 1. Informal leadership in collaborative multinational networks

In general, the phenomenon of informal leadership was recognised in practice. Its formation, utilisation, and effects were also understood to a certain extent. However, a framework for discussing and handling the matter was limited. This could be due to the unfamiliarity with the concept of informal leadership, despite its natural occurrence along with formal leadership [24]. Informal leadership is approached as something built on trust, in a collaborative manner through joint efforts. It is utilised in everyday work to build networks, communicate, and build own knowledge, as well as the knowledge of the group. Taking informal leadership actions and roles had advanced some careers, but not necessarily. Informal leadership is seen to have a link to innovativeness. This connection is combined with openness and acknowledging others' strengths and skills to get the most out of people.

We find no links between the gender, organisation type, or nationality to the views on informal leadership. However, our analysis suggests that an increasing level of understanding of informal leadership results in an increasing openness towards others, the innovative aspect of work, interest in collective leadership, and interest in self-development. Simultaneously, decreasing level of understanding of informal leadership results in a higher reliance on hierarchies, and a reduction in openness toward collective leadership.

3.1 Leading and Being Led

The most important aspect of using collective leadership in collaborative networks is the ability to engage in it. This means the skill of both leading and being led, consisting of a) collective leading, b) understanding leadership, c) leading, and d) being led.

Collective leadership requires the ability to take a role and give a role to others, being able to share issues and leadership in a socially constructed process. A starting point is the ability to rely on others in taking the lead, based on their knowledge and expertise in the subject matter. This giving and taking role includes different practises, for example being flexible in both roles, modifying own behaviour to meet hoped leadership results, waiting and expecting others to take lead in their respective areas, not overstepping or stepping back, realising the need for someone taking over, being invited to participate, and also, if appropriate, being quiet and not participating in order not to get informal leadership responsibilities. All this requires an understanding of leadership and recognising its patterns. Informal leaders aim to learn leadership from others, either by observing others, learning from effective informal leadership practises, improving social skills or by being aware of own strengths:"Leading by example is crucial for informal leadership."

Thus, leading is based on this collectiveness and taking the role when own expertise is invited to lead. It is also about making improvements and engaging with issues, even if they are difficult or require confrontation. Resolving issues and making decisions are essential in this collective endeavour. Role giving happens when someone else has knowledge that is acknowledged to be superior and thus receives the granted position to lead. This requires the stance of being led as well. People who engage in informal leading themselves are also able to be led informally by others. They are open to being influenced by others. They also find it acceptable and useful if someone steps up to lead, as such action is perceived as helpful when based on knowledge:"There are people who have more expertise in some issues, and I can acknowledge that."

3.2 Clear Targets

Clear targets define the joint actions in projects. There are two aspects to this: a) strategic vision, and b) values connecting.

Following the collective leadership approach, also the strategic vision needs to be shared. Getting everyone on the same page is essential in cooperative projects because the vision guides the joint work contributing to both profit and quality. A shared vision eases the workflow and simplifies the resolution of disputes. Also, good fallback methods are created in case of unexpected events. Strategy contributes to the big picture of the project and further to individual responsibilities creating meaning and motivation. Values like reciprocity, honesty, and openness connect the collaborative work by helping participants to create directions for the joint effort:"A very good long term vision helps solve the short term issues."

3.3 Human Relations

Human relations in collaborative project networks rely on a) knowing people, and b) trustworthiness.

An effort is put into building the informal leadership network and gaining influence in it. Also, it is realised that it takes time to build relationships and that it needs to be beneficial to both parties:"We see it as equal parts when it comes to responsibility. It is a collaboration."

It is important to recognise every individual and encounter the relationship building through their personality, knowledge, and strengths. Through this knowing of each persona, trustworthiness is built. In this case, trust implies being trustworthy and trusting, which is aligned with the collective leading approach. Valuing trust means also saying no to pushiness or selfishness:"It's not like I need to keep everything to myself, I can rely on others also."

3.4 Positive and Negative Aspects

Informal leadership is understood and used in collaborative project networks, and there are both positive and negative aspects when engaging in it.

Taking the role of an informal leader is mostly seen as a pleasant task. People enjoy leading through their expertise, improving issues, mentoring others, and also sometimes being promoted due to these activities. Getting recognition and being seen as a person to achieve things is pleasant:"I really enjoyed it and it was energising."

Possibly the most notable negative aspect is handling hierarchy, be it either in own organisation or in a collaborative project. This can be harmful to collaboration as it may unnecessarily delay issues in situations where no hierarchical decisions are required. Sometimes informal leaders get an impression of status threat or ineptitude to handle the phenomenon by the formal leaders. Issues like silencing others, fearing change, and protecting own turf can emerge: "I have an issue with it, especially if it is not merit-based. This informal way of overtaking the projects is not acceptable to me. I felt in the past like someone was stepping on my shoes."

Informal leadership actions can also cause work overload and can result in stepping back. People can experience difficulties in getting their voice heard and valued when informal leadership is happening: "If I see no impact, I tend to withdraw and have not much energy to invest."

4   Discussion

Our analysis of the expressed views of experts who actively participate in collaborative projects and multinational innovation networks helps us propose key aspects in maximising informal leadership in these situations. Our findings show three main approaches that contribute to the maximisation of benefits through the utilisation of informal leadership. As described in the previous chapter and Fig. 1, the most relevant approaches are based on leading and being led, clearly defined and articulated targets, and appropriate human relations. These aspects are in this discussion, and we review the findings regarding their impact, advantages, disadvantages, and suggestions for improvement.

'Leading and being led' aspect requires participants to be willing to engage in collective leading, and be able to both take and give the leading role. This demands an understanding of the social aspect of leadership as well as a willingness to learn about leadership processes. As a consequence, through informal and collective leadership, it is possible to utilise all knowledge available in the group. It is important to understand individuals' roles in advancing issues, as well as acknowledge others' knowledge and learn from them. However, some people can be unable to handle informal leadership, which can harm both personal relationships and the collective work. In these situations, the group's issues may unnecessarily be subjected to formal management decisions. Also, in some cases, informal leadership actions are rejected as they imply an increasing personal workload. To be successful in this and to commit everyone to the task, a clear indication of utilising informal and collective leadership in the collaborative project should be given. Also, from the organisation's side, it is needed to ensure the power, time, and support in this collective work. Eventually, people need to be allowed to be engaged in collaborative network leading and decision-making, as well as trusted in the endeavour. There is a need for people to be aware of informal and collective leadership and its requirements.

'Clear targets' create a shared vision or purpose to guide joint work and help people commit. Defining joint values and the way of working creates unity within the project team. Having clear targets makes collaborative working more efficient and focused. Hence, the joint work becomes rather self-organised based on the expertise and responsibilities, while the joint values work as the glue for the project team. However, if there are no clear targets, everyone may start working based on their personal agendas. In this case, the collaborativeness of the project is rather distant, and simultaneously the link between pre-defined and actual project outcomes may drift farther apart. To avoid this, clear targets with strategies for achieving them and agreeing on joint values should be essential in a collaborative project. If clear targets are not set, efforts can be in vain. Eventually, the meaning of collaboration should be remembered as a value joint working towards a goal and contribution of all participants.

'Human relations' highlights the effort invested in knowing and understanding participants in collaborative projects. Knowing others' skills is key in utilising them to the benefit of the joint work. To be successful in this, one needs to be trustworthy and able to trust others. As a consequence, through honest and sincere cooperation, it is possible to achieve results even above the set targets, when everyone feels free and safe to express their opinions, even if critical. Also, personally knowing each other creates clarity and openness to working. However, if some withdraw from this collective of people, there can be an imbalance in the group, when the commitment of all participants is not seen. Knowing on personal level also can create situations of being excessively involved, and the work issues may be affected by personal matters. Thus, there should be a social balance between of work and people in collaborative projects, so that all issues, both positive and negative, can be addressed constructively. After all, it is everyone's responsibility to understand their input in creating this social balance of a collaborative project network.

5   Conclusions

Informal and collective leadership create knowledge sharing, efficacy, and coherence in collaborative projects and networks. This research contributes to the literature by synthesising the views of those involved in collaborative projects in terms of how they see and use informal leadership, how multinational collaborative projects benefit from it, and what are the best practices.

Our key findings indicate that informal leadership is mostly understood and knowingly used at the managerial level of collaborative projects. However, the absence of a shared framework for understanding it hampers discussing and realising the phenomenon. Collaborative networks benefit from informal and collective leadership. Understanding the variability and reciprocity of leading, the meaning of strategic goals, and investing in human relations are key points. Understanding informal leadership is related to openness towards others, interest in collective leadership, innovativeness, and self-development. Whereas not recognising the informal leadership phenomenon is related to relying on hierarchies and dislike of collective leadership.

The research was conducted with 18 interviewees acting in several international networks. While the amount of data may be limited to yield common generalisations, the focus is placed on people who already operate in collaborative projects and should be used to resourcing informal leadership approaches if they wish to achieve the common purpose. However, the results and recommendations are open to testing in other collaborative projects and networks. As such, they perhaps could contribute to a generalised model as they add value to the previous research. Informal leadership can drive the maximisation of the impact of collaborative projects and networks. It also contributes to the transformation of work in the transition towards Industry 5.0 and Society 5.0, which is a key to the resolution of social problems and a crucial contributor to sustainable development goals.

References

1. Gladden, M.E.: Who will be the members of society 5.0? Towards an anthropology of technologically posthumanized future societies. Soc. Sci. **8**, 148 (2019). https://doi.org/10.3390/socsci8050148
2. Sergi, V., Crevani, L., Aubry, M.: Process studies of project organizing. Proj. Manag. J. **51**(1), 3–10 (2020). https://doi.org/10.1177/8756972819896482
3. Cullen-Lester, K.L., Yammarino, F.J.: Collective and network approaches to leadership: Special issue introduction. Leadersh. Quart. **27**(2), 173–180 (2016). https://doi.org/10.1016/j.leaqua.2016.02.001
4. Chrobot-Mason, D., Gerbasi, A., Cullen-Lester, K.L.: Predicting leadership relationships: The importance of collective identity. Leadersh. Quart. **27**(2), 298–311 (2016). https://doi.org/10.1016/j.leaqua.2016.02.003
5. Friedrich, T.L., Vessey, W.B., Schuelke, M.J., Ruark, G.A., Mumford, M.D.: A framework for understanding collective leadership: The selective utilization of leader and team expertise within networks. Leadersh. Quart. **20**(6), 933–958 (2009). https://doi.org/10.1016/j.leaqua.2009.09.008
6. Zhang, C., Nahrgang, J.D., Ashford, S.J., DeRue, D.S.: The risky side of leadership: Conceptualizing risk perceptions in informal leadership and investigating the effects of their over-time changes in teams. Organ. Sci. **31**(5), 1138–1158 (2020). https://doi.org/10.1287/orsc.2019.1350
7. Cook, A., Meyer, B., Gockel, C., Zill, A.: Adapting leadership perceptions across tasks: Micro-origins of informal leadership transitions. Small Group Res. **50**(2), 227–265 (2019). https://doi.org/10.1177/1046496418810437
8. Fransen, K., Delvaux, E., Mesquita, B., Van Puyenbroeck, S.: The emergence of shared leadership in newly formed teams with an initial structure of vertical leadership: A longitudinal analysis. J. Appl. Behav. Sci. **54**(2), 140–170 (2018). https://doi.org/10.1177/0021886318756359

9. Hong, Y., Catano, V.M., Liao, H.: Leader emergence: The role of emotional intelligence and motivation to lead. Leadersh. Org. Dev. J. **32**(4), 320–343 (2011). https://doi.org/10.1108/01437731111134625/FULL/PDF

10. Pescosolido, A.T.: Informal leaders and the development of group efficacy. Small Group Res. **32**(1), 74–93 (2001). https://doi.org/10.1177/104649640103200104

11. Balkundi, P., Kilduff, M.: The ties that lead: A social network approach to leadership. Leadersh. Q. **16**(6), 941–961 (2005). https://doi.org/10.1016/j.leaqua.2005.09.004

12. Stincelli, E., Baghurst, T.: A grounded theory exploration of informal leadership qualities as perceived by employees and managers in small organizations. Int. J. Bus. Manage. Econ. Res. **5**(1), 1–8 (2014)

13. Bogner, A., Littig, B., Menz, W.: Interviewing Experts. Palgrave Macmillan, UK (2009). https://doi.org/10.1057/9780230244276

14. Nokes-Malach, T.J., Meade, M.L., Morrow, D.G.: The effect of expertise on collaborative problem solving. Think. Reason. **18**(1), 32–58 (2012). https://doi.org/10.1080/13546783.2011.642206

15. McHugh, K.A., Yammarino, F.J., Dionne, S.D., Serban, A., Sayama, H., Chatterjee, S.: Collective decision making, leadership, and collective intelligence: Tests with agent-based simulations and a field study. Leadersh. Quart. **27**(2), 218–241 (2016). https://doi.org/10.1016/j.leaqua.2016.01.001

16. Hajro, A., Gibson, C.B., Pudelko, M.: Knowledge exchange processes in multilcultural teams: Linking organizational diversity climates to teams' effectiveness. Acad. Manage. J. **60**(1), 345–372 (2017). https://doi.org/10.5465/amj.2014.0442

17. Hajro, A., Pudelko, M.: An analysis of core-competences of successful multinational team leaders. Int. J. Cross Cult. Manage. **10**(2), 175–194 (2010). https://doi.org/10.1177/1470595810370910

18. Macher, G., Veledar, O.: Balancing exploration and exploitation through open innovation in the automotive domain – focus on SMEs. In: Yilmaz, M., Clarke, P., Messnarz, R., Reiner, M. (eds.) EuroSPI 2021. CCIS, vol. 1442, pp. 336–348. Springer, Cham (2021). https://doi.org/10.1007/978-3-030-85521-5_22

19. Volpe, M., et al.: Experimentation of cross-border digital innovation hubs (DIHs) cooperation and impact on SME services. In: Camarinha-Matos, L.M., Boucher, X., Afsarmanesh, H. (eds.) PRO-VE 2021. IAICT, vol. 629, pp. 423–432. Springer, Cham (2021). https://doi.org/10.1007/978-3-030-85969-5_39

20. Volpe, M., Rojas, I.G., Veledar, O., Cavallini, S.: Cascade funding as an alternative funding source for innovative investments. In: Proceedings of the 17th European Conference on Innovation and Entrepreneurship (ECIE) (2022)

21. Grenier, R.S., Germain, M.-L.: Expertise through the HRD lens research. In: Chalofsky, N.E., Morris, M.L., Rocco, T.S. (eds) Chapter 11 in Handbook of Human Resource Development. Wiley (2014). https://doi.org/10.1002/9781118839881.ch11

22. Schreier, M.: Qualitative content analysis. In: Proceedings of The SAGE Handbook of Qualitative Data Analysis, pp. 170–183. SAGE Publications (2014). https://doi.org/10.4135/9781446282243.N12

23. Bazeley, P., Jackson, K.: Qualitative data analysis with Nvivo, 3rd ed. SAGE Publications (2019)

24. Denis, J.L., Langley, A., Sergi, V.: Leadership in the plural. Acad. Manag. Ann. **6**(1), 211–283 (2012). https://doi.org/10.1080/19416520.2012.667612

Collaborative Business Models
and Digitalization

The Business Ecosystem Perspective in Digital Strategies

Martin van den Berg[✉] and Klaas Brongers

Utrecht University of Applied Sciences, Utrecht, Netherlands
martin.m.vandenberg@hu.nl, k.brongers@solutions4u.nl

Abstract. According to literature, digital transformation requires an organization to develop a broad, holistic, and business ecosystem perspective on how digital technologies can be used to rethink and improve business models, products, services, and processes. The objective of this research is to empirically explore the claim that the business ecosystem perspective is one of the dominant views in organizations' digital transformation initiatives and more specifically in the digital strategy. We studied seven organizations in the Netherlands through semi-structured interviews and digital strategy documents. These organizations are aware of developments in their business ecosystem. However, their plans, as outlined in their digital strategies, mainly focus on improving internal operations. We also found that collaboration enablers are partially present in digital strategies. Digital strategies and subsequent digital transformations are mainly internally focused. We argue that collaborative business models must be developed at the business ecosystem level rather than at the individual organizational level.

Keywords: Digital strategy · Digital transformation · Business ecosystem · Enablers for collaboration · Collaborative networks

1 Introduction

Digital transformation (DT) is a phenomenon that occupies many organizations and scientists. A systematic literature review demonstrates that the number of publications on DT steadily increased from 2000 to 2018 [1]. The worldwide spending on DT technologies and services in 2022 is projected on USD 1.8 trillion and is expected to increase to USD 2.8 trillion by 2025 [2]. A DT can lead to a significant transformation of an organization or an entire industry [3]. To be successful, a DT must be viewed in a broad, holistic, and organization-transcending perspective [4, 5]. Components, systems, value chains, products, and processes of different organizations become more and more connected [6]. One of the terms that is being used to indicate the interconnectedness of organizations is business ecosystem [7]. While we endorse the importance of this ecosystem, we question the claim that the business ecosystem perspective is one of the dominant views in organizations' DT initiatives. If an organization wants to include the business ecosystem perspective in its DT, the digital strategy (DS) should be the first

© IFIP International Federation for Information Processing 2022
Published by Springer Nature Switzerland AG 2022
L. M. Camarinha-Matos et al. (Eds.): PRO-VE 2022, IFIP AICT 662, pp. 127–140, 2022.
https://doi.org/10.1007/978-3-031-14844-6_11

place to address that perspective. A DS can be seen as the roadmap for a DT [8]. With this empirical study we want to explore the extent to which organizations incorporate the business ecosystem perspective in their DS. Empirical research of digital business ecosystems is needed to validate models and frameworks [9]. We consider our study as an empirical examination of the DS as one of the most prominent places to highlight the role and importance of the business ecosystem perspective.

Our main research question is: *to what extent is the business ecosystem perspective present in digital strategies of organizations*?

This paper is structured as follows: In Sect. 2 we present related work. The research method is explained in Sect. 3. In Sect. 4 we present the results, which are discussed in Sect. 5. Section 5 also describes the limitations. In Sect. 6 we summarize the conclusion.

2 Related Work

Our research focuses on investigating the business ecosystem perspective in DTs. But what is a DT? A DT is completely different from just changing the organizational structure or conducting experiments [4, 10]. Hartl defines a DT as the IT-enabled change in organizations through digitalization of products, services, core processes, customer touch points, and business models [11]. Such a DT has a disruptive effect on organizations. They must rethink their business models, organize the financing of their activities differently, look for new collaboration partners, increase the digital literacy of their employees, and bring about different culture values [11]. To be successful, the general opinion is that a DT must be viewed in a broad, holistic, and organization-transcending perspective [4, 5]. Organizations these days strive for collaborative advantage. According to Roobeek et al. this requires diversity and agility, transparent collaboration in flexible networks, optimal use of competencies in the network, more opportunities to show leadership and entrepreneurship, and more contact with the outside world [12]. This organization-transcending perspective is indicated through terms like business ecosystem, extended enterprise, and collaborative networks [6]. In this research, we will use the term business ecosystem as defined by Peltoniemi and Vuori [7]. They defined a business ecosystem as "a dynamic structure which consists of an interconnected population of organizations".

An important component of a DT is the DS [3]. This strategy functions as a kind of roadmap for the DT and "considers how digital technology can completely reshape the company's relationships—with customers, with employees, with the market as a whole—to create a digital edge, where digital information and physical resources combine in new ways to create value and revenue" [8]. Ideally, a DS should be part of the organizational strategy [13]. Gupta even argues that the DS should not be a separate strategy, but the leading strategy of an organization [10]. This study's focus is on the business ecosystem perspective in the DS as an important step in a DT.

Collaboration in business ecosystems can be enabled in different ways. In this research we used five enablers: 1) culture of collaboration, 2) governance for collaboration, 3) data centricity, 4) speed and boldness, and 5) digital literacy. The first three enablers are essential prerequisites for collaboration. Speed and boldness, and digital literacy are important enablers for DTs, and therefor also for collaboration in business ecosystems. We discuss the enablers one by one.

By a culture of collaboration, we mean a culture in which organizational silos are broken down and data sharing is self-evident. Organizational silos impact business performance and create an inward, rather than an outward, focus [14–16]. A culture of collaboration is a prerequisite for collaboration in a business ecosystem [12].

Secondly, a certain form of governance for collaboration is required with a shift from a control orientation to a collaboration orientation [6]. Organizations often consist of silos. The step that needs to be taken is one towards organizations as collaborative networks. Gray calls this the connected company [17]. An organization that is also characterized as a holarchy or holocracy in which decision-making is pushed to the lowest viable organizational level [4, 17]. An agile way of working is a way to achieve this [4].

In a data-centric architecture data are separated from the application, become the central asset, and move into a network known as a data collaboration platform or data fabric. These platforms allow data to exist as a network, and this networked approach means that data can be shared and reused across various applications without making copies [18, 19]. With data centricity, data copies and integration efforts can be reduced or even eliminated. As a result, collaboration and integration in business ecosystems becomes much easier [19].

DTs also require speed and boldness. Ross et al. distinguish between the operational backbone and the digital platform as two important building blocks that help companies succeed digitally. The operational backbone is "a coherent set of standardized, integrated systems, processes, and data supporting a company's core operations" [4]. The digital platform is defined as a "repository of business, data, and infrastructure components used to rapidly configure digital offerings" [4]. Bossert also distinguishes between a "fast-speed, customer-centric front end and a slow-speed, transaction-focused legacy back end" [20]. The words "rapidly" and "fast-speed" indicate that speed is required. And speed requires agility [4, 20]. Agility can be increased by delegating decision-making and working in an agile fashion. Next to speed, a certain boldness is required. Blackburn et al. demonstrate that a bold approach, in which new technology is used on a larger scale, pays off [21]. Organizations that apply this bold approach grow faster than organizations that work carefully and step by step. The time of cautious experimentation in a remote corner of the organization is over.

Finally, employees of organizations need a certain level of digital literacy. Employees should be encouraged and facilitated in learning and improving their digital skills. This requires actions such as increasing the digital knowledge and skills of employees and establishing DT leadership [22]. Data centricity is only successful if employees embrace it or, better yet, take the lead. Digital literacy is thus a precondition for data centricity. Martin defined digital literacy as "awareness, attitude and ability of individuals to appropriately use digital tools and facilities to identify, access, manage, integrate, evaluate, analyze and synthesize digital resources, construct new knowledge, create media expressions, and communicate with others, in the context of specific life situations, in order to enable constructive social action; and to reflect upon this process" [23].

3 Research Design

Our research follows a qualitative research design and more specifically, an inductive approach in which we study organizations to collect observations as the basis for theories [24]. In line with Morsch, we prefer this approach over a deductive approach, such as how to improve strategy development to incorporate the business ecosystem perspective [25].

To collect observations, we found seven organizations in the Netherlands through our network of the Royal Dutch Computer Association (KNVI), two private and five public, who shared their DS with us. Table 1 contains an overview of the organizations and the interviewees.

We used semi-structured interviews and studied DS documents from the participating organizations. The interviews were held from February to June 2021 with the person responsible for the DT. Each interview was conducted by two researchers and resulted in a report that was supplemented and approved by the interviewee.

The combination of interviews and documents acted as a form of triangulation that allowed us to gather evidence and explanations for the presence of the business ecosystem perspective in the DSs.[1]

Table 1. Organizations and interviewees included in this study.

	Industry	Type	Employees	Interviewee
O1	Healthcare	Public	17,000	IT Director
O2	Insurance	Private	600	CTO
O3	Pensions	Private	1,500	CIO
O4	IT services	Public	170	Director
O5	Hospital	Public	5,500	Head of business intelligence (BI)
O6	Municipality	Public	17,000	CIO
O7	University	Public	4,000	CIO

We wanted to discover to what extent the business ecosystem perspective is present in the DSs of these seven organizations, not primarily by asking for that perspective, but by discussing components of a DS in which that perspective may occur, such as drivers, vision, business model, and operating model.

Furthermore, we discussed five enablers for participating in business ecosystems. These enablers, which we discussed in Sect. 2, are culture of collaboration, governance for collaboration, data centricity, speed and boldness, and digital literacy.

We based the analysis of interview reports and documents on the components of a DS such as drivers, vision, business model, and operating model. These components acted as a-priori themes for analysis purposes to finally determine the presence of the business ecosystem perspective in DSs [26]. The results of this analysis are discussed in

---

[1] Access to the raw material and analysis can be requested from the first author.

Sect. 4.1. Furthermore, we collected evidence from the interview reports and documents to determine the extent to which the enablers for collaboration are present in the DSs. The results of this analysis are discussed in Sect. 4.2.

4 Results

First, we discuss the main characteristics of the DSs of the seven Dutch organizations, including the business ecosystem perspective. Second, we compare the enablers for collaboration one by one across the seven organizations.

4.1 Presence of Business Ecosystem Perspective in Digital Strategies

O1 offers different healthcare services to clients such as nursing, care, home care, mental healthcare, and care to people with a mental disability. At the heart of the DS are events in a client's life from birth to death, described from a business ecosystem perspective. These descriptions provide insight in the way O1 aims to collaborate with organizations like healthcare insurers, instances for childcare, instances for mental diseases, and other providers of healthcare services. Part of the DS are so-called focus areas. One of these focus areas is the way collaboration and the exchange of data should be organized. Some services require different healthcare service providers to collaborate. These service providers must have access to the client's data that are needed to deliver the required service. According to O1's IT Director *"The outcomes of our digital strategy must fit within the healthcare system. We are not free to optimize everything as we see fit. Funding is a permanent issue. There is broad awareness that we depend on collaboration in the sector. We can and must collaborate with other institutions to achieve more."* The introduction of technologies like cloud computing, digital workspace, and intelligent diapers require a certain scale. The best way to introduce such technologies is through an industry association and involving executive managers of associated organizations. These managers can ensure that there is support and funding. O1 is an example of an organization that has embedded the business ecosystem perspective in its DS and establishing concrete links to the client's life events.

O2 positions itself as the legal problem solver and offers legal insurance services. O2's strategy is to become a smart insurer. One of the pillars of this strategy is a DT which has an explicit dependence on the pillar new services and business concepts. A certain digital readiness, including infrastructure, is required to be able to realize new models and concepts. An important part of the DT is a solid foundation. In concrete terms, this means a replacement of legacy working methods. The CTO of O2 indicates the objective of O2: *"To create a digital portfolio of products and services with an ecosystem of partners and by using legal tech."* Currently, its challenge is to adequately serve the business by speeding up the time to deliver solutions and by translating customer demand into the most suitable solution. The switch to IT as an enabler must be made with careful attention to the costs. After all, the costs of IT have a direct effect on returns and premium levels. For the longer term, choices are made based on smart services, smart data, and smart culture. Young people do not want to buy traditional insurance services, which means that O2 must offer new types of services. Insurance services are under pressure anyway. Developing new types of services requires high-quality customer and claims data and a culture that allows O2 to develop and innovate services. O2 is aware that it is part of the criminal justice chain, which is traditional in outlook and has hardly digitized. To sum up, O2 addresses the business ecosystem perspective in its DS. However, this perspective is not yet concrete. The digital readiness of O2 and of the criminal justice chain must be improved first.

O3 provides pension administration services. The Dutch pension sector will soon change over to a new pension system. O3 is preparing for this changing landscape and wants to be at the forefront in terms of customer satisfaction, efficiency, and flexibility. For O3 customers, the new pension system means they need to switch to a new pension scheme by 1 January 2026 at the latest. In terms of strategy, O3 focuses on one sector and no longer on a multi-client approach. O3 also needs to deal with new market entrants that promise a low price per member. The latter aspect has a great impact on O3, which is substantially more expensive than new entrants. The strategy is then translated into financial targets as a dot on the horizon. The collaboration with another pension provider contributes to this. Parties with innovative business models are not yet seen as a threat. A stable IT landscape is a precondition for a DT. O3 achieves this with a cloud-first strategy and by devoting attention to security. According to the O3's CIO, *"The essence of a digital transformation is to find a balance between the business and IT. The role of the CIO is to explain the why, what, and how to all stakeholders. That is a balancing act, also between aspects such as agility, legacy and being in control. Innovation and operations must go hand in hand."* The future of O3 depends on developments in its business ecosystem. It seeks collaboration with another pension administrator and based on its DS it prepares for the new pension system.

O4 is a cooperative that develops IT solutions for providing social benefits. Its IT solutions are used by municipalities. The core system supports the implementation of social benefit laws and income schemes. O4 exchanges data with various organizations in the social benefit domain. O4 is transforming itself from a shared service center to a product supplier. The combination of municipalities acting as both owner and customer used to create tension regarding the provision of services. The outcome of a rethink of its business model is a product vision with a roadmap. According to the director of O4, *"This must lead to a market-compliant organization that must be able to deliver pay per use cloud-based services and enable us to compete with market parties."* The current application silos are transformed into value chains based on operational excellence. Parts of the rethink are divesting the data center, scaling down the organization, and adjusting the governance model. O4 wants to become a learning and scalable organization based on principles of high-performance organizations. The reorganization is a step-by-step process with a reduction of workforce, a focus on internal development capacity, and on both hard and soft skills. The new model offers opportunities for data-driven working and artificial intelligence (AI), such as explainable AI, and proactively approaching citizens with options that they are currently not aware of. In addition, policy effects can be predicted, and data made available to municipalities. O4 is an example of an organization looking to transform and reposition itself in its business ecosystem.

O5 is a hospital with 35 specialisms, and some 580,000 outpatient visits, 40,000 clinical admissions, and 46,000 daily admissions yearly. The hospital strives to provide value driven care in a time of personal and financial scarcity. The DS focuses on 1) the patient experience, 2) ecosystems, 3) the internet-of-things platform, 4) the healthcare information system, and 5) data and analytics. Data and analytics are the core of the DS. The goal of the hospital is to become a data-driven organization that will be able to add value within all hospital processes through insights obtained from data, where data has become a permanent and constant part of the work and is considered of tactical and strategic value. In this way, O5 provides better quality care based on data. According to the head of BI, *"The process information is now correct and 25 care paths and so-called 'patient reported outcome measures' have been elaborated. We are now ready to take the step to medical content data delivery and medical content analysis. This takes shape in a pragmatic way. We support pilots that are well-substantiated. The focus is on the actual usage and demonstrable changes and improvements."* Ambitions can differ greatly per department. The collaboration with external partners, such as providers of medical equipment, requires a focus on data ownership. Health insurers contribute to shaping new business models. Digital skills of employees are initiated through intensive supervision and motivation. There is explicit support from the executive board. The business ecosystem perspective is part of the DS of O5, albeit not the dominant one.

O6 is a municipality that consists of clusters, an administrative and corporate staff, and city districts. The clusters have expertise in a specific area, such as sports, youth, or parking. In the past, the decentralized IT environment consisted of thousands of applications and suffered from continuity problems. At that time, efforts were made to rationalize and consolidate, trimming down to around 1,000 applications and achieving lower costs. For several years now, IT efforts have been concentrated on the task towards reliable digital services. The added value must be recognizable within an extremely political context. Challenges are the accelerated technological developments, the city's tasks, the increased expectations on the part of citizens, an increased risk of cybercrime, and requirements from legislation (such as GDPR). O6 has a strong focus on digital government and digital society, acknowledging that digital is not neutral. There are limitations to the scalability of the infrastructure, limitations in continuity and uniformity, external threats, and the need for digital skills. There is no urgency from a burning platform. This allows a step-by-step approach. The migration to the cloud has started. The data organization is under construction. Deferred maintenance is addressed. Security is a priority. The human side is decisive for successful implementation of the DT. Agile working helps to connect with the line organization. Craftsmanship is the carrier of change. This offers perspective and makes an explicit cultural trajectory superfluous. Some departments work with customer journeys. Cooperation with other cities runs through the so-called common ground initiative of the Association of Netherlands Municipalities. There is awareness that municipalities must each rationalize their own IT landscapes to a minimum and gradually start working together in areas where there are similarities. Collaboration with parties in the business ecosystem, such as municipalities, suppliers, knowledge institutions, and other government bodies, is central to O6.

O7 has an educational model with an international outlook and a multidisciplinary approach: education and research are best organized in teams rather than individually, the notion of diversity and multidisciplinary approaches, and forging links with different stakeholders in the city, the region, Europe, and the rest of the world. A CIO was appointed to bring the position of IT to a strategic level by shaping the DS. The DS focuses on education, research, business operations, and IT. In addition, the DS has three themes: create value, be efficient, and comply and cyber security. The DS touches on three dimensions: people, process, and technology. Updating the DS is now in sync with updating O7's overall strategy. SWOT analyses are used for this purpose. CIOs from other universities are aligned on a common thread and benchmarked. The domain representatives are becoming aware of what digitalization means for them. Everyone now has an opinion and that creates a new dynamic. The customer journeys of the student and the researcher are partly discussed in the DS. The step towards integral support of business operations means a business transformation. The ambition in terms of DT is still modest. Data-driven working and applying AI are in the interest of the research domain. The DS was compared with another university. In terms of content there appeared to be 90% similarity. The CIO points out that *"The content of a digital strategy is not that exciting. The essence is the process of getting the right people together and agreeing on the content of the digital strategy. And that is different in every organization, partly due to cultural differences."* O7's DS demonstrates business ecosystem awareness. For the time being, the focus is on the transformation of the IT function.

4.2   Presence of Enablers for Collaboration in Digital Strategies

In this section we compare the seven Dutch organizations in terms of the extent to which the enablers for collaboration are present in their DSs. More specifically, we judge the degree of activities already performed and planned on the enablers as part of their DSs. The enablers are judged against an ordinal scale following ISO/IEC 33020 [27]. The basis of this judgment is the evidence we found in the interview reports and DS documents. Table 2 contains the results, which are explained in more detail.

Table 2. The extent to which the enablers for collaboration are present in the digital strategies of organizations. N = Not, P = Partially, L = Largely, F = Full, based on [27].

	O1	O2	O3	O4	O5	O6	O7
Culture of collaboration	P	P	P	L	L	P	P
Governance for collaboration	N	P	P	L	P	P	P
Data centricity	P	N	L	N	L	P	N
Speed and boldness	P	N	P	P	P	N	P
Digital literacy	P	P	P	P	P	P	P

Culture of Collaboration. O1 is aware of the need for collaboration. Implementation is still limited. Clients' life events are described from a business ecosystem perspective.

O1 has an eye for broad collaboration in the sector. O2 addresses the business ecosystem perspective in its DS based on customer journeys and wants to move towards a culture of continuous improvement and an agile way of working. These perspectives are not yet concrete. The digital readiness and the criminal justice chain need to be improved first. O3 implemented agile working and BizDevOps. The focus is on the involvement and enthusiasm of employees. O4 moves from silos to value chains, from a government to a market organization. O5 is creating a culture in which agile working, value creation, and data-driven working takes center stage. O6 aspires to achieve coherence, collaboration, and openness. Agile working helps to connect with the line organization. Collaboration with other cities runs through a so-called common ground. O7 organizes collaboration in teams rather than individually with the notion of diversity and multi-disciplinary approaches, and forging links with different. O7 wants to implement agile working and DevOps.

Governance for Collaboration. O1 still needs to address governance aspects. A DS program director has been appointed. O2 moves towards an agile way of working. Empowerment of product owners has started. O3 implemented agile working and BizDevOps to bring people together. O4 works on a fit-for-purpose organization based on value chains within a market-based governance structure, including a supervisory board. O5 implemented agile working and installed an enterprise information steering committee in which different interests are represented and initiatives are prioritized. O6 pays attention to unambiguous and coordinated management, changes in financial management, connection with line management with responsibilities to product owners, the introduction of agile working and DevOps, and the importance of cooperation. O7 integrates processes and technology that support the whole IT value chain and can facilitate agile working, DevOps, and rapid application development. Close multi-disciplinary collaboration is encouraged.

Data Centricity. O1 demonstrates that it is working on this enabler, both within the organization and in the business ecosystem. O1 defined projects on data-driven working, data infrastructure, and data exchange with a standardization committee. O2 sees smart data as a basis for long term choices. Architecture diagrams mainly show an application-centric approach. Change towards a data-centric approach is under preparation. O3 pays a lot of attention to data quality and has a data platform. There are data stewards, a tool for data definitions, and there is a data governance board that anchors ownership of data. A data delivery platform is linked to source systems by which it created a single source of the truth. Algorithms are being used. O4's focus on data is low due to priorities, complexity, and sensitivity. A new set-up of the organization offers future opportunities for data-driven working and AI. O5 has a pragmatic and emerging approach, based on architectural choices and the data-management standard DAMA DMBOK®. Data becomes a fixed part of the work and is of tactical and strategic value. O6 wants to focus on data and AI, including a focus on ethics and privacy. The data organization is under construction. O7 is interested in the research domain for data-driven working and the application of AI. These initiatives are still limited. O7 intends to create a data infrastructure and a data governance with supporting services like data scientists and data stewards.

Speed and Boldness. O1 has little shared sense of urgency to work with new technologies. Gradually, it is realizing that the DS is profitable. O1 demonstrates boldness in taking events in a client's life from birth to death at the heart of its DS. O2's customers feel little urgency to digitize. The strategy has been translated into projects that are in progress. Many legacy systems have been replaced by SaaS. O2 wants to take customer journeys as a starting point. O3 shows boldness in preparing for a changing pension landscape and wants to be at the forefront of pension administration in terms of customer satisfaction, efficiency, and flexibility. O4 shows boldness in transforming itself to a market-compliant organization within a few years. External input is used as a leverage. A roadmap supports the step-by-step change. O5 lends shape to innovation in a pragmatic way based on 25 care paths and patient reported outcome measures. It supports pilots that are well-substantiated. The focus is on actual use and demonstrable changes and improvements. Successful boosters serve as an example. O6 has no urgency from a burning platform, which allows a step-by-step approach. The DS is mainly driven by opportunities for improvement. O7 shows boldness in transforming IT to an enabler. Key for the coming years is to build the foundations for future developments in education and research. This is its first step in its initiatives to change from running the university to differentiating the university.

Digital Literacy. Digital literacy is on everybody's agenda. O1 pays attention to digital skills. Elaboration is ongoing. Digital skills receive ample attention: how can we make work more fun and do it better. It takes language skills into account because of low literacy among employees. O2 pays attention to digital skills as a part of digital readiness. O3 plotted technological developments in the form of a radar to determine the impact of these developments on the organization regarding competencies, both business and IT, including culture and soft controls. O4 changes to a learning organization based on principles of a high-performance organization. The focus is both on hard and soft skills. O5 improves digital skills by intensive guidance and by motivating. Medical staff is committed and open to new technology. There is explicit support from the executive board. O6 uses craftsmanship as a carrier of the intended change. From the viewpoint of professional content, employees are involved in the development of digital skills. O7 trains people to align their mindset and skillset with the IT organization's manifesto. A coaching managerial style and a T-shaped skillset enable working in multi-disciplinary teams with end-to-end process responsibility.

5 Discussion

The results of this empirical research clearly demonstrate the presence of the business ecosystem perspective in DSs of organizations. However, most of these DSs mainly focus on improving internal operations and the IT operating model. The exemption is O4, which will adopt a different business model. The other six organizations do not have plans to change their business model. DSs and subsequent DTs are mainly internally focused. The business ecosystem perspective is not yet dominant. One of the reasons is that the key business functions of some of these organizations, especially the public organizations, are likely to remain stable over time. O7 will continue to offer education and research, O1 and O5 healthcare services, and O6 services for its citizens. Related to this is that all organizations, except O4, have a DS that is aligned with, but not an integral part of, its organizational strategy. Another reason is that some of the organizations, such as O2, O6, and O7, first want to improve their IT operations to get a better starting position for external collaboration. In their book "Designed for Digital", Ross et al. argue that most organizations want to fix their operational backbone before they develop digital offerings [4]. A third reason why the business ecosystem perspective is not yet dominant is that when individual organizations develop strategies, their focus is not primarily on the business ecosystem but on themselves. Each organization has its own purpose and business goals. By developing strategies, they want to achieve these goals. Likewise, a business ecosystem should be viewed as an organization and its purpose, business goals, and strategies must be developed considering distinctive features of a business ecosystem such as more complexity, co-evolution, and more emergent outcomes [7, 28]. We thus argue that collaborative business models must be developed at the business ecosystem level rather than at the individual organizational level [6]. Our view is supported by the growing need for data centricity. This is difficult to achieve for an organization alone and requires collaboration at the business ecosystem level as data flows through ecosystems.

Apart from the extent to which the business ecosystem perspective is present in DSs, it is of importance for individual organizations to prepare for collaboration. The five collaboration enablers we examined show that, on average, these are only partially present in DSs. The importance of collaboration is evident for the organizations we surveyed, and they pay attention to creating a culture of collaboration. They are aware of their place in the business ecosystem and acknowledge that changes in their business processes require a multi-disciplinary approach. This is expressed in approaches such as agile working, BizDevOps, and setting up customer journeys and value chains. These approaches have an accelerating effect in bringing people together. Finding and implementing an appropriate governance for collaboration is proving difficult. Organizations are aware that they need to break down silos and move to collaborative networks. To achieve this, they pushed decision-making powers to lower organizational levels with approaches such as agile working. Governance appears to be a learning process. Data centricity is an existential topic, requires long-term commitment and is gaining in importance, as our research shows. Most of the researched organizations follow a gradual path and work out the consequences of data centricity well. Overall, the seven organizations demonstrate some boldness and less speed. They have taken ambitious steps to adopt digital technologies in their DT with the DS as their compass. Working methods have been adapted to this, as evidenced by a choice for agile working and BizDevOps. The benefits of agile working lie more in the multidisciplinary approach than in speed. In addition, the organizations take the time to properly analyze the consequences of choices for digital technologies. Digital literacy is a topic that is addressed by all organizations, albeit partly. All DSs contain activities to improve digital skills. There is broad awareness that changes in the way of working are only successful if employees embrace them or, better yet, take the lead.

This research has its limitations. Although we studied seven organizations, more research is needed to confirm our proposition that collaborative business models must be developed at the business ecosystem level rather than at the individual organizational level. Furthermore, our sample of seven different organizations may not be fully representative of organizations with DT initiatives and corresponding DSs. The organizations we studied are all based in the Netherlands, and our sample contains more public organizations than private organizations.

6   Conclusion

The organizations we empirically studied are aware of their business ecosystems. However, this research demonstrates that DSs and subsequent DTs of individual organizations are mainly internally focused. Consequently, we argue that collaborative business models must be developed at the business ecosystem level rather than at the individual organizational level.

For researchers, this perspective opens new research avenues. An interesting research question is how collaborative business models can be successfully developed in a business ecosystem. This question is especially interesting for the public sector. Our research shows that organizations in the public sector strongly adhere to the business functions they have been assigned. Who should take the lead in developing collaborative business models in the public sector? Another research question is to which extent the business ecosystem perspective could gain in importance if the digital strategy was a more integral part of the organizational strategy. Our research shows that most digital strategies, although they are aligned with the organizational strategy, they are not yet an integral part of it and are certainly not the leading strategy of the organization. A third research question is what the relationship is between the extent to which the enablers are present in an organizations' DS and the successrate of that organization in collaborating in business ecosystems.

For practitioners, such as DT leads and enterprise architects, this research offers insights in how they could prepare their organizations for collaboration in business ecosystems.

Acknowledgments. We would like to thank Rob Baarda, Frank Brongers, Paul Morsch, Pascal Ravesteijn, Marlies van Steenbergen, and Leon Strous for their review comments.

References

1. Hanelt, A., Bohnsack, R., Marz, D., Antunes Marante, C.: A systematic review of the literature on digital transformation: insights and implications for strategy and organizational change. J. Manage. Stud. **58**(5), 1159–1197 (2021)
2. Spending on digital transformation technologies and services worldwide from 2017 to 2025 (2022). https://www.statista.com/statistics/870924/worldwide-digital-transformation-market-size/
3. Osmundsen, K., Iden, J., Bygstad, B.: Digital transformation: drivers, success factors, and implications. In: Proceedings of Mediterranean Conference on Information Systems, vol. 37 (2018)

4. Ross, J.W., Beath, C.M., Mocker, M.: Designed for digital: How to Architect your Business for Sustained Success. MIT Press (2019)
5. Parida, V., Sjödin, D., Reim, W.: Reviewing literature on digitalization, business model innovation, and sustainable industry: past achievements and future promises. Sustainability **11**(2), 391 (2019)
6. Camarinha-Matos, L.M., Fornasiero, R., Ramezani, J., Ferrada, F.: Collaborative networks: a pillar of digital transformation. Appl. Sci. **9**(24), 5431 (2019). https://doi.org/10.3390/app 9245431
7. Peltoniemi, M., Vuori, E.: Business ecosystem as the new approach to complex adaptive business environments. In: Proceedings of eBusiness Research Forum, vol. 2, No. 22, pp. 267–281. University of Tampere, Tampere, Finland (2004)
8. Gobble, M.M.: Digital strategy and digital transformation. Res. Technol. Manag. **61**(5), 66–71 (2018)
9. Senyo, P.K., Liu, K., Effah, J.: Digital business ecosystem: literature review and a framework for future research. Int. J. Inf. Manage. **47**, 52–64 (2019)
10. Gupta, S.: Driving Digital Strategy: A Guide to Reimagining your Business. Harvard Business Press, Boston (2018)
11. Hartl, E., Hess, T.: The role of cultural values for digital transformation: Insights from a delphi study. In: AMCIS 2017 Proceedings, pp. 1–10 (2017)
12. Roobeek, A., De Swart, J., Van Der Plas, M.: Responsible Business: Making Strategic Decisions to Benefit People, the Planet and Profits. Kogan Page Publishers, London (2018)
13. Bharadwaj, A., El Sawy, O.A., Pavlou, P.A., Venkatraman, N.V.: Digital business strategy: toward a next generation of insights. MIS Q. **37**(2), 471–482 (2013)
14. Gardner, H.K.: Smart collaboration: How Professionals and their Firms Succeed by Breaking Down Silos. Harvard Business Review Press (2016)
15. Tett, G.: The Silo Effect: The Peril of Expertise and the Promise of Breaking Down Barriers. Simon and Schuster (2015)
16. De Waal, A., Weaver, M., Day, T., van der Heijden, B.: Silo-busting: Overcoming the greatest threat to organizational performance. Sustainability **11**(23), 6860 (2019)
17. Gray, D., Vander Wal, T.: The connected company. O'Reilly Media, Inc. (2014)
18. The shift from an app-centric to a data-centric architecture (2021). https://learn.g2.com/data-centric-architecture
19. Martínez, P.L., Dintén, R., Drake, J.M., Zorrilla, M.: A big data-centric architecture metamodel for Industry 4.0. Future Gener. Comput. Syst. **125**, 263–284 (2021)
20. Bossert, O.: A two-speed architecture for the digital enterprise. In: El-Sheikh, E., Zimmermann, A., Jain, L.C. (eds.) Emerging Trends in the Evolution of Service-Oriented and Enterprise Architectures. ISRL, vol. 111, pp. 139–150. Springer, Cham (2016). https://doi.org/10.1007/978-3-319-40564-3_8
21. Blackburn, S., LaBerge, L., O'Toole, C., Schneider, J.: Digital Strategy in a Time of Crisis. McKinsey Digital (2020)
22. Ravesteijn, P., Ongena, G.: The role of e-leadership in relation to IT capabilities and digital transformation. In: Proceedings of 12th IADIS Information Systems Conference, 11–13 April, pp. 188–196. Utrecht, the Netherlands (2019)
23. Martin, A.: Digital literacy and the "digital society." Digit. Literacies: Concepts, Policies, Practices **30**, 151 (2008)
24. Bryman, A., Bell, E.: Business Research Methods, 3rd edn. Oxford University Press, Oxford (2011)
25. Morsch, P.: Innovativeness to enlarge digital readiness-How to avoid digital inertia? J. Int. Technol. Inform. Manag. **30**(4), 157–173 (2021)

26. Brooks, J., King, N.: Doing Template Analysis: Evaluating an End-of-Life Care Service. SAGE Publications, Ltd., 1 Oliver's Yard, 55 City Road, London EC1Y 1SP United Kingdom (2014)
27. ISO/IEC 33020–2019: Process assessment. Process measurement framework for assessment of process capability (2019)
28. Pidun, U., Reeves, M., Schüssler, M.: How do you "design" a business ecosystem? Boston Consulting Group: BCG Henderson Institute (2020). https://www.bcg.com/publications/2020/how-do-you-design-a-business-ecosystem.aspx

Improving Forecasting Capability and Capacity Utilization in Less Digitized Industries Through Participation in the Platform Economy

Jonas Müller[1]([✉]), Julian Lassen[2], Gerrit Hoeborn[1], Ruben Conrad[1], Volker Stich[1], and Nick Lober[1]

[1] FIR e. V. an der RWTH Aachen, Aachen, Germany
{Jonas.Mueller,Hb,Co,Lr9}@fir.rwth-aachen.de
[2] Institute of Mineral Resources Engineering (MRE) RWTH Aachen, Aachen, Germany
Lassen@mre.rwth-aachen.de

Abstract. While digitization is a strategic advantage in numerous industries such as the automotive industry or mechanical engineering, other industries like the German quarrying industry have not yet established a transformation towards a digitized industry. This leads to inefficient work and inaccurate forecasting capabilities. To address these challenges, digital platforms can incentivize digitization by supporting the capacity utilization and forecasting capability of these companies. In this paper, the quarrying industry is analyzed by a morphology and different types of companies are identified. Knowing the digital maturity of these companies and by determining the key factors to forecast demands and the capacity utilization, different operating models are derived. Combined with a morphology and the value creation system, different scenarios for the identification of platform services are examined. These scenarios are weighted in a utility analysis to get an operating model blueprint to develop and establish digital platforms in less digitized industries.

Keywords: Platform economy · Operating models · Digitization · Quarrying industry · Forecasting capability · Optimized capacity utilization

1 Introduction

Many industries, such as mechanical engineering, have been continuously and successively transformed by automation and networking over the past decades. Digitization is an important part of the corporate strategy of companies in these highly developed industries [1]. In addition to the emergence of new, innovative products and services, it has helped to fundamentally change operating principles in these markets. A fundamental driver of this development is the platform economy [2]. In the past decades, the (German) quarrying industry has shown no general trend toward digital transformation [3]. Digital technologies are only integrated to a limited extent due to the industry structure: only a regional market within a 50 km radius is usually served, and more than 40%

of the companies have less than 10 employees [4]. In addition to the use of conventional technologies and insufficient data management, companies in the industry suffer from fluctuations in demand and poor forecasting ability [5].

A suitable platform solution, coupled with the specific capability of suitable data management, can support companies in the industry by improving their forecasting capability and increasing their capacity utilization. The market transparency created comes with advantages for suppliers and buyers and additionally empowers companies to optimize capacity utilization in their operations, which at the same time allows them to act more economically and sustainably.

In this paper, a methodology for a suitable operator model to offer forecasting and capacity utilization optimization services is developed. This enables companies to forecast fluctuating demand more precisely and to react to it with higher capacity utilization. This addresses the structural problem towards digitization in the German quarrying industry with the aim of creating an opportunity for the companies to benefit from the platform economy using a platform solution. The remainder of the paper is organized as follows. Section 2 reviews the relevant theoretical background, and Sect. 3 presents the methodology and study design. Section 4 shows the methodology for establishing a platform operator model. In Sect. 5, the conclusion is provided.

2　Theoretical Background

2.1　Platforms and Platform Ecosystems

In the past decades, digital transformation has significantly changed how firms operate and interact [6]. New business models appeared due to the ubiquity of data storage and processing power available [7]. A new environment for collaboration emerged, forming complex inter-organizational structures. Organizational borders become blurry and value creation is distributed across different actors [8]. Platforms are a new type of value creation systems leveraging these developments. Platforms are an "open architecture with rules of governance designed to facilitate interactions" [9]. The open architecture enables third parties to participate [9] and is the basis for building a platform ecosystem. Existing approaches support the strategic design of ecosystems (e.g. [10]), but mainly focus on transactional platforms (e.g. Amazon, eBay).

Platforms can be differentiated by their purpose and functionality. Whilst digital transactional platforms focus on their role as an intermediate to enable a marketplace, data-centric digital platforms enable the data-based connectivity of different entities. Through a digital data-centric platform, a data-based system is created in which complementary products and services are linked to form a connected overall system, a digital ecosystem [11]. Those platforms are most widely used to connect different entities' respective businesses and therefore are mostly B2B platforms.

2.2　Operating Models for Platforms

The strategy, architecture, and operational actions of platforms are significantly shaped by the underlying operator concept and influence the value proposition [12]. The operator concept of platforms is based on the two central roles, the platform sponsor and the platform manager. The platform sponsor is the owner of the intellectual property of the platform and defines the strategy, target groups, value proposition, and governance [13]. The platform manager acts operationally in the daily business. He also provides the necessary platform components to realize the value proposition [14].

The roles of platform sponsor and platform manager can be fulfilled by one or more organizations. This creates a design space of the operator concept, which contains four prototypical operator models. In the **proprietary model**, both roles are fulfilled by the same organization. Within the framework of this operator model, extraordinary market positions comparable to monopolistic positions are achievable. However, a substantial initial investment on the part of the operators is necessary to achieve this outstanding market position. The **operator scenario** of the joint venture is created by the merger of several organizations on a normative and strategic level, which cooperatively act as shareholders for this joint venture. The joint venture acts largely independently at the operational level distributing the risks of the initial investment evenly among the shareholders. However, this operator model lacks agility at the strategic level after the initial market positioning. Multiple and conflicting shareholder interests can reduce the speed of decision-making. In a **licensing model** with one platform sponsor and multiple platform managers, aggregated customer networks of different organizations prove to be advantageous for the management side. The licensing of several managers, who provide users with access to the platform through various technical solutions, creates competition between the platform managers, which leads to attractive pricing for the platform users. However, this operator model reduces the revenue potential for the sponsor and manager. The **shared model** is created by integrating numerous organizations at the sponsor and management levels. Due to the multitude of actors, a uniform realization is difficult. The openness of these platforms enables low-cost structures. However, revenue potentials for platform sponsors and managers are low and decision-making is significantly more difficult [2].

The normative and strategic platform orientation, therefore, depends on the structural framework defined by the outlined operator scenarios and the specific occupation of the individual roles. This is a critical aspect regarding platform evolution and the offering of various platform services [15].

3 Methodology and Study Design

In the following, methodical foundations for establishing a platform operator model are explained. The action research methodology is a management research approach to bring about a productive synthesis between science and management consulting and meet the requirements of theory and practice [16]. The morphological method is a systematic heuristic creativity technique to systematize inventions. The central element of morphology is the morphological box. First, the problem at hand must be analyzed, then it is fragmented into relevant parameters. These parameters are constituent features of the problem at hand. Subsequently, possible characteristics are identified for each parameter. The characteristic values represent solution variants, from which a preferred solution variant is selected based on a value standard [17].

The utility analysis is a method for the systematic preparation of decisions based on evaluations (benefits) and a selection (ranking of benefits) of optimal alternatives [18]. The degree of fulfillment of each partial benefit is added up to the total benefit [19].

Qualitative interviews allow the capture of rich data but must be carefully conducted to achieve high-quality results [20]. Depending on the interview design, there are several types of qualitative interviews. In this paper, the semi-structured interview is used. The semi-structured interview is held with both prepared questions and improvised questions with a free conversation [20]. This type of interview is following a general outline to gather the necessary information but also gives the researcher enough room to adapt to the interviewees to gather more detailed results [21].

The development and validation of the methodology developed in the paper consider the use of the above-mentioned methods. A rigorous literature review is the starting point for the development of the models, the whole method was validated by 35 experts in several workshops between April 2021 and March 2022.

4   Results

4.1   Methodology for Establishing a Platform Operator Model

The paper proposes a methodology to identify different operator models for the operation of a platform in a less digitized industry. A literature review reveals a lot of research for high digitized industries (e. g. [6, 7, 11, 12]), therefore high digitization within the companies is often assumed. The structure of less digitized industries – as described in Sect. 1 – is very different and leads to the fact that there is hardly any penetration of digital platforms, especially for forecasting and capacity services [22].

To tackle this, a methodology with several steps is developed and explained with an example of the German quarrying industry. For the development, an action research framework is used [16]. Firstly, the value creation system must be designed, the proposed method to use is the value flow model. Secondly, the companies of the industry must be systematically described and characterized. For this, methods like morphology and typification can be used. Thirdly, possible operator concepts have to be identified, they orchestrate the individual actors and define the strategy, the services, and the governance of the platform. For this, a method like the operator concepts classification should be used. Concludingly, an adequate platform operator to offer possible services for the improvement of the forecasting capability and the capacity utilization is determined. The proposed method is a utility analysis, which as a result shows suitable services in dependence on a specific operator. The methodology with the proposed steps and methods is depicted in Fig. 1.

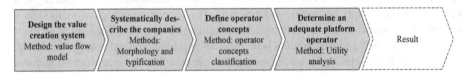

Fig. 1. Methodology for establishing a platform operator model and suitable services

4.2 Platform Operator Model for a Less Digitized Industry like Quarrying Industry

In this section, the different steps for the platform operator model are explained and evaluated with the example of the German quarrying industry.

Value Creation System. Value creation systems consist of complementary nodes and links which enable the interaction between each other [23]. Methods like the "Value Flow Model" provide the possibility to visualize the different roles, their functions, activities, and their core transactions [24]. The value creation system developed focuses on the abstract visualization of the ecosystem from an economic perspective.

The value creation system of the German quarrying industry consists of 15 different roles and their transactional relationships. Raw material extraction companies, which extract large quantities of material, are at the beginning of the value chain [25]. Taking into consideration, that the generally moderately priced (low priced) extracted goods are characteristical by high mass and volume, the transportation distance to the economically accessible market is limited to approximately 50 km [26]. Essentially, a distinction can be made between the extraction of solid rocks (natural stones) and loose rocks (sand & gravel, clay), mostly in opencast mines [27].

For the considered companies, the products are mostly used in the construction industry (approx. 95%). Core areas of the building materials industry are building materials production, building materials recycling, building materials landfilling, and recycling, which are often directly downstream. The remainder is used in different industries such as paper, glass, food, chemicals, fertilizers, iron and steel, and others. Therefore, there are assorted primary products as well as diverse customers [28]. Entrepreneurs or groups of companies fulfill several roles in the value network. A clear demarcation between participants in the building materials industry is therefore becoming increasingly difficult. The products are distributed to consumers and returned as secondary raw materials or as waste materials deriving from demolition and recycling. The transportation occurs either directly, or by means of distribution companies. Machinery and plant manufacturers, as well as blasting service providers, enable the companies to add value. Logistics providers add value by distributing products and waste. Value creation in the industry is regulated by law and standards, public authorities, and auditors. Auditors and testing laboratories ensure the quality of the products. The value creation system is depicted in Fig. 2.

Morphology and Typification of the Companies in the Quarrying Industry. To ensure an adequate application of the morphological method for the characterization and identification of the industry participants of the quarrying industry, a structured decomposition of the problem must be performed. For this, the St. Gallen Management Model can be used as it provides a method to classify a company by key categories [29]. Following the adaptation to manufacturing companies, these key categories can be broken down into in-plant and out-of-plant issues. For the morphology, the dimensions of corporate structure and digital maturity are taken, whereas the focus is on digital maturity [30]. The features and characteristics are derived based on a literature review and were validated in expert interviews (Fig. 3).

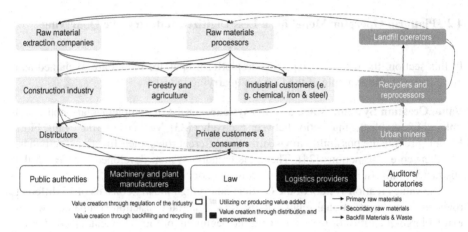

Fig. 2. Value creation system of the German quarrying industry

Type I "Digitally Expandable": This type can particularly be assigned to micro-enterprises and predominantly small groups of companies with annual sales of up to €50 million. They employ less than 100 employees and have less than 5 locations. In the area of digital maturity, the companies work predominantly analog. Data analysis is carried out manually and not on a digital basis. In addition, it was found that recorded data on sales volumes are not evaluated, as the companies operate almost entirely demand-driven. As a result, decisions are made based on experience.

Type II "Digitally Advanced": This type can be assigned to company alliances with up to €150 million in sales, which have up to 20 locations and up to 250 employees. In terms of digital maturity, type II companies record process and status data digitally and automatically using manufacturer platforms. The use of such digital systems enables data to be fed into the internal IT network and diagnostic data analysis. Past events can be looked at intensively to clarify causes and to derive consequences for the future.

Type III "Digital Pioneers": In particular, corporations with annual sales of €50 million or more, more than 20 locations, and more than 250 employees can be assigned to Type III. Process and condition data are collected digitally-automatically via the producer platforms and are partially analyzed descriptively and diagnostically. Available assistance systems cover a wide range, including weighing systems, production monitoring and planning, Excel-based analysis systems, and Material Requirements Planning (MRP II) and Enterprise Resource Planning (ERP) systems.

Operator Concept for the Digital Platform Solution. To identify possible operator models, it is essential to consider the corresponding value network. In addition to private-sector players, the public sector in the form of topic-related authorities as well as associations and cooperative players, for example in the form of industry associations, must also be considered. The number of potential platform operators identified is reduced based on criteria to be selected on an industry-specific basis. By applying the criteria of digital *competencies*, *technical competencies* (mining and mechanical engineering), *network, neutrality,* and *profit orientation*, the potential operator candidates of the *industry association*, a *compendium of equipment manufacturers, technology, and service providers* as well as *a compendium of companies in the quarrying industry* could be identified for the German quarrying industry. The latter would appear in the realization both on the operator level and on the customer level. Furthermore, *downstream players in the value chain* can be considered since the resources used in the primary extraction of bulk raw materials and the downstream construction industry are to a significant extent congruent and the use case of the platform is transferable. In addition, they know the challenges of forecasting and capacity utilization and can address them with proposed solutions. [31].

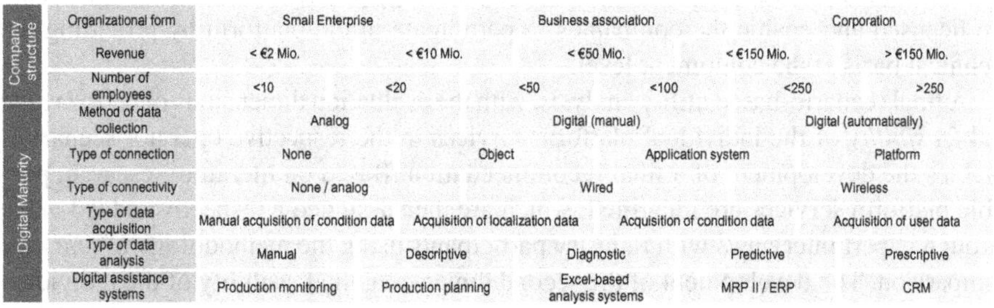
Company structure
Digital Maturity
Organizational form
Small Enterprise
Business association
Corporation
Revenue
< €2 Mio.
< €10 Mio.
< €50 Mio.
< €150 Mio.
> €150 Mio.
Number of employees
<10
<20
<50
<100
<250
>250
Method of data collection
Analog
Digital (manual)
Digital (automatically)
Type of connection
None
Object
Application system
Platform
Type of connectivity
None / analog
Wired
Wireless
Type of data acquisition
Manual acquisition of condition data
Acquisition of localization data
Acquisition of condition data
Acquisition of user data
Type of data analysis
Manual
Descriptive
Diagnostic
Predictive
Prescriptive
Digital assistance systems
Production monitoring
Production planning
Excel-based analysis systems
MRP II / ERP
CRM

Fig. 3. Morphology for less digitized industries at the example of quarrying industry

These identified and filtered candidates are now integrated into the abstracted operator models. After a comparison of the interests of the stakeholder group on the operator side and the user side, five scenarios could be identified. In a further filtering stage, by comparing the interests of the individual stakeholders at the operator and user level, the number of scenarios was reduced to three. These remaining scenarios are presented in Fig. 4 below and classified in the abstracted matrix of operator scenarios.

Scenario 1 "Joint Venture": A union of the corporate associations of the quarrying industry, equipment manufacturers, technology providers, and service providers as well as, if applicable, downstream players in the value chain at the sponsor level realize a joint spin-off in the form of a joint venture for the operational design and management.

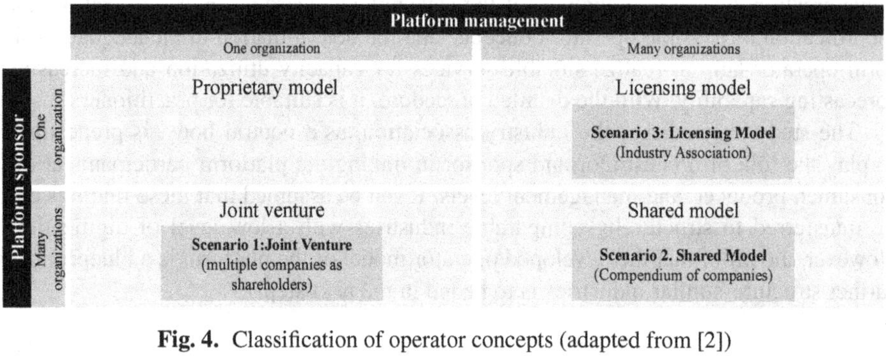
Platform management
One organization
Many organizations
Platform sponsor
One organization
Many organizations
Proprietary model
Licensing model
Scenario 3: Licensing Model
(Industry Association)
Joint venture
Shared model
Scenario 1:Joint Venture
(multiple companies as shareholders)
Scenario 2. Shared Model
(Compendium of companies)

Fig. 4. Classification of operator concepts (adapted from [2])

Scenario 2: "Shared Model": A compendium of companies from the quarrying industry, equipment manufacturers, technology providers, service providers, and downstream players in the value chain defines a standard for sensor-captured data at the sponsor level, as well as standardized APIs to make generated data fully usable. This standard provides the foundation for a company-specific implementation of decentralized platforms, which can be carried out by a variety of independent technology providers and service providers.

Scenario 3 "Licensing Model": The industry association of the German quarrying industry acts on the sponsor level of the operator model and provides a central platform. Furthermore, equipment manufacturers and technology providers, and service providers are licensed and enable the companies to participate in the platform by providing the technical basis at the equipment level.

A final scenario-based utility analysis, with the evaluation dimensions of *added value* and *feasibility* of the individual platform services in the respective operator scenarios, enables the development of a final recommendation. Based on literature research, possible platform services are identified, which are then assigned a respective added value through expert interviews with industry participants using the methodology of pairwise comparison. The development of the second dimension, the feasibility of the individual services in the respective operator scenario, is also based on consultations with industry participants from the quarrying industry and digital transformation experts. The recommendation made by the utility value analysis, based on the procedure of the study, is the implementation of the platform solution through **scenario 3 "Licensing model"**, which is orchestrated by the industry association as platform sponsor.

5   Discussion and Conclusion

The developed procedural model for identifying suitable services for capacity utilization and increasing forecasting capability was explained using the example of the German quarrying industry. It was shown that initial obstacles in digital infrastructure are particularly high in this less digitized industry and reservations about profit-oriented operator models represent a significant hurdle. The approach provides a step-for-step guide to establish a platform operator model. The four steps, consisting of the design of the value creation system, the analysis of the stakeholder regarding their digitization, the identification of possible operator concepts, and the determination of an adequate platform operator help to realize suitable services for capacity utilization and increasing forecasting capability. With the detailed procedure, it is suitable for practitioners.

The study showed that the industry association, as a neutral body, is predestined to play the role of orchestrator and sponsor in linking the platform participants at the consumer, producer, and management levels. It can be assumed that these findings can be transferred to structurally comparable industries with a low level of digitization. However, the proof that the developed operator model of the platform is a blueprint for further structure-similar industries is to be led in the next step.

Acknowledgements. The research project 21480 N is funded by the AiF within the framework of the program for the promotion of joint industrial research (IGF) of the Federal Ministry of Economics and Climate based on a resolution of the German Bundestag. Any opinions, findings, and recommendations expressed in this paper are those of the authors and do not necessarily reflect the views of the correspondent institutions.

References

1. Thurner, M., Glauner, P.: Digitalization in mechanical engineering. In: Glauner, P., Plugmann, P. (eds.) Innovative Technologies for Market Leadership. FBF, pp. 107–117. Springer, Cham (2020). https://doi.org/10.1007/978-3-030-41309-5_9
2. Parker, G., van Alstyne, M., Choudary, S.P.: Platform Revolution: How Networked Markets are Transforming the Economy - and How to Make them Work for You, 1st edn. W.W. Norton & Company, New York, London (2016)
3. Deloitte: Tracking the trends 2018: the top 10 issues shaping mining in the year ahead (2018)
4. Braun, T., Hennig, A.: Untersuchungen zur Betriebsstruktur deutscher Natursteintagebaue. BHM Berg-Huettenmaenn. Monatsh. **161**(4), 181–186 (2016)
5. Agrawal, A.K., Krishnamoorthy, G.: Tomorrow's mine: How Digital can Shape the Future? EY and FIMI (2017)
6. Hanelt, A., Bohnsack, R., Marz, D., Marante, C.A.: A systematic review of the literature on digital transformation: insights and implications for strategy and organizational change. J. Manag. Stud. **58**, 1159–1197 (2021). https://doi.org/10.1111/joms.12639
7. Volberda, H.W., Khanagha, S., Baden-Fuller, C., Mihalache, O.R., Birkinshaw, J.: Strategizing in a digital world: overcoming cognitive barriers, reconfiguring routines and introducing new organizational forms. Long Range Plan. **54**, 102110 (2021). https://doi.org/10.1016/j.lrp.2021.102110
8. Siaw, C.A., Sarpong, D.: Dynamic exchange capabilities for value co-creation in ecosystems. J. Bus. Res. **134**, 493–506 (2021). https://doi.org/10.1016/j.jbusres.2021.05.060
9. Jacobides, M.G., Sundararajan, A., van Alstyne, M.: Platforms and Ecosystems: Enabling the Digital Economy. World Economic Forum (2019)
10. Wieninger, S., Gotzen, R., Gudergan, G., Wenning, K.M.: The strategic analysis of business ecosystems: New conception and practical application of a research approach. In: Co-creating our future: scaling-up innovation capacities through the design and engineering of immersive, collaborative, empathic and cognitive systems: 2019 IEEE International Conference on Engineering, Technology and Innovation (ICE/ITMC): Sophia Antipolis Innovation Park, France, pp. 17–19. IEEE, Piscataway, NJ, pp. 1–8 (2019)
11. von Engelhardt, S., Wangler, L., Wischmann, S.: Eigenschaften und Erfolgsfaktoren digitaler Plattformen: Eine Studie im Rahmen der Begleitforschung zum Technologieprogramm AUTONOMIK für Industrie 4.0 des Bundesministeriums für Wirtschaft und Energie (2017)
12. Meier, P.: Digitale plattformen als innovationstreiber. In: Plugmann, P. (ed.) Innovationsumgebungen gestalten: Impulse für Start-ups und etablierte Unternehmen im globalen Wettbewerb, pp. 207–217. Springer Gabler, Wiesbaden, Heidelberg (2018)
13. Eisenmann, T.R., Parker, G., van Alstyne, M.W.: Opening platforms: how, when and why? SSRN J. 131–162 (2008). Harvard Business School Entrepreneurial Management Working Paper No. 09-030
14. Niebuer, A., Bender, P.: (2020) Akteure und Rollen – Wer macht was bei plattformbasierten Ökosystemen?
15. Gawer, A., Cusumano, M.A.: Industry platforms and ecosystem innovation. J. Prod. Innov. Manag. **31**, 417–433 (2014)

16. Kemmis, S., McTaggart, R., Nixon, R.: The Action Research Planner. Springer Singapore, Singapore (2014)

17. Zwicky, F.: The morphological approach to discovery, invention, research and construction. In: Zwicky, F., Wilson, A.G. (eds.) New Methods of Thought and Procedure, pp. 273–297. Springer, Heidelberg (1967)

18. Dittmer, G.: Nutzwertanalyse. In: Dittmer, G. (ed.) Managen mit Methode, pp. 43–56. Gabler Verlag, Wiesbaden (1995). https://doi.org/10.1007/978-3-663-05929-5_5

19. Thormählen, T.: Der Nutzwert der Nutzwertanalyse. HWWA - Institut für Wirtschaftsforschung Hamburg (1977)

20. Myers, M.D., Newman, M.: The qualitative interview in IS research: examining the craft. Inf. Organ. **17**, 2–26 (2007). https://doi.org/10.1016/j.infoandorg.2006.11.001

21. Liebold, R., Trinczek, R.: Experteninterview. In: Kühl, S., Strodtholz, P., Taffertshofer, A. (eds.) Handbuch Methoden der Organisationsforschung, pp. 32–56. VS Verlag für Sozialwissenschaften, Wiesbaden (2009)

22. Schober, K.-S., Hoff, P., Nölling, K.: Digitalisierung der Bauwirtschaft: Der europäische Weg zu "Construction 4.0". Roland Berger GMBH (2016)

23. Peppard, J., Rylander, A.: From value chain to value network. Eur. Manag. J. **24**, 128–141 (2006). https://doi.org/10.1016/j.emj.2006.03.003

24. den Ouden, E.: Innovation Design. Springer, London, London (2012)

25. Grömling, M.: Volkswirtschaftliches Portrait der deutschen Baustoffindustrie. Bundesverb. Baustoffe - Steine und Erden 2011, Berlin (2016)

26. Grömling, M.: Volkswirtschaftliches Porträt der deutschen Baustoffindustrie. Bundesverband Baustoffe - Steine und Erden, Berlin (2011)

27. MIRO: Die deutsche Gesteinsindustrie: Wirtschaft – Produktion – Anspruch. Bericht der Geschäftsführung, Berlin (2020)

28. Baier, M., et al.: Deutschland – Rohstoffsituation 2020. Bundesanstalt für Geowissenschaften und Rohstoffe (2021)

29. Rüegg-Stürm, J., Grand, S.: The St. Galler Management Modell. Haupt, Bern (2015)

30. Schuh, G., Kampker, A.: Strategie und Management produzierender Unternehmen: Handbuch Produktion und Management 1. SpringerLink Bücher, Berlin Heidelberg (2011)

31. Basten, M.: bbs-Zahlenspiegel 2021: Daten und Fakten zur Baustoff-Steine-Erden-Industrie. Bundesverband Baustoffe – Steine und Erden e. V., Berlin (2021)

A Framework for Collaborative Virtual Power Plant Ecosystem

Kankam O. Adu-Kankam[1,2(✉)] and Luis M. Camarinha-Matos[1]

[1] School of Science and Technology and UNINOVA - CTS, Nova University of Lisbon,
Campus de Caparica, 2829-516 Monte de Caparica, Portugal
k.adu@campus.fct.unl.pt, cam@uninova.pt
[2] School of Engineering, University of Energy and Natural Resources (UENR), P. O. Box 214,
Sunyani, Ghana

Abstract. The notion of Collaborative Virtual Power Plant Ecosystem (CVPP-E) contributes to an effective organization of Renewable Energy Communities (RECs) in such a way that they can act or exhibit the attributes of Virtual Power Plants (VPPs). This concept is derived by merging or integrating principles, organizational structures, and mechanism from the domain of Collaborative Networks (CN) into the area of VPPs. The expectation is that if actors in the RECs engage in collaborative actions this would enable a REC to perform functions that are similar to a VPP. Conceptually, the CVPP-E is constituted of a community manager, a common community energy storage system, prosumers who own a combination of photovoltaic and a battery storage system, and passive consumers, all connected to an energy grid. The key attribute of this proposed ecosystem is that members engage in collective actions or collaborative ventures that are based on a common goal and aimed at achieving sustainable energy generation, consumption, and vending. In this study, we present a high-level model for the aspects of collaboration in the CVPP-E. This involves the compatible/common goals framework, the sharing framework, and the collective actions framework. These frameworks serve as the backbone of the CVPP-E and play a vital role in the modelling of a CVPP-E. Various simulation scenarios are used to assess the proposed model.

Keywords: Collaborative networks · Common goal framework · Sharing framework · Collective action framework · Energy sharing · Energy community

1 Introduction

Until recently, the integration of Photovoltaic (PV) sources from households (HH) into the traditional grid system was negligible [1]. However, several changing factors such as declining prices of solar panels [2], favourable public opinion towards the energy transition [3], coupled with sound governmental policies [4], are changing the narrative. For instance, currently in Europe, the number of HHs with installed PV systems is rising steadily [5]. Concurrently, battery storage technology is also maturing rapidly [6]. This opens the opportunity for individual dwellings as well as communities to incorporate

© IFIP International Federation for Information Processing 2022
Published by Springer Nature Switzerland AG 2022
L. M. Camarinha-Matos et al. (Eds.): PRO-VE 2022, IFIP AICT 662, pp. 151–166, 2022.
https://doi.org/10.1007/978-3-031-14844-6_13

energy storage into their PV systems. A Community Energy Storage System [7] is an energy storage technology that enables energy sharing between members of a community. Available literature suggests that an increasing number of groups of neighbours who are motivated by a common goal such as reduction of their energy costs or promotion of sustainable energy consumption are coming together to form Renewable Energy Communities (RECs). These RECs can operate in stand-alone mode or have a grid-connected architecture [8]. According to [9], a REC can be described as a community that is based on open and voluntary participation. It is usually owned, managed, and controlled by shareholders or members who are autonomous and located within the proximity of the projects. Essentially, members of a REC, who possess roof mounted PV systems can generate renewable energy for their own local consumption and may store, sell, or share the excess with other community members, therefore, acting as prosumers. Other passive members may not generate own energy but may join the REC to enable them consume energy from renewable sources.

Currently, the organization and management of RECs appear as a daunting task due to the complex interaction between multiple and heterogenous actors who are largely autonomous and may have diverse preferences. Many research works have suggested several approaches to the efficient and effective management of the constituent actors of RECs. In [10–12] the authors suggested a collaborative approach which resulted in the proposition of the notion of a Collaborative Virtual Power Plant Ecosystem (CVPP-E) and Cognitive HH Digital twins (CHDTs) in [13]. These concepts are further explained in Sect. 2. The key objective of the CVPP-E and related CHDTs is to approach the management of energy consumption and exchange in a REC from a collaborative point of view.

The purpose of this research is to present a framework that illustrates various collaborative behaviours within a CVPP-E. This objective can be achieved by breaking the various collaborative actions down into discrete steps using the Business Process Modelling Notation (BPMN) language. The framework shall serve as the collaborative component for a prototype model which is intended to be used to study how collaborative actions can facilitate sustainable energy consumption and exchanges in the ecosystem. The following research question is therefore adopted to guide the work:

RQ. What framework can support the modelling of each collaborative behaviour by a population of CHDTs within a CVPP-E?

The considered behaviours are as follows:

a. Communication and information exchange (ComIEx) towards a common goal.

   i. ComIEx towards coalition formation (Joining a Virtual Organization (VO)): In this context, members are expected to have different, but compatible goals. The community manager proposes a goal and through ComIE, members whose preferences are compatible with the suggested goal will accept the invitation and participate in coalition formation towards the achievement *of the proposed goal.*

   ii. ComIEx towards the execution of a specific goal: In this context, the manager proposes a goal and through ComIEx each member who accepts the invitation schedules their appliances and execute the necessary instruction when the time for collective action is due.

b. Sharing common resources: In this context we consider the scenario were CHDTs share energy that is stored in a common community storage.
c. Collective actions. The behaviour exhibited by members when they all act in the same way in order to achieve a collective objective.

2 Background Knowledge and Theoretical Framework

According to the European Parliament and the Council of the European Union [9], a REC is based on open and voluntary participation. It is autonomous and controlled by stakeholders who live in the same proximity. Members of RECs can generate renewable energy for local consumption, and may store, sell, or share the excess with community members. In this context, we attempt to replicate the REC concept by developing a digital twin replica of the community. In our replica model, we represent the community environment as the CVPP-E. The CVPP-E can be described as a form of a Virtual organizations Breeding Environment (VBE), business ecosystem or a community of practice where members approach energy consumption and exchanges from a collaborative point of view. Thus, members engage in collective actions towards the achievement of some goals that may be common to the entire community.

The CVPP-E concept was derived by integrating collaboration principles and mechanisms that were borrowed from the discipline of Collaborative Networks (CNs) into the domain of Virtual Power Plants (VPP). The outcome of this synthesis is a form of REC that adopts collaborative principles and mechanisms in its operations to ensure sustainable energy consumption and exchanges and as well, exhibiting characteristics of a VPP, thus having the capability of aggregating excess energy from the community and have it vended to the grid. In the proposed formulation, a CVPP-E includes: (a) the community manager who promotes collaborative activities and behaviours, (b) multiple actors, thus, a population of prosumer and consumer HHs, each having a different energy use preference. The Prosumers in this case have roof-mounted solar panels and can consume their locally generated energy and share the excess with the community, but the consumers do not. (c) a community owned energy storage system.

In the prototype model, each suggested actor of the CVPP-E is modelled as a software agent that replicates the characteristics and behaviours of the physical actor. These software agents are modelled to reside and interact with each other inside a digital REC environment, namely the CVPP-E. Each HH is represented by a Cognitive HH Digital Twin (CHDT). CHDTs are modelled as software agents possessing some cognitive attributes so that they can act as complementary decision-making agents on behalf of their physical counterparts. These software agents can make rational and autonomous decisions on behalf of their owners. The energy use-behaviours of each physical actor are accommodated in their counterpart CHDT using the notion of a Digital Profile (DP). The DP enables the actors to clearly define their energy use preferences, priorities, and options, that is usually in line with the community goals. The DP is constituted of (a) the Value System (VS), and (b) the Delegated Autonomy (DA) of the actor. The VS describes the values of the actor, which may, for instance, include his/her preferred energy source, which community goal is of priority to him/her, how often his/her resources are available for collaboration, etc. DA, on the other hand, is the instruction or authorisation that is given to the CHDT by the actor, specifying how to carry out or execute the suggested values of the actor. In Fig. 1, we illustrate how a CHDT makes decisions based on its DP. The figure shows a CHDT with three values that are arranged in order of priority. The first priority is 100% consumption from renewable sources, the second priority is to consume from mixed sources and the third is free rider or indifferent option. It also shows three levels of DA, thus (a) delegate (control over) three appliances, (b) delegate two appliances, and (c) delegate one appliance.

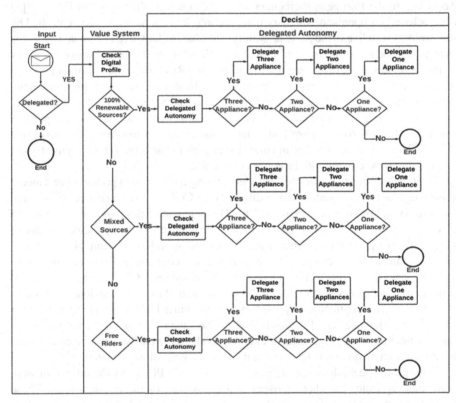

Fig. 1. Decision making based on a CHDTs digital profile

Therefore, by aggregating several CHDTs, each having a different or unique DP, we aim to replicate a physical community in the virtual space (CVPP-E) that has the capacity to accommodate the varied user preferences of each actor or unit of HH. The adoption of agent-based technology allowed the simulation of each HH as a software agent, each having a different DP. By incorporating a level of intelligence into these CHDTs, they could be made to have some cognitive capabilities. Due to their cognitive and decision-making capabilities, these CHDTs are envisaged to have the capability to engage in some collaborative ventures such as pursuing common goals, sharing common resources, mutually influencing one another, as well as engaging in collective actions, without necessarily compromising individual preferences, priorities and options.

The collaborative attributes of CHDTs are envisioned to increase the survivability and sustainability of the CVPP-E. As a community, the diversity in HH sizes, including the number of occupants residing in each HH in the population, is highly essential. To help address this concern, we categorized the constituent HHs (and thus the corresponding CHDTs) into 5 different categories. This categorization and related data were sourced from a survey conducted in [14]. The considered categorization is: (a) HHs with single pensioners, (b) HHs with single non-pensioner, (c) HHs with multiple pensioners, (d) HHs with children, and (e) HHs with multiple persons with no dependent children. The population size of the CVPP-E (community) can always be configured to constitute any number of HH, from each category.

3 Modelling Collaboration Aspects of a CVPP-E

In this section, we present the collaborative framework of behaviours that were mentioned in association to the RQ. We consider the frameworks for (a) common goals, (b) sharing resources, and (c) collective actions. The BPMN language is used to model the various collaborative actions that are considered.

3.1 Modelling Communication and Information Exchange (ComIEx) towards a Common Goal

According to [15] a common goal gives a group of entities a shared purpose. It inspires them to work together as a team to help them achieve the group's objectives. Information exchange for mutual benefit is also a key element of collaboration. Therefore, under this subsection, we consider two cases: (a) ComIEx towards coalition formation (Joining a VO), and (b) ComIEx towards the execution of a specific goal. In the exemplified cases we assume that a CVPP-E was already formed and populated with agents representing the HHs (CHDTs). This ecosystem is a kind of virtual organizations breeding environment where different coalitions of CHDTs (i.e., different virtual organizations, VOs) can be formed to achieve some common goals.

3.1.1 ComIEx Towards Coalition Formation (Joining a VO)

This process is expected to precede a collaborative venture, e.g., minimize energy consumption over a certain period. In other words, it is a process of forming a coalition (a kind of VO) to achieve some goal proposed by the CVPP-E manager. In terms of information exchange, we show the major communication steps that are expected to occur. With reference to the BPMN model of Fig. 2, the following steps are observed:

a) **Invitation**: The community manager extends invitations to achieve goal "x" to the entire community, particularly, prospective CHDTs, whose value system or preferences are in line with this goal "x".

b) **Acceptance/Rejection stage 1**: CHDTs may respond either in the affirmative, expressing readiness to join, or a rejection. The CHDTs shall refer to their digital profile which constitute the users predefined preferences and set of instructions.

c) **Knowledge of coalition conditions**: For CHDTs that accepted the invitation, further information is shared by the community manager, detailing the conditions for the coalition.

d) **Review of the coalition conditions**: The prospective CHDTs may review the conditions and make further decisions whether to pursue or decline joining the coalition.

e) **Acceptance/Rejection stage 2**: The prospective actors will communicate their final acceptance or rejection of the coalition to the community manager.

f) **Confirmation**: The entire process is completed with a confirmation message from the manager.

Throughout these processes, it is observed that information exchange is a crucial prerequisite for coalition formation.

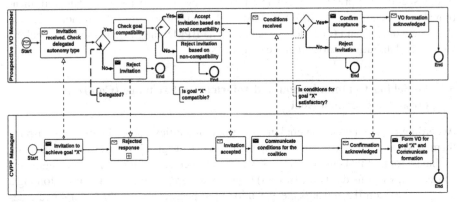

Fig. 2. Process of information exchange towards the formation of a coalition - joining a VO

3.1.2 ComIEx Towards the Execution of a Specific Goal

In Fig. 3 below, we model the processes of information exchange toward the execution of a specific goal. The specific goal, in this example, is to minimize local energy consumption so that unused or saved energy can be vended to the grid. For this to be feasible, the CHDTs may have to engage in some form of collective action based on their individual DPs. This may involve the deferral of the use of either one, two or three of appliances that are considered deferrable. This may include appliances such as washing machines, dishwashers, or tumble dryers, whose delayed use may not affect the quality of service (QoS) to user. This process can also be called delegation of deferrable loads (DDL) as mentioned and discussed in [13]. The key collaborative processes are as follows:

a) **Invitation to pursue a Vending Opportunity (VendOpp)**: The CVPP manager identifies and communicates a VendOpp to community members.
b) **Acceptance or rejection**: CHDT checks their DP assigned to it by its owner. Based on the assigned DP, a CHDT may either accept or decline to participate in the VendOpp.
c) **Scheduling vending**: Upon acceptance, the CVPP-E manager communicates the following vendOpp information to prospective CHDTs: (i) the vending time, (ii) the vending window, and (iii) the duration of vending.
d) **Scheduling the execution of delegated autonomy**: After receiving details concerning the VendOpp, all CHDTs shall schedule themselves in readiness to collectively execute their various "delegated autonomy" actions in line with the vending schedule.
e) **Execution of delegated autonomy**: When the scheduled "vending time" is due, all CHDTs will collectively execute their respective delegated autonomy, thus their DDL. This collective action will result in the general minimization of consumption in the community for the period (vending window). As shown in Fig. 3, for both consumers and prosumers, DDL will result in the minimization of consumption. However, for prosumers, DDL will also result in excess energy from their locally installed PV or storage system.
f) **Sharing unused energy with the community storage**: Thus, the unused energy as a result of reduced consumption shall be sent to the community storage for onward transfer to the grid during the vending window.
g) **Execute VendOpp**: The community manager will ensure that the community storage supplies the grid with the pre-agreed quantity of energy at the proposed time.

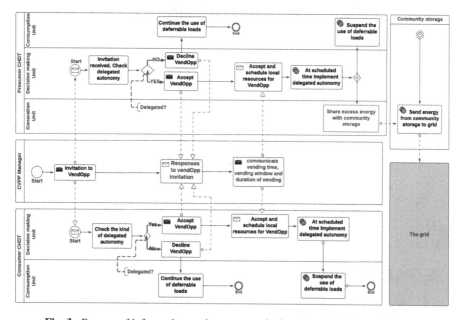

Fig. 3. Process of information exchange towards the execution of a specific goal

3.2 Modelling Sharing of Common Resources

Resource sharing (RS) is a common characteristic of collaborative cases. In the CVPP-E, members engage in resource sharing to help fulfil their collaborative objectives. The case shown in Fig. 4 is used to demonstrate sharing of common resources within the CVPP-E. It demonstrates two modes of sharing (L1RS and L2RS). L1RS refers to sharing excess energy that was produced by prosumer CHDTs with the community storage (charging the community storage). L2RS involves the sharing of energy that was stored in the community storage back with either prosumer or consumers CHDTs (discharging community storage). The following steps are used to describe L1RS and L2RS in detail (also assuming that a VO was previously established for this goal):

i. **L1RS.** Under this mode of sharing, the excess energy from several different CHDTs is shared with the community storage system. This is more of an aggregation process. Referring to Fig. 4, L1RS can be achieved in three major steps:

    a) **Local PV resource availability**: PV availability is a time-dependent event. The CHDT is alerted of the availability of solar energy due to the presence of sunlight.

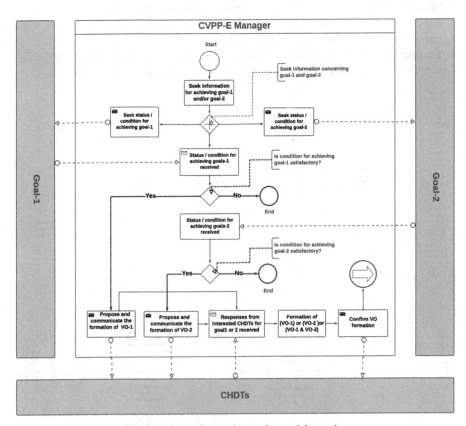

Fig. 4. Information exchange for goal formation

b) **Type of local energy demand:** For this step, the CHDT determines if there is a local demand for the locally generated solar energy (local demand include demand for appliances to use the energy locally or to store it in the local storage). If local demand exists, the generated energy is consumed locally. If otherwise, the generated energy is considered excess it is shared with community storage.

c) **Accept and store:** At this stage of the process, the shared energy is accepted and stored in the common storage system.

ii. **L2RS.** Under this mode of sharing, the energy that was previously stored in the community storage is shared back with community members according to their various needs. The storage capacity is constantly being monitored to determine if the conditions for L2RS are satisfied. Typically, L2RS is enabled when the state of charge (SoC) is greater than a threshold, say $\alpha\%$ of the battery capacity "C". If this condition is satisfied, the energy that was previously stored in the community storage is allowed to flow back into the community. L2RS is terminated when the condition changes, thus, SoC drops below another threshold, say $\beta\%$ of "C", thus, When SoC > $\alpha\%$ of "C", L2RS is enabled, When $SoC < \beta\%$ of "C", L2RS is disabled

3.3 Modelling the Collective Actions Framework

Collective Actions (CA) refer to the actions taken by a collection or group of entities, acting based on a collective decision. CA is also a key component of the collaborative behaviours that are exhibited in the CVPP-E. In Fig. 5 below, we illustrate the CA behaviours of 3 CHDTs that are based on a common goal. The resultant effect of their CA is shown to have a direct impact on the community-owned energy asset (community storage), which subsequently affects the power grid. There are three major steps involved in the CA processes:

(a) **Condition-based decisions**: In this step of the process, a CHDT makes decisions based on some common goal conditions such as VendOpp.

(b) **Execution of assigned delegated autonomy**: If the decision in step (a) is based on some specific goals, all CHDTs will execute their assigned delegated autonomy simultaneously which can result in a common behaviour.

(c) **Appliance use behaviour:** The effect of steps (a) and (b) will have a direct impact on the use-behaviour of the embedded HH appliances in each respective CHDT. The resultant behaviours could also have a direct impact on the community-owned asset (community storage) and subsequently on the grid.

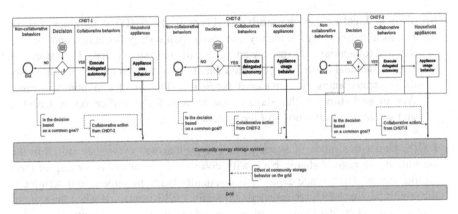

Fig. 5. The process of collective actions towards a common goal

4   How the Collaboration Framework Supports the CVPP-E

Based on the developed prototype, some preliminary partial outcomes have already been demonstrated in [16]. Further demonstration of other behaviours such as modelling "mutual influence" and modelling "delegated autonomy" have also been demonstrated in works that are currently in press awaiting publication. The prototype is constituted of several sub-models that are integrated together to help achieve the desired functionality of the CVPP-E. These sub-models include: (a) The appliance model that is used to model all the embedded HH appliances, (b) The PV model that is used to model the embedded PV systems of prosumers, (c) The community storage model which is also used to model the community storage system, (d) The consumption priority model also used to model (i) The process of initiating the use of an appliance, (ii) The process of selecting a preferred energy source, (iii) the process of having an appliance wait in queue until a preferred energy source is available. Other sub-models include: (d) the consumer/prosumer model that is used to configure a CHDT as either a prosumer or consumer and finally, (e) the influence model that is used to propagate either positive or negative influences from "influencer" CHDTs to "influence" CHDTs.

Depending on the intended purpose, a sub-model could be designed using one of three modelling techniques in AnyLogic. For instance, all models that exhibit dynamic behaviours, thus, having parameters that are constantly changing are modelled using System Dynamics (SD) techniques. Some examples include the community storage sub-model (Fig. 6), the HH appliances sub-model (Fig. 7) and the PV sub-model. Furthermore, all aspects of the model that require systematic procedures and discrete processes are developed using discrete event modelling techniques. One of such examples is the consumption priority model shown in Fig. 8. Finally, all aspects of the model that require the creation of an entity that is endowed with autonomous attributes is achieved using agent-based modelling techniques. Typical examples include prosumer and consumer CHDTs.

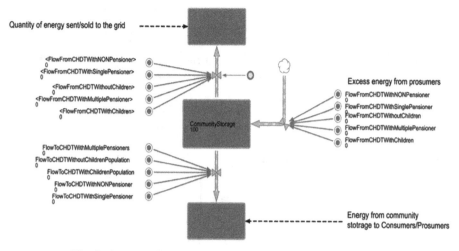

Fig. 6. A system dynamics model of the community storage system

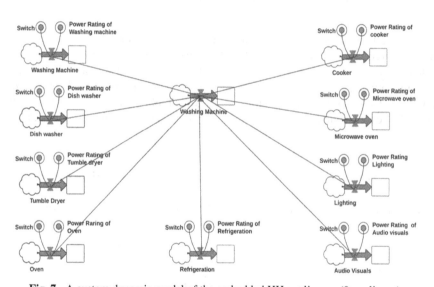

Fig. 7. A system dynamic model of the embedded HH appliances (9 appliance).

In Tables 1 and 2 below, we show some selected scenarios that were used to test the CVPP-E prototype in an earlier study [16]. For instance, the data shown in Table 1 was sourced from [14]. For demonstration purposes, the table (Table 1) shows data for only three out of the nine HH appliances that are embedded in each CHDT. These parameters are used to model each of the appliance's use-behaviour. Furthermore, in Table 2, we consider deferent scenarios of varying prosumer and consumer populations. For each scenario, we tested different degrees of delegated autonomy. Delegation in this sense means that the CHDT have been given authority by their owner to make some rational decisions

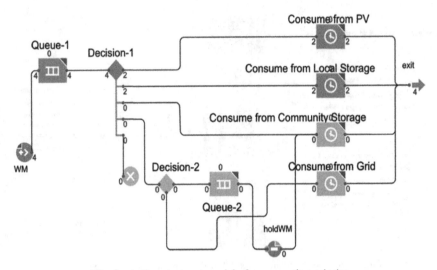

Fig. 8. A discrete event model of consumption priority

on their behalf. In this particular example, the goal was to minimize community consumption within a certain period namely the "vending window" (Fig. 9) so that the saved energy could be vended to the power grid. We tested different delegated autonomy options, i.e., delegating either 1, 2, or 3 of any of the appliances mentioned in Table 1. In Fig. 9 we show the outcome of one scenario, thus, scenario 1 (Table 2). The outcome shows that, within the vending window, the use of all three appliances was suspended resulting in zero consumption (Fig. 9).

Table 1. Distribution of CHDT population from the various category of HH in sample scenario

Type of appliance	Annual Power (kwh)			Peak periods		Number of wash cycles year
	Min	Average	Max	P1	P2	
Washing machine	15.00	178	700	5am–4pm	5pm–2am	284
Tumble dryer	64.25	497	1600	5am–12pm	6pm–11pm	280
Dishwasher	33.32	315	608	5am–3am	6pm–2am	270

Table 2. Population size of the various HH in ample scenario

Scenarios		Degree of delegation	Number of delegated appliances	Percentage of CHDT population (%)	
				Delegated	Undelegated
1	High population of delegated CHDTs	Full	3	100	0
2	Low population of delegated CHDTs	Full	3	10	90
3	High population of delegated CHDTs	Full	3	90	10
4	High population of delegated CHDTs	Partial	2	90	10
5	High population of delegated CHDTs	Partial	1	90	10

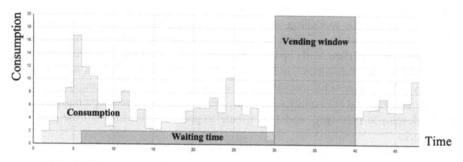

Fig. 9. The outcome of a collective action behaviour for scenario 1 (Table 2)

5   Prerequisite for Implementation and Limitations of the Study

Data from these HH appliances may be collected using IoT sensors, and this data could be transmitted using normal IoT protocols to the cloud where the digital twin may be hosted. In terms of appliance control, IoT actuators could be integrated into the appliances to carry out switching commands of the CHDTs, such as turning the appliances on and off. These commands could also be transmitted using IoT protocols. On the other hand, appliances are becoming more intelligent, embedding computational power. Scheduling and monitoring of these appliances could be done in the cloud by the CHDT. As suggested by [17], a Digital Twin Environment (DTE) is a logical environment in which software and sometimes hardware components interact to simulate an entire digital twin system or subsystem. To help reduce implementation costs, the services of a third-party service provider who provides DTE Platform as a Service could be procured to provide the DTE for the proposed CHDTs. Although this approach may raise some security concerns, a less expensive but effective way could be by embedding a layer of security at the gateway interface between the IoT devices and the DTE.

Limitations. Theoretically, the presented framework only considers four collaborative behaviours although in practice, there could be more. The framework is exemplified with only three deferrable loads. These are washing machines, dish washers, and tumble dryers. In practice, many other appliances could also be used to help achieve similar results. Appliances such as air conditioners, refrigerators, and water heaters, also known as interruptible loads, could be used to achieve similar results.

Prototype. The prototype model was developed using a multimethod simulation app-roach which involves the integration of multiple simulation paradigms such as System Dynamics, Agent-Based, and Discrete Event simulation techniques in a single simulation environment. The Anylogic [18] simulation platform was adopted for this purpose.

6   Conclusion and Future Work

This work is part of an ongoing research that seeks to integrate collaborative behaviours into the domain of RECs to facilitate sustainable energy consumption and exchange. The main objective of this study, as stated in the RQ, was to determine a suitable framework that could support the modelling of the collaborative behaviours of CHDTs within a CVPP-E environment. By adopting the BPMN modelling language, several frameworks have been developed that clearly and systematically outline the collaborative behaviours, key features, collaboration steps, and key roles of the collaborating entities. As discussed, three key collaborative behaviours were identified and modelled: (a) common goals, (b) resource sharing, and (c) collective actions. Demonstration of some partial outcomes for the developed prototype model contribute to point the suitability of the proposed framework.

In future works, other collaborative behaviours like value co-creation (tangible and intangible value) as well as some key performance indicators will be explored further to help access the performance of the model. Other collaborative scenarios such as the case where members could drop in and out of the collaborative, depending on their own strategies, will also be considered.

Acknowledgment. We acknowledge project CESME (Collaborative & Evolvable Smart Manu-facturing Ecosystem and the Portuguese FCT program UIDB/00066/2020 for providing partial financial support for this work.

References

1. Shafiul Alam, M., Al-Ismail, F.S., Salem, A., Abido, M.A.: High-level penetration of renew-able energy sources into grid utility: challenges and solutions. IEEE Access **8**, 190277–190299 (2020). https://doi.org/10.1109/ACCESS.2020.3031481

2. Feldman, D., Ramasamy, V., Fu, R., Ramdas, A., Desai, J., Margolis, R.: U.S. Solar Photo-voltaic System and Energy Storage Cost Benchmark: Q1 2020. National Renewable Energy Laboratory, Golden, CO. https://www.nrel.gov/research/publications.html (2021). Accessed 11 Apr 2022
3. Thomas, M., DeCillia, B., Santos, J.B., Thorlakson, L.: Great expectations: public opinion about energy transition. Energy Policy **162**, 112777 (2022). https://doi.org/10.1016/j.enpol.2022.112777
4. Dobravec, V., Matak, N., Sakulin, C., Krajačić, G.: Multilevel governance energy planning and policy: a view on local energy initiatives. Energy Sustain. Soc. **11**(2), 1–17 (2021). https://doi.org/10.1186/s13705-020-00277
5. IRENA: Future of solar photovoltaic: Deployment, investment, technology, grid integration and socio-economic aspects (A Global Energy Transformation: paper). International Renewable Energy Agency. https://irena.org/-/media/Files/IRENA/Agency/Publication/2019/Nov/IRENA_Future_of_Solar_PV_2019.pdf (2019). Accessed 11 Apr 2022
6. Figgener, J., et al.: The development of stationary battery storage systems in Germany – status 2020. J. Energy Storage **33**, 101982 (2021). https://doi.org/10.1016/j.est.2020.101982
7. Gährs, S., Knoefel, J.: Stakeholder demands and regulatory framework for community energy storage with a focus on Germany. Energy Policy **144**, 111678 (2020). https://doi.org/10.1016/j.enpol.2020.111678
8. Chang, K.C., et al.: Standalone and minigrid-connected solar energy systems for rural application in rwanda: an in situ study. Int. J. Photoenergy **2021**, 1–22 (2021). https://doi.org/10.1155/2021/1211953
9. The European Parliament and the Council of the European Union: Directive (EU) 2018/2001 of the European Parliament and of the Council on the promotion of the use of energy from renewable sources. Official Journal of the European Union. https://eur-lex.europa.eu/legal-content/EN/TXT/PDF/?uri=CELEX:32018L2001&from=fr (2018). Accessed 07 Mar 2022
10. Adu-Kankam, K.O., Camarinha-Matos, L.M.: Towards collaborative virtual power plants: trends and convergence. Sustain. Energ. Grids Netw. **626**, 217–230 (2018). https://doi.org/10.1016/j.segan.2018.08.003
11. Adu-Kankam, K.O., Camarinha-Matos, L.M.: A collaborative approach to demand side energy management. In: Boosting Collaborative Networks 4.0. PRO-VE 2020. IFIP Advances in Information and Communication echnology, vol. 598, pp. 393–405 (2020) https://doi.org/10.1007/978-3-030-62412-5, https://doi.org/10.1007/978-3-030-62412-5_32
12. Adu-Kankam, K.O., Camarinha-Matos, L.M.: A framework for behavioural change through incentivization in a collaborative virtual power plant ecosystem. In: Technological Innovation for Life Improvement. DoCEIS 2020. IFIP AICT, vol. 577, pp. 31–40 (2020). https://doi.org/10.1007/978-3-030-4512, https://doi.org/10.1007/978-3-030-45124-0_3
13. Adu-Kankam, K.O., Camarinha-matos, L.: Towards a hybrid model for the diffusion of innovation in energy communities. In: Technological Innovation for Applied AI Systems. DoCEIS 2021. IFIP Advances in Information and Communication Technology, vol. 626, pp. 175–188 (2021). https://doi.org/10.1007/978-3-030-782, https://doi.org/10.1007/978-3-030-78288-7
14. Zimmermann, J.-P., et al.: Household electricity survey: a study of domestic electrical product usage, Intertek Report R66141. https://www.gov.uk/government/uploads/system/uploads/attachment_data/file/208097/10043_R66141HouseholdElectricitySurveyFinalReportis sue4.pdf. (2012). Accessed 05 Sep 2021
15. Bianca, A.: How does a common goal in an organization help employees shape culture? https://yourbusiness.azcentral.com/common-goal-organization-employees-shape-culture-3311.html (2019). Accessed 13 Apr 2022
16. Adu-Kankam, K.O., Camarinha-Matos, L. M.: Modelling 'cognitive households digital twins' in an energy community. In: Proc. Int. Conf. Electr. Syst. Autom., pp. 67–79 (2022). https://doi.org/10.1007/978-981-19-0039, https://doi.org/10.1007/978-981-19-0039-6_6

17. RED HAT: Understanding digital twin environments. file:///Users/kankamadukankam /Downloads/co-understanding-digital-twin-environments-detail-f30893-202201-en_0.pdf. (2022) Accessed 16 Jun 2022

18. AnyLogic: AnyLogic: Simulation Modeling Software Tools & Solutions for Business. https:// www.anylogic.com/ (2018). Accessed: 27 Apr 2020

Service Design for Society 5.0 and Industry 5.0

From Digitization to Digital Collaborative Service Designs: A Systematic Literature Review on the Categories, Concepts and Constructs of Industry 5.0

Nicola Moosbrugger[✉], Florian Maurer, and Jens Schumacher

University of Applied Sciences Vorarlberg, 6850 Dornbirn, Austria
{nicola.moosbrugger,florian.maurer,jens.schumacher}@fhv.at

Abstract. In the last decade, business and industry put major emphasis on the digitization of its infrastructures, resources, processes and business models. In doing so, managers and organizational decision makers experienced support and guidance from the so-called Industry 4.0 paradigm. At the beginning of the year 2021, the European Commission launched the Industry 5.0 paradigm, an approach, that in comparison to Industry 4.0, puts human-centricity, sustainability, and resilience at the heart of the ongoing digital transition. However, the concept of Industry 5.0 still remains vague. This systematic literature review at hand builds upon this lack of knowledge and inductively investigates into the categories, concepts, and constructs of Industry 5.0. By the use of the Grounded Theory Methodology, a representative sample size of scholarly papers has been analyzed and coded. This process resulted in the emergence of the five categories Governance, Humanness, Technology, Intelligence & proficiency, and Environment. These categories as well as its related concepts and constructs are recognized as the main fields of action in Industry 5.0.

Keywords: Industry 5.0 · Technology · Governance · Humanness · Intelligence and proficiency · Environment

1 Introduction

The digitization of business and industry, especially the digitization of small and medium-sized enterprises, is of major interest to the European Commission and its member states. Digitized enterprises maintain competitive advantages and can provide more efficient, effective, and value-added processes and services to their customers and supply chain stakeholders. However, the speed of digitization has surprised many enterprises. Many businesses and industries are stuck in traditional service provision mechanisms, business models, and processes.

The last decade was highly influenced by the Industry 4.0 paradigm (*Advanced Manufacturing program in the United States*). Industry 4.0 is about the fourth industrial revolution and the transition of traditional processes to digitally supported processes. At

L. M. Camarinha-Matos et al. (Eds.): PRO-VE 2022, IFIP AICT 662, pp. 169–181, 2022.
https://doi.org/10.1007/978-3-031-14844-6_14

the centre of Industry 4.0 is the digitization of enterprises, including its infrastructure, shopfloor, assembly lines, services, processes, business models, etc. Less emphasis is on humans, their creativity and innovativeness as well as the environment. This shall be corrected through the Industry 5.0 paradigm. According to the European Commission [1, 2], which launched their approach towards Industry 5.0 at the beginning of 2021, Industry 5.0 focuses on human-centricity, sustainability and resilience in digitized businesses and industry. Nevertheless, the European Commission as well as other (*scholarly*) sources remain vague in their statement about Industry 5.0. This circumstance motivates us to investigate the paradigm of Industry 5.0. The objective of this systematic literature review at hand is to explore the fields of action of the Industry 5.0 paradigm in more detail. In doing so, the aim is to categorize the fields of action and explore the concepts and constructs which the Industry 5.0 approach is built upon. This systematic literature review is based on the research question "**What are the categories in Industry 5.0, and what are the concepts and constructs?**".

Following Cooper's (1985) taxonomy of literature reviews [3], the focus of this systematic literature review is on practices and applications and the research goal is to identify the central issues of the Industry 5.0 approach. By the application of the Grounded Theory Methodology, the organization of the systematic literature review is conceptual and presents the categories, concepts, and constructs of the Industry 5.0 approach. A representative sample of scholarly papers has been coded and the emerged categories, concepts, and constructs are presented from a neutral perspective. Due to the novelty of the Industry 5.0 approach, the audience of the paper at hand are specialized and general scholars as well as practitioners, policymakers, and the general public.

The paper is organized in four chapters. While chapter 1 introduces the paper and presents the research motivation and the research question, chapter 2 presents the applied research methodology. Chapter 3 introduces the findings of the systematic literature review at hand. It is divided into five sections that present the findings of the identified categories of Industry 5.0: Governance, Humanness, Technology, Intelligence and proficiency, and Environment. Chapter 4 concludes the paper and provides future directions.

2   Research Methodology

The research methodology used in this paper is the Grounded Theory Methodology. The Grounded Theory Methodology (GTM) is a research paradigm for discovery [4]. It is an inductive research methodology [5] and is used in many scientific disciplines, such as Information Systems, Software Engineering, Sociology/Social Sciences, Management [6], as well as for different purposes [4], such as qualitative research, literature reviews [7], etc. The objective of GTM is to build theory from empiricism [4], thus, a theory that is empirically grounded in data (e.g. [4, 5]). The research products of a GTM research are, for example, new core categories [8], models [9], reports, articles, books, etc. that contribute to and extend the ongoing substantive and theoretical conversations from different methodological perspectives [10].

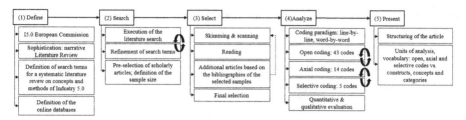

Fig. 1. Research design (*based on:* [7])

As depicted in Fig. 1, Wolfswinkel's et al. (2013) [7] five-stage grounded-theory method framework has been applied. This framework is composed of the stages: (1) define, (2) search, (3) select, (4) analyze, and (5) present. After a narrative literature review and the reading of introductory articles on Industry 5.0 and its emergence from Industry 4.0, published, for example, by the European Commission, the search terms and the online databases have been defined. It was an iterative process and the search terms experienced continuous tailoring, developing from the existing Industry 5.0 understanding. Thereby the conception of the European Commission [1, 2] acted as a basis, determining 3 out of the 4 search terms "Industry 5.0 AND human centricity", "Industry 5.0 AND sustainability" and "Industry 5.0 AND resilience". The fourth research term "Industry 5.0 concepts" was developed to represent the research question. The final literature search was performed from November 2021 to January 2022 and the search terms were applied in Google Scholar and ScienceDirect.

The literature search resulted in the pre-selection of 254 scholarly articles. Following Hart (2003) [11], as next, the pre-selected scholarly articles experienced rigorous skimming and scanning. In doing so, the title, abstract, and conclusion have been read and their appropriateness has been evaluated towards the set research motivation and research question. 27 scholarly articles passed this process and have been chosen for the literature review. Additionally, six papers from the bibliographies of the selected papers have been included. In total 33 papers were selected for the systematic literature review.

The analysis of the selected scholarly articles is based upon the GTM approach of Strauss [12] and applies open coding, axial coding, and selective coding. Open coding is about the close reading of a set of single studies and the early abstracting and categorizing of the hidden aspects of the research topic under exploration and is about the coding of, as important rated, passages (quotes), incl. text, figures, tables, etc. [13]. The objective of open coding is to produce useable and useful abstractions [13]. The applied coding paradigms are line-by-line and word-by-word coding (e.g. [13, 14]). As next, axial coding has been applied. Axial coding is about an intense analysis of the open codes and their further development as well as their alignment to sub-categories. Selective coding is about the identification and development of categories, and the relations between the categories.

3 Findings

The literature analysis resulted in the emergence of five categories of Industry 5.0 that are: Governance, Humanness, Technology, Intelligence and proficiency, and Environment.

Each category describes a selective code that emerged through the application of the Grounded Theory Methodology.

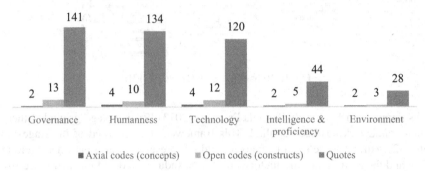

Fig. 2. Code system categories

As presented in Fig. 2, the category "Governance" gained the most quotes and open codes. It is composed of 141 quotes, captured in 13 open codes and 2 axial codes. The following categories are Humanness (4 axial codes, 10 open codes, 134 quotes), Technology (4 axial codes, 12 open codes, 120 quotes), Intelligence and proficiency (2 axial codes, 5 open codes, 44 quotes), and Environment (2 axial codes, 3 open codes, 28 quotes).

The categories are presented in more detail in the following sections. To enable smooth reading and to provide better understanding, in the below paragraphs, the selective codes are called categories, composed of concepts (axial codes) and constructs (open codes).

3.1 Governance

The category "Governance" focuses on the non-technological sides of Industry 5.0, such as management practices, policies, or security, and is composed of two axial codes, formed by 13 open codes and 141 quotes.

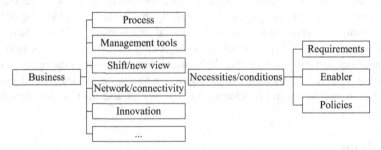

Fig. 3. Category "Governance", its two concepts and most frequently quoted constructs

As depicted in Fig. 3, the concepts (axial codes) are business, and necessities/conditions. The concept business consists of ten constructs (open codes) that cover processes, management tools, methods as well as innovation, and the shift of procedures and a new view on business approaches. The two most frequently mentioned constructs in business are management tools (12 quotes) and processes (13 quotes). While management tools describe different designs, frameworks, or models that support and structure the management (process) in Industry 5.0, processes direct the focus on typical, necessary, or arising types of processes in Industry 5.0. Thereby examples are digitization, continuous improvement process (CIP), or change processes [15–18]. Concerning these two constructs, the constructs methods, standards/rules, and business models are very similar, summarizing requirements and strategies for Industry 5.0 operations. A separately mentioned requirement however is security, which forms a construct covering different types of security such as cybersecurity, access control security, as well as the significance of security in Industry 5.0. The constructs innovation and shift/new view, underline the creative and cutting-edge part of the concept business. This field of interest reflects not only the continuous demand for innovative environments but also a visible transition of (industrial/business) approaches, perspectives, and/or society in the context of Industry 5.0. The centre of attention of the construct network/connectivity is on cooperation and communication rather than on technology. The interaction between employees, stakeholders, machines, and devices is of key importance for Industry 5.0. A prevalently mentioned way of doing this is through a social business network [19].

The concept necessities/conditions includes the constructs policies, requirements, and enabler. The construct enabler examines different enablers for Industry 5.0 from a business viewpoint. This combines various technologies as well as research fields. The business dimension of technologies includes for example organizational impact, process optimization, or change management [20, 21]. Defined business-related research fields are among others bionics, techniques and designs like green computing, or financial systems like fin-tech [20, 22]. The construct requirements consists of 41 quotes, making it one of the biggest and at the same time one of the most varying construct. The only true similarity between the indicated requirements is their necessity. Authors, such as [16, 21, 23, 24] agree on a variety of requirements that need to be fulfilled for Industry 5.0 to evolve. These include, for example, the collection of (big) data, the implementation of strategies, the involvement of external actors, a digital infrastructure, or an increased focus on resilience. A more agreed-upon necessity however is the change or adaption of policies including laws, regulations, and political aspects. Therefore, the third construct is called policies.

3.2 Humanness

The category "Humanness" puts the human and all characteristics that constitute humanity at the centre of attention.

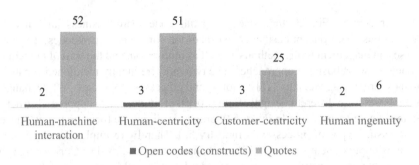

Fig. 4. Category "Humanness" and its code system

As illustrated in Fig. 4, humanness is developed from four axial codes, ten open codes, and 134 quotes, with a focus on human-machine interaction, customer-centricity, human-centricity, and human ingenuity. Thereby human-machine interaction with 52 quotes and human-centricity with 51 quotes, are by far the largest axial codes.

The three constructs (open codes) socio-technical, values, and human-centricity form the concept (axial code) human-centricity and focus on the increased human-centric approach in production/manufacturing. Values, within this concept, include a variety of ethical considerations as well as the creation of values towards internal employees and also external stakeholders like customers. The socio-technical approach supports the social and human side of technologization and directs focus on an increased synergistic relationship between systems and people. Human-centricity not only places the human back on the shopfloor but also shapes all activities around the human. This includes a human-centric design of cyber-physical systems, adaptable technology to the needs of humans, and an increase in human resilience [15, 25–27].

The concept human-machine interaction consists of two constructs, augmentation, and human-machine interaction. Augmentation is mostly about the extension of human abilities through (a human-friendly) technology. The focus lies on enhancement, whereas in human-machine interaction the most important factor is the cooperation between a human and a machine. Thereby the importance of the synergy between humans and machines gets emphasized. It is suggested repeatedly to assign boring or dangerous work to machines and robots and let people unfold their creativity and ingenuity [16, 17, 21, 24, 28–31]. But human-machine interaction even goes one step further and targets the direct cooperation between humans and machines for example a robot acting as a third hand or an exoskeleton enhancing the human's strength.

The concept customer-centricity captures the customers and their demands and preferences. This gets reflected through the three constructs customer, personalization, and customization. The terms personalization and customization describe the Industry 5.0 trend to create products and services that are highly adjusted to a customer's demand. Authors, such as [16, 17, 20, 24, 27, 30, 32], point also in the direction of mass customization/personalization, picturing Industry 5.0 as a way to increase the production, keeping overall costs at a minimum and at the same time including every customer's wish. A few authors, such as [29] consider personalization as an advancement of customization where products and services get adjusted to people's personal needs through the so-called human touch. It is argued that, through human workers on the shopfloor, increased creativity, and human ingenuity incorporated in a product, personalization can be achieved. The construct customer points towards the inclusion of the customer in the design and production process and therefore increasing not only the production of personalized products but also active customer engagement.

The concept human ingenuity emphasizes the human touch as well as creativity and design as two separate constructs. Thereby the possibility for people to engage in creativity, design, innovative ideas, and problem-solving activities is pointed out and described as a crucial difference to the Industry 4.0 paradigm.

3.3 Technology

The category "Technology" describes the technological side of the fifth industrial revolution and is made upon four axial codes named technologies, network and interoperability, robotics, and technologies for energy.

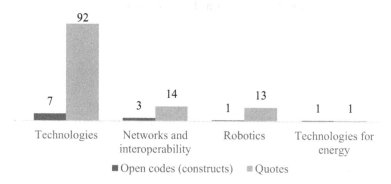

Fig. 5. Category "Technology" and its code system

As depicted in Fig. 5, the most quoted concept (axial code) is technologies, consisting of seven constructs (open codes) and 92 quotes. These constructs however do not describe different types of technology but rather show the current status of technology, for example, future technology, enabling technology, or bio-inspired technology. Thereby the most frequently mentioned technologies are artificial intelligence (AI; 17 quotes), the (Industrial) Internet of Things ((I)IoT; 12 quotes), augmented reality (AR; 5 quotes), cyber-physical systems (CPS; 4 quotes) and robots (13 quotes). A certain consistency can be identified within this data, since a majority of authors [16, 17, 19, 21, 25, 28, 31, 33, 34] mention the same kind of technologies as crucial factors of Industry 5.0 be it as a future necessity or already existing base from the previous industrial revolution, Industry 4.0. It needs to be pointed out that in many journals the term technology is used for a yet unknown development and hence cannot be classified.

The concept robotics was developed separately from the concept technology. The key difference lies in the type of robot described in the selected samples. Whenever the term robot is used in the I5.0 context there is talk of collaborative robots, the cobots.

Cobots are robots that work in tandem with and assist humans on the shopfloor by for example taking over dangerous or boring work [30].

Another focus of technological development in Industry 5.0 lies in networks and the interoperability and connectivity of systems and devices. This concept consists of three constructs of which two describe the smart environment and smart manufacturing, representing the established connection between information, technology, and human ingenuity. The construct network/connectivity includes technological developments like (multiple) networks, platforms, or advanced interconnectivity.

Besides the huge ICT focus of the category "Technology", the fourth concept technologies for energy addresses developments around the energy sector, focusing more on energy efficiency or possibilities to accumulate energy.

3.4 Intelligence and Proficiency

The category "Intelligence and proficiency" captures the work environment including physical and psychological aspects as well as the educational sector. This category is represented through the axial codes work and knowledge/skill.

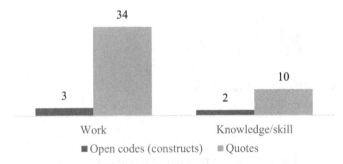

Fig. 6. Category "Intelligence and proficiency" and its code system

As shown in Fig. 6, the concept (axial code) work consists of three constructs (open codes), formed by 34 quotes. The construct new work system/tasks address the question how future work will look like. The focus, on the one hand, is on the transition of the workplace which includes a change of infrastructure on the factory floor (e.g., shared workspaces), as well as a change of established work systems. Due to increased automation, the integration of cobots, and further importance of the wellbeing of workers, work systems and manufacturing processes get rearranged and often become more effective and efficient. On the other hand, the structure of existing jobs changes, and new jobs arise. Especially through new technological achievements, certain jobs become unnecessary whereas new positions are required to use, manage, or design the new technology. A frequently mentioned new position is the Chief Robotics Officer [16, 21, 30, 35] in which the human develops skills in the field of robotics especially cobots, and therefore the interaction between humans and machines. The focus of the construct characteristics of workforce/future work lies in the transformation of the workforce. This includes making the workforce more resilient and skilled. Increased resilience can be achieved through physical, cognitive, and psychological enhancements (e.g. exoskeletons, digital assistance systems, VR) [26]. The Industry 5.0 workforce is also required to upskill which includes being more creative, critically thinking and reasoning, since these are abilities, robots cannot acquire. The construct wellbeing underlines the human-centric approach of Industry 5.0. To operate from a human-centric viewpoint, increase efficiency, creativity, and also resilience, the well-being of the workforce is of crucial importance. Developments to achieve this are people-aware designs of devices [24], inclusive work environments, or work-life balance [25].

The concept knowledge/skill is composed of the two constructs education and research. Education combines all action steps to educate, train or upskill the employees. Having appropriately educated and trained personnel is frequently mentioned as an important factor and advantage to keeping up with the fast pacing digitized and technologized industrial environment [16, 23, 35]. In addition to well-known teaching methods, innovative solutions and new ideas to train employees are for example, modelling and simulation where educational contents are imparted in virtual reality. Besides education, research also plays an important role in Industry 5.0. Fields of application such as agriculture, biology, innovation, economy, etc. are examined, to support and advance the fifth industrial revolution. Additionally, research on Industry 5.0 is conducted to increase the understanding of the fifth industrial revolution.

3.5 Environment

The category "Environment" captures environment-related topics as well as environmental sustainability. This category focuses on ways to operate more sustainably in business and industry, including the scarcity and limitation of resources. The category is composed of two axial codes that are sustainability (1 open code, 15 quotes) and biologizing (2 open codes, 13 quotes) (Fig. 7).

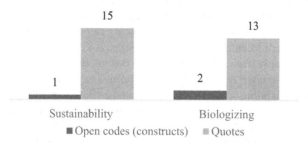

Fig. 7. Category "Environment" and its code system

Sustainability describes several different practices, methods, and ideas to create a more environmentally friendly Industry 5.0. Frequently mentioned are establishing or enhancing a circular economy, waste reduction, better resource efficiency and effectiveness, and production and usage of clean energy [16, 20, 22, 25, 33, 35].

The concept biologizing consists of two constructs bioeconomy (7 quotes) and biology (6 quotes). The construct biology describes the biological direction of research in the Industry 5.0 context. Included are topics that support a more technical approach to finding technical solutions through the help of biology. Tools and methods are, for example, bionics, synthetic biology, biotechnology, or phenomics. Furthermore, bioeconomy investigates the field of biology and economics. The centre of attention hereby is the smart use of biological resources and their transformation into value-added products such as food, bioenergy, or bio-related products.

4 Discussion, Conclusion and Future Directions

This paper at hand presents a systematic literature review of the categories, concepts, and constructs of the Industry 5.0 approach. It responds to the research question about "**What are the categories in Industry 5.0 and what are the concepts and constructs?**" and presents five categories. The first category "Governance" represents the business dimension of Industry 5.0, including processes, management tools, business models, methods but also innovation, and security. The second category "Humanness" directs the focus on human-centricity, resulting in concepts such as human-machine interaction, customer-centricity, human-centricity, and human ingenuity. "Technology" forms the third category, emphasizing the role of different technologies, networks and interoperability, and robotics in Industry 5.0. The fourth category "Intelligence and proficiency" points out the importance of knowledge, skill, and education and also captures the change (needed) in the future of work. The fifth category "Environment" outlines the concepts of sustainability and biologizing, focusing on ways to operate more sustainably in business and industry.

Comparing the findings of this systematic literature review with the Industry 5.0 approach of the European Commission, differences in scope and focus could be identified. The European Commission defined three pillars, human-centricity, sustainability, and resilience [1, 2]. According to the findings of this literature review, the pillar of human-centricity correlates with the category "Humanness". The pillar of sustainability is comparable with the category "Environment" and is additionally represent in other categories and concepts. For the pillar resilience, no equivalent category could be singled out. Following the approach of Maurer (2020) [36], resilience is a capability of a system (e.g. an enterprise, value/supply chain, etc.) and aims to design, develop, and (*re-*) engineer of VRIN-resources, responsiveness capabilities, cognitive capabilities, and dynamic capabilities for system adaption, renewal, innovation, and evolution. Resilience needs continuous attention and refinement and is best reflected in concepts such as business, human-machine interaction, network and interoperability, and work. The remaining three categories "Governance", "Intelligence and Proficiency", and "Technology" can be seen as extensions of the existing Industry 5.0 definition.

Based on the findings and its discussion, the conclusion is that the Industry 5.0 approach extends the Industry 4.0 approach. It not only incorporates the technological dimension but also takes the human, social, governmental and environmental dimensions of business and industry into account. Additionally, Industry 5.0 focuses on the workers' education, wellbeing, and creativity by leveraging and continuously expanding their knowledge, skills, capabilities, and innovativeness. Industry 5.0, thus, is a more symbiotic approach between technology, environment, humans, and society, while considering the scarcity and limitation of (economic) resources and developing a higher degree of robustness and resilience.

This systematic literature review presents a detailed picture of the status quo of the Industry 5.0 approach. Due to the novelty of the Industry 5.0 paradigm, future research is needed in several directions – vertically and horizontally. For example, each category, concept, and/or construct could be examined in more detail by exploring arising artifacts, such as technologies, management frameworks, models, tools, etc. Additionally, further systematic literature reviews and empirical research need to be carried out repeatedly since research and development thus technologies and innovation emerge continuously in both academia and practice.

Acknowledgment. This paper at hand was partly made possible by the financial support of Interreg Central Europe research project »4Steps« (Towards the application of Industry 4.0 in SMEs; project number: CE1492) and the Interreg Alpenrhein-Bodensee-Hochrhein VI-programme project »Data Sharing Framework für KMU« (project number: ABH097).

References

1. European Commission: Enabling technologies for Industry 5.0: results of a workshop with Europe's technology leaders. Publications Office, LU (2020). Accessed: 24 Feb 2022. [Online]. Available: https://doi.org/10.2777/082634
2. European Commission: Industry 5.0: towards a sustainable, human centric and resilient European industry. Publications Office, LU (2021). Accessed: Feb. 24, 2022. [Online]. Available: https://doi.org/10.2777/308407
3. Cooper, H.M.: A taxonomy of literature reviews. In: The Literature Review: Knowledge Synthesis Activities in Education and Psychology, Chicago, pp. 46. [Online]. Available: http://files.eric.ed.gov/fulltext/ED254541.pdf (Mar 1985). Accessed: 11 Dec 2014
4. Walsh, I., Holton, J.A., Bailyn, L., Fernandez, W., Levina, N., Glaser, B.: What grounded theory is…a critically reflective conversation among scholars. Organ. Res. Methods **18**(4), 581–599 (2015). https://doi.org/10.1177/1094428114565028
5. Thornberg, R., Dunne, C.: Literature review in grounded theory. In: Bryant, A., Charmaz, K. (eds.) The SAGE Handbook of Current Developments in Grounded Theory, pp. 206–221. SAGE Publications Ltd, 1 Oliver's Yard, 55 City Road London EC1Y 1SP (2019). https://doi.org/10.4135/9781526485656.n12
6. Kelle, U.: The status of theories and models in grounded theory. In: Bryant, A., Charmaz, K. (eds.) The SAGE Handbook of Current Developments in Grounded Theory, pp. 68–88. SAGE Publications Ltd, 1 Oliver's Yard, 55 City Road London EC1Y 1SP (2019). https://doi.org/10.4135/9781526485656.n5
7. Wolfswinkel, J.F., Furtmueller, E., Wilderom, C.P.M.: Using grounded theory as a method for rigorously reviewing literature. Eur. J. Inf. Syst. **22**(1), 45–55 (2013). https://doi.org/10.1057/ejis.2011.51
8. Hood, J.C.: Orthodoxy vs. power: the defining traits of grounded theory. In: The SAGE Handbook of Grounded Theory. SAGE Publications Ltd, 1 Oliver's Yard, 55 City Road, London England EC1Y 1SP United Kingdom (2010). https://doi.org/10.4135/9781848607941.n9

9. M. H. Kearney, "From the Sublime to the Meticulous: The Continuing Evolution of Grounded Formal Theory," in *The SAGE Handbook of Grounded Theory*, 1 Oliver's Yard, 55 City Road, London England EC1Y 1SP United Kingdom: SAGE Publications Ltd, 2010. doi: https://doi.org/10.4135/9781848607941.n9

10. Lempert, L.B.: Asking questions of the data: memo writing in the grounded theory tradition. In: The SAGE Handbook of Grounded TheorySAGE Publications Ltd, , 1 Oliver's Yard, 55 City Road, London England EC1Y 1SP United Kingdom (2010). https://doi.org/10.4135/978 1848607941.n9

11. Hart, C.: Doing a Literature Review: Releasing the Social Sciene Research Imagination. Sage, London [etc.] (2003)

12. Strauss, A.L.: Grounded Theory Grundlagen Qualitativer Sozialforschung. Beltz, Psychologie-Verl.-Union, Unveränd. Nachdr. Weinheim (1996)

13. Belgrave, L.L., Seide, K.: Coding for grounded theory. In: The SAGE Handbook of Current Developments in Grounded Theory, pp. 167–185. SAGE Publications Ltd, 1 Oliver's Yard, 55 City Road London EC1Y 1SP (2019). https://doi.org/10.4135/9781526485656.n10

14. Kelle, U.: The development of categories: different approaches in grounded theory. In: The SAGE Handbook of Grounded Theory. SAGE Publications Ltd, 1 Oliver's Yard, 55 City Road, London England EC1Y 1SP United Kingdom (2010). https://doi.org/10.4135/978184 8607941.n9

15. Fonda, E., Meneghetti, A.: The human-centric SMED. Sustainability **14**(1), 514 (2022). https://doi.org/10.3390/su14010514

16. Maddikunta, P.K.R., et al.: Industry 5.0: a survey on enabling technologies and potential applications. J. Ind. Inf. Integr. **26**, 100257 (2022). https://doi.org/10.1016/j.jii.2021.100257

17. Yavari, F., Pilevari, N.: Industry revolutions development from industry 1.0 to industry 5.0 in manufacturing. J. Ind. Strateg. Manag. **5**(2), 44–63 (2020)

18. Carayannis, E.G., Dezi, L., Gregori, G., Calo, E.: Smart environments and techno-centric and human-centric innovations for industry and society 5.0: a quintuple helix innovation system view towards smart, sustainable, and inclusive solutions. J. Knowl. Econ. (2021). https://doi.org/10.1007/s13132-021-00763-4

19. Longo, F., Padovano, A., Umbrello, S.: Value-oriented and ethical technology engineering in industry 5.0: a human-centric perspective for the design of the factory of the future. Appl. Sci. **10**(12), 4182 (2020). https://doi.org/10.3390/app10124182

20. Sindhwani, R., Afridi, S., Kumar, A., Banaitis, A., Luthra, S., Singh, P.L.: Can industry 5.0 revolutionize the wave of resilience and social value creation? A multi-criteria framework to analyze enablers. Technol. Soc. **68**, 101887 (2022). https://doi.org/10.1016/j.techsoc.2022.101887

21. Nahavandi, S.: Industry 5.0—a human-centric solution. Sustainability **11**(16), 4371 (2019). https://doi.org/10.3390/su11164371

22. Demir, K.A., Döven, G., Sezen, B.: Industry 5.0 and human-robot co-working. Procedia Comput. Sci. **158**, 688–695 (2019). https://doi.org/10.1016/j.procs.2019.09.104

23. Milisavljevic-Syed, J., Thames, J.L., Schaefer, D.: The digitization of design and manufacturing: a state-of-the-art report on the transition from strategic vision to implementation in industry. Procedia CIRP **93**, 575–580 (2020). https://doi.org/10.1016/j.procir.2020.03.088

24. Aslam, F., Aimin, W., Li, M., Rehman, K.U.: Innovation in the era of IoT and industry 5.0: absolute innovation management (AIM) framework. Information **11**(2), 124 (2020). https://doi.org/10.3390/info11020124

25. Xu, X., Lu, Y., Vogel-Heuser, B., Wang, L.: Industry 4.0 and industry 5.0—inception, conception and perception. J. Manuf. Syst. **61**, 530–535 (2021). https://doi.org/10.1016/j.jmsy.2021.10.006

26. Romero, D., Stahre, J.: Towards the resilient operator 5.0: the future of work in smart resilient manufacturing systems. Procedia CIRP **104**, 1089–1094 (2021). https://doi.org/10.1016/j.pro cir.2021.11.183
27. ElFar, O.A., Chang, C.-K., Leong, H.Y., Peter, A.P., Chew, K.W., Show, P.L.: Prospects of industry 5.0 in algae: customization of production and new advance technology for clean bioenergy generation. Energy Convers. Manag. X **10**, 100048 (2021). https://doi.org/10.1016/j.ecmx.2020.100048
28. Wang, L.: A futuristic perspective on human-centric assembly. J. Manuf. Syst. **62**, 199–201 (2022). https://doi.org/10.1016/j.jmsy.2021.11.001
29. Durmaz, A., Kitapcı, H.: revisiting customer involved value chains under the conceptual light of industry 5.0. Proc. Eng. Sci. **3**(2), 207–216 (2022). https://doi.org/10.24874/PES03.02.008
30. Prassida, G.F., Asfari, U.: A conceptual model for the acceptance of collaborative robots in industry 5.0. Procedia Comput. Sci. **197**, 61–67 (2022). https://doi.org/10.1016/j.procs.2021.12.118
31. Kopacek, P.: Trends in production automation. IFAC-Pap. **52**(25), 509–512 (2019). https://doi.org/10.1016/j.ifacol.2019.12.595
32. Aheleroff, S., Mostashiri, N., Xu, X., Zhong, R.Y.: Mass personalisation as a service in industry 4.0: a resilient response case study. Adv. Eng. Inform. **50**, 101438 (2021). https://doi.org/10.1016/j.aei.2021.101438
33. Fraga-Lamas, P., Lopes, S.I., Fernández-Caramés, T.M.: Green IoT and edge AI as key technological enablers for a sustainable digital transition towards a smart circular economy: an industry 5.0 use case. Sensors **21**(17), 5745 (2021). https://doi.org/10.3390/s21175745
34. Alvarez-Aros, E.L., Bernal-Torres, C.A.: Technological competitiveness and emerging technologies in industry 4.0 and industry 5.0. An. Acad. Bras. Ciênc. **93**(1), e20191290 (2021) https://doi.org/10.1590/0001-3765202120191290
35. Margherita, E.G., Braccini, A.M.: Socio-Technical Perspectives in the Fourth Industrial Revolution - Analysing the Three Main Visions: Industry 4.0, the Socially Sustainable Factory of Operator 4.0 and Industry 5.0, Trento. [Online]. Available: https://hal.archives-ouvertes.fr/hal-03442406 Italy (Oct 2021). Accessed: 24 Jan 2022
36. Maurer, F.: Towards a Strategic Management Framework for Engineering of Organizational Robustness and Resilience. Friedrich-Alexander University Erlangen-Nuremberg, Nuremberg. [Online]. Available: https://opus4.kobv.de/opus4-fau/frontdoor/index/index/docId/14426 (2020)

Customer-Centric Service Design: Featuring Service Use in Life Practices

Garyfallos Fragidis[1][✉] and Dimitri Konstantas[2]

[1] Faculty of Economics and Business, International Hellenic University, Terma Magnisias Campus, Serres, Greece
Gary.Fragidis@ihu.gr
[2] Faculty of Social Sciences, University of Geneva, UniMail en Battelle, Geneva, Switzerland
Dimitri.Konstantas@unige.ch

Abstract. Today digital technologies have become pervasive in human life and shape the everyday life practices of the people. The paper investigates how service design can be used to understand the way that people use services in their everyday life practices and to improve the service value for the people. The purpose of the paper is to advocate the development of a new, customer-centric perspective in service design that is based on the requirements of the user and the use of services in the everyday life practices. The paper discusses the meaning of service design for the customer/user and suggest an alternative approach that emphasizes on design as planning for service use and integrating services in the everyday practices. A holistic service architecture that connects service provision, delivery and use provides insights for the way that services are embedded in the everyday activities and the development of applications and tools that can support the planning of service use and the integration of services in the everyday life practices.

Keywords: Service design · Service architecture · Service integration · Customer-centric · Life practices · Society 5.0

1 Introduction

The rapid evolution of digital technologies has brought drastic changes in every aspect of the business operations and the people's life practices. A variety of new technologies, such as mobile technologies, the Internet of Things (IoT), wearables, artificial intelligence (AI) and machine learning, Big Data, the Cloud, automation and robotics, virtual and augmented reality (VR/AR), stimulate the development cutting-edge innovations that guide the digital transformation of the economy and the society. The continuous progress of digital technologies is accelerating the development of a paradigmatic shift from a product-oriented business logic into a service-oriented logic, according to which service is understood as a perspective of business, rather than a different type of goods [1]. In parallel, the digital technologies boost the development and delivery of online and mobile services and foster service innovation [2], especially with the development

L. M. Camarinha-Matos et al. (Eds.): PRO-VE 2022, IFIP AICT 662, pp. 182–193, 2022.
https://doi.org/10.1007/978-3-031-14844-6_15

of information-intensive services and 'smart services' that are adjusted to contextual parameters [3].

The new technologies promise the development of a smarter, service-based world that will provide opportunities for increased value creation for the people. For instance, 'Smarter Planet' was an initiative of IBM for the development of smarter systems that can achieve sustainable development and societal progress [4]. More recently, the Japanese government introduced 'Society 5.0' as an umbrella initiative for the development of a human-centered information society, as a 'super-smart society' that employs digital technologies for the provision of smart services, so that "people enjoy life to the fullest" [5]. In this realm, transformative service research has been introduced as a research movement that is based on the assumption that service systems have great impact on the way that people live their lives and the quality of life they enjoy and, hence, service research can be used to improve the well-being of individuals and the society [6]. Kristensson [7] suggests the discussion for future service technologies should not focus on the technologies themselves, but on the benefits and the value they create for the user. Likewise, Brenner et al. [8] discuss the importance of the concepts of 'user, usage and utility' in service research.

Today digital technologies have become pervasive in human life and shape the everyday life practices of the people [9]. This brings major changes in the way people use services in their everyday life activities in order to achieve their goals and develop experiences and value. This paper responds to the many calls in the literature for the development of customer-centric approaches in service research that take into account the way that services are embedded and used in people's lifeworld in order to create meaning and value for the people [5, 6, 8, 10–12]. Even though there is a vivid dialog in the service design literature about the embeddedness of services in people's lifeworld, most of the current approaches emphasize on the design of the service, the service system or even the service ecosystem, but they do not extend sufficiently their scope to analyze the use of services in the people's lifeworld.

The paper makes several contributions to the existing service design research. First, it introduces a customer-centric perspective in service design that derives from the concept of the 'customer logic' [10]. Second, it discusses how services are embedded in the sequence of the everyday life practices and the activities of the people. Third, it challenges the conventional approaches of service design that aim at the development of new services or the improvement of existing services and suggests that, seeing service design from the customer's point of view, who uses services to support his life practices, it takes an alternative meaning as conceiving and planning for service use and integrating services to support the implementation of the everyday life practices. Fourth, it develops a holistic service architecture that is based on the customer perspective on service design, that consists of three layers: the customer ecosystem (refers to service use), the service ecosystem (refers to service provision), and the technological ecosystem (refers to service delivery). The holistic approach of the service architecture enables relating service use with service provision in order to develop a complete understanding of service use and service value. The inclusion of the technological ecosystem serves to understand the role of the digital technologies in the provision and use of services. Fifth, the paper provides insights for the use of digital technologies for planning service use and integrating services to support the implementation of the everyday life practices.

2 Service Design and Service Value

Service design can be broadly defined as a human-centered, creative and iterative approach to the creation of new services [14] and it is intertwined with the notions of service innovation, customer experience and value creation [15]. The early approaches on service design aimed at the design of new services or the configuration of service systems and draw attention to the design of the customer experience at the service encounter (e.g., the service blueprint) or at the multiple touchpoints of the service system (e.g., the customer journey). These approaches examined the dyadic relationship and interaction between the customer and the service system as it unfolds in the provider's domain.

The complexity of service systems prompted for the development of multilevel design approaches that integrate the analysis and design of customer experiences at different levels of interest. Characteristic is the Multilevel Service Design (MSD) [16] that consists of three hierarchical levels of service design: the service concept, the service system and the service encounter. Designing at the service concept level requires positioning the service in the customer's 'value constellation experience' and relating it to relevant services that may precede or follow the use of the core service.

With the increasing complexity of the service environment and the fragmented nature of service provision, service design evolved beyond the dyadic customer–provider interaction to develop network approaches that examine the roles and the multilateral relationships of several service actors. These approaches aim at the description of activities and interactions of network actors and the design of services to support these activities. The Service Delivery Network (SDN) is a network of multiple service providers that are together responsible for the provision of a connected, overall service experience [17]. The network can be formed either by the provider's initiative (e.g., an e-commerce company that cooperates with particular partners for payments, delivery, etc.) or by the customer (e.g., holidays that integrate services about accommodation, transportation, entertainment, etc.). Depending on who is the leading actor, the design can reflect a provider-centric or a customer-centric posture in coordination and relationship management. Other service design research emphasized on the mapping of the service network with regard to the participating actors, their roles, services provision and use and the resulted service experiences [12]. Caic et al. [24] performed the mapping of the participants in service networks and recognized patterns with common characteristics.

Service design research has been largely influenced by the concept of service value, as service design aims ultimately at the creation of value for the customer. Major impact has been exercised by the Service Dominant (SD) [1, 18], with service value being always co-created with the customer and determined phenomenologically by the customer when it is used (value-in-use) in the customer context (value-in-context) [1]. The service design research that is inspired by SD logic has as common characteristic the use of oscillating foci in order to address the requirements of analysis at the micro, meso, and macro levels of the overlapping service ecosystems [18]. Vink et al. [19] developed Service Ecosystem Design as a theoretical approach to promote the ecosystemic understanding of service design. Beirao et al. [20] suggested an approach for the study and design of services in healthcare at micro (patient), meso (healthcare provider), and macro level (national health system), noticing that the impact goes both upward and downward, from micro to meso and to macro levels, and the reverse. Likewise, Trischler and Trischler [21] suggest a multi-level approach for public service design.

An alternative perspective on service value is provided by the Customer Dominant (CD) logic [10, 11] that focuses on the customer and his functions for the creation of value in the realm of his life practices. CD logic focuses on the customer, rather than on the provider, the service system or the service itself, and shifts the interest on what the customer is doing with services in his life practices. Service is naturally embedded in customer's life practices and service value is formed in the customer's context when the service is used, influenced and facilitated by the actions of other actors (providers, friends, etc.). In accordance with the CD logic, Becker and Jaakkola [22] suggested the concept of the 'consumer journey' as a next service design level that captures what customers do in their everyday lives to achieve their goals, implying a broader focus than that of the customer journey. Lipkin and Heinonen [23] investigated how the customers, as human actors, shape experiences in customer ecosystems as a result of using services in their own lifeworld. Bettencourt and Ulwick [25] recommended a method to identify what customers try to do and what is needed for the successful implementation of their activities.

3   The Customer Perspective in Service Design

This section presents a holistic approach for customer-centric service design that refers to the way that services are embedded in people's lifeworld and are used in the everyday life practices. The approach is based on the CD logic [10, 11] and introduces the 'customer logic' in service design. The customer logic refers to customer-specific patterns of how customers live their lives, perceive their needs, perform their everyday functions, choose among available offerings and experience the use of service. In order to understand the use and value of a service, it is necessary to develop a holistic understanding of the customer's life, context, practices and experiences, as well as how the service supports customers' life.

The CD logic is based on the value conceptualization of Gronroos and Voima [13] that defines value creation in three spheres: a) the provider's sphere, where the service producer develops and provides the service, b) the customer sphere, where the customer uses/integrates services and potentially adds other self-resources and creates value as 'value-in-use', and c) the co-creation sphere, where the customer interacts with the provider for the co-creation of value, potentially with the participation of other stakeholders. Hence, the focal role goes to the customer, who decides for service use and creates value. The provider can support and influence customers' value creation, directly and indirectly, and service design is a first order opportunity for this.

Service systems are composite configuration of actors and resources that require different perspectives and multilevel design approaches. In this paper, we suggest a holistic approach that involves the perspectives of the customer and the provider in service design, but adopts the 'customer logic' and hence regards service design from the customer's point of view. People's life evolves as a sequence of activities and services can be embedded in these activities to support people in the accomplishment of their goals. The emphasis is put on customer's sphere of value creation, on the activities of the people and the way that services can be embedded in order to provide some benefit. The conceptualization of the customer perspective, as compared to the provider perspective, is depicted in Fig. 1.

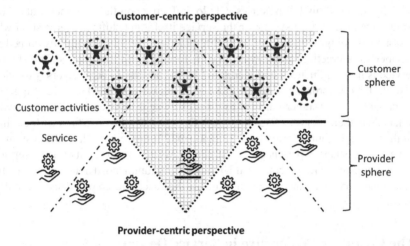

Fig. 1. The customer perspective on service and service design

According to the customer perspective, the attention is on the customer activities, how services can be used to support the customer activities and what is the impact of service use on the other activities of the customer: what else can (not) the customer do, what other activities are (not) compatible and can (not) be used, what opportunities for other activities are effectuated. For example, people that commute to work can take a taxi or use public transport, which entails they can combine different sets of activities (e.g., when going by taxi they save time for some extra activities at home or at work, when going by public transport they can work, communicate with others or surf on the internet). When people telework, they do not need commuting services, but they employ teleworking services and consequently their ecosystem of everyday activities can be shaped in a completely different way (e.g., cook, clean the home, take care other people at home, etc.).

The provider-centric perspective, on the contrary, lays the attention on the service provision, how service can be used to support a particular customer activity and what other services can be triggered by the particular customer activity. For example, the Multilevel Service Design [16], that has exercised considerable impact in the service design literature, requires positioning the service in the customer 'value constellation experience' and relating it to relevant services that precede or follow the use of the core service offering. This perspective is a step forward towards the design of services embedded in the customer's lifeworld, as it places the service into the larger context of the customer experience, but the scope remains restricted around the core service offered by the provider. It can provide several insights for service design; however, it is different from the customer-centric perspective proposed in this paper, which provides a different perspective on service and different insights for service design, as they are presented next.

We know the customer participates regularly in service design projects that follow the conventional approaches, so what is the difference with the proposed customer-centric perspective and what is the role of the customer in it? Service design is a procedure exercised by the service provider for the 'design' of a new service or the improvement of an existing one, that includes as typical phases the ideation, development, prototyping and launch. It is obvious hence that service design reflects the provider's perspective on services and service processes. There are several design approaches that introduce the customer in the design process as co-designer, as evaluator or with other roles, but the goal of customer participation is to support the design process that is organized, implemented and orchestrated by the provider.

The proposed customer-centric perspective on service design does not seek to view simply the same design procedures through the eyes of the customer and to introduce the customer's interest and concerns – it is already done by conventional design methods. It requires to emphasize on the use of service, rather than the development of service, and reinvent the meaning of service design. When the interest is placed in the way services are used in the series of activities performed in the lifeworld of the customer, the design does not refer to actions and decisions about the features of the service, but to the way the customer conceives and plans the use of services in these activities. This conceptualization of service design is compatible with the meaning of the word 'design' (e.g., in Merriam-Webster it is defined as: "to conceive or execute a plan", "to create, fashion, execute, or construct according to plan", "to have as a purpose").

Service design from the customer-centric perspective means the customer decides and plans the use of services in the series of activities performed in the everyday life practices. In particular, as these activities are connected in a timeline, service design means also the customer combines and integrates services. Hence, the service design methods that are required to support the customer-centric perspective of service design should support essentially these two basic functions of the customer: planning for service use and integrating services. Later we discuss how digital technologies can support the development of service design within this perspective.

Figure 2 presents different configurations of service provision and use with regard to the value creation framework of Gronroos and Voima [13]. The customer domain includes the series of people's interconnected (chained) activities, the provider domain refers to service development and provision, and co-creation domain refers to the interaction and collaboration between the customer, service providers and possibly other stakeholders (e.g., friends, family members, community members, social media members, business partners and associates) for the provision and use of services. We distinguish the following types of service configurations: a) Customer activity that is not supported by any service (e.g., going to work on foot or by bicycle). b) Customer activity supported by service offered by the provider (e.g., going to work by taxi). c) Customer activity supported by service co-created by the provider and the customer in the provider's context (e.g., customization of a meal to comply with particular dietary requirements). d) Customer activity supported by service co-created by the customer and the provider in the customer's context (e.g., navigation services adapted to the location and the preferred mode of transport of the customer). e) Customer activity supported by services offered by the provider as a package (e.g. hotel reservation that includes pick-up service from the airport). f) Customer activity supported by two (or more) separate service items provided as an add-on offer (e.g. transportation reservation and hotel reservation). g) Customer activity supported by two (or more) separate service items provided by different providers and combined together by the customer (e.g., separate transportation reservation and hotel reservation). h) Customer activity supported by service developed and offered by the provider with the support of a provider's community (e.g., e-commerce services supported by a community of experts or past users that provide information or solutions). i) Customer activity supported by service developed and offered by the provider with the support of a customers' community (e.g., e-commerce services supported by friends, peers and colleagues that provide information or solutions). j) Customer activity supported by service provided by customers' community (e.g., friends, peers and colleagues that provide information or solutions).

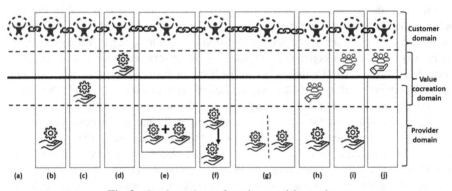

Fig. 2. Configurations of service provision and use

The horizontal axis outlines the timeline of people's practices as a series of activities in a certain part of their everyday life and the way they are interconnected with each other, as well as the services that are used, from several service providers, to support the implementation of these activities. Hence, we can understand better what the user is doing in his life, as well as how services are embedded in these activities and used for the delivery of certain benefits. This analysis can reveal patterns in the lifeworld and the lifestyles of people and in the use of services for the support of their practices. Such patterns, as well as the underlying customer needs and preferences, can be extremely useful for the design of services (according to the conventional, provider-centric perspective) and the development of service models.

The vertical axis describes a particular practice of the user and the potential use of service(s) for the support of this practice. Here the focus is on the dyadic relationship between the user and the provider that can be approached by the micro and meso level design methods that are used in service research for the design of service provision and service experience.

4   A Service Architecture for Customer-Centric Service Design

In Fig. 3 we outline a holistic service architecture that elaborates on the concepts of the customer-centric service design. The architecture consists of three layers: a) the customer ecosystem that refers to service use, b) the service ecosystem that refers to service development/provision, and c) the technological ecosystem that refers to service delivery. This architecture highlights the need for comprehensive approaches that incorporate in the same framework the research about service development/provision, delivery and use in order to support the better understanding of their relations and interdependencies.

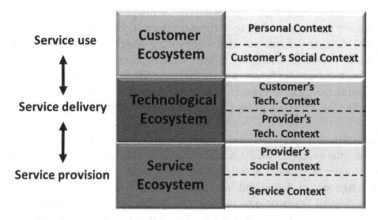

Fig. 3. A service architecture for customer-centric service design

The customer ecosystem is based on the customer logic [10, 11] that refers to user-specific patterns of how people live their lives, perceive their needs, perform their every-day functions, choose among available offerings and experience the use of service. Service use takes place in the customer context that refers to the values of the user (beliefs, attitudes, preferences), the situation of the user (needs, objectives) and the conditions that prevail during service use in the physical and the social environment of the user. The customer's social context refers to the family members, friends and other acquaintances with whom the user is related and interacts, as they can affect the value system and take a role in the everyday life practices of the user.

The service ecosystem is the aggregation of service systems that are available to provide services to the customer. The service context refers to the available services, the requirements and the processes for service design and development, the service/business models employed, the market characteristics, the business relationships and collaborations with other providers, distributors and suppliers. The provider's social context refers to the communities of customers, partners and associates that are developed and coordinated by the provider for the support of service provision, selling and use.

The technological ecosystem refers to the digital technologies that are available for the delivery and use of services by the customers. We distinguish between the provider's and the customer's technological context, with the former referring to the technologies employed for the development and delivery of services by the provider and the latter to the technologies employed for the acquisition and use of services by the customer. The technological ecosystem includes also the capacities and the skills required, the supplementary resources needed and the support models employed for service delivery and use.

The service architecture suggests the need for zooming in the requirements of service design in each particular layer, by exercising available methods and tools from the literature, and zooming out to see how they are relating to and affecting each other, in order to obtain a holistic understanding of service use in the life practices of the customers. The customers may adopt different use patterns according to their particular situations and conditions of their physical, social or technological context. The concurrent examination of the factors in these three layers will provide insights for the relationship between service use and the impact of these particular contexts. For instance, providers sometimes realize their services are not used as they were designed, but the customers invent different uses. The point here is not to alter the design process as flawed, but to learn from the way the users really use services in their life practices. This knowledge can provide insights for the development of alternative service configurations, technologies and service/business models to support the unanticipated preferences and service use patterns.

The inclusion of the technological layer between the customer and the service ecosystems supports the combined analysis of the digital and the physical aspects of services, takes into account the context of the user and service use patterns and provides insights for the development of digital and 'smart services' that are embedded successfully in the life practices of the people to improve the quality of life. Today there are ample opportunities for the development of such services in different environments, such as in 'smart cities', 'smart transportation', 'smart homes', 'smart energy', 'smart/independent living, etc. Not least to mention, it can provide insights for the development of cyber-physical service systems and augmented reality applications that can embed services on the digital or the physical environment of the users.

5 Planning and Integration of Service Use

The customer-centric perspective on service design suggests the key requirement is the understanding of the way customers conceive and plan the use of services in their everyday life practices. Hence, service design research requires the development of new approaches that support the planning of service use in the timeline of customer activities and the integration of services from different service providers. How can existing and new technologies support the understanding of service use in the everyday life activities, the planning of service use and the integration of services?

Service use in customer practices is difficult to be analyzed. Service design research employs a variety of quantitative and qualitative methods (interviews, case studies, ethnographic research, etc.). Even though they are difficult to be implemented, they are extremely useful in order to gain better understanding of the customer logic in service use. Digital technologies can provide additional and more effective methods for the identification of service use patterns at individual and collective level. For instance, tracking and lifelogging technologies and can capture user behavior in digital environments, as well as a variety of data about the user, the contextual parameters and the timeline of service use. Data analytics technologies enable the observation and measurement of human behavior, which can allow the analysis, modeling and experimentation with human behaviors, reveal behavioral patterns and support a dynamic adaptation of service provision. User profiling tools automatically capture the interest, contextual parameters, and past behavior of the user or similar users in order to personalize service experience. All these technologies can provide a basis for the development of tools that support the understanding of the way that people use services and create value in their life practices.

The planning of service use is not supported directly by technologies and tools today. There are personal activity planning tools, like diaries and other particular applications, that focus on the scheduling and organization of the everyday tasks. In addition, there are some applications that can recognize certain services embedded in the everyday schedule of the people, such as in the case of travel services that are automatically included in the digital diaries of the users. All these tools need to be extended and modified in order to include services in a systematic way and relate them to the execution of practices and activities. More importantly, they need visualize the use of services in order to support the planning of service use and the review and evaluation of past service use. This information will provide rich insights for the role of services in the life practices of the people.

The abundance of activities and services makes necessary the facilitation of the user in the integration of services. Today several digital mega-platforms, such as Google, Apple, Microsoft and Facebook, accommodate services from various providers and, more importantly, provide opportunities for single sign-on methods to the services offered by different providers. At the moment the support remains at the access of different services and the integration of these various services remains at minimum level. In the future, it will be required the integration of these services and their connection to the life practices. In addition, it will be required the development of federated platforms that would support the user in the use of a variety of services, seamlessly integrated from different providers.

6   Conclusions

The paper employs the 'customer logic' [10] to study the way that services are embedded and used in people's lifeworld and introduce a customer-centric perspective in service design. Unlike the convectional approaches of service design that aim at the development of new services or the improvement of existing services, the customer perspective in service design explores the meaning of service design for the customer, who uses services to support his life practices. Therefore, the paper suggests a re-conception of service design as conceiving and planning for service use and integrating services to support the implementation of the everyday life practices of the customer. The paper provides also a holistic service architecture for service design that enables seeing and relating service use with service provision and delivery.

The paper provides several research and practical implications for service design. As services are embedded more and more in people's life and affect the practices of the people, the scope of service analysis needs to be extended beyond the direct interaction between customer and provider. Service value can be affected by other services and contextual parameters and it may occur beyond the service interaction, so that it is not directly visible to the provider. In addition, users do not always experience service according to how it is designed by the providers. The customer-centric perspective in service design requires not only to broaden the scope, but to change the lens through which we examine services, and calls for refocusing on the role of services in the series of activities the user performs in his life practices. This way we can understand better what the users are doing and what they wish to achieve, which can be valuable insights for the design of better services.

Future research can address the conceptual elaboration and the further explanation of the customer-centric perspective and the service architecture, the application of these concepts in practical studies for their validation and improvement, and the examination of methods and tools that support the planning of service use and the integration of services. Some particular research questions can refer to the mapping of existing service methods to the service architecture, the investigation of the impact of collaboration and service networks on the customer-centric perspective and the service architecture, the inclusion of the macro level of service design, the analysis and design of applications for the planning of service use and the integration of services.

References

1. Vargo, S.L., Lusch, R.F.: Service-dominant logic: continuing the evolution. J. Acad. Mark. Sci. **36**(1), 1–10 (2008)
2. Huang, M.H., Rust, R.T.: Technology-driven service strategy. J. Acad. Mark. Sci. **45**(6), 906–924 (2017)
3. Wünderlich, N.V., et al.: "Futurizing" smart service: implications for service researchers and managers. J. Serv. Mark. **29**(6/7), 442–447 (2015)
4. Spohrer, J., Maglio, P.P.: Service science: toward a smarter planet. In: Karwowski, Salvendy (ed.) Service Engineering. Wiley, New York (2009)
5. Shiroishi, Y., Uchiyama, K., Suzuki, N.: Society 5.0: for human security and well-being. Computer **51**(7), 91–95 (2018)
6. Anderson, L., et al.: Transformative service research: an agenda for the future. J. Bus. Res. **66**(8), 1203–1210 (2013)
7. Kristensson, P.: Future service technologies and value creation. J. Serv. Mark. **33**(4), 502–506 (2019)
8. Brenner, W., et al.: User, Use and Utility Research. Wirtschaftsinformatik **56**(1), 65–72 (2014)
9. Kunz, W.H., Heinonen, K., Lemmink, J.G.: Future service technologies: is service research on track with business reality? J. Serv. Mark. **33**(4), 479–487 (2019)
10. Heinonen, K., Strandvik, T.: Reflections on customers' primary role in markets. Eur. Manag. J. **36**(1), 1–11 (2018)
11. Heinonen, K., Strandvik, T.: Customer-dominant logic: foundations and implications. J. Serv. Mark. **29**(6/7), 472–484 (2015)
12. Patrício, L., de Pinho, N.F., Teixeira, J.G., Fisk, R.P.: Service design for value networks: enabling value cocreation interactions in healthcare. Serv. Sci. **10**(1), 76–97 (2018)

13. Grönroos, C., Voima, P.: Critical service logic: making sense of value creation and co-creation. J. Acad. Mark. Sci. **41**(2), 133–150 (2013)
14. Ostrom, A.L., Parasuraman, A., Bowen, D.E., Patrício, L., Voss, C.A.: Service research priorities in a rapidly changing context. J. Serv. Res. **18**(2), 127–159 (2015)
15. Yu, E., Sangiorgi, D.: Service design as an approach to implement the value cocreation perspective in new service development. J. Serv. Res. **21**(1), 40–58 (2018)
16. Patrício, L., Fisk, R.P., Cunha, J.F., Constantine, L.: Multilevel service design: from customer value constellation to service experience blueprinting. J. Serv. Res. **14**(2), 180–200 (2011)
17. Tax, S.S., McCutcheon, D., Wilkinson, I.F.: The service delivery network: a customer-centric perspective of the customer journey. J. Serv. Res. **16**(4), 454–470 (2013)
18. Vargo, S.L., Lusch, R.F.: Institutions and axioms: an extension and update of service-dominant logic. J. Acad. Mark. Sci. **44**(1), 5–23 (2016)
19. Vink, J., Koskela-Huotari, K., Tronvoll, B., Edvardsson, B., Wetter-Edman, K.: Service ecosystem design: propositions, process model, and future research agenda. J. Serv. Res. **24**(2), 168–186 (2021)
20. Beirão, G., Patrício, L., Fisk, R.P.: Value Cocreation in service ecosystems: investigating health care at the micro, meso, and macro levels. J. Serv. Manag. **28**(2), 227–249 (2017)
21. Trischler, J., Trischler, J.W.: Design for experience: a public service design approach in the age of digitalization. Public Manag. Rev. 1–20 (2021)
22. Becker, L., Jaakkola, E.: Customer experience: fundamental premises and implications for research. J. Acad. Mark. Sci. **48**(4), 630–648 (2020)
23. Lipkin, M., Heinonen, K.: Customer ecosystems: exploring how ecosystem actors shape customer experience. J. Serv. Mark. **36**(9), 1–17 (2022)
24. Caic, M., Holmlid, S., Mahrz, D., Odekerken-Schroder, G.: Beneficiaries' view of actor networks: service resonance for pluralistic actor networks. Int. J. Des. **13**(3), 69–88 (2019)
25. Bettencourt, L.A., Ulwick, A.W.: The customer-centered Innovation Map. Harv. Bus. Rev. **86**(5), 109 (2008)

Designing Smart Products for Industry 4.0 – An Information Systems Architecture Prototype

Günther Schuh[1], Max-Ferdinand Stroh[1(✉)], and Paul Krüger[2]

[1] FIR, Institute for Industrial Management at RWTH Aachen University, Campus-Boulevard 55, 52074 Aachen, Germany
{Guenther.Schuh,Max-Ferdinand.Stroh}@fir.rwth-aachen.de
[2] RWTH Aachen University, Templergraben 55, 52064 Aachen, Germany
Paul.Krueger@rwth-aachen.de

Abstract. Companies are transforming from transactional sales to providing solutions for their customers. Mostly, smart products, enabling companies to enhance their products by providing smart services to their customers, are a key building block in this transformation. However, the development of a smart product requires many digital skills and knowledge, which regular companies do not have. To facilitate the design and conceptualization of smart products, this paper presents a use-case-based information systems architecture prototype for smart products. Furthermore, the paper features the application and evaluation of the architecture on two different smart product projects. The use of such an architecture as a reference in smart product development serves as a huge advantage and accelerator for inexperienced companies, allowing faster entry into this new field of business.

Keywords: Industry 5.0 · Smart products · Smart services · Digitalization

1 Introduction

The digitalization found its way into the manufacturing environment. Even traditional industries such as mechanical engineering are affected by this trend [1]. The products of mechanical engineering, tools and machines, which previously contained only mechanical parts are becoming smart and connected. In other words, they are enhanced with electronic and digital components such as sensors and microprocessors [2]. The result are smart products. They are based on cyber-physical systems and consist of both physical and digital components [1]. They form the foundation of industry 4.0 and by that, the establishment of collaborative networks [3, 4].

Smart products can be used to generate a competitive advantage by improving the customer's benefit [5]. This is based on an analysis of the gathered field data to better understand the customers' behavior and to create new customer-oriented services tailored to their needs. To do so, smart products require one or more information systems for their development and operation to save, process and use the gathered data along their

© IFIP International Federation for Information Processing 2022
Published by Springer Nature Switzerland AG 2022
L. M. Camarinha-Matos et al. (Eds.): PRO-VE 2022, IFIP AICT 662, pp. 194–205, 2022.
https://doi.org/10.1007/978-3-031-14844-6_16

entire lifecycle. However, since most companies in mechanical engineering are not yet familiar with the use of information systems such as IoT platforms for smart products, they lack the necessary skills regarding the selection, design and adjustment of suitable information systems. [2, 5, 6]

To help overcome this knowledge gap and to empower manufacturers of "non-smart" products to develop their own smart products, more specifically the digital components of a smart product, an information systems architecture is needed providing guidance during a smart product development. Current reference architectures do not sufficiently fulfill this need (see Sect. 2). Therefore, this paper aims at providing a first prototype of a use-case based smart products information systems architecture. Based on the user's selected use-cases it specifies the architectural components necessary for developing a smart product's information system.

In the beginning, the paper gives a definition of the relevant terms regarding smart products, information systems and architecture. Afterwards it presents the general approach for the derivation of the architecture. In section four the authors describe the requirements regarding the architecture and how the requirements are realized by elements. In addition to that, the architecture prototype and its components are described. Subsequently, the resulting architecture is applied and evaluated with two industry use cases. In the end, a summary and an outlook towards the next steps are given.

2   Background and Related Works

Section two provides the necessary definitions for smart products, information systems and (reference) architectures. Next to that, existing reference architectures and their suitability for smart products are evaluated.

2.1   Smart Products in Mechanical Engineering

Smart products are in the limelight of Industry 4.0 and one of the main topics among the smart factory, smart logistic, smart development and others [6]. Based on HICKING'S definition [1, 7] the authors define a smart product as "a product, which consists of both a physical and a digital component. They create value for both, its user (mostly the customer) as well as its manufacturer. For users a smart product's main added value is to provide smart services. For the manufacturer it is the opportunity to learn from its newly generated usage data". Smart services are a data based combination of both digital and physical services provided by smart products [8].

In mechanical engineering there are two main fields of application for smart products: The use of smart products in the own production and the sale of smart products as well as accompanying services [9]. Examples of smart products in mechanical engineering are software applications for a mobile steering of machines or connected machines which are capable of gathering and analyzing production data in real-time [10].

2.2   Information Systems for Smart Products

Smart products require information systems to handle the gathered data. An information system is a socio-technical system which comprises human and machine components or subsystems [11, 12]. It supports gathering, structuring, processing, provision, communication and usage of data [11]. Regarding smart products, the information system enables the networking with other products or systems as well as data processing. Thus, it improves the customer understanding and is the basis to offer value-adding smart services to the customer [5, 6]. Such an information system can be understood as a so called "product cloud" as coined by PORTER & HEPPELMANN [2, 5]. They can be realized through different digital solutions such as IoT platforms, PLM-Systems, or a self-developed software system.

2.3 Architectures and their Reference Character

An architecture is the mapping of functions to elements as well as the description of the element's relationships among each other. The elements are arranged in a structure and create a benefit as a whole [13, 14]. They are used to describe existing systems but are also used for the development and improvement of new systems. Therefore, an information system architecture can be defined as a structured arrangement of an information system's elements and their relationships to each other [15–18].

Some generic architectures are also used as a guidance for the development of concrete product or product line architectures by providing the definitions of relevant terminology, components and structures of the system [19]. In this case, the developed architecture can as a prototype of a reference architecture. A reference architecture describes an architecture which comprises the knowledge about how a concrete architecture for a specific use case must be designed [20]. A generic reference architecture can be used to derive concrete architectures for specific products or product lines [20].

2.4 Existing Reference Architectures

A variety of architectures, which describe and explain the structure and the components of smart products, including their information systems, exist in scientific literature. They can be roughly separated into industry-driven architectures, as well as practical, or software-driven architectures. Among the most common industry-driven architectures are the Technology Stack from PORTER & HEPPELMANN, the Industrial Internet Reference Architecture (IIRA), the Reference Architecture Model Industry 4.0 (RAMI 4.0) and ISO 30141 [2, 19, 21, 22]. Compared to the software-driven Microsoft Azure IoT Reference Architecture, the Amazon AWS well architected framework and the concept of the ADAMOS IoT-Platform [23–27].

These architectures provide guidance for the development and design of IoT and Industry 4.0 applications in general. Nevertheless, existing architectures do not consider the specific requirements and use cases of smart products in mechanical engineering. They also do not include Smart Services. Therefore, a high adjustment effort is inevitable when these architectures are applied in mechanical engineering. To close this gap between the existing architectures, the aim of this research is to provide a practical, use-case based architecture, to allow an intuitive approach to the development of smart products.

3   Description of the Methodology

The approach to create the presented architecture follows the method of KRCMAR ET AL. [28]. This approach is technology-independent and creates an architecture based on the system requirements. Fig. 1 gives an overview of the approach.

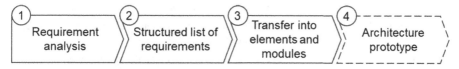

Fig. 1. Research methodology applied in this paper

In the first step, an extensive requirement analysis is conducted. The requirement analysis is based on 12 scientifically derived use cases from HICKING which cover the most common applications of smart products in mechanical engineering [29]. Furthermore, the use cases were complemented by a literature review as well as several interviews and workshops with smart product experts [29–36]. Secondly, all requirements were matched with the 12 use cases, allowing a prioritization of the requirements. The prioritization is used to categorize the requirements into generic and optional requirements. Generic requirements are particularly important for most of the use cases whereas optional requirements are relevant for only a few use cases. The result of this step is a structured requirements list. In the following step, all the requirements of the structured requirements list are transferred into architecture elements and their relationships are described. The identified elements are clustered into modules and form the architecture prototype, as result of the fourth step.

4   Derived Smart Product Reference Architecture Prototype

This chapter presents the results of the methodology. In the beginning, the requirements are described. Then the requirements are transferred into elements and modules of the information system, which are presented afterwards.

4.1   Structured List of Requirements

As discussed previously, 12 use cases, a literature review and several interviews were used to capture all requirements of the information system for smart products in mechanical engineering. In total, 112 different requirements were identified. For a better understanding, they were grouped and summarized into eight different requirement categories. Table 1 gives an overview of the requirement categories.

Subsequently, the requirements were linked to the 12 use cases and categorized as generic and optional requirements. In total, 25 generic requirements were identified, which are particularly important for the majority of the use cases. Some example requirements are: "Gather condition data", "Enable networking" or "Analyze data".

Table 1. Description of the requirement groups

Requirement group	Description
Preparation and development	Includes all requirements that must be met before the operation of the smart product and the information system starts
Networking	Comprises all requirements regarding data transmission and connection of smart products
Product usage and interaction	Describes the requirements that must be met during the usage of the smart product by the customer
Data gathering	Collects all requirements about the data gathering in the smart product, which is the foundation for data analysis and smart services
Data storage and provision	Includes the requirements regarding the short- and long-term storage of data as well as the provision of gathered, stored and analyzed data
Data processing	Describes the requirements about the analysis of gathered and stored data due to statistical evaluations or other methods with the goal of creating new information and knowledge
Smart services	Collects all requirements regarding the services which accompany the physical product and which are based on the gathered data and created knowledge due to data
Data security and access	Comprises all requirements about the security, the protection from unauthorized access and other threats

4.2 Derived Architecture Elements

The requirements of the structured requirements list are transferred into architecture elements. An element can be interpreted as a component of the information system for smart products. The guiding principle for the transfer from requirements to elements was the separation of concern [37]. According to this principle, an element should form a logically self-contained unit and fulfil one function of the system [37, 38]. This means that every requirement is linked to exactly one element. However, an element can realize several requirements. If an element realizes a generic requirement, it automatically becomes a generic element. If an element realizes optional requirements only, it is an optional element.

The optimal realization of the requirements by elements was identified in an iterative process. The result is a list of 49 elements which realize all identified requirements. Similar to the requirements, the elements can be grouped and summarized into groups, the so called modules. Table 2 shows the identified 12 modules.

Like the requirements, the elements were also linked to the 12 use cases. Furthermore, the functional relationships between the elements were examined. These two steps make it possible to derive a specific architecture for smart products in mechanical engineering for each use case, which includes the interdependency of the elements of the information system.

Table 2. Description of the modules

Module	Description
Supporting elements	Includes all elements which support the general development and improvement of the information system but have no direct influence on the functionalities or the customer experience
Connectivity	Contains all elements which ensure the connectivity of the smart product with other objects or systems
Data gathering	Comprises all elements which determine what data needs to be captured and how
Data storage	Includes all elements regarding the storage of gathered and processed data
Data provision	Includes all elements regarding the provision of gathered, processed and stored data
Data analysis	Comprises all elements which enable the information system to process the gathered or stored data
Product usage	Contains all elements which have a direct impact on the product settings and which determine the product's interaction with the customer
Usage analysis	Comprises all elements which enable the tracking, processing and storage of usage data
Documentation	Includes all elements which enable the storage of gathered and processed data in structured and standardized reports
Sales	Contains all elements that support the sales department to handle existing services and to sell new services
Smart services	Comprises all elements with a direct impact on the customer benefit and all elements for which the customer pays
Data security and access	Includes all elements which secure the system's security and protect it from unauthorized access and other threats

4.3 Architecture Visualization

The visualization and presentation of the results is of vital importance for the acceptance and application of an architecture. The results must be presented comprehensible in a way, which allows an unproblematic use in practice. For this, a presentation with different viewpoints is often helpful. A viewpoint highlights certain aspects of a system and allows a contemplation from a specific perspective, e.g. a functional or a technical perspective.[39].

The presented architecture is composed of the 12 modules with the 49 elements from Sec. 4.2. The architecture prototype is displayed in the functional view. The functional view describes the elements, their function and the modules interdependencies. The relationships between the elements are not shown to enhance legibility. Fig. 2 shows the developed architecture prototype.

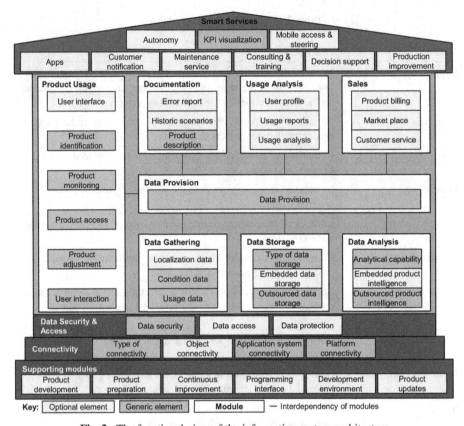

Fig. 2. The functional view of the information system architecture

The functional view is displayed as a house visually emphasizing the character of an architecture. The interdependencies of the modules are displayed with connections between the blocks. In addition, there are three building blocks, which influence most of the other elements. These are the Supporting Elements, Connectivity and Data Security and Access. They form the foundation of the architecture and are displayed at the bottom of the figure.

In the center of the architecture are the elements handling the data. The interpretation of data forms the smart component of a smart product and enables Smart Services providing a benefit for the customer. The data originates mainly in the product use, handled by the homonymous module. The produced data is gathered, stored, analyzed and managed by the modules Data Gathering, Data Storage and Data Analysis. This is often realized by a middleware application that handles the data provision between different subsystems. The results of the data processing need to be documented, which is performed by the element Documentation. To determine individual customer needs and to tailor customer-centric Smart Services, the usage of each product must be captured and assessed. This is the function of the module Usage Analysis. The resulting insights can then be used to create new Services and thus to increase profit. For this, the information system needs to support the Sales department with billing and further customer service, which is executed by the module Sales.

If all these modules work together, a company has the capability to offer value-adding Smart Services to the customer. This module is displayed in the top. Like the roof of a house, this module cannot be realized without the support of the other modules.

The architecture prototype presented in this paper can be used as a reference to derive a concrete product or product line architecture for a specific use case of smart products. This implies a selection and adaption of the containing elements. The first step is to select one of the 12 use cases from HICKING. Based on this, the relevant elements to realize the use case can be identified and eventually customized and detailed. Most use cases do not require all elements but can be realized with a reduced selection of elements. This fulfills the initially mentioned intention of the architecture to identify the architectural components necessary for realizing certain smart product use cases.

5   Application of the Architecture and Discussion of the Results

The purpose of the architecture prototype is to support the derivation of specific architectures for use cases. To verify the results, the architecture was applied to two industry use cases. For the verification process, companies already offering smart products were selected. During the verification process, the developed architecture was applied to the industry use cases, which was then compared to the architecture that was developed in reality, without the architecture prototype. This allows the comparison of the use case's existing architecture and the architecture derived by the presented method.

The developed architecture was applied to the two industry use cases, before familiarizing with the actual realization. This led to the a-priori-architecture. Afterwards, the a-priori-architecture was compared with the actual, existing architecture of the use case. By doing this, the authors examined whether the method supplies useful results and whether the a-priori-architecture determined by the method resembles the actual solution realized in the use case.

The first company is a German SME and founded in 2012. They develop innovative construction machines which produce hoses that are filled with sand or other soil materials. For their smart machines, the company provides a subscription model, which is handled by an information system. The comparison of both architectures is shown in Fig. 3.

The a-priori-architecture shows a high degree of conformity with the company's actual architecture. Out of the 36 selected elements in the a-priori-architecture, only three were not used in the existing architecture. These are product adjustment, product description and customer service. Two other elements were added. These are error reports and historic scenarios.

The second company is a SME, which is a specialist in the glass industry and provides services for glass processing machines since more than 25 years. The objective of their smart product is to increase the product availability by enabling a product monitoring and a notification about occurring issues. For this task, the company requires an information system. The comparison of the a-priori-architecture and the existing architecture is shown in Fig. 4.

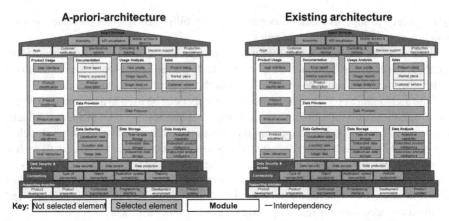

Fig. 3. Comparison of the a-priori-architecture and the existing architecture of the first use case "construction machine"

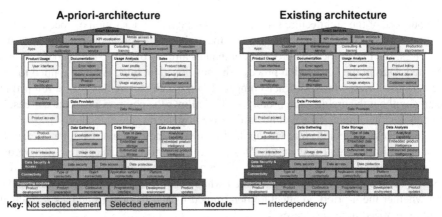

Fig. 4. Comparison of the a-priori-architecture and the existing architecture of the second use-case "glass machine"

Here too, the a-priori-architecture shows a high degree of conformity with the company's actual architecture. Out of the 27 selected elements in the a-priori-architecture, 26 were used in the existing architecture. Only the element production improvement was not used in the existing architecture. Three other elements were added. These are user interface, KPI visualization and mobile access and steering.

The high degree of conformity for both use cases is a promising indicator for the accuracy of the derived architecture prototype. Only small adjustments were needed. Based on the first applications, the architecture prototype presented in this paper appear to be of high accuracy in covering use cases in mechanical engineering.

However, further applications of this architecture are necessary to confirm the results in other companies and to assess its usability. Furthermore, the architecture has not yet been applied on companies from the beginning of a smart product development project. For this, further research with the collaboration of companies from mechanical engineering is necessary. Besides that, the architecture will be displayed in other views as explained in chapter 4 to realize its full potential. These views need to be detailed and will be shown in future publications.

6 Conclusion

This paper introduces an information system architecture prototype for smart products in mechanical engineering. In the beginning, the authors defined the relevant terms regarding smart products, their information systems and architecture. Based on the approach of KRCMAR et al., the requirements related to the information system of smart products were collected. In accordance with the principle of separation of concern, these requirements were transferred into elements and modules which realize the identified requirements. The elements form the resulting architecture prototype, which is shown in a functional view. The functional view describes the elements, their function and their interdependencies. In the end, the architecture's application to two industry use-cases is shown in two industry use-cases.

Acknowledgements. The Cornet project 303 EN of the Research Association FIR e. V. at the RWTH Aachen University is funded via the AiF within the framework of the programme for the funding of cooperative industrial research (IGF) by the Federal Ministry for Economic Affairs and Climate Action (BMWK) on the basis of a decision by the German Bundestag.

References

1. Hicking, J., Zeller, V., Schuh, G.: Goal-oriented approach to enable new business models for SME using smart products. In: Chiabert, P., Bouras, A., Noël, F., Ríos, J. (eds.) PLM 2018. IAICT, vol. 540, pp. 147–158. Springer, Cham (2018). https://doi.org/10.1007/978-3-030-01614-2_14
2. Porter, M.E., Heppelmann, J.E.: How smart, connected products are transforming competition. Harv. Bus. Rev. 1–23 (2014)
3. Camarinha-Matos, L., Fornasiero, R., Afsarmanesh, H.: Collaborative networks as a core enabler of industry 4.0. In: Camarinha-Matos, L.M., Afsarmanesh, H., Fornasiero, R. (eds.) PRO-VE 2017. IAICT, vol. 506, pp. 3–17. Springer, Cham (2017). https://doi.org/10.1007/978-3-319-65151-4_1
4. Abramovici, M., Göbel, J., Savarino, P.: Virtual twins as integrative components of smart products. In: Harik, R., Rivest, L., Bernard, A., Eynard, B., Bouras, A. (eds.) PLM 2016. IAICT, vol. 492, pp. 217–226. Springer, Cham (2016). https://doi.org/10.1007/978-3-319-54660-5_20
5. Porter, M.E., Heppelmann, J.E.: How smart, connected products are transforming companies. Harv. Bus. Rev. 96–112 (2015)
6. Abramovici, M., Gebus, P., Savarino, P.: Engineering Smarter Produkte und Services. Plattform Industrie 4.0 STUDIE, München (2018)
7. Stich, V., Hicking, J.: Smartifizierung von maschinenbauprodukten mittels einer zielorientierten methode. HMD Praxis der Wirtschaftsinformatik **56**(3), 542–556 (2019). https://doi.org/10.1365/s40702-019-00519-4

8. Kampker, A., Frank, J., Jussen, P.: Digitale Vernetzung im Service. WIST **46**, 4–11 (2017). https://doi.org/10.15358/0340-1650-2017-5-4

9. Bauer, W., Schlund, S., Marrenbach, D., Ganschar, O.: Industrie 4.0. Volkswirtschaftliches Potenzial für Deutschland (2014)

10. Kinkel, S., Rahn, J., Rieder, B., Lerch, C., Jäger, A.: Digital-vernetztes Denken in der Produktion. IMPULS-Stiftung für den Maschinenbau, den Anlagenbau und die Informationstechnik, Frankfurt am Main (2016)

11. Krcmar, H.: Informationsmanagement. Springer Berlin Heidelberg, Berlin, Heidelberg (2015). https://doi.org/10.1007/978-3-662-45863-1

12. Abts, D., Mülder, W.: Grundkurs Wirtschaftsinformatik. Springer Fachmedien Wiesbaden, Wiesbaden (2017). https://doi.org/10.1007/978-3-658-16379-2

13. Crawley, E., e al.: The Influence of Architecture in Engineering Systems. MIT ESD (2004)

14. Haberfellner, R., de Weck, O., Fricke, E., Vössner, S.: Systems Engineering: Fundamentals and Applications. Springer International Publishing, Cham (2019). https://doi.org/10.1007/978-3-030-13431-0

15. Tiemeyer, E. (ed.) Handbuch IT-Systemmanagement. Handlungsfelder, Prozesse, Managementinstrumente, Good-Practices, Hanser, München (2016). doi: https://doi.org/10.3139/9783446438156

16. Hoffmann, J.: Informationssystem-Architekturen Produzierender Unternehmen bei Software-Definierten Plattformen. Apprimus, Aachen (2018)

17. Dern, G.: Management von IT-Architekturen. Springer Fachmedien, Wiesbaden (2009)

18. Heinrich, L.J., Stelzer, D.: Informationsmanagement. Grundlagen, Aufgaben, Methoden. De Gruyter Oldenbourg, München (2011)

19. IIC: The Industrial Internet of Things, vol. G1. Reference Architecture (2019)

20. Reidt, A., Pfaff, M., Krcmar, H.: Der referenzarchitekturbegriff im wandel der zeit. HMD Praxis der Wirtschaftsinformatik **55**(5), 893–906 (2018). https://doi.org/10.1365/s40702-018-00448-8

21. International Organization for Standardization: Information technology – Internet of Things Reference Architecture (IoT RA). ISO/IEC CD. https://docplayer.net/45341580-Iso-iec-cd-30141-e.html (2018)

22. Status Report: Reference Architecture Model Industrie 4.0 (RAMI4.0) (2015)

23. Reistad, B.: Microsoft Azure IoT Reference Architecture (2018)

24. Fitzsimons, P., et al.: AWS Well-Architected Framework (2019)

25. AWS IoT Lens (2019)

26. Maschinenbau gestaltet Digitalisierung (2020)

27. ADAMOS GmbH: ADAMOS: Die strategische Allianz im Maschinen- und Anlagenbau. https://www.adamos.com/ueber-uns/ueber-adamos (2020)

28. Krcmar, H., Reidt, A., Duchon, M.: Erstellung einer Referenzarchitektur anhand von individuellen Unternehmensanforderungen. In: Bullinger-Hoffmann, A.C. (ed.) S-CPS: Ressourcen-Cockpit für Sozio-Cyber-Physische Systeme. Abschlussveröffentlichung. Arbeitswissenschaft und Innovationsmanagement, pp. 23–42. aw&I - Wissenschaft und Praxis, Chemnitz (2017). https://doi.org/10.14464/awir.v1i0.105

29. Hicking, J.: Spezifikation von Intelligenten Produkten im Maschinenbau. Apprimus, Aachen (2020)

30. Schlick, J., Stephan, P., Loskyll, M., Lappe, D.: Industrie 4.0 in der praktischen anwendung. In: Bauernhansl, T., ten Hompel, M., Vogel-Heuser, B. (eds.) Industrie 4.0 in Produktion, Automatisierung und Logistik, pp. 57–84. Springer, Wiesbaden (2014). https://doi.org/10.1007/978-3-658-04682-8_3

31. Vogel-Heuser, B.: Herausforderungen und anforderungen aus sicht der IT und der automatisierungstechnik. In: Vogel-Heuser, B., Bauernhansl, T., ten Hompel, M. (eds.) Handbuch Industrie 4.0 Bd.4. SRT, pp. 33–44. Springer, Heidelberg (2017). https://doi.org/10.1007/978-3-662-53254-6_2

32. Vogel-Heuser, B., Bayrak, G., Frank, U.: Forschungsfragen in "Produktionsautomatisierung der Zukunft". Diskussionspapier für die acatech Projektgruppe "ProCPS - Production CPS". acatech Dt. Akad. der Technikwiss, München (2012)

33. Kaidalova, J., Sandkuhl, K., Seigerroth, U.: How digital transformation affects enterprise architecture management – a case study. Int. J. Inf. Syst. Proj. Manag. **6**, 5–18 (2018). https://doi.org/10.12821/ijispm060301

34. Sandkuhl, K., Kaidalova, J., Seigerroth, U.: Towards integration methods of product-IT into enterprise architectures. In: Hallé, S. (ed.) 2017 IEEE 21st International Enterprise Distributed Object Computing Conference workshops - EDOC 2017, pp. 23–28. IEEE, Piscataway, NJ (2017). https://doi.org/10.1109/EDOCW.2017.13

35. Lee, E.A.: Cyber physical systems: design challenges. In: IEEE (ed.) 11th IEEE International Symposium on Object Oriented Real-Time Distributed Computing (ISORC), 2008. 5–7 May 2008, Orlando, Florida, pp. 363–369. IEEE, Piscataway, NJ (2008). https://doi.org/10.1109/ISORC.2008.25

36. Wang, S., Zhang, Y., Yang, Z., Chen, Y.: A Graphical hierarchical CPS architecture. In: IEEE (ed.) 2016 International Symposium on System and Software Reliability. ISSSR 2016: 29–30 October 2016, Shanghai, China, pp. 97–105. IEEE, Piscataway, NJ (2016). https://doi.org/10.1109/ISSSR.2016.17

37. Laplante, P.A.: What every engineer should know about software engineering. Sotware Engineering. Taylor and Francis distributor, Boca Raton, Fla, London (2007)

38. Reidt, A.: Referenzarchitektur Eines Integrierten Informationssystems zur Unterstützung der Instandhaltung. Lehrstuhl für Wirtschaftsinformatik, TU München (2019)

39. Haberfellner, R., Weck, O. de, Fricke, E., Vössner, S.: Systems Engineering. Grundlagen und Anwendung, Orell Füssli, Zürich (2012)

Architectures for Collaborative Enterprise Integration

Design of a Virtual Platform to Counter Economic Recession

Fernando Zatt Schardosin[1]($\boxtimes$), Amanda Lentez[2], Carlos R. De Rolt[2],
and Gabriela Botelho Mager[2]

[1] Federal University of Fronteira Sul (UFFS), Km 405, BR 158, 85.301-970, Laranjeiras do Sul,
Pr, Brazil
`ferzatt@gmail.com`
[2] Santa Catarina State University (UDESC), 2037, Madre Benvenuta, Avenue, 88.035-001
Itacorubí, Florianópolis, SC, Brazil

Abstract. This paper aims to present the proposal of a platform founded on a Virtual Breeding Environment (VBE) as an alternative for resource sharing, survival, and growth of organizations that were impacted by the economic recession caused by COVID-19. Considering this, an informational platform model is presented, based on the theoretical framework of VBE and the potential to meet the needs of actors who are part of this environment. The result is a platform called Collabore. This platform helps with resource sharing between companies and enables the development of new network technologies. It also facilitates the co-creation of value between actors, allows lobby creation to compete with large companies in the global market, ensures new jobs and income generation, and facilitates the collaboration between companies dispersed globally, connected by Information and Communication Technologies (ICTs).

Keywords: Covid-19 · Virtual Breeding Environment · Resource sharing · Ecosystem · Collaborative networks

1 Introduction

With the outbreak of the COVID-19 pandemic, companies worldwide felt the urge to increase the speed of their decision-making process, improve productivity, change their ways to use technology and data, and accelerate their scope and scale of innovation. The management thinking model includes factors such as using talent in new ways, launching new business models, improving productivity, developing new products, and promoting changing operations in various spheres. Therefore, it was necessary to reinvent organizations promptly.

The stimulus for these changes came in a hard way, for the pandemic's consequences are still underestimated. More than 30 million Americans have lost their jobs, and estimates suggest that the unemployment rate in Brazil should reach 14.2% by the end of 2020 [3], while in 2019, studies already pointed out that 68% of small businesses were unprepared for a recession [3].

© IFIP International Federation for Information Processing 2022
Published by Springer Nature Switzerland AG 2022
L. M. Camarinha-Matos et al. (Eds.): PRO-VE 2022, IFIP AICT 662, pp. 209–216, 2022.
https://doi.org/10.1007/978-3-031-14844-6_17

Accordingly, some strategic decisions need to be made, such as determining the position the organization may reach during and after the pandemic and how prepared it is to perform its plans and projects. There is a need to apply intelligent strategic decisions to understand the organization's position in its environment [9] and it's core competencies, performed roles, sold products, and available resources.

In face of the scenario provided by the COVID-19 pandemic, many companies collapsed, mainly small and medium-sized, mostly because they did not have enough resources to remain active during this economic recession. It aggravates unemployment and income reduction, impact sales, and reduces the number of organizations that provide.

Among the alternatives to overcome these problems, emerges the development of a platform to enable new ways of creating products and services, improve productivity, enhance competitiveness, reduce costs [6], generate flexibility, and incite partnerships with other organizations. Due to ecosystems being favorable environments for sharing resources through collaborative networks, that virtuality acts to bring organizations together through Information and Communication Technologies (ICTs), regardless of their geographic location, enabling collaboration between organizations physically located in any country.

The objective of this paper is to present the proposal of a platform founded on a Virtual Breeding Environment (VBE) as an alternative for sharing resources and promote organizations' growth and survival.

This work is divided from this introduction onwards to the theoretical framework where all the concepts necessary to understand the topic are explored, followed by the methodological procedures section, and then the fourth section is the requirements for the platform, next section is where the main research results are presented so that in the last section, the conclusions are presented.

2   Theoretical Framework

The term Business Ecosystem is an analogy to biological ecosystems that are used to explain business environments, which gradually move from a random collection of elements to a more structured community that produces goods and services of value to customers their capacities and roles.

These types of networks seek to preserve local specificities, tradition, and culture, often benefiting from government incentives. A business ecosystem is a cluster or industrial district though it is not limited to a specific sector of activity. It typically promotes standard business processes, providing interoperable collaboration infrastructures and facilitating the building of trust among its members as a prerequisite for any effective collaboration. Thus, defining a common foundation of ICT infrastructure and cooperative business rules between autonomous, geographically distributed, and heterogeneous companies [4]. Trust is a significant component in the configuration of networks. Its shape depends on the environment in which the organizations are inserted, which considers institutionalization, agreements, contracts, standards, and regulations that can favor trust between organizations that are components of the ecosystem [12].

A Virtual Breeding Environment (VBE) is a long-term strategic alliance between organizations, which provides a suitable environment for the rapid formation of goal-oriented networks, such as Virtual Enterprises (VE), targeting specific business opportunities [7]. VBEs are also known as home networks or support networks, designed to offer the necessary conditions (for example, human, financial, social, infrastructure, and organizational) to support virtual companies' fast and fluid configuration [11].

In this structure, all organizations know each other and maintain their activities independently, that is, they buy, produce, and sell products and services that are part of their duties. An information system also stores data about each company's strategy, financial information, production, shareable resources, that they depend on but do not have ownership of, and their primary competencies.

VBE recognizes the market and consumers' needs, and when opportunities arise that an organization cannot undertake individually - either due to a lack of resources or any other factor that does not enable them to meet the fullness of a new project -, a new organizations' network (derived from VBE) is formed, complementing its resources and competences to fulfill the opportunity. This network is called Virtual Enterprise (VE) or Virtual Organization (VO) [5].

Accordingly, while VBE is a long-term strategic network, VE can be conceptualized as a temporary network of organizations gathered through the analysis of essential complementarity competencies. It is a network focused on objectives supported by ICTs. Albeit, the life span of a VE is usually restricted, created for a defined task, and dissolved after its completion [5].

The VE results add value to the client, promote the development of the constituent actors of the VE, and contribute to the VBE. This occurs because after the end of the VE, the actors that constituted it remain in the VBE, ready to compose new VEs, and with each new experience of participation in VEs, the actors become more prepared for this purpose.

The discontinued nature of VE operations increases flexibility, agility, and efficiency in the use of resources, but also causes challenges for their management, such as the risk of increased coordination costs, and loss of information, knowledge, or other resources. Precisely to avoid these problems, the governance within the network needs to be maintained between the different VEs [8].

Before joining the networks, organizations must be prepared for collaboration to be ready to react quickly and take advantage of business opportunities. Romero et al. [11] establish a readiness assessment for organizations that are candidates to take part in VBE and future VEs. It starts with assessing corporate governance by identifying the strategic alignment with the VBE. After this stage, an analysis is performed regarding the organization's past performance in collaborative initiatives. If approved, the organization is admitted to the VBE, being able to form VEs with other organizations, with an analysis of the alignment of the organization's competencies with the competencies required by the VE.

Readiness for collaboration is the organization's ability to lead, support collaborative activities, allocate and assign resources across organizational boundaries, and link to a common ground for successful collaboration (common operating principles, common ontology, interoperable infrastructure, and cooperation agreements) [11]. This evaluation process should be routine for companies that will compose the platform, to make it a successful project.

3 Methodological Procedures

The COVID-19 pandemic has changed the way society is organized and how it works. In the beginning, it was necessary to concentrate efforts to preserve lives and the interruption of activities that were not considered essential was a fact. Consequently, many companies did not survive and ended their activities permanently [2], especially small ones. Those who remained active had their resources reduced, many jobs were lost, and, consequently, income was reduced, even for the most stable workers in the job [1], which in turn reduces consumption. Alternatives need to be considered, seeing this low-income scenario, the lower number of companies, and the increase of unemployed people.

In this scenario, an ecosystem based on VBE was planned, to make it possible to face these problems through:

1. Sharing of resources between the companies that make up the VBE;
2. Development of new ways to create products and services;
3. Co-creation of value between the companies that make up the VBE;
4. Creating a lobby to compete with large companies in the global market;
5. Generation of new jobs and income; and
6. Possibility of collaboration between companies and people dispersed globally, connected by ICTs.

The platform was named Collabore, a derivation of the latin word "Collaborare" that means "work together", in the sense of establishing a connection, which in the universe of the VBE Ecosystem is a connection that is mainly established between the actors on the platform.

A platform design and prototype were developed based on the requirements represented by the needs previously discussed. After suggestions for adjustments were proposed by the authors, the final version of the screens' prototype was prepared, resulting in the main Collabore screen (Fig. 1), dashboard, project list, project overview, partners, and employees. The prototype screens were developed using the Adobe XD® software and can be consulted fully at the following URL: https://bit.ly/3KNxRrj. The results are presented in Sect. 4.

4 Requirements

For the development of the Collabore Platform, it is important to identify and structure the requirements. Among the functional and content requirements, the following stand out:

1. Functional requirement: Partnership management tools for administrators and brokers. Content requirement: Lists of projects, collaborators, and tasks, schedule for carrying out tasks, meeting companies and collaborators in projects.

2. Functional requirement: Sharing of resources and information among companies that are part of Collabore. Content Requirement: List the resources and information that each company has, and their availability, general information about the resources, and the company.
3. Functional requirement: Development of new ways to create products and services. Content Requirement: Make available the possible forms of partnerships among companies, assets, information, and detailed documentation on the competencies and specifications of each company.
4. Functional requirement: Generation of new jobs and income. Content requirement: Detailing the expertise of each company's employees, for possible partnership, efficient search engine for forming partnerships in an agile way, and facilitating meetings of possible partners.
5. Functional requirement: Possibility of cooperation among companies and people located in any region of the world, connected by Information and Communication Technologies (ICTs). Content requirement: Allow the registration of companies from several geographic regions, with a statement of location via GPS, the possibility of searches by distance, in case it is a project that requires proximity among companies.

5 Results

Collabore was planned considering it's lifespan, which involves policy procedures, standards, vision, mission and values, criteria for selecting organizations, and people who meet the readiness and preparedness requirements [11]. The operation stage involves ecosystem governance, as well as conflict resolution, coordination of activities, infrastructure, and technology. The evolution phase is the growth stage, with the formation of an increasing number of VEs, consolidating the model. Lastly, the dissolution stage is when the ecosystem has fulfilled its objectives or has transformed and no longer supports maintaining this model as planned.

The VE broker can be represented by the ecosystem administrator or by any actor who has identified an opportunity, described, and elaborated preliminary planning. The preliminary planning will foresee from the objectives of the VE to the products or services that will be carried out, also going through the search and selection of partners among the members of the ecosystem [10]. Then, together they can prepare more detailed plans, remaining operative at a VE until its dissolution. After the dissolution, the VE heritage will be distributed among the participants, and part returns to VBE [8] for platform maintenance and growth, according to the agreements of which the organizations are signatories. Usually, a VE is established for a short period. However, it may be intentionally planned for a longer-term, in both cases, until reaching the objective that established it [5].

The product or service developed by VE will consider the policies, rules, and regulations that govern all platform participants to improve production processes while developing new products or services to meet the market's needs.

Briefly, the ecosystem administrator or any actor exercising the broker's role will be able to see a problem or an opportunity that will require collective action. The actors will be gathered in VEs from their registered profiles, considering their skills and abilities, starting from an analysis of complementarity made by the administrator or the broker. Based on an information system, Collabore will present a group of actors and each one's percentage in meeting the necessary criteria for a profile or role, based on the information provided in the VE project. It will also have an Artificial Intelligence (AI) system that will learn over time, making the formation of new VEs more intuitive and based on past choices promoted by Brokers.

The platform administrator will validate the registration of new members of the platform according to readiness and preparation criteria based on Romero et al. [11] through the submission of data, documents, and responses from the candidate to a member of Collabore.

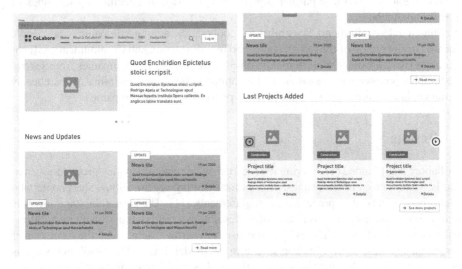

Fig. 1. Collabore main page. Source: Created by the authors.

The main page of Collabore (Fig. 1) will contain a menu with links to the home page, a page about the platform, news, a guide for navigation of the platform, frequently asked questions, and a contact form. It will also have the option to log in with three types of profiles: a) being Collabore administrator, b) an organization, or c) a person component of the platform and client. For each profile, the platform will present the information in a more complete or restricted way, depending on the level of access required by each type of user.

The user with the highest level of access is the platform administrator, who will initially be one of the researchers who envisioned Collabore. However, once the platform is active, the platform administrators will be chosen among its other components for a limited period. As seen in the wireframes (https://bit.ly/Managersboard - Manager´s Board), this user's access has control over all employees and projects (VEs), as well as tasks and execution schedules, thus being able to assist the broker whenever necessary.

The dashboard for projects (VE), as seen in the wireframes (https://bit.ly/Allpro jectsVE - All Projects (VEs) dashboard), offers an overview and allows the management of each project. However, the management of all projects will only be available to

Collabore's administrator, while any organization or person, as a broker, will manage the projects corresponding to their brokerage. The project dashboard will present general information about it, in addition to partners (organizations), collaborators (people involved), tasks, schedules, and documentation (from partners, collaborators, and VE). Both partners and collaborators will be chosen among platform members. Eventually, there may be tasks that are not within the competencies of any component of the platform. In such cases, external members may join the VE to meet the requirements and by individual agreement.

On the dashboard of each project, as can be seen in the wireframes (https://bit.ly/ProjectVE - Project (VE) dashboard – overview), it is possible to obtain an overview of the project, such as tasks, completion rate, requirements, and basic data. It will also be possible to generate different reports regarding the project.

The partners, as can be seen in the wireframes (https://bit.ly/PartnerVE - Partner's Dashboard), will be organizations that are part of the platform (eventually external partners, for some specific task) and have collaborators working on the project. For partners, it is possible to access the data of each partner, such as the business area and the number of collaborators. As a broker or Collabore's administrator, it is also possible to add or remove partners and check the completion status of tasks developed by collaborators.

Collaborators, as can be seen in the wireframes (https://bit.ly/CollabVE - Collaborator's Dashboard), will be individuals who are part of the platform or employed by some organization that is part of the platform and is appointed to exercise some role in the VE, or professionals who, even if not part of the platform, are assigned to exercise any function in the VE, that no other member has the capacity to execute. For collaborators, it will be possible to view the profile, photo, capabilities, and completion status of tasks performed in the project; the broker can also add or remove collaborators from the project.

6 Conclusion

This paper aimed to present a proposal for a platform founded on a Virtual Breeding Environment (VBE) as an alternative for resource sharing, survival, and organizations' growth. The research was stimulated mainly by the severe economic recession that the world is going through due to the COVID-19 pandemic.

Among other elements, the platform presented in this study will contribute to resource sharing between companies that compose it, an important aspect considering the scarcity of resources caused by the pandemic. It will also provide the development of new network technologies among actors that will help supply the society with goods and consumables on which they depend. The co-creation of value between companies and consumers can accelerate this process.

For small and medium-sized companies, stimulating the creation of lobby to compete with large companies in the global market will favor survival and competition on a much larger scale, generating new jobs and income for society. The reach may be increasingly greater, given the possibility of collaboration between companies dispersed globally, since they will be connected by Information and Communication Technologies (ICTs).

This study showcased a prototype of the platform, meaning a practical application and development is still needed.

This research's limitation is the concentration on a specific type of ecosystem, the VBE. Other researchers are welcome to explore other alternatives. More research is needed to determine the level of readiness of organizations to participate in the platform, studies on governance and legal instruments, and the application of this study to other types of crises.

References

1. Almeida, M.: 54% dos funcionários CLT tiveram queda de renda na pandemia (2020). https://exame.com/seu-dinheiro/54-dos-funcionarios-clt-tiveram-queda-de-renda-na-pandemia/ Accessed 19 May 2020
2. Brotero, M.: Mais de 600 mil pequenas empresas fecharam as portas com coronavírus (2020). https://www.cnnbrasil.com.br/business/mais-de-600-mil-pequenas-empresas-fecharam-as-portas-com-coronavirus/ Accessed 20 May 2020
3. Burns, S.: Pandemic Economy Looks Like (2020). https://www.forbes.com/sites/stephanieburns/2020/06/19/what-business-in-a-post-pandemic-economy-looks-like/#713d2286645f Accessed 19 Jun 2020
4. Camarinha-Matos, L.M., Afsarmanesh, H.: On reference models for collaborative networked organizations. Int. J. Prod. Res. **46**(9), 2453–2469 (2008)
5. Duin, H., Thoben, K. D.: Enhancing the preparedness of SMEs for e-business opportunities by collaborative networks. In: E-Business Issues, Challenges and Opportunities for SMEs: Driving Competitiveness, pp. 30–45. IGI Global (2010)
6. Fernández Hurtado, S.R., Castillo Triana, D., Martínez Martínez, L.Á.: Clúster virtual: nueva alternativa a la competitividad eficaz en las empresas. Tendencias. Revista de la Facultad de Ciencias Económicas y Administrativas, pp. 164–186 (2018)
7. Graça, P., Camarinha-Matos, L.M.: Performance indicators for collaborative business ecosystems — Literature review and trends. Technol. Forecast. Soc. Chang. **116**, 237–255 (2017)
8. Karvonen, I., Salkari, I., Ollus, M.: Increasing collaboration preparedness and performance through VO inheritance. Int. J. Ser. Operat. Manage. **6**(3), 293–312 (2010)
9. Pedersen, C.L., Ritter, T.: Preparing Your Business for a Post-Pandemic World (2020). https://hbr.org/2020/04/preparing-your-business-for-a-post-pandemic-world Accessed 21 May 2020
10. Polyantchikov, I., Shevtshenko, E.: Partner selection criteria for virtual organization forming. In: Paper presented at the 9th International Conference of DAAAM Baltic: Industrial Engineering. DAAAM-Baltic (2014)
11. Romero, D., Galeano, N., Molina, A.: Mechanisms for assessing and enhancing organisations' readiness for collaboration in collaborative networks. Int. J. Prod. Res. **47**(17), 4691–4710 (2009)
12. Schardosin, F.Z., De Rolt, C.R., Tezza, R., Cancellier, É.L.P.L.: Mensuração da confiança em organizações e redes interorganizacionais. In: XLIV Encontro da ANPAD – EnANPAD 2020. Evento On-line (2020)

Enterprise Integration and Interoperability in the Footwear Industry: Challenges for Collaborative Digital Manufacturing Networks in Society 5.0

Claudia-Melania Chituc[✉]

DIPF, Rostocker Straße 6, 60323 Frankfurt am Main, Germany
Chituc@dipf.de

Abstract. The footwear manufacturing industry requires high specialization of the operations for the realization of shoe collections, which necessitates a high collaboration among relevant enterprises (e.g., shoe maker, suppliers, sub-contracted companies). This work aims to analyze challenges to ensure interoperability, digital transformation and enterprise integration for the Footwear Digital Manufacturing Networks (FDMNs) towards a collaborative and interoperable Society 5.0. The advances in digital technologies facilitate the emergence of the FDMNs and have the ability to invigorate this manufacturing sector. However, ensuring interoperability and digital transformation is rather challenging. A framework is advanced to address areas where future research and development work can bring significant value in the context of Society 5.0.

Keywords: Footwear digital manufacturing networks · Footwear industry · Interoperability · Enterprise integration · Digital transformation · Society 5.0

1 Introduction

Industrial environments are complex ecosystems, where diverse stakeholders interact and cooperate [1]. The digital collaboration among the enterprises in the footwear manufacturing sector is particularly challenging due to its distinctiveness, and specific technical and business prerequisites [2]. The footwear manufacturing industry distinguishes by a make-to-order manufacturing practice, dynamic season-directed product demand, and the production cycles are rather short; due to the high specialization of the operations involved towards the realization of the final products (e.g., cutting, stitching, finishing, assembly), different companies jointly collaborate to execute specific activities [3].

The up-stream segment in the footwear manufacturing industry comprises the activities primarily executed by three types of companies: the shoe maker (SM) (e.g., the company that creates the finished shoe), Sub-contracted Companies (SCs), and Supply Companies (SPCs); the SCs are enterprises hired by the SM to manufacture pieces of a shoe or the whole shoe, and the SPCs deliver raw and/ or specific shoe components, such

© IFIP International Federation for Information Processing 2022
Published by Springer Nature Switzerland AG 2022
L. M. Camarinha-Matos et al. (Eds.): PRO-VE 2022, IFIP AICT 662, pp. 217–229, 2022.
https://doi.org/10.1007/978-3-031-14844-6_18

as: uppers, heels, or metallic accessories [3]. Interoperability and enterprise integration must be ensured to support the digital collaborations among the different companies in this industry, and to make sure that the data exchanged is interpreted in the same way by the communicating enterprises.

Interoperability commonly concerns the capability of two or more components or systems to transmit/ interchange information and consume it [4]. The absence of interoperability obstructs the enactment of collaborative manufacturing business processes [5]. With the emergence of Industry 4.0 and digital technologies (e.g., Internet of Things (IoT), cloud computing, cyber-physical systems), digital production networks [6] (also called in the literature digital manufacturing networks [7]) emerged. Within the scope of this article, a Footwear Digital Manufacturing Network (FDMN) is a form of collaborative organization (see: [8–11]) that specifically targets the footwear industry, and comprises heterogeneous and geographically distributed enterprises which put together their physical and digital resources and competences to attain a specific goal (e.g., manufacture a shoe collection) in the context of Society 5.0. Aligned with [12], the FDMNs are intended to operate without human interfaces, independently controlling and adapting their activities, e.g., considering external variations. This concept is also aligned with the vision of Society 5.0 reflecting inter-connected systems enacted within the society, merging the physical space and the cyber spaces [13].

Ensuring interoperability in this sector, and, generally, in the fashion industry, is very difficult [2, 14]. The increasing digitalization in manufacturing has further lead to the acknowledgement of concerns for ensuring interoperability in this sector and implementation of Industry 4.0 [1]. Several initiatives exist to address enterprise integration and interoperability in this industry, such as R&D projects, frameworks, standards. However, a recent investigation of interoperability approaches in the up-stream segment footwear manufacturing industry is missing, although very important, and a discussion of challenges towards a collaborative and interoperable Society 5.0 is lacking. This work addresses this gap.

This work aims to analyze challenges for interoperability, enterprise integration and digital transformation in the FDMNs towards the realization of a collaborative and interoperable Society 5.0. The advances in digital technologies facilitate the emergence of the FDMNs and have the potential to reinvigorate this rather traditional manufacturing sector. Areas where future research and development work can bring significant value in the context of Society 5.0 are illustrated, including tackling concerns regarding ethics, data privacy, individualized assessment metrics (e.g., that could be combined with biometrical metrics). Challenging areas that need to be further addressed concern: analytics and artificial intelligence in the IoT-enabled FDMNs; evaluating the efefct of digital transformation; social (footwear) manufacturing; digital twins and artificial intelligence; education/ adequate trained workforce; privacy, trust and ethics.

Due to the extent and diversity of research on enterprise integration and interoperability, researchers, developers, and practitioners would benefit from such a focused analysis on interoperability advances, as well as challenges and enablers for digital transformation in the footwear up-stream segment, and discussion of areas of improvement in this field towards the realization of the collaborative and interoperable Society 5.0. This work contributes to the current literature on interoperability and enterprise integration in the footwear up-stream segment by adding on prior work: (1) it provides an analysis of prior studies tackling interoperability and enterprise integration, and (2) based on the findings of this analysis, a framework is advanced to synthetize the themes that require practitioner´s and scholarly attention to advance the current body of knowledge towards the realization of the collaborative and interoperable Society 5.0. This contribution is constructed by addressing research questions, such as: (**RQ1**) Which are prominent initiatives aimed at ensuring interoperability and enterprise integration in the footwear manufacturing industry up-stream segment? (**RQ2**) Which are enablers for digital transformation in this industry, in the context of FDMNs? (**RQ3**) Which are the emergent challenges that the literature posits concerning interoperability and enterprise integration in this sector? (**RQ4**) Which are the directions for future research and development work that may benefit attaining digital transformation and interoperability in this industry, in Society 5.0?

The reminder of this article is structured as follows. Background information about the footwear manufacturing sector up-stream segment and the FDMSs is introduced next. Section 3 presents the research approach and related work. An analysis of challenges and enablers for digital transformation is presented in Sect. 4, and the proposed framework synthesizing areas to be further addressed. The last section contains concluding remarks.

2 Background

As the footwear manufacturing industry has a season-driven product request with short design and product phases, the SMs often center on executing high-quality high-fashion shoes in rather little amounts, sometimes with an increase in the number of models offered, completed in a make-to-order mode [3]. The diverse activities are often executed by different SCs, e.g., because of the specific craft required for completing each shoe component [15]. The main roles of the companies operating within the up-stream segment of the footwear industry are: buyer, seller, and delivery recipient [3].

This industry is highly fragmented and the realization of the final products requires strong collaborations among these companies [16], which compel adequate Information and Communication Technology (ICT) infrastructures to manage the information and digital production flows, and integrate the different companies in this sector [15]. Thus, it is a strong need to ensure interoperability and enterprise integration in collaborative forms of organization, such as the FDMNs, which are made up of SMs, SCs and SPCs.

The FDMNs, referred in this article in the context of Society 5.0, reflect a collection of enterprises in the footwear industry (e.g., SMs, SCs, SPCs) that join their resources (e.g., manufacturing equipment, software systems, devices, sensors, data) for a specific period of time to attain a specific goal (e.g., manufacture a footwear collection, deliver a digital service), aiming to act with no or minimal human involvement. The FDMNs produce, exchange, collect, archive and share data, and execute complex data and process analytics to accomplish the goal(s) set, acquire an increased revenue, increase the operational efficiency (e.g., of the whole network, and of each individual company), and bring improved customer experience. Aligned with the vision of Society 5.0 in [13], the resulting data, products, and services are relevant for the society.

Specific for the FDMNs is the focus to address interoperability and enterprise integration requirements in the footwear industry, although similarities exist with other forms of collaboration (e.g., virtual enterprises, collaborative networked organization, production networks). The FDMNs make use of the digital technologies in the footwear industry, and focus on the delivery of digital services, and participation in the inter-connected ecosystem, in the interoperable and interconnected Society 5.0. Similar to previous forms of collaboration, the main phases of a FDMN are: set-up, operation, and dissolution. However, the FDMN concept, as defined in this article, emphasizes the digital nature of the intra- and inter-organizational collaborative business activities executed among the networked enterprises in the footwear industry, and the role of dig-ital technologies, interoperability and enterprise integration, in the context of Society 5.0 and recent developments in Industry 4.0. Additionally, interoperability, enterprise integration, and digital technologies are regarded as enablers towards the execution of the collaborative manufacturing activities, supporting the realization of the goals(s) set by the FDMN, by each enterprise, and Society 5.0.

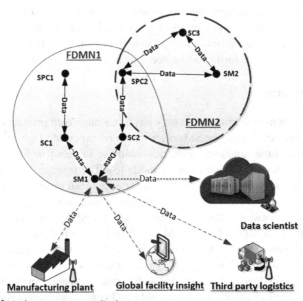

Fig. 1. FDMNs operation – an example

Figure 1 illustrates the operation of two FDMNs and the data flows. The enterprises exchange data and execute cross-organizational business processes (e.g., order manage-ment) towards the realization of a shoe collection. One enterprise (SPC$_2$ in this example) participates simultaneously in more than one FDMNs. The SM stores the operational and other relevant data (e.g., data from the manufacturing plant, third-party logistics collected using different information systems and IoT technologies) on a private cloud, and performs data analytics and process mining, e.g., to support and optimize decision making, identify or diagnose production bottlenecks, monitor the execution of the inter-enterprise business processes.

Figure 2 portrays a simple instantiation of a shoe manufacturing business scenario during the FDMN operation. The SM performs the actual manufacturing of the shoe, using as input shoe components from the SC and data collected from the manufacturing operations (physical layer, e.g., data from manufacturing equipment, hardware, communication interfaces), FDMN connectivity layer, service layer (e.g., data analytics, process mining), application layer (e.g., digital workflow monitoring, data visualization). The data collected by the SM during the FDMN operation phase, from the manufacturing plant and third party logistics (as illustrated in Fig. 1) is stored, cleaned and analyzed, e.g., to identify bottlenecks in the production. During the FDMN operation, the SM, SC and SPC exchange business documents, such as: Submit Order and Accept Order as part of the order management inter-enterprise business process, and Dispatch Advice.

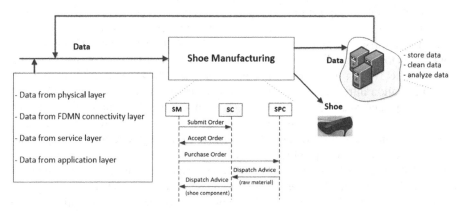

Fig. 2. An instantiation of a shoe collection manufacturing business scenario during a FDMN operation phase

These examples illustrate the need for interoperability and enterprise integration in the context of the FDMNs and Society 5.0.

3   Research Method and Analysis of Related Work

With the goal to determine and analyze prominent interoperability and enterprise integration approaches in the up-stream segment of the footwear manufacturing industry, a literature review has been carried out considering the PRISMA guidelines [17]. The literature search included an analysis of works published between January 2005 and December 2021. The following digital libraries were searched: ACM, Springer, IEEE, Science

Direct/ Elsevier as they constitute major databases in this area. The following keywords were identified: "interoperability", "enterprise integration", "footwear manufacturing industry", "footwear industry", "footwear sector", "infrastructure", "ICT infrastructure", "interoperability framework", "e-business", "digital manufacturing", "digital manufacturing network", "collaborative network", "collaborative networked organization", "IoT", "Industry 4.0". Boolean operators such as OR, AND, NOT have been used to determine works that combine more than one of these topics. Examples of queries include: ("interoperability" AND "footwear industry" AND "digital manufacturing"); ("interoperability" AND "footwear industry" and "IoT"). The list of articles retrieved was very large. Thus, a more elaborated search was performed and different inclusion/ exclusion criteria were set. Firstly, the works written in a language different than English were excluded, as well as the works for which full access has not been granted. Secondly, by reading the title and abstract, the works clearly out of scope were eliminating. The available technical reports (e.g., of R&D projects) and web-sites were also inspected.

The numerous works focusing on ensuring interoperability and enterprise integration in the footwear manufacturing industry reveal the importance of these topics in this sector. The case studies completed either at national level or at a regional level echo the relations among the different enterprises in the footwear manufacturing industry and the need to ensure enterprise integration and interoperability, such as: [18] in Brazil, [2] in the North of Portugal. The R&D projects completed in the past two decades targeting enterprise integration and interoperability in the up-stream segment of the footwear sector include: EFNET-European Network the European Footwear Network for Electronic Trading (cordis.europa.eu/project/id/FP4_28442), with the goal to build a communication infrastructure for information distribution in this sector, SHOENET (cordis.europa.eu/project/id/IST-2001–35393) with the goal to endorse solutions by implementing information systems and novel tools to expand the innovative capabilities of the SMEs in this sector, MODA-ML (www.moda-ml.org), Cec-made-shoe (www. cec-made-shoe.com) with the objective to accomplish seamless interoperability, eBIZ of the eBIZ-TFC project (www.ebiz-tfc.eu), which represents an action for e-business harmonization within the European footwear and textile clothing industry.

While EFNET1 identified national e-commerce initiatives in operational use, EFNET2 tackled data exchanges in the reselling phase contemplating the ebXML (ebxml.org) specifications. EFNET3 focused on the exchange of business data, targeting the first circle of the chain [2]. However, EFNET3 did not register significant implementation [19]. The-XML based Shoe Markup Language (ShoeML) – which represents a framework of XML schemas structured considering the design data storage and exchange needs – has been utilized to collect footwear design data relevant for the EFNET2, EFNET3 schemas [3]. The SHOENET project developed a messaging platform that allows the integration of existing applications or information systems from distinct SMEs in the footwear value chain and the secure exchange of business documents, guaranteeing trackable operations completed; and a collection of 17 XML-established business documents for the footwear industry [3]. The Cec-made-shoe project builds on previous footwear interoperability initiatives, utilizing the SHOENET messaging platform and 17 XML-established business documents; the operational platform deals with business processes involved in different shoe value chain phases, e.g., from the shoe collaborative design to the final shoe delivery [3]. The eBIZ Reference Architecture 4.0 [20] deals with technical, semantic and business aspects of interoperability. However, sparse pilots were completed in this industry to demonstrate their use in digital transformation. Main obstacles in implementing eBIZ 4. (such as: high effort, lack of knowledge) are analyzed in [20].

The use and adoption of standards by the SMEs in the textile-clothing and footwear industry in Europe is analyzed in [21]. The Shoe Process INTeroperability Standard (SPRINTS) – which represents an XML-based language to describe a data exchange protocol between systems and machines in the footwear production domain is presented in [19]. However, the focal point is on CAD communication. A framework and implementation example to ensure interoperability in a collaborative networked environment are advanced in [10] and [22]; the proposed approach relies on the concept of business enabler system, which delivers different services as SaaS (such as: messaging service, performance assessment). However, this solution did not have a broad acceptance.

Standards used for exchanging data or e-documents in the apparel, footwear, and fashion sector include [23]: GS1 EANCOM (www.gs1.org/standards/eancom – which represents a sub-set of the UN/EDIFACT standard) and GS1 XML, PRANKE (pranke.com), eBIZ, Ryutsu Business Message Standards (the Japanese equivalent of a supply and demand chain, www.gs1jp.org/2018/service-and-solution/2_4.html), Universal Business Language (UBL, ubm.xml.org).

Some EU-funded projects focused on distributed control systems for optimizing the transfer of materials from one machine to another machine [24], or on the application of established international standards (such as IEC-61499) to footwear plants automation [25], or personalized shoes. The focal point of the EURO-SHOE project (www.euro-sho e.net) has been the manufacturing of individualized shoes at a reasonable price, akin to mass manufacturing. The aspect of the shoe as well as its adaptation to the real shape of the foot were targeted, having in view of comfortable footwear, easily alterable to anatomical imperfections [19].

There are recent works that reflect the use of digital technologies in selecting specific footwear; for example in [34] is presented the application of artificial neural networks in selecting shoe lasts for citizens with mild diabetes [34]. Endeavors for implementing Industry 4.0 or industrial IoT concepts in the footwear industry are reported in [26, 27]. Several technology enablers in traditional manufacturing industries (such as the footwear manufacturing, clothes or furniture sectors) are discussed in [1]; the authors emphasize the limited capacity to invest in digital production technologies of the enterprises in the traditional industry sectors, which hinders them to take broad advantage of Industry 4.0. Five categories of enablers and challenges to be furthered addressed to attain digital transformation in the footwear manufacturing industry are presented in [28]: networking, digital data and insights, automation, customer-centric manufacturing, digital access.

The analysis of related work revealed that a recent comprehensive analysis of challenges and directions for further R&D work that may benefit attaining interoperability, enterprise integration, and digital transformation in this industry, within the context of Society 5.0 is not available although highly relevant.

4 Analysis, Challenges, and Framework

The above referred initiatives identified (except for EFNET) have a messaging interoperability layer, which enables the exchange of e-documents in the footwear manufacturing sector. However, only supplying a messaging layer is not enough to ensure wide scale interoperability in the FDMNs, as other interoperability dimensions need to also be addressed, such as: the execution and monitoring of operational business processes, the workflow of the documents interchanged, semantic interoperability. By making available a common set of e-documents, the Shoenet approach addresses semantic interoperability, but it does not address the choreography of the e-business documents interchanged. The Cec-made-shoe approach was completed considering the results of previous initiatives, and tackles this gap. However, the solution deployed as the operational ICT messaging infrastructure is proprietary, obstructing interoperability [22]. The eBIZ Reference Architecture 4.0 [20] represents the most developed approach towards attaining interoperability in this sector, addressing technical, semantic and business interoperability challenges. However, scarse pilots exist to depict its role in digital transformation.

There are R&D projects that although did not primarily focus on interoperability in the footwear manufacturing industry they tackled interoperability challenges in this sector, such as: myShopNet (www.myshopnet.eu) which develops a software platform that supports a user to create a complete e-commerce solution within 24 h for the commercialization of customizable goods involving specific modules for footwear, shirts, and high-end fashion, CORENET (cordis.europa.eu/project/id/260169), which addresses customer necessities targeting a wide range of European inhabitants, including aged, obese, disabled or diabetic persons.

The Reference Architecture Model for Industrie 4.0 (RAMI 4.0) was designed to address interoperability for Industry 4.0, which surfaced from the industrial revolution in Germany, with a solid background built on the modeling of industrial norms and standards of the Deutsche Industrie Norm specification [29, 30]. However, scarce solutions exist in the footwear sector that show the adoption of cyber-physical systems for Industry 4.0, although the benefits of their adoption in manufacturing is widely acknowledged, e.g., [31, 32]. The use of the RAMI 4.0 in the footwear industry is discussed in [26]; the authors emphasize the challenges to implement it (e.g., the need to retrofit existing equipment, communication requirements), and advance a methodology aimed to support SMEs in implementing smart machines.

The use of the digital technologies in the selection of specific footwear (for example the application of artificial neural networks in picking shoe lasts for persons with mild diabetes) is described in [34]. However, the adoption of digital technologies in this sector is limited because the SMES in the traditional industries have narrow capabilities to invest in digital production technologies which impedes them to fully benefit of Industry 4.0 advantages [1]. Towards attaining seamless interoperability, enterprise integration and digital transformation in this sector, three challenges are discussed in [28]: analytics in IoT manufacturing, analyzing the effect of digital transformation, social manufacturing.

Summarizing the findings, the following challenges were identified in the literature towards attaining digital transformation in this sector:

- *Restricted ability to spend on digital production technologies* [1]. As most enterprises in the footwear industries are small and medium sized, and the costs associated with digitalization in this sector are high, it is challenging for the enterprises in this sector to make the required investments;
- *Analytics in IoT Manufacturing* [35]. The amount of data required to be archived and managed (e.g., from the physical layer, connectivity layer, service layer, as illustrated in Fig. 2) is increasing with the digital transformation. New applications or software tools need to be designed and implemented to support large scale data/ information management and analytics [35]. Additionally, data in the production processes could be erroneous or noisy (for example: caused by broken equipment or sensors, and cleaning large volumes of data to support accurate analytics is a challenging task. Analytics in the footwear manufacturing and data cleaning are relevant at the enterprise level (e.g., as portrayed in Fig. 2, for the SM), and at the FDMN level (as illustrated in Fig. 1).
- *Analyzing the effect of the digital transformation.* It is important to develop new models to assess the economic impact of digital transformation in this sector, and implement adequate software tools; this allows the quantification and analysis of the benefits and creates advantages over the competitors [1].
- *Social manufacturing* represents a new paradigm for increasing customization accuracy and efficiency, making use of crowdsourcing and big data [36]. Recent advancements in 3D printing and 3D manufacturing enable shoe customization. Nevertheless, it would be relevant to also consider biomedical information for individualized footwear (such as: internal tension) [1], behavior analysis and dynamic netizens [36]. Although some advances exist in this area, for example in the design of orthopedic shoes, it is challenging to automatically construct footwear from a digital foot model, and enterprises continue to concentrate on low-level individualization [1]. Aggregating such data may also rise privacy concerns.
- *Difficulty to implement RAMI 4.0* [26], e.g., it is challenging to retrofit existing equipment, the need to address communication requirements

The visions of Society 5.0 and Industry 4.0 attempt to integrate information between different industries [13]. This requires attaining digital transformation, and addressing societal challenges (e.g., to reconcile individual and societal interests) and technical challenges, e.g., building a technological framework to support the operation of an information integration architecture and data platform that allows to integrate data and information between different sectors, which will supply a knowledge database that links the information from distinct sectors, allowing cross-sector collaboration [37]. Tasks to be tackled towards realizing Society 5.0 include [37]: establishing industry-academia partnerships and developing an adequate collaboration model, develop big data analytics and information integration architecture, digitalization of the different dimensions of life. Towards attaining digitalization in manufacturing, and implementing Industry 4.0, several challenges should be tackled [33], such as: education; interoperability; digital twins, simulation and artificial intelligence; high performance computing platforms, human-machine cooperation; cybersecurity, trust, and privacy; business, society, and ethical issues. Accordingly, adding intelligence in Industry 4.0 or manufacturing (e.g., to support decision making) is an important challenge to be further addressed and integrating simulation in digital twins might be a solution [33].

In the context of footwear manufacturing, especially the topics of education (and providing adequate workforce, with both manufacturing knowledge and computing skills) is very challenging, e.g., due to the high investments that need to be made in continuously training employees, and acquiring adequate software/ technology for digitalization considering the limited resources of the enterprises in this industry. As a technology-enabled data intensive society, Society 5.0 requires highly qualified workforce which surpasses the education necessities of Industry 4.0; the engineering education of Society 5.0 requires not only the knowledge and skills of development of applied technology, but it should also embed the dimensions of ethics and humanism [38].

As the footwear manufacturing industry is expected to be fueled by IoT and artificial intelligence, privacy, ethics and trust issues need to be addressed, e.g., concerning ethical implications of automatic decision making, and their implications on individual citizens and society [39]. While trusting that the artificial intelligence algorithms will make appropriate decisions, it is important to address aspects such as: cultural considerations, ethical frameworks, legal and regulatory compliance, transparency, explainability [40]. As it is expected that by 2023 the digital twin technology will grow by 38% annually [41], it is important that IoT technologies in manufacturing are integrated to allow feeding data into the digital twins [33].

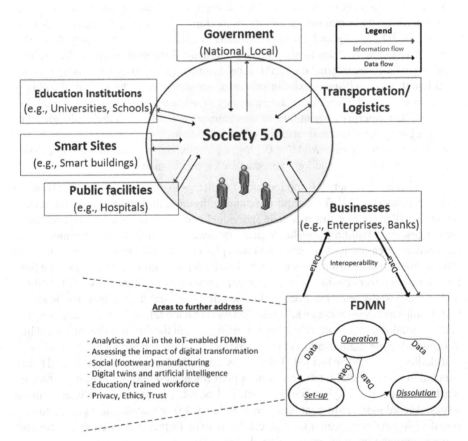

Fig. 3. Areas to further address in footwear manufacturing in the context of Society 5.0

Figure 3 synthesizes the areas that require attention in the context of the FDMNs to advance the current body of knowledge towards the realization of the collaborative human-centric Society 5.0.

5 Conclusions and Future Work

Ensuring interoperability and enterprise integration is essential for the set-up and operation of the FDMNs. The most relevant interoperability approaches targeting the upstream segment of the footwear manufacturing industry include R&D projects, frameworks, architectures, and standards. The digital technologies could reinvigorate this rather traditional sector. However, the lack of resources to invest in adequate technologies [1], and the difficulty to implement Industry 4.0 approaches, such as RAMI 4.0 (e.g., due to the difficulty to retrofit existing equipment, communication needs) [27] represent main obstacles towards digitalization.

Towards realizing the vision of a collaborative and interoperable human-centric Society 5.0, several aspects need to be further addressed in the area of footwear manufacturing, such as: analytics and artificial intelligence; assessing the impact of digital transformation; social (footwear) manufacturing; education/ adequate trained workforce; privacy, trust and ethics.

As Society 5.0 promotes the digitalization of all facets of life and intensive cross-sector collaboration, attaining cross-sector interoperability represent a big challenge. Future R&D work needs to concentrate on the development of interoperability standards and frameworks to address this challenge, and on analyzing the impact of digital transformation in this sector and in Society 5.0. For example, the gains, costs and risks of the digital transformation could be assessed and analyzed at individual level, organization/ enterprise level, industry sector, and societal impact.

References

1. Jimeno-Jimeno-Morenilla, A., Azariadis, P., Molina-Carmona, R., Kyratzi, S.: Technology enablers for the implementation of Industry 4.0 to traditional manufacturing sectors: A review. Computers in Industry **125**, 1003390 (2021)
2. Ribeiro, S.V., Santos, V.R., Pereira, C.S.: Collaborative networks in the Portuguese footwear sector and the cluster of Felgueiras, KMIS, 197--204 (2017)
3. Chituc, C.-M., Toscano, C., Azevedo, A.: Interoperability in collaborative networks: independent and industry-specific initiatives – the case of the footwear industry. Comput. Ind. **59**(7), 741–757 (2008)
4. IEEE: IEEE Standard Computer Dictionary: A Compilation of IEEE Standard Computer Gossaries. Institute of Electrical and Electronics Engineering, NY (1990)
5. Jardim-Goncalves, R., Grilo, A., Popplewell, K.: Novel strategies for global manufacturing systems interoperability. J. Intell. Manuf. **27**(1), 1–9 (2014). https://doi.org/10.1007/s10845-014-0948-x
6. Pereira, A.C., Romero, F., A review of the meaning and implications of the Industry 4.0 concept. Procedia Manufacturing **13**, 1206–1214 (2017)
7. Dakhnovicg, A.D., et al.: Applying routing to guarantee secure collaboration of segments in digital manufacturing networks. Aut. Control and Computer Science **52**(8), 1127–1133 (2016)

8. Camarinha-Matos, L.M.: New Collaborative Organizations and their Research Needs. In: Camarinha-Matos, L.M., Afsarmanesh, H. (eds.) PRO-VE 2003. ITIFIP, vol. 134, pp. 3–14. Springer, Boston, MA (2004). https://doi.org/10.1007/978-0-387-35704-1_1

9. Chituc, C.-M., Toscano, C., Azevedo, A.: E-business and collaborative networks: A service-oriented ICT platform for the footwear industry. IEEE INDIN, 591--596 (2007a)

10. Chituc, C.-M., et al.: Towards seamless interoperability in collaborative networks. In: Camarinha-Matos, L.M. et al. (eds.) Establishing the Foundation of Collaborative Networks. PRO-VE 2007. IFIP, vol. 243, pp. 445–452. Springer, Boston, MA (2007b)

11. Camarinha-Matos, L.M.: Collaborative Networked Organizations: Status and trends in manufacturing. Annu. Rev. Control. 33(2), 199–208 (2009)

12. Erol, S., et al.: Tangible Industry 4.0: a scenario-based approach to learning for the future of production. Procedia CIRP 53, 13--18 (2016)

13. Deguchi A., et al.: What is society 5.0?. In: Society 5.0 A people-centric super-smart society, pp. 1--24. Hitachi-UTokyo Laboratory, Springer Open (2020). Chapter 1

14. Bindi, B., et al.: 2019. eBusiness standards and IoT technologies adoption in the fashion industry: Preliminary results of an empirical research. In: Rindaldi R., Bandinelli R. (eds.) Business models and ICT technologies for the fashion supply chain. In: IT4Fashion 2017. LNEE 525 Springer, pp. 139--150 (2019)

15. Fani, V., Bindi, B., Bandinelli, R.: Balancing assembly line in the footwear industry using simulation: A case study, Communications of the ECMS. In: M. Steglich et al. (eds.) Proc. ECMS 34(1) (2020)

16. Shamsuzzoha, A., et al.: Dynamic and collaborative business networks in the fashion industry. Int. J. Comput. Integr. Manuf. 26(1/2), 125–139 (2013)

17. Moher, D., et al.: Preferred reporting items for systematic review and meta-analyses: The PRISMA statement. PLoS Med. 6(7), e1000097 (2009)

18. Fani, V., et al.: Supply chain structures in the Brazilian footwear industry: outcomes of a case study research. In: XX Summer School "Francesco Turco", pp. 37--42 (2015)

19. Danese, G., et al.: A novel standard for footwear industrial machineries. IEEE Trans. Ind. Inf. 7(4), 713–722 (2011)

20. Bindi, B., et al.: Barriers and drivers of eBIZ adoption in the fashion supply chain: preliminary Results, ICIEA, pp. 555--559 (2018)

21. De Sabbata, P., et al.: Standards creation and adoption for SMEs networks: the experience of the european textile-clothing and footwear industry. In: H. Panetto, et al., (eds.) Interoperability for Enterprise Software and Applications, pp. 41-52. John Wiley & Sons Inc. (2010)

22. Chituc, C.M., Azevedo, A., Toscano, C.: A framework proposal for seamless interoperability in a collaborative networked environment. Comput. Ind. 60, 317–338 (2009)

23. GS1: Implementation of GS1 EDI standards in 2018, Detailed Report (24 April 2019). www.gs1.org/sites/default/files/docs/EDI/edi_implementation_2018_public.pdf (2019)

24. Carpanzano, E., et al.: Development of manufacturing automation systems through object-oriented concepts and international standards. In: IEEE INDIN, pp. 607--611 (2004)

25. Colla, M., et al.: Applying the IEC-61499 model to the shoe manufacturing sector. In: IEEE ETFA, pp. 1301–1308 (2006)

26. Hernández, E., Senna, P., Silva, D., Rebelo, R., Barros, A.C., Toscano, C.: Implementing RAMI4.0 in production - a multi-case study. In: Almeida, H., Vasco, J. (eds.) Progress in Digital and Physical Manufacturing. ProDPM 2019. Lecture Notes in Mechanical Engineering. Springer, Cham, pp. 49--56 (2020)

27. Cunha, B., Hernández, E., Rebelo, R., Sousa, C., Ferreira, F.: An IIoT Solution for SME's. In: Gonçalves, J.A., Braz-César, M., Coelho, J.P. (eds.) CONTROLO 2020. CONTROLO 2020. Lecture Notes in Electrical Engineering, vol. 695, 313--321. Springer, Cham (2021)

28. Chituc, C.-M.: Interoperability in the Footwear Manufacturing Networks and Enablers for Digital Transformation. In: Cherfi, S., Perini, A., Nurcan, S. (eds.) RCIS 2021. LNBIP, vol. 415, pp. 581–587. Springer, Cham (2021). https://doi.org/10.1007/978-3-030-75018-3_39
29. DIN Deutsches Institut für Normung e.V.: DIN SPEC 91345:2016–04: Referenzarchitektur-modell Industrie 4.0 (RAMI 4.0) (2016)
30. Wermann, J., et al.: Using an interdisciplinary demonstration platform for teaching Industry 4.0. Procedia Manufacturing **31**, 302--308 (2019)
31. Wang, L., Törngren, M., Onori, M.: Current status and advancement of cyber-physical systems in manufacturing. J. Manuf. Syst. **37**(Part 2), 517--527 (2015)
32. Pivoto, D.G.S., et al.: Cyber-physical systems architectures for industrial internet of things applications in Industry 4.0: A literature Review. J. Manuf. Sys. **58** (Part A) 176--192 (2021)
33. Leitao, P., Pires, F., Karnouskos, S., Colombo, A.W.: Quo Vadis Industry 4.0? Position, Trends, and Challenges. IEEE Open Journal of Industrial Electronics Society **1**, 298--310 (2020)
34. Wang, C.-C., et al.: Artificial neural networks in the selection of shoe lasts for people with mild diabetes. Med. Eng. Phys. **64**, 37–45 (2019)
35. Dai, H.-N., et al.: Big data analytics for manufacturing internet of things: opportunities, challenges and enabling technologies, Enterprise Information Systems 14 (9–10) (2020)
36. Shang, X., et al.: Moving from mass customization to social manufacturing: a footwear industry case study. Int. J. of Computer Integrated Manufacturing **32**(2), 194–2015 (2019)
37. Deguchi, A., Karasawa, K.: Issues and Outlook. In: Society 5.0 A people-centric super-smart society. Hitachi-UTokyo Laboratory, pp. 155—173. Springer Open, Chapter 8 (2020)
38. Lantada, A.D.: Engineering education 5.0. continuously evolving engineering education. Int. J. Eng. Edu. **36**(6), 1814--1832 (2020)
39. Hurlburt, G.: Toward applied cyberethics. Computer **51**(9), 80–84 (2018)
40. Karnouskos, S.: Self-driving car acceptance and the role of ethics. IEEE Trans. Eng. Manage. **67**(2), 252–265 (2020)
41. Panetta, K.: Top 10 Strategic Technology Trends for 2018" (2017). Available at: www.gartner.com/smarterwithgartner/gartner-top-10-strategic-technology-trends-for-2018

Collaborative Management of Traffic Accidents Data for Social Impact Analytics

A. Luís Osório[1]([✉]), Cláudia Antunes[2], Luis M. Camarinha-Matos[3],
and Carlos Gonçalves[1]

[1] Instituto Superior de Engenharia de Lisboa, Instituto Politécnico de Lisboa, Lisboa, Portugal
{aosorio,cgoncalves}@deetc.isel.ipl.pt
[2] Instituto Superior Técnico, Universidade de Lisboa, Lisboa, Portugal
claudia.antunes@tecnico.ulisboa.pt
[3] School of Science and Technology, NOVA University of Lisbon and UNINOVA-CTS, Lisboa, Portugal
cam@uninova.pt

Abstract. Traffic accidents have a devastating effect on society, and despite the measures taken by transport authorities, numbers still are of concern. As such, various studies emphasize the need for investments in the road infrastructure, vehicle safety, and enforcement measures. However, traffic and accident data are scattered among several stakeholders. Police authorities, emergency agencies, hospitals, road concessions, and the national road safety authorities all hold partial data about accidents and their consequences related to human lives. If such data could become widely available on production time, e.g., when an emergency doctor reports injuries or deaths, a police officer registers the scenario, etc., intelligent analytics could be used on such data towards helpful decision support. To cope with the wide diversity of data sources and ownership, more than data integration, this requires an approach for collaborative data management. Based on previous work on strategies to structure computing and communication artifacts and data science management, we present and discuss a collaborative traffic data management strategy considering the data producers as part of an intelligent traffic collaborative network. The challenge is thus to rethink traffic and accident data collection and management under the responsibility of diverse organizations, keeping their processes and technology culture, but promoting sharing and collaboration. Therefore, the proposed approach considers data analysis performed through business processes executed in the context of virtual organizations.

Keywords: Collaborative networks · Data science and analytics · Distributed systems integration · System of systems integration · Virtual organizations

1 Introduction

Traffic accidents' consequences on human lives are a long-standing problem, which can be derived from the vehicle's construction, drivers' behavior, and quality of road

© IFIP International Federation for Information Processing 2022
Published by Springer Nature Switzerland AG 2022
L. M. Camarinha-Matos et al. (Eds.): PRO-VE 2022, IFIP AICT 662, pp. 230–241, 2022.
https://doi.org/10.1007/978-3-031-14844-6_19

infrastructures. While recent debates discuss the role of autonomous vehicles and their contribution to safety [17], traffic data collection remains an essential source for research about road safety. Investments in road infrastructure quality have proven to be a valuable decision to reduce accidents [6], *"... spending on road maintenance ... contributes to reducing road deaths..."*. Speed enforcement is another typical measure to prevent accidents. For instance, a study from 2005 [11] identifies that the enforcement led to a *"... safety effect ... a reduction of 21% in both the number of injury accidents and the number of serious casualties ..."*. In another study in Lithuania, a couple of years later [10], mentions that *"... vehicles exceeding the speed limit up to 20 km/h decreased from 20.84% to 9.91%, i.e., by 10.93% ..."*, which led to a substantial reduction of accidents with a positive impact on the reduction of traffic causalities. However, one main problem in these and other research works is the lack of more comprehensive data sets.

Moreover, increasing the data quality for traffic safety management is a concern discussed in [21]. This study considers that *"... Ex-ante research only delivers good quality results if good quality road safety data are available ..."*, suggesting the use of safety performance indicators (SPIs) as a step to qualify road safety effects. Nevertheless, the reality is that traffic and accident-related data are scattered among several stakeholders. Road concessions and local and national road safety authorities collect traffic data; police authorities and emergency agencies gather accident data, and hospitals record injured people data. In this manner, each stakeholder has a partial view of the global scenario. Given the difficulties and concerns regarding data sharing, the used decision models, based on partial information, are certainly limited in scope.

Ideally, models for decision support should be trained to identify and understand the causes from and for the globality of collected data. Authorities need to access global injury data to measure the socio-economic impact of traffic accidents. Furthermore, hospitals should assess accident characteristics to determine injury severity, and then being able to predict it. However, data access is often limited due to either the collection process (in many cases, manual or without proper digital tools and data modeling standards) or the lack of sharing mechanisms. An example is the data collected by a fire department or ambulance service where *"... sheets archived within departmental structures and rarely shared ..."* [4], which could be essential sources for global accident data sets.

In this paper, we argue that reliable and up-to-date traffic accident data hold value for analytics if made available and managed in the context of a collaborative data collection network. Due to data privacy concerns in the different contexts, sharing requires extreme safety measures. On the other hand, some behaviors associated to the power of data ownership need to evolve to a culture of collaboration and recognition of the benefits of sharing and reciprocity. Figure 1 illustrates the diversity of potentially interested stakeholders for both roads and urban contexts in the Portuguese case. According to our approach, it is important that they join efforts and make their Information Technology (IT) infrastructures prepared to federate traffic accident data that can then be managed by collaborative analytics business processes.

As such, the main guiding research question is: *In which way can we re-organize distributed traffic accidents data collection and management in order to facilitate better decision-making?*

As a research hypothesis, our approach assumes that a collaborative network among all relevant stakeholders can establish win-win management of distributed accident-related data, supporting a collaborative data analytics system with more value than the sum of its parts. In this way, all stakeholders can get richer insights for improving their efficiency and offer better decision support.

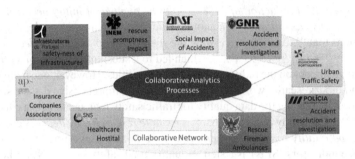

Fig. 1. Example of a potential collaborative network of traffic safety related stakeholders

This assumption is based on and supported by previous work on strategies to structure multi-stakeholder computing and communication artifacts. The approach considers each data source stakeholder as a potential member of an intelligent traffic collaborative network. As such, the challenge is to rethink traffic and accident data collection and management methods, which are performed under the responsibility of diverse organizations, while keeping their own processes and technology culture, but inducing a collaborative spirit. Thus, a collaborative network strategy is suggested to "join" valuable data sources from diverse traffic safety-related stakeholders to create federated data sets with up-to-date data to feed analytic applications. For this purpose, we propose to structure the required technology to be framed as an *Informatics System of Systems* (ISoS) infrastructure [16], where each informatics system (`ISystem`) is a composition of one or more Cooperation Enabled Services (`CES`) abstractions composed of one or more `Services`.

The remaining of this paper is structured as follows: Sect. 2 briefly summarizes and discusses related work; Sect. 3 presents and discusses the adoption of the ISoS framework for collaborative data collection and management. Section 4 discusses data management and analytics under the proposed framework, and finally Sect. 5 presents the conclusions and further research prospects.

2   Traffic and Accidents Data Analytics and Collaboration

An increased interest in exploring artificial intelligence (AI) technologies is reflected in the growth of the range of their applications. For instance, *urban analytics* is one of the fields that has gained track to enhance the understanding of reality in our cities. As an expression of collective behaviors, road traffic is one of the relevant targets in urban analytics. We may identify problematic patterns, find new solutions, and detect alarm situations through such analytics. However, proper data sets for valuable decision support are challenging to collect.

Traditional traffic security analysis used to be developed by specialized studies based on manual forms to collect data from accidents for obtaining statistics like the Abbreviated Injury Scale score (AIS) or the Injury Severity Score (ISS) [9]. The Association for the Advancement of Automotive Medicine (AAAM) maintains the two classification systems. Since in fact many stakeholders are involved in traffic safety, e.g., road authorities, police authorities, emergency rescue service providers, road infrastructure operators, healthcare authorities, and the automotive industry, data collection is challenging and requires an effort to harmonize data collection, from their types to their semantics. The automotive industry, which is also an important stakeholder, has been involved in a related ISO 12353–1:2020 standard (Road vehicles –Traffic accident analysis), addressing the vehicle side. More recently, research on autonomous vehicles also brought in new elements for the discussion. For instance, the report [13] from an OECD workshop points for "... *a proactive safety framework where vehicles are embedded in a communicative network* ...". Indeed, new data sources can be foreseen with autonomous vehicles, as suggested by the study of intelligent accident investigation strategies under driver, car, and infrastructure viewpoints [23].

Considering such multi-stakeholder / multiple data sources contexts, various research works have identified the need and importance of collaboration. For instance, [19] presents a collaborative strategy for data collection, stating that "... *a collaborative environment is necessary, and a web-based solution is ideal for permitting multi-user access and data insertion* ...", and proposing a centralized coordination and management for obtaining data. But many related contributions can be found in the developments from the area of Collaborative Networks in the last decades. For instance, the roots for data federation in collaborative networks can be found in works such as [1, 2, 18].

Collaboration between two or more partners is the strategy for reducing the number of casualties [3]. Therefore, the research challenge is how to develop a technology strategy and architecture through which a group of stakeholders join efforts to reach a comprehensive traffic accidents analytic (T2A) system. This involves a complex socio-technical system where the parts are diverse organizations with their own processes and technology culture, i.e., each component is itself a complex socio-technical system made of persons, organizational models, governance, and technology systems.

To address this challenge, we propose to structure the technology as an Informatics System of Systems (ISoS) infrastructure, establishing what we name the ISoS informatics (or information) technology (IT) landscape. Under this view, an informatics system (ISystem) is a composition of one or more Cooperation Enabled Services (CES) abstractions composed of one or more Services [16].

3   The ISoS Architecture for Collaborative Data Collection

In order to exemplify the proposed approach, let us consider the case of the Portuguese vehicle speed enforcement network (SINCRO), which is part of the National Road Safety Authority (ANSR) IT infrastructure. An existing informatics system (SIGET), responsible for obtaining and validating enforcement events, is planned to evolve to adopt the ISoS framework [16]. To simplify the illustration, we assume that also the remaining stakeholders adopt the ISoS framework. The adoption involves structuring operating computational entities as service abstractions and these as abstractions of informatics systems (ISystem).

Furthermore, all stakeholders participating in some collaborative network [7] are assumed to implement the $ISystem_0$ meta-informatics system responsible for maintaining metadata about the remaining informatics systems, i.e., adopting an ISoS IT landscape.

Another condition in this validation scenario is the adoption of the Enterprise Collaborative Network (ECoNet) framework operationalized by the Enterprise Collaboration Manager (ECoM) informatics system [15]. Nevertheless, adopting the ECoNet CN infrastructure is not mandatory since any ISystem/CES/Service of a stakeholder's ISoS can be discovered through the respective $ISystem_0$, i.e., by default accessing *isos. < stakeholder's public domain server >:2058* endpoint with the proper authentication credentials. A drawback of not using ECoNet is that interactions between service elements are point to point, meaning acquaintances need to understand underlying communication protocols. While adopting ECoNet, acquaintance operating services can use the ECoM's collaboration context (CC) to mediate data and coordination exchanges without being concerned with the underlying communication protocols, including security issues. Furthermore, The Virtual Collaboration Context (VCC) of ECoNet makes it possible to establish multitenant groups where the creator partner can invite other ECoNet nodes to join.

The VCC is based on the Virtual Private Network (VPN) or the more recent concept of Virtual Private Cloud (VPC), wherein we can assume the offer of Virtual Private Cloud services to securely manage resource pools [22]. The ECoM's VCC makes transparent for service elements of an ISoS landscape the exchange or the sharing of application data without any concern with the underlying communication protocols or security mechanisms and policies.

Figure 2 depicts the Traffic Analytics Virtual Organization created for the case of ANSR, presenting an example of a collaborative process – the *"Severity of accidents for the driver, passengers, and pedestrian"* process. The process is enacted by a data analysis informatics system, where process instances handle the data collection and processing towards process objectives. The informatics system that implements the process definition, e.g., embedding an enactment service to execute the *Road Accidents Severity* (RAS) process, is modeled in Business Process Model and Notation (BPMN) using the MagicDraw modeling driven systems engineering tool [5, 12].

The RAS process model has an initial activity to establish a VCC to be created by the ECoM. The process, which is not detailed here, includes the invitation to the National Institute of Medical Emergency (INEM), National Health Service (SNS), and firefighters' federation to join the Traffic Analytics VO sharing all the same CC. A collaboration context makes available domain services specialized in realizing the mission of hiding middleware or infrastructure level mechanisms, e.g., sharing files of any size, authentication, and security. The ECoNet concept is expected to evolve as an adaptive and intelligent layer hiding or making transparent complex distributed systems issues.

One foreseen example is to make failures transparent to some extent by introducing fault tolerance strategies.

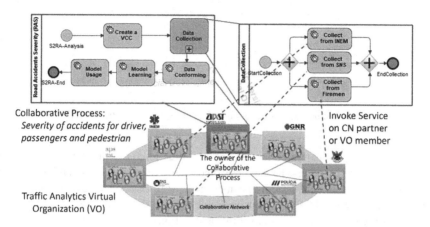

Fig. 2. The traffic analytics virtual organization

Therefore, the proposed system collects the relevant data to feed a traffic analysis system (modeled as a process). Such a system, being a massive data-driven one, shall comprise both descriptive and predictive models, for diagnosis and forecasting purposes, respectively. Moreover, it must be centered on a data management system, able to grant access, protect privacy, and even report unauthorized access attempts.

4   Data Analytics in an ISoS IT Landscape

According to the ISoS architecture, any integrated system becomes interoperable, cooperating with other systems following the same architecture. Although data can be viewed as the oil fueling the systems, data are often centrally managed by some data management system, either a specific database management system from some specific vendor or, more usually, a data management server created to operationally support the rest of the cooperative systems. Note that even distributed or federated databases can be abstracted to this metaphor.

Actually, in a data-driven system, the ISoS architecture may incorporate such a data management ISystem, storing and providing the required data to any other ISystem in the informatics landscape of the collaborative network. We may consider a generic data science system as an ISoS system dedicated to perform all data processing, including data collection, storage, distribution, aggregation, modeling, analysis, and usage. Figure 3 depicts the example of seriously injured victims per road type for 2019, based on data obtained by ANSR [20] from participating collaborative stakeholders.

Our aim is then to design the systems needed to support the analysis and management of traffic and road accidents (DS-TRAM), but also for feeding other systems, in a collaborative network, such as the systems from police authorities and civil protection departments (materializing a perspective of win-win to multiple stakeholders).

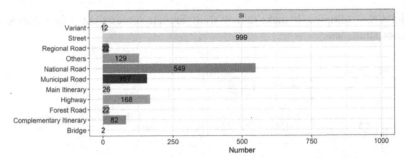

Fig. 3. Number of seriously injured victims per road type, from [20]

Following the ISoS architecture, adding new functionalities through ISystems to DS-TRAM is trivial and can be accomplished at any time. But in the end, the system shall have at least four core systems, besides the $ISystem_0$ and the ECoM ISystem - the data management (DMg), the business intelligence (BI), the diagnosis (Diag), and the forecasting (Frcst) ISystem, as illustrated in Fig. 4.

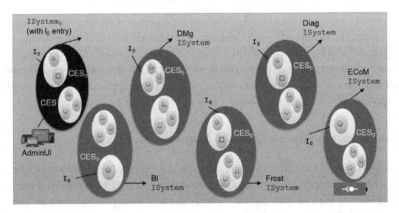

Fig. 4. Organization's ISoS landscape for supporting DS-TRAM

Next, we detail the main functionalities provided by each of the ISystems.

4.1 Data Management ISystem

As a truly ISoS, the internal architecture of the Data Management (DMg) ISystem is not relevant, only its functionalities matter. Indeed, traditionally this would be implemented through a data warehouse and management system. However, it could also be implemented in a distributed way, either in the cloud or any distributed or federated environment. Definitely, in the context of the ISoS architecture, the technology behind the data and its associated models are irrelevant. The key idea is that all services that need to deal directly with the data are contained inside a DBMS service, and all the other services or systems ask it for the required data. The DMg ISystem will support the "Data Collection" and "Data Conforming" elements of the RAS process presented in Fig. 2.

The primary CES in the DMg ISystem is responsible for *retrieving* data from the available data sources. Note that data collection may be distributed under diverse CES, but in order to make it available for the rest of the services and systems, the data shall be managed, but not necessarily stored, centrally. It can more likely follow a federation approach. This service is then responsible for *cataloging* the stored data, and *providing* it whenever required, either for internal or external services in the network.

To accomplish those tasks, the ISystem has another CES to *control access rights*, warranting that only authorized client services receive the data. Of particular importance is the guarantee of data conformance with the privacy policy regulations in force, such as the GDPR in Europe [8]. For example, no prohibited data is processed, and anonymization services are required to feed internal and external data requests.

Being this service accountable for all the data management, machine learning feature engineering tasks shall be under the DMg ISystem. Any feature extracted or generated shall be communicated to the cataloging CES. Indeed, those tasks might be agglomerated under a *feature engineering* CES, that besides feature extraction, generation, and selection, shall be accountable for all data preparation tasks. The DMg ISystem will also function as a feature store [14]. Examples of such tasks are cleaning the data, conforming it to the data structures/models that best suit the analysis tasks (through discretization, dummification, scaling, etc.), and extraction techniques such as principal component analysis (PCA) and discrete Fourier transform (DFT) or aggregation ones.

The last service to consider is a *data profiling* one that shall be kept up to date, supplying a detailed description of the available data, its distribution, granularity, sparsity, and dimensionality. Along with the catalog, they will be used as a showcase for analytic services to consult.

4.2 Business Intelligence ISystem

The Business Intelligence (BI) ISystem has two main responsibilities: i) To give an instant picture of the current scenario; ii) To report summary data of interest for analysis.

Each operational unit (traffic agencies, police units, civil protection, or hospitals) shall have a CES able to display the number and type of occurrences in real-time. This kind of display is known as a *situation dashboard*, and usually, it does not contain any private-sensitive data. A noteworthy ability of such dashboards is showing the data at diverse granularity levels, allowing for navigating through the different levels of detail. Of particular importance is accessing any occurrence in its most atomic detail.

In this context, another CES to consider is the one accountable for *reporting*. Reports reveal analysis and decision support data, giving a clear and effective summary of key performance indicators (KPIs), per time unit, like days, weeks, or months, and any other dimension of interest. Examples of such KPIs are the ones reported in [20].

4.3 Diagnosis ISystem

The third ISystem to consider comprises the different diagnosis (Diag) services running to support the "Model Learning" element of the *Road Accidents Severity* RAS process presented in Fig. 2. These services may be of two main kinds: i) Services to automatically classify or predict situations; ii) Services based on pattern mining and clustering methodologies.

The first kind of service follows a pre-trained model. Examples of such services are the ones for recognizing regular and anomalous situations. Independently of the task at hand, these services involve the existence of a classification or predictive model, pre-learned through some machine learning algorithm and validated against past data. After approved, the model can be put to work, classifying or predicting current situations. However, those models may have different lifespans, from being *timeless* (like disease diagnosis) that needs to be learned once or *ephemeral* (like behavior modeling) that changes over time. Furthermore, the incoming data flow for each one may also be different. Such services must be prepared to evaluate their quality performance and refresh the models whenever they are not accurate enough.

The second kind of service can identify and characterize the set of frequent occurrences and identify cause-effect dependencies.

Nevertheless, with those two kinds of services, the diagnosis ISystem shall comprise as many CES as different diagnosis services running. Indeed, each one shall run, be refreshed, and monitored at its own speed.

4.4 Forecasting ISystem

At last, the fourth considered ISystem comprises the different forecasting (Frcst) services. These services differentiate from the diagnosis ones by their nature. Instead of classifying or describing a given situation, they look at the past data to predict future occurrences. In a manner, they are intrinsically temporal. Despite their differences, they are constructed following similar strategies, and the Forecasting ISystem shall follow an identical structure. This ISystem is responsible for supporting the "Model Usage" element of the RAS process.

5 Discussion

The impact of traffic accidents on society has been recognized to be wide and spreading from personal, both physical and emotional, to social, with evidence on economics in particular [20]. Nevertheless, the quantification of this impact, and subsequent support for decision-making over public road safety policies, depends on the existence of accurate and comprehensive data, in the first place.

As discussed, current technical solutions, lead to data scattered across the diverse stakeholders, who following the rules in place (the GDPR [8], for example) are not allowed to process more than what is strictly required for their operation. Now, the data collected by each partner in the collaborative network respect to the same events – the traffic accidents, viewed from diverse perspectives which make them to be complementary.

Following our proposal thus, several issues are addressed. First, each partner keeps their own data confined to their servers, using their preferred technology. In this manner, nothing changes on their internal activity. Second, each partner controls external access to their data, both by authorizing the access to recognized partners and by negotiating which data to share, in accordance with partners needs and rights (following the regulations in place). Third, and most importantly, each partner accesses more rich data, allowing for a wider view of the situation, and consequently better data to train the analytic models.

From a public point of view, there are also gains, since the data around traffic accidents will be up-to-date and accessible through a single channel. In this manner, studies like the ones mentioned before can be performed more regularly, avoiding the difficulties inherent to the collection of data scattered across different sources.

6 Conclusions

Collecting and managing traffic accident data is an example of challenging application domain which involves a large diversity of stakeholders, each one being responsible for partial subsets of data. In order to be able to make proper decisions, it is important to find ways to collaboratively federate those subsets of data. For this purpose, this paper proposes an approach to establish a network of relevant stakeholders, supporting collaborative analytics business processes.

The work is part of an ongoing initiative that started with a project for the Portuguese national road safety authority and is now being expanded to include other stakeholders in traffic management. Once the aimed collaborative network is established and properly supported by the conceived IT infrastructure, it will be possible to implement sound federated learning mechanisms in support of multiple analytics services according to the interests of the various stakeholders.

Acknowledgments. This work is supported in part by the ANSR/SINCRO project (GIATSI/ISEL/IPL research group) and by the Portuguese FCT programs UIDB/00066/2020 (Center of Technology and Systems – CTS) and VisBig (PTDC/CCI-CIF/28939/2017).

References

1. Afsarmanesh, H., Camarinha-Matos, L.M.: Federated information management for coopera-tive virtual organizations. In: Hameurlain, A., Tjoa, A.M. (eds.) Database and Expert Systems Applications, pp. 561–572. Springer Berlin Heidelberg, Berlin, Heidelberg (1997). https://doi.org/10.1007/BFb0022064
2. Afsarmanesh, H., Garita, C., Hertzberger, L.O.: Virtual enterprises and federated information sharing. In: Quirchmayr, G., Schweighofer, E., Bench-Capon, T.J.M. (eds.) Database and Expert Systems Applications, pp. 374–383. Springer Berlin Heidelberg, Berlin, Heidelberg (1998)
3. Bekefi, T.: The global road safety partnership and lessons in multisectorial collaboration. Technical report, Corporate social responsibility initiative report No 6. Harvard University (2006)
4. Bonnet, E., Nikiéma, A., Adoléhoume, A., Ridde, V.: Better data for better action: rethinking road injury data in francophone west africa. BMJ Glob. Health **5**(5), e002521 (2020). May
5. Browne, D., Kempf, R., Hansen, A., O'Neal, M., Yates, W.: Enabling systems modeling language authoring in a collaborative web-based decision support tool. Procedia Computer Science **16**, 373–382 (2013)

6. Calvo-Poyo, F., Navarro-Moreno, J., de Oña, J.: Road investment and traffic safety: An international study. Sustainability **12**(16), 6332 (2020). Aug
7. Camarinha-Matos, L.M., Afsarmanesh, H.: Brief historical perspective for virtual organizations. In: Virtual Organizations, pp. 3–10. Kluwer Academic Publishers (2005). https://doi.org/10.1007/0-387-23757-7_1
8. European Commission: REGULATION (EU) 2016/679 OF The european parliament and of the council; on the protection of natural persons with regard to the processing of personal data and on the free movement of such data, and repealing Directive 95/46/EC (General Data Protection Regulation) (2016 April)
9. Dove, A.F., Pearson, J.C., Weston, P.A.: Data collection from road traffic accidents. Emergency Medicine Journal **3**(3),193–198 (Sep 1986)
10. Gaveniene, L., Jateikiene, L., Cygas, D., Kasperaviciene, A.: Impact of average speed enforcement systems on traffic safety: evidence from the roads of lithuania. The Baltic Journal of Road and Bridge Engineering **15**(3), 1–18 (2020). Aug
11. Goldenbeld, C., van Schagen, I.: The effects of speed enforcement with mobile radar on speed and accidents. Accident Analysis Prevention **37**(6), 1135–1144 (2005). https://doi.org/10.1016/j.aap.2005.06.011. Epub 2005 Jul 26 PMID: 16051180 Nov
12. Morkevicius, A., Aleksandraviciene, A., Mazeika, D., Bisikirskiene, L., Strolia, Z.: MBSE grid: A simplified SysML-based approach for modeling complex systems. INCOSE International Symposium **27**(1), 136–150 (2017). Jul
13. OECD: Safer roads with automated vehicles? Technical report, International Transport Forum. OECD (2018). https://www.itf-oecd.org/sites/default/files/docs/safer-roads-automated-vehicles.pdf
14. Orr, L., Sanyal, A., Ling, X., Goel, K., Leszczynski, M.: Managing ML pipelines. Proceedings of the VLDB Endowment **14**(12), 3178–3181 (2021). Jul
15. Osório, L.A., Camarinha-Matos, L.M., Afsarmanesh, H.: ECoNet Platform for Collaborative Logistics and Transport. In: Camarinha-Matos, L.M., Bénaben, F., Picard, W. (eds.) PRO-VE 2015. IAICT, vol. 463, pp. 265–276. Springer, Cham (2015). https://doi.org/10.1007/978-3-319-24141-8_24
16. Osório, A.L., Belloum, A., Afsarmanesh, H., Camarinha-Matos, L.M.: Agnostic Informatics System of Systems: The Open ISoS Services Framework. In: Camarinha-Matos, L.M., Afsarmanesh, H., Fornasiero, R. (eds.) PRO-VE 2017. IAICT, vol. 506, pp. 407–420. Springer, Cham (2017). https://doi.org/10.1007/978-3-319-65151-4_37
17. Othman, K.: Exploring the implications of autonomous vehicles: a comprehensive review. Innovative Infrastructure Solutions **7**(2) (Mar 2022)
18. Pang, B., Gou, J., Afsarmanesh, H., Mu, W., Zhang, Z.: Methodology and mechanisms for federation of heterogeneous metadata sources and ontology development in emerging collaborative environment. In: VINE Journal of Information and Knowledge Management Systems (2021)
19. Pirotti, F., Guarnieri, A., Vettore, A.: Road safety analysis using web-based collaborative gis. In: The International Archives of the Photogrammetry, Remote Sensing and Spatial Information Sciences, Vol. 34, Part XXX (2010). https://www.isprs.org/proceedings/xxxviii/4-w13/id_54.pdf
20. Silva, C., Bravo, J., Gonçalves, J.: Social and Economic Impact of Road Crashes in Portugal. Resreport. CEGE - Centro de Estudos de Gestão do ISEG and Autoridade Nacional de Segurança Rodoviária (ANSR) (Oct 2021). http://www.ansr.pt/Estatisticas/RelatoriosTematicos/Documents/estudo%20%E2%80%9CO%20impacto%20econ%C3%B3mico%20e%20social%20da%20sinistralidade%20rodovi%C3%A1ria%20em%20Portugal%E2%80%9D%20ING.pdf
21. Wegman, F., Berg, H.-Y., Cameron, I., Thompson, C., Siegrist, S., Weijermars, W.: Evidence-based and data-driven road safety management. IATSS Research **39**(1), 19–25 (2015). Jul

22. Wood, T., Gerber, A., Ramakrishnan, K.K., Shenoy, P., Van der Merwe, J.: The case for enterprise-ready virtual private clouds. In: Proceedings of the 2009 Conference on Hot Topics in Cloud Computing, HotCloud'09. USENIX Association, USA (2009)
23. Yuan, Q., Peng, Y., Xu, X., Wang, X.: Key points of investigation and analysis on traffic accidents involving intelligent vehicles. Transportation Safety and Environment **3**(4) (Oct 2021)

AI Application in Collaborative Networks

Characterization of the Spatiotemporal Behavior of a Sweeping System Using Supervised Machine Learning Enhanced with Feature Engineering

Bechir Ben Daya[✉], Jean-François Audy, and Amina Lamghari

Business School, UQTR, 3351, boulevard des Forges, (Québec) G8Z 4M3, Trois-Rivières, Canada
{bechir.ben.daya,jean-francois.audy,amina.lamghari}@uqtr.ca

Abstract. This paper focuses on geolocation data processing to infer the behavior of a mechanical sweeping system. A framework based on the feature engineering (FE) and machine-learning (ML) tools for geolocation data processing is proposed. A supervised multi-classification machine learning using a large range of classifiers, input variables, training and data test sets is used to predict the sweeping system behavior. The results showed that Logistic Regression (LR) and Support Vector Machine (SVM) are the best classifiers for predicting the sweeping behavior and some simulated instances constituted the best training sets. The sweeping state prediction accuracy provided with LR and SVM classifiers, when trained with historical data, were in average 86.22% and 86.13%, respectively. These predictions using the same classifiers, when trained with simulated data, were in average 87.40% and 87.22%. These promising results illustrate the potential of integrating FE and simulation to enhance the performance the ML tools when studying the behavior of complex logistics systems.

Keywords: Supervised machine learning · Feature engineering · Multi-classification · Big data processing · Geolocation data · Sweeping system

1 Introduction

Every spring in Canada, a considerable amount of abrasive material applied during winter road maintenance is removed from the road network by mechanical sweeping to increase road safety and reduce environmental impacts. Recently, a small-sized enterprise designed and manufactured a novel broom which significantly changes the road sweeping logistics. Up to known, no evaluation has benne carried out in terms of operational and environmental performance for this novel broom mode. To evaluate and ultimately improve the sustainability of the sweeping system as well as for its virtualization based on AI applications for smart city (e.g., provide information about the progression of the city services to the citizens), a large amount of geolocation data was

L. M. Camarinha-Matos et al. (Eds.): PRO-VE 2022, IFIP AICT 662, pp. 245–261, 2022.
https://doi.org/10.1007/978-3-031-14844-6_20

collected. The streaming data creates its own challenges in terms of how to process the large volume of information collected to determine the simulation parameters while ensuring quality and accuracy. Indeed, rather than visualizing over 400 h of recorded videos, a data analysis approach was developed. The methodology adopted consists in an approach for processing GPS data using Feature Engineering (FE) and machine learning (ML) tools to identify the behavior of the system in order to compute the input parameters for a simulation model. A sample of data was first processing and validating manually for later use as the training and test data sets. In a second step, this data will be used to train classifiers in order to predict, using ML tools, the sweeping behavior over all the collected data.

To achieve the characterization of the sweeping states and its attributes, a wide range of classifiers, input variables and validated training data sets are used. The results show that Logistic Regression (LR) and Support Vector Machine (SVM) are the best classifiers and some simulated instances constituted the best training sets. The sweeping state prediction accuracy provided with LR and SVM classifiers when trained with simulated data were in average 87.4% and 87.22%.

This paper has the following contributions to the study of behavior geolocation data processing using FE tools. First, we propose a smoothing heuristic to the raw data preprocessing stage in order to clearly identify and separate the sweeping states. Second, we propose a classification framework based on two steps, rather than one. The first step classifies the system's states based on the speed variable using appropriate thresholds while the second step makes use of several input variables provided by the first step in its classification. This leads to substantial improvements in the performance of the classification scheme. Third, the accuracy of the prediction using a simulated training data instances gives a better and more stable results than when using historical data. Fourth, a corrective heuristic was proposed to improve the classification of the states of short duration leading to much more accurate results.

The remainder of this paper is organized as follows. A literature review is presented in Sect. 2. Section 3 outlines the methodology followed while Sect. 4 deals with the model building and its application. Finally, a conclusion is provided in Sect. 5.

2 Literature Review

The deployment of the concept of connected vehicles provides a large volume of geolocation data tracked with GPS technology, as noted in [1]. In [2], authors suggested that GPS data analysis could provide a better characterization of the spatiotemporal movement of vehicles. However, the scale of ingested data in the transportation system has become a bottleneck for the traditional data analytics solutions as reported by [3]. ML tools provide data-driven solutions that can cope with the new analysis requirements. It is also noted that the application of ML tools can be used to identify the purpose of a trip and mode of travel on GPS trajectory data according to [4]. However, despite the fact that GPS trackers provide valuable data, they fall short in terms of describing the behavior of a complex system faithfully as noted in [5, 6]. Diverse opportunities to enhance data analytics and applications for logistics and supply chain management, including technology-driven tracking strategies are considered in [7]. Feature engineering tools is an essential discipline to improve the performance of prediction models applied to GPS data to infer the behavior of logistics systems. As noted in [8], FE is a crucial step in the predictive modeling process. It includes building new features from the given data in order to enhance predictive learning performance as suggested in [9]. Similarly, in [10] the author noted that FE as "the task of improving predictive modelling performance on a dataset by transforming its feature space". This discipline "involves domain knowledge, intuition, and most importantly, a long process of trial and error" as reported by [8].

Next, we review the literature dealing with the processing of geolocation data approaches to infer the behavior of transport vehicles.

Using GPS tracking and accelerometer data, authors in [11] focused on how to improve the trip purpose identification technique. The results show that Random Forests (RF) provide robust trip purpose classification with correct predictions between 80% and 85%. This work indicated that ML tools could enhance GPS data using classification in the case of a repetitive trip when data sets used are susceptible to learning. However, for non-repetitive contexts, one can only determine the mode or the state of the system. An innovative methodology for inferring process states from geolocation data is proposed in [12]. Geolocation data can be used to get insight into transportation processes, operations, and service quality, as noted by the authors. The methodology proposed uses the zero-speed threshold to identify stationary and non-stationary events from geolocation data. However, this methodology is more effective in the case where the processes are highly structured and the behavior is well defined and predictable. In [13], authors analyzed the vehicle behavior and extracted operational information using the segmentation of GPS trajectory data generated in logistics transportation. The main contribution is the layout design of convolutional neural network input layer, which represents the fundamental motion characteristics of a moving object including speed, acceleration, jerk, and bearing rates. A highest accuracy of 84.8% has been achieved. This methodology has also been contrasted with traditional ML algorithms.

In [14], authors focused on the segmentation of GPS trajectory data generated in logistics transportation in order to extract operational information related to the vehicle behavior characteristics. The authors noted that the widely applied ML technique K-Nearest Neighbors (KNN) is used to tackle the same trajectory data segmentation problem. The precision and recall for KNN are both 86% to recognize that stopping points are business points. Although KNN performs better in precision compared with probabilistic logic data segmentation problems, it cannot filter out all the real business points. In [4], the application of ML methods to identify the purpose of a trip and mode of travel on GPS trajectory data shows that RF method is more efficient than the decision tree method. The RF and decision tree methods have already proven to be better than some of the other supervised ML methods for the identification of trip purpose as noted in [15].

This literature review shows that very few studies focused on predicting the behavior of an object tracked by GPS using ML, while even fewer studies presented GPS data processing approaches using a FE framework. To the best of our knowledge, no work has addressed the behavior of complex logistics system such as a sweeping system using geolocation data and ML tools with a wide range of multi-classification supervised algorithms. Furthermore, no work has presented a framework based on clustering and multi-classification applied in two successive steps to process real data using classifiers trained with simulated data.

3 Methodology

The study of the sweeping system behavior to evaluate its carbon footprint, to improve its performance, and for its possible virtualization within the framework of a smart city, requires the collection and the processing of real data. To collect the necessary data needed, a set of cameras (front and rear camera) with embedded GPS were installed in the brooms and trucks involved in the sweeping system during a full season of operation. The processing of this large volume of collected data, posed a challenge and call for the development of appropriate methods capable of processing geolocation data in order to infer the behavior of the sweeping system. The methodology adopted consists of developing an approach for processing GPS data using ML tools to identify the behavior of the sweeping system in order to produce the input parameters required for a simulation model and for potential AI-based applications.

3.1 Description of the Sweeping System

The mechanical sweeping system employs a principal broom that continuously loads a dump truck, which is followed by a traditional broom for finishing, as shown in Fig. 1. The behavior of the mechanical sweeping system consists of alternating between different states of sweeping, waiting, or moving:

– *Sweeping state*: when the broom is performing a sweeping operation;
– *Waiting state*: when the broom is in standby mode for various reasons;
– *Moving state*: when the broom is travelling to/from a sweeping area without performing sweeping operations.

Fig. 1. The mechanical sweeping system considered by this study

3.2 Data Processing

A FE framework based on a two-step classification-clustering scheme is conducted to infer the correct behavior of the sweeping system. Figure 2 describes the steps used for data collection and processing. To achieve this objective, we subjected the geolocation data to a set of processing steps. Data collection is followed by data preprocessing, which aims to clean the data by fixing any record errors, especially with regards to time or distance, and splitting this data into different shifts. The objective of the next step is to manually process a batch of data to be used for training and testing the ML classification models. The last two steps relate to the building of an ML classification model and its application to predict the sweeping behavior from the collected data. The classification resulted in a database of sweeping states sorted by their attributes in terms of duration and average speed.

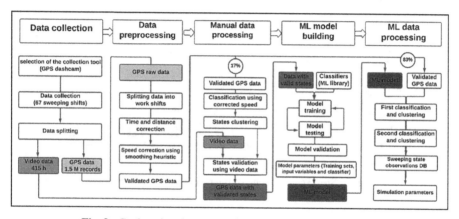

Fig. 2. Geolocation data processing approach reinforced by FE

Data Collection

During the 2019 spring season, over 400 h of recorded video were collected from 67 work shifts for a total size of 3.5 Tb. From the different videos, we have extracted geolocation data. This task was enabled through Dashcam viewer software Version 3.3.2 that extracts maps into KML files and GPS data into CSV files with structured data. Each second of video recording corresponds to a line of the described data and thus generated nearly 1.5 million lines of GPS data.

Data Preprocessing

Data preprocessing involves error and speed correction.

Error Correction

Geolocation data is referenced according to the corresponding work shift and is then structured as a geolocation Excel database. Some errors in recording geolocation data were found. These errors were related to odometer initialization when the broom engine is switched off, some missing recordings of various duration, some redundant recordings, and overlap between shifts. These errors were fixed using appropriate manual processing schemes.

Speed Correction

The speed curve of one shift illustrated in Fig. 3 shows that, when adopting the speed threshold for classification, a large number of states would be obtained with a short and insignificant duration due to the alternating speed between adjacent states. For example, when the broom is in the sweeping state, its speed may increase and cross the threshold between the sweeping and the moving states for a short duration (Fig. 4.a). In this case, the speed classification will produce an alternation between these two states while the broom is always in the sweeping state. The most frequent overlaps are illustrated in Fig. 4 a–d. To remedy this possible misclassification, states that have a small duration should not be classified as separate states, but rather as part of adjacent states. A smoothing heuristic, which will be presented later, is applied to correct the speed in order to minimize these overlaps.

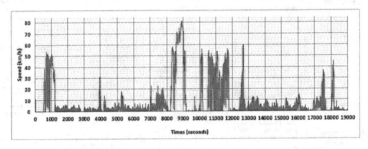

Fig. 3. Speed curve of one shift having a duration of 19000 s

Broom speed differs depending on its state. In the waiting state, the speed is zero, as noted in [14], while in the sweeping state, the speed is lower than in the moving state. In fact, the speed threshold can be used to characterize the various broom states, e.g., in [16], authors classified interstate data into the driver behavior (slow, normal, aggressive) based on the speed thresholds.

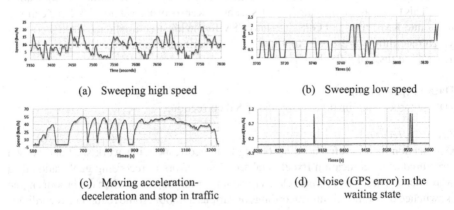

(a) Sweeping high speed

(b) Sweeping low speed

(c) Moving acceleration-
deceleration and stop in traffic

(d) Noise (GPS error) in the
waiting state

Fig. 4. The remarkable overlaps in the speed curve

In order to partially eliminate the interference between states, a smoothing heuristic is built to adjust the speed of each record. This is done by exploring forty-second-records (ten backward and 30 forward around each record). The 40 s duration of the exploration zone is based on experimentation and estimates to the 2/3 of the minimum of the state duration considered. The average speed of each zone is used to adjust the speed of that record in order to minimize the possible overlaps. This heuristic is illustrated in Fig. 5 where S_i is the speed of the record under consideration and AS_i is the average speed of the 40 records around the current record. The adjustment carried out by the heuristic is based on the thresholds between the three states, as mentioned earlier. However, the threshold between waiting and sweeping is adjusted from 1 to 0.4 based on extensive experimentation in order to minimize the number of states in the characterization phase.

ℓ = threshold between waiting and sweeping.
L = threshold between sweeping and moving.
CS_i: corrected speed for record i.

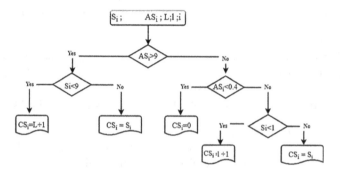

Fig. 5. The heuristic decision tree for correcting the speed

Figure 6 illustrates the speed correction obtained using the smoothing heuristic applied to the time-period of 280 s from 17400 to 17680 of a sweeping shift.

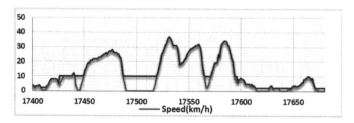

Fig. 6. Smoothing heuristic applied to the speed curve from 17400 to 17680 s

After cleaning and correcting the GPS database, the next step is to characterize the sweeping activity states based on the corrected speed value, since this attribute can be used for classification.

Manual Data Processing
About 17% of the data was processed manually through classification and clustering methods to infer the sweeping states and their attributes. Using the observed data, the broom states are identified based on the speed attribute. Let S be the speed broom in km/h. Then,

- If S in [0, 0.4], the broom is assumed to be in the waiting state to account for the GPS speed error;
- If S in [0.4, 10], the broom is assumed to be in the sweeping state;
- If S ≥ 10, the broom is assumed to be in the moving state.

The thresholds adopted are determined by estimation based on empirical findings.

State Characterizations
The state characterization is a multi-classification of records into various states (sweeping, waiting and moving). This is done according to the thresholds already described using MS Excel. Following this classification, all adjacent records classified into the same state are grouped together and their duration and average speed are calculated.

State Validation Using Video Data
After grouping the states according to the initial classification of the records, a validation of the grouping into states will take place based on the video images. Validation, in this case, serves two purposes. First, it helps verify that the identified states generated correspond to the real situation, otherwise, they are corrected. Second, states with a small duration are attached to adjacent states based on the video images.

Figure 7 illustrates the state characterization example according to the speed value for the period between 17000 and 18000 s.

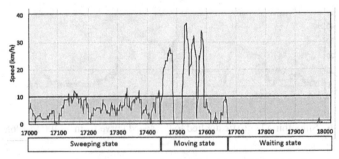

Fig. 7. States characterization according to the speed value validated by video images for the period 17000–18000 s

The validation of the classification based on the video images, as described above, takes a lot of time. This manual data processing was applied to the data from 11 shifts that were classified and validated using video images. Although this exercise proved valuable for understanding the processing of geolocation data, it is not practical for real-life applications given the big data involved. This motivated us to use the manual processed data as an input to train powerful ML classification models. Our objective is to identify the best combination of training sets, input variables and classification algorithms that can be used to deal with the processing of geolocation data to infer the behavior of the sweeping system.

Machine Learning Model Building

While 17% of the data was processed manually, a framework similar to the manual process described above needs to be developed for the remaining data (83%). In practice, it is not possible to make a prediction of the GPS recordings to reach the sweeping states as defined above. FE is essential, in this case, to properly adapt the data for prediction algorithms learning considering the specificities of the GPS data. FE tools allow us to transform the manual procedure of sweeping state characterization into a learning procedure for sweeping behavior prediction. Thus, we will transform the phases of classification and correction into two phases of simultaneous classification-clustering.

Building the ML model based on FE involves four stages:

1. An initial classification of the records is performed based on the corrected speed. The manually processed shift data are used as training and testing sets for the ML classification models;
2. An initial state clustering based on the first classification is performed. In this stage, the duration and the average speed related to each state are computed;
3. A second classification based on the clusters resulting from the previous stage is carried out. The independent variables explored include the initial state, the average speed of the state and its duration;
4. A final state clustering based on the second classification is performed.

First Classification and Clustering

The first supervised classification is based on the corrected speed of the raw geolocation data as an input variable to classify the records into various states. Based on the training sets generated using the manual processing, the LR and the RF classifiers were used to achieve a correct classification. Python 3.7 is used to connect the library of classifiers and the assessment tools, including the confusion matrix and the accuracy indicator.

An initial clustering of states based on the first classification is performed. In this step, the duration and the average speed related to each cluster of states are calculated.

Second Classification and Clustering

The second classification was carried out using two methods. The first method used historical data to train the classifiers. However, the second method performed the training based on simulated data. A simplified simulation model was built based on the 11 manually validated shifts to generate the data instances used for training.

For the first method, the second classification is based on the cluster states generated in the previous clustering step where eleven data sets (shifts) were used for training and testing. Different combinations of input variables (initial state, duration and average speed) were tested to obtain the best results. The two combinations that were retained include either all three variables or duration and average speed. Seven classification algorithms were used. Each of the 11 data sets is used in turn for training and then testing is done using the remaining ten data sets. This operation is performed with the two combinations of variables and uses all the seven classification algorithms leading to 1694 different results. These results are used to identify the best combination of training sets, input variables and classification algorithms in order to build the ML classification model.

For the second method, we have retained as input two variables (the duration and the speed of the state) since the initial state for the simulated shifts is missing. We also used the classifiers which gave the best results of the first method, namely LR and RF, Naive Bays (NB) and SVM algorithms. The selected classifiers were trained by each of the 10 simulated shifts and tested by each of the 11 historical shifts.

A final state clustering similar to the first one is performed based on the result of the second classification. This final step will produce a state database (observations) that provides the description of the sweeping system's behavior during a given shift.

Machine Learning Data Processing

The result obtained when applying building process described above allow the selection of the best classification model and the results of its application to one work shift.

To improve the classification prediction in the case of the last application, we used a corrective heuristic. This heuristic consists in eliminating the states with short duration (<60 s) and assigning them to the nearest adjacent state.

4 Results and Interpretations

4.1 Machine Learning Model Selection

The maximum accuracy allowed when we applied a unique classification of GPS raw data is 49.4%. This level of accuracy is considered insufficient, given the enormous number of misclassified states relative to the GPS data. For this reason, our idea is to carry out the classification in two steps rather than a single one using FE tools. Therefore, the second classification uses several input variables provided by the first classification which increases the prediction capability. This leads to a substantial improvement in the performance of the classification scheme. In this section, we discuss mainly the configuration of the ML classification model for the first and second classification.

First Classification
The first supervised classification is based on the corrected speed of the broom. The prediction of a certain shift proves that at least two classifiers perfectly performed this classification. These are the LR and the RF classifiers.

First Clustering

In this step, the duration and the average speed related to each cluster of states are calculated. This step is advantageous because it allows us to consolidate the second classification to remedy the defects of the classification based on the fixed thresholds.

Second Classification

Using Real Data

Table 1 presents the second classification results of the different combinations of input variables, classifiers and training set data, as explained in Sect. 3.2. Each entry in this table represents the average accuracy obtained using the corresponding shift as training set, the corresponding number of input variables and the corresponding classifier, where all the shifts are used for testing. The results show that the cases involving three independent input variables produce slightly better results than those involving two variables. Shift 11 and Shift 5 offer the best data sets for training in cases involving three and two input variables, respectively. The best classification algorithms are RF and LR in that order. The best result was obtained with Shift 11 as training set, three input variables and the RF algorithm with the accuracy of 86.56% . Table 2 provides the details of the best results in all shifts.

Table 1. The average accuracy of the alternatives explored

Classifiers	Variables	Training data sets										
		Shift 1	Shift 2	Shift 3	Shift 4	*Shift 5*	Shift 6	Shift 7	Shift 8	Shift 9	Shift 10	*Shift 11*
DT	2*	85.72	80.00	72.99	80.67	85.48	74.30	78.47	78.75	77.18	81.36	83.15
	3**	85.66	80.27	74.35	80.23	85.64	74.11	79.19	79.06	77.18	82.31	85.03
KNN	2	79.02	70.59	65.24	73.50	79.07	69.80	71.46	70.96	71.15	76.92	73.05
	3	79.12	71.24	65.51	74.66	79.07	70.39	72.09	71.76	72.16	77.41	74.34
KSVM	2	69.11	69.41	69.41	68.53	69.20	69.08	65.08	69.17	69.11	68.97	25.99
	3	69.11	69.41	69.41	68.49	69.20	69.08	65.07	69.17	69.11	68.97	25.96
LR	2	86.11	84.83	71.95	84.28	*86.22*	71.41	77.01	82.42	73.43	82.66	85.70
	3	86.09	84.75	72.80	84.34	86.37	71.98	77.35	85.20	73.97	83.82	85.92
NB	2	**84.87**	72.02	71.70	81.70	84.73	70.35	72.23	71.79	73.80	73.96	79.50
	3	86.09	84.75	72.80	84.34	86.37	71.98	77.35	85.20	73.97	83.82	85.92
RF	2	84.85	81.80	78.27	84.39	85.97	77.36	82.15	82.76	76.36	83.69	82.12
	3	86.05	81.47	78.50	81.45	**86.13**	78.69	82.76	81.95	76.17	85.40	***86.56***
SVM	2	85.87	79.93	70.85	86.09	*86.13*	71.38	77.10	78.17	73.10	85.06	85.66
	3	86.11	79.74	71.15	86.18	*86.36*	72.14	76.98	77.75	73.12	85.36	85.72

DT: Decision Tree; KNN: K-nearest neighbors; KSVM: Kernel SVM; LR: Logistic Regression; NB: Naïve Bayes; RF: Random Forest; SVM: Support Vector Machine
*: 2 variables – speed and duration of the state; **: 3 variables – initial state, speed and duration of the state

Table 2. The detailed results of the best solution (Training data: Shift 11)

Test data	Shift 1	Shift 2	Shift 3	Shift 4	Shift 5	Shift 6	Shift 7	Shift 8	Shift 9	Shift 10	Shift 11	Average
Accuracy	92.90	81.93	69.03	91.67	92.60	84.12	83.28	81.72	91.54	85.67	97.69	*86.56*

The two configurations retained for the ML classification models are illustrated in the Table 3.

Table 3. ML best classification models

Model	Classifier	Training set	Input variables	Average accuracy
Model 3V	RF	Shift 11	Duration, speed and initial state	86.56%
Model 2V	LR	Shift 5	Duration and speed	86.22%

Using Simulated Data

The manual processed geolocation data for 11 shifts were used to generate parameters for simulating the sweeping system. The simulation model developed was used to generate additional instances for 10 shifts that were used for training purposes.

When simulation data is used for training, only two input variables (speed and duration) were considered since the initial state variable was not available for the simulation data. Also, only the best four algorithms identified using real data were implemented.

Table 4 presents the second classification results obtained using simulated data as training data sets. In this case, we used the following classifiers namely LR, NB, RF and SVM. In this case, the best result is obtained using the 6th shift data set for training, all real data sets for testing and the LR classifier with accuracy 87.4%. Table 5 provides the details of this best result on all shifts. These results show that a better accuracy is obtained compared to the classification using real data sets.

Table 4. The average accuracy using LR, RF, SVM and NB classifier

Classifier	S_shift1	S_shift2	S_shift3	S_shift4	S_shift5	S_shift6	S_shift7	S_shift8	S_shift9	S_shift10	Max	Avg	Rank
LR	87.34	87.02	87.27	83.75	86.73	*87.40*	87.17	87.05	87.21	87.16	87.40	86.81	1
RF	86.57	86.79	85.96	86.89	79.22	75.60	**86.92**	85.62	86.87	86.69	86.92	84.71	3
SVM	87.17	86.37	87.10	83.14	86.19	87.16	86.49	86.96	87.05	*87.22*	87.22	86.49	2
NB	61.65	54.59	73.60	53.73	**82.64**	58.12	57.36	60.35	75.14	54.49	82.64	63.17	4

Table 5. The detail results of the best solution (Training data: S_shift 6)

Test data	Shift1	Shift2	Shift3	Shift4	Shift5	Shift6	Shift7	Shift8	Shift9	Shift10	Shift11	Shift12	Avg
Accuracy	99.33	95.48	81.93	66.79	92.54	94.53	83.87	86.63	81.38	94.86	87.67	83.80	87.40

Second Clustering

A final state clustering is performed based on the result of the second classification. This final step will produce a description of the behavior of the sweeping system on a given shift. Although this second classification provides a categorization of states that is close to reality, some imperfections remain to be eliminated.

4.2 Results Comparison

To assess the prediction quality, the classification accuracy is used to compare the results obtained with real data to those obtained with simulated data as training sets. The prediction accuracy provided with LR and SVM classifiers, when trained with historical data, were in average 86.22% and 86.13%, respectively. These predictions using the same classifiers, when trained with simulated data, were in average 87.4% and 87.22%. Table 6 shows the comparison of this accuracy.

Table 6. Comparison of classification accuracy (%) between real and simulated training sets.

Classifier	Historical training data			Simulated training data		
	Max avg predict. (*)	Standard deviation	Rank	Max avg predict. (*)	Standard deviation	Rank
LR	*86.22*	8.4	1	*87.4*	8.8	*1*
RF	85.97	7.6	3	86.92	9	
SVM	*86.13*	8.4	2	*87.22*	8.9	*2*
NB	84.87	8.9	4	82.64	7.3	4

(*): Average of all data test sets (11 shifts) related to the best shift trainer

FE tools have improved the performance of prediction algorithms in two ways. The first is to adopt two successive clustering-classifications in order to have more explanatory variables after the first classification and the second is to train the algorithms on simulated data. Figure 8 explains the results achieved using the adopted framework.

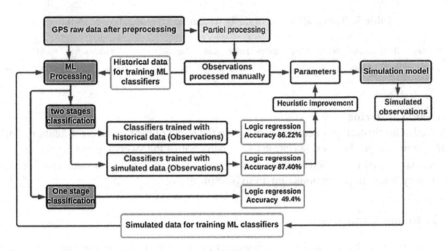

Fig. 8. FE Framework to improve the performance of prediction models

4.3 Corrective Heuristic Impact

In order to evaluate the impact of the corrective heuristic, described above, an application case is tested using a real shift and LR classifier trained with both historical and simulated data. Figure 9 illustrates the first and the second classification result for this particular application (States in the graph is noted 0: for waiting, 1: for sweeping and 2 for moving; the speed is in Km/h).

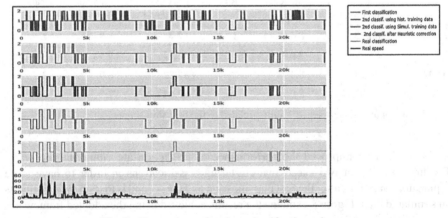

Fig. 9. Comparison of various classification schemes

The single classification has the accuracy of 49.4%. However, the second classification of the two classification model, when trained with historical data, has the accuracy of 95.48% on the training data. Its prediction accuracy is about 93.5%. However, when trained with simulated data, the accuracy on the training data is about 99.33% and its prediction accuracy is about 95.5%. When improved with the corrective heuristic, the classification trained with the historical data gives the accuracy of 98.4%.

The result of the second classification is a set of state observations as illustrated in the Table 7.

Table 7. State observations provided by the considered shift

Ref State	1	2	3	4	5	6	7	8	9	10	11	12	13	14	15	16	
Duration (min)	11.5	3.27	4.45	3.48	4.15	5.83	3.333	4.92	2	8.3	4.05	9.62	1.667	1.28	1.52	7.98	
Avg speed (km/h)	3.13	0.28	2.76	0.19	30.9	0.05	41.44	4.56	28	0.16	18.58	4.42	23.01	7.92	0.12	2.74	
States (*)	1	0	1	0	2	0	2	1	2	0	2	1	2	1	0	1	
Ref State	17	18	19	20	21	22	23	24	25	26	27	28	29	30	31	32	33
Duration (min)	2.15	1.23	77.2	32.7	3.37	3.17	7.967	1.43	18	1.68	37.88	7.47	44	1.53	7.97	2.6	59.2
Avg speed (km/h)	0.72	17.3	5.4	0.3	4.01	0.03	4.15	0.31	2.9	0.03	2.85	0.06	2.74	0.04	2.9	0	3.1
States	0	2	1	0	1	0	1	0	1	0	1	0	1	0	1	0	1

(*): 0: waiting, 1: sweeping, 2: moving

Having the state observation database, we compute the simulation parameters that illustrate the sweeping behavior such as the state's frequency, the average speed and duration as shown in the Table 8. These parameters can be used for simulation if the database has a significant set of shift data.

Table 8. Parameters deduced from the shift observations

State	Number	Average duration (min)	Average speed (km/h)	Frequency (%)	Total duration (min)
0	13	5.8	0.00	39	75.2
1	14	21.1	3.83	42	295.2
2	6	2.7	26.54	18	16.4

4.4 Interpretations

The following observations can be made based on the results obtained:

– The ML tools can describe the behavior of the sweeping system with the accuracy of about 87%;

- Two-step classification-clustering scheme using FE tools improves the accuracy from 49.4% to 87.4%;
- The application of a corrective heuristic allows an improvement of the classification result of 5% when applied to a real shift data;
- Better results, in terms of accuracy and stability, are obtained with simulated training data compared to historical data.

5 Conclusion

This paper focuses on geolocation data processing to infer the behavior of a sweeping system in order to generate the necessary data needed to evaluate its operational and environmental performance using simulation and for potential AI-based applications.

A large range of classifiers, input variables, training and test data sets are used to build the multi-classification ML models. The results showed that LR and SVM are the best classifiers to process GPS data and some simulated instances constituted the best training data sets. The sweeping state prediction accuracy provided with LR and SVM classifiers when trained with historical data were in average 86.22% and 86.13%, respectively. These predictions using the same classifiers when trained with simulated data were in average 87.4% and 87.22%. These accuracy predictions are stable when the classifiers are trained with simulated data.

The main contribution of this paper is the use of the FE tools to transform a manual classification into a classification driven by machine learning algorithms. For predicting the behavior of a logistics system from GPS data, a double classification allows prediction based on attributes other than speed. Compared to the prediction accuracy reported in the literature, as discussed in Sect. 2, the accuracy levels presented in this research are very promising. Such an improvement was possible using a corrective heuristic that enhanced the classification of the sweeping system states. The ability to infer the behavior of the sweeping system, based on geolocation data processing, will form the basis for planning this type of operation in the future, for improving its sustainability and for its possible virtualization based on AI applications within the framework of a smart city.

Acknowledgments. The work in this paper was funded by Fonds de Recherche du Québec - nature et technologies (FRQnet), grant 2019-GS-260551, in partnership with street sweepings service provider (Arseno Sweeping). These supports are gratefully acknowledged.

References

1. Kim, B.S., Kang, B.G., Choi, S.H., Kim, T.G.: Data modeling versus simulation modeling in the big data era: case study of a greenhouse control system. Simulation **93**, 579–594 (2017)
2. Laranjeiro, P.F., et al.: Using GPS data to explore speed patterns and temporal fluctuations in urban logistics: the case of São Paulo Brazil. J. Trans. Geogr. **76**, 114–129 (2019)
3. Servos, N., Liu, X., Teucke, M., Freitag, M.: Travel time prediction in a multimodal freight transport relation using machine learning algorithms. Logistics **4**, 1 (2020)
4. Gong, L., Kanamori, R., Yamamoto, T.: Data selection in machine learning for identifying trip purposes and travel modes from longitudinal GPS data collection lasting for seasons. Travel Behav. Soc. **11**, 131–140 (2018)

5. Pluvinet, P., Gonzalez-Feliu, J., Ambrosini, C.: GPS data analysis for understanding urban goods movement. Procedia. Soc. Behav. Sci. **39**, 450–462 (2012)
6. Shen, L., Stopher, P.R.: Review of GPS travel survey and GPS data-processing methods. Transp. Rev. **34**, 316–334 (2014)
7. Govindan, K., Cheng, T.C.E., Mishra, N., Shukla, N.: Big data analytics and application for logistics and supply chain management. Transp. Res. Part E: Logistics Transp. Rev. **114**, 343–349 (2018)
8. Khurana, U., Samulowitz, H., Turaga, D.: Feature engineering for predictive modeling using reinforcement learning. Proceedings of the AAAI Conference on Artificial Intelligence (2018). https://doi.org/10.1609/aaai.v32i1.11678
9. Khurana, U., Turaga, D., Samulowitz, H., Parthasrathy, S.: Cognito: automated feature engineering for supervised learning. In: 2016 IEEE 16th International Conference on Data Mining Workshops (ICDMW) (2016). https://doi.org/10.1109/ICDMW.2016.0190
10. Nargesian, F., Samulowitz, H., Khurana, U., Khalil, E.B., Turaga, D.: Learning feature engineering for classification. In: Proceedings of the Twenty-Sixth International Joint Conference on Artificial Intelligence Main Track, pp. 2529–2535 (2017). https://doi.org/10.24963/ijcai.2017/352
11. Montini, L., Rieser-Schüssler, N., Horni, A., Axhausen, K.W.: Trip purpose identification from GPS tracks. Transp. Res. Rec. (2014). https://doi.org/10.3141/2405-03
12. Ribeiro, J., Fontes, T., Soares, C., Borges, J.L.: Process discovery on geolocation data. Transp. Res. Procedia **47**, 139–146 (2020)
13. Dabiri, S., Heaslip, K.: Inferring transportation modes from GPS trajectories using a convolutional neural network. Transp. Res. Part C: Emerg. Technol. **86**, 360–371 (2018)
14. Guo, S., et al.: GPS trajectory data segmentation based on probabilistic logic. Int. J. Approximate Reasoning **103**, 227–247 (2018)
15. Feng, T., Timmermans, H.: Comparison of advanced imputation algorithms for detection of transportation mode and activity episode using GPS data. Transp. Plan. Technol. **39**, 1–15 (2016)
16. Bhavsar, P., Safro, I., Bouaynaya, N., Polikar, R., Dera, D.: Machine learning in transportation data analytics. In: Data Analytics for Intelligent Transportation Systems, pp. 283–307. Elsevier (2017). https://doi.org/10.1016/B978-0-12-809715-1.00012-2

Using Evolutionary Algorithms to Promote Sustainable Collaboration Networks Through Partner Selection

Ricardo Santos[1,2(✉)], Poliño F. Katina[3], Jose Soares[4], Anouar Hallioui[5],
Pedro Carmona Marques[2,6], Joaquim Monteiro[2,7], and Ona Egbue[3]

[1] GOVCOPP - University of Aveiro, Aveiro, Portugal
`ricardosimoessantos84@ua.pt`
[2] ISEL-Instituto Superior de Engenharia de Lisboa, Instituto Politécnico de Lisboa, Lisboa, Portugal
[3] Department of Informatics and Engineering Systems, University of South Carolina Upstate, Spartanburg, SC, USA
[4] ADVANCE, ISEG, Universidade de Lisboa, Lisbao, Portugal
[5] Department of Industrial Engineering, Sidi Mohamed Ben Abdellah University, Fez, Morocco
[6] EIGeS, Universidade Lusófona, Lisbon, Portugal
[7] INESC ID IST-UL, Lisboa, Portugal

Abstract. A Collaborative Network (CN), usually arises to achieve a large number of innovations in a short term, by sharing and developing information and competencies, from the interaction of a group of partners involved here. Despite its potential, there are some challenges on deploying this concept into practice, particularly when the purpose is to choose the suitable partner to promote sustainable CNs, regarding the following dimensions of sustainability; Social, Economic and Environment.

Given the lack of methods existent on literature, in this work we propose an approach, which uses multicriteria decision method integrated with evolutionary algorithms (NSGA II) to provide suitable partners for a CN, regarding the three dimensions referred before.

The approach developed here, will be further applied into a real situation, based on an existent CN, in order to provide it with suitable partners, promoting therefore its sustainability over different perspectives.

Keywords: Sustainability · Collaborative networks · Partner's selection · Multicriteria decision-making · Evolutionary algorithms

1 Introduction

Achieving a suitable partner, considering a diversity of knowledge areas to be accounted, is essential to obtain a successful collaborative ecosystem [1, 2].

The last developments, regarding business intelligence, brought many applications for professional use, with some of them, being used by human resource professionals to seek adequate partners to define a project's team [1].

L. M. Camarinha-Matos et al. (Eds.): PRO-VE 2022, IFIP AICT 662, pp. 262–273, 2022.
https://doi.org/10.1007/978-3-031-14844-6_21

However, and despite such achievements, which includes the increase in requirements within SMEs on behalf of social and environmental responsibilities, there are a lack of approaches that allows to support the manager's board on partner's assessment-based criteria, and regarding the three well known sustainability's vectors/dimensions, namely; Economic, Social and Environmental [3].

Therefore, we propose a decision support approach to provide suitable partners for a Collaborative Network (CN) on behalf of the three dimensions referred before.

The framework developed here, uses multicriteria integrated with Multi-Attribute Value Theory (MAVT) methods, and on behalf of the three sustainable dimensions. The decision space, resulted, is then explored by NSGA II in order to find the maximum aggregated value added for a given CN's process, where a set of individual ones are further obtained, concerning each partner's position to be fulfilled, related to each activity.

In addition, the priorities regarding the relative importance, concerning each one of the 3 dimensions, are also considered here, through the use of AHP method.

The obtained results show the versatility of using evolutionary algorithms such as NSGA II, on achieving feasible and alternative solutions, which allows to face contingencies, that might be arise (e.g., resignation of some "elected" candidates to fulfill the partner's position).

The model proposed in this work, will be assessed in terms of its robustness, by using a real situation, relied on a sustainable product, which is developed on behalf of a CN context.

2 Literature Review

An increasingly number of works from the literature, highlights the importance of the collaborative networks, as a mean to rump up SMEs competitiveness, through the innovation achieved through the share of competencies and resources with other partners, on pursuing a common goal such as the development of a new products [3, 4].

Furthermore, the share of information and knowledge with other SMEs, and on behalf of the collaborative networks, has allowed to develop certain skills including expertise among the staff of each SMS's partner involved [5, 6].

Additionally, some studies found on literature (e.g. [1, 7]), states that the high levels of innovation achieved from collaborative networks (CN), is somehow associated with the partner's selection, concerning each activity and process to be considered.

A diversity of studies, focused on partner's selection approaches, has been performed, to increase the CN's innovative performance, with most of them, analyzing the CN created, on behalf of different perspectives such as knowledge relevance (e.g. [6]), key CN available roles (e.g. [8–10]), external assets (e.g. [10, 11]), external cooperation to create new competences or knowledge related to the development of new products (e.g. [11]), between others.

Other works, use Social Networks theory (SN) to map the demanded external assets for SMEs (e.g. [1]). Other works, uses SN to identify expert individuals to be integrated as partners (e.g. [1, 3]).

However, and despite the existence of such studies, there are an absence of approaches that includes sustainable development requirements, increasingly demanded from the SMEs by the society of "today", as well as by the society of "tomorrow".

3 Proposed Approach

3.1 Model's Conceptual Architecture

The approach presented in this section, intends to support the management board of a Collaborative Network (CN), who wants to assess and select a (a set of) of candidates to be partner(s) for an (a set of) activity (ies), related to a (a set of) process(es) on behalf of a CN (Fig. 1).

Each set of candidates (C_{ij}), were previous selected according to a set of CN's pre-requirements and they are related to a given partner's position j, concerning an activity (a_j), which is associated to a given process (n) of the product to be developed. Each set, is associated to a set of possible alternative solutions to be considered, where one solution from each set, will be further selected, relied on the CN's needs and preferences, joined with the correspondent priorities, related to each sustainability's vector. Figure 1, presents the developed approach.

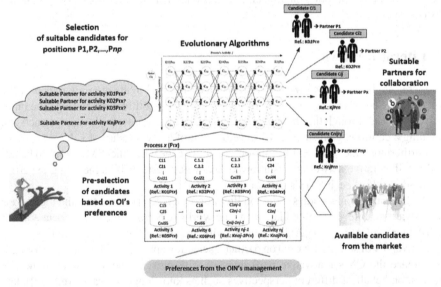

Fig. 1. Model's architecture

Through the observation of Fig. 1, the 1st phase begins with a pre-selection of a set of partner's candidates (x_{ij}) from the market, which is performed according to a set of pre-requirements to be attended, such as the proximity degree, the compliance with the project deadlines, scope and costs, among other factors considered here.

The multi criteria used here, on behalf of the tree dimensions of sustainability, allows to classify each partner's candidate C_{ij}, in order to reduce the decision space, by considering only the candidates, fitted to the needs of collaborative network created here, increasing at the same time the NSGAII's efficiency on getting feasible solutions in less time.

3.2 Criteria Used and Problem's Formulation

The partner's selection for the same CN, arises multiple challenges, especially when it's intended to promote sustainability within the CN itself on developing such products/systems.

According to [12–13], sustainability actions, can be splatted in Social, Economic and Environmental.

Through the literature about partner's selection, it was reached a set of criteria on behalf of the 3 dimensions created before, namely;

- Environmental➜ Regards all the factors that could have an impact on the CN's environmental viability, such as those that are primarily related to the organization's environmental responsibility [3, 5], such as the accreditation for environmental standards, self-energy Greenhouse Gas (GHG) emissions, circular economy policies, soil and water quality, among others.
- Economic➜ Regarding the CN's financial viability and economics. This includes issues relating to the economic well-being of organization [4, 6], such as the supply chain's channels (distribution nodes, transport types/modes, etc.), financial situation as well as the credibility attached to it, operation costs, facility's place, scale (available) of operations, the capacity of facilities, the reliability of feedstock supply, among other related criteria involved.
- Social➜ Relates to all the criteria that could have an impact on the CN's social viability, including problems that are primarily related to the social wellbeing of the organization's stakeholders [6], [12–13], the reputation at stake as well as the knowledge/information sharing concerns, including work conditions, accessibility to knowledge and information sharing, knowledge relevance, reputation, and the number of relationships established with other organizations, among other criteria involved.

Based on that criterion, it was developed a framework to analyze and evaluate each candidate to be included in a CN with concerns to the three dimensions considered before (Table 1), i.e.: ω-Social, λ-Economics and θ-Environmental.

Table 1. Adopted criteria on behalf of the 3 known sustainability's dimensions.

Dimension: Economics (λ)		Dimension: Social (ω)		Dimension: Environmental (θ)	
Designation	Ref.	Designation	Ref.	Designation	Ref.
Financial situation and credibility	λ1	Company's reputation (Transparency)	ω1	Industry's energy dependence level from fossil fuels	θ1
Available assets (€)	λ2	Knowledge relevance	ω2	Compliance with legal requirements regarding environment	θ2
Facility's location	λ3	Work conditions	ω3	Circular economy policies	θ3
Supply chain's channels	λ4	External available resources (social network)	ω4	Environmental standards compliance (accreditation)	θ4
Availability degree (flexibility) to scale operations	λ5	Social responsibility	ω5		
Operations costs to complete the activity/task (€)	λ6	Average deadline to complete activity/task (months)	ω6		
Available funds (€)	λ7	Quality perceived on developing the activities/tasks	ω7		

Based on each sub criteria/attribute presented on Table 1, it was defined a decision variable $\left(c_{ij}^{(D_t)}\right)$, regarding each partner's candidate i, related to a given process activity j. This variable is defined based on each sub criteria/attribute $t\tau$, associated to each activity j and sustainable dimension j (θ -Environment, λ – Economical and ω - Social), namely:

$$D = \{\lambda, \varpi, \theta\} \wedge j = \{1, 2, .., 7\} \wedge \tau = \left\{\{1, 2, ..n_\lambda\} \cup \{1, 2, ..n_\varpi\} \cup \{1, 2, ..n_\theta\}\right\}$$
$$\wedge\ n_\lambda, n_\omega, n_\theta, \tau, j \in \mathbb{N} \tag{1}$$

Based on this notation and through criteria shown on Table 1, it can be established a decision-variable related to each attribute $\left(c_{ij}^{(D_{j\tau})}\right)$, which can be further aggregated into a pay-off table, according to the activity which is demanding for a new partner position, on behalf of process x (K i Pr x) (Table 2 a)).

In order to convert each attribute's value to the same unit's scale $\left(v_{ij}^{D_j}\left(c_{ij}^{(D_{j\tau})}\right)\right)$, we've used the MAVT approach, to uniformize the unit's scale of the attributes involved, by using the following expression:

$$c_{ij}^{(D_\tau)} \longrightarrow \left(\frac{\left|c_{ij}^{(D_\tau)} - c_{ij(worst)}^{(D_\tau)}\right|}{\left|c_{ij(best)}^{(D_\tau)} - c_{ij(worst)}^{(D_\tau)}\right|}\right) \longrightarrow v_{ij}^{(D_\tau)}(c_{ij}^{(D_\tau)}) \tag{2}$$

Table 2 intends to show an example of a table respectively for all $c_{ij}^{(D_\tau)}$ and $v_{ij}^{D_\tau}\left(c_{ij}^{(D_\tau)}\right)$ values.

Table 2. Example of a pay-off table regarding an activity i, related to project j (Ki Prj): (a) $c_{ij}^{(D\tau)}$; (b) $v_{ij}^{D\tau}\left(c_{ij}^{(D\tau)}\right)$.

$c_{i\tau}^{D\tau}$	$\lambda 1$	$\lambda 2$	...	λn_λ	$\omega 1$	$\omega 2$	...	ωn_ω	$\theta 1$	$\theta 2$	...	θn_θ
C_1	$c_{11}^{\lambda 1}$	$c_{12}^{\lambda 2}$	...	$c_{1\lambda}^{\lambda n_\lambda}$	$c_{11}^{\omega 1}$	$c_{12}^{\omega 2}$	...	$c_1^{\omega n_\omega}$	$c_{11}^{\theta 1}$	$c_{12}^{\theta 2}$	...	$c_{1n_\theta}^{\gamma m_\theta}$
C_2	$c_{21}^{\lambda 1}$	$c_{22}^{\lambda 2}$	...	$c_{2n_\lambda}^{\lambda n_\lambda}$	$c_{21}^{\omega 1}$	$c_{22}^{\omega 2}$	...	$c_{2n_\omega}^{\omega n_\omega}$	$c_{21}^{\theta 1}$	$c_{22}^{\theta 2}$	...	$c_{2n_\theta}^{\theta n_\theta}$
...	...	...	...	...	...	...	...	...	...	...	...	...
C_n	$c_{n1}^{\lambda 1}$	$c_{n2}^{\lambda 2}$	...	$c_{nn_\lambda}^{\lambda n_\lambda}$	$x_{n1}^{\omega 1}$	$c_{n2}^{\omega 2}$	...	$x_{nn_\omega}^{\omega n_\omega}$	$c_{n1}^{\theta 1}$	$c_{n2}^{\theta 2}$	...	$c_{nn_\theta}^{\theta n_\theta}$

(a)

$v_{i\tau}^{D\tau}(c_{i\tau}^{D\tau})$	$\lambda 1$	$\lambda 2$	...	λn_λ	$\omega 1$	$\omega 2$	...	ωn	$\theta 1$	$\theta 2$	...	θn
c_1	$v_{11}^{\lambda 1}(c_{11}^{\lambda 1})$	$v_{12}^{\lambda 2}(c_{12}^{\lambda 2})$	...	$v_{1n_\lambda}^{\lambda n_\lambda}(c_{1n_\lambda}^{\lambda n_\lambda})$	$v_{11}^{\omega 1}(c_{11}^{\omega 1})$	$v_{12}^{\omega 2}(c_{12}^{\omega 2})$	...	$v_{1n_\omega}^{\omega n_\omega}(c_{1n_\omega}^{\omega n_\omega})$	$v_{11}^{\theta 1}(c_{11}^{\theta 1})$	$v_{12}^{\theta 2}(c_{12}^{\theta 2})$	...	$v_{1n_\theta}^{\theta n_\theta}(c_{1n_\theta}^{\theta n_\theta})$
c_2	$v_{21}^{\lambda 1}(x_{21}^{\lambda 1})$	$v_{22}^{\lambda 2}(c_{22}^{\lambda 2})$	...	$v_{2n_\lambda}^{\lambda n_\lambda}(c_{2n_\lambda}^{\lambda n_\lambda})$	$v_{21}^{\omega 1}(c_{21}^{\omega 1})$	$v_{22}^{\omega 2}(c_{22}^{\omega 2})$	...	$v_{2n_\omega}^{\omega n_\omega}(c_{2n_\omega}^{\omega n_\omega})$	$v_{21}^{\theta 1}(c_{21}^{\theta 1})$	$v_{22}^{\theta 2}(c_{22}^{\theta 2})$	...	$v_{2n_\theta}^{\theta n_\theta}(c_{2n_\theta}^{\theta n_\theta})$
...	...	...	...	...	...	...	...	...	...	...	...	...
c_n	$v_{n1}^{\lambda 1}(c_{n1}^{\lambda 1})$	$v_{n2}^{\lambda 2}(c_{n2}^{\lambda 2})$	...	$v_{nn_\lambda}^{\lambda n_\lambda}(c_{nn_\lambda}^{\lambda n_\lambda})$	$v_{n1}^{\omega 1}(c_{n1}^{\omega 1})$	$v_{n2}^{\omega 2}(c_{n2}^{\omega 2})$	...	$v_{nn_\omega}^{\omega n_\omega}(c_{nn_\omega}^{\omega n_\omega})$	$v_{n1}^{\theta 1}(c_{n1}^{\theta 1})$	$v_{n2}^{\theta 2}(c_{n2}^{\theta 2})$	...	$v_{nn_\theta}^{\theta n_\theta}(c_{nn_\theta}^{\theta n_\theta})$

(b)

In order to classify each candidate c_{ij}, according to its overall value, based on the value functions $V_{ij}^\lambda\left(C_{ij}^\lambda\right)$, $V_{ij}^\omega\left(C_{ij}^\omega\right)$ and $V_{ij}^\theta\left(C_{ij}^\theta\right)$, considered for each sustainability's dimension D, it was used an additive MAVT model, by aggregating each individual attribute's values $\left(v_{i\tau}^{D\tau}\left(c_{i\tau}^{(D\tau)}\right)\right)$ for each activity j.

In order to obtain the overall function value $\left(V_{ij}(C_{ij})\right)$, used to rank each partner's candidate, a same approach was conducted, by aggregating those values, according to their relative importance, which is expressed by a correspondent factor (α_D), considered for each sustainability's dimension D, i.e.:

$$V_i(C_i) = V_{ij}\left(V_{ij}^\lambda\left(c_{ij}^\lambda\right), V_{ij}^\theta\left(c_{ij}^\theta\right), V_{ij}^\theta\left(c_{ij}^\theta\right)\right) = \alpha_\lambda . V_{ij}^\lambda\left(c_{ij}^\lambda\right) + \alpha_\varpi . V_{ij}^\omega\left(c_{ij}^\omega\right) + \alpha_\theta . V_{ij}^\theta\left(c_{ij}^\theta\right)$$

(3)

Each factor α_D (α_λ, α_ω, α_θ) are obtained by using the Analytical Hierarchical Process (AHP) framework [11], and through the inquiries, conducted to the management board.

Thus, and based on (3), it is obtained the overall objective function to be maximized, composed by individual objectives functions, each associated to a sustainability's dimension.

$$\max \quad V^D(c^D), \qquad w/D = \lambda, \omega, \theta$$

$$\text{subject to } c \in C \qquad w/V^D(c^D) = \left[V^\lambda(c^\lambda), V^\omega(c^\varpi), V^\theta(c^\theta)\right]^T$$

(4)

$$V^D(c^D) = \sum_{j=1}^{n_j}\sum_{\tau=1}^{n_D} v_{j\tau}(c_{j\tau}^{(D\tau)}) \quad w/D = \{\lambda, \varpi, \theta\} \wedge v_{j\tau}(c_{j\tau}^{(D\tau)}) \wedge n_j, n_{D_j}, \tau, j \in \mathbb{N}$$

(5)

where $V_i^\lambda(C_i^\lambda)$, $V_i^\omega(C_i^\omega)$ and $V_i^\theta(C_i^\theta)$ can be obtained by:

$$Economic \ : \ \max V_i^\lambda(c_i^\lambda) = \sum_{j=1}^{n_i} \sum_{\tau=1}^{n_\lambda} v_{ij\tau}(c_{ii\tau}^{(\lambda_\tau)}) \tag{6}$$

$$Social \ : \ \max V_i^\varpi(c_i^\omega) = \sum_{j=1}^{n_j} \sum_{\tau=1}^{n_\omega} v_{ij\tau}(c_{ij\tau}^{(\omega_\tau)}) \tag{7}$$

$$Environmental \ : \ \max V_i^\theta(c_i^\theta) = \sum_{j=1}^{n_j} \sum_{\tau=1}^{n_\theta} \left(v_{ij\tau}(c_{ij\tau}^{(\theta_\tau)})\right) \tag{8}$$

Based on (2), (3) and (5) it is obtained the overall objective function, pondered by a factor (α_D):

$$V_{Total}(c) = \sum_{j=1}^{n_j} \left\{ \begin{array}{l} \alpha_\lambda \cdot \sum_{\tau=1}^{n_\lambda} \left(\dfrac{\left(c_{ij}^{(\lambda_\tau)} - c_{ij(worst)}^{(\lambda_\tau)}\right)}{\left(c_{ij(best)}^{(\lambda_\tau)} - c_{ij(worst)}^{(\lambda_\tau)}\right)} \right) \\[2em] +\alpha_\omega \cdot \sum_{\tau=1}^{n_\varpi} \left(\dfrac{\left(c_{ij}^{(\varpi_\tau)} - c_{ij(worst)}^{(\omega_\tau)}\right)}{\left(c_{ij(best)}^{(\varpi_\tau)} - c_{ij(worst)}^{(\omega_\tau)}\right)} \right) \\[2em] +\alpha_\theta \cdot \sum_{\tau=1}^{n_\theta} \left(\dfrac{\left(c_{ij}^{(\theta_\tau)} - c_{ij(worst)}^{(\theta_\tau)}\right)}{\left(c_{ij(best)}^{(\theta_\tau)} - c_{ij(worst)}^{(\theta_\tau)}\right)} \right) \end{array} \right\} \tag{9}$$

The main function cost, is then subject to a group of constraints, related to the sustainability's vector/dimension, i.e.:

$$r_1 : \sum_{j=1}^{n_j} \left(v_{ij7}(c_{ij7}^{(\lambda_7)})\right) \geq \eta_{min \ imum \ available \ funds} \tag{10}$$

$$r_2 : \sum_{j=1}^{n_j} \left(v_{ij6}(c_{ij6}^{(\lambda_6)})\right) \leq \eta_{max \ imum \ operation \ costs} \tag{11}$$

$$r_3 : \sum_{j=1}^{n_j} \left(v_{ij6}(c_{ij6}^{(\omega_6)})\right) \leq \eta_{max \ imum \ deadline} \tag{12}$$

Given the problem's characteristics, most of all, related with its combinatorial nature, it was used NSGAII's optimization method to solve it, with its individual chromosome presented on Fig. 2.

For the NSGAII's chromosome, it was used real codification, given the nature of each one of decision variable used.

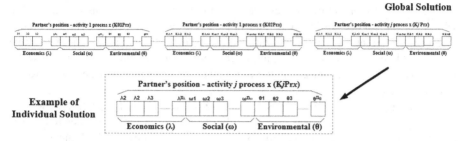

Fig. 2. NSGAII's individual framework.

4 Results and Discussion

In order to evaluate the robustness of the model involved here, it was used a real situation, consisted of the development of an electric vehicle on behalf of a Collaborative Network (CN) established for that purpose.

The main goal was the develop an electric vehicle, to have one of the highest autonomy levels from the market, given its category.

This was done, by optimizing several components of the car (e.g., vehicle's regenerative braking system, battery management system (BMS), aerodynamics, among other innovations). The CN has a total number of 27 Partners, and the framework, used to manage the innovation on CN established here, is based on the work from [7].

On Fig. 3, it is presented part of the table with the different skills and partners involved on this project, as well as part of the correspondent CN.

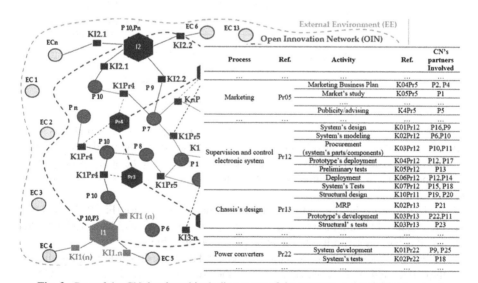

Fig. 3. Part of the CN developed including some of the partners and activities involved

Through the same figure, we can see part of the network created, as well as a table with some of the processes involved. The purpose is to share competencies and resources among the different partners (organizations) involved, to develop a new and innovative product, to better match the client requirements, aiming at the same time, to increase the credibility of the project, attracting therefore other investors that might be interested to fund the project.

Due to the diversity of processes and activities involved on this project, as well as the purpose of this work, it was selected only one process, where it is intended to add new partners on it. Therefore, on Table 3, it is presented the process Pr12, the activities related to it, and its needs in terms of new partners' positions to be fulfilled.

Table 3. Partner's positions to be fulfilled regarding process Pr12.

Process (Prn)	Activity KnPrn	Partner's position (s) needed			
		Current Partner (s)		Partner (s) to full fill	
		Ref.:	Organization type	Ref.:	Organization type
Pr12 Supervision and control electronic system	K01Pr12	P16	University (R&D Group)	P9	University (R&D Group)
	K02Pr12	P6	Company	P10	Company
	K03Pr12	-	-	P10	n.d.
		-	-	P11	n.d
	K04Pr12	-	-	P12	Company
	K05Pr12	-	-	P17	Company
	K06Pr12	-	-	P12	Company
		-	Company	P14	University (R&D Group)
	K07Pr12	-	Company	P15	Company
		P18		-	

n.d. - indifferent/not defined

Through Table 3, it can be seen that some of the positions to be filled, has some specific requirements regarding the type of organization to be included. For instance, while for the positions P10 and P11, the type of organization to be added is indifferent, for the position P14, it is required that the organization to be add should be an University (R&D group).

As it mentioned before and based on the model's architecture (Fig. 1), it was pre-selected from 642 available partners (on total), 198 possible candidates, to be further classified according to multicriteria table, presented on Table 1.

After each candidate c_{ij} being scored on behalf of the three dimensions of sustainability, the correspondent individual solution was then structured according to the NSGAII's individual framework (Fig. 2) and then aggregated, in order to add the maximum value for the process Pr12, based on the three sustainable dimensions discussed before and according to the same framework presented on Fig. 2.

NSGAII approach was then coded into Matlab® software, and runed in a CPU Intel i7, 3.2 GHz, in order to optimize the aggregated value function, presented before.

For the NSGAII's parameters, it was considered the following options/values:

- Selection method: roulette
- Mutation method: normal random
- Mutation rate [%]: 12%
- Initial population: 200 individuals randomly generated
- Elitism: 12 individuals
- Crossover technique: double point
- Crossover rate [%]: 45%
- Stop criteria: 142 generations

Some of these parameters, (including crossover and mutation rates and stop criteria), were previously tunned and obtained from previous tests.

On Fig. 4, it is presented the correspondent Pareto surface.

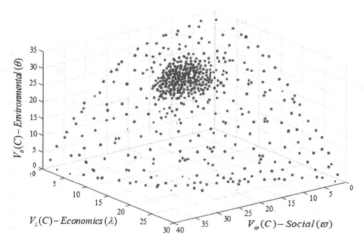

Fig. 4. Pareto Surface, obtained regarding a set of suitable solutions, classified according to the 3 Sustainability dimensions and their relative importance values (respectively for $\alpha_\lambda = 0{,}64$, $\alpha_\omega = 0{,}22$, $\alpha_\theta = 0{,}14$)

Through the Pareto Surface presented on Fig. 4, it can be seen that each point (or node) represents a global solution, consisted in a group of individual solutions c_{ij} (partner's candidates) regarding each activity j, associated to process Pr12 (KjPr12).

Through the same figure, it's even possible the trade-offs between the different sustainability's dimensions.

Based on the Pareto's surface, presented on Fig. 4, and by selecting one of the nodes from the region with more crowding space, it's possible select a suitable solution that allows to promote a high value for the process Pr12 regarding the dimensions of sustainability referred before. One of these nodes is presented on Table 4.

Table 4. Set of solutions achieved, considering $\alpha_\lambda = 0,64$, $\alpha_\omega = 0,22$ and $\alpha_\theta = 0,14$.

Cand.	Suitable for position	Organization type	Partner's candidate							Assigned activity (ies)	
			Average Deadline (months)	Operation Costs (k€))	Available funds (k€)	$v_i^\lambda(c_i^\lambda)$	$v_i^\omega(c_i^\omega)$	$v_i^\theta(c_i^\theta)$	$v_T^\square(c)$	Ref.:	Description
C31	P9	University (R&D Group)	3,0	290	3					K01Pr12	System's design
C52	P10	Company	2,8	1952,8	2000,8					K02Pr12 K03Pr12	System's modeling
C33	P11	Company	4,0	385	400					K03Pr12	Procurement (system's parts/components)
C54	P12	Company	3,7	214	300					K04Pr12	Prototype's deployment
C25	P17	Company	3,1	11253	13000					K05Pr12	Preliminary tests
C16	P14	University (R&D Group)	4,0	325	4000					K06Pr12	Deployment
C37	P15	Company	6,0	658	856,23					K07Pr12	System's Tests
TOTAL			26,6	15077,8	17257,03	19,4	17,5	15,8	52,7		

Therefore, if the CN's board of management choses this solution, presented on Table 4, he can expect to have for the activities regarding the process Pr12, an increase of 26,6 months, 15077800 € and 17257030 €, respectively regarded to the total values of average deadline, operation costs and available funds.

5   Conclusions of the Work

In this work, we've put forth a decision-support technique to choose acceptable partners for a Collaborative Network (CN) on behalf of the three sustainability dimensions, namely economic, social, and environmental.

With regard to the CN's pre-requirements, this method uses a pre-selection stage in which a pool of potential candidates is pre-selected from the market. The decision space, whose global solutions are produced by a set of individual solutions regarding each type of activity, is then determined based on a set of criteria developed on behalf of the three dimensions and by applying MAVT.

In order to optimize the value of each global solution, which is made up of a number of individual candidates, NSGA II was also used.

Each candidate is evaluated in light of a partner's open position as well as an activity connected to a certain procedure.

In addition to classifying each global solution according to the three sustainability dimensions that have been taken into consideration, it is also possible to determine which aspect of sustainability each specific solution scores the highest on and, consequently, which one is best suited to meet a given criterion. In order to tailor the solutions to the CN's objectives, the priorities of the relative importance, given to each of the three sustainability dimensions, can also be altered. For example, approaches like AHP.

The approach created here also enables the selection of partners with the next best score in order to handle potential eventualities that may happen with the candidates chosen to integrate the partnership (such as the unavailability of the selected partner after discussions take place).

The inclusion of evolutionary algorithms, such NSGA II, also makes it possible to have more workable alternatives available, which makes it possible to deal with unforeseen circumstances (like the resignation of some "chosen" candidates to fill the partner's position, for example).

Through the activities/processes taken into consideration here, mainly through its criteria, and its associated attributes as well, the approach proposed here can also be scaled up, to better answer the manager's board needs.

As a future lines of research, and in order to fulfill the needs of the current industry, the model developed here can be enriched with additional attributes, with some of them related to the social networks theory, and whose relevance, was previously discussed on literature review.

References

1. Wei, F., Feng, N., Yang, S., Zhao, Q.: A conceptual framework of two-stage partner selection in platform-based innovation ecosystems for servitization. J. Cleaner Prod. **262**, 121431 ISSN 0959–6526 (2020). https://doi.org/10.1016/j.jclepro.2020.121431
2. Camarinha-Matos, L.M., Afsarmanesh, H.: A comprehensive modeling framework for collaborative networked organizations. J. Intell. Manuf. **5**(18), 529–542 (2007). https://doi.org/10.1007/s10845-007-0063-3
3. Tavana, M., Nasr, AK., Mina, H., Michnik, J.: A private sustainable partner selection model for green public-private partnerships and regional economic development, Socio-Econ. Plann. Sci. 101189 (2021). ISSN 0038–0121 https://doi.org/10.1016/j.seps.2021.101189
4. Santos, R., Matias, J., Soares, J., Marques, P.C., Anes, V.: Using fuzzy-based approaches on partner's selection to promote sustainability on collaborative networks. In: Camarinha-Matos, L.M., Boucher, X., Afsarmanesh, H. (eds.) Smart and Sustainable Collaborative Networks 4.0. IFIP Advances in Information and Communication Technology, vol. 629, pp. 53–64. Springer, Cham (2021). https://doi.org/10.1007/978-3-030-85969-5_5
5. Mansor, N., Yahaya, S.N., Okazaki, K.: Risk factors affecting new product development (NPD). Int. J. Recent Res. Appl. Stud. **27**(1), 18–25 (2016)
6. Januska, M.: Communication as a key factor in virtual enterprise paradigm support. In: Innovation and Knowledge Management: A Global Competitive Advantage, International Business Information Management Association (IBIMA), Kuala Lumpur, pp. 1–9 (2011) ISBN 978-0-9821489-5-2
7. Santos, R., Abreu, A., Anes, V.: Developing a Green Product-Based in an Open Innovation Environment. Case Study: Electrical Vehicle. In: Camarinha-Matos, L.M., Afsarmanesh, H., Antonelli, D. (eds.) Collaborative Networks and Digital Transformation. IFIP AICT, vol. 568, pp. 115–127. Springer, Cham (2019). https://doi.org/10.1007/978-3-030-28464-0_11
8. Tong, L.Z., Wang, J., Pu, Z.: Sustainable supplier selection for SMEs based on an extended PROMETHEE II approach. J. Cleaner Prod. **330** (2022) 129830, ISSN 0959–6526, https://doi.org/10.1016/j.jclepro.2021.129830
9. Xiaoren, Z., Ling, D., Xiangdong, C.: Interaction of open innovation and business ecosystem. Int. J. u-and e-Service. Sci. Technol. **1**(7), 51–64 (2014)
10. Santos, R.S., Soares, J., Marques, P.C., Navas, H.V.G., Martins, J.M.: Integrating business, social, and environmental goals in open innovation through partner selection. Sustainability **13**, 12870 (2021). https://doi.org/10.3390/su132212870
11. Calabrese, A., Costa, R., Levialdi, N, Menichini, T.: Integrating sustainability into strategic decision-making: a fuzzy AHP method for the selection of relevant sustainability issues. Technol. Forecast. Soc. Change **139**, 155–168 (2019). ISSN 0040-1625, https://doi.org/10.1016/j.techfore.2018.11.005

Maturity of Artificial Intelligence in SMEs: Privacy and Ethics Dimensions

Thomas Schuster[iD] and Lukas Waidelich[(✉)] [iD]

Institute of Smart Systems and Services, Pforzheim University of Applied Sciences,
Tiefenbronner Str. 65, 75175 Pforzheim, Germany
{thomas.schuster,lukas.waidelich}@hs-pforzheim.de

Abstract. Artificial intelligence (AI) remains volatile for many companies and
will foster disruptive transformation processes in many industries. Companies
face continuous challenges assessing AI-readiness, current state, and AI-based
requirements for change. Assessment of AI applications, services and products
can be built on maturity models (MM). In this case, specialized AI-based MM
(AIMM) are needed. With this article, we intend to advance the AIMM development. Aspects of small and medium sized companies (SME), privacy, and ethics
are in focus. We will present the current state of AIMM, its interim, and practical
evaluation and an outlook on further AIMM developments.

Keywords: AI · Maturity model · Maturity level · AI privacy · AI ethics

1 Introduction

Digital transformation is advancing and with it the gradual commercialization and rapid
evolution of artificial intelligence (AI). Scientific publications and case studies attest to
significant value creation using AI in private and public institutions. AI is making slow
progress in company-wide adoption. It is currently used in isolated instances and is not
yet a complete solution, but rather a system component.

SMEs in particular need systematic support to introduce AI technologies. So-called
AI maturity models (MM) can represent an approach for determining the state of progress
of AI in a company and serve as a basis for further development activities.

Our previous work [1] revealed a lack of available consistent and applicable AIMM.
Main criticisms are incomplete described AIMM, lack of self-assessment by the user
and not considering relevant thematic dimensions. The underlying data relevant for
AI applications is subject to legal regulations of data protection. Implications of AI
decisions have inherent ethical considerations that need to be considered. This research
gap is addressed in this paper by systematically developing an AIMM that is suitable
inter alia for SMEs. We address the following research questions (RQ):

- **RQ1**: How is the AIMM structured and how is the maturity level determined?
- **RQ2**: How can an interim evaluation of the present state of research be conducted?

L. M. Camarinha-Matos et al. (Eds.): PRO-VE 2022, IFIP AICT 662, pp. 274–286, 2022.
https://doi.org/10.1007/978-3-031-14844-6_22

- **RQ3**: How should a concept for transfer and evaluation be designed?

The paper is structured as follows: First, the scientific basis is explained by a classification of MM and AI in general as well as privacy and ethics context of AI. Then, the research design is presented using a seven-phase process model from the literature on MM development. The transfer of theory to practice on the AIMM topic is described next. This includes the iterative MM development, the attached interim evaluation and the conception of transfer and evaluation. A summary of the work presented, and an outlook of potential further research projects completes this paper.

2 Theoretical Background

2.1 Maturity Model

First theories and applications on MM were published in the early 1990s. MM follow the generally acknowledged target of capturing a specific status quo of a particular area within an organization and supporting its improvement [2]. MM are mainly applied in innovative, novel, and complex disciplines. Due to their systematic and structured approach, MMs enable a first low-threshold involvement with the topic under investigation. Challenging and complex (technologized) fields such as information systems (IS), business process management, digital transformation or AI are described by corresponding MMs [3, 4]. MM concepts and applications have made their way into cross-domain and cross-industry applications [1].

MM are usually divided into different dimensions (also called categories). For each dimension, criteria and associated metrics are defined, which allow a classification per dimension. Approaches are e.g., questionnaires with yes-no questions or the classification by means of Likert scale level. An underlying metric determines a performance level per dimension. The aggregation of these individual categorizations per dimension adds up to an overall result. The outcome is the maturity level. The MM with its maturity levels allows the status quo to be categorized. MM provides two methods for determining the maturity level. Either by working through the question catalog with an expert or by self-assessment. In both cases, the contact person should have an appropriate level of knowledge. In this way, MMs act as an initial indicator for assessing the capabilities of an organization. MMs raise awareness of a topic, provide a valid assessment of the organization's own capabilities, and can trigger innovation processes [5].

2.2 Artificial Intelligence

Historically, the AI concept has existed for about 70 years and is currently experiencing its prime. The AI domain is benefiting from five key developments in particular: The advanced performance and cost-effectiveness of hardware, as well as the combination and further development of different methods and an availability of the required dataset. AI applications are used in almost every industry. Opportunities are offered, for example, by applications in medicine (early disease detection), mobility (autonomous driving) and marketing (chatbots). The discourse of AI mentions risks such as job loss, error-prone algorithms, loss of privacy and violation of ethical code of values [6].

Data is the fuel of AI and thus a basic prerequisite for the use of AI methods. Data processing often involves the processing of personal data or data that can be used to draw conclusions about private behavior patterns. The use of personal data is regulated by strict legislation (EU-GDPR) depending on the geographic location. In the case of the EU GDPR, technical or organizational measures must be taken. According to the area of application, these include activities for pseudonymization and anonymization. When using AI methods, data protection must be taken into account in advance and privacy must be preserved [7, 8].

In accordance with the AI competence area, a self-learning algorithm assesses sensitive situations. The result of an AI operation is a (possibly serious) decision. An ethical dimension arises at the human-machine interface in this case. A scientific consensus on the definition of AI ethics does not exist. The keywords fairness, accountability, and transparency, as well as data protection and privacy, are mentioned in this context [7, 9].

3   Research Design

In this section we define the scientific approach and enrich it with references from additional literature. The practical implementation takes place in Sect. 4. The research work refers to the Design Science Research (DSR) approach [10]. The objective is the profound development of an AIMM based on a conceptual and iteratively evolving design artifact (DA). The methodological framework is provided by a procedure model for the development of MM (see Fig. 1) [11].

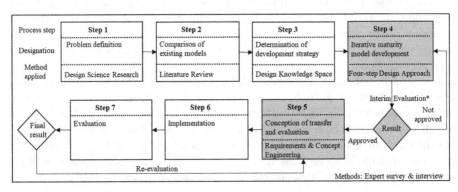

Fig. 1. Adapted procedure model for developing a maturity model based on [11]

In a previous work (see [1]) the steps *(1) Problem Definition, (2) Comparison of existing Models* and *(3) Determination of development strategy* were already addressed. The fourth step has been started and will be processed further in this publication. The current article therefore focuses on the steps: *(4) Iterative maturity model development* and *(5) Conception of transfer and evaluation.* highlights the process steps (gray) that are the focus of this article. The steps *(6) Implementation* and *(7) Evaluation* are currently in progress and will be articulated in future research.

3.1 Iterative Maturity Model Development

Following the procedure model for MM development [11], the main development process proceeds in four iterative sub-steps These include the steps of *(1) select design level, (2) select approach, (3) design model selection* and *(4) test result*. The process step (4) *test result* is emphasized in the procedure model (see Fig. 1) due to its importance The execution of this step will be considered in a separate section (see Sect. 3.2). The first step defines the design level. This includes the architecture and thus the basic structure of the MM. The maturity levels themselves and their structure are to be defined at this stage. The (sub)dimensions and their characteristics for the content of the MM should also be specified. In the second step, the theory suggests two possibilities for designing the characteristics: The bottom-up approach first defines the (sub)dimensions and then infers the maturity levels and their descriptions. The top-down approach proceeds in reverse order and first defines the maturity levels and then specifies the dimensions and their descriptions [5]. The third step is to select a suitable design model for each abstraction level. The process model recommends a literature analysis to identify success factors, comparable models and evaluation criteria for the MM when the topic has reached maturity.

3.2 Interim Evaluation

Step four *(4) test result* is intended to test the developed intermediate result in an interim evaluation. The authors propose three central evaluation requirements: problem adequacy, consistency, and completeness. A case study followed by a questionnaire is an appropriate method. The target group could be students who are familiar with the topic or first experts. The feedback should flow iteratively into process steps 1 to 3. In case of a positive outcome of the intermediate evaluation, the iterative MM-development is completed [11]. This serves as starting point for knowledge transfer, discussion and exchange that follows with the focus group of AI and IT experts to a later stage.

3.3 Conception of Transfer and Evaluation

Once the MM has been developed, both a concept for knowledge transfer and a concept for a final evaluation are to be created in accordance with the MM procedure model [11]. The target group-oriented transfer of knowledge in theory and practice can take different forms. In the referenced literature, document-based checklists or manuals are suggested for this purpose. A tool-supported, internet-based provision of the MM is recommended as technical support [11]. Publications act as an important component of knowledge transfer. The characteristics of the transfer concept determine the possibilities of the evaluation. The final user evaluation should provide a statement on the problem-solving capability of the developed MM. For this reason, the procedure model recommends that feedback possibilities for users should already be considered at the interface of transfer and evaluation concept. (Online) questionnaires in combination with reference to the MM as well as interviews with both quantitative and qualitative characteristics are adequate evaluation methods [5, 11].

4   Results on Development, Interim Evaluation and Conceptions of AIMM

We identified 15 AIMM approaches in our previous literature review. Only three of them [3, 12, 13] were partially convincing according to scientific and practical criteria. The main deficit turned out to be that all three of them cover only a small solution space [14]. Also, they show weaknesses in practical application and evaluation. Also, other criteria remain unconsidered, e.g., AIMM is an important tool for SME, but these were not examined further. The dimensions of privacy and ethics received likewise found little or no consideration. Therefore, we developed our own AIMM approach and are in the process of continuously improving it and testing its suitability for practice.

We first present our approach, and we show how we intend to make AIMM particularly applicable for self-assessment in SMEs. Then, we address open RQs and present the status of our evaluation.

4.1   Iterative Maturity Model Development

The topic of MM development has already been described initially in our previous paper [1]. Our research status shall be described in terms of an iterative procedure. The present status already contains the results of the interim evaluation (see Sect. 4.2). Ideas and suggestions for improvement of the focus group were reviewed for consistency and adopted if positive. Decision made when choosing the *(1) design level* remains in place. In line with the works of Yams et al. [3] and Alsheibani et al. [12] we argue for a concept with multiple AI dimensions. This includes a one-dimensional sequence of discrete stages (Table 1) and multidimensional maturity stages (see Fig. 2).

The bottom-down approach has proven itself analogously in the selection of an implementation approach in step *(2) select approach*. One is that AI dimensions have been identified, analyzed, and evaluated during our preliminary work. This approach is recommended when the research domain has reached a certai level of maturity. This conclusion is supported by both, related work and other AIMM approaches. The definition of the dimensions is based on other AIMM approaches and on identified research gaps being described in detail in our preliminary work. A description of the defined AI dimensions can be found in Table 1 These dimensions comprise the following dimensions: (1) strategy, (2) organization, (3) Culture/Mindset, (4) technology, (5) data, (6) privacy und (7) ethics. The table also includes objectives, scope for action and potential measures for each dimension. An interim evaluation result revealed a shift from an alphabetical order to a hierarchical logical sequence.

Table 1. AIMM dimensions and scope of action

#	Dimension	Objective n	Scope of action and potential measures
1	Strategy	Establishes the strategic enablers for the commercial AI application	• AI vision for AI usage • AI data strategy • AI strategy successfully communicated • AI field and use cases • AI process model
2	Organization	Provides framework conditions (resources and structures) to enable AI application	• AI Experts • AI further education and training • AI incentive system • AI governance structure • AI standard process for projects
3	Culture/Mindset	A workplace culture of innovation and change is created and positive attributed towards AI	• AI information workshop • Leaders promote AI • AI as opportunity • Innovation-friendly atmosphere • AI contact person defined
4	Technology	Delivers technologies and tools that create value using AI	• Access to AI hardware • Access to AI software • Developed and applied AI applications • Usage of AI technologies • Added value through AI
5	Data	Creates foundations to enable AI technologies	• Usage of data management systems • Collecting data for AI usage • AI process pipeline • Available Data for AI • Data quality generate added value
6	Privacy	Added value through AI under the premise of compliant handling of sensitive data	• Awareness AI privacy regulations • Data protection officer in place • Technical and organizational measures regarding AI privacy • Anonymization mechanism for processing personal data • Privacy assurance system
7	Ethics	Addressing ethical concerns when using AI	• Code of (ethic) values • Awareness human-machine relationship • Ethical guidelines/principles for AI • Compliance process with guidelines • Review of AI sensitive and security-related decisions

The AIMM is completed by the definition of AI maturity levels. The model was presented in outline in an earlier work and has been improved punctually. The maturity level designations have been adapted and their descriptions have been revised:

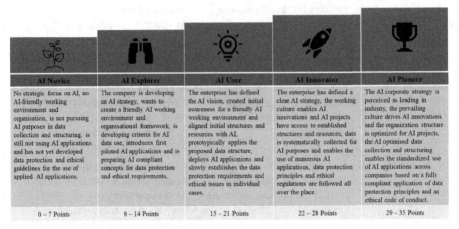

AI Novice	AI Explorer	AI User	AI Innovator	AI Pioneer
No strategic focus on AI, no AI-friendly working environment and organisation, is not pursuing AI purposes in data collection and structuring, is still not using AI applications and has not yet developed data protection and ethical guidelines for the use of applied AI applications.	The company is developing an AI strategy, wants to create a friendly AI working environment and organisational framework, is developing criteria for AI data use, introduces first piloted AI applications and is preparing AI compliant concepts for data protection and ethical requirements.	The enterprise has defined the AI vision, created initial awareness for a friendly AI working environment and aligned initial structures and resources with AI, prototypically applies the proposed data structure, deploys AI applications and slowly establishes the data protection requirements and ethical issues in individual cases.	The enterprise has defined a clear AI strategy, the working culture enables AI innovations and AI projects have access to established structures and resources, data is systematically collected for AI purposes and enables the use of numerous AI applications, data protection principles and ethical regulations are followed all over the place.	The AI corporate strategy is perceived as leading in industry, the prevailing culture drives AI innovations and the organization structure is optimized for AI projects, data collection and structuring enables the standardized use of AI applications across companies based on a fully compliant application of data protection principles and an ethical code of conduct.
0 – 7 Points	8 – 14 Points	15 – 21 Points	22 – 28 Points	29 – 35 Points

Fig. 2. Score-based determination of the AI maturity level

The AI dimensions, their characteristics, the AIMM and the included maturity levels are presented. Step (3) *design model selection* requires detail for each abstraction level. None of the AIMMs identified in advance offer both the possibility of a general classification within their model nor that of a self-classification on a questionnaire basis or information technology DA. In terms of consistent maturity level identification, we are particularly concerned with the explainability of our approach. Organizations should be able to perform the maturity assessment independently, transparently, and comprehensibly. For this purpose, the level of fulfillment of each AI dimension must be determined. The maturity assessment process can be supported by an expert. But a self-evaluation should also be feasible.

Adapted from Gassmann et al. MM [15] from the smart city domain, our AIMM enables a targeted and supported self-assessment based on yes/no questions. For each of the seven AI dimensions, five easy-to-answer yes/no questions were defined in logical order to match the defined maturity levels. One point is scored for each yes-answered question. All points scored are added up. As a result, a total of 35 points can be achieved. Furthermore, specific point ranges were assigned to each of the five maturity levels (see Fig. 2). For example, 18 yes answered questions equals to 18 points, meaning that the *AI User* maturity level has been reached. The questions for the respective AI dimensions are listed in excerpts in Table 2 and are tested by the interim evaluation. The complete AIMM Dimensions and related questions are available online.[1]

---

[1] The latest development status can be found at https://github.com/hochschule-pforzheim/aimm.

Table 2. Exemplary excerpt of the AIMM dimensions and question sets for self-assessment

1. Strategy	
1.1	Is there a company-wide vision for the use of AI?
1.2	Do you have a data strategy that fosters AI?
1.3	Are the AI goals defined and communicated in a way that is understandable to the workforce?
1.4	Are AI fields of business defined and use cases described?
1.5	Is there a process model for the use of AI?
2. Organization	
2.1	Do you have experts / experienced staff in using AI?
2.2	Is further education and training in the AI field supported?
2.3	Are there incentive systems to engage with AI?
2.4	Has a governance structure been created to manage AI development?
2.5	Are standard processes established for AI projects?
...	

4.2 Interim Evaluation

The interim evaluation is part of the iterative AIMM development approach. We prepared a four-step evaluation process to support further development of AIMM. First, the AIMM was designed as digital questionnaire. In addition to the 35 questions, further explanations were given, and the MM was illustrated. In the second step, a set of three different case studies was developed. These case studies describe three different AI maturity levels. Each case study refers to a fictitious company and explains its AI activities. The information contained in the case studies enables the user to assess the AI maturity level independently. In a third step, a feedback questionnaire was created. The overarching evaluation criteria are problem adequacy, consistency, and completeness. These were supplemented by detailed questions (quantitative and qualitative) on the superordinate criteria. In a fourth step, a focus group was defined, and the implementation of the evaluation was organized. Twenty-five students from advanced bachelor's and master's degree programs in information systems and industrial engineering (with AI as specialization) were selected as participants. Students have completed at least one practical phase in companies (practical semester) and are currently working part-time in a company (working students). The survey was carried out anonymously and in compliance with data protection regulations. The findings (see Fig. 3 bis Fig. 5) from the feedback survey are listed as follows:

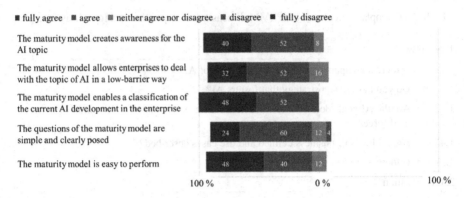

Fig. 3. Evaluation results of the criterion problem adequacy

The participants confirmed the problem adequacy. The MM provides added value in terms of raising awareness. It offers a low-threshold access to the topic of AI. Marginal negative feedback on the clarity of the questions was taken as an opportunity to simplify them once again. For most of the participants conducting the MM was easy (Fig. 3).

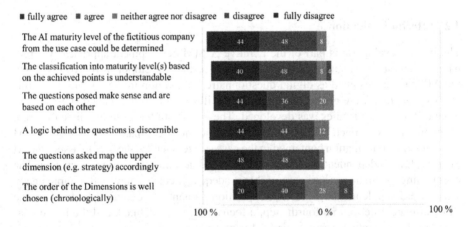

Fig. 4. Evaluation results of the criterion consistency

The consistency criterion was covered by six questions. The participants evaluated this category positively too. Accordingly, the degree of maturity can be determined. A logic in the design is confirmed as well. Criticism was expressed about the chronologically presented order of the dimensions. We see this point of view equally and have made a change to a hierarchical order (see Fig. 4).

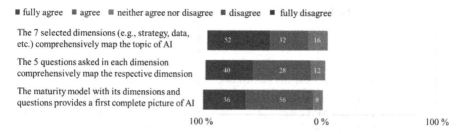

Fig. 5. Evaluation results of the criterion completeness

The findings of the completeness test turn out to be positive. The participants agree with the AI dimensions as well as with the five accompanying questions. The involvement of employees was suggested as a contextual note to the questions. This proposal was considered in dimension 3 Culture/Mindset (see Fig. 5).

In response to the question of what the first overall impression of the MM is, the subjects answered an average of 8.2 on a scale of 0 very poor to 10 very good. The feedback and suggestions for improvement were implemented. The revised status is already presented in Sect. 4.1. We consider the interim evaluation to be predominantly positive and will proceed to the next phase.

4.3 Conception of Transfer and Evaluation

According to the applied methodology [11], a transfer and evaluation concept must be developed in the fifth step. This step is discussed in this section. It addresses the positively evaluated AIMM state of development. The subsequent implementation of the AIMM as DA forms the basis for a final evaluation. The indicated interface between implementation and evaluation should be considered. Table 3 provides an overview of the two conceptions.

The focus groups are identical for both the implementation and the final evaluation. This was already considered in the design phase (see [1]). The technical implementation of the current AIMM online questionnaire into a stand-alone software based AIMM tool will be carried out in the next step. In parallel, a describing AIMM documentation and further focus group-oriented publication will take place. The implemented AIMM tool will be used for the final evaluation with the focus groups. The focus will primarily be on users (mainly organizations in SMEs). After the self-determination of the maturity level, either interviews or (online) feedback questions are envisaged. Evaluation results will provide information on improvement potentials. During a re-evaluation, remarks can be included and the AIMM can reach a higher level of maturity.

Table 3. Characteristics of transfer and evaluation

	Transfer concept for implementation	Evaluation concept for the final evaluation
Focus groups	• Users • AI/IT experts • Scientists	
Input	• AIMM State of development • Online AIMM catalog of questionnaires	• Software-based AIMM tool • Case Study from interim evaluation
Activities	• Technical implementation software based tool • Preparation of AIMM description • Composing documents AIMM knowledge transfer	• Definition of evaluation criteria and questionnaire • Identification of further experts and users • Self-assessment of AIMM maturity level • Conduct questionnaire/interview with focus group
Output	• Software-based AIMM tool • AIMM documentation • AIMM Publication	• Evaluation results • If necessary Re-Evaluation

5 Conclusion and Future Work

As key technology, AI applications will create added value in organizations. To achieve competitive advantages, companies must address this and develop competencies and capacities. We observe that especially SMEs still have difficulties in doing so. Besides a lack of resources and know-how, there are often no initial touchpoints with AI. A lack of adequate getting started offers can be observed (see [1]). Our AIMM development seeks to overcome this issue. Our AIMM encompasses measures of the current situation through self-assessment and furthermore reveals potentials.

We outlined the current design and structure of AIMM, its dimensions and their implications. The iterative development approach we selected favors a progressive maturity of AIMM itself. We set value on the self-assessment of maturity by organizations. For this purpose, we have developed a set of 35 easy-to-answer yes/no questions. This approach offers a good opportunity for the initial classification of AI status quo, a finding we were able to confirm with the interim evaluation. The 35 questions represent a good balance between the time spent on the maturity assessment and the meaningfulness of the results. This way, we respond adequately to RQ1.

The interim evaluation serves as a classification of the state of research. To this end, the current state was depicted as a digital questionnaire. Three designed case studies were processed by 25 participants and the degree of maturity was determined as a result. The state of research was then assessed by means of an anonymous feedback form. Emphasis was placed on the areas of problem adequacy, consistency, and completeness, which were detailed through questions (see Sect. 4.2). Valuable feedback has already been used to improve the AIMM. We consider the results of the interim evaluation positive and respond herewith to RQ2.

The applied methodology [11] describes friction points between later implementation and final evaluation. The intersections should be defined in an early phase. For this purpose, we created a concept describing further procedure for the implementation and its evaluation. In addition to focus groups, we specifically define required inputs, activities, and outputs. The developed concept offers us the possibility to start the implementation work and addresses RQ3.

Our work created a solid foundation for a user-friendly AIMM targeted at SMEs. The conducted interim evaluation achieved positive feedback of the current research state. We are building on this and planning further steps, which can be summarized in two main areas: First, we address incremental improvements to the current state. Our AIMM determines the AI maturity level. Improvement measures based on AI maturity level state cannot be suggest. We want to add this feature. In parallel, the AIMM is to undergo further iteration stages and be continuously enriched with further information. The latest updates will be available online (see GitHub Repository[2]). Second, we plan to apply the developed transfer and evaluation concept in practice as soon as possible. This procedure includes the steps (6) *Implementation* and (7) *Evaluation*. The implementation as a software-based tool is the subsequent objective of our research. Implementation as a standalone tool is a challenge that should be done in a timely manner. As result of this evaluation approach, we expect extensive feedback from our intended target group. A final evaluation with the focus groups of users and IT and AI experts is scheduled as well. In doing so, we also collaborate closely with regional stakeholders to reach the most diverse evaluation group possible.

References

1. Schuster, T., Waidelich, L., Volz, R.: Maturity models for the assessment of artificial intelligence in small and medium-sized enterprises. In: Wrycza, S., Maślankowski, J. (eds.) Digital Transformation. Lecture Notes in Business Information Processing, vol. 429, pp. 22–36. Springer, Cham (2021). https://doi.org/10.1007/978-3-030-85893-3_2
2. Khoshgoftar, M., Osman, O.: Comparison of maturity models. In: 2009 2nd IEEE International Conference on Computer Science and Information Technology, pp. 297–301. IEEE (2009). https://doi.org/10.1109/ICCSIT.2009.5234402
3. Yams, N.B., Richardson, V., Shubina, G.E., Albrecht, S., Gillblad, D.: Integrated AI and innovation management: the beginning of a beautiful friendship. TIM Rev. **10**, 5–18 (2020). https://doi.org/10.22215/timreview/1399
4. Dahlin, G.: What can we learn from process maturity models – a literature review of models addressing process maturity. Int. J. Process Manage. Benchmarking **10**, 495 (2020). https://doi.org/10.1504/IJPMB.2020.110285
5. De Bruin, T., Rosemann, M., Freeze, R., Kulkarni, U.: Understanding the main phases of developing a maturity assessment model. In: 16th Australasian Conference on Information Systems, vol. 109, pp. 8–19 (2005)
6. Richter, A., Gačić, T., Kölmel, B., Waidelich, L.: Künstliche Intelligenz und potenzielle Anwendungsfelder im Marketing. In: Deutscher Dialogmarketing Verband (ed.) Dialogmarketing Perspektiven 2018/2019, pp. 31–52. Springer Fachmedien Wiesbaden, Wiesbaden (2019). https://doi.org/10.1007/978-3-658-25583-1_2

---

[2] Available under https://github.com/hochschule-pforzheim/aimm.

7. Stahl, B.C., Wright, D.: Ethics and Privacy in AI and big data: implementing responsible research and innovation. IEEE Secur. Privacy **16**, 26–33 (2018). https://doi.org/10.1109/MSP.2018.2701164

8. Carr, S.: 'AI gone mental': engagement and ethics in data-driven technology for mental health. J. Ment. Health **29**, 125–130 (2020). https://doi.org/10.1080/09638237.2020.1714011

9. Jobin, A.: Ethische Künstliche Intelligenz. - von Prinzipien zu Prozessen. In: Hengstschläger, M. (ed.) Digitaler Wandel und Ethik, pp. 144–159. Ecowin, Elsbethen (2020)

10. Hevner, A.R., March, S.T., Park, J., Ram, S.: Design science in information systems research. MIS Q. **28**, 75 (2004). https://doi.org/10.2307/25148625

11. Becker, J., Knackstedt, R., Pöppelbuß, J.: Developing maturity models for IT management. Bus. Inf. Syst. Eng. **1**, 213–222 (2009). https://doi.org/10.1007/s12599-009-0044-5

12. Alsheibani, S., Cheung, Y., Messom, C.: Towards an Artificial Intelligence Maturity Model: From Science Fiction to Business Facts. In: PACIS23rd Pacific Asia Conference on Information Systems, vol. 46 (2019)

13. Holmstrom, J.: From AI to digital transformation: The AI readiness framework. Bus. Horiz. **65**(3), 329–339 (2021). https://doi.org/10.1016/j.bushor.2021.03.006

14. vom Brocke, J., Winter, R., Hevner, A., Maedche, A.: Special Issue Editorial –Accumulation and Evolution of Design Knowledge in Design Science Research: A Journey Through Time and Space. JAIS, vol. 21, 520–544 (2020). https://doi.org/10.17705/1jais.00611

15. Gassmann, O., Böhm, J., Palmié, M.F.: Smart City. Innovationen für die vernetzte Stadt - Geschäftsmodelle und Management. Hanser, München (2018)

Dynamic Interplay of Humans and AI in Collaborative Networks

Process Wins and Losses in Dynamic Human-AI Interplay - A Socio-psychological Research Perspective on Collaborative Performance

Kimberly Meyer[(✉)] and Bernd-Friedrich Voigt

South Westphalia University of Applied Sciences, Iserlohn, Meschede, Germany
`meyer.kimberly@fh-swf.de`

Abstract. We analyze socio-psychological process wins and losses in relation to Human-AI collaborative performance. The reported heterogeneous effects of the body of literature on group performance in relation to structural and processual determinants are briefly summarized. Based on this, two of the most relevant socio-psychological aspects of Human-AI collaborative performance are highlighted: Accuracy of the shared mental model and fulfillment of basic human needs. The paper concludes by proposing an empirical and experimental research program that addresses under-researched socio-psychological phenomena in Human-AI collaboration that can be held accountable for process wins and losses.

Keywords: Human-AI interaction · Socio-psychology · Collaborative performance

1 Introduction

While Industry 4.0 emphasized digitization and the associated transformation processes, the current swing toward Industry & Society 5.0 (re)focuses on the social dimension of a solution-oriented integration of humans and technology [1, 2]. At the same time, human-technology interaction further evolves as machines can be designed on anthropomorphic features and be perceived as having human-like attributes or even engaging in social behavior [3]. In practice, human employees are increasingly confronted with outsourcing their tasks to machines, receiving digital support for human weaknesses, and interacting with a team member that has perceived artificial intelligence (AI) instead of human intelligence [4, 5].

The relationship between people and machines is therefore changing. While the machine used to be a tool, AI-based technology is now capable of taking over human competencies such as pattern recognition, planning, and prediction [6]. Consequently, AI-powered applications can be called *intelligent agents*. Intelligent agents are defined as technology that can act and react proactively and autonomously so that interaction with other actors emerges [7].

A key change in human–machine interaction seems to lie in the pursuit of common goals: Humans do *not just use* the intelligent agent but *collaborate* with it in a dynamic

Published by Springer Nature Switzerland AG 2022
L. M. Camarinha-Matos et al. (Eds.): PRO-VE 2022, IFIP AICT 662, pp. 289–302, 2022.
https://doi.org/10.1007/978-3-031-14844-6_23

interplay [8]. Humans need to coordinate with non-human team members, distribute autonomy and make decisions jointly. In this context, the actual technological capabilities of the intelligent agent play a subordinate role. Of primary importance appears to be the team's perception of the non-human team member as intelligent and social [9]. Thus, we argue that real collaboration between humans and intelligent agents is emerging and, that this collaboration is influenced by psychological and physiological human factors, technological requirements of AI, and socio-psychological processes that arise from the interactive nature of collaboration.

Empirical research examining the interplay between humans and intelligent agents has consistently identified socio-psychological processes between the two actors. For example, when interacting with an intelligent agent, people have been found to follow social norms such as politeness [9, 10], establish a trusting relationship [3, 11, 12], and perceive the agent based on the social cognitive dimensions of warmth and competence [13]. However, currently, the evidence gathered in this line of research seems to be heterogeneous and mostly neglects the socio-psychological processes at the group level. An exemption to this is the concept of autonomous agent teammate-likeness [14]. Autonomous agent teammate-likeness relates human attributes to those of the intelligent agent and characterizes the teammate-likeness based on the agentic ability, altruistic intent, task interdependence, task-independent relationship building, depth of communication, and synchronized mental models. Relevant determinants can therefore be captured to distinguish whether technology is an infrastructure element or a social actor. In addition, the concept defines moderators that determine the quality of collaboration (e.g., trust, attribution to failure, human knowledge, skills, and abilities) and its outcomes. Even social group phenomena are already addressed in the representations of these outcomes (e.g., group cohesion that describes the strength of the relationships that bind the members of a group [14]). What remains open is a deeper analysis of the underlying group processes. Which other socio-psychological processes can also be found and held accountable for collaborative performance in human-AI teams? And, by which conditioning factors are they triggered?

With respect to human-only teams, socio-psychological processes have been intensively researched. Various theoretical and methodological approaches have produced a heterogeneous body of knowledge regarding aspects such as (among others) group size and collaborative performance [15], relative richness and evenness of the team composition and the resulting of various outcomes [16], social identity, and the building of ingroups and outgroups [17], group heterogeneity and the building of faultlines in social conflict [18], social influence and the building of trust [19], functional diversity and the building of innovative capacity [20].

In summary team performance is (a) strongly dependent on the task-related variety of characteristics and resources of team members [21] and (b) on structural variables and team processes that support or hinder the utilization of the given resource base [22, 23]. Thus, the underlying body of psychological theories can be sorted into two clusters. Theories, that highlight the value in relative diversity can be attributed to a structural resource-oriented perspective [24]. Theories, that highlight processes wins and losses that effect collaborative performance can be attributed to a transaction-cost perspective

[25]. Even though the literature that relates to these theory families is extensive, it still provides a heterogeneous picture regarding performance outcomes [26].

For a structured exploration of these heterogeneous effects in human-AI teams, we relate to a well-established process-based framework of collaborative performance. From our point of view, Hackman and Morris' [27] framing model of group performance allows to interpret the diversity of findings on traditional human-to-human collaboration and to expand the scope of the model to the newer facets of human-AI-collaboration. The original model defines group performance as the possible performance being the sum of individual group members' potentials minus process losses plus process wins (see Fig. 1).

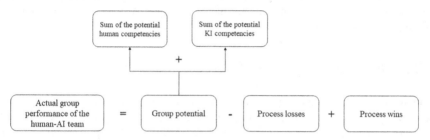

Fig. 1. The concept of group performance by Hackmann and Morris [27]

Process losses are influences that reduce the actual group potential (e.g., poor coordination, loss of motivation). Process wins would allow to harvest or even further increase the actual group potential (e.g., synergies between group members). In the case of human-AI teams, the group potential would be the sum of all the competencies – human as well as artificial competencies. Process losses would correspondingly be coordination or motivation losses triggered by the addition of the intelligent agent to the team. For example, coordination problems with the AI due to a lack of competence in handling or threats to the human identity would be conceivable. On the other hand, there would be process gains resulting from synergies between human and artificial intelligence (e.g., AI has greater memory capacity and quicker accessibility, whereas humans might easier find creative solutions beyond proven setups).

To illustrate this perspective, we introduce a demonstrative example: A team of psychologists has the task of putting together workgroups that have the highest possible fit. Competencies, personality variables, social behavior, likes, dislikes, and past work performances must be considered. The selected employees should fit as well as possible to their task and with the other team members. To solve this task, the team has an intelligent agent that receives information about the different variables and develops team-staffing suggestions. When these are being rejected, the psychologists must provide a rationale so that the intelligent agent can optimize its suggestions. Structural elements in this case would be all conditions that result from the group coming together in this specific context. For example, these would be the skills of the psychologists, the data sources, the structure of the decision situation, the design of the AI, etc. Process elements would arise from the interaction taking place. This could be sympathy effects, the expansion of shared information when a proposal is rejected, or knowledge about the decision behavior of the AI. Whether the respective elements are process gains or losses will be determined during the literature work and further research.

The aim of this paper is to structure human-AI collaboration based on Hackman and Morris' process model of team performance [27] and thus to help categorize existing and future research insights on socio-psychological processes in human-AI interaction as process gains or losses. We considered the model's division into structural and process elements, too, so that a recourse to the underlying theory families of socio-psychology becomes transparent. Therefore, the results of this paper should be considered as initial conclusions on how collaboration in human-AI teams can be structured to be as productive as possible. Based on this, further research gaps could be identified and labelled more systematically across disciplines. This would again allow designing a consistent research program on collaborative performance in human-AI interplay to be pursued in subsequent research activities.

2 Identification of Relevant Research

To identify relevant research in human-AI interaction, we conducted a targeted search for research communities working on this topic. The following communities were identified: *ACM Transactions on Computer–Human Interaction* [4, 14], *Association for the Advancement of Artificial Intelligence* [9, 10] and *Advances in Information and Communication Technology* [28, 29]. In addition, papers regarding socio-psychological processes in human-AI teams have been published in various journals such as *Theoretical Issues in Ergonomics Science* [14], *Scientific Reports* [30], and *Journal of the Academy of Marketing Science* [3]. Within these communities and journals, we identified relevant contributions by theoretical reference to socio-psychological theories or models and then examined them in terms of processual wins and losses in human-AI teams.

2.1 Trust and Relatedness as Basis for Process Wins and Losses

Following the given research foci, a critical element in creating process wins in human-AI teams appears to be the matter of trust [3, 11, 12]. Jennings et al. [8] postulate trust as one of the most important processes in the collaboration between humans and AI. They assume that it is a necessary condition for functions such as coordination, decision-making, and flexible autonomy. Richards and Stedmon also support this assumption [31]. They define trust based on the human understanding of what the machine is currently doing and what it will do next. According to the authors, a shared mental model is created when this information is available. The concept of mental models is used in the understanding of Johnson-Laird [32]. He describes a mental model as an internal representation of integrated information into an inner concept. Through these models, perceptual processes are navigated, new information is categorized, and conclusions are drawn. Takko et al. also describe in their study that shared mental models were able to increase team performance of human-AI teams [30]. Forming a shared mental model, therefore, seems to represent a process win for human-AI group performance. However, it is important to understand that this process win is initially rooted in a structural aspect of team composition because shared mental models are more likely to arise and sustain when team members are similar and form a homogenous group [33]. Paradoxically, shared mental models can also result in process losses. Once a shared mindset evolves, it is secured by a strong social ingroup effect, that tends to negate relevant external information or feedback [34].

We transfer the concept of shared mental models to the exemplary case of the team of psychologists in collaboration with an intelligent agent. The concept implies that a sufficient human-to-human as well as human-to-machine homogeneity is needed across all ties of the team network to enable the expected process wins. Not only need the human team members understand what the machine is currently doing and what it will do next, they also need to feel a shared identity with the AI. In addition to this, the Human-AI team needs to set up adequate measures to ensure that the shared mental model does not lead to the building of dysfunctional subgroups or hinder from seeing and interpreting contradicting external information objectively.

Some studies, which address the structural homogeneity aspect of how to describe the trust relationship in human-AI interaction, examine the influence of anthropomorphic traits. Anthropomorphic traits can be interpreted as a source of both, process losses and process wins. Yet, the effect of these characteristics is not clear. In the studies of Foeher and Germelmann [11] and Pitardi and Marriott [12], the humanization of AI had a positive impact on the trust relationship. However, Ferrari et al. [35] and Mende et al. [36], showed that anthropomorphic AI features posed a threat to human identity. Appel et al. [37] noted a sense of eeriness when service robots exhibited stronger humanization. Finally, Khadpe et al. [13] focused on the nature of humanized traits. To this end, they manipulated the representation of the metaphor through which the AI acted concerning the social-cognitive dimensions of warmth and competence. Individuals were found to have significantly more positive attitudes toward AI when its metaphor was high warmth and low competence.

2.2 Fulfillment of Basic Human Needs as Basis for Process Wins and Losses

According to Fiske et al. [38], the dimensions of warmth and competence are the foundation of social structures because they provide information about competition and status. Warmth is associated with friendly and approachable behavior, and it is considered an indicator, that the other person has good intentions. Competence, on the other hand, is an indicator of whether a person can conduct their good intentions and thus make the interaction successful. In human interactions, people who are rated high on one dimension and low on the other elicit ambivalent reactions. These are expressed, for example, in mixed stereotypes. A common mixed stereotype toward the elderly might be that they are perceived as friendly and open (high warmth), but also as slow, needy, and incapable (low competence) [39].

This ambivalence was not detected in the interaction between humans and AI. On the contrary, if the AI metaphor was a teenager or toddler, the interaction with the AI was rated significantly better than if it was an executive or professor. One assumption could be that the perceived human competence poses a threat to human identity. As research by Mende et al. [36] shows, anthropomorphic characteristics of intelligent agents can cause humans to feel threatened and exhibit more behavior that serves as self-regulation (e.g., purchasing status goods, seeking social affiliation). This behavior ensures the need for competence in comparison to the AI. This would imply that humans compare themselves to AI in terms of competencies if this dimension is humanized. Humanization would therefore lead to a violation of the human need for competence. This again poses a problem because competence, along with social relatedness and autonomy, is considered one of the three basic human needs necessary to ensure elevated levels of performance and well-being. If these needs are not met, defensive needs develop that serve as substitutes but prevent actual need fulfillment [40]. Accordingly, the violation of the basic human need for competence represents a potential process loss not only at the level of competence, but also in terms of autonomy [4, 5].

Incorporating the research of Jiang et al. [4] and Wang et al. [5] into this discussion, one could argue that the participants' expressed desire for full agency may indicate a violation of the autonomy need. In each of these papers, participants were asked about their perceptions of semi-autonomous intelligent agents in their field of work (qualitative research and data science). In both cases, an ambivalent relationship became apparent. While participants assumed that the use increased efficiency, they expressed concerns [4] and a strong need for control, too [5]. Building on the concept of Jennings et al. [8], this desire represents a process loss because the flexible distribution of autonomy is a necessity in a human-AI team. However, the perspective on satisfying human needs in human-AI teams is not exclusively negative. Wynne and Lyons [14] argue that the need for relatedness can have a positive influence on the collaboration in human-AI teams. The intelligent agent is viewed as a social entity and can therefore provide a source of social connection so that the need for relatedness is satisfied. If human team members and non-human intelligent agents share an increased need for social relatedness, this characteristic can constitute a process win for the group's performance.

In addition to the strong need for social relatedness, there are other characteristics of team members that can be valued as process wins. Süße et al. [29] discuss nine human competencies that are beneficial when interacting with an AI. They distinguish between cognitive, emotional, and social competencies. The social competencies refer to communication with the AI. Communication should take place comprehensibly and constantly in the form of an ongoing dialogue. The emotional level also contains a communicative aspect, namely the negotiation of one's rest periods with the AI. The general perception of the AI as a virtual team member is also categorized under emotional competencies. Four competencies are grouped under cognitive competencies, which relate to understanding the AI (cues must be interpreted, abilities must be assessed, and ways of operating must be reflected upon) and dealing with sensitive data. Frequent occurrence of these competencies among human team members thus represents a process gain within human-AI teams. However, it is still unclear, if and to what extend non-human team members are expected to have and show similar competencies through cognitive, social, or emotional team behaviors.

On an interactional level, so far, trust as a process win has been discussed primarily. However, other interaction effects that could represent process losses need also be considered. One of these effects, already well known from human-to-human socio-psychological research, could be the phenomenon of groupthink [41]. Groupthink describes a process that suppresses dissenting opinions for the sake of group harmony, leading to poor decision-making. A group's belief in invulnerability and superior group morality are typical groupthink indicators. Collaborative decisions are collectively justi-fied, and individuals with dissenting opinions are stereotypically perceived. This creates a high pressure to conform, leading to self-censorship, information barriers, and an illu-sion of uniformity [41]. Groups with a high degree of cohesion or a directive leadership style are prone to this phenomenon.

Okamura and Yamada [42] investigated over-trusting in intelligent agents and dis-cussed the resulting security risks. The authors propose so-called trust calibration cues to avoid over-trusting. The authors define over-trusting as the overestimation of the capa-bilities and reliability of intelligent agents. In their study, Okamura, and Yamada show that providing cues of over-trusting to team members significantly aligned trust and the actual capabilities of the AI [42]. Over-trust can be understood considering the group-think phenomenon, especially when it occurs in human-AI teams. The overestimation of the AI's capabilities and thus of the overall group potential could lead to the invul-nerability illusion described above and thus represent a process loss. In the light of this research focus we conclude that the role of intelligent agents as perceived social team members in preventing or upholding groupthink and subsequent performance issues still needs more attention in future research.

3 Preliminary Synthesis of the Underlying Body of Socio-psychological Theorizing

How can socio-psychological process wins and process losses in human-AI teams be sys-temized for a better understanding of team collaborative performance? We approached this question by building on the concept of group performance by Hackman and Morris [27]. First, we argued, that intelligent agents can be seen and perceived as social actors on a team level. Next, we underlined that group performance consists of the potential perfor-mance of the individual human and non-human members minus the process losses plus the process wins. Finally, we identified socio-psychological perspectives in the existing body of human-AI literature and indicated, how they can be related to process wins and/or losses.

Our procedure showed that a socio-psychological perspective is well justified and applicable to research on human-AI collaborative performance. We also showed that the current discussion can be cataloged by two dominant perspectives, namely correlates of shared mental models (e. g. groupthink effects) and effects of basic human needs (e. g. trust). For each of these approaches, we delivered unsolved questions for future research. We synthesized our transfer of socio-psychological approaches to an improved understanding of group performance in Human-AI collaboration as depicted in Fig. 2.

Process wins refer to the accuracy of the shared mental model and the associated explainability and predictability of the AI's actions. In addition, certain human charac-teristics of the AI (e.g., the perception of the AI as warm) promote trust and can promote the satisfaction of the human need for relatedness, especially when individuals exhibit a heightened need in this regard. On the human side, certain competencies are bene-ficial, which positively influence the communication process with AI. These relate to goal-oriented communication and the ability to understand and reflect on the mode of operation of the AI. Process losses also relate to the accuracy of the shared mental model

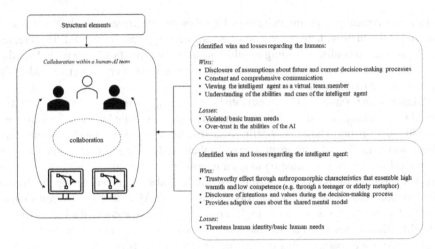

Fig. 2. Visualization of process wins and losses in human-AI teams

and the possibility of satisfying basic human needs. Regarding the shared mental model, there is a risk of over-trusting the AI, which can lead to an illusion of infallibility and thus become a security risk. Furthermore, process losses can occur due to the violation of basic human needs, especially competence and autonomy.

What can be done to counteract these losses and promote benefits? To foster humans' trust in AI, enough information needs to be available so that they can create a mental model that provides reliable information about the current and future actions of AI. Especially the communication of intentions and values during the decision-making process seems to be of importance [14]. In addition, it might be possible to find ways to make the human mental model accessible to the AI and check it for inconsistencies. To ensure this insight, teams should implement structures that promote the sharing of the mental model. For example, after a decision by the AI, team members could be asked for their assumptions about the decision-making process and their hypothesis about future decisions. The AI would integrate all the information into a connected model, thus making a phenomenon that is otherwise only mentally represented a subject of discussion. Inconsistencies, discrepancies, and misconceptions about the decision-making process could be revealed and corrected. This would increase the explainability and predictability of AI behavior, as the shared mental model is increasingly adapted to the actual decision-making process. Okamura and Yamada advocate a similar principle by with their trust calibration cues [42].

Following the work of Khadpe et al. [13], it is also recommended that AI be represented with a metaphor that involves a lot of warmth and little competence, such as children or the elderly. This is believed to spare the human's need for competence. It is also assumed that this will increase the fulfillment of social relatedness. The possible violation of the need for autonomy must also be considered. Team members need to feel that they can make decisions independently while allowing the AI to act (partially) autonomously as well. It is assumed that trust is a key mediator. The explainability and predictability of the AI create reliability, which may lead to overcoming an overbearing need for control and satisfying the actual need for autonomy.

4 Ideas for an Experimental Research Program on Socio-psychological Aspects of Human-AI Collaborative Performance

The theoretical assumptions outlined above need further empirical evaluation in future research. Table 1 provides a list of variables to be tested. We differentiated by structural and process relevance and we referenced the research collected and presented in this paper. Even though closely related to the existing body of literature, the list does not claim to be exhaustive.

Table 1. Selected variables for further research on socio-psychological processes in human-AI teams.

Variables	Refers to Structural or Process Elements	Is Already Studied by
Homogeneity	Structure element	to our knowledge not yet investigated
Diversity	Structure element	to our knowledge not yet investigated
Group Size	Structure element	to our knowledge not yet investigated
Task Requirements	Structure element	e.g., Takko et al. (2021)
Human Factors	Structure element	e.g., Süße et al. (2021)
Features of the Intelligent Agent	Structure element	e.g., Khadpe et al. (2020)
Trust	Process element	e.g., Okamura & Yamada (2020)
Building a Social identity	Process element	e.g., Mende et al. (2019)
Satisfaction of Basic Human Needs	Process element	e.g., Wynne & Lyons (2018)
Resources arising from Collaboration	Process element	e.g., Jennings et al. (2014)
Dysfunctional Group Processes arising from Collaboration	Process element	to our knowledge not yet investigated

4.1 Structural Elements to Be Investigated in Human-AI Teams

Structural elements that should be investigated in human-AI teams with respect to their socio-psychological effects on collaboration are homogeneity, diversity, group size, task requirements, human factors, and features of the intelligent agent.

Some of these variables have already been studied by the authors presented here. For example, Takko et al. [30] show the positive influence of human control on collaboration in a human-AI team. Süße et al. [29] discuss the relevance of communication skills and understanding of the intelligent agent as relevant human factors, and Khadpe et al. [13] point out the relevance of the social-cognitive dimensions of warmth and competence in human-AI interaction.

Here, too, the research could be further intensified to establish a broad empirical basis. In addition, variables that have not been investigated so far (to our knowledge) should also be included in the research, as they prove to be relevant determinants for the functionality of collaboration in human-only teams. One of the determinants is homogeneity. Research in human-only teams shows that similarity in terms of personal variables (e.g., demographic characteristics) [43] is beneficial for effective collaboration. However, a diverse professional background may favor collaboration on tasks that require creativity [22]. Homogeneity is therefore closely linked to diversity and should be examined in dependence. Especially because these effects are dependent on the structure of the task. Adding this observation to human-AI teams it is required to ask the following questions: What similarities and differences do people perceive in human-AI teams? How can they be manipulated? And what group processes are triggered as a result?

Socio-psychology research shows that group size affects collaboration in social groups. These include effects such as the Ringelmann effect (performance decreases in large groups) [44], deindividuation (the person is so immersed in the social role that individual identity is barely perceived) [45], and the bystander effect (the likelihood of helping behavior decreases with group size) [46]. Studies should translate these processes to human-AI teams and answer the question: how would these processes manifest themselves in human-AI teams? A distinction should be made between the number of human team members and the number of artificial team members.

Team performance is highly dependent on task characteristics [26]. Therefore, it could be assumed that the effectiveness of human-AI collaboration varies depending on the task requirements. Here, it could be investigated which tasks can be processed in human-AI teams in a particularly goal-oriented manner and how these tasks are characterized.

4.2 Process Elements to be Investigated in Human-AI Teams

The following socio-psychological processes in human-AI teams should be studied in more detail: Trust, social identity, the satisfaction of basic human needs, resources from collaboration, and dysfunctional group processes from collaboration.

Trust, social identity, and resources generated by collaboration have already been studied [3, 8, 42]. Okamura and Yamada [42] investigated both over-trust and under-trust and established both determinants and possibilities of adjusting the trust level. These findings could be applied to other populations and thus be deepened. Furthermore, processes of trust-building could be characterized in more detail. In this context, dysfunctional group processes, such as groupthink, could also be investigated. The over-trust described by the authors shows similarities with this classical socio-psychological phenomenon. The extent to which this also occurs in human-AI teams remains to be explored.

For functional group processes the work of Jennings et al. [8] may provide some indications. The authors establish a framework for human-AI teams with their HACs concept and define flexible autonomy as a resource in a HAC. Here, it could be investigated more deeply, what team members need to distribute autonomy flexibly and what influence this has on the basic human need for autonomy. According to Deci and Ryan [40], autonomy, competence, and relatedness are fundamental human needs necessary for optimal performance and well-being. The impact of relatedness on human-AI interaction is most notably discussed by Wynne and Lyons [14]. They assume that individuals can satisfy their need for relatedness in human-AI interaction. However, what impact this satisfaction and possible violation of needs may have remained open.

In addition to basic needs, human-AI interaction can also lead to the violation of human identity [36]. According to Tajfel and Turner [47], human identity has not only a personal aspect but also a social one. The latter is comprehensive and includes other group members. In human-AI teams, this would mean that the AI also becomes a part of the group identity. What influence this process has on the threat to human identity and whether this integration of a non-human identity is even possible needs to be investigated.

In addition to the structural and process elements presented here, other variables are conceivable. A standard classification of socio-psychological processes is e. g. social cognition processes, the construction of social identity, the influence of the social other on attitudes and attitude changes, and the accompanying social influence, group dynamics, and the resulting group performance. To profoundly characterize socio-psychological influencing factors in human-AI interaction, research in the relevant areas would be purposeful.

5 Conclusions

The considerations presented are founded conclusions. Although arguments were based on empirical studies, no empirical research was conducted. The structure of the report is based on the best of our knowledge but does not claim to be complete. Especially in interaction processes, additional processes wins and losses may have gone unnoticed. Decision-making processes in human-AI teams could be examined more closely in this context. The evaluation of AI regarding other relevant dimensions could also be of relevance. For example, the influence of perceived similarity between humans and the AI would be an interesting subject of investigation: Is the AI more trusted when perceived similarity increases? If so, which dimensions are decisive for this? Also, the influence of processes between human actors in a human-AI team has been less considered in this paper. Here, the question could be asked: How does the mere presence of an AI influence interpersonal interaction? These questions remain unanswered and require further research. This paper aims to provide a socio-psychological perspective on group performance in human-AI teams that allows to integrate such open research questions more systematically in the future.

In summary, in human-AI teams, human factors, AI factors, and interaction factors simultaneously influence group performance. Group performance can be defined as the summed potential performance of all team members minus process losses plus process wins. Process wins and losses have been focused on in this paper as a group-level output of the dynamic interplay between human and human-like artificial agents. Building on the presented argumentation, the two most important factors seem to be the accuracy of the shared mental model and the possibility of fulfilling the basic psychological human needs. For the shared mental model to be as accurate as possible, communication processes should take place that increases the AI's explainability and predictability. This results in trust, which is considered a crucial process win. To ensure that the basic psychological needs of humans are not compromised, the competence dimension of social cognition should not be represented by humanized features of AI. However, humanizations of the AI that pay into the social cognition dimension of warmth promote the need for social relatedness and improve trust. The reasoning of this paper is conceptual and therefore limited. Moreover, it is a very specific socio-psychological perspective on group performance, which is presumably conditioned by diverse influencing factors. Possibilities for empirical testing of the postulated theoretical considerations are discussed.

References

1. Deguchi, A., et al.: Society 5.0 A People-centric Super-smart Society. Hitachi-UTokyo Laboratory (H-UTokyo Lab.) The University of Tokyo Bunkyo-ku, Tokyo, Japan. Springer open (2020)
2. Özdemir, V., Hekim, N.: Birth of industry 5.0: making sense of big data with artificial intelligence, "the Internet of Things" and next-generation technology policy. Omics: J. Integr. Biol. **22**, 65–76 (2018)
3. Uysal, E., Alavi, S., Bezençon, V.: Trojan horse or useful helper? A relationship perspective on artificial intelligence assistants with humanlike features. J. Acad. Mark. Sci. 1–23 (2022)
4. Jiang, J.A., Wade, K., Fiesler, C., Brubaker, J.R.: Supporting serendipity: opportunities and challenges for human-AI collaboration in qualitative analysis. Proc. ACM Hum.-Comp. Inter. **5**, 1–23 (2021)
5. Wang, D., et al.: Human-AI collaboration in data science: exploring data scientists' perceptions of automated AI. Proc. ACM Hum.-Comp. Inter. **3**, 1–24 (2019)
6. Cichocki, A., Kuleshov, A.P.: Future trends for human-AI collaboration: a comprehensive taxonomy of AI/AGI Using Multiple Intelligences and Learning Styles. Comput. Intell. and Neurosci. (2021)
7. Wooldridge, M.: An Introduction to Multiagent Systems. Wiley, Hoboken (2009)
8. Jennings, N.R., et al.: Human-agent collectives. Commun. ACM **57**, 80–88 (2014)
9. Nass, C., Fogg, B.J., Moon, Y.: Can computers be teammates? Int. J. Hum.-Comp. Stud. **45**, 669–678 (1996)
10. Nass, C., Steuer, J., Tauber, E.R.: Computers are social actors. In: Proceedings of the SIGCHI Conference on Human Factors in Computing Systems, pp. 72–78 (1994).
11. Foehr, J., Germelmann, C.C.: Alexa, can I trust you? Exploring consumer paths to trust in smart voice-interaction technologies. J. Assoc. Cons. Res. **5**, 181–205 (2020)
12. Pitardi, V., Marriott, H.R.: Alexa, she's not human but… Unveiling the drivers of consumers' trust in voice-based artificial intelligence. Psych. Mark. **38**, 626–642 (2021)
13. Khadpe, P., Krishna, R., Fei-Fei, L., Hancock, J.T., Bernstein, M.S.: Conceptual metaphors impact perceptions of human-ai collaboration. Proc. ACM Hum.-Comp. Inter. **4**, 1–26 (2020)
14. Wynne, K.T., Lyons, J.B.: An integrative model of autonomous agent teammate-likeness. Theor. Issues Ergon. Sci. **19**, 353–374 (2018)
15. Biemann, T., Kearney, E.: Size does matter: how varying group sizes in a sample affect the most common measures of group diversity. Organiz. Res. Meth. **13**, 582–599 (2010)
16. Harrison, D.A., Klein, K.J.: What's the difference? Diversity constructs as separation, variety, or disparity in organizations. Acad. Manag. Rev. **32**, 1199–1228 (2007)

17. Chattopadhyay, P., Tluchowska, M., George, E.: Identifying the ingroup: a closer look at the influence of demographic dissimilarity on employee social identity. Acad. Manag. Rev. **29**, 180–202 (2004)
18. Bezrukova, K., Thatcher, S.M., Jehn, K.A.: Group heterogeneity and faultlines: Comparing alignment and dispersion theories of group composition. In: Behfar, K.J., Thompson, L.L. (eds.). (2007). Conflict in Organizational Groups: New Directions in Theory and Practice, pp. 57–92. Northwestern University Press, Evanston, IL (2007)
19. Liotsiou, D., Halford, S. Moreau. L.: Social influence: from contagion to a richer causal understanding. In: Spiro, E., Ahn, Y.Y. (eds.) Social Informatics. SocInfo 2016. LNCS, vol. 10047 pp. 116–132. Springer, Cham (2016). https://doi.org/10.1007/978-3-319-47874-6_9
20. Bunderson, J.S., Sutcliffe, K.M.: Comparing alternative conceptualizations of functional diversity in management teams: Process and performance effects. Acad. Manag. J. **45**(5), 875–893 (2002)
21. Webber, S.S., Donahue, L.M.: Impact of highly and less job-related diversity on work group cohesion and performance: a meta-analysis. J. Manag. **27**(2), 141–162 (2001)
22. Williams, K., O'Reilly, C.: Demography and diversity in organizations: a review of 40 years of research. Res. Organ. Behav. **20**, 77–140 (1998)
23. Joshi, A., Liao, H., Roh, H.: Bridging domains in workplace demography research: A review and reconceptualization. J. Manag. **37**(2), 521–552 (2011)
24. Van Knippenberg, D., Haslam, S.A., Platow, M.J.: Unity through diversity: Value-in-diversity beliefs, work group diversity, and group identification. Group Dyn.: Theory Res. Pract. **11**(3), 207–222 (2007)
25. Milliken, F.J., Martins, L.L.: Searching for common threads: Understanding the multiple effects of diversity in organizational groups. Acad. Manag. Rev. **21**(2), 402–433 (1996)
26. Mannix, E., Neale, M.A.: What differences make a difference? The promise and reality of diverse teams in organizations. Psych. Sci. Publ. Inter. **6**(2), 31–55 (2005)
27. Hackman, J.R., Morris, C.G.: Group tasks, group interaction process, and group performance effectiveness: a review and proposed integration. Adv. Experim. Soc. Psych. **8**, 45–99 (1975)
28. Camarinha-Matos, L.M., Afsarmanesh, H., Antonelli, D. (eds.): Collaborative networks and digital transformation: 20th IFIP WG 5.5 Working Conference on Virtual Enterprises, PRO-VE 2019, Turin, Italy, September 23–25, 2019, Proceedings, vol. 568. Springer Nature. (2019)
29. Süße, T., Kobert, M., Kries, C.: Antecedents of constructive human-AI collaboration: an exploration of human actors' key competencies. In: Camarinha-Matos, L.M., Boucher, X., Afsarmanesh, H. (eds.) Smart and Sustainable Collaborative Networks 4.0. PRO-VE 2021. IFIP Advances in Information and Communication Technology, vol. 629, pp. 113—124. Springer, Cham. https://doi.org/10.1007/978-3-030-85969-5_10
30. Takko, T., Bhattacharya, K., Monsivais, D., Kaski, K.: Human-agent coordination in a group formation game. Sci. Rep. **11**(1), 1–10 (2021)
31. Richards, D., Stedmon, A.: Designing for human–agent collectives: display considerations. Cogn., Tech. & Work. **19**(2), 251–261 (2017)
32. Johnson-Laird, P.N.: Mental Models: Towards a Cognitive Science of Language, Inference, and Consciousness. Harvard University Press (1983)
33. Mathieu, J.E., Heffner, T.S., Goodwin, G.F., Salas, E., Cannon-Bowers, J.A.: The influence of shared mental models on team process and performance. J. Appl. Psych. **85**(2), 273–283 (2000)
34. Matusov, E.: Intersubjectivity without agreement. Mind, Cult. Activ. **3**, 25–45 (1996)
35. Ferrari, F., Paladino, M.P., Jetten, J.: Blurring human–machine distinctions: anthropomorphic appearance in social robots as a threat to human distinctiveness. Int. J. Soc. Robot. **8**(2), 287–302 (2016)

36. Mende, M., Scott, M.L., van Doorn, J., Grewal, D., Shanks, I.: Service robots rising: How humanoid robots influence service experiences and elicit compensatory consumer responses. J. Mark. Res. **56**(4), 535–556 (2019)
37. Appel, M., Izydorczyk, D., Weber, S., Mara, M., Lischetzke, T.: The uncanny of mind in a machine: Humanoid robots as tools, agents, and experiencers. Comp. Hum. Behav. **102**, 274–286 (2020)
38. Fiske, S.T., Cuddy, A.J., Glick, P.: Universal dimensions of social cognition: Warmth and competence. Trends cogn. sci. **11**(2), 77–83 (2007)
39. Cuddy, A.J., Fiske, S.T., Glick, P.: The BIAS map: behaviors from intergroup affect and stereotypes. J. Pers. Soc.. Psych. **92**(4), 631–648 (2008)
40. Ryan, R.M., Deci, E.L.: Self-Determination Theory: Basic Psychological Needs in Motivation, Development, and Wellness. Guilford Publications (2017)
41. Janis, I.L.: Groupthink and group dynamics: a social psychological analysis of defective policy decisions. Policy Stud. J. **2**(1), 19–25 (1973)
42. Okamura, K., Yamada, S.: Adaptive trust calibration for human-AI collaboration. Plos one. **15**, e0229132 (2020)
43. Joshi, A., Roh, H.: The role of context in work team diversity research: a meta-analytic review. Acad. Manag. J. **52**(3), 599–627 (2009)
44. Kravitz, D.A., Martin, B.: Ringelmann rediscovered: the original article. J. Pers. Soc. Psychol. **50**(5), 936–941 (1986)
45. Postmes, T., Spears, R.: Deindividuation and antinormative behavior: a meta-analysis. Psychol. Bull. **123**(3), 238–259 (1998)
46. Latané, B., Nida, S.: Ten years of research on group size and helping. Psychol. Bull. **89**(2), 308–324 (1981)
47. Tajfel, H., Turner, J.C.: The social identity theory of intergroup behavior. In: Worchel, S., Austin, W.G. (eds.) Psychology of Intergroup Relation, pp. 7–24. Hall Publishers, Chicago (1986)

Collaborative System for Question Answering in German Case Law Documents

Christoph Hoppe[1]([✉]), Nico Migenda[1], David Pelkmann[1], Daniel Hötte[2], and Wolfram Schenck[1]

[1] Center for Applied Data Science, Bielefeld University of Applied Sciences, Gütersloh, Germany
{christoph.hoppe,nico.migenda,david.pelkman, wolfram.schenck}@fh-bielefeld.de
[2] Faculty of Business, Bielefeld University of Applied Sciences, Bielefeld, Germany
daniel.hoette@fh-bielefeld.de

Abstract. Legal systems form the foundation of democratic states. Nevertheless, it is nearly impossible for individuals to extract specific information from comprehensive legal documents. We present a human-centered and AI-supported system for semantic question answering (QA) in the German legal domain. Our system is built on top of human collaboration and natural language processing (NLP)-based legal information retrieval. Laypersons and legal professionals re ceive information supporting their research and decision-making by collaborating with the system and its underlying AI methods to enable a smarter society. The internal AI is based on state-of-the-art methods evaluating complex search terms, considering words and phrases specific to German law. Subsequently, relevant documents or answers are ranked and graphically presented to the human. In ad dition to the novel system, we publish the first annotated data set for QA in the German legal domain. The experimental results indicate that our semantic QA workflow outperforms existing approaches.

Keywords: Question answering · Information retrieval · Human-AI interface design · AI-supported decision making · Legal research

1 Introduction

Legal systems are an indispensable pillar in constitutional nations [17]. With the ongoing digitization of the legal system, legal documents are increasingly stored digitally. The question arises of how a legal layperson is supposed to gather information from the overwhelming number of court documents. To extract legal information efficiently a collaborative system is necessary [7]. Traditionally, this meant consulting a specialist, which is neither cheap nor fast. With the rise of large-scale language models and question answering (QA) new opportunities to assist legal laypersons are emerging. Current legal Information Retrieval (IR) systems, databases, and commercial search engines store and process large amounts of legal documents. Unfortunately, extracting a specific passage

L. M. Camarinha-Matos et al. (Eds.): PRO-VE 2022, IFIP AICT 662, pp. 303–312, 2022.
https://doi.org/10.1007/978-3-031-14844-6_24

or answer from a corpus of documents to a posed legal question is either highly time-consuming or impossible, as existing approaches do not provide capabilities for modern QA and semantic search. Moreover, actual research in legal IR and QA shows a lack of sufficient language models and data sets in the German language [22]. This makes it necessary to develop a QA system in the German legal domain that can return a precise answer to a posed question in a corpus of large legal documents, providing collaborative and transparent access to legal information [25].

In this paper, we present a system for semantic QA in German case law documents that follows the guidelines of state-of-the-art search engines. Thereby, our system focuses on human-centered AI collaboration that enables efficient passage retrieval and QA across large-scale legal documents by interacting with humans and autonomously providing suggested answers to legal search queries. We use different retrieval methods as well as a self-trained reader model based on Efficiently Learning an Encoder that Classifies Token Replacement Accurately (ELECTRA) [5]. In order to train and evaluate the presented language models in the field of law, we created a hand-annotated data set consisting of 226 question–answer pairs from German case law documents. In addition, we evaluate multiple end-to-end semantic search workflows consisting of different retriever-reader combinations in comparison to our model. In doing so, we show that fine-tuning a pre-trained language model to a specific domain shows great results even with a small amount of labeled data. Thus, our research bridges the gap between existing legal IR systems and modern human-centered AI technologies. The intelligent system further contributes towards a smarter society. Our approach supports both legal laypersons who need an initial assessment of their problems and legal professionals such as lawyers, who need assistance at their research activities.

2 Related Work

Legal IR systems and databases were originally built to store and retrieve large amounts of various legal documents. *CourtListener* and the *Caselaw Access Project (CAP)* are initial approaches that aim to provide free access to published court decisions of the United States legal system in a uniform format enriched with additional metadata [9, 14]. The two most popular and up-to-date databases for legal research in German language are *Beck Online* and *JURIS*, which publish large collections of court decisions as well as excerpts from legal texts and legal commentaries [1, 8]. The challenge of offering legal documents in machine-readable formats is solved by the legal IR systems *Openlegaldata* and the *Finlex data bank*. Both provide free and public access to legal documents in various data formats and contribute to further machine processing and data analysis in the legal field [15, 18]. However, traditional IR systems are limited in the retrieval of specific passages or answers to a posed question, resulting in imprecise and inefficient results. This has motivated the scientific community to introduce methods that provide QA possibilities for a large amount of legal documents. The majority of recent research in the field of QA generally follows the paradigm of a retriever-reader based search workflow which selects relevant documents and extracts a specific answer to a posed question [4]. Deep learning and large language models represent the given documents as dense vectors, taking their semantics and surrounding context into account. Especially the deep representation of documents [6, 20, 23] leads to first legal QA approaches in the English and Chinese language [2]. Moreover, ontology and knowledge graph-driven methods have been applied in the field of Arabic and Chinese jurisprudence [11, 12, 24].

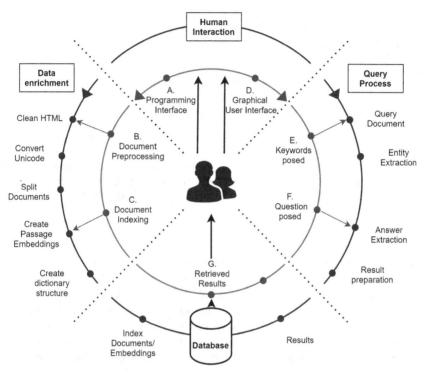

Fig. 1. Presentation of the collaborative QA system. The inner (orange) circle represents the human interaction with the system to either enrich (counterclockwise) or to query (clockwise) the database. The outer (red) circle represents the AI-toolchain to process the human input. Both circles are deeply interlinked. (Color figure online)

3   Human-AI Collaborative QA System

Human-AI collaboration aims to accomplishing a shared goal by deep interaction between humans and AI. Legal laypersons alone are not capable of extracting information from large numbers of law documents. Instead of searching through many documents, the human interacts via a graphical interface with an AI that performs the document search and QA tasks. The AI itself consists of a toolchain of exchangeable statistical and machine learning components to solve the search tasks more efficiently. The system (Fig. 1) consists of two connected and continuously interaction layers: the human layer (front end) and the AI layer (back end).

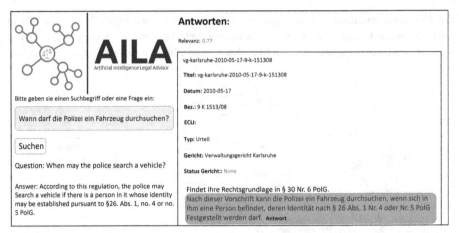

Fig. 2. Section of the graphical user interface. Users can interact with the system and submit a question to the interface (left). Afterwards, they receive back a concrete answer extracted from a legal document (right), enriched with a relevance score and additional metadata.

3.1 Human Interaction

Our system focuses on collaborative interaction between humans and the QA system. For this purpose, humans can engage with various interfaces in order to perform operations on the system (Fig. 1, inner circle). In general, there are two different ways to interact with the system. Initially, it is possible to interact with the AI using the programming interface (Fig. 1, A) to enhance the knowledge base by inserting new legal documents. These are automatically pre-processed, embedded, indexed and saved in the database (no actual programming skills are required). Secondly, a search query can be submitted using the graphical human-AI interface (Fig. 1, D). This query can either consist of individual keywords or contain a specific legal question (Fig. 2). These queries can contain law specific terms (e.g., the § symbol for a paragraph). Depending on the search term, different components of the AI toolchain, which are described in the following Sect. 3.2, are used to find the best matching documents. The top results are then prepared in such a way that the human can directly extract the requested information. In an evaluation loop the presented documents are optionally rated, to enhance the quality of future requests.

3.2 AI Layer

The AI layer is the collection of exchangeable AI components located in the back end of the system (Fig. 1, outer circle). When the human submits a search term, the query process is started via the graphical interface. This triggers the process of retrieving relevant information related to a search query. In a first step, a combination of statistical methods and deep sentence transformer models are used for the task of document retrieval (Fig. 1, E. Keywords posed). To find the most relevant passages, the model transforms a posed question or keywords into a vector of the dimension $d = 768$. This computed vector is mapped to a shared embedding space. Subsequently, the cosine similarity is used to compute the distances between the embedded question or keywords and stored passages. Afterwards, the next $top_k = 10$ relevant passages related to the search request are retrieved [20, 21]. If only single keywords are passed to the system, the retrieved passages are checked for legal entities using a BERT model [6] trained for the task of named entity recognition [13]. Whenever a concrete legal question is passed to the system, the answer extraction method is additionally integrated into the process (Fig. 1, F. Question posed). Therefore, an ELECTRA model is added to the process as a reader. This model receives the relevant passages returned by the retriever as well as the questions posed. In the following, the model extracts the exact answers from the given passages. In our approach, given the $top_k = 10$ passages returned by the retriever, the reader model is advised to extract the $top_k = 5$ answers that are most relevant with respect to the posed question. Finally, the passages or answers found are ranked according to relevance and presented to the human on the graphical human-AI interface.

When the AI is called using the programming interface to enhance the knowledge base, different toolchain components are used. The main tasks of the programming interface are the execution of the document pre-processing and document indexing processes. Their general function is to prepare the raw legal documents within our data set and to store the pre-processed documents inside the database. The document pre-processing (Fig. 1, B Document preprocessing) includes various methods such as the removal of HTML elements from the plain text and the conversion of Unicode symbols. In order to respect the maximum processable token length of different retrieval models and to improve the performance of the retrieval process, long documents are split into passages of 200 words each. Using the indexing method, both the plain text and the metadata are stored in the database (Fig. 1, C Document indexing). Moreover, we generate deep vector representations of the passages with a dimension of $d = 768$ in order to perform a semantic search and QA [20]. These vectors are also stored in the database that acts as a shared embedding space. Once all the texts, metadata and passage vectors in the database have been successfully indexed, the indexing process is complete.

4 Experiments and Results

The experiments compare the performance of our system with different underlying models. We test several pre-trained models as well as s self-trained reader model. Moreover, we introduce the self-annotated data set LegalQuAD for QA tasks in German case law documents.

4.1 Creation of the LegalQuAD Data Set

To evaluate or fine-tune retriever and reader models for the task of QA, annotated data sets consisting of question–answer pairs are necessary. To the best of our knowledge, there is currently no annotated data set published for QA in German legal documents. To overcome this problem, we created a hand-annotated LegalQuAD for training and evaluation purposes. The entire data set consists of 226 question–answer pairs from German case law documents of various legal fields and is structured in the SQuAD format [16, 19]. The data annotation itself was performed by lawyers who are familiar with NLP and have received intensive training on the data annotation process. During the annotation phase, various passages from German case law documents were presented to the lawyers. While reading a passage, the lawyers were asked to formulate a specific question regarding the given passage and highlight a corresponding answer. To ensure the creation of a diversified data set, both complex questions that need to be answered over a span of several sentences as well as shorter questions, that can be answered in a few words are formulated. In addition, the annotators were instructed to rephrase posed questions with synonyms to avoid lexical overlap between question–answer pairs. Furthermore, it was reviewed that all formulated questions are self-sufficient and can be answered completely with the knowledge indicated in the respective text.

4.2 Model Training and Evaluation Metrics

We compared the performance of different combinations of the entire QA workflow introduced in Sect. 3 on our annotated LegalQuAD. Therefore, we selected several publicly available models and tested their performance on our LegalQuAD test data set (see Table 1). Given the results of previous studies, we choose to compare the retrieval methods *BM25* and *MFAQ* in combination with the reader models *GELECTRA-base-GermanQuAD* and *GELECTRA-large-GermanQuAD* [10]. Moreover, we trained our own reader model *GELECTRA-large-GermanQuAD-LegalQuAD* by fine-tuning the pre-trained model *GELECTRA-large-GermanQuAD* [3, 16]. For this purpose, we created a training data set by selecting 200 random question–answer pairs from LegalQuAD. Afterwards, we trained the model for two epochs with a learning rate of $l = 1e - 5$ using Adam as an optimizer and a batch size of $b = 10$ as well as a maximum sequence length of $sl = 256$ tokens. To evaluate the implemented models, we consider several evaluation metrics that show whether the answer span predicted by the model matches the correct answer:

Exact Match (EM) is a metric that measures the proportion of documents where the predicted answer span exactly matches the correct answer span. This metric is very precise and restrictive. For example, a predicted answer *A: "§ 15 BGB."* would result in a score of zero if the answer labeled as correct was *A: "In § 15 BGB."* because this answer span does not match the expected answer exactly. A metric that measures the ratio of overlapping words between the labeled and predicted answer span is the *F1-score*. Thus, this metric is more forgiving than the EM and closer to a human opinion regarding the similarity of two predicted answers [16].

4.3 Results and Discussion

The results of our experiments are presented in Table 1. On the one hand, it has been shown that the combination of the retriever models *MFAQ* and *BM25* in combination with our self-trained reader *GELECTRA-large-GermanQuAD-LegalQuAD* shows the best performance in respect to the EM and F1-scores. On the other hand, it can be observed that the results of pre-trained models is significantly weaker in comparison to our fine-tuned approach.

The results of the experiments indicate that our presented workflow towards a collaborative QA system is functional and able to achieve valuable results compared to state-of-the-art approaches. In particular, it was demonstrated that the human-AI-collaboration regarding the preprocessing and indexing of German legal documents, as well as the query process, is straightforward to manage for both legal laypersons and lawyers, without the need of programming knowledge. In comparison to our fine-tuned model, the pre-trained reader models show weak scores especially in the EM evaluation metric. We argue that the significant increase in the EM score after the fine-tuning process is a result of the fact that law has a very strong and complex domain language which is hard to generalize by pre-trained models.

Table 1. Performance of the QA workflow consisting of retriever and reader models on the LegalQuAD test data set. The results shown were calculated for retriever $top_k = 10$ and reader $top_k = 5$. Model type and training dataset are included in the model name.

Retriever	Reader	Exact match	F1-Score
BM25	GELECTRA-base-GermanQuAD	0.083	0.58
BM25	GELECTRA-large-GermanQuAD	0.12	0.67
BM25	GELECTRA-large-GermanQuAD-LegalQuAD	0.82	0.98
MFAQ (Emb)	GELECTRA-base-GermanQuAD	0.083	0.48
MFAQ (Emb)	GELECTRA-large-GermanQuAD	0.083	0.51
MFAQ (Emb)	GELECTRA-large-GermanQuAD-LegalQuAD	0.5	0.72
MFAQ (Emb) + BM25	GELECTRA-large-GermanQuAD-LegalQuAD	**0.83**	**0.98**

The fact that our reader models show a significant increase in the performance compared to the publicly available models suggests that our research can be beneficial in extracting specific answers from large legal documents in the future. Furthermore, it could be shown that the fine-tuning process of a pre-trained language model can be successfully performed even with a small amount of labeled data. Thus, there is great potential for adapting existing models to a specific domain. As the field of IR moves from statistical document retrieval to AI-based methods, there is a growing need to develop collaborative systems for AI-supported QA and semantic search in the legal domain. With the increasing use of AI, it becomes especially impor tant to bring humans into the center of the process chain and make legal information accessible to both legal laypersons and legal professionals through a human-AI inter- face. The research results presented will enable us to improve existing IR systems from the legal sector like *Beck Online* and *JURIS* and enhance their process with QA functionalities. In doing so, we create transparent and straightforward search capabilities in comprehensive legal documents for all humans, contributing towards a smarter society.

5 Conclusion and Future Work

In this paper, we introduced our approach for a collaborative QA system in German case law documents. We have shown that retrieving information from legal documents and performing extractive QA in the field of German case law are relevant and unsolved problems in the legal system, which can be solved by our semantic search and QA approach. Moreover, we established a human-AI interface and described its applied methods, models and human interactions in detail. To encourage further research in the area of QA in the German language, we hand-annotated and published the data set LegalQuAD, consisting of question–answer pairs derived from German case law documents. To the best of our knowledge, LegalQuAD is the first annotated QA data set for the training and evaluation of legal language models in the German language. Based on this published data set, we evaluated and trained models for the task of QA in German case law documents. Our experiments show that our workflow leads to significantly better results in terms of the EM and F1-score than previously published approaches. Addressing the time-consuming research activities of lawyers, our contribution aims to bridge the gap between modern language technologies and the traditional-oriented field of law. Rationalizing inefficient information seeking for legal professionals allow them to concentrate their work on the actual decision-making processes and find faster conformity of the given cases with specific legal indications. This kind of efficiency may lead to an improvement in the performance of legal professionals which result in a higher quality of their consultation for individuals or entities. Furthermore, we are highly committed to reducing the barriers to society's access to legal information and empowering a smart society to obtain legal information independently from authorities. For this reason, we have ensured that our collaborative QA system can also be used by legal laypersons and enables transparent and straightforward search capabilities in large legal document collections. The code and data set related to the paper can be found at https://www.github.com/Christoph911/Pro-Ve_2022_Appendix.

Acknowledgements. We would like to thank Nicole Salvi for her support of the project by contributing to the annotation of the published dataset and the literature review conducted, as well as providing her excellent knowledge of the legal sector.

References

1. Beck, V.C.: Beck-online - die datenbank. https://beck-online.beck.de. Accessed 17 Feb 2022
2. Chalkidis, I., Fergadiotis, M., Malakasiotis, P., Aletras, N., Androutsopoulos, I.: Legal- BERT: the muppets straight out of law school. In: Findings of the Association for Computational Linguistics (EMNLP), pp. 2898–2904 (2020)
3. Chan, B., Schweter, S., Möller, T.: German's next language model. In: Proceedings of the 28th International Conference on Computational Linguistics (ACL), pp. 6788–6796 (2020)
4. Chen, D., Fisch, A., Weston, J., Bordes, A.: Reading wikipedia to answer open-domain questions. In: Proceedings of the 55th Annual Meeting of the Association for Computational Linguistics (ACL), pp. 1870–1879 (2017)

5. Clark, K., Luong, M.T., Brain, G., Brain, Q.V.L.G., Manning, C.D.: ELECTRA: pre-training text encoders as discriminators rather than generators. In: Proceedings of the 8th International Conference on Learning Representations (ICLR) (2020)
6. Devlin, J., Chang, M.W., Lee, K., Google, K.T., Language, A.I.: BERT: pre-training of deep bidirectional transformers for language understanding. In: Proceedings of the 2019 Conference of the North American Chapter of the Association for Computational Linguistics: Human Language Technologies (NAACL), pp. 4171–4186 (2019)
7. Enders, P.: Einsatz künstlicher intelligenz bei juristischer entscheidungsfindung. Juristische Arbeitsblätter, pp. 721–735 (2018)
8. juris GmbH: Uris - das rechtsportal (2022). https://juris.de/jportal/nav/index.jsp/. Accessed 17 Feb 2022
9. Harvard-Law-School: Caselaw access project (2013). https://lil.law.harvard.edu/projects/caselaw-access-project/. Accessed 05 Mar 2022
10. Hoppe, C., Pelkmann, D., Migenda, N., Hötte, D., Schenck, W.: Towards intelligent legal advisors for document retrieval and question-answering in German legal documents. In: Proceedings of the 4th Artificial Intelligence and Knowledge Engineering Conference (AIKE) (2021)
11. Huang, W., Jiang, J., Qu, Q., Yang, M.: Aila: a question answering system in the legal domain. In: Proceedings of the 29th International Joint Conference on Artificial Intelligence (IJCAI), pp. 5258–5260 (2020)
12. Kourtin, I., Mbarki, S., Mouloudi, A.: A legal question answering ontology-based system. In: Proceedings of the 14th International NooJ Conference, pp. 218–229 (2021)
13. Leitner, E., Rehm, G., Moreno-Schneider, J.: A dataset of German legal documents for named entity recognition. In: Proceedings of the 12th Language Resources and Evaluation Conference (LREC), pp. 4478–4485 (2020)
14. Lissner, M.: Courtlistener: a platform for researching and staying abreast of the latest in the law. Master thesis (2010)
15. Ministry-Justice-Finland: Finlex data bank (2016). https://finlex.fi. Accessed 05 Mar 2022
16. Möller, T., Risch, J., Pietsch, M.: GermanQuAD and germanDPR: improving non-English question answering and passage retrieval. In: Proceedings of the 3rd Workshop on Machine Reading for Question Answering (MRQA), pp. 42–50 (2021)
17. van Opijnen, M., Santos, C.: On the concept of relevance in legal information retrieval. Artif. Intell. Law **25**, 65–87 (2017)
18. Ostendorff, M., Blume, T., Ostendorff, S.: Towards an open platform for legal information. In: Proceedings of the ACM/IEEE Joint Conference on Digital Libraries (JCDL), pp. 385–388 (2020)
19. Rajpurkar, P., Zhang, J., Lopyrev, K., Liang, P.: SQuAD: 100,000+ questions for machine comprehension of text. In: Proceedings of the 2016 Conference on Empirical Methods in Natural Language Processing (EMNLP), pp. 2383–2392 (2016)
20. Reimers, N., Gurevych, I.: Sentence-BERT: Sentence embeddings using siamese BERT-networks. In: Proceedings of the 2019 Conference on Empirical Methods in Natural Language Processing and the 9th International Joint Conference on Natural Language Processing (EMNLP), pp. 3982–3992 (2019)
21. Robertson, S., Zaragoza, H.: The probabilistic relevance framework: Bm25 and beyond. Found. Trends Inf. Ret. **3**, 333–389 (2009)
22. Sugathadasa, K., et al.: Legal document retrieval using document vector embeddings and deep learning. Adv. Intell. Syst. Comput. – Intell. Comput. **857**, 160–175 (2018)
23. Vaswani, A., et al.: Attention is all you need. In: Proceedings of the Advances in Neural Information Processing Systems (NIPS), vol. 30, pp. 5999–6009 (2017)

24. Veena, G., Gupta, D., Anil, A., Akhil, S.: An ontology driven question answering system for legal documents. In: Proceedings of the 2019 2nd International Conference on Intelligent Computing, Instrumentation and Control Technologies (ICICICT), pp. 947–951 (2019)
25. Zhong, H., Xiao, C., Tu, C., Zhang, T., Liu, Z., Sun, M.: How does nlp benefit legal system: a summary of legal artificial intelligence. In: Proceedings of the 58th Annual Meeting of the Association for Computational Linguistics (ACL), pp. 5218–5230 (2020)

How Does the Implementation of AI Agents Affect Human Agents' Job Profiles? Insights from Two Industrial Cases

Antonia Schulte[1]([✉]), Wilhelm Klat[1], and Thomas Süße[2]

[1] CircoVision UG, Elsener Str. 33, 33102 Paderborn, Germany
aschulte@mintkitchen.de, klat@circovision.com
[2] Faculty of Engineering and Mathematics, Bielefeld University of Applied Sciences,
Gütersloh Campus, Langer Weg 9 a, 33332 Gütersloh, Germany
thomas.suesse@fh-bielefeld.de

Abstract. Traditionally, operators, system users as well as other non-management employees have been rarely involved in the design, planning, and construction of machines. With the recent dawn of deep learning ever more AI-based agents enter workplaces across industries. This trend is already affecting the way how employees interact with technology. In this paper we show that operative employees rather become co-creators while collaborating with AI agents. This affects traditional job profiles. The contribution of our research is twofold: Firstly, we discuss a novel approach of systematically evaluating how AI agents affect job profiles based on insights from two real-world industrial cases. Secondly, we provide new research perspectives for AI implementation in collaborative environments as well as for AI-related technological enhancements. These results can be fruitful for firms and decision makers as well as for academia, e.g., in fields like employee training, technology and innovation management, change management, applied machine learning and other.

Keywords: AI agents · Job profiles · Human-AI interaction · AI Support Processes

1 Introduction

Traditionally, operators, system users as well as other non-management employees have been rarely involved in the design, planning, and construction of machines. With the breakthrough of deep learning in 2012 ever more AI-based agents that built on deep neural networks enter workplaces as "open-ended" technologies across industries on a global scale [1]. As AI agents learn tasks from data and can increase their performance with additional training data, recent research in this emerging field identified the need for a closer collaboration between human and AI agents such as "human-AI partnerships" [2]. Although the existing body of research motivates human-AI collaboration with supervision of AI decisions or improving AI systems, it remains to be examined how

© IFIP International Federation for Information Processing 2022
Published by Springer Nature Switzerland AG 2022
L. M. Camarinha-Matos et al. (Eds.): PRO-VE 2022, IFIP AICT 662, pp. 313–320, 2022.
https://doi.org/10.1007/978-3-031-14844-6_25

individual job profiles become affected by the introduction of AI agents in collaborative work. In organizations with higher degrees of labor division and classical hierarchy, various employees with different roles and job profiles are involved in collaborative value creation processes. Thus, we argue that the introduction and implementation of AI agents within such collaborative processes affect job profiles of the involved employees working together with AI. Based on two industrial use cases we seek to reveal that especially operators who are doing the most basic work are experiencing some significant changes in their job profiles.

The contribution of this paper is two fold: Firstly, we provide a first systematization on why and how AI agents affect individual job profiles in collaborative work contexts. Secondly, we derive research perspectives and advice for practice, e.g. in the popular field of AI implementation in organization where a more explicit focus on employees is considered as one success critical element [3, 4].

This paper is structured as follows: Sect. 2 gives an overview of the related research. Section 3 introduces the two industrial use cases and outlines individual job profiles of operators, supervisors and managers. Section 4 discusses the findings and gives for further research and practical relevance of our findings.

2 Related Research

For about three decades there has been a trend emerging in organizations that shows an increasing amount of technologies, particularly computer-based technologies, that are designed and implemented as so-called "open-ended" technologies. A main character-istic of these kinds of modern and more flexible technologies is seen in the fact that they are more adaptable in a sense that they can take up users' input in order to change or improve in a context-specific manner. As a result, further development and adjustments of technologies in organizations is no longer just an exclusive task for developers or designers, but should involve users of such technologies as well [5].

However, in order to foster co-creative and collaborative processes during technical design, development and adjustment there are a number of prerequisites at both sides, the human actor as well as the technology. As mentioned above, on the one hand a critical antecedent for co-creative design and development is that technologies have to become more flexible and adaptable towards various use-cases and use-scenarios. Particularly in that field, the further dissemination of AI-based systems and applications provides promising opportunities as AI-based systems are more often designed in such a way that they can use human actors' input for their own learning and improvement processes. Technically, these processes are often based on machine learning approaches building on the supervised learning concept which demands input from the human counterpart [6]. On the other hand, at the side of the human actor a critical antecedent for the success of supervised learning of AIs demands a shift in the understanding of the human actors role from a user or operator towards a co-creator and collaborator of AI technology. It is not surprising that this shift in the interactional logic between human actors and technologies which goes beyond usage towards a more collaborative form of interaction is of increasing relevance in work environments where AI-based technologies have already been introduced.

Researchers point out that new technologies at work can lead to changes of qualification requirements as well as more skill variety in production environments [7–9]. In addition, an increasing amount of literature is focusing on the readiness of organizations when implementing AI technologies and highlight the upskilling as well as changes of job profiles among employees as a critical success factor [3, 4, 10]. Regarding human employees' shifting role related to successful AI implementation, a number of newly emerging concepts are shaping and supporting the understanding towards a human-AI collaboration in organization. Some of these concepts are outlined in literature as human-AI hybrids [11], human-AI partnerships [2] or human-AI systems [12]. With regards to the changing role of humans required for human-AI collaboration Waefler and Schmid [2] point out that particularly in situations of collaborative decision making between human and AI the human's tasks of verifying AI's decisions, improving the AI system, learning from the AI system as well as taking responsibility for the final decision are gaining increasing importance. In addition, this transformative potential of AI regarding employees' roles and job profiles contributes to the growing importance of collaborative learning capacities as well as creativity and self-organization, to mention just a few [13]. However, these contributions are still on a rather conceptual level and are lacking further reflection in collaborative workplaces in the industry.

3 Changing Job Profiles: Insights from Two Industrial Use-Cases

The introduction of open-ended AI agents into collaborative workplaces is accompanied by a set of new processes we call AI support processes. These new processes are required for performance supervision (Algorithm Supervision Process) and for improving AI performance with additional training data captured during operations. The latter can be divided into training data creation (Data Acquisition Process, Data Labeling Process) and the actual algorithm training (Algorithm Training Process). We illustrate the introduction of open-ended AI agents and AI support procedures with two industrial use cases in which we had a leading role as systems provider. In both cases AI agents took over an assisting role in collaboration with human operators who observe and verify AI decisions. AI agents are designed to acquire the majority of training data required for optimal performance predominantly during operations. Therefore data points automatically collected during operations are permanently stored, labeled and used for algorithm retraining.

3.1 Use Case A: Circular Economy in the Automotive Industry

The first use case is from the automotive industry and the task at hand is a visual inspection of used automotive parts for remanufacturing purposes. The parts need to be sorted into quality categories based on a visual inspection of wear and tear, damage and anomalies. The AI agent is a camera-based machine which uses image classifier algorithms to support the operator with the visual inspection. It judges and pre-sorts parts into categories. Operators can observe the AI decisions in real-time and are tasked to verify the pre-sorted parts. The supervisor is in charge for in-bound and out-bound logistics at this workplace. Finally, the line manager holds full responsibilities for all workplaces in the remanufacturing line including personnel planning and quality control.

3.2 Use Case B: Waste Management Services

The second use case is a communal service in the field of waste management. Garbage trucks collect the contents from garbage bins placed at roadsides. Bins with separated household waste (e.g. paper, organic, plastics) need to be visually checked for contamination by wrong materials to avoid problems in down-stream waste recycling procedures. Garbage truck drivers (operators) are instructed to refuse the collection of highly contaminated bins. An AI agent has been introduced to assist operators with visual inspections of bins. The AI agent is a camera-based system attached to the garbage truck observing the bin contents while being thrown into the truck. The AI agent logs all visual assessments and warns operators in cases of high contamination levels. Operators can observe AI decisions in real-time and have final decision power with regard to refusing garbage collection. Supervisors organize surrounding tasks such as tour planning and deal with customer inquiries. The manager has the authority to change, among others, workplace procedures, truck equipment and contractual agreements with municipalities.

3.3 Factors for Job Profile Changes

Ensuring operational reliability of AI agents and their continuous performance improvement is a crucial challenge for organizations. AI agents, or machine learning teams responsible for their development respectively, have limited means of completing AI support processes without extensive collaboration with operational staff. In the above mentioned use cases, we empirically observed three main reasons favoring the extensive inclusion of operative staff in the co-creation process we call: (1) Ground Truth Proximity, (2) Task Familiarity, and (3) Production Line Insights and Authority.

Ground Truth Proximity. In the field of machine learning, ground truth is often referred to as labels of a data point which are known to be true and of critical importance for algorithm training [14]. The ground truth can be obtained from empirical observation or measurement. In Use Case A, the operator can obtain the ground truth for a data point from physically inspecting the car part including mechanical measurements while it is being processed by the AI agent.

In Use Case B the operator can personally inspect the contents of a garbage bin while it has been photographed and move waste inside the bin to verify a suspected contamination. Access to the ground truth of data points is unequally distributed among human agents. If the ground truth is only accessible temporarily in the moment of data capture then often only operators can access it. In such cases, operators possess a higher degree of ground truth proximity compared to management-oriented colleagues without direct real-time access to the physical objects.

Task Familiarity. Task familiarity includes explicit knowledge about formal decision criteria but also implicit experience from observing vast amounts of data points including their corresponding ground truth. Management-oriented employees and machine learning teams usually have superior explicit knowledge about a task but lack the operator's implicit task familiarity from having personally seen many garbage bins or car parts respectively. This tacit knowledge is of great value for AI development as AI agents possess the ability of replicating this knowledge as abstract features in deep neural networks when trained with data points that have been labeled by humans in possession of tacit task knowledge.

Production Line Insights and Authority. The integration of AI agents into existing workplaces can require changes of established procedures and workplace setups to ensure successful execution of AI support processes. Redesigning processes requires production line authority. A typical change in procedures can be the collection of defective or rare items which previously have been discarded. In Use Case A defective car parts have immediately been discarded for material recycling during inspection. With AI agent introduction, a new process has been implemented to collect certain and rare defective car parts for algorithm retraining.

3.4   Job Profile Analysis

The execution of AI support processes can greatly benefit from co-creation with operational staff. We call this contribution from operational staff 'AI Support Impact'. Due to variations in the degrees of ground truth proximity, task familiarity and production line authority, the potential AI support impact varies among human agents.

Algorithm Support Process (ASP). With regard to performance supervision of AI agents we empirically observed significant effects of the ASP on the operator's job profile. Operators have the highest degree of ground truth proximity and task familiarity which, in both use cases, rendered the inclusion of operators into the ASP mandatory. The job profiles of managers also have been extended to a weaker extent with regard to verifying edge cases. Supervisors can take over a weaker role of first-level support for operators when they request guidance on how to deal with edge-cases or similar.

Data Acquisition Process (DAP). Continuous data acquisition requires human support and supervision to ensure that data points are suitable for algorithm training and the available data is representative in terms of including sufficient and balanced representations of relevant patterns. Ideally the operator's job profile is extended to support the DAP by flagging unsuitable data points on the fly and increasing the availability of e.g. rare patterns in the dataset. Managers with production line authority also play an important role as continuous data acquisition processes usually require a redesign of workplace procedures. Managers need to redesign, communicate and enforce workplace procedures among human agents. Again, supervisors can take over a weaker role of first-level support for operators.

Data Labeling Process (DLP). All human agents with task familiarity are potential contributors in the DLP. While operators can use their implicit task familiarity, supervisors and managers bring knowledge on explicit task requirements and upstream/downstream requirements into the labeling process. A practice-proven division of labeling work is to use supervisors and managers as second-level labelers especially for edge cases.

Algorithm Training Process (ATP). AI agents have shades of being right or wrong as deep neural networks return inferences with almost cardinally scaled confidence levels. Lower confidence decisions, for example, can be the result of algorithm weaknesses. Ground truth proximity can help human agents to identify potential sources of algorithm weaknesses and is therefore of high importance for the AI agents as an open ended technology. The tacit knowledge of operators from collaborating with the AI agents on a regular basis is a critical success factor for retraining AI agents. Their job profiles should be adjusted to become sparring partners in the identification of AI weaknesses (Fig. 1).

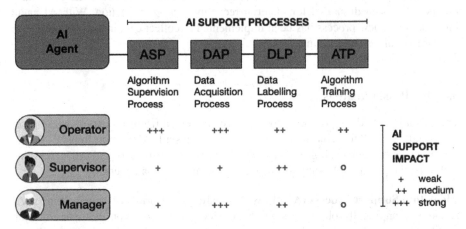

Fig. 1. AI support processes and AI support impact of human agents.

4   Discussion

In collaborative networks, open-ended AI agents require a novel set of operational procedures that we argue can be called co-creative AI support processes. They are required to ensure supervision and continuous improvement of AI agents. When performing AI support processes, machine learning teams can greatly benefit from including operators, supervisors and managers as co-creators. Their inclusion, however, requires changes and extension of their job profiles in different ways. These findings confirm other research contributions in the field of human-AI interaction [2, 7, 8].

Traditionally, operators are rarely involved in the creation process of regular machines. With AI agents present, their relevance increases significantly. As operators may be the only human agents with direct access to the ground truth of data points, we argue that operators should become mandatory co-creators as they may share some of their tacit knowledge with AI agents. As machine learning specialists responsible for the development of AI agents in both industrial use cases presented in this paper we empirically observed tremendous contributions of operators with supervision and improvement of AI agents alike. Operator feedback in both industrial use cases indicates that this new role as co-creators is also beneficial for operators themselves as it enriches the workplace with more responsibility, room for creative problem thinking and task variety.

Managers and supervisors play an important role in the workplace redesign to ensure optimal conditions to execute AI support processes. Especially managers with the authority to change production line procedures require a basic machine learning understanding to correctly redesign workplace procedures. Besides this, their job profile needs to be extended by communication and enforcement tasks as changes in operational procedures can induce human resistance if their purpose is unclear. Supervisor and manager feedback in both industrial use cases indicates the importance of basic machine learning understanding to motivate extensive workplace redesigns.

Our findings also revealed promising research perspectives in the fields of human factors, especially human resources and AI implementation in collaborative workplaces. Firstly, our estimations of the AI support impact of operators, supervisors and managers on AI support processes is derived from few empirical observations in which we introduced AI agents in real-world industrial workplaces. Our first systematization and estimations can be the foundation for extended field research. Secondly, the requirement for extending existing job profiles to accommodate AI support processes raises a variety of research questions on how human agents with different job profiles should be trained and prepared for the future. Thirdly, as ensuring successful implementation of AI support may also require redesigning workplaces, collaboration procedures, production lines and other organizational parts, it remains to be examined how, when and to what extent the various perspectives on collaborative networks should be further adjusted or extended. Finally, we argue that our result should also be recognized by designers of AI agents like digital engineers who have to take into account the important role of operators for learning and improvement of such AI agents in productive environments.

References

1. Russakovsky, O., et al.: ImageNet large scale visual recognition challenge. Int. J. Comput. Vision **115**(3), 211–252 (2015). https://doi.org/10.1007/s11263-015-0816-y
2. Waefler, T., Schmid, U.: Explainability is not enough: requirements for human-AI- partnership in complex socio-technical systems (November 2021)
3. Hamm, P., Klesel, M.: Success factors for the adoption of artificial intelligence in organizations: a literature review (2021)
4. Pumplun, L., Tauchert, C., Heidt, M.: A new organizational chassis for artificial intelligence - exploring organizational readiness factors. In: ECIS (2019)
5. Orlikowski, W.J.: The duality of technology: rethinking the concept of technology in organizations. Organ. Sci. **3**, 398–427 (1992). https://doi.org/10.1287/orsc.3.3.398
6. Zhou, Z.-H.: A brief introduction to weakly supervised learning. Natl. Sci. Rev. **5**, 44–53 (2018). https://doi.org/10.1093/nsr/nwx106
7. Süße, T., Kobert, M., Kries, C.: Antecedents of constructive human-AI collaboration: an exploration of human actors' key competencies. In: Camarinha-Matos, L.M., Boucher, X., Afsarmanesh, H. (eds.) PRO-VE 2021. IAICT, vol. 629, pp. 113–124. Springer, Cham (2021). https://doi.org/10.1007/978-3-030-85969-5_10
8. Pfeiffer, S.: The 'future of employment' on the shop floor: why production jobs are less susceptible to computerization than assumed. Int. J. Res. Vocat. Educ. Train. **5**(3), 208–225 (2018). https://doi.org/10.13152/IJRVET.5.3.4

9. Wegman, L.A., Hoffman, B.J., Carter, N.T., Twenge, J.M., Guenole, N.: Placing job charac-
    teristics in context: cross-temporal meta-analysis of changes in job characteristics since 1975.
    J. Manag. **44**, 352–386 (2018). https://doi.org/10.1177/0149206316654545
10. Ansari, F., Hold, P., Khobreh, M.: A knowledge-based approach for representing jobholder
    profile toward optimal human–machine collaboration in cyber physical production systems.
    CIRP J. Manuf. Sci. Technol. **28**, 87–106 (2020). https://doi.org/10.1016/j.cirpj.2019.11.005
11. Rai, A., Constantinides, P., Sarker, S.: Next generation digital platforms: toward human-AI
    hybrids. MIS Q. **43**, iii–ix (2019)
12. Schelble, B., Flathmann, C., Canonico, L.-B., Mcneese, N.: Understanding human-AI coop-
    eration through game-theory and reinforcement learning models. Presented at the Hawaii
    International Conference on System Sciences (2021). https://doi.org/10.24251/HICSS.202
    1.041
13. Markauskaite, L., et al.: Rethinking the entwinement between artificial intelligence and human
    learning: What capabilities do learners need for a world with AI? Comput. Educ. Artif. Intell.
    3, 100056 (2022). https://doi.org/10.1016/j.caeai.2022.100056
14. Kondermann, D.: Ground truth design principles: an overview. In: Proceedings of the Inter-
    national Workshop on Video and Image Ground Truth in Computer Vision Applications,
    pp. 1–4. ACM, St. Petersburg, Russia (2013). https://doi.org/10.1145/2501105.2501114

The Social Perception of Robots Scale (SPRS): Developing and Testing a Scale for Successful Interaction Between Humans and Robots

Sarah Mandl[1]([✉]), Maximilian Bretschneider[2,3], Frank Asbrock[2], Bertolt Meyer[3], and Anja Strobel[1]

[1] Professorship of Personality Psychology and Assessment,
Chemnitz University of Technology, Wilhelm-Raabe-Str. 43, 09120 Chemnitz, Germany
{sarah.mandl,anja.strobel}@psychologie.tu-chemnitz.de
[2] Professorship of Social Psychology, Chemnitz University of Technology,
Wilhelm-Raabe-Str. 43, 09120 Chemnitz, Germany
{maximilian.bretschneider,
frank.asbrock}@psychologie.tu-chemnitz.de
[3] Professorship of Work, Organizational, and Economic Psychology,
Chemnitz University of Technology, Wilhelm-Raabe-Str. 43, 09120 Chemnitz, Germany
bertolt.meyer@psychologie.tu-chemnitz.de

Abstract. Robots are increasingly populating social settings. Social robots should elicit positive associations to be accepted and integrated into daily lives. Even though social perception is multi-dimensional, available scales do not adequately picture this complexity in the perception of robots. To develop a new scale, we aggregated data on social perception of robots, initially operationalized as competence, sociability, morality, and anthropomorphism from four prior studies. An exploratory factor analysis on a random sample revealed three factors: "anthropomorphism", "morality/sociability", and "activity/cooperation". To validate these results, we performed confirmatory factor analysis (CFA) on the remaining sample and tested for validity and reliability. Reliability was appropriate. We found significant correlations between age, gender, educational level, and factors of the scale. However, missing values interfered with confirmatory and validating analyses. Despite these issues, the scale contributes to future research on social perception of robots.

Keywords: SPRS-social perception of robots scale · Social perception · Robots · HRI · Social robots · Scale construction

1 Social Perception of Robots

Robots have become indispensable assets for simplifying workflows in industrial settings. Smooth integration of robots into the workplace as co-workers is a crucial success factor for the industry of the future [1]. Recently, areas of robotic application have broadened into many settings [2]. Of special interest are social settings, such as health care

L. M. Camarinha-Matos et al. (Eds.): PRO-VE 2022, IFIP AICT 662, pp. 321–334, 2022.
https://doi.org/10.1007/978-3-031-14844-6_26

[3], where socially assistive robots are deployed as interaction partners [4]. Human-Robot Interaction (HRI) is thus multifaceted: Successful HRI should include aspects of the robot (e.g., its design, especially in terms of anthropomorphism, its technical capabilities), the task it is applied in (e.g., military, social), the intended interaction (e.g., type of communication, proximity), and aspects of the user (e.g., affinity for technology interaction, age) [5–7]. With the implementation of robots as social interaction partners, questions of their perception as a precursor for their acceptance need to be evaluated more closely and will be the focus of this study [6]. Social perception of human beings has been investigated in-depth over the last decades [8–12]. Social perception spans two (warmth and competence; [8]) or three (sociability, competence, and morality; [10]) dimensions, respectively. Warmth and competence are the core dimensions of the Stereotype Content Model and convey information about intentions (warmth) and the ability to put these intentions into action (competence) [8]. Furthermore, warmth can be separated into two sub-dimensions: sociability and morality, which provide a deeper understanding of the broad warmth-dimension [10]. Sociability refers to cooperation and forming connections with others, whereas morality is connected to ethics and essential social values [10]. Perceptions of these dimensions form stereotypes and interpersonal impressions [8], which affect emotions and behavior toward interaction partners. Perception of robots is strongly influenced by design aspects such as perceived gender [13], size [14], or anthropomorphism [15]. Additionally, social characteristics should be taken into account [16–18]. Available assessment scales for perceptions of robots include dimensions such as warmth, competence, and discomfort [18], or anthropomorphism, likeability, perceived intelligence, animacy, and perceived safety [19]. These scales depict a multitude of dimensions. Nevertheless, we propose that some relevant aspects are missing to adequately picture the multidimensionality of social perception of robots. Given the relevance of morality for human social perception [10], we posit that a scale measuring social perception of robots also needs to include this concept.

Despite the availability of scales to assess (social) perception of robots [18, 19] or human beings [8–10], we thus propose a new short scale to assess social perception of robots that includes morality, sociability, competence, and anthropomorphism.

The layout of this paper is as follows: in Sect. 2 we summarize the aim of the present study and elaborate on possible associations relevant for the validation of the scale. In Sect. 3 we describe the method of data acquisition, stimuli and items. In Sect. 4, we report results of the exploratory and confirmatory factor analyses as well as reliability and validity of the scale. In Sect. 5, we integrate our findings with prior research, point out limitations, and give an outlook to application and future research directions.

2   The Social Perception of Robots Scale (SPRS)

We aim to develop a short scale for measuring social perceptions of robots that comprises sociability, competence, morality, and anthropomorphism that can be applied to different robots in diverse research settings. We build on findings from social psychology [8, 10] and human-robot interaction [18, 19] that position sociability (the extent to which actors bond with others and hold good [warm] or bad [cold] intentions), competence (the degree to which actors are perceived as being able to put their intentions into action), and morality (the extent to which actors' actions are in line with what is socially acceptable in terms of values and societal rules of ethical conduct) at the core of social perception. We thus include these constructs in our scale on social perceptions of robots and also add anthropomorphism (the extent to which human-like capacities are attributed to the robot [20]).

Social perception of robots is linked to sociodemographic characteristics: Younger people have more positive attitudes toward new technologies [21], as have people with higher education [22]. People identifying as male also have a more positive attitude toward robots in contrast to people identifying as female [23–25]. Personality traits are also related to social perception of robots: Affinity for Technology Interaction (ATI; [26]), the tendency to actively engage with new technologies, is connected to a positive evaluation thereof [27, 28]. ATI is rooted in the construct Need for Cognition (NFC; [29]). NFC is the tendency of an individual to engage in and enjoy thinking. It is connected to the tendency to anthropomorphize [20]. People with higher NFC are less likely to anthropomorphize than people with lower NFC. Consequently, we explore the associations of sociodemographic and personality variables with social perception of robots. In order to provide a concise and valuable instrument, we will test reliability and validity of the newly developed scale.

3 Method

We preregistered the study on OSF (https://osf.io/ymuwr). We aggregated data from four studies (https://osf.io/qz2ca/, https://osf.io/xsn5a/, https://osf.io/ung87/) and reached a total sample size of $n = 1\,532$.

3.1 Participants

The four independent samples were acquired via Social Media, distribution channels of the University, and two online survey platforms, Prolific academic (www.prolific.co; [30]), and clickworker GmbH (www.clickworker.de). The total sample consisted of $n = 1\,532$ participants. From the total sample we drew a random subsample of $n = 500$ as construction sample. The mean age of the sample was $M = 34.48$ ($SD = 13.27$) and consisted of 282 male, 214 female, and 4 non-binary participants. Countries of residence were Germany ($n = 423$), Austria ($n = 26$), and Switzerland ($n = 12$), with 39 participants residing in other countries. The sample was mostly highly educated with 45.6% of the participants having obtained a university degree (high school diploma: 31.4%, other degrees: 22.6%, no degree: 0.4%).

We used the remaining sample ($n = 1\,032$) as validation sample: Mean age was $M = 33.83$ ($SD = 12.66$). The sample consisted of 538 male, 480 female, and 14 non-binary participants. Countries of residence were Germany ($n = 866$), Austria ($n = 70$), and Switzerland ($n = 14$), with 81 participants residing in other countries. 45.1% of the participants having obtained a university degree (high school diploma: 32%, other degrees: 22.5%, no degree: 0.4%).

3.2 Stimulus Material

The stimulus material consisted of three pictures of robots with different levels of anthropomorphism: An industrial robot, which does not possess any human-like qualities such as a face, a social robot, Pepper [31], which possesses a face and mouth with a form resembling a typical human body with head, body, and arms, and an android robot, a still image taken from the movie ROBOLOVE [32], which is almost indiscernible from a human being. Apart from the industrial robot, which was presented in a typical setting, the robots were presented against a neutral background. We presented the pictures in randomized order. In order to assess spontaneous associations participants were asked to rate how they perceive the robot, how they think the robot would act/think/react, even though the first impression might be wrong and revoked later. Below the pictures, we presented twenty-five adjectives on opposing ends of a semantic differential in randomized order, to be rated on a five-point Likert-scale. Additionally, we provided the option for participants to choose 'does not apply to robots in general' and 'does not apply to this specific robot' [33].

3.3 Items

Based on three different instruments [8, 19, 34], we initially composed items to cover the three main dimensions of social perception: competence, sociability, and morality, as well as anthropomorphism.

Competence. Three items covered the dimension of competence (e.g., *competent, able*) which were drawn from previous studies [8, 12, 35].

Sociability. A total of eight items covered the dimension of sociability, taken from three subscales: warmth [8, 12, 35], animacy [19], and likeability [19].

Morality. We adapted eight attributions that people high in Moral Identity possess of the German version of the Moral Identity Questionnaire [34] based on theoretical considerations (i.e., intelligibility and relevance), and chose corresponding antonyms.

Anthropomorphism. We covered the dimension of anthropomorphism by using five items from the Godspeed Questionnaire [19].

Affinity for Technology Interaction. We used the German version of the Affinity for Technology Interaction (ATI) Scale [26]. Nine items were rated on a six-point scale (anchored at *'not true at all'* and *'very true'*) to indicate whether people tend to interact with technological systems (e.g., *I like to try out functions of new technical systems*) and averaged the into a scale.

Need for Cognition. In three studies, we used the German version of the Need for Cognition (NFC) scale [36], comprising sixteen items (e.g., *I consider finding new solutions to problems a fun activity*), to assess NFC. The items were rated on a seven-point scale, anchored at *1 = strong disagreement* and *7 = strong agreement*. We calculated a sum score.

Sociodemographic Data. We assessed age, gender, and educational level as sociodemographic data from the participants.

3.4 Statistical Analysis

We used R (Version 4.1.1) [37] and the Rpackages psych (Version 2.1.6), plyr (Version 1.8.6), openxlsx (Version 4.2.4), corrplot (Version 0.90), ggplot2 (Version 3.3.5), nFactors (Version 2.4.1), dplyr (Version 1.0.7), haven (Version 2.4.3), lattice (Version 0.20-44), and lavaan (Version 0.6-9) for all statistical analyses.

4 Results

We drew a random subsample of $n = 500$ as a construction sample for performing exploratory factor analysis (EFA). On the remaining sample ($n = 1\,032$), we performed a confirmatory factor analysis as we explain below.

4.1 Step 1: Exploratory Factor Analysis

We performed an EFA with the construction sample to identify factors and factor loadings. EFA is a multivariate statistical method, commonly used for the development and validation of psychological theories and measurements [38].

Results. We tested the data for appropriateness for EFA beforehand. Bartlett's test of sphericity was significant χ^2 (276) = 5146.331, $p = .000$), indicating that it was appropriate to use the factor analytic model on this set of data. The Kaiser-Meyer-Olkin measure of sampling adequacy indicated that the strength of the relationships among variables was high (KMO = .82); thus, it was acceptable to proceed with the analysis. We conducted an EFA, performed a Varimax rotation since we expected the factors to be uncorrelated and Weighted Least Squares (WLS) Estimator. To estimate the number of factors, we ran a parallel analysis [39]. Only items with factor loadings above .33 were included. Four factors were extracted. We rejected factor four with an eigenvalue of 1.21 and explaining only 5.03% of the variance in the data due to the small explanative value and limited interpretability. Furthermore, we excluded items that showed factor loadings above .33 on more than one factor. One item did not fit within the context of the factor and was thus rejected due to theoretical considerations. We ran another EFA with the remaining set of 18 variables. The resulting three factors explained a total of 43% of the variance in the data (Table 1).

Table 1. Results from the Exploratory Factor Analysis of the 18 items derived

Item	Factor loading		
	1	2	3
Factor 1: *anthropomorphism*[a]			
humanlike – machinelike	.75		
warm – cold	.68		
natural – artificial	.70		

(continued)

Table 1. (*continued*)

Item	Factor loading		
	1	2	3
real – unreal	.63		
organic – mechanic	.58		
pleasant – unpleasant	.48		
moves smoothly – moves rigidly	.47		
has a consciousness – does not have a consciousness	.45		
Factor 2: *morality/sociability*[b]			
ethical – unethical		.73	
moral – immoral		.68	
honest – dishonest		.64	
good-natured – hostile		.67	
likeable – unlikeable		.60	
polite – impolite		.56	
Factor 3: *activity/cooperation*[c]			
fair – unfair			.63
altruistic – self-serving			.59
diligent – lazy			.59
active – inert			.48
Percentage of Variance explained	17%	15%	11%
Eigenvalue	3.14	2.66	2.06
Cronbach's alpha	.81	.84	.68

Note. $N = 500$. The extraction method was Weighted Least Squares with an orthogonal (Varimax) rotation. Factor loadings below .33 are not shown. Observations with missing values were excluded listwise: [a] $n = 338$; [b] $n = 219$; [c] $n = 285$ (see Appendix, Table A).

Factors one and two showed a marginal positive correlation ($r_{f1,f2} = .11$), Factors one and three showed a marginal negative correlation ($r_{f1,f3} = -.15$). Factors two and three showed a small positive correlation ($r_{f2,f3} = .26$).

Interpretation of the Factors. Factor one, *anthropomorphism*, depicts the feelings toward and morphological perception of robots. It is comparable to the social dimension of *anthropomorphism* [16]. Factor two, *morality/sociability*, reflects how robots are perceived in terms of their 'social personality', comparable to *morality* and *sociability* [16]. Factor three, *activity/cooperation*, is more heterogeneous and comprises attributions that are necessary for smooth interaction, e.g., in work settings.

Hypotheses Derivation for Validity Analyses. To test validity, we chose criteria that were examined in the context of HRI before and assess how these criteria, i.e., age, gender, education, ATI, and NFC, are related to the factors *anthropomorphism, morality/sociability,* and *activity/cooperation.* We posited the following hypotheses:

H1: Age is negatively correlated with factors two and three [21].
H2: People identifying as female have lower ratings of factors one, two, and three, than people identifying as male [23–25].
H3: Lower educational levels correlate with lower ratings of factors one, two, and three [22].
H4: Need for Cognition is negatively correlated with factor one [20].
H5: Affinity for Technology Interaction is positively correlated with factor three [27, 28].
H6: By employing the social dimensions from our prior study (https://osf.io/xsn5a/) [16], we expect the following correlations:

    a)   the social dimension of anthropomorphism is positively correlated with factor one.
    b)   The social dimension of sociability is positively correlated with factor two.
    c)   The social dimension of morality is positively correlated with factor two.

4.2 Step 2: Confirmatory Factor Analysis and Psychometric Properties

Confirmatory Factor Analysis. In order to confirm the factor structure, we performed a confirmatory factor analysis (CFA) on the validation sample ($n = 1\,032$). Observations with missing values were excluded listwise. From the total number of observations ($n = 1\,032$) only 32.4% were used to perform the CFA due to missing values ($n_{f1} = 711$, $n_{f2} = 436$, $n_{f3} = 551$). Hence, model fit indices showed that the data did not fit the model well ($\chi^2(115) = 508.12, p = .000$; RMSEA $= .101$; CFI $= .796$; TLI $= .759$; SRMR $= .096$)[1]. We performed additional exploratory factor analyses to identify a factor structure that would show a better fit. Due to the number of missing values (see Appendix, Table A) we did not find an alternative that would show a better fit and be interpretable in terms of content. Thus, we proceeded with the analyses despite the limitations.

Reliability. We analyzed the internal consistency of the three factors by calculating Cronbach's α [40]. Factors one and two showed a good internal consistency ($\alpha_{f1} = .82$, $\alpha_{f2} = .85$). Factor three showed a lower internal consistency ($\alpha = .64$). At the background of the respective numbers of items and the contents they represent, all reliabilities of the factors can be seen as appropriate.

Validity. To validate the scale by means of construct validity, based on former findings and EFA, we formulated hypotheses and tested them by employing correlational designs (H1, H3–H6) and analysis of variance (ANOVA; H2).

---

[1] RMSEA = Root Mean Square Error of Approximation; CFI = Comparative Fit Index; TLI = Tucker-Lewis Index; SRMR = Standardized Root Mean Square Residual.

Results. Age was not correlated with factors two and three, therefore H1 was rejected. People identifying as female gave significantly lower ratings on factor one than people identifying as male, but not on factors two and three. Therefore, H2 was partly confirmed. Educational levels were correlated with factor one, but not with factors two, or three. Thus, H3 was partly confirmed. Need for Cognition was not correlated with factor one, therefore, H4 was rejected. Affinity for Technology Interaction was not correlated with factor three. Hence, H5 was rejected. The social dimension of anthropomorphism showed a strong positive correlation with factor one ($r = .96$), thus confirming H6a. The social dimension of sociability was strongly correlated with factor two ($r = .70$), confirming H6b. The social dimension of morality was not correlated with factor three ($r = .08$), thus rejecting H6c. The overall results showed that we could only partly validate the SPRS by means of the aforementioned hypotheses. For the results and comparison with the EFA see Table 2.

Table 2. Comparison of the construct validity of the exploratory and confirmatory factor analysis

Hypothesis	Variable	Factor	EFA ($n = 500$)	CFA ($n = 1\,032$)
H1	Age	2	$r = -.27^{**}$	$r = -.02$
		3	$r = -.05$	$r = .04$
H2	Gender	1	$r = .18^{**}$	$r = .16^{**}$
		2	$r = -.05$	$r = .05$
		3	$r = -.11$	$r = -.05$
H3	Educational level	1	$r = -.11^{*}$	$r = -.09^{*}$
		2	$r = -.01$	$r = -.02$
		3	$r = .07$	$r = .01$
H4	NFCa	1	$r = -.11$	$r = -.07$
H5	ATI	3	$r = .09$	$r = .06$
H6a	Anthropomorphism	1	$r = .96^{**}$	$r = .96^{**}$
H6b	Sociability	2	$r = .71^{**}$	$r = .70^{**}$
H6c	Morality	2	$r = .84^{**}$	$r = .87^{**}$

Note. Gender was transformed to a dichotomous variable due to the low count of participants who identified as non-binary (Female = 1, Male = 2). NFC = Need for Cognition; ATI = Affinity for Technology Interaction. * indicates $p < .05$. ** indicates $p < .01$

5 Conclusion

Social perception of robots is a new field of research, which will gain relevance over the following years. By constructing the SPRS, an 18-item questionnaire to assess social perception of robots in a short but comprehensive manner, we add to already available scales on robot perception [18, 19]. We complement these scales by introducing the rather overlooked dimension of perceived morality and sociability, which has a tremendous impact on the overall evaluation of robots as social partners. The construction of the SPRS should therefore be seen as an ongoing process. The EFA did not confirm the four-dimensional approach of social perception of robots which included competence, sociability, morality, and anthropomorphism. Instead, the EFA revealed three dimensions of social perception of robots: anthropomorphism, morality/sociability, and activity/cooperation. The first factor, anthropomorphism, refers to the morphological attributes and feelings toward the robot. The second factor, morality/sociability, depicts the 'social personality' of the robot, Factor three is more heterogenous and includes attributions necessary for cooperation, for example within specific work settings. Even though the factor structure has not yet been fully confirmed, we are confident that this can be achieved in subsequent studies. As can be seen in Table A (Appendix), items especially from the factors morality/sociability and activity/cooperation showed large portions of missing values. All the more interesting are the good reliabilities, which suggest that the subscales do hold merit. Further research on whether the factorial structure can be assumed is needed and should be advanced soon. As for the sample, we need to point out that it is not without bias: For one, our sample is, as is common in this area of research, highly educated with almost half of it (45.6%) having obtained a university degree. Therefore, one limitation of this study is the generalizability. Nonetheless, we suggest that in order to collect more diverse data, the SPRS should be applicated in manifold contexts. As we pointed out earlier, we see the development of this scale as an ongoing process. Secondly, since robots are still somewhat of an exception especially in social settings, we suspect a hypothetical bias, that is, the way in which people are perceiving robots now, without close contact, is not necessarily the way in which they will perceive robots if applied [41]. Therefore, we suggest to apply the SPRS two-fold: Once before the implementation of robots in social settings, and once after a settling-in period. With this approach, pitfalls can be identified and potentially eradicated.

To our knowledge, the Social Perception of Robots Scale is the first of its kind to be constructed by means of exploratory and confirmatory factor analysis and validated with external criteria. We found indications that the construct validity left some things to desire. By comparing the results of the CFA and EFA, results indicate that the sample was not ideal: as we already mentioned, we suspect that missing values had a limiting influence on our approaches to validate the SPRS. Nonetheless, we are confident that future research will fare better at validating the psychometric properties of the SPRS. By taking into account that no other scale was validated along external criteria, we suggest that despite the limitations, the SPRS could serve as a valuable tool complementing existing scales to assess robot perception [18, 19]. Especially in the light of recently published works investigating perceived danger of robots [42] and trust in robots [14] in relation to anthropomorphic design and Robot Acceptance at Work [43], questions of perception, including social perception, need to be considered. We suggest that in order to mitigate possible adverse reactions of users, social perception of the robot in terms of anthropomorphism, sociability/morality, and activity/cooperation should be considered by designers. We suggest applying the SPRS when implementing robots in cooperative work and social settings to prescreen their perception and subsequent acceptance by users who will be in contact with these robots. Even though first steps toward successful integration of robots in cooperative work and social settings were taken, we are confident that a focus on the perception of social dimensions of robots is highly relevant and deserves more recognition.

Acknowledgments. The research was funded by the Deutsche Forschungsgemeinschaft (DFG, German Research Foundation – [Project-ID 416228727 – SFB 1410]).

Appendix

Table A. Percentage of missing values per item, sorted by factors

Item	Missing values in %	
	Sample 1 $n = 500$	Sample 2 $n = 1\,032$
Factor one		
warm – cold	6	7,3
natural – artificial	5,6	5,1
humanlike – machinelike	0,2	0,3
has a consciousness – does not have a consciousness	23,6	21,6
real – unreal	2,4	2,8
moves smoothly – moves rigidly	1,2	1,0
pleasant – unpleasant	6,2	7,0
organic – mechanic	7	6,2
Factor two		
likeable – unlikeable	9,4	10,5
good-natured – hostile	23,4	26,3
polite – impolite	12,2	14,0
moral – immoral	44,6	47,4
honest – dishonest	32,6	31,8
ethical – unethical	41	42,5
Factor three		
fair – unfair	32,8	34,8
diligent – lazy	15,4	21,5
altruistic – self-serving	25,2	28,4
active – inert	6,8	8,3

The Social Perception of Robots Scale (SPRS) – German Version.[2]

Wie schätzen Sie den Roboter in Hinblick auf die angegebenen Merkmale ein? Wie handelt/denkt/wirkt der Roboter aus Ihrer Sicht?

	1	2	3	4	5	
wie ein Mensch	O	O	O	O	O	wie eine Maschine
warm	O	O	O	O	O	kalt
natürlich	O	O	O	O	O	künstlich
echt	O	O	O	O	O	unecht
organisch	O	O	O	O	O	mechanisch
angenehm	O	O	O	O	O	unangenehm
bewegt sich flüssig	O	O	O	O	O	bewegt sich ungelenk
hat ein Bewusstsein	O	O	O	O	O	hat kein Bewusstsein
ethisch	O	O	O	O	O	unethisch
moralisch	O	O	O	O	O	unmoralisch
ehrlich	O	O	O	O	O	unehrlich
gutmütig	O	O	O	O	O	feindselig
sympathisch	O	O	O	O	O	unsympathisch
höflich	O	O	O	O	O	unhöflich
fair	O	O	O	O	O	unfair
uneigennützig	O	O	O	O	O	eigennützig
fleißig	O	O	O	O	O	faul
aktiv	O	O	O	O	O	träge

References

1. Demir, K.A., Döven, G., Sezen, B.: Industry 5.0 and human-robot co-working. Procedia Comput. Sci. **158**, 688–695 (2019). https://doi.org/10.1016/j.procs.2019.09.104
2. Brynjolfsson, E., McAfee, A.: The Second Machine Age: Work, Progress, and Prosperity in a Time of Brilliant Technologies. W. W. Norton & Company Inc, New York, NY, USA (2014)
3. Savela, N., Turja, T., Oksanen, A.: Social acceptance of robots in different occupational fields: a systematic literature review. Int. J. Soc. Robot. **10**(4), 493–502 (2017). https://doi.org/10.1007/s12369-017-0452-5
4. Feil-Seifer, D., Mataric, M.J.: Socially assistive robotics. In: 2005 9th International Conference on Rehabilitation Robotics, ICORR 2005, pp. 465–468. IEEE, Chicago, IL, USA (2005). https://doi.org/10.1109/ICORR.2005.1501143
5. Onnasch, L., Roesler, E.: A taxonomy to structure and analyze human–robot interaction. Int. J. Soc. Robot. **13**(4), 833–849 (2020). https://doi.org/10.1007/s12369-020-00666-5
6. Bishop, L., van Maris, A., Dogramadzi, S., Zook, N.: Social robots: the influence of human and robot characteristics on acceptance. Paladyn J. Behav. Robot. **10**, 346–358 (2019). https://doi.org/10.1515/pjbr-2019-0028

---

[2] Die Items sollten randomisiert vorgegeben werden.

7. Zlotowski, J., Bartneck, C.: The inversion effect in HRI: are robots perceived more like humans or objects? In: 2013 8th ACM/IEEE International Conference on Human-Robot Interaction (HRI), pp. 365–372. IEEE, Tokyo, Japan (2013). https://doi.org/10.1109/HRI.2013.6483611

8. Fiske, S.T., Cuddy, A.J.C., Glick, P., Xu, J.: A model of (often mixed) stereotype content: competence and warmth respectively follow from perceived status and competition. J. Pers. Soc. Psychol. **82**, 878–902 (2002). https://doi.org/10.1037/0022-3514.82.6.878

9. Cuddy, A.J.C., Fiske, S.T., Glick, P.: Warmth and competence as universal dimensions of social perception: the stereotype content model and the BIAS map. Adv. Exp. Soc. Psychol. **40**, 61–149 (2008). https://doi.org/10.1016/S0065-2601(07)00002-0

10. Kervyn, N., Fiske, S., Yzerbyt, V.: Forecasting the primary dimension of social perception: symbolic and realistic threats together predict warmth in the stereotype content model. Soc. Psychol. **46**, 36–45 (2015). https://doi.org/10.1027/1864-9335/a000219

11. Abele, A.E., Ellemers, N., Fiske, S.T., Koch, A., Yzerbyt, V.: Navigating the social world: toward an integrated framework for evaluating self, individuals, and groups. Psychol. Rev. **128**, 290–314 (2021). https://doi.org/10.1037/rev0000262

12. Fiske, S.T.: Stereotype content: warmth and competence endure. Curr. Dir. Psychol. Sci. **27**, 67–73 (2018). https://doi.org/10.1177/0963721417738825

13. Ernst, C.-P.H., Herm-Stapelberg, N., Mainz, J.G.-U.: Gender stereotyping's influence on the perceived competence of Siri and Co. In: Proceedings of the Americas Conference on Information Systems (AMCIS), AMCIS 2020, Salt Lake City, Utah, USA (2020). https://aisel.aisnet.org/amcis2020/cognitive_in_is/cognitive_in_is/4

14. Schaefer, K.E., Sanders, T.L., Yordon, R.E., Billings, D.R., Hancock, P.A.: Classification of robot form: factors predicting perceived trustworthiness. Proc. Hum. Fact. Ergon. Soc. Ann. Meet. **56**, 1548–1552 (2012). https://doi.org/10.1177/1071181312561308

15. de Visser, E.J., et al.: Almost human: anthropomorphism increases trust resilience in cognitive agents. J. Exp. Psychol. Appl. **22**, 331–349 (2016). https://doi.org/10.1037/xap0000092

16. Mandl, S., et al.: Embodied digital technologies: first insights in the social and legal perception of robots and users of prostheses. Front. Robot. AI. **9**, 787970 (2022). https://doi.org/10.3389/frobt.2022.787970

17. Sauppé, A., Mutlu, B.: The social impact of a robot co-worker in industrial settings. In: Proceedings of the 33rd Annual ACM Conference on Human Factors in Computing Systems, CHI 2015, pp. 3613–3622. ACM Press, Seoul, Republic of Korea (2015). https://doi.org/10.1145/2702123.2702181

18. Carpinella, C.M., Wyman, A.B., Perez, M.A., Stroessner, S.J.: The robotic social attributes scale (RoSAS): development and validation. In: Proceedings of the 2017 ACM/IEEE International Conference on Human-Robot Interaction, pp. 254–262. ACM, Vienna Austria (2017). https://doi.org/10.1145/2909824.3020208

19. Bartneck, C., Kulić, D., Croft, E., Zoghbi, S.: Measurement instruments for the anthropomorphism, animacy, likeability, perceived intelligence, and perceived safety of robots. Int. J. Soc. Robot. **1**, 71–81 (2009). https://doi.org/10.1007/s12369-008-0001-3

20. Epley, N., Waytz, A., Cacioppo, J.T.: On seeing human: a three-factor theory of anthropomorphism. Psychol. Rev. **114**, 864–886 (2007). https://doi.org/10.1037/0033-295X.114.4.864

21. Broadbent, E., Stafford, R., MacDonald, B.: Acceptance of healthcare robots for the older population: review and future directions. Int. J. Soc. Robot. **1**, 319–330 (2009). https://doi.org/10.1007/s12369-009-0030-6

22. Scopelliti, M., Giuliani, M.V., Fornara, F.: Robots in a domestic setting: a psychological approach. Univ. Access Inf. Soc. **4**, 146–155 (2005). https://doi.org/10.1007/s10209-005-0118-1

23. Arras, K.O., Cerqui, D.: Do we want to share our lives and bodies with robots? A 2000-people survey. Swiss Federal Institute of Technology Lausanne, EPFL, Lausanne, Switzerland (2005)

24. Schermerhorn, P., Scheutz, M., Crowell, C.R.: Robot social presence and gender: do females view robots differently than males? In: Proceedings of the 3rd International Conference on Human Robot Interaction, HRI 2008. ACM Press, Amsterdam, The Netherlands (2008). https://doi.org/10.1145/1349822.1349857

25. Kuo, I.H., et al.: Age and gender factors in user acceptance of healthcare robots. In: The 18th IEEE International Symposium on Robot and Human Interactive Communication, RO-MAN 2009, pp. 214–219. IEEE, Toyama, Japan (2009). https://doi.org/10.1109/ROMAN.2009.532 6292

26. Franke, T., Attig, C., Wessel, D.: A personal resource for technology interaction: development and validation of the affinity for technology interaction (ATI) scale. Int. J. Hum.-Comput. Interact. **35**, 456–467 (2019). https://doi.org/10.1080/10447318.2018.1456150

27. de Graaf, M.M.A., Allouch, S.B.: Exploring influencing variables for the acceptance of social robots. Robot. Auton. Syst. **61**(12), 1476–1486 (2013). https://doi.org/10.1016/j.robot.2013. 07.007

28. Heerink, M.: Exploring the influence of age, gender, education and computer experience on robot acceptance by older adults. In: Proceedings of the 6th International Conference on Human Robot Interaction, Lausanne, Switzerland, pp. 147–148 (2011). https://doi.org/10. 1145/1957656.1957704

29. Cacioppo, J., Petty, R.E.: The need for cognition. J. Pers. Soc. Psychol. **42**, 116–131 (1982). https://doi.org/10.1037/0022-3514.42.1.116

30. Palan, S., Schitter, C.: Prolific.ac—a subject pool for online experiments. J. Behav. Exp. Finan. **17**, 22–27 (2018). https://doi.org/10.1016/j.jbef.2017.12.004

31. SoftBank Robotics: Pepper. https://www.softbankrobotics.com/emea/en/pepper. Accessed 11 Nov 2021

32. Arlamovsky, M.: ROBOLOVE. NGF - Nikolaus Geyrhalter Filmproduktion (2019)

33. Chita-Tegmark, M., Law, T., Rabb, N., Scheutz, M.: Can you trust your trust measure? In: Proceedings of the 2021 ACM/IEEE International Conference on Human-Robot Interaction, HRI 2021, Boulder, Colorado, USA (2021). https://doi.org/10.1145/3434073.3444677

34. Aquino, K., Reed, A.: The self-importance of moral identity. J. Pers. Soc. Psychol. **83**, 1423–1440 (2002). https://doi.org/10.1037//0022-3514.83.6.1423

35. Meyer, B., Asbrock, F.: Disabled or Cyborg? How bionics affect stereotypes toward people with physical disabilities. Front. Psychol. **9**, 2251 (2018). https://doi.org/10.3389/fpsyg.2018. 02251

36. Bless, H., Wänke, M., Bohner, G., Fellhauer, R.F., Schwarz, N.: Need for cognition: a scale measuring engagement and happiness in cognitive tasks. Zeitschrift für Sozialpsychologie. **25**, 147–154 (1994)

37. R Core Team: R: A language and environment for statistical computing. R Foundation for Statistical Computing, Vienna, Austria (2021)

38. Watkins, M.W.: Exploratory factor analysis: a guide to best practice. J. Black Psychol. **44**, 219–246 (2018). https://doi.org/10.1177/0095798418771807

39. Horn, J.L.: A rationale and test for the number of factors in factor analysis. Psychometrika **30**, 179–185 (1965). https://doi.org/10.1007/BF02289447

40. Cronbach, L.J.: Coefficient alpha and the internal structure of tests. Psychometrika **16**(3), 297–334 (1951)

41. Buckell, J., et al.: Hypothetical Bias (2020). https://catalogofbias.org/biases/hypothetical-bias/

42. Müller, B.C.N., Gao, X., Nijssen, S.R.R., Damen, T.G.E.: I, robot: how human appearance and mind attribution relate to the perceived danger of robots. Int. J. Soc. Robot. **13**(4), 691–701 (2020). https://doi.org/10.1007/s12369-020-00663-8

43. Turja, T., Oksanen, A.: Robot acceptance at work: a multilevel analysis based on 27 EU countries. Int. J. Soc. Robot. **11**(4), 679–689 (2019). https://doi.org/10.1007/s12369-019-005 26-x

AI and Digital Tools for Collaborative Healthcare Networks 5.0

Care Pathway as the Basis for Collaborative Business Model Innovation in Healthcare

Julius Francis Gomes[1], Marika Iivari[1(✉)], Timo Koivumäki[1], Milla Immonen[2], Miia Jansson[1], Minna Pikkarainen[3], Kirsi Rasmus[1], and Yueqiang Xu[1]

[1] University of Oulu, Oulu, Finland
{julius.francisgomes,marika.iivari}@oulu.fi
[2] VTT Technical Research Centre of Finland, Oulu, Finland
[3] Oslo Metropolitan University, Oslo, Norway

Abstract. Digital transformation has disrupted various healthcare domains, yet we are just starting to witness the enrollment of digital solutions enabled by technologies such as artificial intelligence and machine learning. Stroke is one of the leading causes of death and permanent disability globally. Research evidence suggests a need for newer technology-enabled collaborative service models that will not only improve stroke care but are economically viable for stakeholders (i.e., service providers, patients, and payers). A new collaborative service model equally requires the development of new collaborative business models in the stroke care cycle. In a large-scale research ecosystem in Finland, the stroke care pathway is utilized to identify the scope of digitalization in early stroke diagnosis, treatment, rehabilitation, and secondary prevention. This study presents how the stroke care pathway has been used as the basis for new collaborative business models and healthcare service innovation.

Keywords: Collaborative business model · Healthcare innovation · Artificial intelligence · Care pathway · Stroke

1 Introduction

The disruption caused by the use of data in the healthcare sector, e.g. the availability of biomedical data and the genetic makeup, has been compared with how information and communications technologies changed our society in the past decades [1]. Various forms of data and digital disruptions in healthcare help not only overcome existing long-term challenges in the domain (i.e., ageing population, growing non-communicable disease patient group) but also create novel vertical solutions [2, 3]. Furthermore, the immersion of ICT in the health sector has enabled people to acquire care outside hospitals and control and share their personal health information and user-generated content for more personalized care [4]. Nevertheless, we are only starting to witness the enrollment of digital solutions enabled by technologies such as artificial intelligence (AI) and machine learning (ML) [5]. One of the reasons for the inertia in embracing the possibilities of these new technologies is that the successful utilization of AI and ML technologies requires a

© IFIP International Federation for Information Processing 2022
Published by Springer Nature Switzerland AG 2022
L. M. Camarinha-Matos et al. (Eds.): PRO-VE 2022, IFIP AICT 662, pp. 337–347, 2022.
https://doi.org/10.1007/978-3-031-14844-6_27

holistic understanding of the implications of these technologies. The findings in Blomster and Koivumäki [6] suggest that the capability to understand the requirements for the data, the impact of the technology adoption on the service and business environment and rigorous business processes and management procedures to support data governance are the most crucial competencies of successful AI-based business model innovation.

AI-driven innovations are crucial for healthcare organizations in bridging the gap between future possibilities and healthcare delivery [4]. Especially innovations related to new approaches to preventing [7] and managing illness call for new technology-enabled solutions. Stroke is a medical condition caused by poor blood flow to the brain, and it is one of the leading causes of death and permanent disability globally. The scope of digitalization in stroke diagnosis, treatment, rehabilitation, and secondary prevention has different implications and needs for recovering patients and care providers. Therefore, we need to draw attention to patient care pathways and how digital solutions utilize data for the most optimal decision-making during the treatment continuum. Trans-ischemic attack (TIA) is called a "mini-stroke", where the blood supply to the part of the brain is temporarily disrupted. TIA patients have a higher risk of having a stroke soon after TIA. On the other hand, usually, TIA patients do not have any symptoms after 24 h of the attack, and they do not need any care or rehabilitation afterwards, only lifestyle changes and preventive medication. In this article, we focus only on the stroke care pathway.

Research evidence suggests [5] that there is a need for newer technology-enabled collaborative service models that will not only improve health care but are also economically viable for stakeholders (i.e., service providers, patients, and payers). This calls for the development of new collaborative business models in the care cycle that are based on patient care pathways. This single case study focuses on understanding *"how to use care pathway as a basis for collaborative business models in data-intensive healthcare innovation"*. This is done by examining the challenges and success factors when a care pathway is used as a baseline for business model innovation in the ecosystem that is collaborating to create a collaborative business with data-intensive innovations for stroke diagnosis, treatment, rehabilitation, and secondary prevention.

The research is structured as follows. First, the literature on patient care pathways is reviewed in connection with digitalization. Then, we will explore how business models are conceptualized in a collaborative healthcare setting. Then we will present our empirical case, explain the empirical findings and relate them to academic discussions in the final chapter.

2 Care Pathways and Patient Journey in Digital Health

2.1 Care Pathways and the Patient Journey

A patient care pathway acts as a template of the care to be offered to a specific group of patients; however, it is not intended to compromise clinical judgement. A care pathway is a complex plan to support the mutual decision-making and organization of care processes for a well-defined group of patients, in most cases in a well-defined period [8]. One of the critical aims of building care pathways is to improve the quality of care across the treatment continuum. Care pathway has its roots in various management concepts and terms, such as the critical path method, the six sigma method, business process redesign and the theory of constraints [9]. However, works on care pathways have primarily focused on care "process" improvement and related innovation. Existing literature somewhat overlooks the need for improvement and innovation of care "products" and "systems" that can further improve the overall care pathway performance. Patient care pathways are often finalized as a formal document presenting steps in the care process, the period in each step that the treatment will require or even the period that needs to be elapsed before the next step can be started. Although formally organized care pathways become an integral part of the selected patient groups' treatment once implemented, the unformalized care pathways can often be used as a tool for innovation and unit of analysis [10]. The concept of patient journey maps is closely tied to such unformalized patient care pathways. Patient journeys emphasize user centrism and how it could impact designing future care pathways and solutions for healthcare [11]. Patient engagement and input about patients' expectations of solutions can enhance the acceptance of new medical and non-medical devices and systems [12]. In the scope of this paper, we use the terms patient care pathway and patient journey interchangeably.

2.2 Digitalization in Modern Healthcare

According to Standell and Wolff [13], the total number of people aged over 65 in the 28 EU states is expected to peak at 149.2 million in 2050 from 101.2 million in 2018. World Health Organization (WHO) [14] states that among six WHO regions, the European region has the highest number of patients affected by non-communicable diseases. Together, these five significant conditions account for 77% of diseases and 86% of deaths in the European region.

Data-intensive digitalization in healthcare focuses on solving problems for the ageing society and non-communicable diseases [2, 15]. Within this scope, data becomes a vital resource, which is available for collection, but in the healthcare domain, it is often unavailable for analysis, innovation, and commercialization purposes. Data analytics and visualization techniques help in better decision-making for individual patient treatment [16, 17] and can also help create better health policies for the population. AI capabilities and its application in healthcare as a medical device, still have different hurdles such as legitimacy, ethical use, standardization and regulatory approval. To enable AI deployment and governance for healthcare, a collaboration between policymakers, healthcare professionals, technology developers and researchers is needed, as well as international cooperation and coordination [18].

While low- and middle-income societies lack direct financial resources to be invested in the healthcare systems, higher-income societies also face a lack of other human and technological resources. Data can be used as resources for better-personalized healthcare services that help patients get better care and allow healthcare professionals to organize their care. Automatic data collection and standardized interfaces are among key technological success factors for new services in healthcare [19]. To manage the various challenges in future healthcare, digital-intensive health solutions can be developed to optimize access, sharing, analysis and usage of collected data [15]. Future digital-intensive solutions are envisioned to bring together patients, doctors, nurses, and other healthcare professionals. The secure and proper data channeling between various stakeholders can be completed according to the MyData principle [20].

3 Towards Collaborative Business Models in Healthcare

3.1 Business Model Innovation

Business models are often imposed by technological innovation that creates the need to bring discoveries to market and the opportunity to respond to unmet customer needs. Hwang and Christensen [21] claimed that disruptive technologies should match innovative business models. Christensen et al. [22] conceptualize business models to be made of four elements: 1) a value proposition for customers; 2) resources (e.g., people, money, technology); 3) the processes used by the organization to convert inputs to finished products or services; and 4) the profit formula dictating the margins, asset velocity, and scale required to achieve an attractive return [30, p. 33]. These elements are interdependent and must be compatible for the business model to function [22]. The business model needs to describe how the solution brings value to its customers in a profitable way and how this value is delivered to the customers.

The health sector has long been criticized for lacking innovation in the business models [21]. This resonates with academic research on business model innovation in the healthcare context. First, it is important to acknowledge that business models are not static descriptions of elements but evolve, requiring constant innovation and experimentation [23]. Adding to the complexity of business model innovation in healthcare, it is also important to note that creating business models for new ventures emphasizes a different focus than developing business models for more mature organizations. Therefore, business model innovation can be defined as the design of novel business models for newly formed ventures (BMD) or the reconfiguration (BMR) of existing business models [24] to explain the two types of business model innovation. While BMD refers to the entrepreneurial activities of creating, implementing, and validating; BMR involves reconfiguration requires shifting from an existing model to a new one through gradual to radical degrees of change in the new business model. In the case of business model reconfiguration, the innovation in the business model often has an epicentre. As the business model is assumed to have a customer side, a resource and capabilities side, a value proposition element, and a cost and revenue element, the business model innovation can be driven by any one or more of these "epicentres".

3.2 Collaborative Business Models in Healthcare

Traditionally, healthcare systems have suffered from fragmentation and a low innovation capacity, where challenges related to balancing the allocation of resources and performance [4, 25]. The innovation process in healthcare increasingly requires access and combinations of knowledge from different departments and sectors; innovators are pushed towards collaboration [4, 5] with various types of actors to overcome these challenges. However, how organizations manage this collaboration and co-develop their capabilities to build mutually beneficial relationships becomes a central question [26]. Complementarities in resources and alignment in objectives, opportunities and advantages can create a basis for collaboration in healthcare business ecosystems [3]. Also, complementary strategic goals, opportunities, and combined advantages allow collaborating business entities to co-create and co-capture greater value [27].

Newer conceptualizations of business models take the external environment and ecosystem into account and emphasize collaboration, synergy and compatibility [27]. Business models can be used as tools to bend the boundaries of organizations [28], where a collaboration of the focal organization with its network can be considered one of the main functions of the business model [29]. Therefore, understanding how business models can be utilized as tools for developing and streamlining collaboration, more specifically the co-creation, co-capture and co-development of capabilities, opportunities and eventually solutions, becomes central. The search for collaboration, synergy and compatibility puts even more pressure on innovators of healthcare solutions. In addition to internally matching the different business model elements, they also need to ensure their business model is compatible with the partners in the process. Therefore, this kind of interplay between the design and reconfiguration perspectives of business model innovation, coupled with collaboration, is of crucial importance to academic discussion on business models and practitioners.

4 Research Approach

4.1 Stroke-Data Project

The research data for this study is primarily collected from a Business Finland-funded Smart Life R&D project consortium titled "Stroke-Data". The consortium comprises various stakeholders from industry and academia; five active industry partners are involved in the project, and three industry partners complement the project as affiliates. The overall setup of the industry partners has a mix of SMEs and larger organizations in the ecosystem. In addition, the research consortium includes three research organizations and three hospital organizations. Among the hospital organizations, two tertiary level hospitals are responsible for population healthcare for large areas of the country. The third hospital organization involved in the project is a privately functioning rehabilitation hospital. Among the industry partners, different partners focus on digital health solution design and development, medical device production for clients, medical data platform creators, and remote monitoring device and service producers. Together, the stakeholders form a specialized data-intensive healthcare ecosystem, with a mutual goal to create ways to provide better patient care through the co-creation of novel data-intensive innovations for stroke identification, treatment, diagnosis, and rehabilitation.

While the R&D project primarily aims to create new data-intensive solutions for TIA and Stroke care to provide better care and save health costs, the consortium also creates an ecosystem of stakeholders working towards implementing research results for the future healthcare market. The R&D actions include business model ideation, business model innovation with partners, co-creation of solution ideas, and conceptualizing ecosystemic collaborative business models for Stroke-Data.

4.2 Data Collection

The co-creation of data-intensive innovations in healthcare requires clinical data. The project consortium initially aimed to obtain datasets from real-life situations along the care path of stroke and TIA patients. The data used for research and creating data-intensive innovations comes from a local birth cohort, the Northern Finland Birth Cohort (NFBC), and by collecting new data sets with various sensors and devices at two hospitals and one rehabilitation hospital. The data collection at hospitals happened, with patients' consent, after the patients had received the most acute treatment and were in the ward for follow-up. In addition, the collected data sets allowed the consortium to focus on co-creating solutions for the phases in the care path after stroke, such as rehabilitation.

This research was constructed as a qualitative single case study [30]. First, during the early stages of the joint effort, six semi-structured interview sessions with industry partners focused on Stroke-Data objectives, technical infrastructure, existing business models, and co-creation opportunities, among other topics. Further, a scenario mapping workshop was organized as a part of service ideation and innovation; this workshop was co-organized with medical professionals who are experts in the field of Stroke treatment and diagnosis, technology developers from multiple industry partners, and researchers. There were altogether 27 participants in this workshop. The results of the scenario workshop helped to identify the current state of technology, data utilization and the patient journey in the studied context and the preferable and probable scenarios for the future. Based on the workshop results, the needs and challenges of the current patient journey were identified, which helped draft an initial set of high-level requirements for the future preferable patient journey. From there, coupled with requirements and opinions from clinical experts, the research team in the Stroke-Data project started working on identifying a more detailed set of user needs and requirements, which were further validated in the project workshop.

Altogether, 157 high-level user needs were identified in this task that can be developed through software solutions. In addition, the second round of business model-focused interviews were conducted with all the industry partners that raised issues such as data security, privacy, access, innovation in healthcare, and collaborative activities within the ecosystem. Altogether 10 follow-up interviews were conducted in this phase. The follow-up interviews also covered challenges in inter-organizational collaboration, data-related issues in digital healthcare innovation, and validating the data collection approach.

5 Findings and Analysis

Stroke, one of the leading causes of permanent disability and death globally, has a broad impact on societies. The patient journey or the care pathway has been identified as a critical basis of service innovation in the context of this R&D project. However, it is understood from the research data that the contributors agree to observe the patient journey on a general level, which will enable service creation opportunities to be broader. The generic stroke patient journey can be perceived to have five stages where medical assistance can be provided to the patient: 1) the scene of the stroke event and the ER, 2) The intensive care and surgery facilities, 3) post-surgery care and Stroke ward, 4) rehabilitation in-hospital care, and 5) rehabilitation in home-care.

The 157 user needs covered the phases of prediction, emergency care, diagnosis, and rehabilitation of stroke patients. Further, these high-level user needs were defined for both users who are healthcare professionals and lay people.

Initial interviews revealed that among all the industry partners in the ecosystem, some had clear research and development plans in the domain of digital health, which contributes to the stroke patient care pathway. Some of the industry partners brought special skills and long-term goals aligned with the public research program's aims. In addition, the Small and Medium Enterprises (SME)s involvement in the project is for new solution development and validated references to their solutions. Most industry partners involved are not generic stroke or neuro care providers. Hence, the devices and services created in the program context significantly differ from the usual offerings for most industry partners. The same can be argued about the business models for each industry partner involved in the case.

The original objectives of the research project included clinical data collection and research of new services in four out of the five stages of the stroke patient journey. Data collection from the intensive care and surgery facilities was identified outside the scope of the project's onset. However, during the Covid-19 pandemic, clinical data collection using new devices for foundational research proved unfeasible, especially for stroke patients who are often highly vulnerable. Hence, the clinical data collection was planned to be reduced to stroke ward patients and rehabilitation hospital patients, besides data from control groups. While the clinical data is not the subject of this paper, the clinical data collection and research on new services affect the co-creation and collaboration outcomes.

The industry partners in the stroke data project used the care pathway and business model workshops organized in the project as a baseline to identify the key focus areas of their stroke-related services and businesses in overall stroke care. One of the partners decided to focus on pre-hospital care. In contrast, two of the partners in the ecosystem concentrated their efforts more on the rehabilitation of stroke patients dividing their businesses into one vertical solution including two perspectives 1) rehabilitation decision support and 2) personalized data-intensive service innovation for the stroke rehabilitation patients. Although the two companies focusing on rehabilitation cases have a clear distinction in the offering or basic value proposition and customer segments they are serving; the partners agreed to co-create one "vertical solution" for the involved rehabilitation hospital having separate interfaces instead of creating two "horizontal solutions" which could potentially become competitors. The research data suggests that the decision to make one "vertical solution" was as much a "business model decision" as it was a "technology decision" by the industry partners involved in the case (Fig. 1).

From the collaborative business model perspective, we can observe that both partners targeted the same "phase/stage" of the stroke patient journey. However, their targeted end-users group are different but working together in such a way that these end-user groups are constantly connected for the whole care cycle to be completed is bringing them additional value compared to their competitors in the market. Further, from the value proposition elements, the partnering players identified complementarities in such a way by not only creating value for customers but also by reducing future competition among themselves. A coherent technology strategy means reduced technical infrastructure costs for both parties. Although the vertical solutions are closely integrated, they can also be sold as standalone systems to different customers where the need is such. However, the closely integrated solutions also bring the opportunity of "piggybacking" sales for

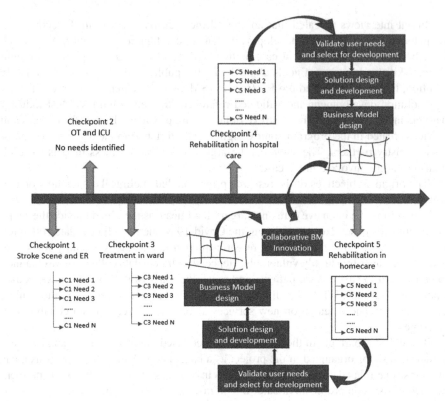

Fig. 1. The Stroke-Data process: from patient care pathways to collaborative business models.

both partnering players; a new sale made by one partner can bring new customers to the partner organization.

While looking closely at the collaboration between these two companies, a few essential continuous efforts have helped this collaboration succeed thus far. First, the partners have agreed on specific resource sharing between themselves. This indicates that both the partners are willing to identify the strength and expertise of the other side's organization and utilize the collective strength. The resources not only include human or financial resources, but they can also include technology know-how, a specific skill set and expertise. Second, both partners have actively participated in customer case meetings to ideate, identify, and develop the solution on a regular schedule. Precise goal setting and following through with checkpoints have helped the collaboration smoother. Third, when it comes to solution testing, the organizations adopted an "open" strategy to allow the other party to test the solutions as standalone and build modular services. Fourth, seamless communication between partnering organizations has been identified as a key to inter-organizational collaboration. Fifth, although the companies are not yet in the commercialization phase, there are early discussions within the organizations on value-sharing models that can benefit both parties.

Data-intensive innovation in the healthcare domain in the current European market is challenging due to data protection regulations if the innovating organizations are looking to use actual patient data for development. The original aim of this collaborative solution for the Stroke-data rehabilitation case included data analytics and AI capabilities applied to actual patient data collected in the scope of the research project. However, current data protection regulations and the test use of the developed solution with actual patients meant that such analytics and AI capabilities could not be trialled in the first phase. In the current scope, the collaborating partners agreed the vertical solutions would create a seamless communication channel between rehabilitating Stroke patients and healthcare professionals to track their rehabilitation process digitally. The inclusion of data analytics, AI and ML capabilities will be done in the future phases of the collaboration.

Looking at the Stroke-Ward phase of the studied case, although the clinical data collection and data-oriented medical research are being conducted, they are currently conducted as foundation research only. Only public organization (University and Hospital) researchers are permitted to access and analyze the collected clinical data for any potential ML or AI algorithms. Any personnel from organizations with commercial objectives will only be given access to an anonymized and aggregated data set with no identifiable variables available. This prolongs the product-to-market timeline for the participating partners in this phase.

6 Discussion and Conclusions

In this study, we looked at the Stroke-Data ecosystem, where multiple research organizations, hospitals and industry partners combined efforts to co-create data-intensive solutions to improve the current state of early stroke treatment, diagnosis, rehabilitation, and secondary prevention. From a business model innovation perspective, the case shows how a patient journey or care pathway can be used as a unit of analysis to locate the "epicentre of innovation". Our findings suggest that collaborating partners not only utilized these "epicentres" for innovation but further deepened the collaboration between them. The complementarities of resources and alignment of objectives also enable creating such collaborative business models [26, 27]. We also observed in this case that the same epicentres could enable collaboration between multiple organizations. This collaboration can take various forms: resource sharing, skill and expertise exchange, business case development, and business model co-development, among other things. The care pathway approach for collaborative business model innovation is not only meant to identify the initial epicentre of collaboration but instead, continuously supports collaboration throughout the development cycle. This is important so that the developed solutions will address the needs of the "patient care pathway" besides the needs of the patient in the specific phase of the pathway.

Some of the identified benefits of this approach realized during this exercise include a clear and empirically validated value that the newly created solutions will have; as solutions developed in this approach are based on actual user needs and requirements, close cooperation means a faster development cycle, continuous customer feedback in the development cycle also improves the solution outcome. As one of the challenges of this approach, these activities seem to be individual-oriented. Changes in personnel in partnering organizations can impact collaboration. Also, organizational objectives, resources, and objectives are essential in addressing specific pathway needs.

Another challenge in such activities is the strict regulations on data usage by commercial organizations and the lack of collaboration with healthcare professionals.

The identified limitations of this study include the research data is gathered from a single project. Although rich and diverse in qualitative terms, it is challenged by generalizability. Current data protection regulations stand, private organizations with commercial goals are not permitted to access and analyze personal data which are not "fully anonymized". To develop such solutions, the innovating companies need to test the developing solutions with a "synthetic data set". The result is that even digital solutions that require certification as a "medical device" will need to go through formal clinical trials. Using a "synthetic data set" in the development rounds can end up being unrepresentative of the actual use case in various ways, resulting in unreliable trial attempts. Hence the cycle from idea to product to implementation can be significantly longer than expected. Future research is called on tackling how to speed up the commercialization of data-driven healthcare solutions and how collaborative methods can help validate especially personal data at an individual level and scale these solutions for broader industry use. We also need to increase our understanding of the companies' challenges when making AI-driven innovations in the ecosystems creating certified medical solutions.

References

1. Horgan, D., Romão, M., Torbett, R., Brand, A.: European data-driven economy: a lighthouse initiative on personalised medicine. Heal. Policy Technol. 3(4), 226–233 (2014). https://doi. org/10.1016/j.hlpt.2014.10.007
2. Blake, B.: Healthcare and the Promise of Digitization. Gartner.com (2017). https://www.scm world.com/healthcare-promise-digitization/
3. Gomes, J.F.: Exploring connected health business ecosystems through business models (2020)
4. Hyrkäs, P., Haukipuro, L., Väinämö, S., Iivari, M., Sachinopoulou, A., Majava, J.: Collaborative innovation in healthcare: a case study of hospitals as innovation platforms. Int. J. Value Chain Manag. 11(1), 24–41 (2020). https://doi.org/10.1504/IJVCM.2020.105475
5. Kraus, S., Schiavone, F., Pluzhnikova, A., Invernizzi, A.C.: Digital transformation in healthcare: Analyzing the current state-of-research. J. Bus. Res. 123, 557–567 (2021). https://doi. org/10.1016/j.jbusres.2020.10.030
6. Blomster, M., Koivumäki, T.: Exploring the resources, competencies, and capabilities needed for successful machine learning projects in digital marketing. Inf. Syst. e-Bus. Manage. 20(1), 123–169 (2022). https://doi.org/10.1007/s10257-021-00547-y
7. Iivari, M., Pikkarainen, M., Gomes, J.F., Ranta, J., Ylén, P.: Toward Open inz novation and data-driven health policymaking, June 2021, pp. 199–225 (2019). https://doi.org/10.1142/978 9813271647_0007
8. Middleton, S., Barnett, J., Reeves, D.S.: What is an integrated care pathway? Hayward Med. Commun. 3(3), 1–8 (2001)
9. Schrijvers, G., van Hoorn, A., Huiskes, N.: The care pathway concept: concepts and theories: an introduction. Int. J. Integr. Care 12(6), e192 (2012)
10. Olsson, L.-E., Hansson, E., Ekman, I., Karlsson, J.: A cost-effectiveness study of a patient-centred integrated care pathway. J. Adv. Nurs. 65(8), 1626–1635 (2009)
11. Simonse, L., Albayrak, A., Starre, S.: Patient journey method for integrated service design. Des. Heal. 3(1), 82–97 (2019). https://doi.org/10.1080/24735132.2019.1582741
12. Trebble, T.M., Hansi, N., Hydes, T., Smith, M.A., Baker, M.: Process mapping the patient journey: an introduction. BMJ 341, c4078–c4078 (2010)

13. Strandell, H., Wolff, P.: "Ageing Europe: Looking at the lives of older people in the EU," Luxembourg (2019). https://doi.org/10.2785/26745
14. WHO: Non-communicable diseases. World Health Organization (2022). https://www.euro. who.int/en/health-topics/noncommunicable-diseases/noncommunicable-diseases. Accessed 25 Apr 2022
15. Chouvarda, I.G., Goulis, D.G., Lambrinoudaki, I., Maglaveras, N.: Connected health and integrated care: toward new models for chronic disease management. Maturitas **82**(1), 22–27 (2015). https://doi.org/10.1016/j.maturitas.2015.03.015
16. Do Nascimento, I.J.B., et al.: Impact of big data analytics on people's health: overview of systematic reviews and recommendations for future studies. J. Med. Internet Res. **23**(4), e27275 (2021). https://doi.org/10.2196/27275
17. Johnson, K.B., et al.: Precision medicine, AI, and the future of personalized health care. Clin. Transl. Sci. **14**(1), 86–93 (2021). https://doi.org/10.1111/cts.12884
18. Morley, J., Murphy, L., Mishra, A., Joshi, I., Karpathakis, K.: Governing data and artificial intelligence for health care: developing an international understanding. JMIR Form. Res. **6**(1), 1–13 (2022). https://doi.org/10.2196/31623
19. Pikkarainen, M., Huhtala, T., Kemppainen, L., Häikiö, J.: Success factors for data–driven service delivery networks. J. Innov. Manag. **7**(4), 14–46 (2019). https://doi.org/10.24840/ 2183-0606_007.004_0003
20. Gomes, J.F., Pääkkönen, J., Iivari, M., Kemppainen, L., Pikkarainen, M.: 'MyData' potential in public health decisions. In: EDSI Conference 2018, pp. 2–6 (2018)
21. Hwang, J., Christensen, C.M.: Disruptive innovation in health care delivery: a framework for business-model innovation. Health Aff. **27**(5), 1329–1335 (2008). https://doi.org/10.1377/hlt haff.27.5.1329
22. Christensen, T.B., Van Bever, D.: The hard truth about business model innovation @BUL-LET reading time: 30 min recommended harnessing the best of globalization designing and developing analytics-based data products unleashing creativity with digital technology. MIT Sloan Manag. Rev. **58**(1), 31–40 (2016)
23. Chesbrough, H.: Business model innovation: opportunities and barriers. Long Range Plann. **43**(2–3), 354–363 (2010). https://doi.org/10.1016/j.lrp.2009.07.010
24. Massa, L., Tucci, C.: Business model innovation. In: The PDMA Handbook of New Product Development, pp. 68–81 (2013). https://doi.org/10.1002/9781118466421.ch4
25. Dias, C., Escoval, A.: The open nature of innovation in the hospital sector: the role of external collaboration networks. Heal. Policy Technol. **1**(4), 181–186 (2012). https://doi.org/10.1016/ j.hlpt.2012.10.002
26. Gomes, J.F., Iivari, M., Pikkarainen, M., Ahokangas, P.: Business models as enablers of ecosystemic interaction: a dynamic capability perspective. Int. J. Soc. Ecol. Sustain. Dev. **9**(3), 1–13 (2018). https://doi.org/10.4018/IJSESD.2018070101
27. Jansson, N., Ahokangas, P., Iivari, M., Perälä-Heape, M., Salo, S.: The competitive advantage of an ecosystemic business model: the case of OuluHealth. Interdiscip. Stud. J. **3**(4), 282–295 (2014)
28. Zott, C., Amit, R.H., Massa, L.: The business model: recent developments and future research. J. Manage. **37**(4), 1019–1042 (2011)
29. Pikkarainen, M., Koivumäki, T., Iivari, M.: Seizing the business opportunities of the MyData service delivery network: transforming the business models of health insurance companies. J. Bus. Model. **8**(2), 39–56 (2020)
30. Yin, R.K.: Case Study Research and Applications: Design and Methods. Sage Publications (2017)

A Semantic-Based Collaborative Ambient-Assisted Working Framework

Turgut Cilsal[1]([✉]), Daniele Spoladore[1,2], Alberto Trombetta[2], and Marco Sacco[1]

[1] Institute of Intelligent Industrial Technologies and Systems for Advanced Manufacturing (STIIMA), National Research Council of Italy (CNR), via G. Previati 1/E, 23900 Lecco, Italy
{turgut.cilsal,daniele.spoladore,marco.sacco}@stiima.cnr.it
[2] Department of Pure and Applied Sciences, Insubria University, via Ottorino Rossi 9, 21100 Varese, Italy
alberto.trombetta@uninsubria.it

Abstract. Over the last two decades an utmost interest has been shown to Ambient Intelligence (AmI), with most of the related applications focusing on home settings. However, considering the ever-increasing number of ageing people occupied in the workforce, the Ambient-Assisted Working (AAW) is arguably at the beginning of its development. For an effective development and integration of AAW systems, cooperation among and shared knowledge from different stakeholders are required. This work proposes an AmI framework leveraging on Semantic Web technologies to foster employees' wellbeing. The AAW framework makes use of a domain ontology, outcome of the cooperation between different stakeholders (employer, employees and environment) to adjust, modify and correct indoor comfort metrics in workplaces. In this paper, the proposed framework's architecture and its underlying ontology are described, along with a use case scenario that illustrates how collaboratively modelled data can actively support ageing workers.

Keywords: Ambient intelligence · Ambient-assisted working · Collaborative design · Ontology-based decision support system · Society 5.0

1 Introduction

The aging workforce is defined as "workers over 55 years old", characterized by age-related impairments, such as in visual and/or hearing capabilities, muscular deterioration, and chronic diseases related to their cardiovascular, respiratory, endocrine, or cognitive systems; these impairments may hinder workers' harmony with the natural flow of daily work requirements [1]. This group of employees represents a relevant portion of the total workforce in EU, with an increase from 14% in 2004 to 20% in 2019 [2]. As this share is expected to raise significantly in the upcoming years, it is essential to take measures to foster the wellbeing of aging workforce in their workplaces. In order to adapt a workplace for such needs in an optimal manner, it is crucial to ensure an eminent level of collaboration between different stakeholders, namely the employer, the employees and the surrounding environment – i.e. the devices for the improvement

L. M. Camarinha-Matos et al. (Eds.): PRO-VE 2022, IFIP AICT 662, pp. 348–355, 2022.
https://doi.org/10.1007/978-3-031-14844-6_28

or maintenance of employees' wellbeing, such as HVAC systems, illumination sources, sensory equipment, etc. The essential factor for a successful collaboration is that all these devices can be clustered around an application that enables context-aware functionality and intercommunication, which can otherwise be connoted by the concept of Internet of Things (IoT). A promising solution to achieve this goal is Ambient Intelligence (AmI), that enables environment responsiveness to the needs of people in a non-invasive, adaptive, anticipatory and personalized fashion by means of embedded, unobtrusive, smart devices [3]. AmI is widely investigated for the care-taking of elderly population in their residences, generally referred as Ambient Assisted Living (AAL). On the other hand, Ambient Assisted Working (AAW) applications are still at the beginning and low in number compared to AAL studies. Therefore, this field is avid for novel and diverse approaches.

In this work, an AAW framework founded on an ontology-based Decision Support System (DSS) is introduced, which does not only aim for safer accommodation of aging workforce via avoiding exacerbation on their health conditions, but also for an increase in efficiency of the business via reducing sick leaves and injuries. This method leverages on the collaboration among different stakeholders, by representing the employees and their relevant characteristics, the partaking utilities and devices, the environmental metrics to be kept record of and controlled, and all of the interactions between these distinct elements. While providing this cooperation, it also contributes to the non-invasiveness principle of AmI by not constantly monitoring the workers but taking necessary actions according to their representations in the ontology. The AAW framework general approach leverages on previous AAL research projects [4, 5] and introduces collaboration as a means to increase the system's scalability for multiple workers in the same workplace.

This paper is organized as follows: Sect. 2 surveys the previous works related to AAW; Sect. 3 illustrates the ontology underlying the DSS and its collaborative ontology engineering process; in Sect. 4, a use case scenario is depicted with preliminary results; lastly, in the conclusion and future works are addressed.

2 Related Work

Following the developments in fields like IoT and AmI, AAW solutions are investigated as a means for providing necessary attention to increasing number of ageing workers in workplaces.

Several studies are mainly focused on continuous monitoring of workers via a variety of smart devices: Sun et al. [6] introduced Healthy Operator 4.0, where an ontology-based DSS drives a health management scheme, withdrawing the required data through smart wearables. Pancardo et al. [7] used a wristband along with an accelerometer for keeping track of workers' stress levels and cardiac status against the effects of heat, while Rick et al. [8] exploited the information retrieved by facial recognition, movement tracking, EEG and ECG devices for observing the physical status and mood variations of employees. Kiyokawa [9] leveraged on worker's concentration and sleepiness monitoring to actuate lighting and speaker system housed on the worker's chair for optimizing his/her performance.

The above-mentioned works either aim at individuals' monitoring and adjustments, lacking non-invasiveness, or offer very generalized solutions that would not be sufficient to enhance the indoor comfort of a workplace; all works miss considering the cooperative nature of a working environment. On the contrary, this paper presents a framework that provides personalized settings without being invasive, leveraging on a cooperative approach for multiple workers working in the same area.

3 Collaborative AAW Framework

In this section, the framework's architecture is explained. The framework is composed of a collaboratively-engineered ontology layer, which needs to determine essential health and environment-related information. Leveraging on sensors, fundamental comfort metrics are monitored and fed to the ontological model, so that reasoning processes can trigger the appropriate actuation to avoid any exacerbation on workers' health issues. In this way, the framework provides a less-invasive system that relies on the workers' location in the workplace and his/her characteristics to provide tailored services, without actively monitoring him/her.

3.1 Ontology Layer

The ontology needs to model the essential health information, used to represent the workers' conditions and to adapt the working environment for each worker, along with the relevant ambient measures. As foreseen in collaborative ontology engineering, stakeholders adopting the ontology and its results should be involved in its development [10]. The AAW framework foresees workers (with the cooperation of their clinicians, who determine the health condition), the employers and the working environment to identify relevant information with the aim of developing an ontology able to actuate the environment, so that it is possible to avoid any environmental condition that would result in an exacerbation of the worker's health issues. Together with the employer, this information is used to define the optimal metrics of the environment for the general wellbeing of all workers. Also, sensors placed in the working environment monitor the defined comfort metrics, while DL reasoning techniques [11] are adopted to detect risk situations and to trigger actuations.

The definition of worker's health condition is performed reusing the International Classification of Functioning, Disability and Health (ICF) and the International Classification of Diseases (ICD10) ontologies [12, 13], since they describe the functional impairments of the worker and provide a common language to foster cooperation among different health stakeholders [14]. Environmental metrics are identified reusing ComfOnt [5], which provides the means to represent measures like CO_2 concentration, humidity rate, temperature, and indoor illuminance – indoor comfort metrics that can act as risk factors for many chronic health conditions [15–18]. The thresholds for each indoor comfort metric and for each specific condition (asthma, COPD, cataract, low vision acuity, etc.) are also modelled in separate modules in guidance of healthcare professionals. Since ComfOnt reuses the Smart Appliance REFerence (SAREF) ontology [19] and parts of Sensor, Observation, Sample, and Actuator ontology (SOSA) [20], both models are reused to represent sensors, the measurements they perform in the working environment, and the actuators.

The resulting ontology is developed with Resource Description Framework (RDF) [21] and Ontology Web Language (OWL) [22], with rules in Semantic Web Rule Language, and hosted on a semantic repository – queryable with SPARQL [23]. As further illustrated in Sect. 4, workers – aware of their health conditions and supported by their clinicians – and employers – leveraging on their knowledge on the working environment – cooperate to define the relevant comfort metrics and actuations to enhance environmental metrics and conditions for aging workforce, thus selecting those concepts and relationships modelled in the ontology and necessary to provide the actuations.

3.2 Components of the Framework

As illustrated in Fig. 1, the AAW Framework is completed with sensors and actuators, as well as a middleware accounted for receiving measurements from sensors, inserting them in the ontology, and triggering reasoning. The prototypical version of the AAW Framework relies on a thermo-hygrometric sensor (AM2320 Digital Temperature and Humidity Sensor), an illuminance sensor (TSL2561 Digital Luminosity/Lux/Light Sensor), a CO2 reader (3709 Adafruit SGP30 Air Quality Sensor), with a RFID Reader to localize the worker.

4 Use Case

The use case foresees a clothing retail company with operations taking place in different countries, where the environmental conditions are different. Two different sales offices in different clothing factories are populated with some ageing workers characterized by varying health conditions, to demonstrate how the level of collaboration between different modules of the ontology is implemented for different situations and to show how the cooperation among employer, employees and the AAW system can produce working conditions' enhancement for different workers.

The first office is situated in Novosibirsk, Russia, characterized by winter temperatures with peaks of $-15\,°C/-20\,°C$, with average humidity equal to 80%, and daylight is available only for limited periods [24]. The second sales office is in Doha, Qatar. In this city, temperature in summer ranges between $35\,°C$ and $40\,°C$. Humidity rate is attested lower than 40% [25]. Company's management values its ageing workforce's expertise, therefore they implemented the AAW framework with the aim of improving the comfort of the employees and avoiding any exacerbation on their health conditions by providing them the most suitable environmental metrics. Both offices are equipped with a thermo-hygrometer, a CO_2 sensor, and an illuminance sensor. There exist a HVAC system that operates for the entire room, a number of general-purpose illumination sources and desks for each employee. Each desk is equipped with an RFID reader, a workstation in which a software that sends the particular worker relative notifications is present, and a minor illumination source for personal use. The workers introduce their RFIDs to their desk-readers to identify themselves.

In Novosibirsk office there are 4 workers, with names and conditions as follow:

- Alex (male, 61 years-old), affected by COPD (ICD J44.9).

- Liza (female, 55 years-old), affected by adult-onset asthma with acute exacerbation (ICD J45. 901).
- Sergei (male, 53 years-old); affected by age-related incipient cataract (ICD H25.0), which causes impairments in glare sensitivity (ICF b21020 "Light sensitivity")
- Nina (female, 26 years-old), no particular health condition.

On the other hand, in Doha office there are 5 workers, defined by following characteristics:

- Khalid (male, 61 years-old), affected by COPD (ICD J44.9).
- Mohamad (male, 57 years-old), affected by low visual acuity (ICF b21002 "Binocular acuity of near vision"); he wears corrective eyeglasses.
- Noora (female, 49 years-old); affected by adult-onset asthma with acute exacerbation (ICD J45. 901).
- Aisha (female, 34 years-old), no particular health condition.
- Nasser (male, 32 years-old), no particular health condition.

Employers in each factory acquire workers' health condition and, by working together with them, leverage on the AAW ontology to identify the optimal indoor comfort metrics for each worker. Leveraging on reasoning and on workers' ICF and ICD health models, each health condition mentioned above can be tackled specifically: Alex and Khalid's statuses (COPD) require ideal indoor comfort to be specified as a CO_2 concentration lower than 800 ppm [26], temperature lower than 22 °C and the humidity rate up to 40% [27]. On the other hand, Noora and Liza – both suffering from asthma – can take advantage of a maximum CO_2 concentration of 700 ppm, a maximum temperature of 21.6 °C and humidity rate no higher than 45% [28, 29]. These comfort metrics are inferred in the ontology layer leveraging on both the health conditions and the best environmental conditions modelled in the semantic model. Considering the workers' respiratory conditions, the ontology CO_2 module is required to be implemented for both locations, while the inferences regarding humidity rate for Doha and indoor temperature for Novosibirsk can be disregarded in the summer months, as the average values never exceed the defined thresholds to trigger exacerbation of health conditions of workers.

Regarding workers characterized by visual impairments, Sergei would benefit from working in a low illuminance area, whereas Mohamad needs a higher amount of illuminance to feel comfortable working. The ontology infers for Sergei a maximum illuminance of 650 lx, while the suggested illuminance for Mohammad is set to 750 lx. Under these circumstances, the employers can decide on not to include the module that is related to visual-aid adaptations. This is because the daylight levels in Novosibirsk is generally limited which is preferable for Sergei and they are always high in Doha which is preferable for Mohamad. If the health conditions were the opposite, the use of visual-aid module would be inevitable in both locations.

In this scenario, employees and employers cooperate to define the ontology modules that can be adopted to actuate the tailored indoor comfort metrics. While temperature and humidity rate modules are active for most of the year in both regions, the adoption of other modules – tackling different health conditions – needs to be decided by all involved stakeholders.

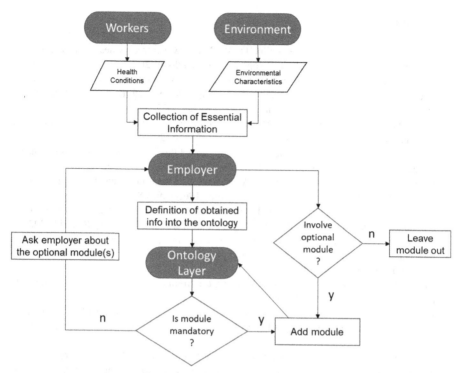

Fig. 1. Flowchart of the collaborative process from the acquisition of information to selection of modules.

5 Conclusion

This paper introduced an ontology-based DSS for a healthier aging workforce by means of an AmI framework. It is shown how the collaborative ontology engineering allows a comprehensive yet personally tailored AAW framework for maintaining the wellbeing of each employee in a workplace. In addition, this is accomplished in a less-invasive and discrete manner thanks to the holistic functioning of the system. Leveraging on the interactions among employer, employees and environment, cooperative ontology-supported decisions are made to provide comfort for workers as required, without any implementation of an unnecessary measure.

Aprototypical testing on the use case given above is projected in STIIMA-Lecco, Smart Environments Laboratory. Through this application, it is planned to validate the applicability and scalability of the system, and to address privacy concerns, principally the data security as it is stored in the ontology. Among other future works there are the examination for further limits of expansion of collaborative ontologies with the target of comprising more comfort metrics, by inclusion of all the stakeholders that take part in the system and implementation of stress monitoring via providing workers and employers with blind data regarding stress, in order to provide further tailored suggestions (breaks, dedicated training on specific activities, etc.).

References

1. Yaldiz, L.M., Fraccaroli, F., Truxillo, D.M.: Aging workforce issues from a multilevel approach. In: Oxford Research Encyclopedia of Psychology (2017)
2. Eurostat. Ageing Europe - statistics on working and moving into retirement (2020). https://ec.europa.eu/eurostat/statistics-explained/index.php?title=Ageing_Europe_statistics_on_working_and_moving_into_retirement. Accessed 14 Jan 2022
3. Gams, M., Gu, I.Y.H., Härmä, A., Muñoz, A., Tam, V.: Artificial intelligence and ambient intelligence. J. Ambient Intell. Smart Environ. **11**, 71–86 (2019)
4. Spoladore, D., Mahroo, A., Trombetta, A., Sacco, M.: DOMUS: a domestic ontology managed ubiquitous system. J. Ambient Intell. Humaniz. Comput. **13**, 3037–3052 (2022)
5. Spoladore, D., Mahroo, A., Trombetta, A., Sacco, M.: Comfont: a semantic framework for indoor comfort and energy saving in smart homes. Electronics **8**, 1449 (2019)
6. Sun, S., Zheng, X., Gong, B., Garcia Paredes, J., Ordieres-Meré, J.: Healthy operator 4.0: a human cyber–physical system architecture for smart workplaces. Sensors **20**, 2011 (2020)
7. Pancardo, P., Acosta, F.D., Hernández-Nolasco, J.A., Wister, M.A., López-de-Ipiña, D.: Real-time personalized monitoring to estimate occupational heat stress in ambient assisted working. Sensors **15**, 16956–16980 (2015)
8. Rick, V.B., et al.: WorkingAge: Smart Working Environments for AllAges. Universitätsbibliothek der RWTH Aachen (2019)
9. Kiyokawa, K., et al.: Owens Luis—a context-aware multi-modal smart office chair in an ambient environment. In: 2012 IEEE Virtual Reality Workshops (VRW), pp. 1–4. IEEE (2012)
10. Spoladore, D., Pessot, E.: Collaborative ontology engineering methodologies for the development of decision support systems: case studies in the healthcare domain. Electronics **10**, 1060 (2021)
11. Sirin, E., Parsia, B., Grau, B.C., Kalyanpur, A., Katz, Y.: Pellet: a practical owl-dl reasoner. J. Web Semant. **5**, 51–53 (2007)
12. BioPortal. International Classification of Functioning, Disability and Health (ICF) Ontology (2012). https://bioportal.bioontology.org/ontologies/ICF. Accessed 04 Apr 2022
13. BioPortal. International Classification of Diseases (ICD-10) Ontology (2021). https://bioportal.bioontology.org/ontologies/ICD10. Accessed 04 Apr 2022
14. Spoladore, D., Mahroo, A., Sacco, M.: Fostering the collaboration among healthcare stakeholders with ICF in clinical practice: EasyICF. In: Camarinha-Matos, L.M., Boucher, X., Afsarmanesh, H. (eds.) PRO-VE 2021. IAICT, vol. 629, pp. 623–631. Springer, Cham (2021). https://doi.org/10.1007/978-3-030-85969-5_58
15. Lowther, S.D., et al.: Low level carbon dioxide indoors—a pollution indicator or a pollutant? A health-based perspective. Environments **8**, 125 (2021)
16. Ye, X., Wolff, R., Yu, W., Vaneckova, P., Pan, X., Tong, S.: Ambient temperature and morbidity: a review of epidemiological evidence. Environ. Health Perspect. **120**, 19–28 (2012)
17. Contin, M.A., Benedetto, M.M., Quinteros-Quintana, M.L., Guido, M.E.: Light pollution: the possible consequences of excessive illumination on retina. Eye **30**, 255–263 (2016)
18. Perlmutter, M.S., Bhorade, A., Gordon, M., Hollingsworth, H., Engsberg, J.E., Baum, M.C.: Home lighting assessment for clients with low vision. Am. J. Occup. Ther. **67**, 674–682 (2013)
19. Daniele, L., den Hartog, F., Roes, J.: Created in close interaction with the industry: the smart appliances reference (SAREF) ontology. In: Cuel, R., Young, R. (eds.) FOMI 2015. LNBIP, vol. 225, pp. 100–112. Springer, Cham (2015). https://doi.org/10.1007/978-3-319-21545-7_9
20. Janowicz, K., Haller, A., Cox, S., Le Phuoc, D., Lefrancois, M.: SOSA: a lightweight ontology for sensors, observations, samples, and actuators. J. Web Semant. **56**, 1–10 (2019)

21. Pan, J.Z.: Resource description framework. In: Staab, S., Studer, R. (eds.) Handbook on Ontologies. IHIS, pp. 71–90. Springer, Heidelberg (2009). https://doi.org/10.1007/978-3-540-92673-3_3

22. Antoniou, G., van Harmelen, F.: Web ontology language: owl. In: Staab, S., Studer, R. (eds.) Handbook on ontologies, pp. 67–92. Springer, Heidelberg (2004). https://doi.org/10.1007/978-3-540-24750-0_4

23. Perez, J., Arenas, M., Gutierrez, C.: Semantics and complexity of SPARQL. ACM Trans. Datab. Syst. **34**, 1–45 (2009)

24. Novosibirsk climate: Average Temperature, weather by month, Novosibirsk weather averages - Climate-Data.org (2022). https://en.climate-data.org/asia/russian-federation/novosibirsk-oblast/novosibirsk-459/. Accessed 11 Apr 2022

25. Doha climate: Average Temperature, weather by month, Doha water temperature - Climate-Data.org (2022). https://en.climate-data.org/asia/qatar/doha/doha-6368/. Accessed 11 Apr 2022

26. Kurmi, O.P., Lam, K.B.H., Ayres, J.G.: Indoor air pollution and the lung in low- and medium-income countries. Eur. Respir. J. **40**(1), 239–254 (2012). https://doi.org/10.1183/09031936.00190211

27. Mu, Z., et al.: Synergistic effects of temperature and humidity on the symptoms of COPD patients. Int. J. Biometeorol. **61**(11), 1919–1925 (2017). https://doi.org/10.1007/s00484-017-1379-0

28. Hayes, D., Jr., Collins, P.B., Khosravi, M., Lin, R.-L., Lee, L.-Y.: Bronchoconstriction triggered by breathing hot humid air in patients with asthma: role of cholinergic reflex. Am. J. Respir. Crit. Care Med. **185**, 1190–1196 (2012)

29. Azuma, K., Kagi, N., Yanagi, U., Osawa, H.: Effects of low-level inhalation exposure to carbon dioxide in indoor environments: a short review on human health and psychomotor performance. Environ. Int. **121**, 51–56 (2018)

Simulation of Patient-Centred Scenarios for the Improvement of Transportation Service in Hospitals

Rossana Fulgenzi[1,2], Simone Gitto[2], Gianluca Murgia[2], and Elena Pessot[2,3(✉)]

[1] Department of Computer, Control, and Management Engineering , Sapienza University of Rome , Rome, Italy
rossana.fulgenzi@uniroma1.it
[2] Department of Information Engineering and Mathematics, University of Siena, via Roma 56, 53100 Siena, Italy
{simone.gitto,gianluca.murgia,elena.pessot}@unisi.it
[3] Institute of Intelligent Industrial Technologies and Systems for Advanced Manufacturing, National Research Council of Italy, via Alfonso Corti 12, 20133 Milan, Italy

Abstract. Hospitals and healthcare facilities are increasingly challenged to ensure an efficient use of resources while achieving a high quality in their services that also maximizes the patients' safety. This is especially important in the case of transportation of patients whose health conditions require the use of appropriate procedures and tools. This work employs a simulation approach to propose solutions for hospitals to improve the organization of the patient transportation service. Resulting solutions are based on the perspective of the service provider and especially driven by patients' needs. By using the Arena software, we analysed the service model in an Italian hospital and the variations in the human, physical and intangible resources that could improve the service performance, with a focus on the operations adding value in terms of time and collaborative behaviours among patients and operators.

Keywords: Simulation scenario · Healthcare services · Transportation service improvement

1 Introduction

Hospitals and healthcare facilities are increasingly challenged to ensure an efficient use of resources while achieving a high quality in their services that also maximizes patients' safety. Different hospital services and tasks can now leverage a tremendous amount of data collected on daily operations, services, and resources, to be analysed with digital and computerized tools for enhancing the management process [1].

The provision of adequate service quality is especially important in the case of transportation of patients whose health conditions require the use of appropriate procedures and tools. This service uses specialized staff and appropriate tools, such as wheelchairs,

© IFIP International Federation for Information Processing 2022
Published by Springer Nature Switzerland AG 2022
L. M. Camarinha-Matos et al. (Eds.): PRO-VE 2022, IFIP AICT 662, pp. 356–365, 2022.
https://doi.org/10.1007/978-3-031-14844-6_29

stretchers, and hospital beds, which should be assigned in accordance with the health condition of the patients. The limited number of these resources, together with the scarce predictability of the demand for this service and the constraints provoked by the hospital infrastructure (e.g., the limited availability of elevators), makes the optimization of internal transportation extremely important in several hospitals [2]. For these reasons, the (in-hospital) transportation service is often outsourced to service providers. This choice allows hospitals to concentrate their internal resources on their core activities, such as patients' health, and to take advantage of the economies of specialisation and scale obtainable by the companies that specifically deal with these services [3].

The service provider should guarantee that all transfers are performed in the greatest safety and with the highest degree of care for the patient, as well as in the shortest possible time, with a propensity to optimising and standardising routes and in compliance with current company procedures. To ensure the accomplishment of quality performance, the management and the improvement of the service should take into account the potentialities of digital and computer-based tools. Different patient-centred scenarios that evaluate both the waiting times and the safety of patients could be considered. In this sense, this study aims to understand how the service level for patients is affected by the amount of resources available to the transportation system, and to identify the possible strategies for managing the service demand. To this aim, we defined different patient-centred scenarios according to the variations in the human, physical and intangible resources in the service model of an Italian hospital.

2   The Application Context

2.1   Models for Patient Transportation Services Improvement

The studies on (in-hospital) patient transportation try to optimize the use of physical and human resources involved in the transportation of patients between different hospital units, such as wards, treatment rooms, and operating theatres. Among the operations management approaches proposed in the literature, both Hanne et al. [4] and Kuchera and Rohleder [5] present a software solution that heuristically solves the Dial A Ride problem, thus supporting a more efficient scheduling of the staff involved in in-hospital transportation. Séguin et al. [6] adopt a mixed-integer model to minimize the cost of staff assignment based on a high decentralization, in which the employees are assigned to specific routes, rather than to a more generic area. To reduce both the waiting time of the patient and the related waste of resources involved in internal transportation, Schmid and Doerner [7] propose a systematic and cooperative approach that jointly optimizes the scheduling of operating rooms and transportation services.

While these studies are based on optimization techniques, Segev et al. [8] deal with in-hospital transportation problems by using simulation. They develop an Arena model to estimate the right number, type, and location of the elevators dedicated to internal transportation, other than to study the performance and the robustness of this service in accordance with a different number of elevators. Although simulation may provide a relevant contribution to the analysis of in-hospital transportation, its application in the literature is still limited.

2.2   The Patient Transportation Service of the Santo Stefano Hospital in Prato

The Santo Stefano Hospital in Prato is one of the 13 hospitals belonging to the Azienda USL Toscana Centro (AUSL TC), based in Italy. The centre was created in 2016 following a deep reorganisation of the health service in the Region of Tuscany. The Santo Stefano hospital includes:

- the hospital building, which has 540 beds, 20 short intensive observation areas, 40 dialysis spots, 15 operating theatres, 6 labour rooms and 4 delivery rooms, boasted high diagnostic technology and is organised to meet the different patients' care needs;
- the service building, which is mainly dedicated to logistics, technology centres and laboratories.

The patient transport service consists in transferring the patient, with any aids (infusion pumps, oxygen cylinders, etc.), and the related documentation (medical records, authorisations necessary for diagnosis and treatment purposes etc.), to the ward/service of destination indicated, in most of the hospitals of the AUSLTC. It can be performed using means of transport such as wheelchair, stretcher, bed and corpses trolley. Moreover, it can belong to the categories of scheduled, non-scheduled or urgent transport service, depending on the advance notification of the request by the department to the provider and the maximum time allowed for delivery.

The patient transport service in Santo Stefano hospital is completely outsourced to a Facility Management corporation. The most critical issues that emerged in the analysis of the service include: the presence of delays, highlighted in the majority of the centres of AUSL TC; the limited availability of the service, only at certain times; the lack of service traceability and execution errors. In order to overcome these critical points, an increase in the resources available for the service, a more systematic (and collaborative) organisation, and the adoption of digital tools to monitor the requests for the service were evaluated in this study.

3   The Innovation in the Patient Transportation Service Model

This section describes the steps followed to develop a simulation- and collaboration-based solution for the improvement of the patient transportation service model in the Santo Stefano Hospital in Prato.

3.1   Organisational Analysis of Transportation Service Operations

The requests for patient transportation service in the Santo Stefano di Prato hospital are performed with a centralised process, summarized in Table 1. This process is managed by an Operations Centre (headquarter), made up of porters and telephone operators, who are responsible to forward the requests via mobile phones received from the departments to fellow porters. The advantage of this method, if compared to the other processes that are generally performed in hospitals decentralised general process, semi-centralised process, and decentralised specialized process, is the higher awareness of the Operations Centre of all the information necessary to choose the most suitable operator to satisfy the request.

The first step of the study was the organisational analysis of the operations belonging to the patient transportation service. Table 1 summarises the main features of operations that occur or could occur in the process, and distinguishes them into value-added (VA) and non-value-added (NVA) activities.

Table 1. The centralised process for requests in patient transportation service.

Operations	Execution time	Human resources	Tangible assets	Operations type
Ward contacts headquarters	50–60 s	1 telephone operator; 1 ward supervisor	2 telephones	NVA
Headquarters contact operator	50–60 s	1 or 2 operators; 1 telephone operator	1 telephone; 1 mobile phone	NVA
The operator carries out transport	12 min	1 or 2 operators; 1 patient	0 or 1 transport vehicle	VA

For example, the first operation is mapped as NVA, considering that queues and long waits are very likely to be generated if several transport requests arrive simultaneously from different wards and/or services, thus affecting services' performance. These activities increase the duration of transport and the number of resources used. They cannot be easily eliminated in the short term, thus they need to be addressed by medium-/long-term improvement plans or major change management activities.

3.2 The Patient Transportation Service Model of the Santo Stefano Hospital

As introduced in the previous section, the patient transport service carried out within the Santo Stefano hospital in the Prato district area is a centralised and outsourced process. The switchboard operators of the Operations Centre handle the sorting of requests, which are both scheduled and unscheduled equally distributed (the latter also includes urgent ones) and are received every day from 08:00 to 18:00. The calls which are not included in this time interval are diverted directly to the porters on duty. In addition, the Operations Centre has 24 porters and 4 wheelchairs available to process requests.

The type of equipment required for transport includes stretchers, beds and corpse trolleys and they are owned by the Healthcare Public Body of the centre of Tuscany, totalling the amount of 150,600 and 2 respectively. The most used type of transportation is the stretcher, located in the Radiology department. Whenever the porter has to carry out a transport, it is necessary that he/she first goes to the Radiology department, and then transfers to the patient's department. This causes an average increase in travel time of about 4 min, representing a clear waste in the service. The transport carried out with the bed requires two porters, while the transport of corpses is carried out with a single porter, as the latter is helped by the mortician.

Finally, with regard to the optimisation policies, the switchboard operators are the ones having a broad knowledge of the precise locations of departments/services and the movements of porters, thus able to choose the best route in terms of time and resources.

Based on data collected on the average number of requests, use of resources along with operations, and average percentages of routings of patients, we created with Arena Simulation the simulation model of the patient transportation service, shown in Fig. 1.

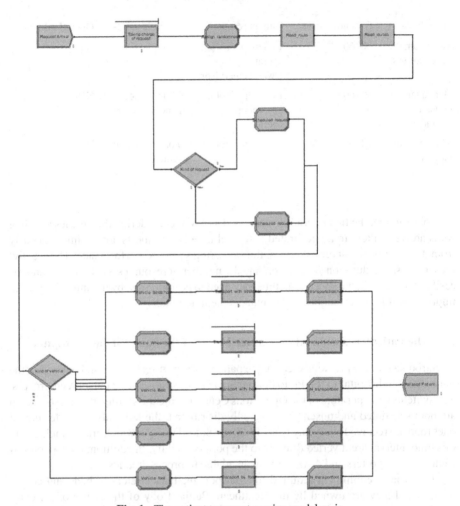

Fig. 1. The patient transport service model as-is.

This starts with the request arrives at the Operations Centre, and ends with the release of the patient. Based on data collected, the type of vehicles used were divided according to the percentage of assignments for transportation as: 65% of the probability that entities are routed towards the stretcher, 15% towards the wheelchair, 17% towards the bed, 1% towards the corpse trolley and by the remaining 2% towards transport without any assistance. The simulation model allows to evaluate the strengths and weaknesses, and thus to improve the organization of the patient escorting service in the hospital, based on the perspective of multiple stakeholders and especially driven by patients' needs. Specifically, main areas of improvement concerned the delays, the limited availability of the service, and the lack of service traceability and execution errors. It emerged the need to evaluate how the amount of human, physical and intangible resources could improve the transportation service level, and to simulate the possible strategies into different patient-centred scenarios.

The as-is model was validated by comparing the results obtained from the simulation with real data. Table 2 below categorises the results by transportation means.

Table 2. Validation of the service model as-is

Simulation results			Reality
Statistic name	Arithmetic average	Geometric average	
Number of bed transports	16.50	16.50	31.12
Number of corpse trolley transports	960.00	960.00	278.00
Number of foot transports	1.95	1.95	1.94
Number of stretcher transports	62.92	62.92	58.57
Number of wheelchair transports	14.50	14.50	11.44
Number of arrival request (IN)	96.84	96.84	104.21
Number of arrival request (OUT)	96.83	96.83	104.21

4   Simulation Results and Improvement Proposal

The results obtained by the simulations address the main critical issues identified in Sect. 2. The main criticalities include: the waiting times of the entities in the various processes of the service model, and especially the waiting time for requests before being accepted; the time required to complete the execution of the various transports; and the average usage of all the resources necessary to accomplish the performance of the service, especially in terms of the difference between the number of transports with stretcher started and finished and the number of transports with stretcher started, but not finished.

The results were divided into Entities, Processes, Queues and Resources for analysis, as shown in Table 3.

Table 3. Results of the simulation for patient transportation service.

	Results
Entities	A request awaits about 5 min, before being processed
Processes	• The taking over of requests by the switchboard operator causes a waiting time of about 5 min • The VA Time necessary to carry out a transport with a stretcher is on average about 14 min, because the porter has to retrieve the stretcher in the radiology ward and then carry out the transport
Queues	The average number of requests waiting to be accepted is equal to 4 units
Resources	• The most used human resources during the execution of the service are porters (48%) and telephone operators (74%) • The most used material resources are the telephone (74%) and the wheelchair (25%) • The critical resources are the telephone and the switchboard operator, slowing down the process execution as they are not able to accommodate multiple requests at the same time • Hiring new human resources could be unprofitable, as less than half of porters are in activity at a precise moment in time

Table 4 shows the confidence intervals for the most significant results regarding Entities, Processes and Resources of the model in Arena.

Table 4. Confidence intervals for results of the simulation.

Arena modules' statistics	Confidence interval 95%	
Entity Wait Time	5.00	6.01
Process - Taking charge of request - NumberInQueue	4.02	4.89
Process - Taking charge of request, Queue, WaitingTime	5.00	6.00
Process - Taking charge of request - WaitTimePerEntity	5.00	6.00
Process - Transport with stretcher - TotalTimePerEntity	14.35	14.43
Resource - Operator.Utilization	47.81	48.58
Resource - Telephone Operator.Utilization	36.75	37.30
Resource - Telephone.NumberBusy	73.51	74.60
Resource - Telephone.Utilization	73.51	74.60
Resource - Wheelchair.Utilization	25.01	25.98

The results highlighted some problems in the current configuration of the service and allowed the development of some improvement strategies. By making some changes to the system, it was possible to reduce both the number of requests in the queue and the duration of their processing, and the time required to carry out a transport by stretcher.

The strategies consider the essential role of collaborative participation of the service provider personnel, and the need to define patient-centred scenarios, as follows.

First Scenario. The first scenario aims to increase the number of transports by stretcher completed and generally to reduce the time required to carry out a transport with this transportation. By allocating the 150 stretchers currently available in a proportionate way in the various wards/services, porters can carry out the transport in a shorter time. From a modelling point of view, it was sufficient to eliminate from the duration of the "Transport with stretcher" process, the part of time dedicated to the recovery of the transportation. With this change the average time to carry out a transport by stretcher has decreased by 4 min, becoming just over 10 min, and the average number of transports completed by stretcher has increased by 2 units. In addition, this variation has caused a further reduction in the percentage of use by stretcher, from 5% to 3.6%. A final observation concerns the Radiology ward. If the stretchers were no longer stationed in this ward, but were allocated directly at the departure and destination wards/services, there would be an important recovery of physical space and a clear improvement in the working conditions of the healthcare personnel.

Second Scenario. The second scenario aims to further modify the first one, in order to reduce the waiting time required to accept a request. The first solution consists in adding one more material resource than the one already present. To do this, it is satisfactory to increase the capacity of the "Telephone" resource by one unit. Having two phones instead of one, the waiting time would be reduced by a considerable amount. Furthermore, it would not be necessary to hire a new human resource, as those already present would be sufficient to guarantee the reception of requests, also coming from the second telephone. Thus, in this way, the workload of the two human resources would be equally distributed. With the addition of the new resource, the waiting time needed to accept a request became approximately 8 s (before this change it was 5 min). In addition, the number of received and fulfilled requests, increased by 2 units and the number of Work in Progress requests decreased by 6 units. Finally, the results in terms of instant use of resources, show how well the switchboard operators' workload is balanced, as their occupation is 37%.

Third Scenario. The third scenario suggests an alternative solution to the waiting time problem for receiving a request. The basic idea is the following: if the distinction between scheduled and unscheduled requests were made prior or sufficiently in advance, the queue in the reception would be almost completely extinguished. In this way, only unscheduled requests would be accepted by telephone, while those scheduled would be communicated by means of a paper sheet. To implement this solution, it was necessary to make some changes to the model by eliminating the block decide "Kind of request" and halving the amount of incoming requests per time interval. As regards to human and material resources, the following considerations were made:

- the human resource responsible to accommodate unscheduled requests by telephone, remains one, while the second resource deals with the organisation of scheduled transport;
- on the other hand, the capacity of the carrier and transportation resources remain unchanged, as the unscheduled request always takes priority over the scheduled one.

Also with this alternative, the waiting time to accept a request is equal to 21 s, slightly higher than that of the second scenario but in any case, much better than the real one. What improves compared to the real model and compared to the second scenario is the difference between the number of requests accepted and completed and the number of requests accepted, but not completed, which is approximately equal to 3 units. Finally, as in the case of the second, the results in terms of instantaneous use of resources show how much the workload of the switchboard operators is balanced, as their employment is 37%.

Results of Improvement Scenarios. Figure 2 highlights the key improvements in terms of waiting times in the second and third scenarios. The proposed scenarios were evaluated by the staff of the patient transportation service provider, and was characterised by a continuous questioning between them. Moreover, they performed systematic questioning aimed at checking that the patient's safety and his/her life were considered absolute and inviolable priorities.

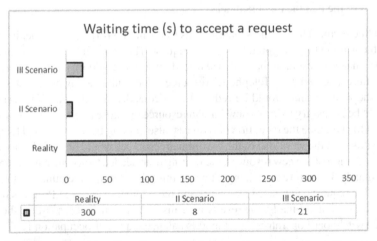

Fig. 2. Comparison of waiting times (in seconds) for accepting a request in reality (model as-is) and in the two proposed improvement scenarios.

5   Conclusions

This work presented a simulation-based approach for identifying possible improvements in the patient transportation service in hospitals. By using the Arena software, we analysed the service model in an Italian hospital and the variations in the human, physical and intangible resources that could improve the service performance, with a focus on the operations adding value in terms of time and collaborative behaviours among patients and operators. Results show the importance of analysing the organisation and management of transportation service operations with the collection of multiple data, and to consider the collaborative behaviours between the operators and the patients in the accommodation of requests.

Despite the limited generalizability of the detailed data of a single case, the results of the model in terms of Entities, Processes, Queues and Resources can be adopted for the analysis of different hospital services. The application of the simulation in the literature on in-hospital patient transportation service is still limited, but the exploitation of this tool in a participated development project allows to collect several data on service operations from multiple sources, and to map different scenarios according to the organisation's objectives and improvement areas.

Acknowledgments. The authors wish to thank Eng. Alberto Coppi of Azienda USL Toscana Centro (AUSL TC) and the team of Santo Stefano Hospital for the precious support in data collection.

References

1. Oliver, N., Arnesh, T., Tak, I.: Smart hospital services: health 4.0 and opportunity for developing economies. In: Pretorius, L., Pretorius, M.W. (eds.) Towards the Digital World and Industry X.0 - Proceedings of the 29th International Conference of the International Association for Management of Technology, IAMOT 2020, pp. 345–361 (2020)
2. Naesens, K., Gelders, L.: Reorganising a service department: central patient transportation. Prod. Plan. Control **20**(6), 478–483 (2009)
3. Mariani, P., Falotico, R., Zavanella, B.: Outsourcing services in the Italian National Health Service: the evaluation of private and public operators. Procedia Econ. Financ. **17**, 256–264 (2014)
4. Hanne, T., Melo, T., Nickel, S.: Bringing robustness to patient flow management through optimized patient transports in hospitals. Interfaces **39**(3), 241–255 (2009)
5. Kuchera, D., Rohleder, T.R.: Optimizing the patient transport function at Mayo Clinic. Qual. Manage. Healthc. **20**(4), 334–342 (2011)
6. Séguin, S., Villeneuve, Y., Blouin-Delisle, C.H.: Improving patient transportation in hospitals using a mixed-integer programming model. Oper. Res. Health Care **23**, 100202 (2019)
7. Schmid, V., Doerner, K.F.: Examination and operating room scheduling including optimization of intrahospital routing. Transp. Sci. **48**(1), 59–77 (2014)
8. Segev, D., Levi, R., Dunn, P.F., Sandberg, W.S.: Modeling the impact of changing patient transportation systems on peri-operative process performance in a large hospital: insights from a computer simulation study. Health Care Manag. Sci. **15**(2), 155–169 (2012)

Digitalization in Professional Football: An Opportunity to Estimate Injury Risk

Laurent Navarro[1](✉), Pierre-Eddy Dandrieux[1,2], Karsten Hollander[3], and Pascal Edouard[2,4]

[1] Mines Saint-Etienne, INSERM, U 1059 Sainbiose, CIS, Univ Lyon, Univ Jean Monnet, Saint-Etienne, France
navarro@emse.fr
[2] Inter-University Laboratory of Human Movement Biology, Univ Lyon, UJM-Saint-Etienne, EA 7424, 42023 Saint-Etienne, France
[3] Institute of Interdisciplinary Exercise Science and Sports Medicine, MSH Medical School Hamburg, Hamburg, Germany
[4] Department of Clinical and Exercise Physiology, Sports Medicine Unit, University Hospital of Saint-Etienne, Saint-Etienne, France

Abstract. Digitalization in the field of sport has already been a reality for a number of years. The growing increase in the volume of data that can be acquired on athletes today makes its use possible mainly for performance enhancement and also for injury prevention. We propose in this paper to evaluate the possibility of including Artificial Intelligence (A.I.) through Machine Learning (ML) as a mean for estimating injuries in professional football, by 1) discussing the addition of ML information in the interaction between stakeholders through graph network representations, and 2) presenting the injury risk estimation through two ML techniques adapted to the characteristics of data from players. We first constructed an elementary representation for an athlete and his/her environment, and we then created a complex network of 23 professional football players. We discussed the implication of ML methods for stakeholders such as coaches, players or medical staff. Regarding injury risk estimation, we focused on methods allowing 1) to work with few data and 2) to have a certain level of explainability to avoid the well-known "black box" effect. In particular, we used decision tree and logistic regression methods to predict the occurrence of hamstring injuries in 284 professional footballers for whom baseline data, as well as sprint acceleration mechanical output measurements taken from one football season were available. The results show that the estimation of injury risk is possible to a certain extent, and that the centrality of the technical team is crucial when incorporating such methods in team sports.

Keywords: Injury risk estimation · Machine learning · Professional football · Sports science · Sports medicine · Social networks

L. M. Camarinha-Matos et al. (Eds.): PRO-VE 2022, IFIP AICT 662, pp. 366–375, 2022.
https://doi.org/10.1007/978-3-031-14844-6_30

1 Introduction

Digital data has regularly been used to monitor, track, guide, and direct the training of athletes. A strong emphasis is placed on sports performance, but the use of this data for injury prevention and injury risk estimation seems to represent an opportunity. At the research level, the use of databases to make predictions is increasing [1]. Indeed, medical data is often used after the injury, for diagnosis, but not for prevention or injury risk estimation. However, A.I., and more specifically Machine Learning (ML), now offers the possibility to create a form of "digital twin" [2] for athletes. Complete integration is possible thanks to sensors and questionnaire inputs. This "digital twin" theoretically makes it possible to obtain incomplete but useful models of the athlete, ahead of time, that can help reducing the occurrence of injuries.

Training rules are created from a complex and informal interdisciplinary decision-making. It is a team effort that we believe can be aided by A.I. usage with data from the athletes. This data is mainly of two types: objective and subjective. Objective data often results from sensor data, such as heart rate sensors, mechanical data from mechanical tests during training, timed data, etc. Subjective data are often provided by the athlete orally or via questionnaires on paper or via web or smartphone applications. One of the difficulties when collecting subjective data is the level of interaction that exists between the athlete and the various other stakeholders. The use of graph network representations allows to understand the different interactions between the stakeholders by formalizing interactions through mathematical rules. Consequently, a social network type approach can be envisaged [3], and the role of A.I., more precisely ML, can be understood within the decision-making process.

In addition, explainable ML is an interesting opportunity for this type of problem. Indeed, the often denounced black box effect on ML models is partly solved by models that have good explainability [4, 5]. In particular, decision tree or logistic regression type models have this characteristic: the importance of the input parameters for the prediction can be quantified for example.

In this paper we propose the use of digital data to help estimate injury risk in football players. Therefore, we implemented a micro/macro type approach based on the use of an elementary social network type model of the interactions between the athlete and his/her environment that we replicated to create complex networks. We then analyzed these complex networks using graph representations and betweenness centrality measures [6, 7]. In particular, the importance of stakeholders is shown and discussed. We then used as an example of the potential of ML techniques to estimate injury risk, a database of 284 players from 16 professional football teams for which training data and hamstring injury occurrence data are recorded. We first implemented two ML algorithms on the data to predict hamstring injury occurrence: decision tree and logistic regression. Then we addressed the questions of the place of this tool through the analysis of different graphs, and the relationships between social network analysis and importance of ML parameters.

2 Graph Description of the Problem

In this section, we used a graph network approach. The idea was to create a micro-scale model of the athlete, which described all interactions between an athlete and his immediate environment. Then, a macro model connected a number of micro systems to observe the importance of the different stakeholders as well as the place of the athletes in a network. In this model, the nodes correspond to the different stakeholders, and the edges correspond to the interactions between them. An interaction corresponds to a relationship between two stakeholders, through which the behaviors of these individuals influence each other and change accordingly. The edges are therefore all considered to be bidirectional. We considered two types of interactions: human/human interactions and human/machine interactions (A.I.).

We describe an example of an elementary system for one athlete (Fig. 1) for illustration purpose, which is not exhaustive. However, it is still fairly representative to the athlete's environment. The different stakeholders that we chose to describe in this system are: athlete, technical team, medical staff, social life, family, work (which can correspond to school or higher education depending on the age of the athlete), administrative leaders, and finally A.I. and Data Scientists. Some interactions ("research only") appear in red

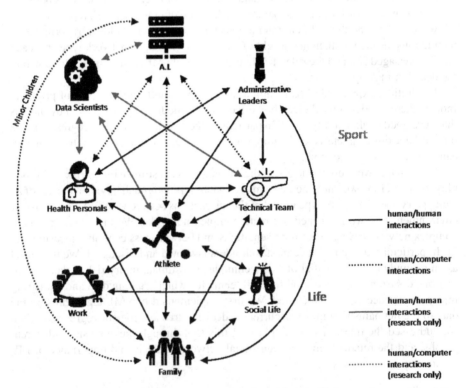

Fig. 1. Proposed elementary system representing the athlete in his/her environment, and the interactions with the stakeholders.

color. These interactions are provisional, they are active in the research phase for the construction of the A.I. system, but are intended to be deactivated in routine operation.

We constructed two types of graphs: a first type of graph comprising only one (minor) athlete (Fig. 2) and a second containing 23 adult players (Fig. 3), which corresponds to the standards for the number of players in a professional football team before 2020. These graphs are simulated ones, and edges values have all been set to 1, as we consider binary interactions between nodes for the sake of simplicity, but also because objective data about the importance of these interactions do not exist at this time.

For the professional adult players, we removed the node "Work", and the edges between the nodes "Family" and "A.I.". We also created recursive links between social lives, families and athletes to illustrate the dense social interactions existing in professional sports environments. Each type of graph is declined in three cases: the classic case (classic) where there is no A.I., the case with A.I. and the research case with A.I. and data scientist (Data Sc.).

We chose to analyze the graphs in terms of betweenness centrality, both for nodes [6] and edges [7]. Betweenness centrality is equal to the number of times one node (or edge) is on the shortest path between any two other nodes in the graph. On the graphs, the greater the diameter of a node, the greater its betweenness centrality, and the thicker an edge, the greater its betweenness centrality.

Colors correspond to the type of nodes: blue for athletes, yellow for sports professionals or A.I. stakeholders, and red for life environment.

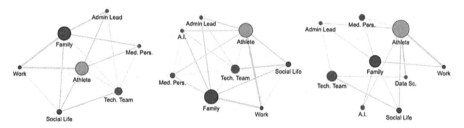

Fig. 2. Graphs of the three cases for one minor athlete: classic (left), with A.I. (middle) and research with A.I. and Data Scientist (right).

Table 1 gives the normalized (on a [0,1] range) betweenness centralities of the different types of nodes in the graphs. In the 23 players case, the betweenness is considered for one athlete, one family and one social life, as these are the same for the 23. Technical team, medical personal, A.I., administrative leaders and data scientists are unique for each graph. Work has been removed for the 23 players graphs (Fig. 3).

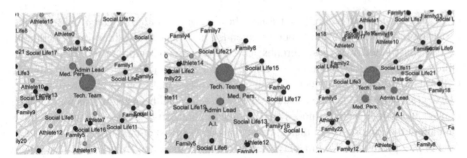

Fig. 3. Graphs of the three cases for 23 professional adult football players: classic (left), with A.I. (middle) and research with A.I. and Data Scientist (right).

Table 1. Normalized betweenness values of nodes of the two different graphs. Max values are indicated in **bold**.

	Classic	A.I.	A.I. and D.S.	Classic	A.I.	A.I. and D.S.
Stakeholder	Single athlete			23 Football players		
Athlete	**0.1333**	**0.1468**	**0.1845**	0.0050	0.0052	0.0054
Family	**0.1333**	**0.1468**	0.1101	0.0050	0.0049	0.0047
Tech. Team	0.0444	0.0595	0.0833	**0.1826**	**0.1851**	**0.1873**
Med. Pers.	0.0000	0.0119	0.0298	0.0407	0.0426	0.0444
Social Life	0.0222	0.0159	0.0119	0.0059	0.0057	0.0056
A.I.	N/A	0.0000	0.0089	N/A	0.0000	0.0000
Admin Lead	0.0000	0.0000	0.0000	0.0407	0.0396	0.0385
Work	0.0000	0.0000	0.0000	N/A	N/A	N/A
Data Sc.	N/A	N/A	0.0000	N/A	N/A	0.0000

We observed that in the single athlete's case, the athlete has the most important betweenness centrality, which means that his relative "power" or influence is high. Its value is shared with family for the classic and A.I. cases. Concerning the 23 players case, the technical team has in any case a way more important betweenness centrality, followed by the medical team and the administrative leaders.

3   Machine Learning on Real-World Data

This section aims to highlight the potential of ML techniques to estimate injury risk in sports. We chose an approach mostly presented in the current literature: estimation of injury risk during the season based on baseline data (i.e., data at the start of the season). As mentioned above, explainability is crucial when it comes to including A.I. algorithms in a network composed mainly of humans who are used to interacting in a system that already works. Also, we chose two methods for their relative explainability: decision trees and logistic regressions. For these two methods, we can compute the weight of each parameter in the final prediction, so feedback other than the final prediction can be provided to the stakeholders concerned.

For this example, we used a dataset from 284 male football players from 16 professional football teams from three countries (Japan, France and Finland) over one season. More details, as well as statistics about these data can be found in [8]. The outcome was the occurrence of hamstring injuries during the season. At the end of the season, 47 hamstring injuries affected 38 players. At the start of the season, all players performed a 30 m sprint to measure sprint acceleration. Data for each athlete included: binary coded country group (country), age, height, body mass, training volume, history of hamstring injuries (previous season), and data recorded during training sessions: horizontal force production capacity (FH0 and V0), the maximum power, the force-speed profile, the time at 5 m, the time at 10 m, the time at 20 m, and the maximum speed [8]. Thus, all these data constitute the inputs of the model, and the output is the outcome, i.e. the occurrence of hamstring injuries during the season.

For the hyperparameters tuning, we followed the principle of nested cross-validation, which limits the bias on small datasets [9]. For each of the two models (i.e., decision trees and logistic regressions), 200 nested cross validation iterations were carried out. Here, the dataset was divided into 10 equal parts, nine of which (train) are used for hyperparameter selection. Then, this 90% of the dataset were further divided into 10 parts and 9 of them were used to predict the 10th. Hyperparameter optimization was performed during this operation, with a grid-search algorithm. Then, the performance evaluation of the model was carried out on the first of the 10 initial parts which have been left out. There are therefore 10 scores for each iteration, i.e., $200 \times 10 = 2000$ sets of hyperparameters.

Table 2 presents the performance results for the two methods, namely decision tree and logistic regression. The mean and standard deviation of the recall, specificity, precision, accuracy and ROC-AUC parameters are specified. It is interesting to observe that these parameters have a very precise explanation with respect to the estimation of the risk of injury occurrence. The recall parameter indicates the ability of the model to detect injuries. The specificity parameter indicates the ability of the model to detect non-injured. The precision parameter indicates the proportion of injured among positive predictions. The accuracy parameter indicates the ability of the model to make good predictions of injured and non-injured. Finally, the ROC-AUC parameter represents the overall measure of the model's performance.

Table 2. Performance parameters for the two methods tested 200 times wit mean and std.

Model	Recall (mean ± std)		Specificity (mean ± std)		Precision (mean ± std)		Accuracy (mean ± std)		ROC-AUC (mean ± std)	
Decision Tree	0.58	0.07	0.67	0.04	0.22	0.03	0.66	0.03	0.65	0.04
Logistic Regr.	0.69	0.03	0.76	0.01	0.32	0.02	0.75	0.01	0.77	0.01

Figure 4 shows the importance of features for both models in injury risk estimation. Since logistic regression has a better performance, we base our analysis on the latter in the following paragraphs. We noted that the most influential parameters on the injury were height, followed by the fact of belonging to the Finland country group, followed by the time at 20 m, followed by the fact of belonging to the France country group, followed by the fact of belonging to the Japan country group.

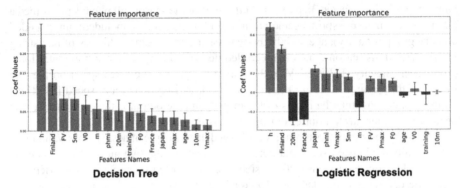

Fig. 4. Importance of features for the two methods tested.

Height is an intrinsic non-modifiable parameter of an adult athlete and is not controllable but must be taken into account by all stakeholders. Indeed, although it is non-modifiable, better management of the other modifiable parameters should be proposed. The time at 20 m parameter is related to sprint performance, and this implies that the technical team must take this parameter into account when building their training programs. A discussion between the technical team and the medical staff is thus recommended. Belonging to a specific country group seems to be a very important parameter. With all the precautions that must obviously be taken, this data raises the legitimate question of the training methods used by each country group.

4   Discussion

In all network representations with multiples athletes, the technical team occupies a central position, with a node of the highest betweenness centrality. This centrality is not a surprising phenomenon. Coaches in particular have a central position in the lives of athletes. However, the athlete must be at the center of the process, as shown in the graph Fig. 1.

Sections 2 and 3 raised the question of the place of artificial intelligence in sport, by first proposing a network model, and an example of machine learning on real-world data. The confrontation of these two approaches shows that the technical team, in the case of a professional football team, carries a great responsibility in the overall process, and therefore the occurrence of injuries. ML seems capable, to a certain extent, of predicting the possible occurrence of injuries. It is then the role of the technical team to take the prediction results into consideration when creating training programs.

If one normalizes the importance of the parameters by the betweenness centralities (by simple multiplication, like done in Table 3) in the classic case, one can see what are the real means of action on the occurrence of injuries. Indeed, since one isolated athlete has a very low betweenness centrality compared to the doctor and the technical team, all the parameters specific to him (age, height, body mass, FH0 and V0, maximum power, force-speed profile, time at 5 m, time at 10 m, time at 20 m, and maximum speed) are not controllable. The means of action that are relegated to the technical and medical teams, and therefore preponderant, are: the country, which is linked to the training programs, the history of hamstring injuries, and the volume of training.

Table 3. Example of correction of feature importance with betweenness centralities. The last column corresponds to the product of first column and fourth column.

Feature importance	Feature	Most infuencal Stakeholder	Betweenness centrality	Corrected value
0.680472408	h	Athlete	0.0050	0.003395516
0.451034408	Finland	Tech. Team	0.1826	**0.082378062**
−0.294332569	20 m	Athlete	0.0050	−0.001468702
−0.279330584	France	Tech. Team	0.1826	**−0.051017642**
0.247351867	Japan	Tech. Team	0.1826	**0.045176969**
0.194580992	phmi	Med. Pers.	0.0407	**0.007924184**
0.1935081	Vmax	Athlete	0.0050	0.000965594
0.159192767	5 m	Athlete	0.0050	0.000794362
−0.15626462	m	Athlete	0.0050	−0.000779751
0.139131464	FV	Athlete	0.0050	0.000694258
0.135991412	Pmax	Athlete	0.0050	0.000678589
0.116354602	F0	Athlete	0.0050	0.000580602
−0.039871139	Age	Athlete	0.0050	−0.000198955
0.033002423	V0	Athlete	0.0050	0.00016468
−0.029759597	Training	Tech. Team	0.1826	**−0.005435368**
−0.004197034	10 m	Athlete	0.0050	−2.09429E−05

There can exist some tension between the technical team and the medical staff when it comes to injury prevention [10]. The technical team is looking for performance, which influences the risk of injury. The medical staff tries to avoid injuries, that is their main goal. We are therefore in the presence of a dual performance/injury prevention objective. As the example on our athlete database shows, performance tends to be correlated with the risk of injury [11]. Thus, the overall problem can be seen as an optimization problem, under constraints of increasing performance and decreasing injury risk.

In our models, the importance of the interactions was not specified, this is one of the limitations. It is obvious that the interactions do not have the same importance between the different stakeholders. In addition, its importance can vary according to the situation and the athlete's personality. A model integrating the importance of the interactions would make it possible to calculate the importance of the nodes differently. We could therefore understand more precisely what actions could be put in place to put the athlete back at the center of the process and partially reduce the centrality of the technical team. The place of A.I. in this operation could be decisive. Indeed, the transmission of information and the restriction according to the positions of the stakeholders could enable to control the importance of the interactions, via a mediation between the different stakeholders.

5 Conclusion

We proposed in this paper to study two approaches related to digitalization in sport for the estimation of injury risk: graph social networks, and ML. These two approaches are complementary, the first allowing to understand the importance of stakeholders in a sports context, and the second allowing to assess the possibility of predicting the risk of injury using athlete's data. It is the combination of these two approaches that is interesting, as it shows how the integration of artificial intelligence in sport can influence the risk of injury. In particular, the role of the technical team is crucial, and it appears to be its responsibility to integrate the results of artificial intelligence predictions for the construction of training programs.

Future work will focus on the specification and improvement of the two proposed approaches. Networks embedding the weight of the nodes and the importance of the edges will be developed through the use of questionnaires. This will allow a finer understanding of the interactions. The explainable machine learning approach will also be developed through the construction of algorithms truly adapted to the world of sport. These specific models will be developed in a multidisciplinary framework involving sports scientists, sports doctors, sports scientists, and engineers.

References

1. Van Eetvelde, H., et al.: Machine learning methods in sport injury prediction and prevention: a systematic review. J. Exp. Orthop. **8**(1), 1–15 (2021)
2. Barricelli, B.R., et al.: Human digital twin for fitness management. IEEE Access **8**, 26637–26664 (2020)
3. Wäsche, H., et al.: Social network analysis in sport research: an emerging paradigm. Eur. J. Sport Soc. **14**(2), 138–165 (2017)
4. Burkart, N., Huber, M.F.: A survey on the explainability of supervised machine learning. J. Artif. Intell. Res. **70**, 245–317 (2021)
5. Lundberg, S.M., et al.: From local explanations to global understanding with explainable AI for trees. Nat. Mach. Intell. **2**(1), 56–67 (2020)
6. Freeman, L.C.: A set of measures of centrality based on betweenness. Sociometry 35–41 (1977)
7. Girvan, M., Newman, M.E.J.: Community structure in social and biological networks. Proc. Natl. Acad. Sci. **99**(12), 7821–7826 (2002)

8. Edouard, P., et al.: Low horizontal force production capacity during sprinting as a potential risk factor of hamstring injury in football. Int. J. Environ. Res. Publ. Health **18**(15), 7827 (2021)

9. Vabalas, A., et al.: Machine learning algorithm validation with a limited sample size. PloS One **14**(11), e0224365 (2019)

10. Ekstrand, J., et al.: Communication quality between the medical team and the head coach/manager is associated with injury burden and player availability in elite football clubs. Br. J. Sports Med. **53**(5), 304–308 (2019)

11. Chapon, J., Navarro, L., Edouard, P.: Relationships between performance and injury occurrence in athletics (track and field): a pilot study on 8 national-level athletes from sprints, jumps and combined events followed during at least five consecutive seasons. Front. Sports Active Living 176 (2022)

Contribution of Digital Transformation to Sustainable Supply Chains

The Role of Visibility and Trust in Textile Supply Chains

Ricardo Zimmermann[1]([⊠]), César Toscano[1], João Oliveira[2],
and Antonio Carrizo Moreira[1,3]

[1] INESC TEC, Porto, Portugal
{ricardo.a.zimmermann,cesar.toscano}@inesctec.pt
[2] CITEVE, Vila Nova de Famalicão, Portugal
joliveira@citeve.pt
[3] University of Aveiro and GOVCOPP, Aveiro, Portugal
amoreira@ua.pt

Abstract. The increasing complexity and dynamism of business environments
has led to a significant growth in the risks related to the management of supply chain relationships. Trust and visibility between supply chain partners have
been increasingly considered paramount aspects to manage these relationships and
reduce risks. This paper aims to analyze and discuss the role of trust and visibility
in supply chains, considering the complexity of multi-tier supply chains and multi-
aspects visibility. Two cases of the textile sector from Portugal have been studied.
After the analysis of the level of visibility and trust, a set of recommendations is
provided.

Keywords: Supply chain visibility · Supply chain trust · Information sharing ·
Textile

1 Introduction

Current supply chain (SC) environments are characterized by growing complexity and
dynamism, challenging companies to develop effective and innovative solutions to contemporary challenges [1, 2]. Besides increasingly common social, environmental, economic and political issues, the rapid evolution of digital technologies has a major influence on the way companies interact with suppliers and customers [3]. As companies
increasingly share information and infrastructures with different partners, a crucial aspect
to accomplish an effective management of SCs consists in developing trust; considered
a fundamental aspect to build collaborative partnerships [4].

The increasing complexity of business environments has led to a significant growth
in the risks related to the management of relationships [5]. Recent events and developments – such as the COVID 19 pandemic, the effects of the Russian invasion of Ukraine
and the growing awareness of the impacts of climate and social crises – are recent and
expressive examples of such risks, leading SC managers to seek information that allows

L. M. Camarinha-Matos et al. (Eds.): PRO-VE 2022, IFIP AICT 662, pp. 379–389, 2022.
https://doi.org/10.1007/978-3-031-14844-6_31

them to have greater visibility of the factors that affect both demand and supply [6, 7]. An increasing number of authors argue that many of the problems faced by companies in these and other current issues are related to low levels of SC visibility [8].

Previous studies have highlighted that the visibility between SC partners is a crucial aspect to be managed in order to improve decision making and performance [9–12]. SC visibility is understood as the ability of companies to have and/or provide access to the necessary and relevant information, at the right time and to the right partners to support decision making [11, 13]. Recent studies highlight that visibility is a critical factor for increasing the resilience and sustainability of SCs [12, 14].

Although the relationship between trust and visibility is recognized in the literature, few studies have assessed the two aspects together [15]. Moreover, the visibility of SC partners is typically analyzed including two factors to be made visible, such as demand and inventory levels [11].

This paper aims to bridge these gaps by considering the relationship between trust and visibility and by including several types of information to be shared in the assessment of SC visibility. Thus, the aim of this paper is to analyze and discuss the role of trust and visibility in SCs, considering the complexity of multi-tier SCs and multi-aspects visibility. Two cases of the textile sector from Portugal have been studied. The paper contributes to theory by advancing the literature on trust and visibility; and to practice by providing guidance to managers on how to assess and manage visibility and trust in order to improve decision making.

2   Theoretical Background and Literature Review

This paper uses the Organizational Information Processing Theory (OIPT) as the theoretical basis. According to the OIPT, a company must have the capabilities to collect the necessary information, inside and outside its borders, and be able to interpret, synthesize and coordinate these information [6, 16, 17]. Thus, based on the OIPT, this paper considers that companies benefit from the ability of sharing information with SC partners, which has the potential to improve trust and visibility levels; and from the ability of using the information collected to inform the decision-making process.

The concept of trust plays an important role in many contexts [18] and has been studied in different disciplines over time, including psychology, sociology, management, economics and information technology. In the social perspective, trust is the basis for people to engage in any kind of social interaction, and is related to the expectation of cooperative and supportive behavior [19]. To psychology, trust results from the cognitive learning derived of past experiences with others. In the context of economics and management, trust helps to explain the behavior of companies regarding their relationships [19, 20] and is based on calculated incentives for alternative behaviors [19]. In this sense, trust is related to the expectation of a certain behavior, and the development of trust relationships reflects a judgment on the ability, honesty, and reliability of a partner to deliver expected outcomes [20].

The effectiveness of information sharing in SCs strongly depends on the level of trust between its members. Trust in SCs can be understood as the ability of a company to fulfill what was agreed with another partner [4, 19]. Trust, in general, can be based on "benevolence" in personal relationships and on the capacities (intention and abilities) to create trust. However, trust between SC partners is basically dependent on: (1) the ability to generate/demonstrate commitment and (2) the ability to achieve the expected performance [4, 21]. Thus, on one hand companies must invest in skills that allow them to improve performance and, on the other hand, in skills that support them to demonstrate commitment. These efforts allow SC partners to move from a limited level of trust to a level of collaborative trust [4].

From a performance point of view, companies must be able not only to deliver expected and agreed-upon performance, but also to communicate performance effectively [20]. An effort by SC partners to unify the metrics facilitates the sharing of information and ensure the effectiveness of communication.

When it comes to commitment, it is essential to understand that a relationship of trust can take time to be built. In this sense, the short-term view – usually based solely on costs – tends to be an obstacle to the establishment of trust relationships. If the only thing that matters is price, why should a manager invest time and energy to (1) develop the people skills needed to foster collaboration and (2) invest in building trust-based relationships with other members of the chain? Two other key aspects for increasing trust between SC partners are: the establishment of common goals, which is translated into the alignment of expectations and incentives (governance, balance of power, service level agreements); and the openness to share information [4].

The concept of visibility is closely linked to information sharing. The conditions that facilitate the sharing of information (including resources, skills and cultural aspects) are paramount to increasing visibility [9], which also contributes to foster transparency, traceability and trust between SC partners. Rogerson and Parry [22, p. 602] state that "efficient supply chains require managers to have the ability to process the enormous volume of data generated to make decisions".

Visibility is the result of the quantity, quality (accuracy/absence of errors) and "opportunity" (information made available at the right time) of information sharing. It demands the development and continuity of close relationships with all relevant partners. To have access to accurate, timely and usable information is beneficial to companies in many aspects [22]. However, the level of visibility with each partner varies depending on aspects such as: the perception of the importance of the relationship, the implementation of resources (technological and non-technological), the time spent on developing the relationship, informal/formal procedures, trust and commitment [9]. On the other hand, some aspects hinder visibility, such as: the lack of common metrics [23, 24], the lack of coordination of information and collaboration between partners [9, 24] and the incompatibility of the information systems used [9].

Thus, the ability to increase the level of visibility depends basically on two factors: (1) the adoption of information technology and systems that facilitate the sharing of information and the organizational capacity to implement them; and (2) the construction of value-added networks (including the adoption and development of processes and routines that allow partners to work towards the same goals) that include internal and external partners (upstream and downstream) and, preferably, for beyond the first level of relationships [26–28]. The level of visibility between SC partners is often analyzed including two aspects, such as demand and inventory levels. However, several authors propose metrics to assess the level of visibility a company has over its SC, upstream and downstream, considering a broader range of aspects [13].

3   Methodology

Data were collected through interviews with multiple respondents from two companies operating in the sector of textiles and clothing in Portugal (focal firms) and through the application of an online-based questionnaire to representants of SC partners (downstream and upstream) of the focal firms. The data collected included aspects related to trust and visibility considering the relationship between the focal companies and their SC partners.

Two large companies operating in the sector of textile and clothing in Portugal were selected as the case studies. The first company (Company A) is a family-owned business, with over 50 years of experience, that exports ready-made textile products worldwide. The second company (Company B) has more than 40 years of experience and also exports to countries around the globe. Both companies are currently investing in innovation and digitalization.

The data were collected in April 2021. Representants from the focal firms and their partners were identified and contacted. The respondents of the focal firms were asked to provide information relating to a minimum of three main customers and three main suppliers. The questionnaire link could be shared and answered by different people within the company, as multiple replies were allowed. Five-point Likert scales were used for all questions. Additional information was collected through interviews with the contact persons in each focal company.

The first part of the questionnaire aimed to classify companies as customers or suppliers of the focal company, as well as to identify the duration of the relationship (less than one year to more than ten years). This part of the questionnaire allows an analysis of the type of relationship existing between the partners.

Regarding trust, companies were invited to inform, with regard to the relationship with each partner, to what extent they agree or disagree with the following statements:

1. Expectations for excellent performance in commercial transactions are high
2. Expectations for future investments are high
3. The company works towards building a stronger future relationship
4. There is a high level of trust, which is the basis for a high-intensity relationship
5. Innovative collaboration opportunities are identified and leveraged to generate collaborative advantage

Subsequently, respondents were asked to classify a set of information types that could be shared between SC partners according to their importance. Focus companies should assess the importance of sharing each type of information with each of their key partners. Companies could also inform other types of information that they consider relevant. The types of information evaluated were: (1) Production capacity; (2) Production process; (3) Inventory; (4) Buy and sell orders; (5) Traceability (track and trace); (6) Contracts (governance) - supplier, customer, logistics; (7) Alternative suppliers; and (8) Market (changes, threats, opportunities).

Following, based on the model presented by Messina et al. [13], interviewees evaluated the sharing of information with their main partners in order to allow the analysis of SC visibility. The visibility metric considers the quantity and quality of information shared [13, 26]; where quality is obtained as a combination of precision (accuracy or absence of errors) and timeliness (degree to which information is available at the right time) [13, 25, 26]. The following questions were answered to each relationship:

(1) How do you classify the amount of information shared with the partner company?;
(2) How do you classify the quality/accuracy/absence of errors of the information shared with the partner company?; and
(3) Is relevant information shared or received in a timely manner?

From the answers of the questions, a visibility indicator is calculated by averaging the visibility index of each of the evaluated aspects and is classified as:

- High visibility greater than or equal to 4),
- Medium (visibility greater than or equal to 3 and less than 4), and
- Low (visibility less than 3).

4 Results and Discussion

The focal companies, as well as their main customers and suppliers, were interviewed and answered the questionnaire made available on the online platform. The focal companies provided information on 20 SC partners, nine related to their main customers and 11 related to their main suppliers. 22 responses were received from the partner companies.

The responses indicated that most of the relationships evaluated are long-term. 70% of the partnerships are more than five years old, and 20% of these are more than ten years old. Only 10% of the partnerships evaluated has less than one year. These numbers show that companies consider the partners with whom they interact over extended periods of time as the main ones, indicating that trusting relationships take time to build.

Regarding the types of information considered most relevant to companies, the information related to routine trade operations and exchanges are the most valued. 100% of respondents say that sharing purchase and sales order information with their partners is critical to their business. Information regarding the production process, contracts and product traceability are considered important by 95% of respondents and production capacity by 90%. On the other hand, information regarding alternative suppliers, inventory and market information are considered less important.

The relevance of track and trace of goods is highlighted by the respondents, even though this type of information is still seldom shared and with great opportunities for improvement – especially with the application of new digital technologies. Track and trace have been aspects widely valued by companies for their potential operational management impact, but also by customers and other stakeholders due to social and environmental aspects of supply chains.

4.1 Company A

Company "A" evaluated its relationship with its four main suppliers and three main customers. Among the partners evaluated by the company, only the relationship with one client (client 3) is less than 5 years old, which shows that the company values building long-term relationships. Regarding the degree of visibility with partners, the answers indicate a high degree of visibility with all three customers evaluated, as well as a high overall index of visibility with the main customers (4.56). On the other hand, company "A" has a medium level of visibility with three of its main suppliers (the global index of visibility with the main suppliers is equal to 3.58).

These numbers can be interpreted from the point of view of the companies' technological "maturity", often directly linked to size. In a traditional sector such as textiles and apparel, smaller companies tend to have lower investments in technology, a factor highly related to the level of visibility, as demonstrated in Sect. 2. Thus, the larger size of company "A" customers compared to its suppliers helps to explain the levels of visibility presented and indicate the need for investment in technology as a way of strengthening SCs, especially upstream (Table 1).

Table 1. Visibility assessment Company A

Partner	Relationship duration	Visibility level
Supplier 1	More than 10 years	4.00
Supplier 2	5 to 10 years	3.67
Supplier 3	5 to 10 years	3.33
Supplier 4	More than 10 years	3.33
Client 1	5 to 10 years	4.33
Client 2	5 to 10 years	4.67

| High visibility level | Medium visibility level | Low visibility level |

The SC of company "A" presents high levels of trust, both in the relationship with suppliers and with customers, as shown in Table 2. The numbers may reflect a company's strategy of investing in the relationship with a reduced number of partners (the company evaluated the relationship with a relatively low number of customers and suppliers), but with a high degree of trust and a long-term strategy.

Table 2. Trust assessment Company A

Partner	Relationship duration	Trust level
Supplier 1	More than 10 years	4.20
Supplier 2	5 to 10 years	4.40
Supplier 3	5 to 10 years	5.00
Supplier 4	More than 10 years	5.00
Client 1	5 to 10 years	5.00
Client 2	5 to 10 years	5.00

High level of trust   Medium level of trust   Low level of trust

4.2 Company B

Company "B" evaluated its relationship with its top five suppliers and its top eight customers. Only one of the suppliers has had a relationship with the company for more than ten years, while two relationships evaluated are less than one year old. The relationship with most of the analyzed clients is between five and ten years.

The analysis of visibility in the supply chain of company "B" (Table 3) clearly demonstrates the need for improvement in two "nodes" of the chain: supplier 1 (2.67) and customer A (2.00). The answers indicate that the company is not satisfied with the quality, quantity and "opportunity" of exchanging information with these two partners. There are also average levels of visibility in three suppliers (two of them in the lower limit, 3.00) and four customers (one of them in the lower limit of 3.00). The exchange of information is satisfactory in the relationship with one supplier and three customers.

The global visibility indicator with the main suppliers is equal to 3.20 and the global visibility indicator with the main customers is 3.58. As with company "A", the numbers demonstrate a greater need for improved visibility with suppliers, although there are also problems in exchanging information with some of the main customers.

Analysis of the trust levels of company "B" (Table 4) helps to demonstrate the relationship between trust and the development of long-term relationships. Two of the company's suppliers (supplier 1 and supplier 4), whose relationship has existed for less than a year, have low levels of trust (2.80 and 2.40 respectively). The same occurs with supplier 5, even though the relationship has been in existence for over 5 years. The relationship with four of the eight clients analyzed shows medium levels of trust, showing the opportunity for improvement in existing relationships.

Table 3. Visibility assessment Company B

Partner	Relationship duration	Visibility level
Supplier 1	Less than 1 year	2.67
Supplier 2	5 to 10 years	3.33
Supplier 3	More than 10 years	4.00
Supplier 4	Less than 1 year	3.00
Supplier 5	5 to 10 years	3.00
Client 1	5 to 10 years	2.00
Client 2	5 to 10 years	3.00
Client 3	5 to 10 years	3.67
Client 4	5 to 10 years	3.67
Client 5	5 to 10 years	4.33
Client 6	5 to 10 years	4.33
Client 7	5 to 10 years	4.00
Client 8	5 to 10 years	3.67

High visibility level   Medium visibility level   Low visibility level

Table 4. Visibility assessment Company B

Partner	Relationship duration	Trust level
Supplier 1	Less than 1 year	2.80
Supplier 2	5 to 10 years	3.40
Supplier 3	More than 10 years	4.00
Supplier 4	Less than 1 year	2.40
Supplier 5	5 to 10 years	2.60
Client 1	5 to 10 years	3.60
Client 2	5 to 10 years	3.20
Client 3	5 to 10 years	3.00
Client 4	5 to 10 years	4,20
Client 5	5 to 10 years	4,00
Client 6	5 to 10 years	4,40
Client 7	5 to 10 years	4,20
Client 8	5 to 10 years	3,40

High level of trust   Medium level of trust   Low level of trust

5   Discussion

Both companies present higher degrees of visibility with customers than with suppliers. These results can be interpreted from the perspective of the technological maturity level. In a traditional sector such as textile, smaller companies tend to have lower investments in technology. Thus, the larger size of customers compared to suppliers helps to explain the levels of visibility presented and indicates the need for investment in technology as a way to strengthen visibility. In terms of trust, one company presents high levels in the relationships with suppliers and customers, reflecting the company's strategy of investing in close relationships with a reduced number of partners, with high degrees of trust and with a long-term strategy. In the other company, the suppliers whose relationships last for less time present the lowest levels of trust.

The diagnosis of the levels of visibility and trust can be analyzed and used by the companies for the development of actions to improve trust and visibility. Specific action for each partner (according to the results of the assessment) or general action can be developed.

Additionally, based on the information collected and the theoretical analysis, a set of recommendations can be developed to companies seeking to improve trust and visibility with their SC partners, such as:

(1) implementing a tool for the self-assessment of trust and visibility with SC partners;
(2) adoption of a SC visibility index as an indicator of the companies' strategic performance;
(3) development of action plans to implement improvements in information sharing practices with the partners with indexes classified as "medium" or "low";
(4) automation of processes and the integration of information systems in order to improve the sharing of information in the necessary quantity, with the necessary quality (accuracy/absence of errors) and at the right time;
(5) standardization of performance metrics between SC partners;
(6) adoption of a routine of benchmarking among suppliers.
(7) involvement of strategic partners in the decision-making; and
(8) definition of the end-to-end visibility as a vision for the future.

6   Conclusions

This paper uses cases from the textile sector in Portugal to analyze the role of visibility and trust in the management of SCs. Based on the OIPT, this paper considers that companies benefit from the ability of sharing information with SC partners, which has the potential to improve trust and visibility levels; and from the ability of using the information collected to inform the decision-making process.

The analysis of the two cases suggests that trust is closely related to the duration of the relationships and to long-term strategies, while visibility reflects the capacity of companies to share information; which is directly related to their technological maturity level and to companies' size. The results also suggest a relationship between trust and visibility, as many of the partnerships that present lower levels of trust also tend to have lower visibility. This paper shows that carrying out trust and visibility level assessments can help companies to improve their practices but also to improve their relationship with specific partners based on their characteristics. In the long run, companies must seek visibility across the entire chain - end-to-end.

The paper contributes to theory by analyzing and discussing the role of visibility and trust in SCs and by highlighting the relationships between: trust and the duration of partnerships; visibility and technological maturity level and companies' size; trust and visibility. This paper also contributes to practice as it shows that carrying out trust and visibility level assessments can help companies to improve their practices and their relationship with specific partners based on their characteristics and by presenting a set of recommendations for companies seeking to improve trust and visibility with their SC partners.

Acknowledgments. This study was developed in the scope of the STVgoDigital project - PPS2 Digitization of the STV value chain (POCI-01-0247-FEDER-046086), co-financed by COM-PETE2020, under the Competitiveness and Internationalization Program, through Portugal 2020 and the European Regional Development Fund (FEDER).

References

1. Swift, C., Guide, V.D., Jr., Muthulingam, S.: Does supply chain visibility affect operating performance? Evidence from conflict minerals disclosures. J. Oper. Manag. **65**(5), 1–24 (2019)
2. Zimmermann, R., Ferreira, L.M., Moreira, A.C.: How supply chain strategies moderate the relationship between innovation capabilities and business performance. J. Purch. Supply Manag. **26**(5), 100658 (2020)
3. Raj, A., Dwivedi, G., Sharma, A., Jabbour, A.S., Rajak, S.: Barriers to the adoption of industry 4.0 technologies in the manufacturing sector: an inter-country comparative perspective. Int. J. Prod. Econ. **224**, 107546 (2020)
4. Fawcett, S.E., Jones, S.L., Fawcett, A.M.: Supply chain trust: the catalyst for collaborative innovation. Bus. Horiz. **55**(2), 163–178 (2012)
5. Wieland, A., Durach, C.F.: Two perspectives on supply chain resilience. J. Bus. Logist. **42**(3), 315–322 (2021)
6. Williams, B.D., Roh, J., Tokas, T., Swink, M.: Leveraging supply chain visibility for responsiveness: the moderating role of internal integration. J. Oper. Manag. **31**(7–8), 543–554 (2013)
7. Bastas, A., Garza-Reyes, J.A.: Impact of the COVID-19 pandemic on manufacturing operations and supply chain resilience: effects and response strategies. J. Manuf. Technol. Manag. (2022). https://doi.org/10.1108/JMTM-09-2021-0357
8. Kalaiarasan, R., Olhager, J., Agrawal, T.K., Wiktorsson, M.: The ABCDE of supply chain visibility: a systematic literature review and framework. Int. J. Prod. Econ. **248**, 108464 (2022)
9. Barratt, M., Oke, A.: Antecedents of supply chain visibility in retail supply chains: a resource-based theory perspective. J. Oper. Manag. **25**(6), 1217–1233 (2007)
10. Francis, V.: Supply chain visibility: lost in translation? Supply Chain Manag. Int. J. **13**(3), 180–184 (2008)
11. Zhang, A.N., Goh, M., Meng, F.: Conceptual modelling for supply chain inventory visibility. Int. J. Prod. Econ. **133**(2), 578–585 (2011)
12. Busse, C., Schleper, M.C., Weilenmann, J., Wagner, S.: Extending the supply chain visibility boundary: utilizing stakeholders for identifying supply chain sustainability risks. Int. J. Phys. Distrib. Logist. Manag. **47**(1), 18–40 (2017)
13. Messina, D., Soares, A.L., Barros, A., Zimmermann, R.: How visible is your supply chain? A model for supply chain visibility assessment. Supply Chain Forum: Int. J. (2022). https://doi.org/10.1080/16258312.2022.2079955

14. Cao, A., Bryceson, K., Hine, D.: Improving supply chain risk visibility and communication with a multi-view risk ontology. Supply Chain Forum: Int. J. **21**(1), 1–15 (2020)
15. Brookbanks, M., Parry, G.: The impact of a blockchain platform on trust in established relationships: a case study of wine supply chains. Supply Chain Manag. Int. J. **27**(7), 128–146 (2022)
16. Burns, L.R., Wholey, D.R.: Adoption and abondonment of matrix management programs: effects of organizational characteristics and interorganizational networks. Acad. Manag. J. **36**(1), 106–138 (1993)
17. Srinivasan, R., Swink, M.: An investigation of visibility and flexibility as complements to supply chain analytics: an organizational information processing theory perspective. Prod. Oper. Manag. **27**(10), 1849–1867 (2017)
18. Baah, C., Acquah, I.S.K., Ofori, D.: Exploring the influence of supply chain collaboration on supply chain visibility, stakeholder trust, environmental and financial performances: a partial least square approach. Benchmark. Int. J. **29**(1), 172–193 (2022)
19. Jiang, R., et al.: A trust transitivity model of small and medium-sized manufacturing enterprises under blockchain-based supply chain finance. Int. J. Prod. Econ. **247**, 108469 (2022)
20. Andras, P., et al.: Trusting intelligent machines: deepening trust within socio-technical systems. IEEE Technol. Soc. Magaz. **37**(4), 76–83 (2018)
21. Poppo, L., Zhou, K.Z., Li, J.J.: When can you trust? Calculative trust, relational trust, and supplier performance. Strateg. Manag. J. **37**(4), 724–741 (2016)
22. Rogerson, M., Parry, G.C.: Blockchain: case studies in food supply chain visibility. Supply Chain Manag. **25**(5), 601–614 (2020)
23. Saint McIntire, J.: Supply Chain Visibility: From Theory to Practice. Routledge, London (2014)
24. Somapa, S., Cools, M., Dullaert, W.: Characterizing supply chain visibility – a literature review. Int. J. Logist. Manag. **29**(1), 308–339 (2018)
25. Barratt, M., Barratt, R.: Exploring internal and external supply chain linkages: evidence from the field. J. Oper. Manag. **29**(5), 514–528 (2011)
26. Caridi, M., Crippa, L., Perego, A., Sianesi, A., Tumino, A.: Do virtuality and complexity affect supply chain visibility? Int. J. Prod. Econ. **127**(2), 372–383 (2010)
27. Yu, M.-C., Goh, M.: A multi-objective approach to supply chain visibility and risk. Eur. J. Oper. Res. **233**(1), 125–130 (2014)
28. Brusset, X.: Does supply chain visibility enhance agility? Int. J. Prod. Econ. **171**, 46–59 (2016)

Impacts of Digital Transformation on Supply Chain Sustainability: A Systematic Literature Review and Expert Assessment

Martha Orellano[✉] and Sanaa Tiss

Direction Recherche & Innovation, Capgemini Engineering, 31700 Blagnac, France
{martha-stefany.orellano-carrasquilla,sanaa.tiss}@capgemini.com

Abstract. The current industrial context is characterized by the integration of digital technologies to improve process efficiency and Supply Chain agility to better respond to market volatility and customer needs. Digital transformation could contribute to the transparency, integration, connectivity, and flexibility of Supply Chains, enabling autonomous management and decision-making decentralization. Nevertheless, in addition to efficiency and agility, current and future Supply Chains should be sustainable, regarding the economic, environmental, and social pillars. In this paper, we analyzed the positive and negative impacts carried out by digitalization on the sustainability performance of Supply Chain activities, using the SWOT matrix method and the SCOR model. From a methodological point of view, a systematic literature review of 35 publications was performed and complemented by the expert consultation approach, involving a panel of experts in the fields of Supply Chain Management, digitalization, and sustainability.

Keywords: Digital transformation · Industry 4.0 · Sustainable supply chain · Supply chain management · Systematic literature review

1 Introduction

In the last few years, national and international standards and policies have been implemented to guide and incite companies to integrate sustainable development considerations into their activities. Also, the health crisis triggered by Covid 19 has accentuated the need to design flexible, resilient, and responsible logistics systems. Thus, the economic factors related to the increase of productivity within the Supply Chain (SC) are no longer the only concerns nor the only criteria ensuring the sustainability of SC activities. Rather, the integration of social and environmental considerations is becoming a key factor for SC sustainability and for gaining competitive advantage.

Furthermore, customers' needs become increasingly challenging, especially in terms of product customization. To keep up with the market dynamics and meet its new and growing standards, the adoption of digital transformation technologies is seen as a key asset. The adoption of these technologies in logistics and Supply Chain Management activities has led to the emergence of Logistics 4.0 and Supply Chain 4.0.

© IFIP International Federation for Information Processing 2022
Published by Springer Nature Switzerland AG 2022
L. M. Camarinha-Matos et al. (Eds.): PRO-VE 2022, IFIP AICT 662, pp. 390–405, 2022.
https://doi.org/10.1007/978-3-031-14844-6_32

The impacts of the adoption of these technologies in the SC have been considered positive regarding the pillars of sustainability, since it allows companies to improve their productivity, master their CO_2 emissions and improve their working conditions. However, the risks and negative impacts involved in the integration of these technologies are less emphasized in the literature.

In this paper, we study the impacts of new technologies on sustainable Supply Chain by relying on the state-of-the-art and expert opinions within the consulting firm Capgemini Engineering. First, we introduce the theoretical background on Supply Chain 4.0, and Sustainable Supply Chain. Then, we present our methodological approach, which combines a systematic literature review and expert consulting. After that, we present the main results of our work. Finally, we present the conclusions.

2   Theoretical Background

2.1   Logistics and Supply Chain 4.0

The notion of Industry 4.0 is generally used to characterize a system integrating digital technologies to autonomously collect, analyze, and evaluate data in real time and then decide and communicate with other systems, equipment, and humans [1, 2]. The application of Internet of Things (IoT)-based technologies is one of the key features of this industry phase (4.0) [3]. Industry 4.0 technologies allow the digital transformation of information, processes, and businesses to make information available anytime, anywhere, and in any context on different devices [4]. Different characteristics are used to describe the capabilities of digital transformation technologies. For instance, Junge [5] proposes the following characteristics to describe sustainable digital technologies: (1) elaborateness for more accurate and robust tools, (2) transparent structures for more technical openness, (3) comprehensive structure to be easily assimilated by humans and machines, (4) distributed location.

The adoption of industry 4.0 technologies in logistics and Supply Chain Management has led to the new concepts of logistics 4.0, Supply Chain 4.0, and Supply Chain Management (SCM) 4.0. Those technologies were adapted for logistics applications to better meet the volatility of today's market and respond more efficiently to individualized customers' demands [6, 7]. From an operational perspective, the use of intelligent et interconnected systems enhances the analytical and operational capabilities and thus optimizes Supply Chain activities [8–10]. The use of industry 4.0 technologies in Supply Chain Management allows accessing data in real time, promoting transparency between Supply Chain actors, and enhancing agility [4, 11].

2.2   Sustainable Logistics and Supply Chain Management

Nowadays, sustainability is one of the major concerns of manufacturers and SC managers. Ahi et C. Searcy [12] define Sustainable Supply Chain Management (SSCM) as "the creation of coordinated Supply Chains through the voluntary integration of economic, environmental, and social issues with inter-organizational business systems, to efficiently manage the material, information, and capital flows over the SC, to meet stakeholder requirements and improve the profitability, competitiveness, and resilience of the organization over the short and long-term".

Besides, sustainable logistics is used as an interchangeable term for SSCM and can be defined as "the strategic and transparent integration and realization of social, environmental and economic objectives throughout the SC thanks to the systemic coordination of inter-organizational processes, enabling the economic performance of all the actors over the long term" [13]. Peng et al. [14] consider that sustainable Supply Chain Management is achieved through the following capabilities: sustainable strategy and governance, sustainable data collection and sharing, training and benchmarking, sustainable reporting, sustainable risk analysis, and sustainable innovation.

Particularly, environmental aspects in the logistic systems take a great extent in the contemporary debates and companies' initiatives mostly related to transportation, warehousing, supplier selection, and product return management issues [15, 16]. In this line, Green Logistics is another notion that focuses on measuring and minimizing the impact of logistics activities from an ecological perspective [17].

Regarding the social aspects, the ISO 26000 standard [18] defines the main social categories as governance of organizations, working conditions, Human Rights, consumer protection, fair practices, and development of local communities. Yet, the social dimension of sustainability remains the most difficult to apprehend in sustainable SC, which is probably linked to the difficulty of measuring the intangible aspects related to the human factors [15]. Thus, new paradigms such as Society 5.0 and Industry 5.0 are emerging to emphasize the need to integrate social aspects by involving SC stakeholders benefiting from digital technologies, adapting and improving the SC organization, strengthening SC linkages, and capitalizing on the creativity of human experts in collaboration with intelligent machines [19, 20].

3   Research Methodology

3.1   Systematic Literature Review

We conducted a preliminary step concerning a bibliometric analysis, then we followed the steps of the PRISMA framework [21] (Fig. 1). The bibliometric analysis allows identifying the main trends, keywords and authors in the searched domain over time, to refine the research scope [22]. A systematic literature review is a well-structured and rigorous process that should be reliable and repeatable over time. It allows summarizing and analyzing relevant literature about a subject and identifying the research gaps [23]. To conduct this research, we mobilized two bodies of literature, one concerning logistics 4.0 or Supply Chain 4.0, and the second one referring to sustainable Supply Chain. The following research questions guided this research: (1) What are the technologies involved in logistics 4.0 or Supply Chain 4.0? (2) How does the use of new technologies in Supply Chain activities impact positively and negatively the sustainability pillars?

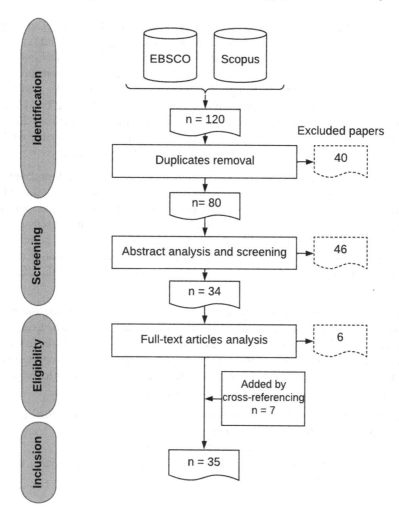

Fig. 1. Systematic literature review according to the PRISMA framework.

Preliminary Bibliometric Analysis. We applied the following keyword combination in Scopus database: ("logistics" OR "Supply Chain Management") AND ("corporate social responsibility" OR "sustainability") AND ("4.0 technolog*" OR "digital*" OR "smart"). The search was performed between 2000 and 2022. Three major periods characterize the evolution of the academic literature that links Supply Chain Management, sustainability, and 4.0 technologies. First, the emergence of this research field coincides with the appearance of the Industry 4.0 notion in 2011 [7]. Then, between 2014 and 2018, the subject gained a slight interest, reaching an accelerated growth after 2018. We selected 2011–2022 as a representative time span to perform the successive steps of the systematic literature review process.

Source Identification. A set of keywords was defined based on the research questions, addressing two bodies of literature corresponding to logistics 4.0 and sustainable Supply Chain. Using Boolean operators, the keywords include the combination of ("logistics" OR "Supply Chain Management") AND ("corporate social responsibility" OR "sustainability") AND ("4.0 technolog*" OR "digital*" OR "smart"). We used Scopus and EBSCO databases and performed advanced research by "Title" and "Field". Moreover, considering the bibliometric analysis, we defined a time span between 2011 and 2022. Peer-reviewed journals, conferences, and book chapters were considered. Only English-written articles were included. This step resulted in 80 papers.

Screening. An abstract analysis of the retained papers was performed throughout three screening criteria: i) the paper discusses at least one Supply Chain activity (i.e., SCOR model [24]: source, make, deliver, return, and plan); ii) the paper analyses the application of at least one technology 4.0 in Supply Chain activities; iii) the paper discusses either the environmental or the social pillar of sustainability. Two researchers performed an independent abstract analysis. Only the papers matching at least two out of the three criteria were included for full-text analysis. 34 papers were gathered at the end of this step.

Eligibility. Depth analysis of the screened papers was done considering the type of methodology implemented, the Supply Chain activity considered according to the SCOR model, and the pillar of sustainability addressed. Six articles were removed at this step because of their poor or no contribution to the research questions. Moreover, a cross-reference analysis was performed, from which seven papers were added to the sample. This step resulted in the consolidation of a relevant sample of 35 papers.

Included Papers. Most of the included publications take place between 2017 and 2021, and the sample is composed of 27 journal articles [3, 5, 7, 8, 10, 16, 17, 22, 25–43], six conferences [4, 5, 9, 14, 44, 45], and two book chapters [6, 46].

54% of the papers adopt a theoretical approach, 32% apply survey research, and 14% combine literature review and expert consulting.

3.2 Expert Assessment

The literature that crosses the applications of Industry 4.0 technologies in the Supply Chain and the dimensions of SC sustainability is very limited and particularly rare for those that deal with the negative impacts involved in the use of these technologies at the social and environmental level. We have relied on the experience of consultants within Capgemini Engineering to deal with these limits of the state-of-the-art. This investigation was conducted using a brainstorming approach and semi-structured interviews with experts in logistics and digitalization.

4 Results and Discussion

4.1 Results of the Systematic Literature Review

A content analysis of the articles was performed according to the Supply Chain activities defined by the SCOR (Supply Chain Operations Reference) model [24]. This model is used by scientists and practitioners alike. This model classifies and describes the different levels of logistics processes as Source, Make, Deliver, Return, and Plan [24]. The articles were analyzed according to these SC processes while considering the use of new technologies and their sustainability impacts.

Sustainable Source 4.0. Gottge et al. [37] highlight the sourcing and purchasing challenges related to the management of an enormous mass of data, which is difficult to process using traditional methods. Big data analytics (BDA) enable an accurate analysis of a big volume of data at a high velocity [28]. Sun et al. [25] discuss the use of Artificial Intelligence (AI) for data analysis and risk anticipation, allowing companies to be more reactive in the face of threats. Furthermore, Sun et al. [25] evoke cloud computing as a useful technology to support buyer-supplier transactions and data sharing, since it enables centralized storage of data while providing autonomy and decentralized data access to each actor. Finally, Blockchain is evoked as a promising technology to assure data security in buyer-supplier transactions [27, 40, 41].

From an economic perspective, AI and BDA enable the analysis of market trends and suppliers' patterns, which favors the formulation of effective sourcing strategies [25, 28, 37]. Cloud computing and Blockchain facilitate data sharing and increase buyer-supplier trustworthiness. In particular, Blockchain can be used to create smart contracts, which eliminate the intermediation of transactions, reducing costs while improving data security [27, 40, 41]. Some economic shortcomings have been slightly discussed in the literature, concerning the high costs of system acquisition, management, and maintenance, and the risks of having technical problems [41].

From an environmental perspective, new technologies allow verifying suppliers' compliance with environmental regulations and tracking their environmental impacts [40]. It also promotes paperless operations [41]. In contrast, high energy consumption is needed for data storage and computation, and big amounts of electronic waste are generated from data centers [41]. Finally, considering the social issues, Blockchain improves data transparency, reducing the risk of corruption along the Supply Chain and contributes to tracing and tracking the ethical behavior of suppliers [27].

Sustainable Make 4.0. Junge [5] considers that real time, decentralization, and automation are the main capabilities of industry 4.0 technologies that allow for reducing the cycle time and the efficient use of resources. Those capabilities can be provided by the combined use of autonomous robots and IoT which allows high connectivity and automation in smart production systems and thus more flow fluidity and real-time communication [25]. Using sensors for data acquisition in manufacturing systems allows for agility, better product quality, and thus better customer service rate [17, 38].

The use of Artificial Intelligent (AI) and cloud computing in connection with IoT-embedded systems is essential for effective planning and real-time work visualization and thus better process control [3, 25, 39]. Besides, Additive Manufacturing (AM) enables increasing customization capabilities and makes it easier to involve customers in product design and also the implementation of JIT [25, 33]. Blockchain allows the integration of information and material flow within the manufacturing system [25]. This integration facilitates information sharing, increases data security, reduces costs, and increases organizational efficiency [40]. Finally, simulation and Digital Twin (DT) can be used to handle emergency problems and enhance process efficiency [26, 35, 46].

Although there are various economic advantages of digitizing factories, it involves some business-related shortcomings. For instance, significant efforts and investments are needed for the implementation and integration of these technologies to ensure their interoperability and communication with the existing systems and equipment [17, 25].

Regarding the environmental pillar, using real-time data collection provides an opportunity for controlling energy usage and for efficient waste management [39]. Also, digitalization and automation of production systems allow waste minimization and paperless operations [38]. For example, AM makes it possible to use waste to make new value-added products [33]. Digital Twin can be used to detect and remove products or processes damaging environmental aspects [46]. However, the use and integration of these technologies imply different challenges and risks to the environment related to the lifecycle impact of the equipment [25]. For instance, Tran-Dang [17] highlight the significant energy consumption of IoT devices due to their permanent activity to fulfill real-time data collection requirements. Also, the use of AM can generate hazardous waste linked to the chemical consumables used in the transformation process [33].

From a social perspective, the features and services provided by Industry 4.0 technologies can lead to a better work environment by improving safety and reducing the work arduousness, while providing better visibility of accomplishments and progress to operators and managers [25, 38, 41]. Thanks to real-time monitoring, scraps and rework expenses and the associated workload can be reduced [39]. Furthermore, the application of Blockchain in manufacturing systems can be a useful tool for better assurance of human rights, especially those related to data privacy. Moreover, technologies like simulation can provide opportunities for operators' training in a safe environment. However, within digital and automated systems, the knowledge requirements will be higher, and this can cause job loss and anxiety [10, 25, 33].

Sustainable Deliver 4.0. Delivering-related technologies consist of IoT devices to track and trace products (e.g., RFID, scanning devices, intelligent goods), voice-guided picking systems, Intelligent Transport Systems (ITS), and Transport Management Systems (TMS), among others. The sustainability implications of those technologies have been discussed in recent literature, focusing on their positive aspects.

From an economic perspective, Nantee and Sureeyatanapas [10] and de Vass et al. [38] highlight the use of IoT devices in warehousing to facilitate order picking accuracy throughout the implementation of RFID and scanning devices. In the same line, Barreto et al. [9] and Sajjad et al. [39] argue that IoT devices improve operational performance and traceability accuracy thanks to real-time data collection. Specifically, in transport operations, TMS and ITS enable interactions with the warehouse management system, the track and trace of freights, and improve routing optimization [9, 10]. As stated by Nantee and Sureeyatanapas [10], TMS and ITS contributes increasing customer satisfaction by reducing lead time and improving shipping and information accuracy, and better responsiveness. Nevertheless, the high costs of investment and use constitute a barrier to the broad adoption of these intelligent systems.

From the environmental perspective, ITS and TMS allow the reduction of CO_2 emissions thanks to routing optimization, provide eco-efficient driving support, and enable the planning of multimodal transport [9, 10, 42]. In complement, the use of sensors enables real-time monitoring of CO_2 emissions [38]. However, the use of these devices constitutes a source of electronic waste and requires a huge amount of energy.

Finally, concerning the social issues, digital technologies can improve the working experience. In the transport sector, it helps to increase the safety and comfort of drivers by facilitating traffic analysis, providing driving guidance, monitoring fatigue, and controlling security devices [10, 42]. In warehousing activities, IoT devices contribute to improving health and safety in the workplace through the use of sensors and fatigue analysis [38]. Furthermore, technology adoption in delivery operations can promote the acquisition of new IT skills [35]. However, some negative impacts can be indicated. Adopting new technologies can lead to the loss of manual jobs, and generate a feeling of work uncertainty among the employees [4, 10]. Moreover, human-machine excessive collaboration can provoke skills degradation. Finally, the data collection made throughout the delivery applications can lead to data privacy vulnerabilities.

Sustainable Return 4.0. The main technologies supporting return activities are tracking devices and Blockchain. For instance, Sajjad et al. [39] put forward the notion of a "recycling center", which operates thanks to tracking technologies based on IoT, such as RFID and intelligent containers. The idea behind those recycling centers is to track the products until their end of life, identify the recycling products' parts, and enable optimal inventory management of returned products. Besides, regulatory return policies can be defined within smart contracts enabled by the Blockchain.

From an economic perspective, the use of new technologies in return activities contributes to improving customer satisfaction and gaining a competitive advantage throughout business model innovation [33]. Concerning the environmental issues, these technologies enable close-loop Supply Chains, improving the efficient management of waste, defective products, maintenance flows, and excess Supply Chain products [41]. Furthermore, it allows for mastering the product's lifecycle information and the traceability of reusable containers [39]. From a social point of view, tracking technologies in reverse logistics allow information sharing transparency between the Supply Chain actors, including suppliers and customers [27].

Sustainable Supply Chain Management 4.0. The generalization of the use of IoT-based technologies throughout the Supply Chain, not only allows to improve traceability within this chain [37, 39], but also the agility thanks to an efficient process of risk management [14, 25, 31]. For instance, the use of cloud-based information systems allows centralizing and facilitating the exchange of data between SC actors and thus reducing the synchronization cycle time, while respecting the autonomy of each actor [47]. This allows aligning the decisions of the SC actors and optimizing the flows through the SC [10, 39]. In this context of massive real-time data sharing, a primary concern is the quality and security of the shared data. Blockchain can help secure the data and improve cooperation between the various SC actors by eliminating intermediation [40], thus reducing the cost and time of transactions [27].

From an environmental perspective, tracking technologies and Blockchain can enable tracking products from their origin and along all their lifecycle and tracking their carbon footprint. This provides an opportunity for the development of effective eco-friendly products and thus avoid greenwashing issues [27]. As well, advanced information and communication systems help promote sustainability among SC actors (e.g., Social plastic or Recycle to Coin programs [27]) and align their visions toward a responsible logistics system. From a social perspective, Blockchain and smart contracts can improve reliability and contribute to developing sustainable and trustworthy relationships between SC actors [27, 40]. This reduces the risk of corruption and opportunistic and unethical behavior within the SC [48].

4.2 Results of the Expert Assessment

Beyond the elements identified from the literature review, the brainstorming and interviews carried out with the experts at Capgemini Engineering led to relevant insights related to industrial applications of new technologies.

For instance, the voice picking system was identified as a new technology being implemented in the "Deliver" phase of the Supply Chain. This technology supports the operators to perform the picking operation through the voice instructions to indicate the right location, quantity, and reference of articles to perform the order preparation. Besides, related to the sustainability impacts of new technologies, most of the elements evoked by the experts correspond to economic and social aspects, whereas the environmental one was less addressed.

Among the economic impacts indicated by the experts, we count the costs of subcontracting IT and system adaptation for an IoT-based system. It was highlighted that this adaptation can aim even at a conception of new equipment to optimize the Process Cell for MES (Manufacturing Execution System). Furthermore, the technological interfacing cost, the management of special stock related to the use of new technologies (e.g., chemical consumables for additive manufacturing), and the reduction of the labor costs in manual operations were also evoked.

Concerning the social aspects, some threats such as the distrust in the algorithms, the gap between IT and real business practices, and the risk of losing autonomy in the case of IT outsourcing were indicated. Moreover, the imbalance in the technological maturity of the collaborators in the Supply Chain was indicated as a general feature in Supply Chains. Finally, "greenwashing" and "sustainability marketing" remain crosscutting issues that threaten the integration of sustainability concerns in logistics systems, identified as major challenges according to the experts [16].

4.3 SWOT Analysis

The literature findings were summarized into a SWOT matrix, structured according to the activities of the SCOR model, the relevant technologies used in each of these activities, and their sustainability-related impacts. The sustainability impacts were summarized and categorized thanks to a thoughtful analysis of the literature. An initial SWOT matrix based on the literature insights was presented to the experts to have their validation and appreciation. Then, we completed the SWOT matrix with the experts' insights from their industrial experience (Tables 1, 2, and 3).

Table 1. Environmental impact analysis of 4.0 Technologies in Supply Chain activities.

	Technologies	Sustainability	
		Environmental pillar	
		Negative impacts	Positive impacts
Source	AI Big data analytics Cloud computing Blockchain	• Data center locations (Use of space) • Energy consumption from the servers • Electronic waste generation	• Supplier selection and purchasing strategy oriented towards eco-responsibility • Reducing pollution thanks to paperless operations
Make	Autonomous robots IoT systems AI AM DT	• Energy consumption • Life cycle impacts of equipment • Hazardous waste generation linked to the chemical consumables used in AM • Electronic waste generation	• Equipment maintenance cycles • Low raw material volume used in AM • Waste reduction • Reduction of remanufacturing, thus energy saving
Deliver	Tracking tech. ITS Voice picking	• Electronic waste generation • Energy consumption	• Mastering and reduction of CO_2 emissions thank to routing optimization and planning of multimodal transport
Return	Data-driven marketplace Tracking tech. Blockchain	• Massive product labeling packaging • Long-distance returns • Electronic waste	• Product lifecycle information • Increasing recycling efficiency • Closed-loop SC
SCM	Blockchain Cloud	• Carbon footprint of information system technologies	• Tracking the entire product life cycle impacts

SCM = Supply Chain Management

Table 2. Economic impact analysis of 4.0 Technologies in Supply Chain activities.

	Technologies	Sustainability	
		Economic pillar	
		Negative impacts	Positive impacts
Source	Artificial Intelligence (AI) Big data analytics Cloud computing Blockchain	• Cost of system management and maintenance • Subcontracting cost and high dependency • (If IT outsourcing) • Risk of sharing sensible data	• Analysis of market trends and purchasing patterns • Effective planning • Reduction of errors linked to manual data entry and processing • Risk management
Make	Autonomous robots IoT systems AI Additive manufacturing (AM) Digital Twin (DT)	• Investment costs on equipment acquisition • Cost of system use • Cost of system maintenance • Cost of system interfacing • Management of stocks of chemical consumables for AM	• Process performance improvement • Real-time process monitoring • Reduction of labor costs in manual operations • Increasing customization capabilities • Ease to involve customers in product design
Deliver	Tracking technologies Intelligent Transport Systems (ITS) Voice picking	• Cost of equipment acquisition • Cost of system management and maintenance • Cost of systems use • Recharging time of electrical equipment	• Process performance improvement • Traceability accuracy • Process flexibility • Customer satisfaction • Reduction of manual labor costs • Stability of delivery costs
Return	Data-driven marketplace Tracking tech. Blockchain	• High investment cos • Cost of system management	• Customer satisfaction • Competitive advantage throughout innovation • Traceability of reusable containers
SCM	IoT Blockchain Cloud	• Cost of enforcing technological adoption • Loss of collaborators (resistance to change)	• Virtual currency transactions • Secure access to data • Improving marketing and strategic planning • Data-driven business

Table 3. Social impact analysis of 4.0 Technologies in Supply Chain activities.

	Technologies	Sustainability	
		Social pillar	
		Negative impacts	Positive impacts
Source	Artificial Intelligence (AI) Big data analytics Cloud computing Blockchain	• Distrust in the algorithms • Gap between IT and real business practices • IT staffing shortage • If IT outsourcing, loss of skills and autonomy • Loss of purchasing jobs	• Transformation of job profiles (IT and decision-oriented) • Autonomy given data decentralization • Buyer-supplier transparency
Make	Autonomous robots IoT systems AI Additive manufacturing (AM) Digital Twin (DT)	• Several applications and tools to master and handle • Layoff on manual jobs • Feeling of job uncertainty • Stress linked to high productivity exigence • Perception of autonomy loss • Reduction of human relationships • Hazardous waste generation	• Reduction of work arduousness • Transformation of job profiles (from manual/technique to engineering/decision profiles) • Creation of new job profiles (IT and decision-oriented)
Deliver	Tracking tech. ITS Voice picking	• Layoff on manual-related jobs • Feeling of job uncertainty • Increasing stress linked to high productivity exigence • Competences and skills degradation • Data privacy vulnerability	• Improvement of delivery working experience • Adaptable equipment/vehicles (ergonomics) • Improvement of work safety (e.g., fatigue analysis)
Return	Data-driven marketplace Tracking tech. Blockchain	• Customer data privacy vulnerability	• Improvement of flow transparency
SCM	IoT Blockchain Cloud	• Data privacy vulnerability • Interest conflicts	• Trustworthy business environment

5 Conclusion

In this article we address the impacts of the adoption of industry 4.0 technologies in Supply Chains. We answered two research questions: What are the technologies involved in logistics 4.0 or Supply Chain 4.0? How does the use of new technologies in Supply Chain activities impact positively and negatively the sustainability pillars?

To answer those questions, we confronted the applications of different technologies in each of Supply Chain activities and studied their positive and negative impacts simultaneously on each of the pillars of sustainability (economic, environmental, social) within a SC. We relied on an analysis of the state-of-the-art, then we validated and completed this analysis with a panel of experts in the fields of digitalization and logistics. Finally, we summarized the results of this analysis using a SWOT matrix that crosses the different studied dimensions of SC activities using the SCOR model.

Based on the literature, we have detailed the applications of the different technologies in each of the SC activities according to the SCOR model. Data analytics and cloud computing technologies are significantly addressed at the level of purchasing and procurement activities of companies to improve the accuracy of forecasts and to assist the decision-making process. Additive manufacturing technologies and autonomous systems are also being used extensively in manufacturing systems to improve productivity and reduce production cycle times for customizable products. IoT devices and TMS (Transport Management Systems) are used in delivery and distribution activities to improve reactivity thanks to real-time data, and to control and optimize CO_2 emissions. These technologies are used to manage return flows, which enables closed-loop supply chains. Lastly, the management of transactions and data sharing using blockchain and IoT-based technologies enable a secure and efficient exchange of data between SC actors in an agile and trusted collaborative environment.

The collection of experts' opinions mainly contributed to identifying and analyzing practically the observed negative effects of 4.0 technologies according to their experience as implementers or users of these technologies. This allowed us to complete our analysis of the positive and negative impacts of 4.0 technologies on the SC sustainability, that are not well covered in the literature. The experts agreed with the fact that social factors are crucial to ensuring the effective integration and use of technologies to improve the efficiency and productivity of SC activities. They identified the necessary adaptation of usual processes for the integration of new technologies as the most constraining factor impacting the acceptability by users. Also, operators might feel a loss of autonomy in their interactions with these new technologies. On the economic pillar, the cost of integration is very high and mainly constrained by the significant efforts required to adapt existing tools and information systems. Furthermore, regarding the use of IoT-based technologies for the collection and analysis of real-time data, we stress that quantitative analyses are required to estimate the contribution of these technologies in comparison to the associated energy consumption due to their permanent running.

Finally, in the obtained SWOT matrix, we observe potential compensations between positive and negative impacts (e.g., new job profiles versus the loss of manual jobs). It will be possible to tackle this effect by assigning weights to the impacts using multicriteria analysis.

References

1. Thoben, K.-D., Wiesner, S., Wuest, T.: "Industrie 4.0" and smart manufacturing - a review of research issues and application examples. Int. J. Automat. Technol. **11**(1), 4–16 (2017)
2. Ghobakhloo, M.: Industry 4.0, digitization, and opportunities for sustainability. J. Clean. Prod. **252**, 119869 (2020)
3. Çınar, Z.M., Zeeshan, Q., Korhan, O.: A framework for industry 4.0 readiness and maturity of smart manufacturing enterprises: a case study. Sustainability **13**(12), 6659 (2021)
4. Kayikci, Y.: Sustainability impact of digitization in logistics. Proc. Manuf. **21**, 782–789 (2018)
5. Junge, A.L.: Prospects of digital transformation technologies (DTT) for sustainable logistics and supply chain processes in manufacturing. In: Leiras, A., González-Calderón, C.A., de Brito Junior, I., Villa, S., Yoshizaki, H.T.Y. (eds.) POMS 2018. SPBE, pp. 713–720. Springer, Cham (2020). https://doi.org/10.1007/978-3-030-23816-2_70
6. Demir, S., Yilmaz, I., Paksoy, T.: Augmented reality in supply chain management. In: Logistics 4.0. CRC Press (2020)
7. Winkelhaus, S., Grosse, E.H.: Logistics 4.0: a systematic review towards a new logistics system. Int. J. Prod. Res. **58**(1), 18–43 (2020)
8. Strandhagen, J.O., Vallandingham, L.R., Fragapane, G., Strandhagen, J.W., Stangeland, A.B.H., Sharma, N.: Logistics 4.0 and emerging sustainable business models. Adv. Manuf. **5**(4), 359–369 (2017)
9. Barreto, L., Amaral, A., Pereira, T.: Industry 4.0 implications in logistics: an overview. Proc. Manuf. **13**, 1245–1252 (2017)
10. Nantee, N., Sureeyatanapas, P.: The impact of Logistics 4.0 on corporate sustainability: a performance assessment of automated warehouse operations. Benchmark. Int. J. **28**(10), 2865–2895 (2021)
11. Oleśków-Szłapka, J., Stachowiak, A.: The framework of logistics 4.0 maturity model. In: Burduk, A., Chlebus, E., Nowakowski, T., Tubis, A. (eds.) ISPEM 2018. AISC, vol. 835, pp. 771–781. Springer, Cham (2019). https://doi.org/10.1007/978-3-319-97490-3_73
12. Ahi, P., Searcy, C.: A comparative literature analysis of definitions for green and sustainable supply chain management. J. Clean. Prod. **52**, 329–341 (2013)
13. Carter, C.R., Rogers, D.S.: A framework of sustainable supply chain management: moving toward new theory. Int. J. Phys. Distrib. Logist. Manag. **38**(5), 360–387 (2008)
14. Peng, X., Kurnia, S., Cui, T.: IT-enabled sustainable supply chain management capability maturity. In: Proceedings of the 54th Hawaii International Conference on System Sciences (2021)
15. Roussat, C., Fabbe-Costes, N.: Logistique durable du futur: etat des lieux en France et pistes de recherche. Logist. Manag. **22**(1), 19–34 (2014)
16. Schiffer, M., Dörr, D.M.: Development of the supply chain management 2040 – opportunities and challenges. In: Proceedings of the Conference on Production Systems and Logistics: CPSL 2020 (2020)
17. Tran-Dang, H., Krommenacker, N., Charpentier, P., Kim, D.-S.: The Internet of Things for logistics: perspectives, application review, and challenges. IETE Tech. Rev. **39**(1), 93–121 (2020)
18. ISO 26000. Guidance on Social Responsibility, 1st edn. vol. 22 (2010)
19. Fornasiero, R., Zangiacomi, A.: Reshaping the supply chain for society 5.0. In: Dolgui, A., Bernard, A., Lemoine, D., von Cieminski, G., Romero, D. (eds.) APMS 2021. IAICT, vol. 632, pp. 663–670. Springer, Cham (2021). https://doi.org/10.1007/978-3-030-85906-0_72
20. Maddikunta, P.K.R., et al.: Industry 5.0: a survey on enabling technologies and potential applications. J. Indust. Inf. Integrat. **26**, 100257 (2022)

21. Moher, D., et al.: Preferred reporting items for systematic review and meta-analysis protocols (PRISMA-P) 2015 statement. System. Rev. **4**(1), 1 (2015)

22. Frazzon, E.M., Taboada Rodriguez, C.M., Meireles Pereira, M., Cardoso Pires, M., Uhlmann, I.: Towards supply chain management 4.0. Brazil. J. Oper. Prod. Manag. **16**(2), 180–191 (2019)

23. Xiao, Y., Watson, M.: Guidance on conducting a systematic literature review. J. Plan. Educ. Res. **39**, 93–112 (2017)

24. Stadtler, H., Kilger, C., Meyr, H. (eds.): Supply Chain Management and Advanced Planning. STBE, Springer, Heidelberg (2015). https://doi.org/10.1007/978-3-642-55309-7

25. Sun, X., Yu, H., Solvang, W.D., Wang, Y., Wang, K.: The application of Industry 4.0 technologies in sustainable logistics: a systematic literature review (2012–2020) to explore future research opportunities. Environ. Sci. Pollut. Res. **29**(7), 1–32 (2022)

26. Zhong, R.Y., Xu, X., Klotz, E., Newman, S.T.: Intelligent manufacturing in the context of Industry 4.0: a review. Engineering **3**(5), 616–630 (2017)

27. Saberi, S., Kouhizadeh, M., Sarkis, J., Shen, L.: Blockchain technology and its relationships to sustainable supply chain management. Int. J. Prod. Res. **57**(7), 2117–2135 (2019)

28. Wang, G., Gunasekaran, A., Ngai, E.W.T., Papadopoulos, T.: Big data analytics in logistics and supply chain management: certain investigations for research and applications. Int. J. Prod. Econ. **176**, 98–110 (2016)

29. Beske, P., Seuring, S.: Putting sustainability into supply chain management. Supply Chain Manag. Int. J. **19**(3), 322–331 (2014)

30. Montreuil, B.: Toward a physical internet: meeting the global logistics sustainability grand challenge. Logist. Res. **3**(2–3), 71–87 (2011)

31. Giannakis, M., Papadopoulos, T.: Supply chain sustainability: a risk management approach. Int. J. Prod. Econ. **171**, 455–470 (2016)

32. Rajeev, A., Pati, R.K., Padhi, S.S., Govindan, K.: Evolution of sustainability in supply chain management: a literature review. J. Clean. Prod. **162**, 299–314 (2017)

33. Nascimento, D.L.M., et al.: Exploring Industry 4.0 technologies to enable circular economy practices in a manufacturing context: a business model proposal. J. Manuf. Technol. Manag. **30**(3), 607–627 (2019)

34. Marshall, D., McCarthy, L., Heavey, C., McGrath, P.: Environmental and social supply chain management sustainability practices: construct development and measurement. Prod. Plan. Control **26**(8), 673–690 (2015)

35. Bag, S., Telukdarie, A., Pretorius, J.H.C., Gupta, S.: Industry 4.0 and supply chain sustainability: framework and future research directions. Benchmark. Int. J. **28**(5), 1410–1450 (2021)

36. Kumar, G., Subramanian, N., Maria Arputham, R.: Missing link between sustainability collaborative strategy and supply chain performance: role of dynamic capability. Int. J. Prod. Econ. **203**, 96–109 (2018)

37. Gottge, S., Menzel, T., Forslund, H.: Industry 4.0 technologies in the purchasing process. Indust. Manag. Data Syst. **120**(4), 730–748 (2020)

38. de Vass, T., Shee, H., Miah, S.J.: Iot in supply chain management: a narrative on retail sector sustainability. Int. J. Log. Res. Appl. **24**(6), 605–624 (2021)

39. Shokouhyar, S., Pahlevani, N., Sadeghi, F.M.M.: Scenario analysis of smart, sustainable supply chain on the basis of a fuzzy cognitive map. Manag. Res. Rev. **43**(4), 463–496 (2019)

40. Khanfar, A.A.A., Iranmanesh, M., Ghobakhloo, M., Senali, M.G., Fathi, M.: Applications of blockchain technology in sustainable manufacturing and supply chain management: a systematic review. Sustainability **13**(14), 1–20 (2021)

41. Groschopf, W., Dobrovnik, M., Herneth, C.: Smart contracts for sustainable supply chain management: conceptual frameworks for supply chain maturity evaluation and smart contract sustainability assessment. Front. Blockchain **4**, 506436 (2021)

42. Reyes-Rubiano, L., Serrano-Hernandez, A., Montoya-Torres, J.R., Faulin, J.: The sustainability dimensions in intelligent urban transportation: a paradigm for smart cities. Sustainability **13**, 10653 (2021)
43. Govindan, K., Kilic, M., Uyar, A., Karaman, A.S.: Drivers and value-relevance of CSR performance in the logistics sector: a cross-country firm-level investigation. Int. J. Prod. Econ. **231**, 107835 (2021)
44. Kusters, A.C.: Relating Digitization, Digitalization and Digital Transformation: A Maturity Model and Roadmap for Dutch Logistics Companies. University of Twente (2022)
45. Ethirajan, M., Kandasamy, J., Dhinakaran, V., Kumaresan, G., Raju, R.: Assessment of sustainability in supply chain management for industry 4.0 requirements. AIP Conf. Proc. **2283**(1), 1–7 (2020)
46. Kim, G.-Y., Flores-García, E., Wiktorsson, M., Noh, S.D.: Exploring economic, environmental, and social sustainability impact of digital twin-based services for smart production logistics. In: C-PALs IFIP Advances in Information and Communication Technology (2021)
47. Paksoy, T., Kochan, C.G., Ali, S.S.: Logistics 4.0: Digital Transformation of Supply Chain Management. CRC Press (2020)
48. Bag, S., Telukdarie, A., Pretorius, J.-H., Gupta, S.: Industry 4.0 and supply chain sustainability: framework and future research directions. Benchmark. Int. J. **28**(5), 1410–1450 (2018)

Meeting the Challenges of Collaborative Network Compliance – An Exemplary View

Oyepeju Oyekola[(⊠)], Lai Xu[(⊠)], and Paul de Vrieze[(⊠)]

Computing and Informatics, Bournemouth University, Poole BH12 5BB, Bournemouth, UK
{ooyekola,lxu,pdvrieze}@bournemouth.ac.uk

Abstract. Ensuring the conformance of an organization's processes to certain rules and regulations has become a major issue in today's business world. As non-compliance with these regulations could cost organizations a considerable sum of money in fines or litigation or even loss of company reputation. Recently, the intelligent connectivity of collaborative networks of people, organization, machines, and smart things has become a high potential for value creation, and at the same time bring about some compliance challenges. Ensuring compliance in such a collaborative network environment (i.e., a dynamic and networked environment) is complicated due to its design principle for decentralized decision-making. To meet up with the various challenges of collaborative networks, this paper reviews an existing compliance approach, using a decomposition approach with eCRGs (extended Compliance Rule Graph) as a specification language. A real-world collaborative case is used to examine which compliance properties can be checked using the decomposition approach and which compliance properties cannot be checked yet. We further explore how to extend the approach to meet up with the identified challenges of collaborative network compliance, which served as a base for supporting the automated compliance checking of the Collaborative Process either at design time or run-time.

Keywords: Collaborative process · Collaborative network · Business compliance rules · Global compliance rule · Decomposition rule

1 Introduction

Ensuring the conformance of processes to certain rules and regulations has become a major issue in today's business world. As non-compliance with these regulations could cost organizations a considerable sum of money in fines or litigation or even loss of company reputation. Recently, the intelligent connectivity of collaborative networks of people, organization, machines, and smart things has become a high potential for value creation, and at the same time bring about some compliance challenges. For instance, Collaborative networks/processes present unique attributes such as the need to conform to security and privacy requirements, the need to conform to various regulatory requirements as a cross border organizations, as well as conforming to the constant changes in policies and regulations (e.g., COVID-19, BREXIT), presents a unique challenge.

L. M. Camarinha-Matos et al. (Eds.): PRO-VE 2022, IFIP AICT 662, pp. 406–419, 2022.
https://doi.org/10.1007/978-3-031-14844-6_33

While several compliance verification approaches have been addressed in the literature, these approaches still lack the support for the automated compliance checking of collaborative processes to the full extent. The compliance checking for the collaborative process should be designed to fully support the different process perspectives in terms of control flow, data flow, resource flow, and time perspective. In our previous paper [1], we identify some of the different challenges as a requirement needed to support the automated compliance checking of collaborative processes. We used a motivating use case of a collaborative process involving five partners adapted from [2], and a few of the key challenges is checking the compliance of processes involving a high level of dependency and response between each partner activity and data condition. As well as detecting the imminent violation of instance execution as well as the potential violators.

Generally, the Business Process Compliance lifecycle involves different compliance strategies: the design-time (preventive approach) and run-time compliance checks (monitoring approach) [3]. Based on the literature, compliance monitoring has been identified as an important building block in the process lifecycle [17]. The reality is that even if a business process has been checked during design time (before execution), there is no certainty that the corresponding running process instance will be compliant due to human and/or machine-related errors [1]. This implies that after designing a process model and the actual execution of a process is initiated, the running process instances need to be constantly monitored to detect any inconsistencies or violations early. As well as providing a reactive and proactive countermeasure i.e., recommending what next to do and predicting what will happen in the future instances of execution.

This research paper aims to support the compliance of the collaborative process with the varied requirement from multiple process perspectives i.e., control flow, data flow, resource flow, and time perspective. To support this functionality, the paper intends to follow the following process: (i) review an existing compliance approach for Collaborative processes i.e., decomposition approach [4, 5] using eCRG as a specification language. (ii) Use a real-world collaborative case to examine which compliance properties can be checked by the decomposition approach and which compliance properties cannot be checked yet, and (iii) explore how to extend the approach to meet up with the identified challenges of collaborative network compliance.

The rest of the paper is structured as follows: Sect. 2 describes the case description used in identifying some of the challenges of the collaborative process adapted from [2]. Section 3 explores and discusses the eCRG approach and its applicability to our use case. In Sect. 4, we examine which compliance properties can be checked by the decomposition approach and which compliance properties cannot be checked yet using the use case. Lastly, Sect. 5 gives the summary of the paper, and we highlight the challenges of collaborative networks as well as our future research.

2   Case Description

A motivating use case of a collaborative process involving five partners is adapted from [2] depicted in Fig. 1. The process starts with the insurance policyholder who reports a claim in case of any damage to the issued car. Euro Assist is the company that receives the report from the policyholder via the telephone, registers the claim received, and encourages approved garages. Euro Assist sends the claim to AGFIL which is the insurance company that underwrites the car policy and decides whether the reported claim is valid or not. If the claim is valid, AGFIL will make payment to all parties involved. Lee Consulting Services (CS) works on behalf of AGFIL and manages the day-to-day emergency service operation. Lee CS access and determine whether the car requires an assessor after the assigned Garage estimated the repair cost, i.e., an assessor would be assigned to assess the damage of the car only when the repair cost exceeds a certain amount. They control how quickly garages will receive payment, as all invoices received from the Garage are sent through Lee CS, and further present the invoice to AGFIL to process the payment while ensuring that repair figures align with industry norms. The approved garages are then responsible for repairing the car after Lee CS has agreed upon the repair. The repair work must be conducted quickly and cost-effectively.

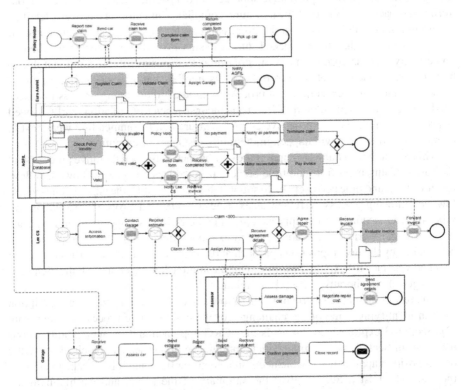

Fig. 1. Collaborative model for insurance case [1, 2]. (Color figure online)

3   Compliance Rule Language

Compliance rules must be comprehensible and at the same time should have precise semantics to enable automated processing and avoid ambiguities [3]. Therefore, the identification of suitable compliance rule language that can support all multiple process perspectives i.e., support control flow, data, resource, time, and interactions with process partners remain important. Several approaches for the formal specification of compliance rules have been identified in the literature using languages such as the FCL (Formal Contract Language), LTL (Linear Temporal Logic), CTL (Computation Tree Logic), or other text-based languages, but since these formal languages are complex and error-prone, some researchers like [8–11] suggested the idea of specifying compliance rule using visual notation such as BPSL [13], Compliance Rule Graph (CRG) [12], BPMN-Q [6], etc. The visual approach to compliance rules is flexible and aids comprehensibility for domain experts [7]. However, it is worth noting that most of these existing visual languages do lack the full support of all the various process perspectives as it solely focuses on the specification of the control flow perspective and an aspect of the data flow. For instance, CRG supports solely the control flow perspectives while BPMN-Q supports control flow and data conditions.

To support the specification of the different process perspectives, [7, 15] presents an extended Compliance Rule Graph (eCRG) i.e., an extension of CRG to visually model compliance rules and to enable the full support of multiple process perspectives regarding the control flow, data, time, and resource perspectives as well as the interactions of a process involving different partners [4]. It allows detecting compliance violations at run-time, as well as visually highlighting their causes. Additionally, it allows providing recommendations to users to proactively ensure a compliant continuation of a running business process [4]. The specification of an eCRG consists of a precondition and a postcondition. The former specifies when the compliance rule shall be applied or triggered, and the latter needs to be met to satisfy the compliance rule. Accordingly, the edges and nodes of an eCRG are partitioned into an antecedence pattern (precondition), and a related consequence pattern (postcondition) [7]. The eCRG semantics is formally specified through a translation of eCRGs into FOL (First Order Logic) expressions based on completed process logs. The feasibility of eCRG was scientifically evaluated in [15] using a different approach such as a proof-of-concept prototype, empirical evaluations, its applicability to real-world cases, as well a systematic comparison with LTL and compliance patterns. Based on the benefits of eCRG and the scientific evidence of eCRG, this study supports the use of eCRG for its compliance rule specification language.

3.1   Collaborative Business Process Models in eCRG

Since the focus of this study is on Collaborative Processes (CP), then this section reviews a few works of CP that based their language specification on eCRG. Supporting cross-organizational processes involving multiple partners concerning GCR (Global Compliance rule) is addressed in [14] using eCRG to specify the asserted rules and GCRs (Global Compliance Rules). The paper checked the compliance rules that needed to be rechecked after a change in CPs. The algorithm developed was used to detect the impact of CP changes on GCR. In [4], the authors describe how the global compliance rule of process choreographies could be verified in a decentralized manner by each partner in the process collaboration and deal with the restricted visibility of process activity. The approach uses a decomposition-based approach i.e., the decomposition of GCR into a set of an assertion that can be checked by each partner locally making sure the privacy of each partner is not violated. The work was further extended in [5], with more complex rules with multiple antecedence patterns, extensions of theorem proofing and illustrations as well as the extension of the decomposition algorithm. The feasibility of the approach was based on a prototypical implementation, which includes the use of a model checker to verify the correctness of the decomposition. Due to the feasibility of their approach (i.e., support for privacy requirements among partner processes and the language specification), this paper explores how the decomposition approach could be applied to more complex CPs.

3.2 Decomposition Approach

This section looked at the decomposition approach as described in [4, 5]. The decomposition approach is applied when a GCR involves a private activity of one or several partners in a process collaboration. In such a situation, each partner's private activities remain invisible to the other partner, and no information about when or how these activities are executed and, therefore, cannot identify the dependencies between each activity involved in the GCR. As such, the original GCR is split into a set of assertions that are checked locally by each partner and combined to generate the behavior of the original GCR. The decomposition process is based on a well-grounded theorem, representing a decomposition of a given compliance pattern. A decomposition algorithm is presented using transitivity properties to break down the initial GCR into derived assertions. Once the GCR is decomposed and the corresponding assertions are derived, each partner locally checks its derived assertions at runtime.

4   Declarative Representation of GCR Using Decomposition Approach

The applicability of the decomposition approach is demonstrated using the Car Insurance Case depicted in Fig. 1. Using the use case, we examine which compliance rules can be checked by using the decomposition approach and which compliance rules cannot be checked yet. The plan is to optimize this approach to fully support the automated compliance checking of the collaborative process. In general, the collaborative model involves the choreography model, public model, and private model. The choreography model describes the global view of interactions among the partners in the collaboration (see Fig. 2). The public model describes the message interaction between the collaborative partners. Lastly, the private model includes tasks that are not visible to others in the collaboration (see blue boxes depicted in Fig. 1). The process model is subject to various global compliance rules that stem from various policies and regulations as shown in Table 1.

Table 1. Global compliance rule for car insurance.

	Global compliance rule	GCR conditions
GCR 1	The garage must receive and confirm payment from AGFIL within a specific period	AGFIL makes reconciliation and payment to the garage only when: • Policyholder assures that a completed form will be returned to AGFIL within a specific period • Lee CS assures invoice is forwarded to AGFIL within a specified period
GCR 2	Once Euro assist notifies AGFIL of any claim, AGFIL assures a claim form is sent to the Policyholder within a specified period if only the claim is valid	The claim form will only be sent to the policyholder only when claim validity is checked, and the DATA OBJECT is and remain in the state "Valid" or otherwise the process end

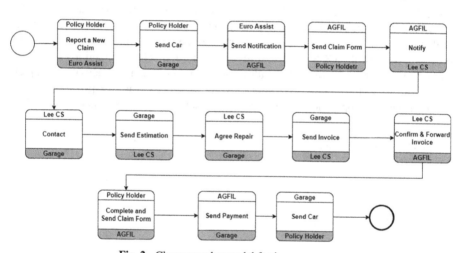

Fig. 2. Choreography model for insurance case

4.1 GCR 1

GCR 1 as shown in Table 1, involved the choreography, public as well as private tasks/activity of the partners involved in the GCR as Table 2.

Table 2. Tasks/activities of partners involved in GCR 1

GCR 1	Choreography task (see Fig. 2)	Private task (See blue boxes in Fig. 1)	Public task (See Fig. 1: message interactions between partners)
Tasks/activity	Send payment (Between AGFIL and Garage)	Pay invoice (AGFIL) Complete claim form (Policyholder) Evaluate invoice (Lee CS) Confirm payment (Garage)	Return completed claim form (Policyholder) Forward invoice (Lee CS)

For instance, in Fig. 1, the private task "pay Invoice" is invisible to the other partner and cannot have an idea of when the task is completed or not. However, there are a few complexities as regards this GCR as it involves some conditions that also need to be verified first. The private activity "pay Invoice" involves a high level of dependency on the activity of one or several other partners in the collaboration making it difficult to decompose just the GCR 1 without the sub condition. These conditions need to be verified first to ensure compliance with GCR 1. And note that, the activity "complete claim form" for Policyholder and Evaluate Invoice from Lee CS are also private activities. Hence the need to apply the decomposition approach to ensure compliance.

Global Compliance rule for GCR 1   Assertions (A)

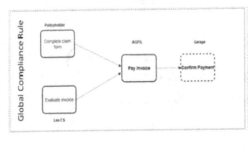
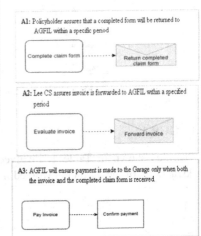

Fig. 3. GCR 1 and its Assertion

To decompose GCR 1 into assertion as shown in Fig. 3, Policyholder assures that a completed form will be returned to AGFIL (A1), Lee CS assures that the invoice will be forwarded to AGFIL (A2) and, AGFIL assures payment is made to the Garage upon receiving both the invoice and completed claim form (A3).

We illustrate the decomposition process of GCR 1 using two scenarios to ensure simplicity and readability depicted in Fig. 4. The decomposition of GCR1 includes (a) the sub-conditions that needed to be satisfied first and (b) the rule that needed to be satisfied afterward.

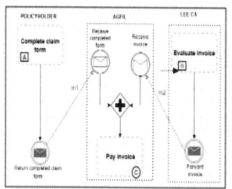 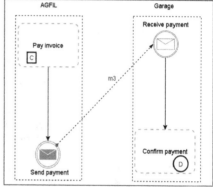

(a): Decomposition scenario of GCR condition for GCR1   **(b)**: Decomposition scenario of GCR 1

Fig. 4. Decomposition of GCR 1

The scenario in (a) explains that if C is executed, then both A and B should have been executed before, and both m1 and m2 are successfully received by AGFIL.

$$A \rightarrow m1 \wedge B \rightarrow m2 \Rightarrow m1 \wedge m2 \rightarrow C$$

It is worthy to note that the execution of just A and the successful receiver of m1 does not mean C will always be executed and the same with B. Though, there is no interaction between Lee CS and Policyholder.

In addition, the scenario in (b) explains that there is a message exchange between AGFIL and Garage which satisfies that the message m3 sent by AGFIL will be received correctly by Garage.

$$C \rightarrow m3 \text{ and } m3 \rightarrow D \Rightarrow C \rightarrow D$$

This means that the execution of C and the successful receiver of m3, will lead to the execution of D. Once the decomposition as depicted in (**a**) and (**b**) in Fig. 4 is verified, then we can ensure the correctness of GCR 1, that is:

$$A \wedge B \rightarrow C \text{ and } C \rightarrow D \Rightarrow A \wedge B \rightarrow D$$

4.1.1 The Applicability of the Decomposition Algorithm to GCR 1

This section analyses the capabilities of the algorithm presented as Algorithm 1 in [5], in the Car Insurance Case. We aim to check the applicability and complexity of the algorithm by analyzing whether the algorithm can handle a complex collaborative process with a high level of dependency on the partner's process and data conditions.

Table 3 depicts the application of the algorithm in [5] to GCR 1 to derive the assertions using transitivity is shown below:

Table 3. Application of the algorithm to derive assertion for GCR 1

Algorithm [5]	Derivation of assertion for GCR 1
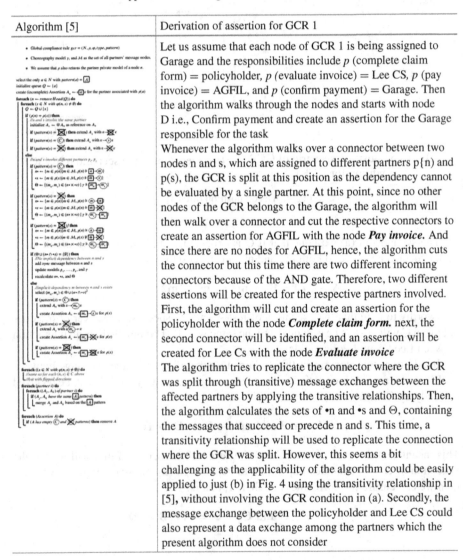	Let us assume that each node of GCR 1 is being assigned to Garage and the responsibilities include p (complete claim form) = policyholder, p (evaluate invoice) = Lee CS, p (pay invoice) = AGFIL, and p (confirm payment) = Garage. Then the algorithm walks through the nodes and starts with node D i.e., Confirm payment and create an assertion for the Garage responsible for the task
	Whenever the algorithm walks over a connector between two nodes n and s, which are assigned to different partners p{n} and p(s), the GCR is split at this position as the dependency cannot be evaluated by a single partner. At this point, since no other nodes of the GCR belongs to the Garage, the algorithm will then walk over a connector and cut the respective connectors to create an assertion for AGFIL with the node *Pay invoice*. And since there are no nodes for AGFIL, hence, the algorithm cuts the connector but this time there are two different incoming connectors because of the AND gate. Therefore, two different assertions will be created for the respective partners involved. First, the algorithm will cut and create an assertion for the policyholder with the node *Complete claim form*. next, the second connector will be identified, and an assertion will be created for Lee Cs with the node *Evaluate invoice*
	The algorithm tries to replicate the connector where the GCR was split through (transitive) message exchanges between the affected partners by applying the transitive relationships. Then, the algorithm calculates the sets of •n and •s and Θ, containing the messages that succeed or precede n and s. This time, a transitivity relationship will be used to replicate the connection where the GCR was split. However, this seems a bit challenging as the applicability of the algorithm could be easily applied to just (b) in Fig. 4 using the transitivity relationship in [5], without involving the GCR condition in (a). Secondly, the message exchange between the policyholder and Lee CS could also represent a data exchange among the partners which the present algorithm does not consider

Based on [5] explanation, the decomposition of the GCR into a set of assertions is subjected to a well-grounded theorem such that if a conjunction of hypothesis is true (i.e., the assertions), then the conclusion is true as well (i.e., GCR). Proving a set of theorems to ensure the correctness of the decomposition process for Fig. 4, we realized that the eight proofed theorems (Transitivity, Zig-zag transitivity, Rightward chaining transitivity, Generic rightwards chaining transitivity, between pattern 1, Between pattern 2, Between pattern without loops, requires transitivity) described in [5] cannot be applied to GCR 1. Hence, we propose the need to extend the algorithm and provide formal proof for the transitivity relationship. Such that if the decomposition in Fig. 4 is verified to be true, then we can ensure the correctness of GCR 1. That is:

$$\mathbf{A} \wedge \mathbf{B} \rightarrow C \text{ eventually lead to the execution of } \mathbf{D}$$

Does the successful execution of $\mathbf{A} \wedge \mathbf{B} \rightarrow C$ will eventually lead to the execution of **D** always? The answer here is No. For example, if the claim form by the Policyholder and the Invoice by Lee CS is successfully received by AGFIL but AGFIL forgot to send payment to Garage within the specified period. Or when neither of the partners fulfills their obligations. In such an instance, there is a need to provide a solution that can detect: (1) what is expected from a partner in the future (2) which partner must be reminded of their obligation (3) which partner is the potential violator.

4.2   GCR 2

Expressing GCR 2 (see Table 2) is also complicated because of the data condition associated with the rule. The rule refers to the choreography, and public and private tasks of the partner as shown in Table 4:

Table 4. Tasks/activities of partners involved in GCR 2

GCR 2	Choreography task (see Fig. 2)	Private task (see blue boxes in Fig. 1)	Public task (see message interaction in Fig. 1)
Tasks/activity	Send notification	Check policy validity	Send claim form

Though the GCR could be verified on the choreography model, the condition also depends on the private activity of AGFIL, hence the reason to decompose the GCR. To decompose GCR 2 into assertion as shown in Fig. 5, Euro Assist assures that a claim will be forwarded to AGFIL (A1), and AGFIL assures that a claim form will be sent to the policyholder only if the data object is in state valid (A2) and, the policyholder assures that the claim form will be completed (A3).

Global Compliance Rule for GCR 2   **Assertions**

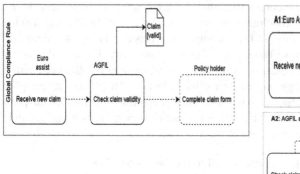

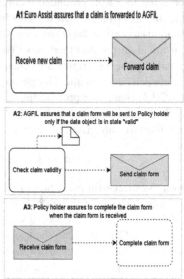

Fig. 5. GCR 2 and its Assertion

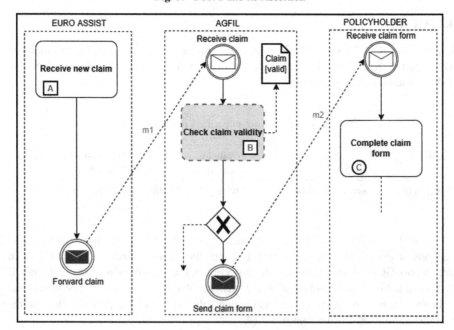

Fig. 6. Decomposition scenario of GCR 2

For this scenario, there is a message exchange between Euro Assist and AGFIL through m1, and the successful receiver of m1 will bring about the execution of B. when B is executed, we want to make sure that the state of the data object "Claim" will always be valid for m2 to be executed i.e. if the data object is in state invalid then the process stops. Therefore, if C is executed, then B would have been executed before and the state of the data object "Claim" must always remain valid (see Fig. 6). Once the decomposition in Fig. 6 is verified, then we can ensure the correctness of GCR 2.

4.2.1 The Applicability of the Decomposition Algorithm to GCR 2

Applying the algorithm in [5], the algorithm starts with the node **A** "Receive new claim" from Euro Assist, and an assertion is created, them a connector is identified, and the algorithm cut the connector and creates a new assertion for the node "check claim validity" for AGFIL. Expectedly, the algorithm will spot a connector to create a new assertion for the Policyholder. However, this cannot happen as there is a data condition that needs to be satisfied before an assertion is created for the Policyholder. As the data condition will determine the decision of the OR gateway. In case the data condition remains to be invalid because of the execution of **B**, no assertion is needed for the policyholder. However, when B is executed and the data object remains in the state "valid," then the algorithm can create an assertion for the node "Complete claim form" for the policyholder. Hence, the algorithm is not applicable in such a scenario. This scenario is common for a typical collaborative process. To fully support the compliance check of a collaborative process, there is also a need to extend the approach in [5] to support the compliance patterns that deal with data flow and data conditions.

To prove a set of theorems that is required to ensure the correctness of the decomposition method above, it is possible to apply the leftwards chaining Transitivity [5] to this scenario but with the data condition, such that the antecedent of A and B will eventually lead to C only when the data object is in the state "valid".

$$A \to m1, m1 \to B \text{ and } B \text{ (Claim is in state "valid")} \to m2, m2 \to C \Rightarrow A \to C$$
$$\forall a, b, c \ (a = b) \land (b = c) \Rightarrow a = c$$

Hence, there is a need to check whether data validation could be embedded into the different proofed theorems in [5] to support data conditions and data flow in CP.

Overall, it is worthy to note that message interactions among partners in the collaboration could also represent a set of data objects. For instance, in GCR 1, m1 and m2 are effectively data, the message exchange for m1 involves a completed claim form (data) being sent to AGFIL and m2 which include an invoice (which is also a data) sent to AGFIL. As a result, the compliance checking approach must be able to consider not just the message flow or interactions among partners but must consider messages as valid data as well as the states the relevant data objects can adopt during the process execution. Hence, for this current approach, there is an assumption that all messages are valid data. That is, we will treat all message interactions between partners as valid data.

5   Conclusion and Future Works

This paper intends to review existing compliance i.e., the decomposition approach as described in [4, 5] to examine its applicability and complexity demonstrated using a real-world collaborative case i.e., a car insurance case. We examine which compliance properties could be checked and which cannot be checked yet. We further explore how the decomposition algorithm set out in [4], and [5] could be applied to our case. Based on our analysis, compliance rule patterns that involve a high level of dependency between more than two partners as well as the data flow pattern between partner processes, which could involve the private model remains a challenge with this approach. And as a result, our future work plan to optimize their approach to support this limitation. And in this instance, the research on commitment [2, 13, 16] and the use of BPMN-Q [6] could be embedded in this approach to help solve the identified gaps. Lastly, we intend to use the application of the optimized algorithm to further explore how to detect future violations as well as to detect any potential violator and provide the main cause of the violation. This is important because if something goes wrong, the whole business process can become more complex. This will help to add more complexity to the approach and meet up with the challenges of a collaborative process.

Acknowledgments. This research is part of the FIRST project that has received funding from the European Union's Horizon 2020 research and innovation programme, the Marie Skłodowska-Curie grant agreement No. 734599.

References

1. Oyekola, O., Xu, L., de Vrieze, P.: Compliance checking of collaborative processes for sustainable collaborative network. In: Camarinha-Matos, L.M., Boucher, X., Afsarmanesh, H. (eds.) PRO-VE 2021. IAICT, vol. 629, pp. 301–310. Springer, Cham (2021). https://doi.org/10.1007/978-3-030-85969-5_27
2. Xu, L.: A multi-party contract model. SIGecom Exchange 13–23 (2004). https://doi.org/10.1145/1120694.1120697
3. Oyekola, O., Xu, L.: Verification and compliance in collaborative processes. In: Camarinha-Matos, L.M., Afsarmanesh, H., Ortiz, A. (eds.) PRO-VE 2020. IAICT, vol. 598, pp. 213–223. Springer, Cham (2020). https://doi.org/10.1007/978-3-030-62412-5_18
4. Fdhila, W., Rinderle-Ma, S., Knuplesch, D., Reichert, M.: Decomposition-based verification of global compliance in process choreographies. In: IEEE 24th International Enterprise Distributed Object Computing Conference (EDOC), pp. 77–86 (2020)
5. Fdhila, W., Rinderle-Ma, S., Knuplesch, D., Reichert, M.: Verifying compliance in process choreographies: foundations, algorithms, and implementation. 101983 (2022)
6. Awad, A., Weidlich, M., Weske, M.: Specification, verification and explanation of violation for data aware compliance rules. In: Baresi, L., Chi, C.-H., Suzuki, J. (eds.) ICSOC/ServiceWave -2009. LNCS, vol. 5900, pp. 500–515. Springer, Heidelberg (2009). https://doi.org/10.1007/978-3-642-10383-4_37
7. Knuplesch, D., Reichert, M.: A visual language for modeling multiple perspectives of business process compliance rules. Softw. Syst. Model. **16**(3), 715–736 (2017)
8. Dwyer, M.B., Avrunin, G.S., Corbett, J.C.: Property specification patterns for finite-state verification. In: Proceedings of the Second Workshop on Formal Methods in Software Practice, pp. 7–15 (1998)
9. Ramezani, E., Fahland, D., van der Aalst, W.M.P.: Where did I misbehave? Diagnostic information in compliance checking. In: Barros, A., Gal, A., Kindler, E. (eds.) BPM 2012. LNCS, vol. 7481, pp. 262–278. Springer, Heidelberg (2012). https://doi.org/10.1007/978-3-642-32885-5_21

10. Ramezani Taghiabadi, E., Fahland, D., van Dongen, B.F., van der Aalst, W.M.P.: Diagnostic information for compliance checking of temporal compliance requirements. In: Salinesi, C., Norrie, M.C., Pastor, Ó. (eds.) CAiSE 2013. LNCS, vol. 7908, pp. 304–320. Springer, Heidelberg (2013). https://doi.org/10.1007/978-3-642-38709-8_20

11. Turetken, O., Elgammal, A., van den Heuvel, W.-J., Papazoglou, M.P.: Capturing compliance requirements: a pattern-based approach. IEEE Softw. **29**(3), 28–36 (2012)

12. Ly, L.T., Rinderle-Ma, S., Dadam, P.: Design and verification of instantiable compliance rule graphs in process-aware information systems. In: Pernici, B. (ed.) CAiSE 2010. LNCS, vol. 6051, pp. 9–23. Springer, Heidelberg (2010). https://doi.org/10.1007/978-3-642-13094-6_3

13. Montali, M., Plebani, P.: IoT-based compliance checking of multi-party business processes modeled with commitments. In: De Paoli, F., Schulte, S., Broch Johnsen, E. (eds.) ESOCC 2017. LNCS, vol. 10465, pp. 179–195. Springer, Cham (2017). https://doi.org/10.1007/978-3-319-67262-5_14

14. Knuplesch, D., Fdhila, W., Reichert, M., Rinderle-Ma, S.: Detecting the effects of changes on the compliance of cross-organizational business processes. In: Johannesson, P., Lee, M.L., Liddle, S.W., Opdahl, A.L., López, Ó.P. (eds.) ER 2015. LNCS, vol. 9381, pp. 94–107. Springer, Cham (2015). https://doi.org/10.1007/978-3-319-25264-3_7

15. Knuplesch, D., Reichert, M., Ly, L.T., Kumar, A., Rinderle-Ma, S.: Visual modeling of business process compliance rules with the support of multiple perspectives. In: Ng, W., Storey, V.C., Trujillo, J.C. (eds.) ER 2013. LNCS, vol. 8217, pp. 106–120. Springer, Heidelberg (2013). https://doi.org/10.1007/978-3-642-41924-9_10

16. Telang, P.R., Singh, M.P.: Specifying and verifying cross-organizational business models: an agent-oriented approach. IEEE Trans. Serv. Comput. **5**(3), 305–318 (2012). https://doi.org/10.1109/TSC.2011.4

17. Ly, L.T., Rinderle-Ma, S., Knuplesch, D., Dadam, P.: Monitoring business process compliance using compliance rule graphs. In: Meersman, R., et al. (eds.) OTM 2011. LNCS, vol. 7044, pp. 82–99. Springer, Heidelberg (2011). https://doi.org/10.1007/978-3-642-25109-2_7

Agile and Responsive Supply Chains

Becoming an Agile Organization: Development of a Morphology for Strategic Agile Management Systems

Clara Herkenrath[✉], Ruben Conrad[✉], and Volker Stich[✉]

Institute for Industrial Management at RWTH Aachen University, Campus-Boulevard 55, 52074 Aachen, Germany

{Clara.Herkenrath,Ruben.Conrad,Volker.Stich}@fir.rwth-aachen.de

Abstract. Driven by different trends, such as digitalization, the number of companies aiming for successful business transformation is increasing, while new structures and systems are paving the way. Strategic agile management systems offer significant potential benefits given the increasing speed of the evolving environment in which organizations find themselves these days. To select and implement the appropriate strategic agile management system, companies need to understand the underlying theoretical principles to be able to select the most suitable for the respective company and to introduce it based on individual adaption. Within this paper, a morphology is presented to improve theoretical knowledge about strategic agile management systems. Creating a common understanding of strategic agile management systems and their current areas of application creates a suitable frame of reference for future research projects.

Keywords: Strategy · Agile management systems · Morphology · Taxonomy

1 Introduction

1.1 Initial Situation and Relevance of the Topic

Ongoing globalization and digitalization are confronting companies with an environment that is becoming increasingly dynamic. The speed and unpredictability of the corresponding conditions in question are shaping the dynamics of the economic environment. While the socioeconomic framework presents itself as volatile and complex in ambiguous interdependencies [1], the controversy over how to respond appropriately to the uncertainties is becoming a constant presence. The onset of digitalization at the beginning of the new millennium caused a profound paradigm shift [2], which has become even more pronounced in recent years due to the Covid-19 pandemic [3]. Organizations that operate in an agile manner are sensitive to change, with a framework for continuously identifying adjustments. Hence, a key component in this process is the need to transform into an agile organization that enables agile development, planning, and implementation of the organization's internal objectives and orientation [4].

© IFIP International Federation for Information Processing 2022
Published by Springer Nature Switzerland AG 2022
L. M. Camarinha-Matos et al. (Eds.): PRO-VE 2022, IFIP AICT 662, pp. 423–433, 2022.
https://doi.org/10.1007/978-3-031-14844-6_34

The organization's strategy provides a long-term path to ensure the organization's economic success [5]. Conventional strategic management systems are not capable of the fast decision-making and action capability that is required and are pushed to their limits when it comes to meeting the need for responsiveness [6]. Structures and processes that incorporate the dynamic environment in an agile manner must be implemented to achieve the strategic goal. Strategic agile management systems provide the framework and foundation for successful collaboration in organizations through shared strategic alignment.

1.2   Object of Study

An intensive examination and introduction of the strategic agile management systems suitable for the organization is an indispensable approach to becoming an agile organization. To select the most suitable strategic agile management system, the various approaches and their theoretical foundation need to be analyzed and evaluated in a systematic way. This paper aims to provide a fundamental understanding of the underlying theories from an empirical perspective using a unified reference base. Approaches are identified and researched for this purpose using a systematic literature search. Articles from science and practice are described, highlighting the research gap. This allows to uncover commonalities and differences between existing approaches and to draw a holistic picture of the current state of research. The relevant features and corresponding characteristic expressions are summarized in a morphology. Based on the developed morphology it will be possible to distinguish strategic agile management systems on a shared base. This represents the starting point for increasing the integration level and the coalition type of the organization using common goals and joint identities for collaborative networks. Based on the above discussion, the objective of the paper is to answer the following research question:

What are the relevant features and characteristics that differentiate strategic agile management systems applied in practice on the theoretical foundation?

2   Relation to Existing Works and Theories

2.1   Definition of Strategic Agile Management Systems

Agility is a concept that originated in the field of software development and represents a contrarian approach to the classic planning methods. Being agile is the dexterity or mobility of organizations and people as well as structures and processes [7]. It contradicts the linear and sequential approach, where individual steps are executed one after the other [8]. Furthermore, a management system is defined by its sub-components management and system [9]. Its related system thinking is seen as a discipline for examining holistic patterns of change and interrelationships rather than static moments in time [10]. Systems thinking is widely seen as critical to managing the complexity that confronts the world in the present [11] by defining systems with respected sub-systems thus making them manageable in the first place. The successful implementation of the organization's strategy ensures long-term survival in the market and the sustainable achievement of corporate goals [12]. Strategic agile management systems are therefore characterized as a system for the agile implementation of corporate strategies as a multidimensional relationship from initial actions and plan to the final success through target fulfillment. An organization's management system can address a specific function as well as an entire organization.

2.2 Theoretical Differentiation of Strategic Agile Management Systems in Use

To create a morphology for the evaluation of practically relevant strategic agile management systems, the systems used in practice are first identified. The different strategic agile management systems applied in the field represent the object of study to identify relevant features and characteristics in the further course of the study. Based on the definition of strategic agile management systems given in Sect. 2.1, agile management systems that address and actively incorporate the design of the strategy are considered below. Neither agile management systems nor methods focusing on the operative implementation will be considered.

Among the pioneers of modern management, the theory is Drucker [13], who presented *Management by Objectives* (MbO) as a holistic approach to the strategic implementation picture. By translating business goals into personal goals for each employee through the direct link between top-level strategy and lower-level operational strategy a blueprint for multiple modern strategy agile management systems was built. Since the early 1990s, the *Balanced Scorecard* (BSC) has been based on the challenge of breaking down strategic objectives to the individual levels of an organization in the form of measurable indicators [14]. The *Objectives and Key Results* (OKR) approach is a continuous process that manifests itself through cyclical goal setting, assessment, and commitment to annual targets [15], built on the idea of MbO. Developed by Benioff and Adeler [16], the *Vision, Value, Methods, Obstacles, Measures* (V2MOM) approach specifically addresses the optimization of goals and strategies and promotes the alignment of an organization [16] and presents a further approach. The *Agile Objectives, Goals, Strategies, and Measures* (OGSM) typically align an organization for up to five years, addressing intra-organizational transparency and interdisciplinary communication [17]. It forms a strategic agile management system designed to guide companies in forcing an overall organizational alignment and linking long-term visions and strategies with short- and medium-term goals and measures [18]. Inspired by MbO, the *Hoshin Kanri* (HK) approach provides a transparent and measurable approach that aligns the continuous improvement cycles to force the agility of an organization [14] and achieve breakthrough goals as annual targets at the lower levels [19]. Finally, *the 4 Disciplines of Execution* (4DX) is the most recently developed approach, in which operational tasks focus the attention of managers on monthly and quarterly targets to achieve strategic goals [20]. However, this approach does not encompass all dependent elements of an organization, as only parts of the organizational environment are considered.

The approaches listed above form the common basis for a coherent comparison. In practice, the choice of selecting a strategic agile management system is based on the company's orientation, the skill set of the employees, and the target system. Choosing the suitable strategic agile management system is challenging for companies, as the theoretical basis is the starting point for the implementation and individual adjustment in the practical application.

3 State of the Art

3.1 Process of Literature Review

The conducted systematic literature review illustrates the relevance of the morphology, as a key element. Based on the cumulative approach, new knowledge is generated by interpreting and combining existing knowledge [21]. The literature review process is understood as the synthesis of a subject area that supports the identification of different research questions [22]. Both the validity of the search process and scientific rigor are central to the discovery of relevant sources and the reproducibility of the search process [21]. Implementation of this process is achieved by retrieving information from scientific databases [23], following the research process according to vom Brocke [21].

3.2 Results of the Literature Review

Within the scope of this research, the process is composed of a systematic literature search in three online databases as well as a keyword search and a forward-backward analysis [23]. The broad spectrum of scientific publications was covered using the three online libraries Scorpus, Springer Link, and IEEE Explore, to support the identification of relevant works for the development of the morphology. Table 1 shows the selected queries that ensure the reproducibility of the systematic literature search. additional search strings were examined to identify further approaches. To identify related concepts, the search term "taxonomy" was added to the term "morphology".

Based on the identified queries, 158 publications were identified that offer a wide range of contributions on the topic. A review of the literature shows an absence of a morphology of strategic agile management systems based on their underlying theory. On the one hand, the papers cover a systems-based approach for organizations to achieve greater adaptability and thus agility yet provide little focus on the agile implementation of strategy [24–26]. On the other hand, specific fields, such as increasing the innovation capability of the R&D department [27], packaged enterprise systems [28], or a service-oriented portfolio [29], are explored in detail.

The characteristics generally show overlap. However, they do not cover the entire complexity of implementing corporate strategy through strategic agile management systems. This underlines the importance of the research question addressed above. Hence, this paper offers additional insights for science and practice through the aggregated view of strategic agile management systems based on the theoretical framework. Collaboration in Society 5.0 can be deepened by strengthening the collaborative approach through the alignment of a shared understanding of strategy.

Table 1. Queries for the systematic literature review

Data base	Queries	Number of publications
Scopus	TITLE-ABS-KEY (strategic AND agile management AND system AND taxonomy OR morphology)	16
Springer Link	"Strategic" AND "Agile Management" AND "System" AND ("taxonomy" OR "morphology")	116
IEEE Explore	("Abstract":Agile Management) AND ("Abstract":Strategic) AND ("Abstract":System) OR ("Document Title":Agile Management) AND ("Document Title":Strategic) AND ("Document Title":System) AND ("All Metadata":Strategic Agile Management Systems) AND ("All Metadata":taxonomy OR "All Metadata":morphology)	26

3.3   Research Approach: Morphology Development

To answer our research question, the paper strives for the development of morphology. A morphology is concerned with the structure and arrangement of parts of an object and is applied to provide conceptual guidance to the research object [30]. To develop the morphology, the authors apply seven steps with a focus on the empirical-to-conceptual approach from Nickerson et al. [31]: 1) define meta-characteristics, 2) determine ending conditions, 3) decide on an empirical-to-conceptual or conceptual-to empirical approach, 4) identification of sub-set of objects, 5) identification of common characteristics, 6) grouping of characteristics and 7) test for ending conditions. Based on the step-by-step approach of Nickerson et al. [31], the morphology was designed using the empirical-conceptual approach.

4   Morphology Development

Based on the strategic agile management systems in use, eight different features and corresponding characteristics were identified to describe strategic agile management systems. Concerning the underlining theoretical framework and other authors in this field, the features and characteristics are explained below (see Fig. 1). The morphology forms the basis for the systematic analysis and the selection and comparison of the various strategic agile management systems regarding the theoretical foundation. The morphology unfolds its potential in its holistic form, with the core lying in the combination of the features and characteristics. Interaction and interdependencies must be considered in the overall context.

Features	Characteristics		
Superordinate focus	Purpose, Vision, Mission, Strategy		Strategy
Incentives for employees	Intrinsic motivation		Extrinsic motivation
Level of objective-precision	Personal level	Team level	Corporate level
Structure of the goal-setting process	Top-Down		Sideways (Top-Down und Bottom-Up)
Reflectionprocess of attainment	All levels		Executive level
Risk propensit of objective setting	Ambitious	Risik-averse	Nonspecitic
Type of objective setting	Qualitativ	Quantitativ	Combination of qualitativ and quantitativ
Time dimension	Specific		Nonspecific

Fig. 1. The strategic agile management system morphology

(1) **Superordinate Focus**

The corporate strategy determines the direction of the company's actions. Based on the differentiation between strategy definition and strategy [32], there are two ways in which strategic management can derive the objectives. On the one hand, the derivation of purpose, vision, and mission, the strategy is understood as an overall picture. On the other hand, the defined strategy exclusively serves as the starting point for implementing in an agile way. The strategic agile management system is structured on an overall understanding, which is mutually dependent [16, 33].

(2) **Incentives for Employees**

There are two ways in which the agile management system can enhance the motivation of employees in their day-to-day work. Firstly, the system can be extrinsically motivated, usually driven by direct monetary stimuli [34]. Secondly, employees can be incentivized using intrinsic motivation. Additionally, such participation reduces the uncertainty of one's role and, consequently, the commitment to the organization [35].

(3) **Level of Objective-Precision**

The degree of detail in the specification of objectives is broken down to different levels in the organizational structure. A greater level of detail can increase employee loyalty and commitment [36]. The theories examined above break down the goal definition based on a tree structure from the corporate level [14] through the team level down to the personal level [15, 17]. A strategic agile management system theory deviates here from the practice implementation and is frequently adjusted in practice [37].

(4) **Structure of the Goal-Setting Process**

The goal-setting process is based on the organizational levels, with the corresponding theories distinguishing between the two approaches. On the one hand, a top-down approach is chosen, which focuses on reflection processes within the organizational level [14]. On the other hand, the top-down approach is extended by a bottom-up reflection [15, 33]. Although the MbO approach forms the starting point for the reflection, the feedback is not reflected explicitly at higher levels. In later approaches, this extension was actively integrated [20].

(5) **Reflectionprocess of Attainment**

The reflection process of attainment is related to the structure of the goal-setting process, given the degree of participation in the reflection. Transparent communication at all levels leads to a great expenditure of resources. In addition, collaboration reduces the uncertainty of one's role and, as a result, commitment to the organization [35]. If synchronization takes place at the management level, implementation is leaner due to fewer communication channels. At the same time, less employee involvement reduces the level of self-commitment.

(6) **Risk Propensit of Objective Setting**

Essential for identifying with the organization is an intensive examination of the organizational goals, which does not occur with a simple distribution of tasks [38]. Objectives should be defined distinctively and explicitly, leaving no uncertainty for misinterpretation by the individual. The scientific literature shows a consensus on the benefits of defined specific goals for performance and goal commitment [39, 40]. Individual theories examine the definition of goals in greater depth and can be divided into ambitious and risk-averse objectives.

(7) **Type of Objective Setting**

The objectives defined in strategic agile management systems can be distinguished between qualitative and quantitative objectives [41]. This distinction arises in the precise terms of definition and may differ in individual details. Quantitative objectives are understood as objectively measurable goals, while qualitative objectives are understood as difficult to measure and quantify directly. With qualitative objectives, transferred criteria are usually used to achieve measurability [33]. By combining qualitative and quantitative goals, subjectivity can be reduced without excluding subjects [16, 20].

(8) **Time dimension**

The agile management system is characterized by flexible adaptation to the dynamic environment, with tasks being aligned in different time segments. The length of these cycles or segments is specified or is determined individually and therefore nonspecific. Predefined cycles or periods are usually quarterly [15, 20].

Collaboration in Society 5.0 is focused differently on the individual features and corresponding characteristics. the example of Level of Objective-Precision shows that breaking down the strategy to team level challenges collaboration in a different way than it does to the personal level. the insights of the morphology support the targeted selection of the strategic agile management system, considering collaboration in society 5.0.

4.1 Visualization of OKR Morphology

Based on the example of OKR, the suitability of the theoretical principles can be examined for an organization. For visualizing the proposed model, the strategic agile management morphology is applied to describe OKR (see Fig. 2).

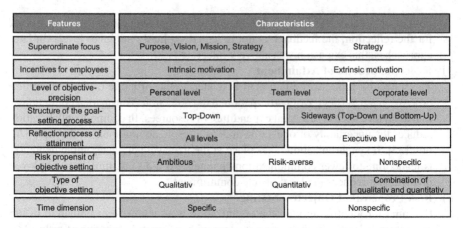

Fig. 2. OKR described in the strategic agile management system morphology

According to Doerr, the OKR approach not only specifies which goals are to be achieved but also how these goals can be achieved [33]. The OKR approach starts with the strategy, which is derived from the overarching mission, vision, and purpose using a pyramid structure. Breaking down the objectives and key results from the purpose paves the way for intrinsically motivated employees who can assign the daily work to the overarching picture [15]. Based on the OKR theory, objectives and key results are broken down from the corporate level to the team level and down to the individual level. To implement these, the structure of the goal-setting process is first mirrored top-down and then mirrored bottom-up with the inclusion of employee feedback in a V-shape. This encourages transparent communication at all levels, with ambitious goals targeted using so-called moonshots [15]. The objectives and corresponding key results are broken down into quarters [33] and determined in an agile manner quarterly. Qualitative objectives are broken down into key results, which are measurable and quantitative [15]. Using the example of OKR, the model's successful use along the features and characteristics is visualized.

5   Conclusion

In this paper, we have shown that for the purposeful selection and implementation of strategic agile management systems, a distinction based on their underlying theoretical foundation is required. By conducting a systematic literature review, it was determined that there is no systematic overarching model that differentiates strategic agile management systems based on the theoretical foundation. Therefore, a morphology was developed using features and characteristics to close the research gap and answer the research question, what are the relevant features and characteristics that differentiate strategic agile management systems, applied in practice on the theoretical foundation are. The morphology contains eight features with corresponding characteristics. Based on the theoretical foundation, the morphology provides the foundation for the systematic analysis and comparison of the different strategic agile management systems. As a result, the core of morphology lies in the combination of the characteristics and properties in their holistic form, interdependencies being considered in the overall context. The application of morphology was exemplified by the strategic management system OKR.

One major advantage of the model is its expandability to include potential new strategic management systems in use by extending the characteristics of the morphology without great challenges. Furthermore, the extension of the characteristics to include the company-specific adaptation of the strategic agile management systems provides a perspective for further research e.g., the bottom-up structure of the goal-setting process may offer a characteristic that is necessary for practice.

Acknowledgments. This research is a part of the findings of the research project "OKReady". The IGF project 21740 N of the Forschungsgemeinschaft Research Foundation FIR e. V. at RWTH Aachen University, Campus-Boulevard 55, 52074 Aachen, is funded by the AiF within the scope of the program for the promotion of industrial joint research (IGF) by the Federal Ministry for Economic Affairs and Climate Action (BMWK) based on a decision of the German Bundestag. Responsibility for the content of this publication lies with the authors. On behalf of the authors, we would like to thank the AiF for the support within the scope of this project.

References

1. Buchholz, U., Knorre, S.: Interne Kommunikation in agilen Unternehmen. Springer Fachmedien Wiesbaden, Wiesbaden (2017)
2. Valenduc, G., Vendramin, P.: Digitalisation, between disruption and evolution. Trans. Eur. Rev. Labour Res. **23**, 121–134 (2017). https://doi.org/10.1177/1024258917701379
3. Almeida, F., Duarte Santos, J., Augusto Monteiro, J.: The challenges and opportunities in the digitalization of companies in a post-COVID-19 world. IEEE Eng. Manage. Rev. **48**, 97–103 (2020). https://doi.org/10.1109/EMR.2020.3013206
4. Pries-Heje, J., Krohn, M.M.: The SAFe way to the agile organization. In: Proceedings of the XP2017 Scientific Workshops, Article 18. Association for Computing Machinery, Cologne, Germany (2017). https://doi.org/10.1145/3120459.3120478
5. Hanelt, A., Bohnsack, R., Marz, D., Antunes Marante, C.: A systematic review of the literature on digital transformation: insights and implications for strategy and organizational change. J. Manag. Stud. **58**, 1159–1197 (2021). https://doi.org/10.1111/joms.12639
6. Japing, T.A.: Steuerungsmechanismen Agiler Prozesse (2018)
7. Bendel, O.: Was ist "Agilität"? (2019). https://wirtschaftslexikon.gabler.de/definition/agilit aet-99882/version-368852
8. Habermann, F.: Hybrides Projektmanagement — agile und klassische Vorgehensmodelle im Zusammenspiel. HMD **50**, 93–102 (2013). https://doi.org/10.1007/BF03340857
9. Petersen, S.: Führung in Managementsystemen. Der Faktor Mensch in der ISO 9001, ISO 14001 und OHSAS 18001. Hanser, München (2015)
10. Senge, P.: The fifth discipline: the art and practice of the learning Organizationsenge. Hum. Resour. Manage. **29**, 343 (1990)
11. Arnold, R.D., Wade, J.P.: A definition of systems thinking: a systems approach. Proc. Comput. Sci. **44**, 669–678 (2015). https://doi.org/10.1016/j.procs.2015.03.050
12. Kreikebaum, H., Gilbert, D.U., Behnam, M.: Strategisches Management. Kohlhammer Verlag, Stuttgart (2018)
13. Drucker, P.F.: The Practice of Management. Harper & Row (1954)

14. Kudernatsch, D.: Balanced scorecard als steuerungsinstrument — Direkt Anlage Bank. In: Engelbach, W., Meier, R. (eds.) Customer Care Management. Lernen von den Besten aus den USA und Deutschland. Springer eBook Collection Business and Economics, pp. 161–176. Gabler Verlag, Wiesbaden (2001). https://doi.org/10.1007/978-3-322-88933-1_8

15. Niven, P.R., Lamonte, B.: Objectives and key results. In: Driving Focus, Alignment, and Engagement with OKRs. Wiley, Hoboken (2017)

16. Benioff, M.R., Adler, C.: Behind the cloud. In: The Untold Story of How Salesforce.com Went from Idea to Billion-Dollar Company--and Revolutionized an Industry. Jossey-Bass, San Francisco (2010)

17. Lafley, A.G., Martin, R.L.: Playing to Win: How Strategy Really Works. Harvard Business Press (2013)

18. Bickelmann, R.: Key Account Management. Gabler Verlag (2001)

19. Klesse, P.: Best Practice im Vertrieb Durch Hoshin Kanri. Springer Fachmedien Wiesbaden, Wiesbaden (2019)

20. McChesney, C., Covey, S., Huling, J.: The 4 disciplines of execution. In: Make Your Most Wildly Important Goals Happen. Free Press, New York (2012)

21. vom Brocke, J., Simons, A., Niehaves, B., Riemer, K., Plattfaut, R., Cleven, A.: Reconstructing the giant: on the importance of Rigour in documenting the literature search process. In: Proceedings of the 17th European Conference on Information Systems, vol. 1, pp. 2206–2217 (2017)

22. Rowley, J., Slack, F.: Conducting a literature review. Manag. Res. News 27, 31–39 (2004). https://doi.org/10.1108/01409170410784185

23. Webster, J., Watson, R.T.: Analyzing the past to prepare for the future: writing a literature review. MIS Q. 26 (2002)

24. Cross, S.E.: A model to guide organizational adaptation. In: 2013 International Conference on Engineering, Technology and Innovation (ICE) & IEEE International Technology Management Conference, pp. 1–11 (2013). https://doi.org/10.1109/ITMC.2013.7352653

25. Nicoletti, B.: Agile procurement. In: Agile Procurement, pp. 15–42. Springer, Cham (2018). https://doi.org/10.1007/978-3-319-61082-5_3

26. Zykov, S.V.: The agile way. In: Managing Software Crisis: A Smart Way to Enterprise Agility. SIST, vol. 92, pp. 1–33. Springer, Cham (2018). https://doi.org/10.1007/978-3-319-77917-1_1

27. Kuhn, M., Dölle, C., Riesener, M., Schuh, G.: Concept for Organizational Structures of Agile Development Networks Production at the Leading Edge of Technology, pp. 653–662. Springer, Heidelberg (2019). https://doi.org/10.1007/978-3-662-60417-5_65

28. Wang, Q., Ren, C., Chen, F.: Achieve agile enterprise system through collaboration with BPMS. In: 2012 Annual SRII Global Conference, pp. 494–501 (2012). https://doi.org/10.1109/SRII.2012.61

29. Hannay, J.E., Brathen, K., Mevassvik, O.M.: Agile requirements handling in a service-oriented taxonomy of capabilities. Requir. Eng. 22(2), 289–314 (2016). https://doi.org/10.1007/s00766-016-0244-8

30. Ritchey, T.: Problem structuring using computer-aided morphological analysis. J. Oper. Res. Soc. 57, 792–801 (2006). https://doi.org/10.1057/palgrave.jors.2602177

31. Nickerson, R.C., Varshney, U., Muntermann, J.: A method for taxonomy development and its application in information systems. Eur. J. Inf. Syst. 22, 336–359 (2013). https://doi.org/10.1057/ejis.2012.26

32. Andrews, K.R.: The Concept of Corporate Strategy. Dow Jones-Irwin, Homewood (1971)

33. Doerr, J.E.: Measure what matters. In: How Google, Bono, and the Gates Foundation Rock the World with OKRs. Portfolio/Penguin, New York (2018)

34. Ignatius, A.: Time to kill forced rankings? Harv. Bus. Rev. 93, 1 (2015)

35. Luft, J., Shields, M.D.: Mapping management accounting: graphics and guidelines for theory-consistent empirical research. Acc. Organ. Soc. **28**, 169–249 (2003). https://doi.org/10.1016/S0361-3682(02)00026-0

36. Kaplan, R.S., Norton, D.P.: Balanced scorecard. In: Strategie Erfolgreich Umsetzten. Schäffler-Poeschel Verlag, Stuttgart (1997)

37. Ematinger, R., Schulze, S.: Spielend Ziele setzen und erreichen. Objectives and Key Results mit LEGO SERIOUS PLAY. Springer Fachmedien Wiesbaden; Springer Gabler, Wiesbaden (2020)

38. Gary, M.S., Yang, M.M., Yetton, P.W., Sterman, J.D.: Stretch goals and the distribution of organizational performance. Organ. Sci. **28**, 395–410 (2017). https://doi.org/10.1287/orsc.2017.1131

39. Locke, E.A., Latham, G.P.: Building a practically useful theory of goal setting and task motivation: a 35-year odyssey. Am. Psychol. **57**, 705–717 (2002). https://doi.org/10.1037/0003-066x.57.9.705

40. Wright, P.M., Kacmar, K.M.: Goal specificity as a determinant of goal commitment and goal change. Organ. Behav. Hum. Decis. Process. **59**, 242–260 (1994). https://doi.org/10.1006/obhd.1994.1059

41. Janeš, A., Faganel, A.: Instruments and methods for the integration of company's strategic goals and key performance indicators. Kybernetes **42**, 928–942 (2013). https://doi.org/10.1108/K-08-2012-0022

A Decision Support System for Better Qualitative Supply Chain Diagnoses

Anthony Fouqué[1], Matthieu Lauras[2]([✉]), Frederick Benaben[2],
and Hamideh Afsarmanesh[3]

[1] AGILEA, Rue Michel Larousse, 31100 Toulouse, France
anthony.fouque@agilea-group.com
[2] IMT Mines Albi, Industrial Engineering Center, Route de Teillet, 81013 Albi, France
{matthieu.lauras,frederick.benaben}@mines-albi.fr
[3] University of Amsterdam, 1012 WX Amsterdam, The Netherlands
h.afsarmanesh@uva.nl

Abstract. In the current supply chain world where instability and variability are the norm, being able to efficiently identify/diagnose the root causes of non-performance is of prime importance. Although numerous methods exist to support quantitative diagnosis step, there are very few materials regarding the qualitative dimension of diagnosis. Additionally, the rare existing methods are very time-intensive, need scarce expertise and often produce poor results. In a such context, the problem is how to make supply chain qualitative diagnoses impactful and fast. Practically, this paper develops a business process and its associated knowledge-based system, inspired by the theory of constraints' thinking processes approach, to effectively support practitioners in their qualitative diagnosis step. A set of real industrial application cases is analyzed to discuss the implications of the contribution. It notably demonstrates that the proposal supports both increasing the impact of the diagnosis and reducing the time of the process by almost 80% .

Keywords: Supply chain · Qualitative diagnosis · Theory of constraints · Thinking processes · Decision support system

1 Introduction

As [1] said, "a good doctor is not the one who first knows well all medications or who masters all healing techniques, but the one who is able to quickly make a proper diagnosis". A right diagnosis will allow you to choose the right medication that is to say the right tool and so caring. Make a wrong diagnosis, can even cause amplification of the problem. The point is exactly the same for Supply Chain (SC) improvement step. SCs are under pressure due to the high level of uncertainty and variability they have to cope with and as a consequence, they have to be able to adapt themselves quickly if they do not want to die prematurely. To reach such a goal, SC practitioners need to develop several abilities and notably ones to detect rapidly and effectively potential weaknesses

L. M. Camarinha-Matos et al. (Eds.): PRO-VE 2022, IFIP AICT 662, pp. 434–446, 2022.
https://doi.org/10.1007/978-3-031-14844-6_35

in their organization. This is generally supported by a diagnosis step which tries to assess objectively the forces and the weaknesses of the existing SC.

But as demonstrated by [2], these methods are generally large, quantitative, expert-oriented and time-consuming. [2] also indicated that most of them do not allow producing a relevant analysis to support improvements of the SC. Let's now take time to analyze these issues and to fix the problem statement of this research work.

Basically, most of the quantitative diagnosis techniques such as Cause and Effect Diagram or Interference Diagram need long time to gather, classify and analyze data. This is nowadays particularly problematic as the data sources are numerous and as SC features change so quickly. As a consequence, these approaches often deliver obsolete conclusions. Finding a solution to speed up the diagnosis process appears now as mandatory. An approach to solve this issue might consist in supporting the step within a dedicated decision support system able to assist properly the SC practitioners.

Regarding the relevance of the SC diagnosis, authors like [3] showed that using qualitative approach might be powerful. However, despite their potentialities, [3] indicated that these qualitative approaches are very time-consuming. They also explained that only very well-trained experts are able to use this kind of approach effectively. These techniques are then poorly spread among SC practitioners. As a consequence, a solution able to make the use of qualitative diagnosis easier seems to be required by SC practitioners.

To sum up, there is a need for a SC qualitative diagnosis method that would bring relevant analysis in a very short time. The research question can then be formulated as: how to process and support a fast and relevant SC qualitative diagnosis?

To answer this question, the remainder of the paper is presented in four sections. First, an analysis of the literature will be developed to identify existing methodologies and to conclude about good practices and gaps. Second, the proposed decision support system will be developed by focusing on the business process and on the associated knowledge-based system. Third, the paper will describe and analyze a set of real industrial application cases to demonstrate the potential benefits of using such a system and to discuss about its limitations. Fourth, the paper will end up by summarizing the contributions and developing avenues for future research.

2 Background

Most of the SC diagnosis methodologies are generally linked to automatic control and systems theory on one hand, and continuous improvement methodologies such as Lean Manufacturing, 6 Sigma, Supply Chain Operations Reference (SCOR) or Balanced Scorecard on the other hand. In the following, we first discuss the features of them before diving in the details of the existing qualitative approaches.

2.1 Quantitative Diagnosis Methodologies

Quantitative methods were among the first to emerge in systems theory in the seventies. Nowadays, most of the quantitative diagnosis methods come from the field of automatic control and the fault detection [4]. They are generally based on control and statistical decision theories. As shown by [5], these approaches are based on the following requirements: Early detection of small faults with short time behavior, diagnosis of faults, detection of faults in closed loops and supervision of processes in transient states. The goal is then to detect on-the-fly "potential failures to react quickly by making decisions such as reconfiguration, maintenance or repair" [5]. Obviously, these approaches are working on dedicated systems and often do not consider the interactions between them [4]. As a consequence, it is not possible to support any diagnosis step within such an approach in the context of complex systems such as SCs, or any industrial organization.

Another spectrum of quantitative diagnoses is proposed by continuous improvement approaches as the first stage of such a process is systematically a diagnosis stage. Among all the continuous improvement approaches, Lean Manufacturing is probably the most famous one. Lean Manufacturing is considered as the most effective methodology for productivity improvement in any kind of organization [6]. The main idea of Lean Manufacturing consists in managing flows in order to better satisfy the customer demand. Particularly, it focuses on the time spent by the different operations of the process in order to reduce it by eliminating wastes [7]. According to [7], Lean Manufacturing is mainly a philosophy which includes a specific toolbox able to evaluate and improve any kind of system.

Within a management control perspective, we also must consider the Balanced Scorecard approach which was created in the early 1990s by [8]. The Balanced Scorecard should be designed as "a day-to-day diagnosis tool to guide executive actions" as mentioned by [9]. On their side, [10] indicated that Balanced Scorecard can be considered as a diagnosis control system as it might be used to monitor the organizational outcomes to correct deviations from pre-set standards of performance. However, they highlighted some limits of such an approach and notably the fact that Balanced Scorecard needs frequent and regular attention from operating managers at all levels, huge amount of data regularly refreshed to be relevant, and a point of reference (to compare) must be set up a priori to any diagnosis consideration.

Additionally, Supply Chain Operations Reference (SCOR) has received a lot of attention from scholars and practitioners during the past decades for supporting continuous improvement approaches in the context of supply chain management. The SCOR model [11] provides a unified representation of SC activities with six general activities: Plan, Source, Make, Deliver, Return and Enable. Each activity can be refined into sub-activities, which are themselves decomposed into sub-sub activities, and so on. Several quantitative key performance indicators are associated to each activity in order to assess the performance of the SC and make a diagnosis. Although these performance indicators are attached to activities and well formulated, they remain very difficult to set up a proper diagnosis within an existing SC. If the decomposition process on a macroscopic level is quite generic and can be applied to a lot of industrial cases, the detailed levels might be difficult to use, due to the granularity and specificities of activity representation [12]. In addition, the SCOR model does not "try to close the loop", and there is no suggestion that the indicators should be used to manage the system. Thus, it could be rather difficult – even random in some cases – to define, the necessary corrective actions on this basis alone [12].

As we reminded in this section, the main features of quantitative based diagnosis approaches and their limits, it is now time to extend our analysis in direction of qualitative diagnosis methodologies.

2.2 Qualitative Diagnosis Methodologies

Within a qualitative perspective, we identified three main methodologies in the literature:

- Cause and Effect Diagram (CED),
- Quick Scan (QS),
- Current Reality Tree (CRT).

CED are usually represented through an Ishikawa Diagram. The main idea of this methodology is to collect facts which may explain the connection between a potential root cause of the current situation and the noticed symptom. Usually, CED is composed of the following steps:

- Recording consciously each defect occurring in the company.
- Identifying the potential root causes associated to the event.
- Classifying the root causes.
- Visualizing the root causes by putting them into an Ishikawa Diagram.

CED has several advantages. The implementation is quick (only few hours are needed), participative and quite easy to get [13]. However, there is one major drawback as CED is poorly consistent in terms of diagnosis results. [13] demonstrates that for a same problem, different teams never get the same results when using CED approach. This is why we could not consider CED has good enough to reach our goal of improving the efficiency of diagnosis.

QS can be defined as a robust diagnosis methodology developed to assess the current performance of an organization's SC [14]. The core of the methodology consists in conducting the QS itself through four sources of data: attitudinal and qualitative questionnaires, process maps, semi-structured interviews and archival information [14]. Typically, the QS methodology implies a mixed approach that consider both qualitative and quantitative insights and try to make the link between them. We must also highlight that QS is an iterative process which required approximately two weeks to be executed (for the whole process). Some authors such as [15] propose to enrich the QS methodology by adding a dynamic Bayesian network to elaborate on the causal relationships previously extracted. In addition, [15] highlight several drawbacks regarding QS implementations. They notably mentioned that QS is time consuming comparing to other diagnosis methods and needs a very important expertise and experience to be used efficiently. They also indicate that the methodology is very sensitive to the completeness and freshness of the data used. In a variable world as we know in modern SCs, this is definitely a critical limitation.

The CRT methodology is based on the Theory of Constraints (TOC) body of knowledge. The TOC has been developed by [16] through a novel book named "The Goal". As for Lean Manufacturing, the TOC is also a philosophy and a toolbox which can be applied for production, distribution, project and problem-solving issues. Regarding our problem statement, we focus on the last domain of application and more specifically on what is called the Thinking Processes which are a set of logic tools able to support the problem-solving issue [16]. The Thinking Processes involve five basic logic tools. As explained by [17], these tools use logic to help managers understand why desirable or undesirable situations occur, to ascertain the impact of interventions designed to elimi-nate undesirable conditions and to offer guidance on how to manage the change required for improved performance. The five tools are current reality tree (CRT), evaporating or conflict cloud, future reality tree, prerequisite tree and transition tree. In the TOC philos-ophy, the Thinking Processes should not only focus on the improvement of the system but also consider the change management issues. Basically, this methodology implies three major components to support efficiently the change: agree on the problem, agree on the solution and agree on the way to implement it. The Thinking Processes put a huge emphasis on the diagnosis step which is necessary to agree on the problem. In practice, this step is supported by the CRT tool. As for QS and CED, CRT is a cause-and-effect approach, but it focused on "conflicts". A conflict is a combination of two opposite actions which theoretically contribute to the same goal but do not get the same results. For example, a purchasing team can be in the following conflict: buy large quantity to save money on fixed-costs or buy just the required quantity even if fixed-costs are impor-tant. The two actions are opposite. When you buy higher quantity to scale, you decrease the purchase price which may results in more money. But when you buy only what is required, you may have less inventory which increase the cash availability. These are two opposite actions which might help the company to make money and to be more or less profitable. CRT implementation is quite similar to QS and CED in terms of process. It consists in identifying symptoms (also called undesirable effects) which are limiting the performance of the system [17]. CRT logically linked the identified symptoms through a series of intermediate entities that specify prevailing relationships downward to a core problem [17]. According to [17], the first step of CRT process consists in examining the different symptoms for possible cause-effect relationships using "if-then" logic and make appropriate logical linkages between them. Then, it consists of enhancing the link-ages by introducing additional insights to ensure that the resulting relationships are clear and sufficient. As for QS and CED, CRT has some drawbacks as it is time consuming and needs high level of expertise and experience to be performed. However, CRT has a huge advantage compared to others which is its robustness. As mentioned in [3], when different teams work on the same list of symptoms with this approach, they achieved systematically the same root causes. Moreover, [3] also demonstrated through a specific experience that consisted of submitting a same problem to three different teams using CED, QS and CRT to solve it. It appeared that only CRT approach allowed finding the real root causes of the undesirable effects.

To sum up, the results of this approach can be described with the following chart (Table 1):

Table 1. Qualitative diagnosis methodologies comparison.

	CED	Quick Scan	CRT
Ability to make robust diagnosis	Low	Medium	High
Level of experience and expertise required	Low	High	High
Time to perform	Fast	Long	Medium

2.3 Problem Formulation

According to the previous table, there is no methodology which provides full benefits in the qualitative diagnosis approach. The first consideration of any diagnosis is to make sure that the results are pointing to real root cause. Consequently, the CRT is probably the best tool to use when you want to focus on qualitative information. However, there are several drawbacks in the process to build a CRT efficiently: The high level of competencies, the time to perform it, the visibility of the results and the capacity to use it easily. The question we are trying to answer in this study is finally: how can we speed up the process of CRT's diagnosis while improving usability of it? To reach such a goal, we propose to build an innovative decision support system (DSS) as described in the next section.

3 Decision Support System Proposal

This section develops the features of the Decision Support System we suggest to better benefit from the CRT methodology to support a SC diagnosis step. Practically, this section gives first an overview of the Decision Support System and explains how to use it concretely. Then it explains the functional architecture of the DSS and its key components: the key algorithms and the core knowledge base. Finally, some information about the technical architecture used to run the DSS is presented.

3.1 Overview of the DSS

As demonstrated in the previous section, one major issue with CRT methodology is the process is long to execute, particularly regarding the time needed to build the CRT itself. This is mainly explained by the fact that the combination of potential symptoms, facts or conflicts is huge and depending of numerous features and behaviors of the studied company. Consequently, our proposal suggests speeding up the process consists in questioning the user in order to focus only on symptoms, facts and conflicts which could occur regarding the gathered knowledge about the studied system. In essence, the DSS will start by asking some key features about the company to the user. This information is mainly about name of the company, scope of the improvement project and material-flow strategy (Make-To-Stock, Make-To-Order, Engineering-To-Order). Then, the DSS will ask questions to the user in order to help him/her identifying symptoms, facts and potential conflicts. A first set of questions will be generating based on the key features indicated during the first step. Then, questions will be adapted on-the-fly depending of the answers given by the user in order to avoid orienting user on useless directions. This is made to optimize the time needed to gather the necessary information to build the CRT. When, the DSS gets enough information to set up the CRT of the studied system, then it will automatically build it up and display it. The user will have the possibility to update the result by modifying directly the CRT (e.g., add/withdraw some elements) or by going back to the previous step in order to indicate additional symptoms, facts or conflicts. Finally, based on the obtained CRT, the user will have the opportunity to formulate his/her qualitative diagnosis to support his/her SC improvement step. Figure 1 summarizes the DSS steps and the following sub-section will give more information about how technically this DSS runs to get such a result.

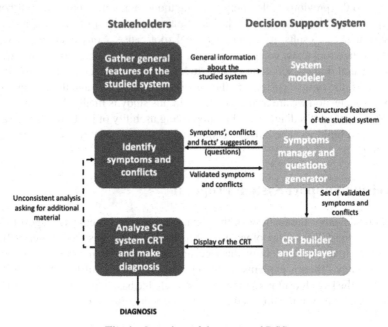

Fig. 1. Overview of the proposed DSS

3.2 Functional Architecture of the DSS

As mentioned on Fig. 2, the functional architecture is composed of 3 types of components: interface, services and database.

- The interface component is about the necessary User Interface functionalities as for any kind of DSS. There is no specific innovation on this part.
- The services' components include some important contributions through specific algorithms allowing to gather and exploit the useful knowledge for an automatic generation of the CRT. This is one of the main contributions of the proposal.
- The database components are in the core of the device as it includes some usual database for the storage of the collected information, but also because it includes a

specific database called "Generic Reality Tree". This is another major contribution of the proposal.

Let's start by presenting the Generic Reality Tree database. This database is a knowledge base which represents all the possible connections which can exist in a Make-To-Stock environment between symptoms, facts and conflicts. This knowledge base has been established conceptually by the "web of conflicts" proposed by [18] and recently enriched by [19] based on a review of both practices and literature. In this paper we did not try to challenge the content of this knowledge base but only tried to instantiate it practically through our DSS. However, we must give some insights regarding the content of this database to well understand how the DSS runs. Basically, the Generic Reality Tree database makes the link between the current major conflicts which can exist in a production environment (e.g., buy in volume vs buy only what's needed; run larger batches vs run smaller batches; authorize overtime vs do not authorize overtime, etc.) and the undesirable effects, called symptoms (e.g., too much inventory, bad quality of service, machines/tools which are not used by shopfloor, etc.). In [19], the authors suggest to represent this knowledge base through a logic graph. Practically, the Generic Reality Tree database is the pivot of the DSS as it will be used to select the questions that the system must ask to confirm or infirm the existence of this or that symptom. Basically, the DSS will travel across the graph to automatically ask additional questions in order to close potential options or at the opposite, confirm some other ones. The final CRT that the DSS will build up will be composed of all validated symptoms, facts and conflicts for the studied system as well as all the validated connections. The diagnosis will be based on this mapping of the current situation.

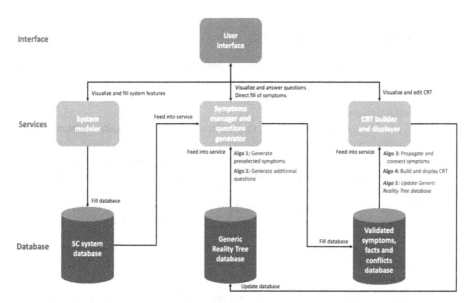

Fig. 2. Functional architecture of the DSS

Obviously, the knowledge base is not enough to get such a result. Some value-added services are needed to exploit properly the knowledge of the Generic Reality Tree on one hand, and the knowledge given by the user about the studied system on the other hand. In our proposal, four main algorithms have been developed and implemented as shown on Fig. 2. Practically, these algorithms manage the following issues:

- Algorithm 1 is about generating the first set of potential symptoms and conflicts that the studied system should occur based on the key features of the system indicated by the user and of course, the Generic Reality Tree database.
- Algorithm 2 is about travelling across the knowledge base function of the answers given by the user to both confirm / reject potentialities and ask for new questions able to open on new set of potentialities according to previous ones.
- Algorithm 3 is about sorting and extracting the valid set of symptoms and conflicts as well as all associated connections in order to build the CRT up.
- Algorithm 4 is about building the CRT itself and displaying it in order to allow the user analyzing it on one hand, and potentially editing it to help interpretation along on the other hand.

In addition to the algorithms previously described, we also considered the possibility for the user to fill information directly into the system without following automatic recommendations. To support this additional way to gather relevant information, some syntactic algorithms have been developed to recognize proximity between the terms that a user can choose to express a given symptom. For instance, the DSS should have been able to identify that "high inventory" and "high stock" are two different wordings for a same symptom.

3.3   Technical Architecture of the DSS

The DSS has been designed as a Software as a Service developed using Java languages. Basically, there are 5 technical components which are:

- User Interface based on ReactJS.
- Rest API for managing the security of the application based on Spring web and Spring security
- Core services for supporting the main functionalities based on Java coding.
- Relational database for managing standard database through object-relational mapping and data access object (MyBatis).
- Graph database for managing logic graphs that CRT methodology requires through object-relational mapping and graph data access object (OrientDB).

4   Application Case

The developed DSS has already been experimented on more than 50 real industrial cases during the last few months. Among them, we decided to present the case of a SME (55 persons) from the industrial sector which manufactures springs for aeronautics, railways and nuclear, oil & gas. The production is divided into two segments: short springs and long springs. The industrial process can be summarized as described in the following Figure (Fig. 3).

Fig. 3. Industrial case process

Practically, the diagnosis operating process based on the proposed DSS is defined through the five steps described on Fig. 4. The setting-up has been conducted via 5 interviews covering production, supply, planning and quality functions.

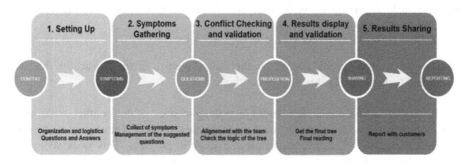

Fig. 4. Operating process

In the context of these exchanges, we were able to note the following symptoms:

– Suppliers are often late;
– The production system is obliged to incur additional expenses to deliver on time (overtime, temporary workers, subcontracting);
– The sales order book is decreasing;
– The company buys quantities of raw materials in excess of its needs;
– The stock (raw material, in-progress, finished product) is increasing;
– Team productivity is decreasing;
– Priorities in the workshop change regularly.

The list of symptoms was integrated into the proposed DSS as outlined in previous sections. At this stage, the DSS has been able to generate a set of questions to refine and consolidate the initial diagnosis. Basically, the tool automatically generated 57 questions as shown in the Fig. 5. To answer these questions, we brought together the 5 people initially interviewed to collectively answer each of the proposed questions. Once all the questions had been dealt with, and therefore all the symptoms had been validated, we were able to display the complete tree. Given the richness of this tree (difficult to read in the format of this document), we only propose a quick snapshot of it on Fig. 5

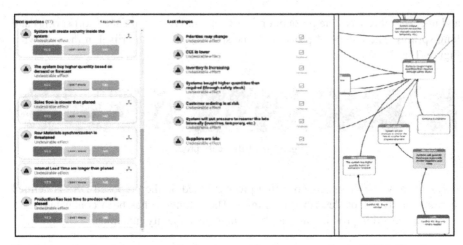

Fig. 5. Sample of questions automatically generated for the company by the DSS (left) and extract from the automatically deduced tree (right).

and discuss several specific extracts without displaying it in full. Basically, the tool highlighted automatically three major conflicts:

– The conflict between making to order or making to stock. If this conflict exists, then the system will seek to protect itself through stock or time. These protections will generate more stock of raw materials and work in progress. This stock will slow down the flow and therefore increase manufacturing cycles when, at the same time, it generates a greater risk of obsolescence;
– The conflict between buying the necessary quantities or buying more than needed. The point is the quantity bought is large then it will generate stock. And this stock generation will lead to an increase in cycles and thus impact the entry of cash flow significantly;
– The conflict between producing large or small batch sizes. Through this conflict, the tree suggests that the increase in batch sizes generates an increase in the stock of raw materials and therefore purchases in higher quantities. These purchases in higher quantities increase variable costs and invariably impact the company's income statement.

These 3 conflicts have been validated by the practitioners and used for developing a concrete improvement plan for the company that is currently ongoing. In terms of implementation, it took half a day to conduct the interviews and visit the company. Entering the information into the tool took 23 min (answers to suggested questions). Reading, interpreting and sharing the diagnosis (the resulting tree) took 1 h. To compare with the days and weeks usually need with the existing methods.

5 Conclusion and Perspectives

In the work carried out in this paper, we found that most of the existing SC diagnostic methods were based on quantitative data which unfortunately now tend to be valid only for very short periods. Other approaches advocate conducting the SC diagnoses mainly through qualitative approaches. Unfortunately, the findings are not much more satisfactory than for quantitative methods. Indeed, the existing methods also require a significant amount time to implement. In addition, they often require technical expertise and very significant business experience. Finally, they have the disadvantage of having a very low level of quality, and are highly dependent on the people who carry out the diagnoses. To solve this issue, we designed, structured and developed a decision support system (DSS) to carry out organizational diagnoses of SCs based on qualitative data. This DSS, directly inspired by the Thinking Processes, includes a functional dimension, an implementation process and a complete technical architecture, instantiated in the framework of a software prototype. The relevance and the usability of the proposal have been tested on more than 50 real industrial cases among which the one of a springs production company which was used as an illustration in this paper. We noticed that the conversion rate to the improvement stage for these cases were 70% on average whereas it was only 37% for all other diagnoses (about 100) made during the same experiment without our DSS. We also noticed that the consultants who used our DSS needed 32 min for making a diagnosis while days were needed for the others.

Many research avenues arise from this research work. Indeed, the use of the DSS is quite significant and regular with users. Thus, the knowledge base of the DSS is developing. One line of research could be to study the recurrences of symptoms and conflicts according to the typologies of companies diagnosed. These analyses could lead to the consolidation of the knowledge base and perhaps to its development as well. Another one is related to the resulted trees deduced by the DSS which can be likened to neural networks. We could imagine utilizing this information network in order to influence the questioning even more with users. In addition, we could imagine the DSS being linked to market trend information that would help identify potential symptoms. This would give users the opportunity to anticipate the actions to be implemented.

References

1. Ben Fredj-Ben Alaya, L.: VSM a powerful diagnostic and planning tool for a successful Lean implementation: a Tunisian case study of an auto parts manufacturing firm. Prod. Plann. Control 27(7–8), 563–578 (2016)
2. Foggin, J.H., Mentzer, J.T., Monroe, C.L.: A supply chain diagnostic tool. Int. J. Phys. Distrib. Logistics Manage. 34(10), 827–855 (2004)
3. Doggett, A.M.: Root cause analysis: a framework for tool selection. Quality Manage. J. 12(4), 34–45 (2005)
4. Ribeiro, L., Barata, J.: Re-thinking diagnosis for future automation systems: an analysis of current diagnostic practices and their applicability in emerging IT based production paradigms. Comput. Ind. 62(7), 639–659 (2011)
5. Isermann, R.: Supervision, fault-detection and fault-diagnosis methods—an introduction. Control. Eng. Pract. 5(5), 639–652 (1997)

6. Urban, W.: The lean management maturity self-assessment tool based on organizational culture diagnosis. Procedia Soc. Behav. Sci. **213**, 728–733 (2015)
7. Womack, J.P., Jones, D.T., Roos, D.: The Machine that Changed the World: The Story of Lean Production–Toyota's Secret Weapon in the Global Car Wars that is Now Revolutionizing World Industry. Simon and Schuster, New York (2007)
8. Kaplan, R.S., Norton, D.P.: Using the balanced scorecard as a strategic management system. Calif. Manage. Rev. **39**, 53–79 (1996)
9. Williams, K.: What constitutes a successful balanced scorecard? Strateg. Finance **86**(5), 19 (2004)
10. van Veen-Dirks, P., Wijn, M.: Strategic control: meshing critical success factors with the balanced scorecard. Long Range Plan. **35**(4), 407–427 (2002)
11. Huan, S.H., Sheoran, S.K., Wang, G.: A review and analysis of supply chain operations reference (SCOR) model. Supply Chain Manage. Int. J. **9**(1), 23–29 (2004)
12. Lauras, M., Lamothe, J., Pingaud, H.: A business process oriented method to design supply chain performance measurement systems. Int. J. Bus. Perform. Manag. **12**(4), 354–376 (2011)
13. Park, J., Nam, G., Choi, J.: Parameters in cause and effect diagram for uncertainty evaluation. Accred. Qual. Assur. **16**(6), 325–326 (2011)
14. Naim, M.M., Childerhouse, P., Disney, S.M., Towill, D.R.: A supply chain diagnostic methodology: determining the vector of change. Comput. Ind. Eng. **43**(1–2), 135–157 (2002)
15. Childerhouse, P., Towill, D.R.: Effective supply chain research via the quick scan audit methodology. Supply Chain Manage. Int. J. **16**(1), 5–10 (2011)
16. Goldratt, E.M., Cox, J.: The Goal: a Process of Ongoing Improvement. Routledge, New York (2016)
17. Kim, S., Mabin, V.J., Davies, J.: The theory of constraints thinking processes: retrospect and prospect. Int. J. Oper. Prod. Manage. **28**, 155–184 (2008)
18. Smith, D.: The Measurement Nightmare: How the Theory of Constraints Can Resolve Conflicting Strategies, Policies, and Measures. CRC Press, Cambridge (1999)
19. Fouque, A., Lauras, M., Afsarmanesh, H., Benaben, F.: Toward automated qualitative supply chain diagnoses. In: ILS 2018–7th International Conference on Information Systems, Logistics and Supply Chain, p. p-296 (2018)

Blockchain Implementation Process Model for Supply Chains - From Technology Awareness to Scaling

Marc Hübschke[(⊠)], Eugen Buss, Stefan Lier, and Elmar Holschbach

Department of Engineering and Business Administration, South Westphalia University
of Applied Sciences, Meschede, Germany
{huebschke.marc,buss.eugen,lier.stefan,
holschbach.elmar}@fh-swf.de

Abstract. This contribution proposes a new blockchain implementation process model which closes identified gaps of existing models such as the lack of supply chain management focus, guidance on scaling or performance measurement. In particular, existing models do not provide a sufficiently detailed approach. To prove this, we develop criteria for a blockchain implementation process model in supply chains and systematically compare existing process models in this context. In order to identify a suitable use case for companies, to plan its implementation and to measure its impact on the company performance, we develop a new implementation process model. Furthermore, this process model supports the roll-out of the blockchain use case to other partners along the value chain, thereby increasing scalability.

Keywords: Blockchain · Blockchain implementation process model · Supply chain management

1 Introduction

Companies operating in globalized supply chain networks experience increasing competitive pressure driven by an accelerated business pace [1]. A large amount of data is exchanged along the supply chain, but there is often a lack of trust between the parties involved [2]. Companies are concerned that information could be leaked to a competitor or company confidential information could be made public. This leads to data exchange being prevented and to some information received not being trusted. In this context, blockchain technology has the potential to simplify collaboration in supply chain networks by addressing the trust issues between the stakeholders [3]. Blockchain technology is one of today's most promising technological innovations and, due to its characteristics, provides many advantages, especially in supply chain management [4, 5]. Some of it's benefits include data integrity through immutability of information, network resilience through decentralized structures, cost reduction due to process automation and secure as well as transparent supply chain data exchange among companies [6, 7]. Despite these

L. M. Camarinha-Matos et al. (Eds.): PRO-VE 2022, IFIP AICT 662, pp. 447–460, 2022.
https://doi.org/10.1007/978-3-031-14844-6_36

numerous advantages and exploitable potentials, only a few companies have used the technology yet. Small and medium-sized enterprises (SME) in particular are reluctant to use the technology due to existing barriers. A detailed literature review has shown that no holistic blockchain implementation model exists offering companies a step-by-step guide from the initial idea of the blockchain to the identification of a suitable use case and then to actual implementation and scaling. The objective of this paper is to develop a model for the integration of blockchain technology in companies and in particular small and medium sized enterprises for supply chain management.

2 Background

In this section, the relevant theoretical backgrounds such as supply chain management and blockchain technology including their definitions are introduced to achieve a common understanding.

2.1 Supply Chain Management

According to the Council of Supply Chain Management Professional (CSMCP), supply chain management (SCM) is defined as the planning and management of all activities involved in sourcing and procurement, conversion and other logistics management activities. This essentially includes coordination and collaboration with partners, which can be suppliers, intermediaries, third-party providers and customers [8]. The main objective of supply chain management, according to Muchna et al., is to use information and coordination mechanisms to manage supply chain processes in such a way that supply and demand are synchronized as much as possible [9]. As a result of an increasing division of labor, supply chain networks are becoming more and more complex [9] leading to our current day situation where it is not individual companies, but rather entire supply chain networks are competing with each other [9]. The reciprocal exchange of information between supply chain participants is recognized not only as a crucial activity of SCM [10], but also as the management of these networks [11]. Sharing information is essential to ensure coordination among partners, build an integrated supply chain and meet customer demands [12]. The reciprocal sharing of information such as forecasts, inventory levels and track-and-trace data reduces uncertainty amongst supply chain partners and can finally create a more effective supply chain [13].

2.2 Blockchain in Supply Chain Management

For the supply chain management and related collaborative information, sharing is important. Increasing this can significantly improve the efficiency of supply chains [14]. Companies often share only a certain amount of information with each other because of concerns about other partners in the supply chain [15]. To strengthen collaboration, blockchain provides a secure, more direct and decentralized infrastructure even in non-trusted environments [15]. According to Lee Kuo Chuen, the blockchain can be defined as a decentralized, constantly growing list of entries, called blocks, which are interconnected in an equal network and secured by cryptography. To form a network or chain, each block contains a cryptographic hash of the previous block with a timestamp and transaction data, as well as information of all previous blocks and transactions. Once the information has been processed by the blockchain, all computers in the network lock in. At the same time, a permanent digital record is created that is hard to alter [16]. Most blockchains today include smart contracts that allow business logic to be implemented [17]. This enables complex applications and services between users [17]. The technical architecture of the blockchain offers several advantages. These include tamper resistance, transparency through chronological storage, reduction of transaction costs through intermediation, automation of processes with smart contracts and high network resilience [15]. This results in a broad field of application for supply chain management. Among the most important applications of blockchain in supply chain management are easing paperwork processes, identifying counterfeit products, facilitating tracking and tracing, and monitoring the condition of products through the internet of things [18]. Despite the opportunities that blockchain offers for supply chain management, they often cannot be exploited. Companies, and small and medium size enterprises in particular, have difficulties in adopting and implementing blockchain technology [19]. The reasons for this are manifold. Many managers lack a strong knowledge of the technology and its possibilities [20]. Furthermore, the impact of the technology on all areas is not predictable [17]. To take advantage of the benefits, the supply chain network should be extensive. In this context, one of the biggest challenges of a successful use case with blockchain is scaling [21].

3 Methodology

A large number of Blockchain implementation models already exists in the academia. For this reason, a literature research and analysis of existing models will be conducted to obtain an overview. This literature analysis is conducted according to Webster & Watson (2002) [22]. For the research the databases IEEE, Web of Science, Elsevier, Scopus, Springer Link and Google Scholar were used. The basic requirement is that the models are written in the English or German language.

In the first step, a list of the blockchain implementation models found has been created. A total of 29 different models have been found whose focus is on the introduction of blockchain technology in businesses. To generate high scientific standard peer-reviewed articles are prioritized in the selection of articles, but to obtain a wider range of models relevant to practice, models in scientific textbooks are also included. Gray literature is excluded because it does not fulfill the scientific standard due to a lack of peer reviews or originates from companies with commercial interests and is often not described in detail. In addition, these are not listed in common databases. Eleven models remain. In the next step, all models are filtered out that are not generally applicable but relate to a specific use case (e.g. electronic voting system or energy sector). In total, there are seven models that relate to the general adoption of blockchain in enterprises. Figure 1 shows the literature selection procedure in detail black and white.

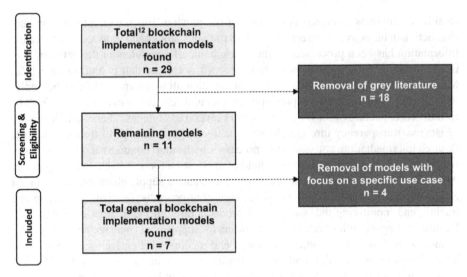

[1] databases: IEEE, Web of Science, Elsevier, Scopus, Springer Link, Google Scholar
[2] search strings: Blockchain Process Model, Blockchain Implementation Model, Blockchain Process Implementation Model,
Blockchain Model, Blockchain Supply Chain Process Model, Blockchain Step-by-step-guide

Fig. 1. Overview of the literature selection process

3.1   Existing Blockchain Implementation Models

The remaining seven identified process models are the subject of analysis in this paper. These are the following process models:

1. Model for integrating blockchain technology in supply chain according to Guerpinar et al. [23]
2. Path to blockchain enterprise adoption according to Arun et al. [24]
3. Blockchain implementation phases according to Attaran and Gunasekaran [25]
4. Selection process to identify application opportunities for blockchain technology according to Werner et al. [26]
5. Three pillars for realizing a successful blockchain use case according to Urban [27]
6. Process model for the implementation of blockchain in companies according to Wittenberg [6]
7. Conceptual stage model for blockchain implementation in Supply Chains according to Vu et al. [28]

The first model consists of six phases defining multiple activities and milestones [23]. The model framework covers the whole process starting with the evaluation of the use case and ending with the evaluation of the implementation results. A special characteristic of the model is that the processes are partly executed iteratively and that repetitive cross functions are described. Arun's et al. model describes four phases from use case identification to enterprise integration. Specific activities are also defined within the model [24]. The Blockchain implementation phases model according to Attaran and Gunasekaran contains three phases also starting with the finding of a suitable use case and ending with the implementation in the company. The authors also mentioned the importance of continuous improvement afterwards [25]. According to Werner et al. two different stages are to be considered: The selection of the use case and the implementation afterwards. These two phases are enriched by several phases [26]. Urban's model consists of three pillars each defining a different model starting with the first idea of implementation and finishing with the integration of blockchain in future usage [27]. Wittenberg's model consists of four different phases with each model defining a milestone after completing the activities. The model analyses the whole process from finding a suitable use case to maintaining the implemented blockchain solution inside the company [6]. Due to Vu et al. three stages with different factors need to be taken into account when implementing a blockchain. These factors need to be considered in each phase making the model also iterative. The model starts with the initiation and ends with the implementation [28].

3.2 Requirements for Blockchain Implementation Models

This section, we highlight requirements from the literature for a process model for blockchain implementation. Five requirements (**RQ**) emerged from a combination of different research. First, they originate from the project experience of an ongoing Blockchain implementation project. In addition to this, the requirements have been included from discussions with German small and medium sized enterprises at various events, which thereby have a high practical relevance. This is due to the high density of hidden champions in the North Rhine-Westphalia region, which is representative of small and medium-sized enterprises in Germany. The listed requirements do not claim to be complete and represent a current status at the time of publication. These requirements are briefly described below, based on the literature:

RQ1 Creating a Technology Insight: For many companies and in particular SMEs, blockchain is an innovative but also complex technology [27, 29]. In order to develop and subsequently implement suitable use cases, both the opportunities and the limitations of the technology should be fundamentally understood [20, 21, 29]. In addition, when designing your own use cases, you benefit from knowing about existing use cases. The results must be easy to understand so that they can also be discussed in interdisciplinary teams [30].

RQ2 Holistic Perspective: The second requirement is a holistic perspective on implementation. In this paper, we understand holistic perspective on the one hand as a socio-technical perspective, with the consideration of technical and organizational aspects and the human factor and their interactions, as generally recommended for digitization projects [31]. The organizational aspects include processes and responsibilities in companies [32]. The technical aspects involve systems and interfaces, data standards, a smart contract concept and permissions [23]. For the human factor, competencies and work routines must be considered and onboarding focused [33, 34]. In addition, legal [21, 25] ecological [35, 36] and strategic aspects [37, 38] should also be taken into consideration in order to gain a holistic perspective.

RQ3 Iterative and Agile Approach: In IT project management, agile methods are regularly used in an iterative way [39]. These methods combine speed with flexibility and can react effectively to changing requirements [40]. Guerpinar et al. also take this into account in their implementation model by allowing phases to take place repeatedly [23]. During development, a simple result should be aimed for as a minimum viable product [6, 41]. Feedback should be allowed and taken into account at every stage [23].

RQ4 Impact Analysis and Performance Measurement: The frequently assumed disruptive character of blockchain is based on its fundamental changes for companies, their value creation and their business model [42]. In order to successfully roll out blockchain, Dutta et al. recommend detailed analysis of the impact on the company and its supply chain [43]. The use of qualitative (e.g. improvement of transparency) and quantitative methods [6, 27, 44, 45] for performance measurement should also be considered during implementation. This requires the determination of the impact on all areas according to RQ2 and a method-based detailed analysis depending on the area.

RQ5 Scaling to Further Business Partners: In supply chains, value creation is achieved across multiple companies [46] and requires optimized information flows in addition to optimized material and cash flows [9]. Therefore, supply chain management is the collaboration of companies to fulfill customer needs [47]. If blockchain is used as an infrastructure for the exchange of information and intangible assets, it requires a sufficient number of participating companies. Blockchain will strengthen supply chain management when sufficient scale has been achieved [21, 46]. For this purpose, partners have to be evaluated according to their maturity level (e.g. business relationships, contacts, similar use case) and afterwards the network can be expanded.

4 Evaluation

In the following, the process models for implementation selected in Sect. 3.1 are compared with the requirements identified in Sect. 3.2. Each of the process models has been evaluated along the guiding question "To what extent does the process model in the row meet the requirements of the column?". The evaluation examines whether a model fulfills the respective requirement. The evaluation indicates "fulfilled", "partially fulfilled" and "not fulfilled", but no process model completely fulfills a requirement. The entire evaluation is shown in Fig. 2.

The requirement **RQ1** "Creating a technology insight" is partially fulfilled by four process models and not fulfilled by the remaining models. All process models start with either the identification of a use case or an evaluation of it. A specific phase for providing BC knowledge is not found in any model. The process model according to Attaran and Gunasekaran partially fulfills the requirement because questions about their current business model are used to familiarize managers with the technology [25]. Urban gives BC knowledge using a self-developed and detailed decision model for the use of the technology and shows alternatives when a BC is not suitable [27]. Starting with an open collection of use cases, these are evaluated according to Werner et al. and the list is gradually reduced until only one suitable use case remains. The reduction follows

Evaluation of the researched approaches according to the set requirements. **Question:** To which extent does the researched approach in the row meet the requirements of the process model in the column? **Rating scale:** ○ = not fulfilled ◐ = partially fulfilled ● = fulfilled	Requirements (RQ)				
	Creating a technology insight	Holistic perspective	Iterative and agile approach	Impact analysis and performance measurement	Scaling to further business partners
	RQ1	**RQ2**	**RQ3**	**RQ4**	**RQ5**
Model for integrating blockchain technology in supply chain according to Gürpinar et al.	○	●	●	◐	◐
Path to blockchain enterprise adoption according to Arun et al.	○	◐	○	○	○
Blockchain implementation phases according to Attaran and Gunasekaran	◐	●	○	○	○
Selection process to identify application opportunities for blockchain technology according to Werner et al.	◐	◐	◐	○	○
Three pillars for realizing a successful blockchain use case according to Urban	◐	◐	○	●	○
Process model for the implementation of blockchain in companies according to Wittenberg	○	●	◐	●	○
Conceptual stage model for Blockchain implementation in Supply Chains according to Vu et al.	◐	◐	○	○	◐

Fig. 2. Evaluation of the analyzed models in terms of the requirements for the implementation of blockchain technology in enterprises

an evaluation and examination of the use case. In workshops, basic knowledge is thus provided through iterations [26]. Vu et al. identify a lack of knowledge as a barrier to successful implementation and highlight this as a task in their initiation phase [28]. How they provide this knowledge is not described in detail.

The second requirement (**RQ2**) is partially fulfilled by every process model, since at least one process and one technology perspective are always taken into account during implementation. Only three models fulfill this requirement in its entirety and consider the levels of people, organization and processes. These three process models have certain aspects that they particularly emphasize. Wittenberg, for example, also considers the legal aspects [6]. In contrast, Guerpinar et al.'s process model focuses on the human factor in addition to organizational aspects during the integration phase [23]. Attaran and Gunasekaran also include all levels and provide a very detailed description of them [25].

Only one of the process models follows an iterative and agile approach according to **RQ3**, two others in divisional, while the other process models are executed linearly, phase by phase. The process model of Guerpinar et al. as the only one has an iterative continuous improvement and support phase and goes through its first preliminary phase once and therefore defines the use case in general terms. Each subsequent phase can be cycled to continuously gather feedback and make necessary changes [23]. As described above, Werner et al. approach the most appropriate use case iteratively [26] in their process model, while implementation is linear without feedback. Wittenberg uses agile IT project management methods in his process model to develop and improve the prototype. Before the prototype goes live, it is tested repeatedly [6]. There is no loop back to a previous phase in the model.

An impact analysis and performance measurement (**RQ4**) are a prerequisite for evaluating the implementation. Only two of seven process models fulfill this requirement. Both Wittenberg and Urban use scoring models [6, 27] to determine the value added by the Blockchain. They visualize the new business relationships using either BPMN or their own representation consisting of material flows, cash flows, and information flows [6, 27]. Guerpinar et al. is the only process model with an additional quantitative analysis approach, but it is not described in detail and for this reason is only classified as partially fulfilled [23].

The fifth requirement "Scaling to further business partners" (**RQ5**) is only partially fulfilled by two process models. While the remaining process models state the importance of scaling, they do not provide any information on its achievement and conclude with implementation [6, 24–27]. Guerpinar et al. include the scalability of the use case in their integration planning phase in order to minimize the effort involved in transferring it to further partners [23]. By analogy with Guerpinar et al., Vu et al. refer to so-called system-related barriers in their initiation phase, which also include scalability. A detailed description of how scaling can succeed is missing [28]. A subsequent phase for scaling the blockchain solution is missing in all process models. After comparing the process models with the identified requirements, it can be concluded that no existing process model fulfills all requirements. Consequently, a new process model needs to be developed that meets these requirements.

5   Results

In the following section, the developed blockchain implementation model is presented in detail including the individual tasks and results. This model is intended to provide companies with a step-by-step guide to overcome the barrier of blockchain adoption and accelerate digitization. Especially for small and medium-sized enterprises, which have great difficulties with such complex projects. Figure 3 shows the model in its completeness:

The first phase of the model is called introduction to blockchain systematics. The purpose of this phase is to gain a deeper understanding of blockchain technology, as this knowledge is essential for selecting a suitable use case. Only if the basics are understood it is possible to build a custom use case. Therefore, the use of experiential knowledge is particularly important. This understanding will be provided during workshops. In addition, possible application fields are examined with best practices based on already existing use cases. The result after completion of the first phase is a Blockchain Technology Insight and therefore the fulfillment of the first requirement (**RQ1**).

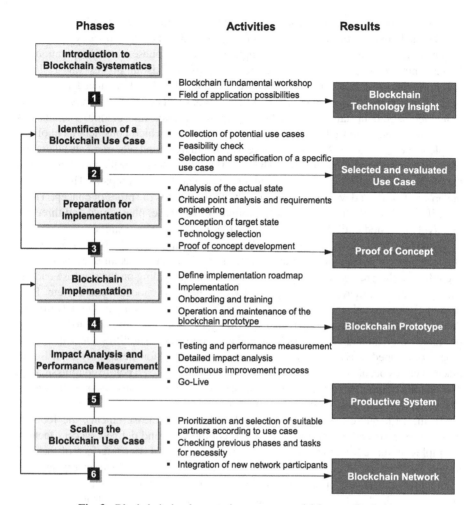

Fig. 3. Blockchain implementation process model for supply chains

In the second phase, the blockchain use case is identified. For this process, potential use cases are collected in the company using creativity techniques (e.g., brainstorming). The use cases are subsequently examined in detail for technical, economic and legal feasibility. Once a use case has been found, it is specified in precise terms. An assessment framework is developed for this purpose. This is used to evaluate, for example, compatibility with the existing business model, the expected economic benefit and the non-economic benefit (e.g. increased transparency). The assessment framework can be designed for the following three use case dimensions: Data, Processes, and Systems. All information is described in a formalized way in a Blockchain Canvas. Possible content includes which blockchain system should be used, which supply chain partner should participate, and which technology should be used as a complementary tool (e.g., Internet of Things). The second phase allows the model to also fulfil the second Requirement (**RQ2**), the holistic perspective. The result is a selected and evaluated Use Case.

Once the second phase has been completed, the third phase starts: Preparation for Implementation. The focus is on the current state of the existing process and IT landscape. At the same time, the processes are operationalized and enhanced with costs, times, participants and, if necessary, CO_2 consumption. The IT systems are expanded to include data, data standards, interfaces and other relevant information. The analysis of the current situation takes a socio-technical approach which considers technology, people and organization. Afterwards, a weak point analysis and requirements elicitation with success factors are carried out. The final step is the design of the target state with the blockchain solution as an implementation roadmap for the company. This includes the proof of concept development. The result of this phase is the proof of concept. However, if no applicable use case has been found in this phase, phases two and three are iteratively repeated until this is done. Thereafter, the fourth phase starts.

This fourth phase is called blockchain implementation and aims to develop a Blockchain prototype. For this purpose, the right Blockchain technology is selected according to the previously identified requirements. Depending on the use case and the specific demands, there are three types of Blockchains to choose from: Private, Public and Permissioned. In the same way, the roles and permissions in the network are defined. This includes assigning read and write permissions, deciding which data should be stored on-chain and which off-chain, and allocating responsibilities. Once the prototype is developed, it will be implemented and onboarding for the employees will take place. If errors occur during user training, they must be corrected before commissioning. The operation and maintenance of the blockchain prototype are also tasks in this phase. The result is the finished blockchain prototype.

In the fifth phase (impact analysis and performance measurement), the focus is on measuring success according to fulfilled requirements and defined success factors. Examples of success factors are the usability and graphical user interface of the prototype, the increase in efficiency that has been achieved and cost and energy savings. Another particularly important aspect of this phase is the comparison of target and actual processes. A GAP analysis is used for this purpose. The gaps identified from the analysis are worked out in detail. The whole process takes place as a continuous improvement process. Finally, a deduction and definition of measures for improvement potentials takes place. With the go live the result of this phase is the finished productive system. Through a detailed performance measurement, impact analysis and a multi-method approach, the model also fulfills the requirement **RQ4**.

The final phase of the model is scaling the blockchain use case. During this phase, the company has to decide how to scale the network. The question must be answered in which order which customer or supplier should be added to the Blockchain network. A strategy also needs to be developed as to how the customers of the customers and the suppliers of the suppliers can be integrated. In the process of connecting new partners, it is important to check which phases in the model need to be iterated again. Phases one to three are skipped because a productive system is already in place and only the network needs to be expanded. Accordingly, an iteration also takes place in this last phase. It is also necessary to check whether there are any termination criteria for the connection of new partners. After the successful connection of business partners, the result at the end of the phase is the finished blockchain network. The last phase of the model leads to the fulfillment of requirements **RQ3** (iterative approach) and **RQ5** (scaling to further business partners). Therefore, the model fulfills all requirements for a Blockchain implementation model and advances both science and practice.

6 Conclusion

An increasing challenge in supply chain management is the exchange of information. Global division of labor is creating supply chain networks rather than individual supply chains. It is the supply chain networks and not the individual companies that are competing against one another, and they are competitive when the exchange of information between the individual companies is efficient. Blockchain technology provides an approach to transmit information rapidly, encrypted and tamper-proof within the supply chain. Currently, small and medium sized enterprises in particular struggle with the implementation of blockchain technology, as it is an extremely complex technology. To simplify the implementation for companies, a large amount of blockchain implementation models can be found. In a comprehensive literature review, the existing models were compiled and analyzed. Subsequently, five requirements were identified from the literature, from project experience with SMEs and from discussions with companies, which apply to blockchain implementation models. The collected models were compared and evaluated based on the requirements. The result is as follows: while none of the models meets all the requirements, some of them meet them partially and others do not meet them at all. Therefore, a model for the introduction of blockchain technology is developed that fulfils all the five requirements. This model is intended to provide companies with a guideline for the implementation of blockchain technology, starting with the identification of a use case and ending with the scaling to other business partners and post-implementation monitoring.

Based on this study, it is necessary to examine if the implementation model also leads to positive results in practice. For this purpose, at least partial aspects of it should be implemented, evaluated and continuously developed further at the beginning. Several German SMEs have agreed to participate in the evaluation and subsequent validation after implementation of the process model. The findings and requirements collected will also be validated by experts in the future in order to be able to assess the suitability of the model. It will be helpful in the next step to include grey literature in the analysis as well in order to gain even more approaches and scientific legitimacy for the developed model. In the future, more models will be developed, which should also be included in the evaluation. A constant adaptation of the requirements will also be necessary, as they may change due to the disruptive and ever-changing nature of the subject. The last point to mention is that the process model follows a multi-method approach, for which additional tools still need to be developed for the quantitative assessment of blockchain projects and their impact.

References

1. Connelly, B.L., Ketchen, D.J., Hult, G.T.M.: Global supply chain management: towards theoretically driven research agenda. Glob. Strateg. J. **3**(3), 227–243 (2013)
2. Chen, S., Shi, R., Ren, Z., Yan, J., Shi, Y., Zhang, J.: A blockchain-based supply chain quality management framework. In: 2017 IEEE 14th International Conference on e-Business Engineering (ICEBE), pp. 172–176. IEEE, November 2017
3. Treiblmaier, H.: The impact of the blockchain on the supply chain: a theory-based research framework and a call for action. Supply Chain Manage. Int. J. **23**(6), 545–559 (2018)
4. Wang, H., Zheng, Z., Xie, S., Dai, H.N., Chen, X.: Blockchain challenges and opportunities: a survey. Int. J. Web Grid Serv. (IJWGS) **14**(4), S.352 (2018)
5. Rawat, D.B., Chaudhary, V., Doku, R.: Blockchain: emerging applications and use cases. arXiv preprint arXiv:1904.12247 (2019)
6. Wittenberg, S.: Blockchain für Unternehmen: Anwendungsfälle und Geschäftsmodelle für die Praxis. Schäffer-Poeschel (2020)
7. Gentemann, L.: Blockchain in Deutschland–Einsatz, Potenziale, Herausforderungen. In: Bitkom e.V., Berlin (2019)
8. Szymczak, M., Szuster, M., Wieteska, G., Baraniecka, A.: Supply chain management. In: Szymczak, M. (ed.) Managing Towards Supply Chain Maturity, pp. 9–44. Palgrave Macmillan UK, London (2013). https://doi.org/10.1057/9781137359667_2
9. Muchna, C., Brandenburg, H., Fottner, J., Gutermuth, J.: Grundlagen der Logis-tik. Begriffe, Strukturen und Prozesse. Springer Gabler, Wiesbaden (2018). https://doi.org/10.1007/978-3-658-18593-0
10. Cooper, M.C., Lambert, D.M., Pagh, J.D.: Supply chain management: more than a new name for logistics. Int. J. Logistics Manage. **8**(1), 1–14 (1997)
11. Liebetruth, T.: Prozessmanagement in Einkauf und Logistik. Springer Fachmedien Wiesbaden, Wiesbaden (2016). https://doi.org/10.1007/978-3-658-09759-2
12. Stevens, G.C.: Integrating the supply chain. Int. J. Phys. Distrib. Mater. Manage. **19**(8), 3–8 (1989)
13. Salcedo, S., Grackin, A.: The e-value chain. Supply Chain Manage. Rev. **3**(4), 63–70 (2000)
14. Guggenberger, T., Schweizer, A., Urbach, N.: Improving interorganizational information sharing for vendor managed inventory: toward a decentralized information hub using blockchain technology. IEEE Trans. Eng. Manage. **67**(4), 1074–1085 (2020)
15. Abeyratne, S.A., Monfared, R.P.: Blockchain ready manufacturing supply chain using distributed ledger. Int. J. Res. Eng. Technol. **5**(9), 1–10 (2016)
16. Chuen, D.L.K. (ed.): Handbook of Digital Currency: Bitcoin, Innovation, Financial Instruments, and Big Data. Academic Press, Amsterdam (2015)
17. Swan, M.: Blockchain: Blueprint for a New Economy. O'Reilly & Associates, Sebastopol (2015)
18. Hackius, N., Petersen, M.: Blockchain in logistics and supply chain: trick or treat? In: Digitalization in Supply Chain Management and Logistics: Smart and Digital Solutions for an Industry 4.0 Environment. Proceedings of the Hamburg International Conference of Logistics (HICL), vol. 23, pp. 3–18. epubli GmbH, Berlin (2017)
19. Henke, M., Schulte, A.T., Jakob, S.: Blockchain-basiertes supply chain management. In: ten Hompel, M., Bauernhansl, T., Vogel-Heuser, B. (eds.) Handbuch Industrie 4.0, pp. 599–615. Springer, Heidelberg (2020). https://doi.org/10.1007/978-3-662-58530-6_116
20. Verhoeven, P., Sinn, F., Herden, T.T.: Examples from blockchain implementations in logistics and supply chain management: exploring the mindful use of a new technology. Logistics **2**(3), 20 (2018)

21. Wang, Y., Han, J.H., Beynon-Davies, P.: Understanding blockchain technology for future supply chains: a systematic literature review and research agenda. Supply Chain Manage. Int. J. **24**, 62–84 (2018)
22. Webster, J., Watson, R.T.: Analyzing the past to prepare for the future: writing a literature review. MIS Q. **26**, 8–23 (2002)
23. Guerpinar, T., et al.: Blockchain technology: Integration in supply chain processes. Data science and innovation in supply chain management: how data transforms the value chain. In: Proceedings of the Hamburg International Conference of Logistics (HICL), vol. 29. epubli GmbH, Berlin (2020)
24. Arun, J.S., Cuomo, J., Gaur, N.: Blockchain for Business. Addison-Wesley Professional, New York (2019)
25. Attaran, M., Gunasekaran, A.: Applications of Blockchain Technology in Business: Challenges and Opportunities. Springer, Cham (2019). https://doi.org/10.1007/978-3-030-277 98-710.1007/978-3-030-27798-7
26. Fill, H.-G., Meier, A.: Blockchain. Springer Fachmedien Wiesbaden, Wiesbaden (2020)
27. Urban, N.T.: Blockchain for Business. Springer, Cham (2020). https://doi.org/10.1007/978-3-658-29822-7
28. Vu, N., Ghadge, A., Bourlakis, M.: Blockchain adoption in food supply chains: a review and implementation framework. Prod. Plann. Control 1–18 (2021)
29. Dujak, D., Sajter, D.: Blockchain applications in supply chain. In: Kawa, A., Maryniak, A. (eds.) SMART Supply Network. E, pp. 21–46. Springer, Cham (2019). https://doi.org/10.1007/978-3-319-91668-2_2
30. Queiroz, M.M., Telles, R., Bonilla, S.H.: Blockchain and supply chain management integration: a systematic review of the literature. Supply Chain Manage. Int. J. **25** (2019)
31. Dispan, J., Schwarz-Kocher, M.: Digitalisierung im Maschinenbau. Entwicklungstrends, Herausforderungen, Beschäftigungswirkungen, Gestaltungsfelder im Maschinen-und Anlagenbau (No. 94). Working Paper Forschungsförderung (2018)
32. Mendling, J., et al.: Blockchains for business process management-challenges and opportunities. ACM Trans. Manage. Inf. Syst. (TMIS) **9**(1), 1–16 (2018)
33. Sternberg, H.S., Hofmann, E., Roeck, D.: The struggle is real: insights from a supply chain blockchain case. J. Bus. Logist. **42**(1), 71–87 (2021)
34. Morabito, V.: Business Innovation Through Blockchain. Springer, Cham (2017). https://doi.org/10.1007/978-3-319-48478-5
35. Saberi, S., Kouhizadeh, M., Sarkis, J., Shen, L.: Blockchain technology and its relationships to sustainable supply chain management. Int. J. Prod. Res. **57**(7), 2117–2135 (2019)
36. Kshetri, N.: 1 Blockchain's roles in meeting key supply chain management objectives. Int. J. Inf. Manage. **39**, 80–89 (2018)
37. Weking, J., Mandalenakis, M., Hein, A., Hermes, S., Böhm, M., Krcmar, H.: The impact of blockchain technology on business models–a taxonomy and archetypal patterns. Electron. Mark. **30**(2), 285–305 (2020)
38. Chong, A.Y.L., Lim, E.T., Hua, X., Zheng, S., Tan, C.W.: Business on chain: a comparative case study of five blockchain-inspired business models. J. Assoc. Inf. Syst. **20**(9), 9 (2019)
39. Highsmith, J.: Agile Project Management: Creating Innovative Products. Pearson Education, Boston (2009)
40. Saghiri, A.M.: Blockchain architecture. In: Kim, S., Dek, G.C. (eds.) Advanced Applications of Blockchain Technology, pp. 161–176. Springer, Singapore (2020). https://doi.org/10.1007/978-981-13-8775-3_8
41. Osterland, T., Rose, T.: From a use case categorization scheme towards a maturity model for engineering distributed ledgers. In: Treiblmaier, H., Clohessy, T. (eds.) Blockchain and Distributed Ledger Technology Use Cases. PI, pp. 33–50. Springer, Cham (2020). https://doi.org/10.1007/978-3-030-44337-5_2

42. Iansiti, M., Lakhani, K.R.: The truth about blockchain. Harv. Bus. Rev. **95**(1), 118–127 (2017)
43. Dutta, P., Choi, T.M., Somani, S., Butala, R.: Blockchain technology in supply chain operations: applications, challenges and research opportunities. Transp. Res. Part E Logistics Transp. Rev. **142**, 102067 (2020)
44. Qu, Y., et al.: An integrated framework of enterprise information systems in smart manufacturing system via business process reengineering. Proc. Inst. Mech. Eng. Part B J. Eng. Manuf. **233**(11), 2210–2224 (2019)
45. Platt, M., et al.: Energy footprint of blockchain consensus mechanisms beyond proof-of-work. arXiv preprint arXiv:2109.03667 (2021)
46. Perboli, G., Musso, S., Rosano, M.: Blockchain in logistics and supply chain: a lean approach for designing real-world use cases. IEEE Access **6**, 62018–62028 (2018)
47. Chen, I.J., Paulraj, A.: Understanding supply chain management: critical research and a theoretical framework. Int. J. Prod. Res. **42**(1), 131–163 (2004)

Risk and Resilience in Collaborative Networks

A Simulation Framework Dedicated to Characterizing Risks and Cascading Effects in Collaborative Networks

Tianyuan Zhang[(✉)], Jiayao Li, and Frédérick Bénaben

Centre Génie Industriel, IMT Mines Albi-Carmaux, 81000 Albi, France
{tianyuan.zhang,jiayao.li,frederick.benaben}@mines-albi.fr

Abstract. Cascading effects describe risk interdependencies, whereby the occurrence of one risk may trigger one or more risks with potential propagation chains in complex systems. In this study, on the basis of a formalized model namely *danger-risk-consequence* chain, a generic simulation framework is proposed to characterize risk causal processes and cascading effects within collaborative networks. Risk-related components and the causal relationships between them are visualized by abstractly representing the instantaneous state of the considered collaborative network as a directed graph. Furthermore, the simulation of trajectories of the state evolution over time is realized by knowledge-driven automatic inference of causal chains and propagation chains, thus enabling the tracing of cascading effects within complex systems. The presented simulation framework provides a solid foundation for a systemic understanding of risks, which implies an innovative tool that helps decision-makers to identify, prevent and mitigate cascading effects within collaborative networks (e.g., supply chains).

Keywords: Simulation · Cascading effect · Risk interdependency · Collaborative network · Framework

1 Introduction

Over the past decades, participation in collaborative networks has become a vital avenue for any organization to improve profitability through sharing competencies and resources [1]. Organizations in collaborative networks are more exposed to risks since they are interdependent [2, 3]. In the context of enterprise collaboration, the risk of an individual company is no longer confined to its own risk; it is in fact the risk of all partners [4]. *Cascading effects* are implied by such risk interrelations. Specifically, as described by Buldyrev et al. [5], "*the occurrence of one risk can trigger further risks, thus creating cascading effect*". It signifies a high vulnerability to perturbations with amplifying impacts. Therefore, it's important to identify, prevent and mitigate cascading effects within collaborative networks for enterprises.

To date, risk interdependencies and cascading effects have attracted extensive attention in academic research. The vast majority of studies fall within the context of the

© IFIP International Federation for Information Processing 2022
Published by Springer Nature Switzerland AG 2022
L. M. Camarinha-Matos et al. (Eds.): PRO-VE 2022, IFIP AICT 662, pp. 463–474, 2022.
https://doi.org/10.1007/978-3-031-14844-6_37

supply chain, which can be regarded as a typical collaborative network. The available studies can be broadly classified into three categories according to their purposes: 1) vulnerability analysis in the context of cascading effects; 2) evaluation of the impact of cascading effects; 3) conceptual modeling of cascading effects [6–9]. Among the above research, simulation approaches were adopted in most of the studies for the following reasons:

First, cascading effects are caused by low-frequency high-impact disruptions in most cases [10, 11]. There are fewer real cases and data available for study. Simulation can be used to address this rareness.

Second, the ultimate goal of studying cascading effects is to find prevention and mitigation strategies. Simulation can provide a risk-free environment for testing different prevention and mitigation measures.

Third, cascading effects are dynamic processes. Simulation is dedicated to tracking the evolution and characterizing the dynamic nature, and thus helping to understand the triggers and mechanisms of cascading effects [12].

Although simulation methods are widely used in cascading effects research, most of the studies use simulation only as a tool to simulate the behavior of complex systems experiencing cascading effects in a specific context, or for a specific case. There is a lack of a generic simulation framework dedicated to characterizing risks and cascading effects in collaborative networks. This study aims to address this absence by constructing a novel simulation framework on the basis of a formalized model namely *danger-risk-consequence* chain.

The article is organized as follows. Section 2 presents a literature review of cascading effect simulation-based modeling and highlights the limitations of existing research. Section 3 provides a brief introduction of the preliminary work, mainly the *danger-risk-consequence* chain model. Section 4 introduces the proposed simulation framework and Sect. 5 presents an illustrative use case based on the proposed framework. The final section concludes the contributions and limitations of this work, as well as the future directions.

2   Literature Review

The term of cascading effect has been introduced into academic literatures over the last two decades and has received significant attention in a wide range of enquiries. According to [13], cascading effect is consistent with the metaphor of topping dominoes, that is, the first domino is pushed down, it crashes into the next domino and keeps pushing down to the end of the sequence. FEMA describes cascading effect as a universal dynamic form that may multiply the impact of combinations of hazards from a perspective of emergency management [14]. Cascading effect is also related to ripple effect that concerns disruption propagation in supply chains [15]. Generally speaking, this effect is *"the dynamics present, in which an initial impact can trigger other phenomena that lead to consequences with significant magnitudes"* [16].

As suggested by Helbing et al. [3], cascading effects can be considered as a direct output of the evolution of complex systems, which means that they change constantly over time. Hence, simulation-based modeling naturally performs an important role on cascading effect studies, given its ability to cope with time-dependent risk analysis, vulnerability analysis and performance impact [15].

LIaguno et al. [10] proposes a conceptual framework to present the characteristics of ripple effect in supply chains, which is validated by a system dynamics simulation model. Ghadge et al. [12] utilizes system dynamics approach to simulate different types of risks and cascading effects. Besides, agent-based simulation and discrete-event simulation have been widely used to model cascading effects and their resilience performance. For example, Lohmer et al. [17] quantitatively presents an agent-based simulation model to analyze ripple effects and the impact of introducing blockchain technology on supply chain resilience. Ivanov [18] simulates a coronavirus outbreak case by using discrete-event modeling, which demonstrates how simulation-based methodology can be used to predict the impacts of disruptions and cascading effects. Furthermore, in addition to the simulation methods introduced above, graph-based studies also need to be named for cascading effect analysis [15]. For instance, Khakzad and Reniers [6] proposes a set of graph metrics and measurements for vulnerability analysis of process plant, given that cascading effects are represented as a directed graph.

To summarize, significant strides can be recently witnessed from academic literatures to cascading effect simulation-based modeling. However, on one hand, most of studies focus on utilizing the simulation methods to analyze resilience and robustness performance for a considered complex system in the light of cascading effects [10, 17, 19], instead of simulating cascading effects. On the other hand, there are plenty of simulation models proposed either in the context of a specific domain (*e.g.*, supply chains [12, 15]) or on a specific case [18]. In such cases, we argue that such simulation tools are lack of university and flexibility, which may be hard to reuse or reproduce under other contexts. In a nutshell, there is a lack of a more generic simulation framework dedicated to characterizing the causes and propagation processes of cascading effects. Our study aims to bridge this research gap.

3 Preliminary Work

To simulate risks and cascading effects within collaborative networks, a formalized model that can characterize the risk causal processes and propagation processes is needed. A conceptual approach, namely *danger-risk-consequence* chain [9, 20, 21], dedicated to modeling risks and cascading effects within complex systems is adopted as the basis of the proposed simulation framework.

As shown in Fig. 1, the *danger-risk-consequence* chain was firstly introduced in [20] as a formal description of risk dependencies. To conceptualize the risk causal processes, five risk-related components (*danger, stake, risk, event*, and *consequence*) are identified to represent the internal causal mechanism of risks [9, 21]. The definitions of the five risk-related components used in the *danger-risk-consequence* chain are stated as follows.

Danger is defined as the hazardous characteristic or situation of the considered collaborative network that may lead to undesirable negative impacts. *Stake* is defined following the instruction of ISO 7010:2019, as "*an item, thing or entity that has potential or actual value to a considered system or its environment*" [22]. Compared with the conceptual description, *risk* is further clarified as the latent effect of a *danger* acting on

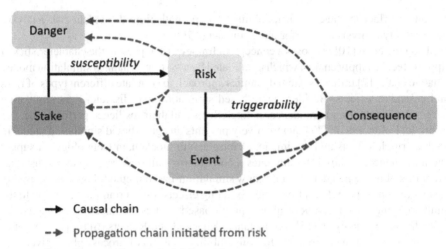

Fig. 1. The formalized *danger-risk-consequence* chain model [9, 21]. (Color figure online)

a *stake*. *Event* can be seen as a fact that has occurred or a condition that has been fulfilled, marking the transition of a *risk* from a potential state to a realized state. *Consequence* can be defined as the undesirable negative impacts caused by the realization of the *risk* [9, 21]. Compatible with the broad understanding of risks, *danger* can be regarded as the source of *risk*, *stake* can be considered as the *risk*-bearing entity, *event* can be seen as the trigger of *risk*, while *consequence* can be described as the impacts of *risk*.

By breaking down the complex concept of risks into five risk-related components, the *danger-risk-consequence* chain summarized the causal mechanism of risks into two ternary relations: *susceptibility* and *triggerability*. *Susceptibility* describes the causal relationship between *danger*, *stake*, and *risk*, that is, a *stake* is susceptible to a *danger* and thus generates a *risk*. Similarly, *triggerability* defines the causal relationship between *risk*, *event*, and *consequence*, that is, an *event* triggers a *risk* and thus realizes a *consequence* [9, 21]. In summary, the causal processes of risks are formally described through the two causal chains (i.e., *susceptibility* and *triggerability*) in the *danger-risk-consequence* chain model.

In addition to risk causal processes, the *danger-risk-consequence* chain model characterizes the cascading effect by introducing the propagation chain to represent the risk propagation processes. *Risk* and *consequence* can be regarded as the results in causal chains, on the contrary, these two components are treated as the causes that generate impacts on *danger*, *stake*, and *event* in propagation chains. Therefore, risk propagation processes are formalized as the potential propagation connections initiated from *risk* (blue connections in Fig. 1) and *consequence* (red connections in Fig. 1), respectively. It is worth noting that the source and target of the propagation chain may belong to the same causal chain or be separated into different causal chains. A series of potential propagation chains being activated means that the cascading effect takes place.

Compared with the descriptive definitions of risks and cascading effects, the *danger-risk-consequence* chain model provides a highly formalized tool that can be used to simulate the risk causal processes and propagation processes. Furthermore, instead of modeling the collaborative networks, the *danger-risk-consequence* chain model directly interprets risk causal mechanism and propagation phenomena, thus enables the direct simulation of risks and cascading effects.

4   The Proposed Simulation Framework

Based on the preliminary work, especially the *danger-risk-consequence* chain model, a generic simulation framework is proposed to simulate the risk causal processes and cascading effects in collaborative networks. Inspired by the philosophies of agent-based modeling and graph theory, the proposed simulation framework is designed as a hybrid approach through object-oriented design (OOD) and is implemented with the python (version 3.10.0) programming language.

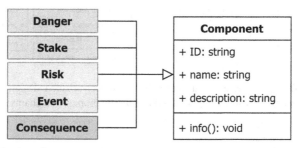

Fig. 2. The UML class diagram that illustrates the OOD of the proposed simulation framework regarding the five risk-related components.

4.1   The OOD of the *Danger-Risk-Consequence* Chain Model

As the basis of the proposed simulation framework, the *danger-risk-consequence* chain model is implemented first, which defines the core elements that the simulation framework can operate on. As shown in Fig. 2, the five risk-related components of the *danger-risk-consequence* chain model are defined as five classes that inherit from the same class: "Component". Thus, the five classes ("Danger", "Stake", "Risk", "Event", and "Consequence") share the same attributes: "ID", "name", and "description". It is important to note that each instance has a unique "ID", but different instances can have the same "name" and "description". Sharing the same "name" and "description" means that two different instances belong to the same identified risk-related component, but the different "IDs" indicate that they may exist in different time and space and are different instances. In addition to the attributes, all five classes provide the method "info()" to obtain corresponding information.

Apart from the five risk-related components, the proposed simulation framework implements the risk causal chain and propagation chain as two packages respectively.

The "Causal Chain" package contains two classes: "Susceptibility" and "Triggerability". Each class has three attributes to record all known components, and an additional attribute to record the existence of causal relationships corresponding to all possible combinations of these components. Similarly, the "Propagation Chain" package also contains two classes: "Creation" and "Deletion". The "Creation" class describes the propagation relationship that a *risk/consequence* might create a *danger/stake/event*, the "Deletion" class describes the propagation relationship that a *risk/consequence* might delete a *danger/stake*. An *event* cannot be deleted because it represents a fact that has occurred or a condition that has been fulfilled. All these four classes provide the method "check()" to check whether the corresponding causal or propagation chain exists (Fig. 3).

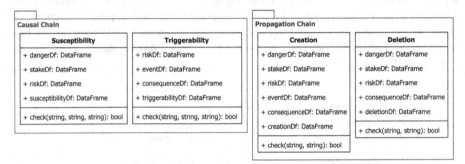

Fig. 3. The UML class diagram that illustrates the object-oriented design of the proposed simulation framework regarding the risk causal chains and propagation chains.

4.2 The OOD of the Proposed Simulation Framework

After defining the core elements that can be manipulated, the proposed simulation framework is designed to consist of four classes: "KnowledgeBase", "State", "Action", and "Experiment". Figure 4 illustrates the overall picture of the whole framework, which describes the relationships between these four classes. The "KnowledgeBase" class is designed to store all the knowledge of the simulated collaborative network, which involves all the identified risk-related components as well as causal and propagation chains between them. Therefore, the "KnowledgeBase" can be used to characterize the simulated system and drive the simulation process.

With the support of knowledge, the "State" class is defined to describe an instantaneous state of the simulated collaborative network. Each instantaneous state is formalized as a directed graph derived from the *danger-risk-consequence* chain model. For causal chains, the binary relations are adopted to replace the ternary ones in the original model for better compatibility with the form of directed graphs (see Fig. 5). More specifically, *susceptibility* is split into 3 binary relations: a *stake* is susceptible to a *danger*, a *danger* generates a *risk*, and a *risk* concerns a *stake*. Similarly, *triggerability* is split as follows: an *event* triggers a *risk*, a *risk* defines a *consequence*, and a *consequence* is realized by an *event*. The directed graph describes all risk-related components present in the collaborative network at the moment, and the causal chains between them. In addition, for

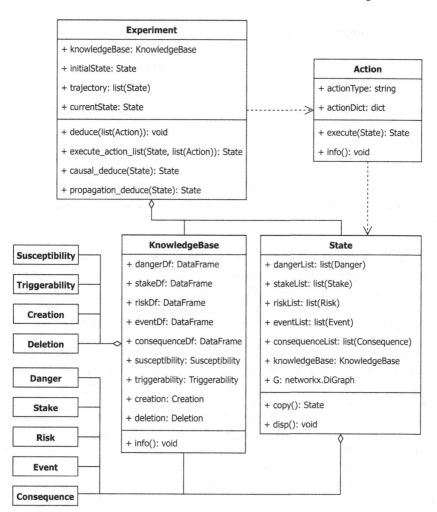

Fig. 4. The UML class diagram that illustrates the OOD of the whole proposed simulation framework.

propagation chains, the binary relation "Creation" is also recorded in the "State" class and presented in the directed graph to better visualize and track cascading effects. The python package NetworkX (version 2.6.3) is used for implementing the directed graph [23].

Apart from the "KnowledgeBase" and "State" class, the proposed simulation framework also provides an "Action" class to capture the actual situation that a collaborative network might face disruptions and interventions. The "Action" class has a method "execute()" that takes a "State" as input and returns a "State" as the result after the disruption or intervention has been executed. This class can be used to break the stable state of the system during a simulation or to test the impact of risk management measures on the system.

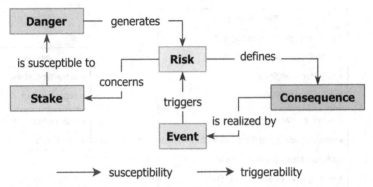

Fig. 5. Illustration of the binary causal relationships between five risk-related components in the directed graph.

Aggregating and depending on the above three class, the "Experiment" class is designed for implementing the simulation experiment given a specific collaborative network. The "knowledgeBase" attribute provides knowledge of the considered system for driving the inference, the "initialState" and "currentState attribute represents the starting point and the status of the simulated system respectively, while the "trajectory" attribute is composed of a series of states and records the state evolution over time. The "Experiment" class provides a method "deduce()" to perform the automatic knowledge-driven deduction. Each deduction step consists of three sub-steps: first, a list of actions is executed to inject disruptions or intervention into the simulated system; second, the causal relationships are inferred based on the identified causal chains in the knowledge base, new *risk/consequence* are be generated; third, new danger/stake/event are created, or existing danger/stake are deleted according to the known propagation chains in the knowledge base. After each deduction step is completed, the resulting instance of "State" will be added to the "trajectory" attribute, and the "currentState" attribute will be updated.

It is worth noting that risks as well as cascading effects in a collaborative network are largely determined by properties of the network itself, such as the structure of the network. Therefore, the simulation framework proposed in this study defines the "knowledgeBase" attribute to describe the related characteristics of the considered system as knowledge to support the simulation of risks and cascading effects. Furthermore, the "trajectory" attribute and the "deduce()" method are implemented to capture the dynamic nature of interdependent risks and the cascading effects. Instead of simulating how a collaborative network behaves, the proposed simulation framework directly simulates risk causal and propagation processes, thus provides a powerful tool for better understanding the trigger and mechanism of risks and cascading effects from both the macro- and micro-level perspectives.

5   An Illustrative Use Case

For illustrative purposes, a use case is simulated using the proposed framework in a scenario of construction supply chain, which can be considered as a classical collaborative network. The simulated supply chain consists of three stakeholders: the material supplier, subcontractor, and contractor. The subcontractor needs to pay the material supplier in advance and to receive the payment from the contractor only after the delivery is completed. Therefore, the subcontractor's cash flow is an important indicator of the status of this supply chain. However, with only one material supplier in the initial supply chain, the network faces the intrinsic risk of supply delays or disruptions. Once this risk is triggered, potential cascading effects will be activated, ultimately resulting in the tightness of subcontractor's circulating assets and the break of the stable status of the collaborative network.

Table 1. Identified risk-related components of the simulated construction supply chain.

Type	Name	Description
Danger	D1	Single source of supply on cements
	D2	Temporary procurement from a new supplier
	D3	The subcontractor pays before receiving required materials
Stake	S1	Subcontractor
	S2	Material Supplier
	S3	Contractor
Risk	R1	Supply delay or disruption
	R2	The quality of cements can't be guaranteed
	R3	The after-sale service can't be guaranteed
	R4	Unable to recover the advance payment
Event	E1	The production of the cement supplier is interrupted
	E2	The rate of defective products is too high
	E3	The new supplier refuses of return
	E4	The material supplier refuses to refund advance payment
Consequence	C1	The subcontractor fails to deliver on time
	C2	Return is needed
	C3	The new supplier fails to deliver all the required cements
	C4	Bad debts, tightness of circulating assets

To characterize the construction supply chain and drive the simulation of risks and cascading effects considering the above context, a series of risk-related components are extracted based on expertise and historical data (see Table 1). These components are organized using the *danger-risk-consequence* chain model, and the causal chains and propagation chains between them are also identified as knowledge.

The initial state of the simulated system consists only two components: D1 and S1. Driven by the knowledge base, a simulation experiment is performed. There are two disruptions (E1 after State 1 and E2 after State 3) injected into the system during the simulation. The resulting trajectory of the state evolution over time is shown in

Fig. 6. After each automatic deduction, the directed graph representing the instantaneous state becomes more and more complex. New components are added according to the simulated risk causal processes, and multiple risk propagation processes are activated during the state evolution. In contrast to other commonly used simulation methods, the risk causal relationships are initiatively visualized, and the underlying cascading effect are successfully simulated and tracked through the proposed simulation framework.

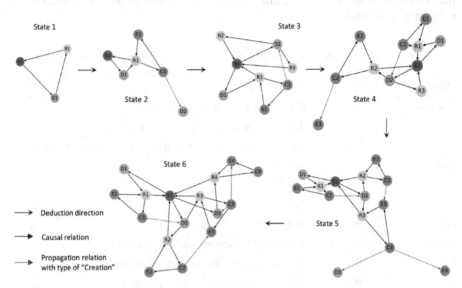

Fig. 6. The simulated trajectory of the state evolution over time.

6 Conclusion and Future Work

This study proposes a generic simulation framework dedicated to characterizing risks and cascading effects in collaborative networks. Based on a formalized *danger-risk-consequence* chain model, the presented framework is able to simulate risk casual processes and propagation processes and thus can directly simulate cascading effect itself, rather than reflecting it indirectly by simulating the behavior of a considered system. Furthermore, the static knowledge base in the framework can be used to organize the risk-related characteristics of the considered systems, while the dynamic trajectories obtained from simulations can be used to capture the dynamic nature of cascading effect. The simulation framework is implemented with the python (version 3.10.0) programming language, thus is easy to be coupled with other powerful tools in domains, such as scikit-learn for machine learning and pandas for data sciences.

The future work will aim to make the proposed simulation framework easier to apply in practice, with the following directions to be explored:

1) Automatic mapping the considered collaborative network as a static knowledge base following the form defined by the *danger-risk-consequence* chain model;

2) Identifying and mining of the causal relationships and propagation relationships among risk-related components;
3) Refining the current simulation framework, introducing stochasticity regarding the occurrence of disruptions, providing tools for testing human intervention measures and evaluating the impacts of cascading effects.

References

1. Camarinha-Matos, L.M., Afsarmanesh, H., Galeano, N., Molina, A.: Collaborative networked organizations - concepts and practice in manufacturing enterprises. Comput. Ind. Eng. **57**, 46–60 (2009). https://doi.org/10.1016/j.cie.2008.11.024
2. Wulan, M., Petrovic, D.: A fuzzy logic based system for risk analysis and evaluation within enterprise collaborations. Comput. Ind. **63**, 739–748 (2012). https://doi.org/10.1016/j.com pind.2012.08.012
3. Helbing, D.: Globally networked risks and how to respond. Nature **497**, 51–59 (2013). https://doi.org/10.1038/nature12047
4. Hallikas, J., Varis, J.: Risk management in value networks. In: Zsidisin, G.A., Ritchie, B. (eds.) Supply Chain Risk: A Handbook of Assessment, Management, and Performance, pp. 35–52. Springer, Cham (2009). https://doi.org/10.1007/978-0-387-79934-6_3
5. Buldyrev, S.V., Parshani, R., Paul, G., Stanley, H.E., Havlin, S.: Catastrophic cascade of failures in interdependent networks. Nature **464**, 1025–1028 (2010)
6. Khakzad, N., Reniers, G.: Using graph theory to analyze the vulnerability of process plants in the context of cascading effects. Reliab. Eng. Syst. Saf. **143**, 63–73 (2015). https://doi.org/10.1016/j.ress.2015.04.015
7. Li, Y., Chen, K., Collignon, S., Ivanov, D.: Ripple effect in the supply chain network: forward and backward disruption propagation, network health and firm vulnerability. Eur. J. Oper. Res. **291**, 1117–1131 (2021)
8. Ma, G., Wu, Z., Jia, J., Shang, S.: Safety risk factors comprehensive analysis for construction project: combined cascading effect and machine learning approach. Saf. Sci. **143**, 105410 (2021)
9. Li, J., Bénaben, F., Gou, J., Mu, W.: A proposal for risk identification approach in collaborative networks considering susceptibility to danger. In: Camarinha-Matos, L.M., Afsarmanesh, H., Rezgui, Y. (eds.) PRO-VE 2018. IAICT, vol. 534, pp. 74–84. Springer, Cham (2018). https://doi.org/10.1007/978-3-319-99127-6_7
10. Llaguno, A., Mula, J., Campuzano-Bolarin, F.: State of the art, conceptual framework and simulation analysis of the ripple effect on supply chains. Int. J. Prod. Res. (2021). https://doi.org/10.1080/00207543.2021.1877842
11. Kinra, A., Ivanov, D., Das, A., Dolgui, A.: Ripple effect quantification by supplier risk exposure assessment. Int. J. Prod. Res. **58**, 5559–5578 (2020). https://doi.org/10.1080/00207543.2019.1675919
12. Ghadge, A., Er, M., Ivanov, D., Chaudhuri, A.: Visualisation of ripple effect in supply chains under long-term, simultaneous disruptions: a system dynamics approach. Int. J. Prod. Res. (2021). https://doi.org/10.1080/00207543.2021.1987547
13. May, F.: Cascading disaster models in postburn flash flood. In: Butler, B.W., Cook, W.C. (eds.) The Fire Environment–Innovations, Management, and Policy; Conference Proceedings, 26–30 March 2007; Destin, FL. Proceedings RMRS-P-46CD. Fort Collins, CO: U.S. Department of Agriculture, Forest Service, Rocky Mountain Research Station, CD-ROM, pp. 443–464, 046 (2007)

14. FEMA: Principles of Emergency Management. Washington, DC (2006)
15. Ivanov, D.: Simulation-based ripple effect modelling in the supply chain. Int. J. Prod. Res. **55**, 2083–2101 (2017). https://doi.org/10.1080/00207543.2016.1275873
16. Pescaroli, G., Alexander, D.: A definition of cascading disasters and cascading effects: Going beyond the "toppling dominos" metaphor. Planet@Risk, vol. 3 (2015)
17. Lohmer, J., Bugert, N., Lasch, R.: Analysis of resilience strategies and ripple effect in blockchain-coordinated supply chains: an agent-based simulation study. Int. J. Prod. Econ. **228**, 107882 (2020). https://doi.org/10.1016/j.ijpe.2020.107882
18. Ivanov, D.: Predicting the impacts of epidemic outbreaks on global supply chains: a simulation-based analysis on the coronavirus outbreak (COVID-19/SARS-CoV-2) case. Transp. Res. Part E Logistics Transp. Rev. **136**, 101922 (2020). https://doi.org/10.1016/j.tre.2020.101922
19. Giannoccaro, I., Iftikhar, A.: Mitigating ripple effect in supply networks: the effect of trust and topology on resilience. Int. J. Prod. Res. **60**, 1178–1195 (2022). https://doi.org/10.1080/00207543.2020.1853844
20. Bénaben, F., Barthe-Delanoë, A.-M., Lauras, M., Truptil, S.: Collaborative systems in crisis management: a proposal for a conceptual framework. In: Camarinha-Matos, L.M., Afsarmanesh, H. (eds.) PRO-VE 2014. IAICT, vol. 434, pp. 396–405. Springer, Heidelberg (2014). https://doi.org/10.1007/978-3-662-44745-1_39
21. Li, J.: Cascading effects of risk dedicated to collaborative networked organizations. Doctoral dissertation, Beijing Jiaotong University, Beijing (2020)
22. ISO/TC 145/SC 2 - Safety identification, signs, shapes, symbols and colours. https://www.iso.org/cms/render/live/en/sites/isoorg/contents/data/committee/05/26/52692.html. Accessed 5 May 2022
23. NetworkX—NetworkX documentation. https://networkx.org/. Accessed 5 May 2022

A Risk Model to Promote Collaborative Logistics Networks

Vitor Anes[1,3](✉), António Abreu[1,2], Ana Dias[1], and João Calado[1,3]

[1] Instituto Superior de Engenharia de Lisboa, Instituto Politécnico de Lisboa,
Rua Conselheiro Emídio Navarro, 1, 19559-007 Lisbon, Portugal
`vitor.anes@isel.pt`
[2] CTS - Uninova, Lisbon, Portugal
[3] IDMEC, Instituto Superior Técnico, Universidade de Lisboa, Av. Rovisco Pais, 1,
1049-001 Lisbon, Portugal

Abstract. One of the most common wastes in the transportation of goods is empty transportation. In recent years, collaborative network models have shown promising results in reducing the waste caused by empty transport. However, despite the associated benefits, adherence to these logistical models is far from the expected due to the associated risks. In order to encourage new collaborators to join collaborative networks in the freight transportation sector, this work developed a model for assessing and managing reputational risk, with the aim of making the whole process of managing collaborative networks clearer, more efficient, and more predictable. The developed model was implemented in an illustrative case study in which collaborators of a collaborative network were prioritized according to their reputation risk. The results show that the developed model enables collaborators of a network to participate in the selection of their respective partners according to their reputational risk.

Keywords: Reputational risk · Risk assessment and management ·
Collaborative logistics networks · Partner selection · Logistic sector

1 Introduction

The logistics sector plays a key role in the economy. Products, goods, and services are fundamental to the growth and maintenance of a society's prosperity, therefore, negative impacts in this sector also have negative impacts on society. In particular, negative impacts on the freight transport sector have an almost immediate effect on the end consumer. This sector is highly dependent on fuel prices, which translates into rising operating costs. Indeed, the price of fuel results from two aspects: on the one hand, the relationship between supply and demand and, on the other, regulatory measures aimed at regulating the consumption of fossil fuels through ever higher taxes in order to promote environmental sustainability. In this sense, it is important to reduce waste in freight transport in order to reduce both the operating costs and the environmental footprint of

L. M. Camarinha-Matos et al. (Eds.): PRO-VE 2022, IFIP AICT 662, pp. 475–487, 2022.
https://doi.org/10.1007/978-3-031-14844-6_38

the sector. In fact, reducing the sector's environmental footprint should also be a concern for this industry, in order to promote potential relief from fuel tax restrictions.

One of the most consequential wastes in the freight sector is the empty return of a logistics mission. To reduce waste, a logistics mission optimizes delivery routes, selects the vehicle with the appropriate load capacity, and packages freight in a way that fully utilizes the available load capacity and aligns freight organization with the delivery route. However, in the return to the company for a new logistics job, the vehicle returns empty and without freight, which incurs costs. These costs can be broken down into vehicle wear and tear, fuel costs and costs for unproductive driver activities.

Recently, collaborative networks have been shown to be a solution to reduce empty vehicle waste [1]. However, despite the benefits, the adoption of this new logistics model is not as high as expected. In general, this type of collaborative network is managed by virtual companies that collect operational information from their collaborators and distribute logistics orders to them based on the information exchanged between the collaborators and the virtual company. In practice, the virtual enterprise aims to reduce idle transportation using the information at its disposal through multi-criteria decision making.

For example, if a particular collaborator in the collaborative network has an order to transport goods from the south to the north, the transport will be empty when he returns. To avoid this waste, the virtual enterprise checks if the transport of goods from north to south is performed by another collaborator. If this is the case, the collaborator who would drive empty from north to south will transport these goods. The network collaborator who placed the logistics order from north to south will receive the corresponding payment from his customer, and the collaborator who transported the goods will have a future transport credit that can be executed by another collaborator under the same conditions. This approach not only reduces waste, but also enables faster delivery of goods, which somehow promotes the link between the supplier and the end customer.

1.1 Industrial Need

These collaborative networks must have a large number of collaborators in order for their benefits to be more prominent, i.e., the larger the number of collaborators in the network, the more attractive it becomes to belong to the network. In this sense, the larger the number of collaborators, the less likely those collaborators will experience empty run events, and the less operational waste they will have. However, there are some operational aspects of this type of collaborative network that have caused some mistrust among potential collaborators, which is why the adoption of this logistical model has not been as expected.

The most sensitive issues are the disclosure of information to the virtual company and the possible negative impact on the satisfaction of logistics customers due to the quality of the transport services provided by third parties (other network collaborator). The exchange of operational information between collaborators is a very delicate point, since the collaborators of the network have the same field of activity and compete with each other.

It is the virtual company's responsibility to ensure that each collaborator's information is managed securely and confidentially to promote the sustainability of each collaborator, thus preventing collaborators from leaving the collaborative network. However, despite the fundamental role that the virtual enterprise plays in information management, potential collaborators find it difficult to share their operational information because of the risks involved. In addition, the execution of their logistical tasks by other collaborators can have a negative impact on reputation.

A customer portfolio is built on the basis of trust and the quality of the service provided, being necessary a customer satisfaction-based process to construct a successful portfolio which takes a long time to build. In this sense, the provision of logistics services by third party collaborators can have an impact on the reputation of the collaborator who placed the logistics order, resulting in the loss of logistics customers and consequently a decrease in the company's business volume. These fears are justified, and if there is no effective control over them, collaborators can have a negative impact that could jeopardize the survival of their company.

It is incumbent upon the virtual enterprise to develop prevention and mitigation measures to protect the interests of network collaborators in a reliable and resilient manner. However, it appears that in current models of collaborative networks in logistics, these barriers are not yet clear and effective enough to reassure both collaborators who are already part of the collaborative network and potential collaborators, especially in terms of reputational impacts, as these impacts may come not only from the virtual company but also from other collaborators in the network.

1.2 Research Question

Consistent with solving the industrial problem described, this work aims to develop a decision support model to help select collaborative partners in a collaborative logistics network. The purpose of this model is, first, to quantify the reputational risk that a collaborator takes when it awards a particular logistics contract to another collaborator at a particular time, and second, to allow the virtual enterprise to manage the reputational risk of each collaborator. The goal of the proposed model is not to reduce waste, because there are already models for collaborative networks proposed by several authors for this purpose [1, 2].

The problem is that the collaborative network must have a critical size, i.e., it must have a number of collaborators that allows the network to function efficiently.

However, in practice, it is difficult to achieve this number of collaborators due to uncertainties related to reputational risks, such as the impact that a particular logistics order may have on the end customer, which in turn may have an impact on the supplier and finally on the collaborator. In this sense, the proposed model aims to reassure the collaborator by providing information about the reputational risk of the other collaborators in the network. In this sense, the collaborator that places a logistics order can cancel the order if the collaborator that will execute the logistics order has a higher reputation risk. This capability makes the collaborative network much more attractive and shares decision-making responsibilities between the virtual enterprise and its collaborators. This encourages the recruitment of new collaborators and the retention of those who are already part of the collaborative network.

1.3 Managerial Insights

In practice, the model developed should make it possible to clarify the level of risk to which each collaborative network collaborator is exposed, to clarify the understanding of the prevention and mitigation barriers developed and implemented in the collaborative network, to enable each collaborator to, query the reputational risk of each collaborator in the network, enable the collaborator placing the logistics order to query the level of reputational risk of the collaborator to whom the logistics order was placed, and in this way enable the collaborator placing the logistics order to review the placement of the order.

The model described in this work allows the collaborator who places the logistics order to be involved in the selection of the network collaborator who will execute it. In this way, risks with potential impact on the collaborators of the network should be minimized. This promotes compliance of the collaborative network, increases its efficiency in reducing empty transport waste and reduces the environmental footprint of freight transport.

1.4 Paper Structure

This paper is divided into 5 sections, beginning with the introduction, which describes the research context through a holistic approach, the research question, and the practical applications of the research findings. Then, the literature review briefly reviews recent work on risk assessment and risk management in collaborative networks. In the third section, the model of reputational risk is presented. In the following section, a hypothetical case study is used to illustrate the application of the model and the analysis of the results obtained. Finally, the last section presents the conclusions of the paper and future work to be conducted following this research.

2 Literature Review

2.1 Collaborative Networks

The first studies of collaborative networks in the literature date back to the 1990s [3]. Since then, research in this area has increased and currently includes about 60,000 scientific articles in a variety of research areas, including sociology, agriculture, medicine, engineering, and others. The benefits of this type of management and decision making are undeniable, with the most obvious benefits being resource sharing and risk sharing [4, 5].

It is interesting to note that patterns of cooperation can even be observed in nature, such as protocooperation between animals of the same species, as in the case of ants working together to carry objects much larger than themselves, bees through task sharing, birds and fish working together to protect themselves from predators. There is also cooperation between animals of different species, also called facultative mutualism, as in the case of the crab and the sea anemone, where the crab carries the sea anemone, and the sea anemone protects the crab from predators. It appears that the survival of these species, which are endangered in some sense, depends on their ability to cooperate.

Similarly, collaborative networks aim to bring companies together with a common goal, resulting in benefits that would otherwise be difficult for these companies to achieve. The increasingly demanding challenges in the modern economy threaten the survival of lower capacity companies in some ways, and the collaborative approach is a natural survival solution [6].

Because of the transversality of the concept, there are different types of collaborative networks, such as social networks, virtual organizations, virtual enterprises, and agile enterprises. Each type of collaborative network has its specifics, but there are certain basic requirements common to all types of networks that must be ensured for the proper functioning of a given collaborative network [7]. Essentially, these requirements are the sharing of information, decision making with consideration of the other participants in the collaborative network, the promotion of trust, the sharing of resources, and the application of integrative strategies.

In many situations, these requirements are compromised by a lack of trust, the adoption of inconsistent business strategies, the absence of a holistic view of business strategy, and insufficient information. These issues have hampered the effectiveness of collaborative networks, particularly the lack of trust, and have contributed to few new collaborators joining because the risk of sharing sensitive business information with third parties can threaten the survival of the organization [2]. In this sense, risk analysis and management in collaborative networks is a recurring research topic. The fundamental goal is to support the decision-making process of the network's collaborators.

For example, the literature contains work on risk analysis and risk management in collaborative networks related to open innovation [8], project management [9], information sharing [10], information management [11], and the sharing of human and material resources [12]. It can be concluded that risk analysis and risk management play a key role in managing collaborative networks.

2.2 Reputational Risk

Nobanee et al. [13] developed a bibliometric analysis focused on reputational risk in 2021. The study analyzes the 88 major publications that appeared between 2001 and 2020 and concludes that the amount of work done in this area is very small compared to the need and that more research needs to be done to meet existing operational needs. Indeed, a company's reputation is its most valuable asset. If this reputation is compromised, the resulting negative effects can threaten the survival of the company. In this sense, reputational risk can be considered as the damage caused to the company if it fails to meet the expectations placed on it. Reputational risk analysis and management models can be an extremely useful tool to minimize or even eliminate these impacts and strengthen the resilience of companies that are highly exposed to this type of risk.

One of the risk factors with the greatest impact on the proper functioning of collaborative networks is also reputational risk [14]. Impacts to a particular company's reputation can lead to irreversible damage or even destruction of the company. With this in mind, companies are increasingly concerned about their image and reputation when interacting with their customers [15, 16]. In collaborative logistics networks, this interaction with the customer is lost, since the company who executes the logistics order is a company working together in the collaborative network, rather than the company that has a relationship with the customer who needs the logistics service. In this sense, companies have concerns about joining collaborative logistics networks because it could have a negative impact on their reputation.

However, for collaborative networks to be effective, they must have a sufficient number of collaborators so that the benefits justify the risk taken. This indicates that there is a real need to develop models for risk analysis and risk management related to reputational risk in collaborative logistics networks [3]. There are a large number of models in the literature for reputational risk in different activity domains. However, for collaborative logistics networks, to the best of the authors' knowledge, there is no systematic and effective approach to assess and manage reputational risk. In this sense, this work aims to fill this knowledge gap and contribute to the sustainability of collaborative networks.

3   Reputational Risk Model for Collaborative Networks

The strategy for developing the reputation risk model is based on the analysis of supplier and customer satisfaction in the provision of the logistics service. In this sense, the development of the model begins with the identification of the most important factors in the assessment of customer satisfaction, followed by the identification of logistics operations with potential negative impact on these factors. Then, the causal relationships between customer satisfaction and logistics operations are identified. To quantify the impact of each logistics operation on customer satisfaction, an impact table is developed and later used to assess reputational risk. Then, based on causal diagrams, reliability theory, event trees, and fault trees, a mathematical expression is developed to evaluate the reputation risk of each collaborator in the network. Finally, the expression developed in conjunction with the Monte Carlo model is used to prioritize the collaborators in the network according to their respective reputation risk.

Figure 1 shows the logistical operations that affect customer satisfaction factors. These operations are divided into 3 major groups, namely OP-order processing, shown in Sub-fig. 1 a), WH -warehousing, shown in Sub-fig. 1 b), and T-transportation, shown in Sub-fig. 1 C).

Customer satisfaction factors are divided into 4 groups, namely SQ for service quality, DSQ for distribution service quality, CSQ for customer service quality, and finally CBSQ for quality of services provided when transporting goods abroad.

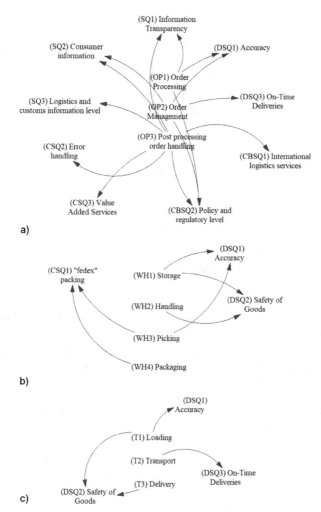

Fig. 1. Causal relationships between logistical processes and factors influencing customer satisfaction. a) Causal relationships during processing b) Causal relationships during storage c) Causal relationships during transport of goods. (SQ - service quality, DSQ - distribution service quality, CSQ - customer service quality, CBSQ - quality of services provided when transporting goods abroad)

Table 1 shows the impact of each customer satisfaction factor. These values were qualitatively assigned on a scale of 1 to 3. In this sense, the factor with the greatest impact has a rating of 3 and the factor with the least impact has a rating of 1.

Based on the diagrams shown in Fig. 1 and the classifications given in Table 1, and taking into account reliability theory, fault trees, and event trees, the expressions (Eqs. 1–3) that allow risk assessment for each of the previously mentioned groups of logistics operations were determined. In this formulation (Eqs. 1–3), the probability of failure of a particular collaborator in the logistics operations is represented by P_{FOP},

Table 1. Factors that influence customer satisfaction and respective impact scores.

Area	Item	I_Score
Service quality	Information transparency	2
	Consumer information security	3
	Logistics and customs information level	1
Distribution service quality	Accuracy	2
	Safety of goods	3
	On-time deliveries	3
Customer service quality	fedex packing	2
	Error handling	3
	Value-added services	1
Cross-border service quality	International logistics services	3
	Policy and regulatory level	2

P_{FWH} and P_{FT}. These probabilities were considered along with the probability of failure of prevention barriers, represented by P_{PB}, and the probability of failure of mitigation barriers, represented by P_{MB}. In addition, in this formulation, the variables beginning with "I" represent the influence that each customer satisfaction factor described in Table 1 has on overall satisfaction. The values of these variables are taken from Table 1.

$$
OP_{risk} =
\begin{aligned}
&P_{FOP1} \cdot P_{PB\_OP1} \cdot \left(P_{MB\_SQ1} \cdot I_{SQ1\_score} + P_{MB\_DSQ1} \cdot I_{DSQ1\_score}\right. \\
&\left. + P_{MB\_CBSQ2} \cdot I_{CBSQ2\_score}\right) \\
&+ \\
&P_{FOP2} \cdot P_{PB\_OP2} \cdot \left(P_{MB\_SQ2} \cdot I_{SQ2\_score} + P_{MB\_DSQ1} \cdot I_{DSQ1\_score}\right. \\
&\left. + P_{MB\_DSQ3} \cdot I_{DSQ3\_score} + P_{MB\_CBSQ2} \cdot I_{CBSQ2\_score}\right) \\
&+ \\
&P_{FOP3} \cdot P_{PB\_OP3} \cdot \left(P_{MB\_SQ1} \cdot I_{SQ1\_score} + P_{MB\_SQ2} \cdot I_{SQ2\_score}\right. \\
&+ P_{MB\_SQ3} \cdot I_{SQ3\_score} + P_{MB\_CSQ2} \cdot I_{CSQ2\_score} + P_{MB\_CSQ3} \cdot I_{CSQ3\_score} \\
&\left. + P_{MB\_CBSQ1} \cdot I_{CBSQ1\_score} + P_{MB\_CBSQ2} \cdot I_{CBSQ2\_score}\right)
\end{aligned}
\tag{1}
$$

$$
WH_{risk} =
\begin{aligned}
&P_{FWH1} \cdot P_{PB\_WH1} \cdot \left(P_{MB\_DSQ1} \cdot I_{DSQ1\_score} + P_{MB\_DSQ2} \cdot I_{DSQ2\_score}\right) \\
&+ P_{FWH2} \cdot P_{PB\_WH2} \cdot P_{MB\_DSQ2} \cdot I_{DSQ2\_score} \\
&+ \\
&P_{FWH3} \cdot P_{PB\_WH3} \cdot \left(P_{MB\_DSQ1} \cdot I_{DSQ1\_score} + P_{MB\_CSQ1} \cdot I_{CSQ1\_score}\right) \\
&+ P_{FWH4} \cdot P_{PB\_WH4} \cdot P_{MB\_CSQ1} \cdot I_{CSQ1\_score}
\end{aligned}
\tag{2}
$$

$$
T_{risk} =
\begin{aligned}
&P_{FT1} \cdot P_{PB\_T1} \cdot \left(P_{MB\_DSQ1} \cdot I_{DSQ1\_score} + P_{MB\_DSQ2} \cdot I_{DSQ2\_score}\right) \\
&+ \\
&P_{FT2} \cdot P_{PB\_T2} \cdot P_{MB\_DSQ3} \cdot I_{DSQ3\_score} + P_{FT3} \cdot P_{PB\_T3} \cdot P_{MB\_DSQ2} \cdot I_{DSQ2\_score}
\end{aligned}
\tag{3}
$$

Equation 4 is used to assess reputational risk, where the sum of the risks of each group identified in Eqs. 1 through 3 represents the total reputational risk. Equation 4 allows network collaborators to be prioritized according to their respective reputational risk. These results can also be used as an indicator of the quality of each employee in the network and can be used in continuous improvement initiatives.

$$Risk_{reputation} = OP_{risk} + WH_{risk} + T_{risk} \tag{4}$$

4 Illustrative Case Study

This section illustrates the applicability of the model described in the previous section. To this end, we consider two network collaborators, companies X and Y. The first step in applying the model is to determine the failure probabilities for each company for both the logistic operations and the respective prevention and mitigation barriers. Tables 2 and 3 show these probabilities, taking into account the mean and the respective standard deviation. The actual collection and analysis of these data requires a separate study, which is not part of the objectives of this study and is referred to future work. With this in mind, it is assumed that the data in Tables 2 and 3 represent the performance of individual companies.

Table 2. Logistic process and preventive barriers failure probabilities for companies X and Y.

	Company X				Company Y			
	Normal distribution for failures in logistic processes		Normal distribution for failures in **preventive barriers**		Normal distribution for failures in logistic processes		Normal distribution for failures in **preventive barriers**	
	μ	σ	μ	σ	μ	σ	μ	σ
(1) Order processing	0,4	0,1	0,3	0,1	0,3	0,2	0,4	0,2
(2) Order management	0,3	0,1	0,4	0,15	0,35	0,1	0,4	0,15
(3) Post processing	0,42	0,2	0,2	0,1	0,4	0,2	0,3	0,1
(1) Storage	0,3	0,2	0,4	0,2	0,3	0,1	0,5	0,2
(2) Handling	0,4	0,15	0,5	0,1	0,35	0,15	0,6	0,2
(3) Picking	0,35	0,1	0,4	0,2	0,6	0,1	0,3	0,2
(4) Packaging	0,4	0,2	0,4	0,1	0,4	0,2	0,4	0,2
(1) Loading	0,6	0,2	0,6	0,1	0,3	0,14	0,5	0,1
(2) Transport	0,4	0,2	0,3	0,1	0,5	0,2	0,2	0,1
(3) Delivery	0,2	0,1	0,5	0,2	0,3	0,1	0,3	0,1

Normal distributions were used for the failure probabilities presented in Tables 2 through Table 4 because they apply relatively well to failures associated with human performance. The inclusion of the standard deviation along with the mean serves to account for the variability that is always present in the scenarios used to evaluate the failure probabilities.

To account for the variability in failure probabilities, a Monte Carlo simulation was performed, updating the average values of Tables 2 and 3 over 10000 iterations. Equation 4 was evaluated and plotted for each iteration. Based on these results, the respective average value of reputational risk and the respective standard deviation for each company were determined. Table 4 shows these results.

Table 3. Mitigation barriers failure probabilities for companies X and Y.

	Impact score	Company X		Company Y	
		Normal distribution for failures in **mitigation barriers**		Normal distribution for failures in **mitigation barriers**	
		μ	σ	μ	σ
(1) Information transparency	2	0,2	0,1	0,5	0,1
(2) Consumer information security	3	0,3	0,2	0,6	0,1
(3) Logistics and customs information level	1	0,4	0,1	0,3	0,1
(1) Accuracy	2	0,5	0,1	0,3	0,1
(2) Safety of goods	3	0,3	0,1	0,3	0,1
(3) On-time deliveries	3	0,5	0,1	0,4	0,1
(1) "fedex" packing	2	0,3	0,1	0,3	0,1
(2) Error handling	3	0,2	0,1	0,4	0,2
(3) Value-added services	1	0,5	0,1	0,5	0,1
(1) International logistics services	3	0,3	0,1	0,6	0,1
(2) Policy and regulatory level	2	0,2	0,1	0,5	0,1

Table 4. Results for companies X and Y regarding their reputational risk.

Company X Reputational risk		Company Y Reputational risk	
μ	Σ	μ	σ
2,73	0,63	2,90	0,81

The results presented in Table 4 cannot be used directly to prioritize companies according to their respective reputational risk, as the respective standard deviation must also be taken into account in addition to the average value of the reputational risk. With this in mind, and based on the results of the Monte Carlo simulation, the relative risk between the two companies was determined. Table 5 shows the results of this analysis. It can be seen that the probability that the reputational risk of company Y is greater than the reputational risk of company X, i.e., company X is the company with the lowest reputational risk.

Table 5. Relative reputational risk between companies X and Y.

>	Company X	Company Y
Company X	0	0,40
Company Y	0,58	0

The model described relates a set of logistical operations related to freight transportation to the factors that have the greatest impact on customer satisfaction. By combining this relationship, the reputational risk of a particular partner in the network is obtained, which allows ranking between pairs.

These factors for logistics operations and customer satisfaction were identified through a literature review and correlated in this paper. Although the structure of the model is predefined, it is possible to make adjustments as needed by updating Eqs. 1–3 and also the scores presented in Table 1. In this sense, the described model is versatile enough to be adapted over time.

The implementation of the model in practice is simple and fast and can be implemented both in customized computer applications and in commercial software such as Excel, which means that the entire model can be automated, requiring only the introduction or updating of the information related to the failure probabilities of each network member. Capturing the probabilities of failure associated with the reality of the partner companies is critical in order to take advantage of the inherent benefits of the model described. At the beginning of the company's participation in the collaborative network, this information can be obtained through questionnaires sent by the virtual company to the newly added collaborating company. With the participation of this company, questionnaires can be sent to customers (suppliers and end customers) over time to update the failure probabilities.

5   Conclusions

In this article, the problem of the lack of collaborators in collaborative logistics networks is analyzed. It is shown that reputational risk is one of the main reasons for this limited accession. As a result, the efficiency of these networks is affected by the uncertainty about the potential impact on the reputation of their collaborators. In this sense, and in order to encourage the joining of collaborators to the network, this work has developed a methodology for the analysis and management of reputational risk through the theory of reliability, failure tree analysis, event trees, and the Monte Carlo method. The model developed is qualitative and allows adjustments during its application in practice. The model developed is intended to reduce uncertainty about reputational risk and allow network collaborators to participate in the selection of the network collaborator that will perform the logistical task they specify. In this way, the participation of collaborators in the network becomes more transparent, which encourages the participation of existing and future collaborators in the network which increases the size of the network, and consequently increases its efficiency. The developed model can be easily implemented in practice and can be used as an indicator of the quality of the network's collaborators. It can be used not only in the selection of the collaborator for a particular logistical task, but also as a tool for continuous improvement. In the future, it is expected that the methods for evaluating the probability of failure of each collaborator in the different areas of the model will be improved. This improvement, based on new information technologies, includes the introduction of online questionnaires for both suppliers and end users.

Acknowledgments. This work was supported by the Polytechnic Institute of Lisbon through the Projects for Research, Development, Innovation and Artistic Creation (IDI&CA), within the framework of the project ReEdIA—Risk Assessment and Management in Open Innovation, IPL/2021/ReEdIA_ISEL. This work was also supported by FCT, through CTS, project UIDB/00066/2020.

References

1. Vargas, A., Fuster, C., Corne, D.: Towards sustainable collaborative logistics using specialist planning algorithms and a gain-sharing business model: a UK case study. Sustainability **12**, 6627 (2020)
2. Akintoye, A., Main, J.: Collaborative relationships in construction: the UK contractors' perception. Eng. Constr. Archit. Manage. **14**, 597–617 (2007)
3. Camarinha-Matos, L.M., Afsarmanesh, H.: Collaborative networks: a new scientific discipline. J. Intell. Manuf. **16**, 439–452 (2005)
4. Romero, D., Galeano, N., Molina, A.: Mechanisms for assessing and enhancing organisations' readiness for collaboration in collaborative networks. Int. J. Prod. Res. **47**, 4691–4710 (2009)
5. Feiock, R.C., Lee, I.W., Park, H.J.: Administrators' and elected officials' collaboration networks: selecting partners to reduce risk in economic development. Public Adm. Rev. **72**, S58–S68 (2012)
6. Pan, S., Trentesaux, D., Ballot, E., Huang, G.Q.: Horizontal collaborative transport: survey of solutions and practical implementation issues. Int. J. Prod. Res. **57**, 5340–5361 (2019)
7. Asadifard, R., Chookhachi Zadeh Moghadam, A., Goodarzi, M.: A model for classification and study of success factors in international collaborative networks. Innov. Manage. J. **5**, 129–150 (2023)
8. Santos, R., Abreu, A., Dias, A., Calado, J.M., Anes, V., Soares, J.: A framework for risk assessment in collaborative networks to promote sustainable systems in innovation ecosystems. Sustainability **12**, 6218 (2020)
9. Nunes, M., Dias, A., Abreu, A., Martins, J.D.M.: A predictive risk model based on social network analysis. In: Modelling and Simulation, pp. 82–88 (2020)
10. Alawamleh, M., Popplewell, K.: Risk in collaborative networks: relationships analysis. Int. J. Serv. Oper. Manage. **12**, 431–446 (2012)
11. Durugbo, C.: Managing information for collaborative networks. Ind. Manage. Data Syst. **20**, 1207–1228 (2014)

12. Camarinha-Matos, L.M., Fornasiero, R., Ramezani, J., Ferrada, F.: Collaborative networks: a pillar of digital transformation. Appl. Sci. **9**, 5431 (2019)
13. Nobanee, H., Alhajjar, M., Abushairah, G., Al Harbi, S.: Reputational risk and sustainability: a bibliometric analysis of relevant literature. Risks **9**, 134 (2021)
14. Scott, S.V., Walsham, G.: Reconceptualizing and managing reputation risk in the knowledge economy: toward reputable action. Organ. Sci. **16**, 308–322 (2005)
15. Petersen, H.L., Lemke, F.: Mitigating reputational risks in supply chains. Supply Chain Manage. Int. J. **20**, 495–510 (2015)
16. Blom, T., Niemann, W.: Managing reputational risk during supply chain disruption recovery: a triadic logistics outsourcing perspective. J. Transp. Supply Chain Manage. **16**, 13 (2022)

Resilience and Sustainability of Freight Transport: A Comprehensive Review

Nesrine Kharrat[1,2,3], Nadia Hamani[2(✉)], Mounir Benaissa[3], and Lyes Kermad[1]

[1] Laboratory of QUARTZ, University of Paris 8, 140 Rue de la Nouvelle France, Montreuil, France
nesrine.kharrat@etud.univ-paris8.fr, l.kermad@iut.univ-paris8.fr
[2] Laboratory of Innovative Technologies, University of Picardie Jules Verne, 48 Rue d'Ostende, Saint-Quentin, France
nadia.hamani@u-picardie.fr
[3] OASIS (Optimization and Analysis of Industrial and Service Systems) Laboratory, University of Sfax, Sfax, Tunisia
mounir.benaissa@isgis.usf.tn

Abstract. Market disruption has made the freight transport (FT) activities more complex. In this context and for competitive reasons, companies must operate in more resilient manner to solve problems related to changes without damaging their economic, environmental and social performance. Therefore, a communicative indicator used to monitor the performance of FT and enhance development by prioritizing improvements is crucial. However, the resilience measures of FT were not widely studied in the literature. In this paper, we propose a systematic review of FT resilience by defining it, identifying its indicators and focusing on its synergies with sustainability and collaboration. This work provides a comprehensive view of resilience and the new directions for future research works.

Keywords: Resilience · Freight transport · Key performance indicators · Sustainability · Collaboration

1 Introduction

Good movement is fundamental to the economic vitality [1]. Despite its important role in sustaining a given area, FT is widely recognized for its unsustainable consequences. In fact, it is the source of several economic, environmental and social disturbances that threaten the citizens' quality of life. With the unexpected changes, these harmful impacts are constantly increasing. Thus, setting up a resilient system has become important. Nowadays, the application of the concept of resilience in FT worldwide is increasingly necessary due to the disastrous effects of the COVID-19 pandemic [2].

Faced with the rise of vulnerability to risk and the accumulation of FT impacts, FT operators should deal with what we adopt or change into something new and better [3]. To deal with this issue, many questions arise:

© IFIP International Federation for Information Processing 2022
Published by Springer Nature Switzerland AG 2022
L. M. Camarinha-Matos et al. (Eds.): PRO-VE 2022, IFIP AICT 662, pp. 488–500, 2022.
https://doi.org/10.1007/978-3-031-14844-6_39

- *What is resilience? what are its main characteristics and its assessing indicators in FT?*
- *How can resilience contribute to the sustainability of FT?*
- *How can collaborative strategy lead to a resilient system?*

The present work aims at identifying communicative resilient indicators that monitor and defining the barriers to FT development. It also emphasizes the importance of using them to improve FT sustainability and addresses the importance of collaboration in building a resilient FT system.

This manuscript is organized as follows. The next section describes the adopted research methodology. In Sect. 3, the definitions of resilience are presented. In Sect. 4, we extract the FT resilience indicators from literature. The importance of resilience to achieve the sustainability of FT is addressed in Sect. 5. In Sect. 6, we highlighted the importance of collaboration to make the system more resilient. In the last section, the conclusion and the future directions are presented.

2 Research Methodology

To provide a guideline to firms and states and help them understand the importance of resilience in the FT system, we conducted a comprehensive review to define resilience, present its characteristics and indicators and determine its relation with sustainability. This is to point out significant findings and prospects research in the FT field.

The systematic literature review comprises five steps inspired from [4]. These steps are: (1) defining research question formulation, (2) keywords definition, (3) presenting inclusion and exclusion criteria, (4) searching database and collecting data, and (5) analyzing and discussing the obtained results. The proposed approach is presented in Fig. 1.

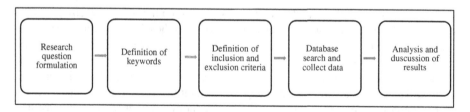

Fig. 1. Research approach.

To select papers, we conducted a search by using the identified keywords: "Resilience", "Collaboration", "Sustainability", "Performance", "Assessment", "Indicators", "Transport" and "Freight". For this, we chose the most widely used databases such as: Google scholar, Science direct and ResearchGate.

In this bibliographic search, we adopted certain inclusion and exclusion criteria defined to refine the literature search. Three inclusion criteria were adopted:

- Selecting the most recent study

- Focusing on works peer-reviewed academic journals
- Considering resilience in all fields

Only articles written in English and French languages were included. A set of 46 papers were selected for the analysis.

3 Resilience Definitions

Risk management is an area of early research. It is the process of identifying, evaluating and controlling undesirable events that may affect the achievement of an organization's goals. This process is the best way to prepare eventualities. It could improve the operational efficiency, safety and security of the system and allows achieving competitive advantages. Recently, with the emergency of the resilience paradigm, risk management has never been more important. Indeed, many practitioners have considered it as a part of resilience management [5]. Comtois al. [6] described resilience as the capacity to increase resilience and generate technical and social systems. Although the resilience concept has appeared 40 years ago, FT has not received much attention. In this section, we review the definitions given in literature defining resilience and we present its characteristics.

Resilience has become wide-ranging and multidisciplinary which is described in several domains. Because of the multiple definitions of resilience and its related concepts, researchers cannot give a universal definition. In fact, to deal with disruptions, several keywords could be used (e.g. resilience, transformative resilience and antifragility) [7]. Resilience is defined as the capacity of a system to recover from a shock. This concept has been used in different contexts. Hosseini [8] classified resilience into four types, namely organizational, social, economic and engineering. First, the organizational domain is the capability to cope with unanticipated shocks and learn after they become manifest. Sheffi et al. [9] linked resilience to companies that consider resilience as the stability and the speed at which companies could return to their normal performance level. In social domains, resilience is tied to individuals, groups, communities and environmental capacities. However, economic resilience is described as the inherent ability and adaptive response that enable companies and regions to limit their losses [10]. On the other hand, in engineering, it is a new concept compared to other fields. According to [11], resilience is the intrinsic ability of a system to adjust its functionality in the presence of disturbances and unanticipated changes. In literature, we can distinguish between adaptive and transformative resilience. Indeed, adaptive resilience aims at resisting a disruption and maintaining the existing structure, while transformative resilience aims at reorganizing, reconfiguring, restructuring and reinventing the system when it is important [12]. It is a radical change. However, antifragility differs from resilience. Indeed, the resilient resists shocks and stays the same, while the antifragile improves [13]. It also refers to the survival of a system facing a disruption. It is a convex response resulting in a positive sensitivity to increased volatility.

In our perspective, FT is considered as a part of engineering. Zhou et al. [14] defined resilience in the transport sector based on the transportation mode. The authors affirmed that all definitions are based on the same general idea whose objective is to quantify resilience as a function of the ability of a system to maintain its functionality under disruptions and determine the required time and resources to restore the performance level after disruptions. In the field of FT, Ta et al. [15] defined resilience as the ability of the system to reduce the consequences and the impacts of disruptions and maintain freight mobility.

Any disrupted system has four main states [16]: preparation, absorption, recovery and adaptation state (See Fig. 2).

Preparedness State ($t_0 \rightarrow t_d$): In this phase, the system operates under normal conditions. The anticipation of a disruptive event could lead to the preparation of preventive actions. Therefore, the use of historical data to predict system damage is important.

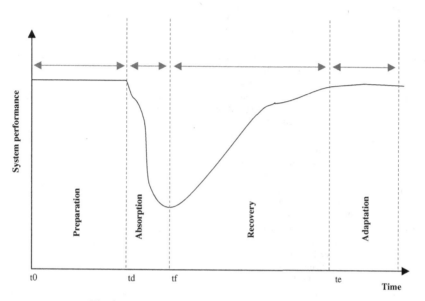

Fig. 2. Resilience performance in function of time.

Absorption State ($t_d \rightarrow t_f$): When a disruptive event occurs, the system must absorb the damage. In this way, the potential impact may exceed the threshold estimated in the preparation phase. Therefore, the system performance will be reduced. In this regard, the system must absorb the shocks without destroying the structures and the relationships between the system components and its performance.

Recovery State ($t_f \rightarrow t_e$): It is the state of the system transition from its damaged state to its steady state. To do so, it is important to set up a resource management process to respond and restore the system operations and service availability to their pre-event capacity and efficiency.

Adaptation State: It occurs immediately after the restoration of the damaged system when the recovery state is over. It consists in learning from unpredictable event and improving the adaptability of the system that makes it more flexible to future disturbances.

Each state incorporates many characteristics of resilience to understand the resilience term and assess the system performance. In Table 1, the most frequently used terms are presented.

Table 1. Resilience key characteristics.

Characteristic	Definition	State				Reference
		Prepara-tion	Dis-turbed	Re-covery	Adapta-tion	
Anticipation	The capacity to learn, adapt, take precautions, persist, and return the system to normal state after a disruption	✓				[17]
Absorption	The ability of a system to absorb, resist and mitigate the consequences of disturbance		✓	✓		[17]
Adaptability	The capacity of a system to absorb perturbations and to adapt to unexpected conditions by accepting certain adjustments		✓	✓	✓	[17, 18]
Recoverability	The capacity to recover, repair and restore damage to return to a stable state of functionality		✓	✓		[17]
Reliability	The probability that a system will continue to operate after a disruptive event	✓				[19]
Redundancy	The capacity of certain components of a system to take over the functions of failed components without degrading the system performance		✓			[3, 17, 18, 20]
Robustness	The capacity of the system components to resist and tolerate certain constraints without degrading the system		✓	✓		[14, 17, 18, 20, 21]
Vulnerability	It expresses the susceptibility of critical components of a transmission system and generally represents the operational performance of the system		✓			[3, 19]
Preparedness	The preparation of some measures before the interruption	✓			✓	[18]
Flexibility	The ability of a system to respond to disruptions and adapt to changes through contingency plans that are put in place after disruptions		✓	✓	✓	[3, 18, 21]

(continued)

Table 1. (*continued*)

Characteristic	Definition	State				Reference
		Prepara-tion	Dis-turbed	Re-covery	Adapta-tion	
Rapidity	The ability to respond to priorities and meet targets in a timely manner to limit losses and avoid future disruption		✓	✓		[18, 20]
Resourcefulness	The capacity to diagnose and prioritize problems and implement solutions by determining the material, monetary, informational, technological and human resources required			✓		[14]
Interdependence	It designates the connections of the components of the system or its dimensions		✓	✓		[18]
Survivability	The ability to resist unexpected disruptions while meeting the original requirements	✓	✓			[22]
Responsiveness	It increases costs while improving the level of service		✓			[17]

4 Identification of Resilience FT Indicators

Resilience is one of the most interesting topics in FT field. The evaluation of resilience is crucial to determine the system performance, which helps to understand its complexities and investigate different impacts of environmental, social and economic factors on resilience. Indicators are the best tools for decision making as they promote the monitoring of resilience and point out weaknesses of FT. Based on the literature results, the

Table 2. Summary of resilience indicators.

Dimensions	Indicators	Transport field					Other fields			
		[19]	[20]	[21]	[23]	[24]	[17]	[25]	[26]	[27]
Environment	Air quality									✓
	Use of natural resources									✓
	NO/SO2 emission									✓
	GHG emissions									✓
	Increase in global temperature									✓
Economic	Cost of disruption/damage	✓								
	Transport cost before and after disturbance	✓			✓					

(*continued*)

Table 2. (*continued*)

Dimensions	Indicators	Transport field					Other fields			
		[19]	[20]	[21]	[23]	[24]	[17]	[25]	[26]	[27]
	Recovery budget	✓								
	Energy consumption					✓				
	Infrastructure cost: cost of rebuilding the road	✓				✓				
	Loss rate						✓			
	Alternative modes		✓							
Social	Unemployment rate					✓				
	Equity of distribution									✓
	Social commitment									✓
	Density of the road network									✓
	Rate of increase of accidents									✓
	Road safety									✓
	Distance to nearest transport network									✓
	Level of accessibility	✓	✓	✓						
	Self-administered evacuation plans				✓					
	Integral part of disaster relief and recovery plan				✓					
	Availability of resources (human and material) to deal with disturbances		✓							

indicators of resilience in FT have not yet been studied. In this section, the indicators that are most frequently used to assess FT sector resilience are identified.

To develop a resilience evaluation process, the identification of useful resilience indicators has a crucial role. The resilience FT indicators are extracted from literature and summarized in Table 2.

A comprehensive review was conducted by [19] to compile an overview of the resilience measurement parameters that could be used to formulate resilience quantification and improve the strategies of the transportation system. Leobons et al. [20] used a set of indicators to measure the resilience of transport systems by focusing on urban mobility. To do so, a bibliometric analysis was carried out to reveal the influence of the ecological, social and economic domains of resilience on the transport domain. Roosta et al. [21] examined the resilience of the street network in three types of urban fabrics (a new street network, an old network and an average network). A formal network resilience indicator was identified based on previous studies. The work of Azad et al. [23] was performed in the field of FT to minimize the total cost after disruption. A decision framework was also proposed to determine the optimal measures to be adopted after a disruption to return the normal performance at the lowest possible cost. Fu and

Wang [24] proposed an Integrative Urban Resilience Capacity that integrates individual, economic, ecological, social and institutional indicators. It helps all stakeholders to take the most preferred scenario.

The context is not a barrier to get a comprehensive set of indicators, that is why we search other contexts to identify resilience indicators. Ahmadi et al. [17] pointed out that the energy performance, total cost, repair time, and damage performance are the key metrics used to analyze the energy system resiliency. In the context of community resilience, Yoon et al. [25] developed a methodology to construct a series of indicators utilized to assess the sustainability community resilience index (human, social, economic, environmental and institutional). The aim of the article [26] is to discuss the difficulty of identifying complex networks failures and predicting their environmental impacts on urban area. The manuscript presented an assessment flood indicators and mapped resilience levels by considering critical infrastructure networks as risk propagators at different spatial scales. Assarkhaniki et al. [27] conceptualized five key dimensions among twenty-one dimensions considered as frequently-addressed dimensions: economic, environmental, social, institutional and infrastructural.

According to the state of the art on FT, several studies have recently dealt with the issue of resilience. The present work defines the resilience concept, the type of resources and the characteristics that a transport system must have in order to be resilient.

In addition, we note that few studies identified indicators of resilience to respond to economic, environmental and social requirements in the FT sector.

5 Importance of Resilience to Sustainable FT: Similarities and Synergies

The existing literature defined a sustainable system as that meeting the needs of people and societies to satisfy the requirements of future generations. In literature, several definitions of sustainability were presented. In this study, we focus on the definitions that link sustainability to risk concepts.

Sustainability was defined as the system potential to maintain a desirable state or function over time [28]. Generally, sustainable systems are those that can be adapted to the changing circumstances [29]. Similarly, Milman and Short [30] pointed out that sustainability indicators should measure the system ability to adapt to unpredicted change and continue to operate over time. A performance indicator must take into consideration the risks and uncertainties that affect significantly the system [31]. These sustainability definitions include elements of resilience that can lead to the fuzzy understanding of sustainability and resilience.

The combination of sustainability and resilience has emerged in the literature under two main categories [32]: (i) the two concepts are synonymous and used indifferently [33] and (ii) resilience is a critical component of sustainability.

The sustainability of each activity is strongly related to the life-support ecosystems. In addition, if a development strategy is not resilient, it is not sustainable. However, the two concepts focus on survivability under disturbances events [3].

The literature indicated the lack of a conceptual framework for consolidating sustainability and resilience. In this regard, Marchese et al. [34] studied 17 frameworks. Three main integrations were identified:

- Resilience is an element of sustainability,
- Sustainability is an element of resilience,
- Sustainability and resilience have distinct goals.

The first framework considers resilience as a small part of a broader field of sustainability. In this state, the enhancement of resilience can make a system more sustainable. Conversely, increasing the sustainability of a system does not necessarily improve its resilience. As resilience is a support to the achievement of the sustainability goals set [35] a non-resilient system leads to sustainable fragility. Therefore, after any disturbance, a system is susceptible to recover its original stable state. Several works proposed a framework to assess sustainability and resilience performance by integrating economic, environmental and social indicators in the urban water sector. The second framework presents resilience as the goal of the system where sustainability is presented as a determinant of resilience. Indeed, increased sustainability makes the system more resilient. However, the reverse is not necessarily correct. In the third framework, sustainability and resilience are either complementary or competing. In this context, resilience does not promote sustainability and vice versa.

6 Importance of Collaboration to Build Resilient FT Network

Collaborative network is a novel emerging discipline focusing on the improvement of the network dynamism through collaboration between partners to better achieve common and compatible goals. It was defined, in [36], as a means that two or more independent firms work and plan jointly. There are two main types of collaboration categories: vertical collaboration, focusing on synchronization and coordination of the actors' operations [37], and horizontal collaboration occurring between actors that do not belong to the same supply chain but operating at the same level.

Several authors linked the concept of collaboration networks and resilience in the same definition. According to [38], risk management and collaboration are integrated. In fact, the resilience in the risk management field is presented as the mitigation risk process based on collaboration and coordination. In addition, Barratt [37] defined collaboration as the sharing of benefit and risk between partners by sharing information. Whipple and Russel [39] considered collaboration as an enabler to the synergy's development among stockholders by planning jointly and exchanging real-time information required to prepare, respond and recover in the face of disruptions. In a recent study, Poberschnigg et al. [40] have presented collaboration as a capability of resilience.

The more important question arising in this context is: "How collaborative strategy can lead to a resilient system?". To respond to this question, we are interested in literature highlighting the importance of collaboration to build resilient systems. Christopher and Peck [41] showed the importance of collaboration to build a resilient supply chain. They defined collaboration as glue that makes organizations work together in a crisis. Ergun et al. [42] stated that collaboration and information sharing contribute to faster risk response processes. Scholten and Schilder [43] identified the role of collaboration in improving resilience by increasing visibility, flexibility and velocity. Hendry et al. [44] showed that horizontal and vertical collaboration between stockholders is the best strategy to build supply chain resilience. Comtois et al. [6] emphasized the importance of collaboration and networked integration of information and operations to ensure that the transportation system is resilient and competitive in the marketplace. Lotfi and Larmour [45] found that collaboration helps supply chains be more resilient by improving anticipation, adaptation, response, recovery and learning from a disturbance. Azadegan and Dooley [46] explained the typology of resilience strategies related to different types of collaboration in the supply chain networks. They presented resilience in supply networks at the micro-level (between buyers and suppliers to recover the risk of the network), at the macro-level (between competing companies and government that manage together the risks on long-term) and at the meso-level when several supply networks collaborate on short and medium-term supply risks.

7 Discussion

We now give a summary discussion based on the various observations and insights gained from the literature review:

1. From the proposed definitions of resilience, we conclude that a clear and universal definition of resilience is required.
2. In literature, few studies identified resilience indicators in the FT sector. Our study fills this gap by determining economic, environmental and social indicators.
3. More research is needed to manage FT and build a sustainable and resilient system ([2] and [47]). Clearly, this is an important avenue of foundational research study that should be followed to minimize conflicts and maximize synergies between the two concepts based on a well-defined set of indicators.
4. Performance indicators are important to identify the best practices and strategies to improve the resilience of FT.
5. Combination of resilience and collaborative strategy is needed to create more synergies and improve the networks ([40, 43] and [46]).
6. Selection of solutions and strategy to improve sustainability and resilience of FT using tools integrating stakeholders in the decision-making process.

8 Conclusion

Recently, the efforts of assessing resilience in FT systems have become important in the presence of radical changes. The performance evaluation can help stockholders understand the state of resilience and highlight the need to enhance resilience abilities.

The aim of our work was to conduct a comprehensive review to: (1) understand resilience of FT; (2) identify the major indicators of resilience FT that influence the economic, environmental and social aspects; and (3) investigate the resilience importance in sustainable FT system by identifying the similarities and differences. This paper proposed a novel direction for the performance assessment of FT. Consequently, it is needed to introduce sustainable and resilient composite indicators that aggregate several indicators to control and monitor the actual state of performance. The development of a sustainable and resilient framework is also important to help decision-makers make the best decisions and improve the sustainability and resilience of the FT system by applying efficient strategies.

References

1. Muñuzuri, J., Larrañeta, J., Onieva, L., Cortés, P.: Solutions applicable by local administrations for urban logistics improvement. Cities **22**(1), 15–28 (2005)
2. Roostaie, S., Nawari, N.: The DEMATEL approach for integrating resilience indicators into building sustainability assessment frameworks. Build. Environ. **207**, 108113 (2022)
3. Lew, A.A., Ng, P.T., Ni, C.C., Wu, T.C.: Community sustainability and resilience: similarities, differences and indicators. Tour. Geogr. **18**(1), 18–27 (2016)
4. Durach, C.F., Kembro, J., Wieland, A.: A new paradigm for systematic literature reviews in supply chain management. J. Supply Chain Manage. **53**, 67–85 (2017)
5. Louisot, J.P.: Risk and/or resilience management. Risk Govern. Control Financ. Mark. Institutions **5**(2), 84–91 (2015)
6. Comtois, C.: Changements dans les conditions du marché international: essai sur la résilience des ports de vrac et perspectives à la Canada (2020)
7. Zitzmann, I.: How to cope with uncertainty in supply chains? – Conceptual Framework for agility, robustness, resilience, continuity and anti-fragility in supply chains. In: Kersten, W., Blecker, T., Ringle, C.M. (eds.) Next Generation Supply chains: Trends and Opportunities, pp. 361–377. Springer, Berlin (2014)
8. Hosseini, S., Barker, K., Ramirez-Marquez, J.E.: A review of definitions and measures of system resilience. Reliab. Eng. Syst. Saf. **145**, 47–61 (2016)
9. Sheffi, Y.: Resilience reduces risk. LogistQ, vol. 12, p. 1 (2006)
10. Rose, A., Liao, S.Y.: Modeling regional economic resilience to disasters: a computable general equilibrium analysis of water service disruptions. J. Reg. Sci. **45**(1), 75–112 (2005)
11. Prologue, H.E.: the scope of resilience engineering. In: Hollnagel, E., Paries, J., Woods, D.D., Wreathall, J., (eds.) Resilience Engineering in Practice: A Guidebook. Ashgate Publishing Company, USA (2010)
12. Ramezani, J., Camarinha-Matos, L.M.: Approaches for resilience and antifragility in collaborative business ecosystems. Technol. Forecast. Soc. Chang. **151**, 119846 (2020)
13. Taleb, N.N.: Antifragile: Things That Gain from Disorder. Random House Publishing Group, New York (2012)
14. Zhou, Y., Wang, J., Yang, H.: Resilience of transportation systems: concepts and comprehensive review. IEEE Trans. Intell. Transp. Syst. **20**(12), 4262–4276 (2019)
15. Ta, C., Goodchild, A.V., Pitera, K.: Structuring a definition of resilience for the freight transportation system. Transp. Res. Rec. **2097**(1), 19–25 (2009)
16. Sharifi, A., Yamagata, Y.: Principles and criteria for assessing urban energy resilience: a literature review. Renew. Sustain. Energy Rev. **60**, 1654–1677 (2016)
17. Ahmadi, S., Saboohi, Y., Vakili, A.: Frameworks, quantitative indicators, characters, and modeling approaches to analysis of energy system resilience: a review. Renew. Sustain. Energy Rev. **144**, 110988 (2021)
18. Gonçalves, L.A.P.J., Ribeiro, P.J.G.: Resilience of urban transportation systems. concept, characteristics, and methods. J. Transp. Geogr. **85**, 102727 (2020)
19. Ahmed, S., Dey, K.: Resilience modeling concepts in transportation systems: a comprehensive review based on mode, and modeling techniques. J. Infrastruct. Preserv. Resilience **1**(1), 1–20 (2020). https://doi.org/10.1186/s43065-020-00008-9
20. Leobons, C.M., Campos, V.B.G., de Mello Bandeira, R.A.: Assessing urban transportation systems resilience: a proposal of indicators. Transp. Res. Procedia **37**, 322–329 (2019)
21. Roosta, M., Javadpoor, M., Ebadi, M.: A study on street network resilience in urban areas by urban network analysis: comparative study of old, new and middle fabrics in Shiraz. Int. J. Urban Sci. **26**, 309–331 (2021)

22. Wan, C., Yang, Z., Zhang, D., Yan, X., Fan, S.: Resilience in transportation systems: a systematic review and future directions. Transp. Rev. **38**(4), 479–498 (2018)
23. Azad, N., Hassini, E., Verma, M.: Disruption risk management in railroad networks: an optimization-based methodology and a case study. Transp. Res. Part B Methodol. **85**, 70–88 (2016)
24. Fu, X., Wang, X.: Developing an integrative urban resilience capacity index for plan making. Environ. Syst. Decis. **38**(3), 367–378 (2018). https://doi.org/10.1007/s10669-018-9693-6
25. Yoon, D.K., Kang, J.E., Brody, S.D.: A measurement of community disaster resilience in Korea. J. Environ. Planning Manage. **59**(3), 436–460 (2016)
26. Serre, D., Heinzlef, C.: Assessing and mapping urban resilience to floods with respect to cascading effects through critical infrastructure networks. Int. J. Disaster Risk Reduction **30**, 235–243 (2018)
27. Assarkhaniki, Z., Rajabifard, A., Sabri, S.: The conceptualisation of resilience dimensions and comprehensive quantification of the associated indicators: a systematic approach. Int. J. Disaster Risk Reduction **51**, 101840 (2020)
28. Maclaren, V.W.: Urban sustainability reporting. J. Am. Plann. Assoc. **62**(2), 184–202 (1996)
29. Jeffrey, P., Seaton, R., Parsons, S., Stephenson, T.: Evaluation methods for the design of adaptive water supply systems in urban environments. Water Sci. Technol. **35**(9), 45–51 (1997)
30. Milman, A., Short, A.: Incorporating resilience into sustainability indicators: an example for the urban water sector. Glob. Environ. Chang. **18**(4), 758–767 (2008)
31. Loucks, D.P.: Quantifying trends in system sustainability. Hydrol. Sci. J. **42**(4), 513–530 (1997)
32. Derissen, S., Quaas, M.F., Baumgaertner, S.: The relationship between resilience and sustainability of ecological-economic systems. Ecol. Econ. **70**(6), 1121–1128 (2011)
33. Walker, B., Holling, C.S., Carpenter, S.R., Kinzig, A.: Resilience, adaptability and transformability in social–ecological systems. Ecol. Soc. **9**(2), 1–10 (2004). http://www.ecologyandsociety.org/vol9/iss2/art5/
34. Marchese, D., Reynolds, E., Bates, M.E., Morgan, H., Clark, S.S., Linkov, I.: Resilience and sustainability: similarities and differences in environmental management applications. Sci. Total Environ. **613**, 1275–1283 (2018)
35. Ahern, J.: Urban landscape sustainability and resilience: the promise and challenges of integrating ecology with urban planning and design. Landscape Ecol. **28**(6), 1203–1212 (2013)
36. Simatupang, T.M., Sridharan, R.: The collaborative supply chain. Int. J. Logist. Manag. **13**(1), 15–30 (2002)
37. Barratt, M.: Understanding the meaning of collaboration in the supply chain. Supply Chain Manage. Int. J. **9**(1), 30–42 (2004)
38. Safyalioglu, K.: The selection of global supply chain risk management strategies by using fuzzy analytical hierarchy process a case from Turkey. Procedia – Soc. Behav. Sci. **58**, 1448–1457 (2012)
39. Whipple, J.M., Russell, D.: Building supply chain collaboration: a typology of collaborative approaches. Int. J. Logistics Manage. **18**(2), 174–196 (2007)
40. da Silva Poberschnigg, T.F., Pimenta, M.L., Hilletofth, P.: How can cross - functional integration support the development of resilience capabilities? The case of collaboration in the automotive industry. Supply Chain Manage. Int. J. **25**(6), 789–801 (2020)
41. Christopher, M., Peck, H.: Building the resilient supply chain. Int. J. Logistics Manage. **15**(2), 1–14 (2004)
42. Ergun, Ã., Heier Stamm, J.L., Keskinocak, P., Swann, J.L.: Waffle House Restaurants hurricane response: a case study. Int. J. Prod. Econ. **126**(1), 111–120 (2010)

43. Scholten, K., Schilder, S.: The role of collaboration in supply chain resilience. Supply Chain Manage. Int. J. **20**(4), 471–484 (2015)
44. Hendry, L., Stevenson, M., MacBryde, J., Ball, P., Sayed, M., Liu, L.: Local food supply chain resilience to constitutional change: the Brexit effect. Int. J. Oper. Prod. Manag. **39**(3), 429–453 (2019)
45. Lotfi, M., Larmour, A.: Supply chain resilience in the face of uncertainty: how horizontal and vertical collaboration can help?. Continuity Resilience Rev. **4**, 37–53 (2021)
46. Azadegan, A., Dooley, K.: A typology of supply network resilience strategies: Complex collaborations in a complex world. J. Supply Chain Manag. **57**(1), 17–26 (2021)
47. Lizarralde, G., Chmutina, K., Bosher, L., Dainty, A.: Sustainability and resilience in the built environment: the challenges of establishing a turquoise agenda in the UK. Sustain. Cities Soc. **15**, 96–104 (2015)

A Path Forward Towards the Green Deal

A Framework of Collaborative Multi-actor Approach Based Digital Agriculture as a Solution for the Farm to Fork Strategy

José Barata[1,2(✉)], Javad Jassbi[1,2], and Sanaz Nikghadam-Hojjati[1,2]

[1] UNINOVA - Centre of Technology and Systems (CTS), FCT Campus, Monte de Caparica, 2829-516 Caparica, Portugal
{jab,j.jassbi,sanaznik}@uninova.pt
[2] NOVA University of Lisbon, Monte de Caparica, Lisbon, Portugal

Abstract. The Agri-food sector is tied to food and national security. Regardless of the circumstances, the degree of economic justification, and territorial readiness, all governments are investing to make sure that at least they could meet the local demand. But challenges in front of the Agri-food sector making this difficult. The suggested solution is collaborative multi-actor approach-based agriculture, which could be reached by utilizing emerging technologies. Smart or Precise agriculture are not new concepts, but most of the cases are still demonstration and not feasible on a large scale. In this paper, the concept of "Collaborative Multi-Actor Approach based Digital Agriculture" (CMDA) would be discussed from different perspectives, and the architecture of technology, business challenges of Implementation, and the Impacts would be analysed. The output will provide a framework of "Collaborative Digital Agriculture" as a solution for the European Farm to Fork strategy.

Keywords: Emerging technology · Collaborative Digital Agriculture · Agri-food industry · Farm to forks strategy · Multi-actor approach · Digitalization · United Nations Sustainable Development Goals

1 Introduction

The agri-food sector is crucial not only from an economic point of view but from political, social, health, and environmental [1]. Food security is part of any plan, which plays an essential role in regional and national security [2]. Covid-19 Pandemic once again shows the importance of the Agri-food industry and the potential consequence risk of failure in the Food Value Chain (FVCs) [3]. In the European Union (EU), with more than 22 Million agricultural workers [4], including farmers and 4 million staff in food and drink industries, the Agri-food sector plays a vital role in the economy [5]. European Commission released the "European Green Deal," which gives a broader perspective cover different domains to transform the EU into a fair and prosperous society [6, 7]. The introduced "Farm-to-Fork" strategy with a holistic approach is the heart of the European

L. M. Camarinha-Matos et al. (Eds.): PRO-VE 2022, IFIP AICT 662, pp. 503–518, 2022.
https://doi.org/10.1007/978-3-031-14844-6_40

Green Deal, targeting fair, healthy, and environmentally-friendly food systems [8]. This means the FVC from farming to processing, transportation, and retailers, and finally, consumption by the final user would be considered in any plan. On the other hand, Sustainable Development Goals (SDGs) proposed by the UN, dealing closely with the agri-food industry, and the goals would be highly affected by this industry. The agri-food industry is still stuck to the traditional ways and needs a paradigm shift to cope with all the mentioned challenges [9]. Digitalization is the central pillar, and emerging technology is a solution to achieve the goals [10]. Concepts such as "Smart Agriculture", "Precise Agriculture," and "Agriculture 4.0", are used to show this digital transformation in the agri-food industry. The "4.0" trend is almost in all industries with many success cases, but the nature of the agri-food industry made this transition difficult. There are many scientific articles discussing technology assessment, acceptance, and adoption in the agri-food industry (e.g. [11–16]) focused on emerging technologies such as big data(e.g. [17]), artificial intelligence(AI) (e.g. [18, 19]), UAVs (e.g. [19]), robots (e.g. [20]), self-driving systems (e.g. [21]), Internet of Things (e.g. [22]), and blockchain (e.g. [23]), and the barriers are identified and ranks in different research works. The challengers could be categorized in different ways, but one of the main issues is the nature of agriculture, such as distributed small farmers, seasonal mode, price sensitivity. All these characteristics lead us to new models, which are known as "Collaborative Agriculture", "CoFarming", "Cooperative Agriculture", "Crowd Farming" and similar ones [24]. Although they are not with precisely the same meaning but all common in Collaboration.

In this paper, we would like to discuss *"Collaborative Digital Agriculture"* from a *holistic perspective*. The result is from a qualitative research methodology and via the in-depth interviews, open-ended questionnaires, and several facilitated and guided meetings in different formats with different actors in the agri-food industry and ecosystem. Organizations, advocate associations, farmers, distributors, technology developers/providers/enablers, and research centres from different countries, including Portugal, Spain, Italy, Romania, France, Germany, Switzerland, Emirates, and Turkey, Iran, Tunisia were involved in this research. The main concentration was to know "How to develop a long-term strategy for the successful implementation of technology in FVC align with the Farm to Fork strategy?" Also, this exploratory study investigated impact of the CDA application outcomes on the 17 United Nations Sustainable Development Goals (UN-SDGs).

2 Holistic Perspective

Collaborative Digital Agriculture (CDA) is an ideal solution for most of the challenges of the agri-food Industry. This strategy vertically connects the nodes but should also horizontally cover all the processes to change the traditional dominant game. CDA is not just a technological challenge but a multidimensional dilemma in which a holistic approach is essential. In this section, beyond the technology itself, the main concerns and challenges are discussed and evaluated in a systematic way to understand how the digitalization process in the agri-food sector could impact the stakeholders involved in each of the life cycle phases and the society. The approach is based on the "Technology

Assessment" models and theories to making sure the short and long-term consequences in different areas such as societal, economic, political, business ethical, legal, would be considered. Figure 1 shows the holistic view of CDA.

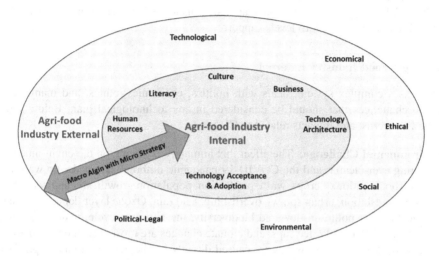

Fig. 1. The holistic view of Collaborative Digital Agriculture

As could be seen, there are two main clusters, internal and external Agri-food industry, while the macro and micro strategy should support each other and be aligned to make CDA happens. In the following, the most critical issues of each one, extracted from interviews and meetings, are discussed.

2.1 Micro vs Macro Strategy

A wide range of innovative and affordable technologies have emerged to facilitate the creation, expansion, and streamlining of FVCs [25]. To successfully disseminate these technologies, entrepreneurs need to have Micro and Macro levels perspective to design-related strategies [26]. Successful business cases show new innovative technology would be successfully implemented when the micro and macro strategies meet each other. Considering the different nature of the micro and macro environments, having both strategies that suit each other and create synergy is great support for any business leader in the industry. CDA could not happen without these top-down, down-top aligned strategies. For example, technological innovation is the fuel that can run the engine of the agri-food business. The new technological solutions can build a smart agri-food value chain, while agri-food-tech start-ups are a meaningful solution across the agri-food value chain. They can provide a product, a service, or even an application that helps in the agri-food sector. The idea of empowering start-ups working on technology brings in a lot of insight, interest, and innovation in any industry. Agri-food is no exception. Agri-food-tech start-ups face problems such as rigid old business models, lack of commercial guidance, investor apathy, lack of subject matter experts or mentors, application of technology, urban investors' lack of understanding, climate change, etc. [27]. Some of these problems are so fundamental that they need a deeper cultural shift, which can also happen by a start-up movement. Starting a start-up movement is a significant challenge that requires an organized effort by a large group of people that includes Businesses, Digital Innovation Hubs (DIHs), Governmental Organizations, Consumers, etc. But start-up movement needs both macro and micro levels support.

2.2 Agri-Food Industry External

CDA, as a complex system, deals with politics, economics, ethics, and many other macro challenges that should be considered in any technological plan. Below some issues, concerns, and impacts related to CDA:

Environmental Challenge: The effect that humanity is having on the environment is becoming ever-clearer, and the COVID-19 pandemic outbreak is a wake-up warning! Genetic modification of crops, waste production, population growth, soil and water pollution, deforestation, urban sprawl, overfishing, acid rain, Ozone layer depletion, ocean acidification, air pollution, lowered biodiversity, the Nitrogen cycle, natural resource use, transportation, polar ice caps, and climate changes are most critical environmental issues [28]. Most of these issues are caused directly by the agriculture and Agri-food sectors. Soil and Water Pollution by Pesticides and Agricultural Waste are important issues among global warming, which should be considered in any technology plan for the agri-food industry. It is estimated that about 998 million tons of agricultural waste are produced yearly [29]. According to an estimate made by the Plant Protection Department (PPD), about 1.8% of the chemicals remain in their packaging [30]. These wastes have the potential to cause unpredictable environmental consequences such as food poisoning, unsafe food hygiene, and contaminated farmland due to their potentially lasting and toxic chemicals [31]. At every stage, food provisioning releases greenhouse gases into the atmosphere. Agriculture accounted for 10% of the EU's total greenhouse-gas emissions in 2012 [32]. This means CDA which is a Farm-to-Fork strategy-based solution should be evaluated precisely to measure it's positive and negative impacts while it is expected to have a positive impact on mentioned issues such as waste production, water pollution, deforestation, air pollution, natural resource use, transportation, soil degradation, and climate change.

Economical: CDA, more than a technology solution, is an economical solution. It supports small farms on large scale to be connected, benefits from emerging technology, and changes the lifestyle. The collaboration will give power to small players to be active, which will support regional and local development as well as increasing the share of the Agri-food industry in GDP and job creation. The horizontal collaboration will help for the natural optimization of FVC in the processes to elevate the productivity in this sector [33]. CDA also will empower farmers by involving them in digital data business while their products more than agricultural products will be information that could be used cooperatively and add value for the farmers to cover the cost of new technologies. This will support the democratization of information and, consequently, the regional farmer-driven development (down top approach).

Politics: CDA, such as any technological development, could bring risk for the agri-food ecosystem and different players. It seems that between different players, farmers are the most vulnerable one in terms of the risk of adopting new technologies [34] and this should be managed at the macro-level while the solution would be more politically, Governments would find a solution for it. CDA will help countries with unsuitable and poor conditions to employ technology that could guaranty minimum food security of different regions, and this would be important in a difficult situation such as COVID-19 while the logistics and supply chains are not working properly. It is also important to understand how to support small farms vs. dominant giant agri-food companies and avoid worsening of the farmer debt/income crisis, which could exclude small, peasant farmers from the Agri-food production network [35, 36]. CDA will help governments to have access to dynamic data from the Agri-food process in detail, which could give them power for estimation of demand & supply, supporting clean business against the black market in the Agri-food industry.

Legal: Using emerging technology, including intelligent systems and robotics, is challenging and could raise legal issues [37], specifically when the data would have a major role in the future of the Agri-food industry. The nature of collaboration on a large-scale causes' problems. For instance, CDA could cause a question of responsibility as in case of any problem in the quality of the farms' product, it would create confusion about who will take responsibility and how the potential support by governments could be managed. Technology providers, technology enablers, and farmers are all in the process, which makes the judgment very difficult. The crystal process in FVC could also bring advantages and disadvantages simultaneously, which could lead to a legal fight!

Ethics: CDA could make confusion in terms of "Data Justice" for farmers, and it should be cleared and guaranteed fairness and social justice into digital agriculture to protect the most vulnerable in the agri-food industry. CDA is based on new emerging technology, while data is the most valuable asset. This would raise concerns about the privacy and cyber security issue, which could be seen from the perspective of practical ethics of digital agriculture and should be addressed in any technological development project dealing with agri-food, including the food supply chain. Fair Trade is also a critical issue as it supports the right of the people, including invisible agri-food workers. CDA will create a traceable digital passport among collaborators that could increase the level of fair trade in different aspects, from resource to market, including laborers and their rights.

2.3 Agri-Food Industry Internal

Alongside external components in the agri-food industry, here are important concerns in the internal agri-food ecosystem. Below some of them are introduced while two crucial components of the *Business Model* and *Technology Architecture* would be discussed in separate sections following section two.

Culture: The Agri-food industry has a particular culture with specific characteristics. The number of invisible staff, seasonal workers, and low-skill persons are among these characteristics. Comparing with other sectors, the penetration rate of technology is low, and in most countries, it is still a family business. It is claimed that although women have an essential role, especially in rural agriculture and in developing and underdeveloped countries [38], they are not visible, and they do not have normal rights such as insurance or retirement benefits [39]. CDA hopes to change the agri-food industrial culture dramatically, including the working environment. It will help to attract more intelligent and high qualified people in this industry and make it a prestigious cluster to work for high tech companies and talented people. Technology will change the types of needed skills as well as the visibility, models of collaboration, and responsibility, which means a new working environment for Agri-food stakeholders and players.

Technology Acceptance and Adoption: One of the main challenges of CDA is the problem of real cases and the rate of penetration. The acceptance of technology is more than just the technology itself and how it is advanced, but it's about successful technology deployment, which needs a strategy. Many papers are discussing the barriers to justify the lack of technology in the agri-food industry (e.g. [40–43]), but most of them are focusing on the traditional criteria. Interviewing different FVC chain players shows us that the main problem is the collaboration model. Most of the other factors are derived from weak Collaborative Networks (CNs). Analysing the agri-food industry as an ecosystem from the point of view of CN, the main causes such as inappropriate typology of the network, lack of synergy, and weak cooperation to share the resources and increase productivity and finally, lack some critical nodes of the supply chain are recognized. Also, the vertical development to connect the process from farm to fork is not yet fully supported by existing technology.

Human Resources and Literacy: Agri-food-tech businesses are aware that the technical and soft skills of their employees directly influence business performance and, consequently, improving these skills will enhance the effectiveness, efficiency, and sustainability of their business [44]. They also are informed that the lack of knowledge, lack of technical skills for working with new technologies, lack of awareness, and social ignorance about new methods, technologies, and processes are some of the most critical adapting barriers of their products and services by consumers, market and society which cause resistance. In this regard, Literacy is not just crucial to agri-food-tech businesses, but vital [45]. One main issue which would be a crucial challenge that should be addressed in any technological project in the agri-food industry is the level of technology literacy of stakeholders, mainly farmers and the leading agriculture field players [46]. This would be one of the primary and critical issues to guaranty the use, manage, understand, and assess technology.

3   Reference Architecture Model

The proposed digital ecosystem for CDA focuses on delivering an autonomous and fully interoperable environment taking advantage of the European investments on platforms such as FIWARE and Arrowhead tools, intending to optimize the agri-food chain (from farming to processing and distribution) in a modular and open way. This is possible with the aid of core technologies and proved tested through pilot demonstrators that embed within real environments. The proposed reference model for CDA shows in Fig. 2.

The CDA ecosystem addresses the combination of robotics at scale with IoT devices, big data, and AI applications to bring added value into the agri-food chain across its different phases, following the Farm-to-Fork vision represented by the yellow arrow in Fig. 2. This implies that several of the actors are transversal to the lifecycle, with the context of their intervention changing depending on the phase in question from *farming* to *processing*, *distribution*, and finally, the *consumer*.

Throughout the different phases, the key for the interoperability of the ecosystem is the CDA middleware, built on top of the FIWARE platform. First, a multiagent-based IoT layer is responsible for the interaction and acquisition of data from the field level, namely interacting with existing legacy equipment (using appropriate adaptors) and the CDA robotic systems, as well as external data sources such as the Copernicus observation satellites and state of the art ground data sensors (Humidity, geo-localization) or meteorology services. This layer interacts with the FIWARE Orion Context Broker following the Next Generation Services Interface (NGSI) specification, managing, and facilitating the access to the information flowing through the platform. This allows the management of the entire lifecycle of context information (including updates, queries, registrations, and subscriptions), using an NGSI v2 interface. The adoption of FIWARE will be leveraged to speed-up the design and implementation of the ecosystem, as it offers a catalogue of components known as Generic Enablers, along with a set of reference implementations that allow the instantiation of functionalities such as Big Data analysis, development of context-aware applications, connection with different IoT devices or external systems.

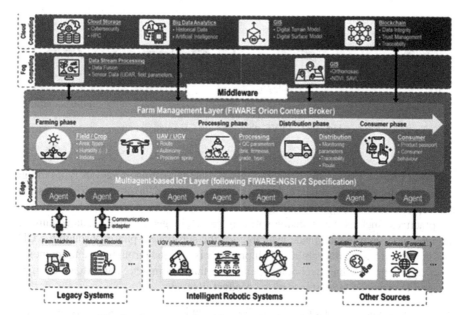

Fig. 2. A conceptual architecture for the CDA ecosystem

On top of this, several applications can be plugged at different levels to bring added functionality and value to the ecosystem. A fundamental characteristic of the CDA ecosystem is the low-code approach for the configuration of the information flow and interaction with the platform. The advantages of such an approach are two-fold, firstly it ensures that stakeholders, particularly farmers, do not require expert knowledge to interact with the platform. Secondly, it facilitates the rapid configuration and deployment of intelligent robotic solutions using the CDA ecosystem in different scenarios. Also, while FIWARE will be regarded as a core enabling technology, CDA will exploit the connections within the consortium to maximize compatibility and compliance with other major platforms as part of the development cycle of the modular software applications. One such case will be the connection to the Arrowhead Framework through the mutual STM partner, which is being actively developed and exploited across multiple EU projects for building IoT-based systems-of-systems.

Three distinct levels of computation are considered across the lifecycle, namely edge, fog, and cloud computing. At the edge level, the multiagent IoT layer ensures that not only the data acquisition takes place, but also that some computation can be performed to address the real-time requirements, with the added flexibility of such an approach (i.e., plug and play deployment of smart drop-in sensors). At the fog level (for instance at IoT gateways) some stream processing can be performed, along with the fusion of data from the different sources at the field level and computations that can be too heavy to perform at the edge, but do not necessarily require the computational power of cloud resources (e.g., calculation of varied indexes). Finally, several services can be made available at the cloud level, including robust and secure data storage, big data analytics, and blockchain services to ensure the traceability and integrity of all transactions being carried out. The lifecycle addressed in CDA is shown in Fig. 3 and expected to flow as follows:

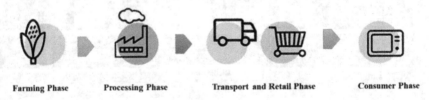

Farming Phase   Processing Phase   Transport and Retail Phase   Consumer Phase

Fig. 3. The FVC phases in the CDA ecosystem

Farming Phase: During the "Farming Phase", the harvesting of various types of agricultural products, which can be either manual or automated, takes place. This phase also encompasses the management of the fields and crops with the use of different farming practices, such as the precision spraying case. The geo-reference data acquired by the robotic system is then made available for the subsequent phases through the CDA middleware. Besides, traceability of all products is enabled through the employment of a new type of blockchain technology, ensuring that a complete, contextualized digital passport is provided at all stages of the product lifecycle.

Processing Phase: Afterwards, in the "Processing Phase", an improved resource allocation strategy is made possible due to all the newly available data, with CDA supporting decision-making based on the analysis of historical data and forecasting applications. Harvested products are then submitted to automated, non-destructive quality control during grading, as opposed to the current manual and more subjective approach, which is often tedious and error prone. To achieve this, data from the different phases can be combined and processed by a data analytics module which can either be embedded onto the flexible robotic platform in an in-door setting or onto quality control check-point stations. In the case of the former, the AGV can navigate from pallet to pallet as they arrive at the processing facility, performing the quality assessment with the assistance of a mounted manipulator and the embedded AI application. In both scenarios, the emphasis is on sustainability, as the approach reduces the amount of wasted product due to its non-destructive nature, whilst reducing the time required for testing (in some instances manual testing can currently take up to a few hours) and thus increasing the number of items that can be tested to improve the overall process. Moreover, in contrast to destructive methods, this solution enables products to be tested multiple times, including for instance both before and after storage, hence providing a better indication of the evolution or possible degradation of the associated quality.

Retail Phase: Then, during the "Retail Phase", once more products can be monitored enroute to retail through the IoT layer, ensuring that appropriate conditions are maintained during transportation with data being recorded into the passport of the product, increasing the transparency, and promoting trust along the value chain.

Consumer Phase: Finally, at the "Consumer Phase", CDA aims to tackle one of the big challenges being currently faced in the agri-food sector, which is the lack of visibility at this stage, which contributes heavily to the problem of food waste and loss. This will be addressed with the employment of gamification strategies to promote the engagement of consumers with the CDA ecosystem. On the one hand, it will create the means for consumers to provide feedback on the perceived product quality and safety, contributing to the continuous improvement of the automated processes in the previous phases. On the other, it will contribute directly to the mitigation of the food loss and waste problem, by rewarding users for logging their consumer behaviour, fully consuming products before their expiration date, and providing suggestions to better manage their inventory at home.

These different phases are perfectly aligned with the Farm to Fork strategy, from sustainable food production to processing, distribution, and consumption, promoting responsible behaviour towards the reduction of food loss and waste.

4 Business Model

The sharing Economy paradigm has changed the principles of business, and it helps technology providers to commercialize their technology. In different ecosystems, the most successfully implemented technology uses the business layer, which is called "Service Enabler." They are a group of entities that could connect supply and demand in the market and give the right service to potential clients without involving them in the complicated world of technology. Despite the success of technology providers in terms of implementation and usage, in the agri-food industry, sophisticated technologies have not yet found their market. Technology literacy, price, and cost, economy scale, permanent use due to the seasonal process, and other criteria lead us to the fact that it would be challenging to connect suppliers to the final user of technology in the agri-food value chain. In this regard, connecting the providers of these services to the targeted consumers, including smallholder farmers through a service enabler platform, is vital. This platform includes a network of organizations and businesses involved in the delivery of specific agri-food technology-related services through a technology-based platform. Due to the absence of this platform and its framework in the agri-food sector, in the first place, proposing a framework for such a network is fundamental. This platform would be based on the sharing economy model, which is an economic model defined as a peer-to-peer (P2P) based activity of acquiring, providing, or sharing access to goods and services that is often facilitated by a community-based online platform. Figure 4 shows the business model of Collaborative Digital Agriculture.

Fig. 4. Technology enabler as a key chain in CDA business model

As it could be seen, CDA as a collaborative network includes different players, and here the roles and categories are described: i) **Technology Providers**: Technology is the trigger of CDA. This group includes companies that are developing and selling technologies using different models. ii) **Technology R&D Partners**: The R&D units are the engine of innovation and work with the value chain to support the R&D needs. iii) **Technology Enabler**: Technology enablers are the heart of this business, which is missing in the Agri-food industry now. One of the main concerns in CDA should be developing a "Technology Enabler Ecosystem". This ecosystem is vital for the successful implementation of any strategy related to Smart Agriculture, including CDA. iv) **Technology User/Market**: Any technology at the end needs to have an end-user, and the users are not just companies working in any specific part of the agri-food industry, but the entities involved in the value chain and from farm to fork, including farmers, transporting companies, distribution, and retailers and so on. Technology users are the final client whose needs must be addressed and their challenges to be met.

Table 1 is the initial Canvas model as a general framework to understand the business side of CDA:

Table 1. Canvas model for CDA as a business

Key Partners	Key Activities	Value Proposition	Customer Relationship	Customer Segments
-Agri-food associations -Local Governors and mayors -Big retailers	- Developing Technology - Develop standards for Agri-food technology - Develop Technology Enabler ecosystem for the Agri-food industry	CDA will propose a cooperative network using emerging technologies	Technology enabler system will develop Agri-food technology Club to make an international network of stakeholders	Agri-food Industry
	Key Resources - Knowledgeable and experienced team both in technology and Agri-food industry - Partnership with relevant entities	This will support the Agri-food value chain from farm to fork.	**Channels** The services and technologies would employ usual strategies such as social media, website, etc, but mainly will approach its target group by being active in related fairs, arranging workshops, and events. Also, policymakers at state and national levels who are looking for new technology in Agri-food are the potential target to catch and present the work.	
Cost Structure Cost of business includes: - Technology Development - Service Customization & Project Implementation - Hi qualified HR			**Revenue Streams** The revenue streams would be different for different partners in this ecosystem, but the main revenue stream would be based on Technology as a service (TaaS).	

In Table 2, SWOT analysis of future potential business according to the information from the Portuguese team working in SFColab and the initial investigation is presented. The SWOT table shows the main strategies which could be similar for many entities looking to this business to develop a CDA ecosystem.

Table 2. SWOT analysis to identify strategies of CDA as a business

SWOT Strategies	Strength a) Presence of High qualified teams in this area b) Developing a new business model based on technology that would be unique and competitive c) Knowing types of merging technologies and working with agricultural entities d) Diversity of the team to make sure all aspects and needs are covered	Weaknesses a) Lack of collaboration with different entities in this scale b) lack of Financial strength comparison with American companies in the industry
Opportunities 1. Very large and committed potential market 2. Support of European Commission for the renovation of Agri-food industry 3. The rising importance of the local Agri-food industry as a national security 4. The decreasing trend of Technology-based solutions in the Agri-food industry 5. Technology as a recognized solution to deal with the challenge f radical change in the world population and its consequences (Food, water ...) 6. EU is one of the world's leading producers and exporters of agricultural products	**SO** 1. Working on R&D projects and use potential resources from universities including professors, researchers, and students 2. Develop different platform of collaboration to Keep the team 3. Protect the technology and CDA know-how by using strategies such as patent registration	**WO** 1. Using financial instruments of EC to leverage the work and continue developing the technology 2. Target countries with the non-suitable situation for agriculture using the high-level European delegation to penetrate their market
Threats 1. The agri-food industry is a price-sensitive industry in which costs of new expensive technologies will not be readily accepted 2. Lack of standardization in the Agri-food industry 3. Lack of Technology Enablers in the Agri-food industry 4. Nature of Agri-food industry with an unbalanced load of work in the year 5. Variety of processes to be covered in the Agri-food value chain 6. 6. The dominant position of Political economy in the Agri-food industry	**ST** 1. Finding a supplier for different modules in the solution to have a competitive price 2. Develop a Start-up ecosystem 3. Develop a Technology enabler system in the Agri-food Industry 4. Increasing our mobility and agility to meet the unbalanced seasonal business of Agri-food	**WT** 1. Negotiating with investors and financial organizations to have financial support for the competition 2. Work with the European Commission to develop the international market using a unified approach 3. Negotiate with the standard organizations/ Companies and related authority in European Commission to establish standards of Technologies in Agri-food Industry

As it could be seen, all the aspects of the business are promising. Potentially it shows that the investment in CDA is a very wise and smart move not only in terms of business but to guaranty, the future of the agri-food industry in Europe aligns with the CDGs of the United Nations and to increases the share of European entities, worldwide in the agri-food industry.

5 Impacts

In this section, the main idea is to understand the impact of a CDA solution based on SDGs that meet the urgent social, environmental, political, and economic challenges facing our world. Social and Environmental Impact is the effect on people, communities, and environments that happens as a result of an action or inaction, an activity, project, program, or policy. Investigating social and environmental impact in any activities, such as technological development, business activities, social movement, etc., is a priority to help to achieve the mission of that activity, attracting additional funding, ensuring avoiding from any environmental harm, improving society, improving effective communication, demonstrating value for money, understanding better the strengths and weaknesses of the activity, and improving the activity.

Fig. 5. CDA potential impact on UN-SDGs

The advantage of the proposed model called "Collaborative Digital Agriculture" was discussed in the previous section, and here the aim is investigating the expected impact of CDA outcomes on 17 UN-SDGs. To do that, questionaries were designed and distributed between large-scale potential clients in different FVC processes and asked them to justify the impact of CDA based on their existing businesses and situation by giving a number from 0 to 10. Figure 5 shows the result of aggregated data after collecting the questionnaires, merging different potential implementation cases to analyse the data.

According to Fig. 5, the six most significant impacts will be on the Partnerships for the goals, Industry, Innovation, and Infrastructure, Zero Hunger, Good Health and Well-being, Decent Work and Economic Growth, and No poverty. CDA outcomes will have the lowest impact on Life Below Water, Peace, Justice, and Strong Institutions, Reduced Inequalities, Life on the Land, and Gender Equality. The CDA application outcomes will have a positive impact on Climate Action.

6 Discussion and Conclusion

New emerging technologies will boost effectiveness and reduce risks of the agri-food industry. This would be a shifting paradigm in this sector, which will dramatically change farms and food processing industries. The increasing demand for food, which is estimated to be doubled by 2050 due to population growth and the rising importance of food security pushing the agri-food industry to increase its productivity. This will be impossible without employing new technologies and creating different ways of managing the FVC. Considering all challenges and dilemmas, "Collaborative Digital Agriculture" seems the most promising model to achieve this goal. In this paper, CDA was discussed as a multidisciplinary concept, and the main challenges from various points of view were brought up. Then two crucial issues, the business model to tackle exiting barriers and the technical architecture to develop the core technology, were introduced separately as a framework of CDA. On the other side, dealing with SDGs and social impact is the driver in the sector, and the impact of CDA on SDGs was evaluated. The main output of this paper could be listed as below: i) "Technology Enabler" is an essential missing ring in the food value chain to employ emerging technologies and make it feasible and attainable. ii) The success of CDA depends on the alignment of the Micro and Macro strategy to tackle challenges and dilemmas. iii) The appropriate Technology architecture is proposed to be used in the framework of CDA.

The article is the first step to shape the new strategy, which could support the shift of the agri-food industry to the new paradigm. Still, it needs further research to understand the operational barriers, the role of local ecosystems as well as developing the typology of the collaborative network to have a better picture of this new paradigm of agriculture align with the Farm to Fork strategy.

Acknowledgement. This work was supported by the project SMARTFARM 4.0 – Soluções inteligentes para uma agricultura sustentável, preditiva e autónomas (Intelligent Solutions for a Sustainable, Predictive and Autonomous Agriculture) – Project Number POCI-01-0247-FEDER-046078.

References

1. Esposito, B., Sessa, M.R., Sica, D., Malandrino, O.: Towards circular economy in the agri-food sector. A systematic literature review (2020). https://doi.org/10.3390/SU12187401
2. Main, S.J.: Food policy and food security. Putting food on the Russian table. Eur. Asia. Stud., 331–332 (2019). https://doi.org/10.1080/09668136.2019.1584461

3. FAO Data Lab: FAO Big Data tool on Covid-19 impact on food value chains (2020). https://www.fao.org/family-farming/detail/en/c/1271571/
4. Euronews: What will be the new face of European agriculture in the coming years? 28 April 2021. https://www.euronews.com/green/2020/03/02/what-will-be-the-new-face-of-european-agriculture-in-the-coming-years
5. EUROSTAT: Performance of the agricultural sector 13 April 2021. https://ec.europa.eu/eurostat/web/products-eurostat-news/-/ddn-20210413-2
6. Ossewaarde, M., Ossewaarde-Lowtoo, R.: The EU's green deal: a third alternative to GreenGrowth and Degrowth? Sustainability 12, 9825 (2020)
7. The European Commission: A European Green Deal 11 December 2019. https://ec.europa.eu/info/strategy/priorities-2019-2024/european-green-deal_en
8. The European Commission: Farm to Fork Strategy – for a fair, healthy and environmentally-friendly food system 20 May 2020. https://eur-lex.europa.eu/legal-content/EN/TXT/?uri=CELEX%3A52020DC0381
9. Herren, H.R., Haerlin, B.: IAASTD+10 Adviso Group: Transformation of our food systems: the making of a paradigm shift. Zukunftsstiftung Landwirtschaft (Foundation on Future Farming) (2020)
10. Tang, S., Zhu, Q., Zhou, X., Liu, S., Wu, M.: A conception of digital agriculture. In: International Geoscience and Remote Sensing Symposium (IGARSS) (2002). https://doi.org/10.1109/igarss.2002.1026858
11. Kabbiri, R., Dora, M., Kumar, V., Elepu, G., Gellynck, X.: Mobile phone adoption in agri-food sector: are farmers in Sub-Saharan Africa connected? Technol. Forecast. Soc. Change. 131, 253–261 (2018). https://doi.org/10.1016/j.techfore.2017.12.010
12. Frewer, L.J., et al.: Consumer response to novel agri-food technologies: implications for predicting consumer acceptance of emerging food technologies (2011). https://doi.org/10.1016/j.tifs.2011.05.005
13. Pappa, I.C., Iliopoulos, C., Massouras, T.: What determines the acceptance and use of electronic traceability systems in agri-food supply chains? J. Rural Stud., 123–135 (2018). https://doi.org/10.1016/j.jrurstud.2018.01.001
14. Handford, C.E., Dean, M., Henchion, M., Spence, M., Elliott, C.T., Campbell, K.: Implications of nanotechnology for the agri-food industry: opportunities, benefits and risks (2014). https://doi.org/10.1016/j.tifs.2014.09.007
15. Schiefer, G.: New technologies and their impact on the agri-food sector: an economists view. Comput. Electron. Agric., 226–241 (2004). https://doi.org/10.1016/j.compag.2003.12.002
16. Carmela Annosi, M., Brunetta, F., Capo, F., Heideveld, L.: Digitalization in the agri-food industry: the relationship between technology and sustainable development. Manag. Decis., 1737–1757 (2020). https://doi.org/10.1108/MD-09-2019-1328
17. Belaud, J.P., Prioux, N., Vialle, C., Sablayrolles, C.: Big data for agri-food 4.0: application to sustainability management for by-products supply chain. Comput. Ind., 41–50 (2019). https://doi.org/10.1016/j.compind.2019.06.006
18. Di Vaio, A., Boccia, F., Landriani, L., Palladino, R.: Artificial intelligence in the agri-food system: rethinking sustainable business models in the COVID-19 scenario. Sustainability (2020). https://doi.org/10.3390/SU12124851
19. Miranda, J., Ponce, P., Molina, A., Wright, P.: Sensing, smart and sustainable technologies for Agri-Food 4.0. Comput. Ind. (2019). https://doi.org/10.1016/j.compind.2019.02.002
20. Newswire, P.R.: Agricultural Robots and Drones 2017–2027: Technologies, Markets, Players (2017)
21. Duong, L.N.K., et al.: A review of robotics and autonomous systems in the food industry: from the supply chains perspective (2020). https://doi.org/10.1016/j.tifs.2020.10.028

22. Boursianis, A.D., et al.: Internet of Things (IoT) and agricultural Unmanned Aerial Vehicles (UAVs) in smart farming: a comprehensive review. Internet Things (2020). https://doi.org/10.1016/j.iot.2020.100187

23. Caro, M.P., Ali, M.S., Vecchio, M., Giaffreda, R.: Blockchain-based traceability in Agri-Food supply chain management: a practical implementation. In: 2018 IoT Vertical and Topical Summit on Agriculture - Tuscany, IOT Tuscany 2018 (2018). https://doi.org/10.1109/IOT-TUSCANY.2018.8373021

24. Adamashvili, N., Fiore, M., Contò, F., La Sala, P.: Ecosystem for successful agriculture. Collaborative approach as a driver for agricultural development. Eur. Countrys., 242–256 (2020). https://doi.org/10.2478/euco-2020-0014

25. Suffian, S., Reus, A.D., Eckard, C., Copley, A., Mehta, K.: Agricultural technology commercialisation: stakeholders, business models, and abiotic stressors - part 1. Int. J. Soc. Entrep. Innov., 415–437 (2013). https://doi.org/10.1504/ijsei.2013.059314

26. Cunningham, J.A., O'Reilly, P.: Macro, meso and micro perspectives of technology transfer. J. Technol. Transf. 43(3), 545–557 (2018). https://doi.org/10.1007/s10961-018-9658-4

27. Masterfox Consulting Group (MCG): Current Challenges Addressing the Landscape of Agritech Startups and Their Probable Solutions 27 December 2019. https://m.facebook.com/pages/category/Business-Consultant/MCG.Insights/posts/

28. Ecavo.com: Top 17 Environmental Problems 4 December 2016. https://ecavo.com/top-environmental-problems/

29. Obi, F., Ugwuishiwu, B., Nwakaire, J.: Agricultural waste concept, generation, utilization and management. Niger J. Technol., 957–964 (2016). https://doi.org/10.4314/njt.v35i4.34

30. Dien, B.V., Vong, V.D.: Analysis of pesticide compound residues in some water sources in the province of Gia Lai and DakLak. Vietnam Food Adm. (2006)

31. Zakaria, Z.A. (ed.): Sustainable Technologies for the Management of Agricultural Wastes. AESESF, Springer, Singapore (2018). https://doi.org/10.1007/978-981-10-5062-6

32. EEA: Agriculture and climate change (2015)

33. Yuan, Y., Viet, N., Behdani, B.: The impact of information sharing on the performance of horizontal logistics collaboration: a simulation study in an agri-food supply chain. IFAC-PapersOnLine (2019). https://doi.org/10.1016/j.ifacol.2019.11.619

34. Cafer, A.M., Rikoon, J.S.: Adoption of new technologies by smallholder farmers: the contributions of extension, research institutes, cooperatives, and access to cash for improving tef production in Ethiopia. Agric. Hum. Values 35(3), 685–699 (2018). https://doi.org/10.1007/s10460-018-9865-5

35. Cornelis (Kees), L.J., Van, D.M.: Exclusion from coordinated supply chain. Agro-food chain. Netw. Dev., 209–217 (2006)

36. Huang, F., Wu, Y., Rozelle, S.: Marketing China's fruit: are small, poor farmers being excluded from the supply chain? In: The Transformations of Agri-food Systems: Globalization, Supply Chains and Smallholder Farmers (2008)

37. Leenes, R., Palmerini, E., Koops, B.J., Bertolini, A., Salvini, P., Lucivero, F.: Regulatory challenges of robotics: some guidelines for addressing legal and ethical issues. Law, Innov. Technol., 1–44 (2017). https://doi.org/10.1080/17579961.2017.1304921

38. FAO: Women in agriculture (2022). https://www.fao.org/reduce-rural-poverty/our-work/women-in-agriculture/en/

39. IFPRI: Closing gender gaps in agriculture (2022). https://www.ifpri.org/closing-gender-gaps-agriculture

40. Sutrisno Hadi Purnomo, K.: Barriers to acceptance of information and communication technology in agricultural extension in Indonesia. Inf. Dev. 35.4, 512–523 (2019). https://doi.org/10.1177/0266666918767484

41. Yadav, V.S., Singh, A.R., Raut, R.D., Govindarajan, U.H.: Blockchain technology adoption barriers in the Indian agricultural supply chain: an integrated approach. Resour. Conserv. Recycl., 104877 (2020). https://doi.org/10.1016/j.resconrec.2020.104877

42. Long, T.B., Blok, V., Coninx, I.: Barriers to the adoption and diffusion of technological innovations for climate-smart agriculture in Europe: evidence from the Netherlands, France, Switzerland and Italy. J. Clean. Prod., 9–21 (2016). https://doi.org/10.1016/j.jclepro.2015.06.044

43. Ebrahim, Z., Irani, Z.: E-government adoption: architecture and barriers. Bus. Process Manag. J., 589–611 (2005). https://doi.org/10.1108/14637150510619902

44. Gaspar, P.D., et al.: Training requirements for the agro-food industry in Portugal. Int. J. Food Stud., 12–28 (2015). https://doi.org/10.7455/ijfs/4.1.2015.a2

45. Frick, M., Kahler, A.: A definition and concepts of agricultural literacy. J. Agric. Educ., 49–57 (1991). https://doi.org/10.5032/jae.1991.02049

46. Trendov, N.M., Varas, S., Zeng, M.: Digital technologies in agriculture and rural areas. Briefing Paper FAO (2019)

Collaborative Optimization Tool for Sustainable Planning of an Agricultural Supply Chain Preserving Farmers' Independence

Ana Esteso[1]([✉]), M. M. E. Alemany[1], Ángel Ortiz[1], and Mario Lezoche[2]

[1] Research Centre on Production Management and Engineering (CIGIP),
Universitat Politècnica de València, Camino de Vera S/N, 46022 València, Spain
{aesteso,mareva,aortiz}@cigip.upv.es
[2] Université de Lorraine, CNRS, CRAN, Nancy, France
mario.lezoche@univ-lorraine.fr

Abstract. Farmers often decide independently when and how much area to plant each crop. As farmers unknow the demand for crops, they tend to plant the most profitable crops from the previous year. If all farmers reproduced this behavior, they would overproduce the most profitable crops and underproduce the least profitable ones, leading to a supply-demand imbalance and price fluctuations. To solve this problem while maintaining farmers independence, a collaborative optimization-based tool is proposed that allows to centrally define the minimum and maximum proportion of area to be planted with each crop and in each period to be sustainable in terms of profits, waste, and unmet demand, and to use this proportions to independently define the planning of planting, harvesting and crop distribution for each farmer. The proposed tool is assessed by determining and comparing what the supply chain outcomes would be if farmers used the collaborative tool or not.

Keywords: Collaborative · Crop planning · Agri-food · Perishable · Optimization

1 Introduction

In the agri-food sector, farmers usually make decisions about how much area to plant each vegetable and/or fruit and when to plant them independently and without considering the decisions made by other farmers [1]. As farmers have no information about the demand and supply for the crops when making such decisions, they tend to plant those crops that had a higher economic margin in the previous year [2].

If all farmers act in this way, there will be an oversupply of those crops that were most profitable in the previous year and a shortage of those that were not so profitable [3]. This imbalance of supply and demand results in the wastage of some crops and the impossibility of meeting the full demand for others, which negatively affects the environmental and social sustainability of the supply chains (SCs). In addition, crop prices fluctuate according to the balance between demand and supply, rising when supply

L. M. Camarinha-Matos et al. (Eds.): PRO-VE 2022, IFIP AICT 662, pp. 519–532, 2022.
https://doi.org/10.1007/978-3-031-14844-6_41

is lower than demand and falling when there is an excess of crop over demand [4], which also impacts on the economic sustainability of the SC.

There are multiple mathematical programming models that support the crop planting planning process that aim to balance supply and demand. However, most proposals rely on centralized decision-making in which farmers lose independence in crop planting [5–7]. Up to our knowledge, only [1] propose distributed models for crop planting planning, concluding that their results are not sustainable for the SC.

In this context, it is intended to answer the following research question: Is it possible to establish a collaborative tool to balance crop supply and demand and increase the SC sustainability while maintaining farmers' independence?

To solve this question, a collaborative tool based on multi-objective mixed integer linear programming models is proposed. This tool establishes in a first step the minimum and maximum proportion of area to be planted with each crop and in each planting period to balance crop supply and demand and to achieve economic, environmental, and social sustainability. In a second step farmers independently choose the area to be planted with each crop, respecting the proportions set in the first step.

This approach is common in some countries, where government agencies advise farmers on the areas to be planted with each crop and in each planting period to have a greater control over markets and prices.

In addition, this paper assesses the results obtained with the collaborative tool and compares them to those that would be obtained if farmers acted completely independently, thus validating the proposed tool and showing its main advantages.

The rest of the article is structured as follows. Section 2 describes the problem under study. Section 3 proposes the collaborative tool and the resolution methodology. Section 4 validates the collaborative tool through its application to a case study and tests the advantages of implementing the proposed tool. Finally, Sect. 5 outlines the main conclusions and future lines of research.

2   Problem Description

The problem addressed in this paper is the collaborative planning of planting, harvesting, distribution and sale of crops in a SC composed of multiple farms and markets. The SC commercialises multiple crops that have a limited shelf life. Markets require crops to have a minimum shelf-life at the time of sale to be accepted.

Figure 1 shows the composition of the SC as well as the main decisions or activities, carried out by each of its actors, that are considered in this paper. Thus, farmers are responsible for planting, cultivating, harvesting the area defined for each crop, storing, and packing the harvested crops, and transporting them to markets. Once they reach the markets, the crops are sold to the final consumers.

In addition, if the shelf-life of the product is shorter than required by the market during storage or while they are on the market, they are wasted. On the other hand, if the supply of the product is less than the demand, unsatisfied demand is generated.

Moreover, the following assumptions are considered:

- The area available on the farms can be planted in different weeks in the same year but can only be planted once.

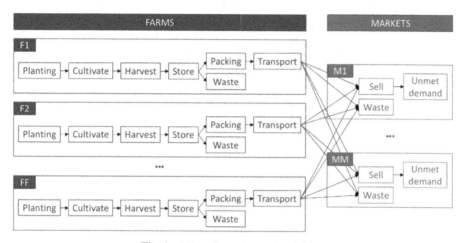

Fig. 1. SC configuration and activities.

- The planting, cultivation and harvesting calendar is known for each type of crop. The cultivation and harvesting periods are dependent on the planting period.
- The yield of the plants is known and depends on the planting and harvesting period of the plants.
- Once harvested, crops have a limited shelf-life.
- Harvested crops can be stored on farm until their shelf-life is lower than the required by the markets.
- The crops are packed on the farms and transported to the markets in the same period of their packing.
- All crops that reach the market are sold if supply is less than or equal to demand. In this case, unsatisfied demand could be generated.
- If the supply of crops in the markets is higher than the demand, wastage is generated in the markets.
- The aim is to achieve planning sustainability by maximizing profits, minimizing wastage, and minimizing unsatisfied demand.

3   Collaborative Tool

This section proposes a collaborative tool to plan the planting, harvesting, distribution and sale of multiple crops that allows balancing supply and demand of multiple crops in a sustainable way while preserving farmers' individually.

The tool is composed of three stages (Fig. 2). For the first stage, a centralized mixed integer linear programming model is formulated to plan the planting, harvesting, distribution, and sale of the crops and to establish the minimum and maximum proportion of area to be planted with each crop and in each planting period in order to balance supply and demand. This model aims for sustainability of the SC by maximizing profit (economic), minimizing waste (environmental), and minimizing unsatisfied demand (social).

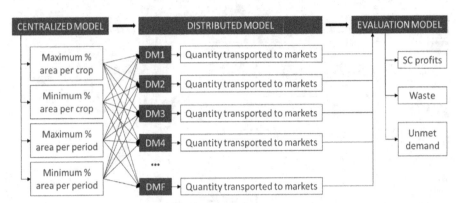

Fig. 2. Collaborative tool

For the second stage, a distributed mixed integer linear programming model is formulated that allows farmers to plan the planting, harvesting, distribution and sale of crops separately and independently. This model considers the minimum and maximum proportion of area to be planted with each crop obtained in the first stage as an input. Therefore, farmers' independence is not unrestricted but controlled. Since at this level farmers have no information on market demand and supply from other farmers, it is assumed that all crops transported from farms to markets are sold.

Given that the entire quantity transported may not be finally sold to the markets due to existing demand, and to test the validity and advantages of the proposed collaborative tool, an assessment model is formulated. This model draws on the quantities of crops that farmers have decided to transport to the markets and derives what the actual profits, wastage and unsatisfied demand in the SC will be.

3.1 Centralized Model Formulation

Table 1 shows the notation used to formulate the centralized model to define the minimum and maximum proportion of area to be planted with each crop and in each planting period.

The model has three objectives aligned with the three pillars of sustainability. The economic objective is to maximize profits from the SC and consists of sales and costs related to planting and cultivation of crops, storage, and transport (1). The environmental objective is the minimization of waste generated and consists of crop waste at farms and at markets (2). The social objective consists of minimizing the unsatisfied demand for crops (3), ensuring the meeting of the human needs, and increasing the consumers' satisfaction.

$$Max\ Z_{ECC} = \sum_c \sum_m \sum_{h\in H_c} \sum_t sp_{cm}^{tx=sl_c+h-t} \cdot QS_{cm}^{ht} - \sum_c \sum_f \sum_{p\in P_c} cpc_c \cdot AP_{cf}^p$$
$$- \sum_c \sum_f \sum_{h\in H_c} \sum_t ch_c \cdot I_{cf}^{ht} - \sum_c \sum_f \sum_m \sum_{h\in H_c} \sum_t ct_{cfm} \cdot QT_{cfm}^{ht} \quad (1)$$

$$Min\ Z_{ENVC} = \sum_c \sum_f \sum_{h\in H_c} \sum_t WF_{cf}^{ht} + \sum_c \sum_m \sum_{h\in H_c} \sum_t WM_{cm}^{ht} \quad (2)$$

Table 1. Notation for the centralized model.

Indices	
c	Crop $(c = 1, \ldots, C)$
p	Planting period $(p = 1, \ldots, P)$
h	Harvest period $(h = 1, \ldots, H)$
t	Time period $(t = 1, \ldots, T)$
f	Farm $(f = 1, \ldots, F)$
m	Market $(m = 1, \ldots, M)$
x	Freshness of crop $(x = sl_c + h - t)$
Set of indices	
P_c	Set of periods p in which the crop c can be planted
H_c	Set of periods h in which the crop c can be harvested
PC_c^p	Set of periods t in which crop c is to be cultivated (activities related to irrigation, application of phytosanitary products, among others) if it is planted in period p
PH_c^p	Set of periods h in which crop c is to be harvested if it is planted in period p
HP_c^h	Set of periods p in which crop c can be planted to be harvested in period h
Parameters	
a_f	Area available for planting on farm f
am_c	Minimum area to be planted with crop c in case of planting due to technical reasons
ma	Maximum difference between the minimum and maximum planting area ratio
y_c^{ph}	Yield of crop c if planted in period p and harvested in period h
sl_c^h	Shelf-life of crop c if harvested in period h
msl_c	Minimum shelf-life required by the markets for the sale of crop c
d_{cm}^t	Demand for crop c in market m and in period t
sp_{cm}^{tx}	Selling price of a kilogram of crop c with freshness x on market m in period t
cpc_c	Cost of planting and cultivating one hectare of crop c
ch_c	Cost of inventorying one kilogram of crop c during a period
ct_{cfm}	Cost of transporting one kilogram of crop c between farm f and market m
Decision variables	
AP_{cf}^p	Area planted with crop c on farm f in planting period p
$AMinc_c$	Minimum proportion of the area to be planted with crop c
$AMaxc_c$	Maximum proportion of the area to be planted with crop c
$AMinp_p$	Minimum proportion of the area to be planted in planting period p
$AMaxp_p$	Maximum proportion of the area to be planted in planting period p

(continued)

Table 1. (*continued*)

YP^p_{cf}	Binary variable with value 1 if crop c is planted on farm f in period p, and 0 if not
AC^t_{cf}	Area planted with crop c on farm f cultivated in period t
AH^{ph}_{cf}	Area planted with crop c on farm f in period p and harvested in period h
QH^h_{cf}	Quantity of crop c harvested on farm f in harvest period h
QP^{ht}_{cf}	Quantity of crop c harvested on farm f in period h and packed in period t
WF^{ht}_{cf}	Quantity of crop c harvested on farm f in period h and wasted in period t
I^{ht}_{cf}	Quantity of crop c harvested on farm f in period h and inventoried in period t
QT^{ht}_{cfm}	Quantity of crop c harvested on farm f in h and transported to market m in period t
WM^{ht}_{cm}	Quantity of crop c harvested on market m in period h and wasted in period t
QS^{ht}_{cm}	Quantity of crop c harvested in period h and sold at market m in period t
U^t_{cm}	Quantity of unsatisfied demand for crop c at market m in period t

$$Min\ Z_{SOC_C} = \sum_c \sum_m \sum_t U^t_{cm} \tag{3}$$

The centralized model is subject to the following constraints.

The area planted on each farm with all crops in all planting periods cannot exceed the area available on the farm (4).

$$\sum_c \sum_{p \in P_c} AP^p_{cf} \leq a_f \qquad\qquad \forall f \tag{4}$$

The total area panted with each crop on each farm must be between the minimum and maximum area ratio defined for each crop (5).

$$a_f \cdot AMinc_c \leq \sum_{p \in P_c} AP^p_{cf} \leq a_f \cdot AMaxc_c \qquad \forall c, f \tag{5}$$

The total area planted in each period on each farm must be between the minimum and maximum area ratio defined for each planting period (6).

$$a_f \cdot AMinp_p \leq \sum_c AP^p_{cf} \leq a_f \cdot AMaxp_p \qquad \forall f, p \tag{6}$$

The ratio of minimum area to be planted will all crops (7) and in all planting periods (8) must be less than unity, which is equivalent to the total area to be planted.

$$\sum_c AMinc_c \leq 1 \tag{7}$$

$$\sum_p AMinp_p \leq 1 \tag{8}$$

The difference between the maximum and minimum proportion of area to be planted with each crop (9) and in each period (10) may not exceed the fixed limit.

$$AMaxc_c - AMinc_c \leq ma \qquad \forall c \tag{9}$$

$$AMaxp_p - AMinp_p \leq ma \qquad \forall c \tag{10}$$

In case it is decided to plant a crop in one period, a minimum area must be planted due to technological reasons (11).

$$am_c \cdot YP_{cf}^p \leq AP_{cf}^p \leq a_f \cdot YP_{cf}^p \qquad \forall c,f, p \in P_c \tag{11}$$

The entire planted area must be cultivated (12) and harvested (13) in the required periods, which depend on the planting period.

$$AC_{cf}^t = \sum_{p \in PC_c^t} AP_{cf}^p \qquad \forall c,f,t \tag{12}$$

$$AH_{cf}^{ph} = AP_{cf}^p \qquad \forall c,f, p \in P_c, h \in PH_c^p \tag{13}$$

The quantity of harvested crops depends on the yield of the plants, which is different depending on the planting and harvesting period and the crop (14).

$$\sum_{p \in HP_c^h} y_c^{ph} \cdot AH_{cf}^{ph} = QH_{cf}^h \qquad \forall c,f, h \in H_c \tag{14}$$

The harvested crops can be stored, packed, or wasted (15). These crops can be kept in storage until the shelf-life of the crops is less than that required by the markets (16), at which point they cannot be inventoried (17).

$$I_{cf}^{ht} = QH_{cf}^h - QP_{cf}^{ht} - WF_{cf}^{ht} \qquad \forall c,f, h \in H_c, t = h \tag{15}$$

$$I_{cf}^{ht} = I_{cf}^{ht-1} - QP_{cf}^{ht} - WF_{cf}^{ht} \qquad \forall c,f, h \in H_c, h < t \leq h + sl_c^h - msl_c \tag{16}$$

$$I_{cf}^{ht} = 0 \qquad \forall c,f, h \in H_c, t = h + sl_c^h - msl_c \tag{17}$$

The packed crops are transported within the same period of their packing to the markets (18), where they can be sold or wasted (19).

$$QP_{cf}^{ht} = \sum_m QT_{cfm}^{ht} \qquad \forall c,f, h \in H_c, h \leq t \leq h + sl_c^h - msl_c \tag{18}$$

$$\sum_f QT_{cfm}^{ht} = QS_{cm}^{ht} + WM_{cm}^{ht} \qquad \forall c, m, h \in H_c, h \leq t \leq h + sl_c^h - msl_c \tag{19}$$

In the case of insufficient crop availability to serve the demand, unsatisfied demand is produced (20).

$$\sum_{h \in H_c} QS_{cm}^{ht} + U_{cm}^t = d_{cm}^t \qquad\qquad \forall c, m, t \qquad\qquad (20)$$

Finally, the nature of the decision variables is defined (20).

$$AP_{cf}^p, AC_{cf}^t, AH_{cf}^{ph}, QH_{cf}^h, I_{cf}^{ht}, QP_{cf}^{ht}, QT_{cfm}^{ht}, QS_{cfm}^{ht}, WF_{cf}^{ht}, WM_{cm}^{ht}, U_{cm}^t \; CONTINUOUS \qquad (21)$$
$$YP_{cf}^p \qquad\qquad\qquad\qquad\qquad\qquad\qquad\qquad\qquad\qquad\qquad\qquad\qquad BINARY$$

3.2 Distributed Model Formulation

Table 2 shows the additional notation used to formulate the distributed model for planning the planting, harvesting, distribution and sale of crops on a farm.

Table 2. Notation added for the distributed model

Parameter	
a	Area available for planting on farm
ct_{cfm}	Cost of transporting one kilogram of crop c between farm f and market m
Decision variables	
AP_c^p	Area planted with crop c in planting period p
YP_c^p	Binary variable with value one if crop c is planted in period p, and zero if not
AC_c^t	Area planted with crop c cultivated in period t
AH_c^{ph}	Area planted with crop c in period p and harvested in period h
QH_c^h	Quantity of crop c harvested in harvest period h
QP_c^{ht}	Quantity of crop c harvested in period h and packed in period t
WF_c^{ht}	Quantity of crop c harvested in period h and wasted in period t
I_c^{ht}	Quantity of crop c harvested in period h and inventoried in period t
QT_{cm}^{ht}	Quantity of crop c harvested in period h and transported to market m in period t

The distributed model considers the economic and environmental objectives analogous to those of the centralized model but focused on a single farm. The economic objective is to maximize the farmer's profit, which is made up of sales and costs related to planting and cultivating crops, storage, and transport (22). The environmental objective is to minimize waste generated on the farm (23). The social objective of minimizing unsatisfied demand is not considered at this stage as farmers do not have information on market demand.

$$Max \; Z_{EC_D} = \sum_c \sum_m \sum_{h \in H_c} \sum_t sp_{cm}^{tx=t-h} \cdot QT_{cm}^{ht} - \sum_c \sum_{p \in P_c} cpc_c \cdot AP_c^p$$

$$-\sum_c \sum_{h \in H_c} \sum_t ch_c \cdot I_c^{ht} - \sum_c \sum_m \sum_{h \in H_c} \sum_t ct_{cm} \cdot QT_{cm}^{ht} \tag{22}$$

$$Min\ Z_{ENV_D} = \sum_c \sum_{h \in H_c} \sum_t WF_c^{ht} \tag{23}$$

The model is subjected to the constraints (24)–(35) which are analogous to those in the centralized model (4)–(6), (11)–(19). In these constraints, $AMinc_c, AMaxc_c, AMinp_p$, and $AMaxp_p$ act as parameters and not as decision variables. The nature of the variables is defined (34).

$$\sum_c \sum_{p \in P_c} AP_c^p \leq a \tag{24}$$

$$a \cdot AMinc_c \leq \sum_{p \in P_c} AP_c^p \leq a \cdot AMaxc_c \qquad \forall c \tag{25}$$

$$a_f \cdot AMinp_p \leq \sum_c AP_c^p \leq a_f \cdot AMaxp_p \qquad \forall f, p \tag{26}$$

$$am_c \cdot YP_c^p \leq AP_c^p \leq a_f \cdot YP_c^p \qquad \forall c, p \in P_c \tag{27}$$

$$AC_c^t = \sum_{p \in PC_c^t} AP_c^p \qquad \forall c, t \tag{28}$$

$$AH_c^{ph} = AP_c^p \qquad \forall c, p \in P_c, h \in PH_c^p \tag{29}$$

$$\sum_{p \in Hp_c^h} y_c^{ph} \cdot AH_c^{ph} = QH_c^{ph} \qquad \forall c, h \in H_c \tag{30}$$

$$I_c^{ht} = QH_c^h - QP_c^{ht} - WF_c^{ht} \qquad \forall c, h \in H_c, t = h \tag{31}$$

$$I_c^{ht} = I_c^{ht-1} - QP_c^{ht} - WF_c^{ht} \qquad \forall c, h \in H_c, h < t \leq h + sl_c^h - msl_c \tag{32}$$

$$I_c^{ht} = 0 \qquad \forall c, h \in H_c, t = h + sl_c^h - msl_c \tag{33}$$

$$QP_c^{ht} = \sum_m QT_{cm}^{ht} \qquad \forall c, h \in H_c, h \leq t \leq h + sl_c^h - msl_c \tag{34}$$

$$\begin{aligned} &AP_c^p, AC_c^t, AH_c^{ph}, QH_c^h, I_c^{ht}, QP_c^{ht}, QT_{cm}^{ht}, WF_c^{ht}\ CONTINUOUS \\ &YP_c^p \qquad\qquad\qquad\qquad\qquad\qquad\qquad\qquad\quad BINARY \end{aligned} \tag{35}$$

3.3 Evaluation Model Formulation

To assess the impact of farmers' independent decisions on SC outcomes, a third evaluation model is defined, that is composed of the objective functions defined in the centralized model (1)–(3) and the constraints (19) and (20) that regulate the sales of the crops that are transported to the markets from farms. Therefore, the model receives as input data the values of AP_{cf}^p, QT_{cfm}^{ht}, I_{cf}^{ht} and WF_c^{ht} obtained in the distributed models that are needed for the calculation of the real sales and values of the objective functions.

3.4   Resolution Methodology

To solve the multi-objective models, the weighted sum method is used. This consists of assigning weights to the objectives according to their relative importance in order to construct a single objective function. The weights assigned to the objectives must add up to 100%. Thus, w_{EC} is the weight assigned to profit maximization, w_{ENV} is the weight assigned to waste minimization, and w_{SOC} is the weight assigned to minimizing unsatisfied demand. In addition, since each objective has a different order of magnitude, each of its values is divided by the maximum value that it can acquire so that the values obtained are between zero and one.

Thus, the centralized model would be as follows:

$$Max\ Z_C = w_{EC_C} \cdot \frac{Z_{EC_C}}{maxZ_{EC_C}} - w_{ENV_C} \cdot \frac{Z_{ENV_C}}{maxZ_{ENV_C}} - w_{SOC_C} \cdot \frac{Z_{SOC_C}}{maxZ_{SOC_C}} \quad (36)$$

Subject to: (4)–(21)
The formulated of the distributed model would be as follows:

$$Max\ Z_D = w_{EC_D} \cdot \frac{Z_{EC_D}}{maxZ_{EC_D}} - w_{ENV_D} \cdot \frac{Z_{ENV_D}}{maxZ_{ENV_D}} \quad (37)$$

Subject to: (24)–(35)
And finally, the evaluation model would be:

$$MaxZ_C$$

Subject to: (19) and (20)

$$QS_{cfm}^{ht},\ WM_{cm}^{ht},\ U_{cm}^{t} \qquad CONTINUOUS \qquad (38)$$

4   Application to the La Plata Tomato SC

The proposed collaborative tool is validated through its application to the case study of the production of different tomato varieties in La Plata region of Argentina. The SC consists of ten farms and two markets and commercializes three tomato varieties (round, pear, and cherry) with a shelf-life of two weeks [1].

To show the functioning of the designed tool, it is tested for the case where equal relative weight is given to all objectives. That is, 33% is assigned to profit maximization, waste minimization and minimization of unsatisfied demand in the case of the centralized and evaluation models, and 50% is assigned to profit maximization and waste minimization in the case of the distributed model.

The first block of Fig. 3 (Centralized) shows the range of area to be planted for each tomato variety and in each planting period. These ranges are determined by the minimum and maximum proportion of area obtained by the centralized model for these cases. These values are employed in the distributed models as an input.

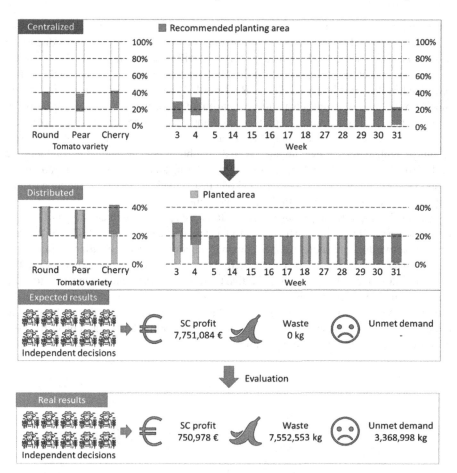

Fig. 3. Collaborative tool application and results.

The second block of Fig. 3 (Distributed) shows in addition to the recommended area range for each tomato variety and planting period (green), the proportion of area that farmers have decided to plant independently (yellow) and which is obtained after running the distributed model for the ten farmers and aggregating the results obtained. In addition, the aggregated results of the profits and waste that farmers expect to obtain by making their decision in a distributed way are displayed. To obtain these values, the profits and wastage that each farmer expects to obtain after running the distributed model were added together.

As for the proportion of area planted with each crop and in each planting period, these coincide in all the farms, this being the mix that optimizes the objectives set. In this case, all farmers decide to plant the maximum recommended area ratio with round and pear tomatoes, because they offer the highest economic margin. In the case of cherry tomatoes, only the minimum recommended area ratio is planted. As for the planting periods, it is shown that in some of them it is decided not to plant, while in others the minimum recommended, the maximum recommended, or an area between these two values is planted. The farmers expect to obtain more than seven million euros due to the sale of the entire harvest, which means that there will be no waste.

However, after the evaluation of the distributed decisions, it can be seen in the results presented in the third block of Fig. 3 (Real results) that the real profits of the SC are much lower than expected, also suffering an increase in waste and the generation of unmet demand. This is because supply and demand for crops are still not fully balanced.

To test the advantages of using the collaborative tool versus not using it, the real results previously shown are compared with those obtained by not using the collaborative tool. To do this the distributed model is used considering that the minimum and maximum proportion area to be planted are zero and one respectively in all cases, and then results are aggregated and assessed with the evaluation model.

Figure 4 compares the proportion of the total area planted with each type of tomato by farmers according to the distributed models and the real economic (SC profit), environmental (waste), and social (unmet demand) outcomes for the SC after evaluation of the distributed decisions for the cases where the collaboration tool is and is not used.

In the case of not using the collaborative tool, farmers decide independently to plant only the tomato variety that was the most profitable in the previous year, in this case, the round tomato. In contrast, when using the collaborative tool, farmers decide to plant all three tomato varieties respecting the areas recommended by the tool and planting more of those varieties that are more profitable.

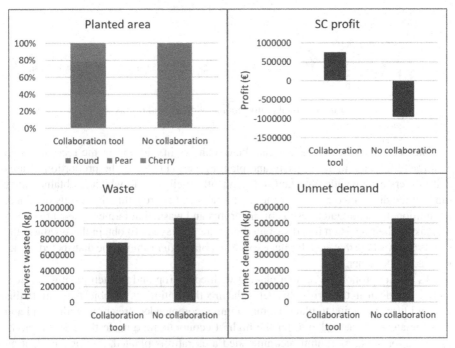

Fig. 4. Comparation of SC results using the collaboration tool or not.

When assessing the impact of these decisions on the SC by not using the collaborative tool, the chain suffers large economic losses due to the costs of planting, storing, and transporting round tomatoes that cannot be sold because there is not enough demand. This causes the wastage of a large quantity of tomatoes. Also, the entire demand for pear and cherry tomatoes cannot be met since they are not produced, being represented as unmet demand.

On the contrary, when the collaborative tool is used, a better balance between demand and supply is achieved. This has a positive impact on the sustainability of the SC economically, environmentally, and socially. Thus, farmers already benefit economically from their decisions while maintaining their independence in decision-making, and tomato waste and unmet demand are reduced.

4.1 Computational Efficiency

The optimization program MPL Modeling System® Release 5.0.8.116 with the solver Gurobi Optimization 9.1.1 has been used to implement and solve the proposed models in a computer with two processors Intel® Xeon® CPU E5–2640 v2 @ 2.00 GHz 2.00 GHz, an installed capacity of 32 GB and a 64-bit operating system. In addition, databases created in Microsoft Access Database have been used both to import the input data for the models and to export the values obtained for the decision variables.

Table 3 shows the size and resolution time of the models for the presented case study. Given that the distributed models are run once per farmer up to a total of ten runs, the lowest and highest resolution time is shown for these models.

Table 3. Computational efficiency.

Scenario	Model	Constraints	Continuous variables	Binary variables	Resolution time (seconds)
Collaboration tool	Centralized	16658	20696	390	1.45
	Distributed	1590	1956	39	0.10–0.17
	Evaluation	708	1104	–	0.06
No collaboration	Distributed	1558	1956	39	0.12–0.25
	Evaluation	708	1104	–	0.07

5 Conclusions and Future Research

In this paper, a collaborative tool based on optimization models has been proposed that allows farmers to individually plan the planting, harvesting and distribution of crops by providing a better balance between crop supply and demand than that obtained when farmers make decisions completely independently (without the collaborative tool). A model has also been proposed to evaluate the performance of the decisions made by farmers when using or not using the collaborative tool.

The results show that by using the proposed tool, more crops are planted, and the sustainability of the SC is increased due to increased profits (economic aspect), reduced waste (environmental aspect) and reduced unsatisfied demand for crops (social aspect).

In the future, the proposed collaborative tool could be extended by using different artificial intelligence algorithms such as reinforcement learning to establish the minimum and maximum proportion of area to be planted with each crop and the minimum and maximum proportion of area to be planted in each planting period. In this way, through an iterative process, it would be possible to better adjust these ratios to achieve a better balance between supply and demand, while maintaining individuality in the farmers' decision-making.

On the other hand, the proposed tool has been used for the case where equal weight is assigned to the three objectives (maximising profit, minimising waste, and minimising unsatisfied demand). In future work, a sensitivity analysis could be carried out on the weights assigned to the objectives and the impact this has on the plannings obtained by the tool.

Acknowledgments. We acknowledge the support of the project 691249, RUCAPS: "Enhancing and implementing knowledge based ICT solutions within high risk and uncertain conditions for agriculture production systems", funded by the European Union's research and innovation programme under the H2020 Marie Skłodowska-Curie Actions.

References

1. Alemany, M.M.E., Esteso, A., Ortiz, Á., del Pino, M.: Centralized and distributed optimization models for the multi-farmer crop planning problem under uncertainty: application to a fresh tomato Argentinean supply chain case study. Comput. Ind. Eng. **153**, 107048 (2021). https://doi.org/10.1016/j.cie.2020.107048
2. Tweeten, L., Thompson, S.R.R.: Long-term global agricultural output supply-demand balance and real farm and food prices. Farm Policy J. **6**, 1–16 (2009)
3. Zaraté, P., Alemany, M.M.E., del Pino, M., Alvarez, A.E., Camilleri, G.: How to support group decision making in horticulture: an approach based on the combination of a centralized mathematical model and a group decision support system. In: Freitas, P.S.A., Dargam, F., Moreno, J.M. (eds.) EmC-ICDSST 2019. LNBIP, vol. 348, pp. 83–94. Springer, Cham (2019). https://doi.org/10.1007/978-3-030-18819-1_7
4. Huka, H., Ruoja, C., Mchopa, A.: Price fluctuation of agricultural products and its impact on small scale farmers development: case analysis from Kilimanjaro Tanzania. Eur. J. Bus. Manag. **6**, 155–160 (2014)
5. Ahumada, O., Villalobos, J.R., Mason, A.N.: Tactical planning of the production and distribution of fresh agricultural products under uncertainty. Agric. Syst. **112**, 17–26 (2012). https://doi.org/10.1016/j.agsy.2012.06.002
6. Najafabadi, M.M., Ziaee, S., Nikouei, A., Ahmadpour Borazjani, M.: Mathematical programming model (MMP) for optimization of regional cropping patterns decisions: a case study. Agric. Syst. **173**, 218–232 (2019). https://doi.org/10.1016/j.agsy.2019.02.006
7. Esteso, A., Alemany, M.M.E., Ortiz, A., Liu, S.: Optimization model to support sustainable crop planning for reducing unfairness among farmers. Cent. Eur. J. Oper. Res. **30**, 1101–1127 (2022). https://doi.org/10.1007/s10100-021-00751-8

Collaborative Eco-Industrial Networks: A Case Study

Ovidiu Noran[✉]

IIIS Centre for Enterprise Architecture Research and Management, Griffith University,
Brisbane, Australia
O.Noran@griffith.edu.au

Abstract. Circular Economy is the typical industry response to climate change - the ubiquitous and urgent problem of our times. Previous work has presented a multidisciplinary approach towards the optimal enactment of Circular Economy through Eco-Industrial Networking, able to deal with its many-faceted and complex aspects. This paper takes this work further by investigating the practical use of the relevant concepts within a real-world case study followed by drawing conclusions and proposing potential improvements. A concise theoretical background is followed by the explanation of the scenario and of the proposed concepts' application in practice, including challenges and benefits of the chosen approach. Finally, a reflection is carried out and conclusions are drawn, followed by proposals for future applications and development of the method.

Keywords: Collaborative networks · Eco-industrial networking · Enterprise architecture · Green virtual enterprise

1 Introduction

The increasingly ubiquitous impact of climate change, biodiversity loss, waste, and pollution have brought forward the need for urgent and meaningful action [1]. Among the possible avenues for tackling these problems, the circular economy (CE) [2] initiative features prominently due to its potential to address the root causes of the above-mentioned challenges, by aiming to share, lease, reuse, repair, refurbish and recycle existing materials and products for as long as possible [3]. As shown in previous work [4, 5], CE can be more effectively enacted in a structured collaborative environment by adopting the Eco-Industrial Network (EIN) approach [6], which in turn builds on Environmental Management concepts applied to proven Collaborative Networking (CN) paradigms [7]. In order to deal with complexity and emergent behaviour aspects that typically manifest themselves in the EIN endeavour, some authors [8–10] have proposed adopting a multidisciplinary stance that provides a holistic approach considering all aspects relevant to the specific EIN endeavour.

This paper describes a practical EIN case study which has been tackled using this multidisciplinary paradigm while laying more emphasis on the Enterprise Architecture and Collaborative Network artefacts; the focus is on the application and benefits of the approach in practice, while observing challenges encountered and lessons learned.

© IFIP International Federation for Information Processing 2022
Published by Springer Nature Switzerland AG 2022
L. M. Camarinha-Matos et al. (Eds.): PRO-VE 2022, IFIP AICT 662, pp. 533–542, 2022.
https://doi.org/10.1007/978-3-031-14844-6_42

2 Background

The industrial application of Circular Economy, namely Industrial Ecology (IE) provides the model for the formation and operation of the EIN. IE supports moving from a linear progression of the resources through the system to an integrated and circular so-called 'industrial eco-system', optimizing all relevant resource flows (including information and knowledge) to up- and down-cycle them. As they become inputs for new processes, such resources are fully utilized and thus support reducing the dependence on non-renewable natural resources [11].

The practical manifestation of Industrial Ecology, Industrial Eco-systems (IES), typically subsume a plethora of autonomous entities that in turn possess interrelated and interdependent components within their 'techno-sphere' (man-made technological systems) and their 'biosphere' (natural ecosystems) [12]; as the boundary between these components are often blurred, and in the context of the Internet of Things (IoT), IES are nowadays becoming complex cyber-physical systems (CPS).

The capability to promptly bid for and win large grants and/or projects requires an adequate set of competencies and resources; often, this is beyond the capabilities of most companies taken in isolation. Therefore, companies often form 'alliances' taking forms of Collaborative Networks (CNs) such as Breeding Environments (BE) which are set up so as to achieve the required preparedness to promptly create Virtual Enterprises (VEs) able to bid for projects as described above [13]. Typically, CNs feature one or more lead partners which orchestrate the BE and VE efforts and one or more brokers whose role is to identify and acquire new collaboration opportunities and negotiate with potential participants [14]. If successful in bidding, the VEs then build and manage projects while also possibly using resources outside the CN.

Moving on to the next knowledge area, namely Enterprise Architecture (EA), Gartner Research [15] sees it as representing a holistic change management paradigm connecting management and engineering best-practice, providing requirements, principles and models that describe future state of the enterprise. This paradigm includes humans, processes, information and technology within the enterprise, together with their internal and external relationships; according to the definition above, it can be considered that EA represents in fact the 'ontology of change'.

Typically, such viewpoints are structured in EA frameworks (EAF). Several such artefacts are currently in use worldwide, depending on various factors; in order to ensure the most relevance and coverage to the problem at hand, the author has decided to adopt a framework that represents and generalizes several mainstream EAFs, namely the Generalized Enterprise Reference Architecture and methodology (GERAM), which is described in Annex A of the ISO15704 Standard [16]. This EAF includes a reference architecture (GERA) containing a modelling framework (MF) which integrates aspects deemed of the most importance for the EIN problem at hand. An important aspect is the presence of the life cycle concept, which is absent from the majority of other approaches [17, 18] and can be used as a background to all the other viewpoints, as shown in Fig. 1, left on the vertical axis.

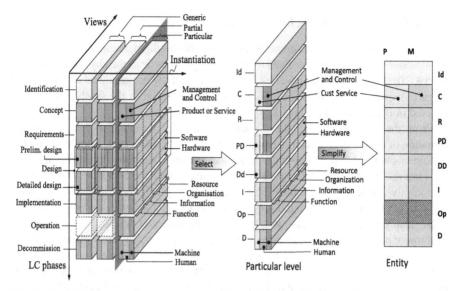

Fig. 1. Deriving the modelling constructs used to analyze specific viewpoints in the case study.

Note that the proposed MF defines requirements for the expressiveness of the candidate languages, rather than enforcing specific selections; in addition, it also integrates viewpoints present in other disciplines relevant to EIN in a multi-dimensional framework as shown in Fig. 1, left. This enables multiple analyses in a consistent manner, by allowing selected viewpoints to be examined separately at any one time, as shown in Fig. 1 right and further in Sect. 3.

For the reasons above, it is hereby argued that EA, as a provider of useful artefacts, is an ideal companion to the CN approach involved in this case study analysis.

3   A Collaborative Eco-Industrial Network

3.1   Situation

A large company and developer aimed to diversify its investments by creating an industrial precinct; the decision was taken to adopt a recycling-based strategy, so as to minimize waste and pollution and realise savings on raw materials. The strategy was to attract various participants to the precinct and then get selected members to form a recycling-based environment based on their potential and willingness to connect their relevant inputs and outputs. However, there was a need a) for guidance as to how to select these partners in the initial and continuing stages and b) to define the kind of association these partners were to enter and furthermore the various ways they could connect in order to realise the circularity concept – more specifically, the various configurations the partner association would create. In view of the above narrative, it became apparent that the theoretical background presented in Sect. 2 could be used to provide guidance towards the set-up and operation of the envisaged network.

3.2 Setting up the Breeding Environment

The above situation matched a combined CE and CN paradigm, namely the closed-loop logistics and integrating forward and reverse supply chains described by various authors [12, 19, 20]. In the particular case described, in view of the geographical co-location of the participants, the specific type of EIN envisaged was that of the symbiosis network depicted in Patala et al.'s [10] work.

From the point of view of the CN knowledge area, the situation was akin to the formation of a so-called 'Green' Breeding Environment (GBE) [12], a pool of potential participants which are pre-qualified (for instance, all the cooperation protocols and contracts are pre-established and negotiated) and thus achieve the necessary preparedness to promptly participate in various joint ventures (aptly called 'Green' Virtual Enterprises, or GVEs) as required to bid for- and win project opportunities and/or grants. The initial 'lead partner' in this case was the large company and developer; subsequently, other major participants followed: a telecommunications company ensuring the essential infrastructure (data centre and 'lake') and a tertiary education institution contributing the necessary research and innovation resources. The selection of these lead partners has been a result of investigating the relevant areas that needed to be addressed by potential partners (using the EA MF viewpoints, namely Information and Resource). Further on, several other participants have been identified and qualified as GBE members using the same multi-disciplinary approach, as shown in Fig. 2.

The qualification process was based on several criteria; a first qualifying condition was the initial preparedness to participate in the Circular Economy-based GBE, i.e. whether the aspiring participants had any existing or potential inputs or outputs that could connect with other GBE members. This initial analysis has involved using the IE-inspired technical and organisational domains, encompassed and complemented by the EA MF Function, Information, Resource and Organisation (FIRO) viewpoints.

A further qualifying criterion for BE membership from the point of view of SoS has been the commitment to build up adequate connectivity preparedness by developing and maintaining a 'digital twin' [21] for the potential input/output connections that could develop between the GBE members. The concept of digital twin has been used before in EIN [22]; in this case study, it was necessary in order to start quantifying the inputs and outputs of the various 'exchange streams' participants (not performed in previous cases as erroneously being deemed not necessary). Measuring the amount of matter, information and energy involved in the streams was paramount to their proper setup and operation (also involving trading) that underpinned the entire Eco-Industrial Network paradigm. From the CN point of view, the situation looked as per Table 1:

Table 1. CN specifics of the case study

Generic CN notion	Practical manifestation
Breeding environment	Qualified network participants
Virtual enterprise	Lead partner, Telco, Education
Broker	Green virtual enterprise
Streams	Exchanges via interfaces
Reference model	Interface templates

EA MF viewpoints have been used to detail streams; thus, e.g. functional and informational criteria have been used to elicit which exchange activities must be modelled and what data is needed to describe relevant properties of the exchanges, respectively.

3.3 Building the Virtual Enterprise

The lead partners within the GBE have decided to allocate resources to a workgroup whose tasks are to create input/output streams connecting GBE members and also to apply for government and private funding supporting EIN endeavours. According to the CN body of knowledge, a suitable materialisation of such a workgroup is a VE; however, in this case study, this entity is expected to have a lasting presence and take on other tasks which are not assigned to it in the typical CN realm.

The initial models had the format shown in Fig. 2, requiring a separate diagram for each exchange so as to ensure readability.

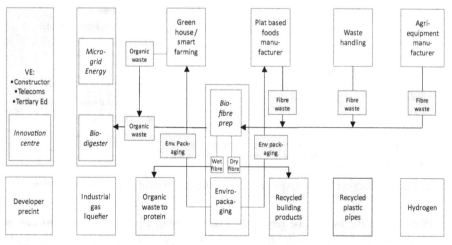

Fig. 2. Extract from the set of initial EIN Models including the BE, VE and the Streams.

This meant that showing potential relations between streams was very difficult and required shuffling between diagrams which was very awkward for stakeholders. In addition, many essential aspects such as life cycle of the BE participants, VE and the streams and the potential relations between them could not be meaningfully represented. According to the concepts described in the theoretical background section and previous successful life cycle-based endeavours in the area of environmental management [23, 24], it has been proposed to use the modelling constructs proposed in Sect. 2 and analyse the results.

Figure 3 shows the same situation in a 'business model' using the EA modelling construct derived as shown in Fig. 1, which allows a richer representation considering the life cycles of the participants and management/production (or service) aspects.

The arrows between entities represent the role played by the originating entity in the life cycle/s of the destination entity. Note that some arrows originate from- and point to the same entity (e.g. in the case of the VE and the streams S1 and S2); this is to indicate the capacity of the entity to change itself to a certain extent (adaptation/agility), as further explained. Various line types and colours are also used as illustrated in the same figure, in order to better represent possible scenarios or behaviours.

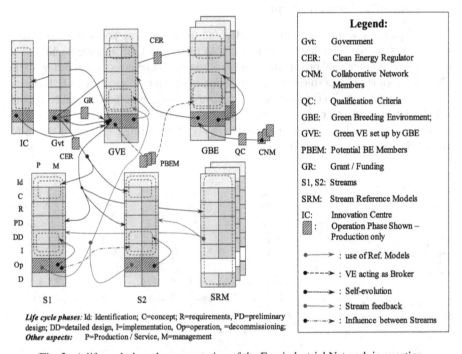

Life cycle phases: Id: Identification; C=concept; R=requirements, PD=preliminary design; DD=detailed design, I=implementation, Op=operation, =decommissioning; *Other aspects:*   P=Production / Service, M=management

Fig. 3. A life cycle-based representation of the Eco-industrial Network in question

Should specific aspects be required to be represented, various viewpoints can be selected from the MF shown in Fig. 1 left. For example, if the contents of the streams need to be shown, the Information viewpoint may be selected and an appropriate language such as Entity Relationship- or UML Class Diagrams can be used; if the flow of data or sequence of activities within a stream need to be represented for analysis and costing, the Function viewpoint may be selected and a view created using a language such as IDEF0 or UML Activity Diagram may be used. While one can use such languages independently of employing an (EA) MF, the advantage here is that all the viewpoints represented are linked via the framework through a common meta-model and as such, the consistency of the complete model can be intrinsically maintained.

In Fig. 3, one can see the role of governmental agencies such as the Clean Energy Regulator (CER) in the early life cycle phases (identification, concept) of the GBE and the Streams, in order to abide by the rules and qualify for potential funding (see operating 'CER' on arrow originating from the Government Operation phase going to GBE and Streams' Identification and Concept life cycle phases). The Government also influences the GVE(s) created by the GBE by means of funding ('GR' in the figure).

A GVE is set up by the GBE for several reasons, such as: a) to bid for government grants and other types of funding for CE initiatives b) to set up the interfaces displayed to BE members for stream creation and operation and c) to act as a broker for the CN, investigating the market for new potential participants and bringing them in the GBE.

In the figure, the above facts are shown as follows: a) an arrow going from the GVE to the Government management (lobbying and applying for funding), b) arrows going to the Identification through Detailed Design life cycle phases of the streams and c) arrow containing PBEM (Potential BE Members) going from the GVE to the Identification through to Detailed Design life cycle phases of the GBE, respectively.

The GVE may also create and maintain a set of Stream Reference Models (SRM in Fig. 3), which will be used to store and reuse accumulated knowledge from the creation and operation of previous streams in view of accelerating the creation of new streams. The reference models can be e.g. partially instantiated interfaces presented to GBE members; they can also be used to prepare new entrants for GBE membership.

Notably (and in a deviation from the canonical CN concepts), a so-called 'Innovation Centre' (IC) was also created by the GVE using the capabilities of its tertiary education lead partner, so as to be able to discover and manage new stream possibilities that did not fit any existing/reusable knowledge, while at the same time enabling the continuous improvement of the existing streams and the EIN in general.

Figure 3 also shows how Collaborative Network members (represented as 'CNM') may contribute to the GBE if they satisfy the Qualification Criteria (shown as 'QC'), importantly including adequate preparedness to participate in Streams and agreement to develop Digital Twins.

3.4 Setting up and Operating the Streams

The streams' interfaces are designed by the GVE according to criteria that are mostly specialisations of fundamental viewpoint types present in the above-mentioned MF. When joining the GBE, the assenting CN participants create Digital Twins, which are then employed to quantitively assess their participation in Streams. For example, if within a stream a participant needs CO_2 of certain parameters delivered in a certain manner one can use the Information, Function and Resource viewpoints respectively to model this aspect as required, while the Organisation view may depict the managerial changes required for this stream to occur. The automation viewpoint (see 'machine' and 'human' depictions in Fig. 1) may be used to define any necessary human, machine, or combination thereof trait of the processes involved [25]. Furthermore, the Management vs. Production distinction present in the EA MF can also be used such as for example in Fig. 3 in order to represent how the management of the stream supports its own evolution (within limits shown as the circled life cycle phases).

Figure 3 also depicts the relations between the streams and with the managing GVE in the context of their life cycles. This enables the analysis of alternative forms of such relations, possibly uncovering emergent features that did not exist in the participants, and their positive or negative effects. Thus, Fig. 3 shows how feedback from stream operation analyses can flow back to- and influence the GVE (arrows in the figure from stream operation to GVE detailed design life cycle phase), which may result in restructuring so as to optimise the streams in question.

Note that in the process of stream operation there may be emergent unpredicted optimisations, which may result in autonomous changes (self-evolution) up to a certain level (shown in Fig. 3, as arrows from Management side of Operation up to Detailed Design and Implementation life cycle phases), beyond which the GVE has to be involved in the redesign effort. For example, in the particular case study, there may adjustments in concentration and composition of the gases' production and delivery which can be handled by the stream; however, any major change (e.g. 'blue' rather than 'green'-produced hydrogen for economic reasons) will need to be handled by the GVE.

The streams can also influence each other (see e.g. the dash-dot arrow from Stream 1 to Stream 2 in Fig. 3); for example, in the specific case study if fibre waste is collected from several outputs using shared infrastructure, optimisations may be possible but also bottlenecks may occur. These situations may be modelled showing the extent of the affected life cycle phases (with other viewpoints added as required) and suitable action can be designed and assigned to streams'- or to GVE management, depending on the importance of the issue as previously described.

4   Conclusions and Further Work

This paper has aimed to apply previous research investigating the use of several knowledge areas in EIN to a real-world case study, while laying emphasis on the CN and EA-specific artefacts. Thus, various cohesive models of the EIN have been created and assessed in contrast with the previous approach featuring limited clarity and usability; unfortunately, the available space has limited the number of perspectives that could be exemplified in this paper.

The conclusion has been that EA-based artefacts have enabled a rich and integrated representation of all the required aspects of the relevant entities within the project, especially life cycle, which has facilitated stakeholder synergy underpinned by a common understanding of the present and future situations. Thus, a major contribution of this paper is in the assistance it provides to stakeholders by providing a more coherent, life cycle-based and overarching view of complex projects, enhancing agility and future-proofing by its ability to seamlessly integrate present and emerging modelling concepts.

Beyond reinforcing and refining the application of CN and EA concepts in more case studies, further work may also include incorporating a supporting artefact enabling the creation of directly applicable stream setup, operation and overhaul methods for specific EIN scenarios, such as a meta-methodology [26]. This would provide additional guidance and user friendliness to practitioners seeking to apply the proposed EA artefacts in their projects.

References

1. Manisalidis, I., Stavropoulou, E., Stavropoulos, A., Bezirtzoglou, E.: Environmental and health impacts of air pollution: a review. Front. Public Health **8**(14) (2020). https://doi.org/10.3389/fpubh.2020.00014. PMID: 32154200; PMCID: PMC7044178
2. Brennan, G., Tennant, M., Blomsma, F.: Business and production solutions: closing the loop. In: Kopnina, H., Shoreman-Ouimet, E. (eds.) Sustainability: Key Issues, pp. 219–239. EarthScan (2015)
3. European Parliament: Circular economy: definition, importance and benefits, October 2021. www.europarl.europa.eu
4. Romero, D., Noran, O.: Green virtual enterprises and their breeding environments: engineering their sustainability as systems of systems for the circular economy. IFAC Papers Online **48**(3), 2258–2265 (2015)
5. Halog, A., Balanay, R., Anieke, S., Yu, T.Y.: Circular economy across Australia: taking stock of progress and lessons. Circ. Econ. Sustain. **1**(1), 283–301 (2021). https://doi.org/10.1007/s43615-021-00020-5
6. Yedla, S., Park, H.-S.: Eco-industrial networking for sustainable development: review of issues and development strategies. Clean Technol. Environ. Policy **19**(2), 391–402 (2016). https://doi.org/10.1007/s10098-016-1224-x
7. Camarinha-Matos, L.M., Afsarmanesh, H., Galeano, N., Molina, A.: Collaborative networked organizations - concepts and practice in manufacturing enterprises. Comput. Ind. Eng. **57**(1), 46–60 (2009). https://doi.org/10.1016/j.cie.2008.11.024
8. Haskins, C.: Multidisciplinary investigation of eco-industrial parks. Syst. Eng. **9**(4), 313–330 (2006)
9. Noran, O., Romero, D.: A pluralistic approach towards sustainable eco-industrial networking. IFAC Proc. Vol. **47**, 4292–4297 (2014)
10. Patala, S., et al.: Towards a broader perspective on the forms of eco-industrial networks. J. Clean. Prod. **82**, 166–178 (2014)
11. International Society for Industrial Ecology (IS4IE): Definition of Industrial Ecology (2013). http://www.is4ie.org
12. Romero, D., Molina, A.: Green virtual enterprise breeding environments: a sustainable industrial development model for a circular economy. IFIP AICT **380**, 427–436 (2012)
13. Afsarmanesh, H., Camarinha-Matos, L.M.: A framework for management of virtual organization breeding environments. In: Camarinha-Matos, L.M., Afsarmanesh, H., Ortiz, A. (eds.) PRO-VE 2005. ITIFIP, vol. 186, pp. 35–48. Springer, Boston, MA (2005). https://doi.org/10.1007/0-387-29360-4_4
14. Camarinha-Matos, L.M., Afsarmanesh, H., Ollus, M.: Ecolead: a holistic approach to creation and management of dynamic virtual organizations. In: Camarinha-Matos, L.M., Afsarmanesh, H., Ortiz, A. (eds.) PRO-VE 2005. ITIFIP, vol. 186, pp. 3–16. Springer, Boston, MA (2005). https://doi.org/10.1007/0-387-29360-4_1
15. Gartner Research: IT Glossary (2012). http://www.gartner.com/technology/it-glossary/enterprise-architecture.jsp. Accessed 2012
16. ISO/IEC, Annex B: GERAM, in ISO/IS 15704:2019: Industrial automation systems - Enterprise Modelling and Architecture - Requirements for Enterprise-Referencing Architectures and Methodologies (2019)

17. Clark, T., Sammut, P., Willans, J.S.: Applied Metamodelling: A Foundation for Language Driven Development, 3rd edn. ArXiv arXiv:1505.00149 (2015)
18. Nwokeji, J., et al.: A modelling technique for enterprise agility (2017)
19. Meade, L., Sarkis, J., Presley, A.: The theory and practice of reverse logistics. Int. J. Logist. Syst. Manag. 3(1), 56–84 (2007)
20. Srivastava, S.K.: Green supply-chain management: a state-of-the-art literature review. Int. J. Manag. Rev. 9(1), 53–80 (2007)
21. Negri, E.: A review of the roles of Digital Twin in CPS-based production systems. Procedia Manuf. 11, 939–948 (2017)
22. Rojek, I., Mikołajewski, D., Dostatni, E.: Digital twins in product lifecycle for sustainability in manufacturing and maintenance. Appl. Sci. 11, 31 (2021)
23. Noran, O.: Towards an environmental management approach for collaborative networks. In: Camarinha-Matos, L.M., Boucher, X., Afsarmanesh, H. (eds.) PRO-VE 2010. IAICT, vol. 336, pp. 17–24. Springer, Heidelberg (2010). https://doi.org/10.1007/978-3-642-15961-9_2
24. Lewis, H., Demmers, M.: Life cycle assessment and environmental management. Australas. J. Environ. Manag. 3(2), 110–123 (1996)
25. Bichraoui, N., Guillaume, B., Halog, A.: Agent-based modelling simulation for the development of an industrial symbiosis - preliminary results. Procedia Environ. Sci. 17, 195–204 (2013)
26. Noran, O.: A Meta-methodology for Collaborative Networked Organisations: Creating Directly Applicable Methods for Enterprise Engineering Projects. VDM Verlag Dr. Müller, Saarbrücken (2008)

Shaping Values Through Collaborative Work

Conceptualizing Sustainable Artificial Intelligence Development

Christian Zinke-Wehlmann[1]([✉]), Julia Friedrich[1], Amit Kirschenbaum[1],
Mandy Wölke[1], and Anja Brückner[2]

[1] Institute of Applied Informatics, University of Leipzig, Leipzig, Germany
{zinke,friedrich,Kirschenbaum,woelke}@infai.org
[2] University of Leipzig, Leipzig, Germany
anja.brueckner@uni-leipzig.org

Abstract. The next level of digitalization in (smart) manufacturing will be the broad implementation of Artificial Intelligence (AI). As in every evolutionary step, AI will not only affect the processes it is implemented in but will also have an impact on the way employees and organizations work. The paper underpins the importance of changing the collaboration schema with the development of AI – and its social impact. Nevertheless, technological innovation is mainly driven by economic pressure nowadays, but the demand for sustainability and ethical development of AI has become of significant importance, especially for the manufacturing sector. With this paper, we would like to offer a conceptual approach on how sustainability issues can be brought together with AI development in the industry to create ecological, economic, and social value. Based on Design Science Research, a concept is developed that illuminates the possibilities of sustainable AI development at the different impact levels.

Keywords: AI · Sustainability · Value in work · Value from AI

1 Introduction

Within the last 25 years, digitalization processes, including platform economy, the Internet of Things or Big Data technologies, have already changed the way people live and work. Industry 4.0 is the next evolutionary step in this technology-driven transformation, and it comes along with novel business models and collaboration approaches, supported by developments of collaboration networks, as shown in [1]. This next wave of digitalization has already started, bringing methods and tools of Artificial Intelligence (AI) into practice – with a huge impact on Industry and Society – as Makridakis predicted by stating that the "AI revolution aims to substitute, supplement and amplify practically all tasks currently performed by humans" [2]. Further, AI is mainly understood as "systems that display intelligent behavior by analyzing their environment and taking action—with some degree of autonomy—to achieve specific goals." [3]. Thus, by definition, AI will act within manufacturing and industrial processes – consequently, it will

L. M. Camarinha-Matos et al. (Eds.): PRO-VE 2022, IFIP AICT 662, pp. 545–554, 2022.
https://doi.org/10.1007/978-3-031-14844-6_43

also have an impact on collaboration as well as the value (co-)creation within manu-facturing. Nowadays, methods of AI are already a crucial part of smart manufacturing and the evolution of Industry 4.0, focusing mainly on process optimization, predictive maintenance, quality control as well as human-robotic interaction and ergonomics [4]. These AI development activities are mostly driven by economic benefits (e.g., quality raise, novel business models or speed up manufacturing by automation/optimization of routines). Human or ecological factors are considered at most secondarily, often only in the context of implementation.

However, while novel AI technology pushes industry into novel innovation tracks, customers pull with a growing demand for sustainability [5] in products, services as well as supply chains.[1] Sustainability issues and AI developments address "all layers of the manufacturing systems, from the shop floor to the production management systems and value-chain networks" [1]. Thus, both forces should be taken into consideration for future developments in collaborative networks. Reaching a sustainable industry and society is a global task with many implications and necessary actions on different levels – society, industry, and politics. Since AI has the potential to enable and support sustainable development, especially in the manufacturing industry, the question is how to conduct sustainable AI development. Current discussions in AI development focus on ethical developments [6] and the human-centered use of AI [7] as well as the top-level impact of AI [8]. Up to now, there is no systematic linkage between concrete values, their impact on work tasks or human level and, more generic, descriptions of values and impacts on the society, organizations, or collaborative networks. For a broader view of sustainability in concrete AI development, synergies between existing approaches must be exploited. As an example, prioritizing the human perspective or society in AI development may lead to environmentally unsustainable behavior within the organization or collaborative network - e.g., due to high energy consumption, AI continues deployment processes in work tasks with little relief. The conflicting goals between ecological, social, and economic values in AI development processes on different levels must be brought into focus and awareness must also be raised in the scientific discussion. Therefore, the paper aims to analyze the link between sustainability issues and AI development, highlighting the different levels of analysis (micro-, meso- and macro). Therefore, the research interest is to explore the dimensions and potential methods for sustainable AI development processes.

2 Methodological Remarks

Methodologically, this is a conceptual and positioning paper bridging sustainability mod-els, collaborative networks, and AI development to finally lay the ground for the analysis, design and evaluation of sustainable AI solution development within industries. Further, the overall methodology is conducted within the Design Science Research strongly linked to the development of novel socio-technical systems [9]. Following Hevner and Gregor [10], the paper focuses on the development of a descriptive knowledge base, by systematical synthesis, describing the different phenomena and building a theoretical

---

[1] See also recent marketing studies from Simon & Kucher "Global Sustainability Study" https://www.simon-kucher.com/sites/default/files/studies/Simon-Kucher_Global_Sustainability_Study_2021.pdf.

background for defining solutions objectives as well as design principles for sustainable AI development. Thus, the new design research contribution is an important extension of an existing artifact or the application of an existing artifact in a new application domain. To do so, we explore the theoretical dimensions of sustainable AI by doing a review using "sustainable AI" as a search string in EBSCO Discovery Service - a bibliographic search system – we identify only 4 papers with the search string in the title with significant relevance for our research question. In the next step, we screen relevant literature taking sustainability or sustainability aspects as well as AI development and design into consideration by using different search strings combining "sustainability", "AI" as well as "AI development" on EBSCO and Google Scholar (publications not older than 5 years with relevant title and abstract). The screening has the goal to give a brief overview of relevant topics and approaches and not to do a full systematic review of all research trees.

3   Theoretical Review and Background

A definition of the concept of sustainable AI is still in process. Bjørlo et al. [11] define it as "the extent to which AI technology is developed in a direction that meets the needs of the present without compromising the ability of future generations to meet their own needs.", which goes along with Halsband's [12] conclusion "that recent calls for more sustainable AI are based on a narrow understanding of sustainability, it instructed a return to intergenerational justice as a central ethical dimension of sustainability". A broader (re-)view can be found in [13]. The authors review seven definitions of sustainable AI with a focus on the public sector, identifying "diversity, capacity for learning, capacity for self-organization common meaning, and trust" as boundary conditions for sustainable AI.

However, to ensure completeness and better understanding, we provide the general ideas of AI before focusing on sustainable AI. Following AI Watch [10] and the High-Level Expert Group on Artificial Intelligence [11], AI can be defined as follows: "Artificial intelligence (AI) systems are software (and possibly also hardware) systems designed by humans that, given a complex goal, act in the physical or digital dimension by perceiving their environment through data acquisition, interpreting the collected structured or unstructured data, reasoning on the knowledge, or processing the information, derived from this data and deciding the best action(s) to take to achieve the given goal. AI systems can either use symbolic rules or learn a numeric model, and they can also adapt their behavior by analyzing how the environment is affected by their previous actions." [10]. The broad definition opens space for different AI domains and subdomains. They can be divided into two subsections - the core (goal-oriented) and transversal (supporting, supplementing) section [10]. Core AI sections are: Reasoning, Planning, Learning, Communication, and Perception. Transversal sections are: Integration and Interaction, Services, Ethics, and Philosophy. While Ethics refers to a humanized point of view on AI, sustainability is not yet mentioned as a transversal section for AI. Sustainability has three related dimensions: economic, social and ecological, which are collectively termed Triple-bottom-line, and can be combined/synthesised with the Sustainable Development Goals (SDG) [14].

"That AI will have a major impact on society is no longer in question. The current debate turns instead on how far this impact will be positive or negative, for whom, in which ways, in which places, and on what timescale" [6]. As Vinuesa et al. [15] analyze, AI can support 134 targets (79%) across all Sustainable Development Goals (e.g., in SDG 1 - no poverty or SDG 4 - quality education), but also has the potential to negatively impact 59 SDG targets (35%) – e.g., by requiring huge natural resources on runtime, by biased models reject gender equality (SDG 5) or by supporting anti-democratic nations [15]. However, in smart manufacturing, AI may have many positive effects in addition to the SDG – such as productivity, energy-saving, and saving scarce resources [4]. On the other hand, studies in other domains like the financial sector[2] show that AI may displace jobs [8]. AI brings a change in value creation, labor, labor market, and economy – and therefore has the potential to change skill demands and job opportunities [16]. The implementation and (sustainable) success of AI technologies depend on context and usage. It may have unintended consequences – which is why all those factors need to be considered in AI development processes.

Nevertheless, it is important to shape our digitized society and the associated forward-looking technologies based on sustainability values, such as human dignity, diversity, participation, well-being, and quality of life [17]. To do so and enhance individual and societal well-being, human-centered approaches for AI rise up [7]. Human-oriented AI is a design approach that focuses on the human being with all his needs, emotions, motivations, and perspectives [7]. As an answer to the dystopian ideas, in which machines handle tasks completely autonomous and humans lose control over AI and will ultimately become dominated by it, the concept of human-centered AI describes the prospect of humans being empowered in the exercise of their cognitive abilities through the use of AI methods [18]. AI supports the individuum through robotics and intelligent assistance systems by taking over physically and mentally stressful routine tasks. Human-centered AI fosters the idea of maximizing human control and autonomy of decisions and the benefits of machine autonomy and automation through AI [19]. Human-centered AI materializes the ethical dimensions/principles of being beneficial to humanity, being non-maleficence, supporting human autonomy, addressing the principle of justice, and holding explicability (incl. intelligibility and accountability) [20]. Both AI ethics, which provides a broader view of AI impacts (at the macro level), and human-centered AI, focusing on concrete AI embeddings, explicitly reference sustainability in a broader sense (e.g., the triple bottom line). Consequently, the human-centered AI development process should undergo a systematic extension of sustainable AI development. As a result, AI development should be understood as a multi-level process, where work processes (collaboration and tasks) will be redesigned with the help of AI, in which human, technical and organizational aspects (HTO) take place within an economic, social, and environmental context.

---

[2] "Goldman Sachs employed six hundred traders in 2000, the corporation was able to reduce their number of human traders to two by 2017 because of advances in narrow AI" [8].

4 AI Development in Industry – A Sustainable Approach

On the one side, sustainable AI development in manufacturing/industries needs to be aware of the changes and impacts on micro-level (e.g., concrete humans, material flows, emissions by work tasks), meso-level (e.g., processes, organization, and collaboration, pollution) and on macro-level (e.g., industries/economy, society, eco(logical)-system), which comes along with AI implementation. On the other side, there are driving and regulating forces from the macro-level, which are highly relevant for the sustainable AI development process. Therefore, we suggest a conceptual model (Fig. 1) for the development of sustainable AI, which includes a selection of the major perspectives that are displayed in the contemporary scientific debate. The model represents the forces at the level described below.

There are mainly four forces spanning from macro-level through meso-level to micro-level. (1) The **industry** or sector pushes the organization to be competitive, in two major directions: First to be competitive on market by AI-driven rationalization or product/service enrichment and second to be competitive in the war for talents, having an attractive and future-oriented work environment. (2) In addition, there is a growing demand for **sustainability**, e.g., offering eco-friendly solutions, pushing the organization to explore the potentials of AI development (e.g., in material loss or emission reduction). (3) From the **political side**, a lot of initiatives to regulate the operation of AI are ongoing. (4) Those regulations are built on works about the **ethics** of AI and AI usage – which is broader and less formalized than the law, regulations and standards [21] – but is also a driving force in AI development. Both ethics and politics targeting on the humanization of AI-based collaboration and work. Its three levels resp. perspectives are explained in the following:

Micro-level of Sustainable AI Development
While human-centered AI approaches place humans at the center of AI development, the Human-Technologies-Organization (HTO) approach complements this approach by analyzing and developing socio-technical systems and emphasizing the importance of the work task which bridges the comprehensive intertwining of humans, technology, and organization [22]. This also includes the role of the machine, as a novel actor in tasks (see definition above). Finally, AI developments are creating novel technical actors (see AI definition) and thus novel collaboration schema on the micro-level. Consequently, in order to analyze the impact and design of the use of AI technologies on a micro-level in a sustainable way, one needs to be aware of the strong links between humans and their tasks, the collaborations, incl. to autonomous tasks taken by AI, within the organization.

The idea of sustainable AI development is to enhance the flexibility, resilience, autonomy, and efficiency of organizational processes (economical value) and reduce the ecological impact (e.g., emissions) while keeping the independence of human decisions within the tasks or processes (social sustainability). All targets may be contradictory. Therefore, the development process needs to be multi-disciplinarity (e.g., HTO, human-centered approaches, sustainability measures), including different measures to analyze and develop novel organizational, technical as well as human capabilities, and partici-pative, involving stakeholders and maximize the values in a sustainable way. Collabora-tion among the various stakeholders is particularly important, both in terms of external influences and within the organization (e.g., inclusion of different employee groups). Aspects of team design, task design, and work practices are related to human-centered collaboration - e.g., how to incorporate machine team members into existing collaborative processes [23]. This requires bringing together expert knowledge from science (e.g., industrial psychology) and practical use cases from companies. Finally, sustainable AI development is a pathway of finding measures to minimize negative impacts and maximize values for all.

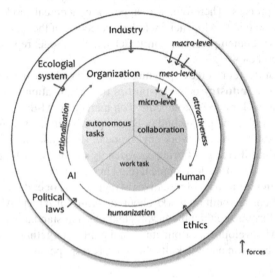

Fig. 1. Conceptualization of the levels of sustainable AI development

Meso-level of Sustainable AI Development

On the meso-level, analytically, AI development has two directions. While AI development is on the one hand, a rationalization process toward automation and autonomization of processes within an organization or in collaborative networks, it is on the other hand, a mechanism that can foster the humanization of work (fostering well-being), focusing on the human-oriented design of work systems. While the first aspect (rationalization) is mainly driven by economic factors of the organization, the second (humanization) is primarily driven by social demands and requirements (e.g., law or culture). On the meso-level, the above described four main forces are getting operand. AI development can act like a catalysator for realizing aspects of sustainability on the macro-level (e.g., reducing material loss in manufacturing, which goes along with economic factors and helps to support SDG 12 [24]).

Macro-level of Sustainable AI Development

SDG has been adapted in several ways in the European Union, e.g., by the Green Deal [25] or the Annual Sustainable Growth Strategy 2020 [26]. A combination of reports, regulations, and recommendations of the EU high-level expert group [27] as well as the presented political frame for sustainability builds the backbone of the macro-level. Eurostat has developed several indicators to measure the sustainable impact [28]. Besides the ethical and political dimension, the macro-level also includes the societal and economical forces on the market described above.

To assess sustainable AI development at different levels, the interplay needs to be considered. The identification of trade-offs between the indicators is always important for the analysis and development. As an example: AI-enabled eco-efficient production lines (less material as well as input and costs per product) may foster, on the macro-level, unemployment (meso-level also loss of capability and knowledge) or repetitive, non-creative work and therefore violate the decision-making autonomy of employees and increase psychological strain (micro-level) [29]. It also may lead to a higher production rate (more products and more material input and respectively more waste) – thus, the end-of-life and business models came into focus. Table 1 presents some quintessential examples of measures for the levels of sustainable AI development and depicts the interlinkage among them.

Table 1. Exemplary methods for measuring sustainable AI

Methods (examples)		Impact and value perspective
To identify and measure concrete values for all stakeholders, value mapping tools [30] can be used to describe created, destroyed, and not-realized values. Also, the human-centered design of work systems with digital work equipment approaches can be used (see also DIN EN ISO 6385 2016; DIN EN ISO 9241-11 2018)	Micro-level	AI developments have an impact on work tasks and concrete collaborations. There are concrete values and effects on the ecological and economical side, as well as consequences for direct or indirect involved actors that need to be analyzed. Design and development include measures to maximize stakeholder values and avoid one-sided misuse
Lifecycle costing and assessments are common tools for sustainable developments [31]. To assess the value for this triple-bottom-line of sustainability, a 3D vector may be used [32], but a multidimensional vector with industrial and case-specific indicators is also possible. Further a sustainable value mapping or similar approaches can be employed [33]	Meso-level	The organizations and collaborative networks are the binding links between task level and multi-national sustainability goals. Indicators need to summarize the micro-level impacts in a proper way all over the product lifecycle and the supply network
In addition to the SDG and its European realization mentioned above, several works/methods with specific indicators, like the GRI (Global Report Initiative), ISO 26000, EMAS (Eco-Management and Audit Scheme) can be used	Macro-level	AI developments all over the product lifecycle and supply network will have an impact on economic growth, ecological and social aspects. Here, sustainable AI development needs to link the indicators on the meso-level with the indicator developments on the macro-level

AI will cause changes within the whole product lifecycle – from cradle to cradle – and the supply network. Consequently, sustainable AI development must be aware of its prerequests (e.g., data acquisition and data sovereignty of all stakeholders), consequences (e.g., on workforces and competencies), and (if predictable) rebound effects (more products without end-of-life integration) within the product lifecycle [34] also shown in [24].

5 Conclusion and Outlook

Due to the potential negative impacts of AI, the application of AI encounters ethical, political, and organizational resistance. For example, there is currently a lack of uniform, European-level recommendations with a focus on human-centered and ethical AI [6]. To counteract these, the possible values, as well as the potential value destruction, on all levels need to be understood. The approach developed here provides a conceptual framework that places sustainable and human-centered AI in the focus of design research. This combines approaches from different domains (see e.g., [7]). Due to its rapid development, AI has a decisive influence on the achievement of the 2030 Agenda, and in this context, can influence the goals both positively and negatively [15]. Its sustainability considerations and interdisciplinarity, the presented concept may serve as a starting point to using AI as a positive driver for the achievement of the Sustainable Development Goals and for creating relevant contexts.

However, at this stage, the concept has its limitations, e.g., effectiveness in practical applications. In this context, the concept needs to be implemented and evaluated in practice [9]. Therefore, the long-term goal must be to apply and adapt the concept to various practical use cases. Due to different legal regulations, cultural values, and organizational structures, there are also certain differences between countries and regions in terms to the practical problems in the introduction of AI [15].

Furthermore, the paper focuses on the impact of AI in processes/value chains/networks within the industries and not on AI development for products or services. Maybe the approach is also adaptable, but we focus on the organizational value chain at this point. In summary, the presented approach provides a basis for combining the factors of technology, human, and organization when using AI. In the future, the concept needs to be expanded based on ongoing research projects as well as practical evaluations. Therefore, further work will e.g., require to administer standardized interviews and the assessment of an AI-readiness questionnaire to evaluate the concept in a practical environment.

Acknowledgments. This research and development project is funded under the funding measure "Future of Work: Regional Competence Centers for Work Research - Artificial Intelligence" in the program "Innovations for Tomorrow's Production, Services and Work" of the Federal Ministry of Education and Research (BMBF) and supervised by the Project Management Agency Karlsruhe (PTKA). Fund. No.: 02L19C500.

References

1. Camarinha-Matos, L.M., Fornasiero, R., Ramezani, J., et al.: Collaborative networks: a pillar of digital transformation. Appl. Sci. **9**, 5431 (2019). https://doi.org/10.3390/app9245431
2. Makridakis, S.: The forthcoming Artificial Intelligence (AI) revolution: its impact on society and firms. Futures **90**, 46–60 (2017). https://doi.org/10.1016/j.futures.2017.03.006

3. EC: Coordinated Plan on AI (2018). https://eur-lex.europa.eu/legal-content/EN/TXT/HTML/?uri=CELEX:52018DC0795&rid=3#:~:text=Artificial%20Intelligence%20refers%20to%20systems,or%20speak%20with%20digital%20assistants. Accessed 05 Apr 2022
4. Cioffi, R., Travaglioni, M., Piscitelli, G., et al.: Artificial intelligence and machine learning applications in smart production: progress, trends, and directions. Sustainability **12**, 492 (2020). https://doi.org/10.3390/su12020492
5. Hong, Z., Guo, X.: Green product supply chain contracts considering environmental responsibilities. Omega **83**, 155–166 (2019). https://doi.org/10.1016/j.omega.2018.02.010
6. Floridi, L., et al.: AI4People—an ethical framework for a good AI society: opportunities, risks, principles, and recommendations. Mind. Mach. **28**(4), 689–707 (2018). https://doi.org/10.1007/s11023-018-9482-5
7. Auernhammer, J.: Human-centered AI: the role of human-centered design research in the development of AI. In: DRS2020: Synergy. Design Research Society (2020)
8. Goralski, M.A., Tan, T.K.: Artificial intelligence and sustainable development. Int. J. Manag. Educ. **18**, 100330 (2020). https://doi.org/10.1016/j.ijme.2019.100330
9. Hevner, A.R., March, S.T., Park, J., et al.: Design science in information systems research. MIS Q. **28**, 75 (2004). https://doi.org/10.2307/25148625
10. Gregor, S., Hevner, A.R.: Positioning and presenting design science research for maximum impact. MIS Q. **37**, 337–355 (2013). https://doi.org/10.25300/MISQ/2013/37.2.01
11. Bjørlo, L., Moen, Ø., Pasquine, M.: The role of consumer autonomy in developing sustainable AI: a conceptual framework. Sustainability **13**, 2332 (2021). https://doi.org/10.3390/su13042332
12. Halsband, A.: Sustainable AI and intergenerational justice. Sustainability **14**, 3922 (2022). https://doi.org/10.3390/su14073922
13. Wilson, C., van der Velden, M.: Sustainable AI: an integrated model to guide public sector decision-making. Technol. Soc. **68**, 101926 (2022). https://doi.org/10.1016/j.techsoc.2022.101926
14. Shevlin, H., Vold, K., Crosby, M., et al.: The limits of machine intelligence: despite progress in machine intelligence, artificial general intelligence is still a major challenge. EMBO Rep. **20**, e49177 (2019). https://doi.org/10.15252/embr.201949177
15. Vinuesa, R., Azizpour, H., Leite, I., et al.: The role of artificial intelligence in achieving the sustainable development goals. Nat. Commun. **11**, 233 (2020). https://doi.org/10.1038/s41467-019-14108-y
16. Frank, M.R., Autor, D., Bessen, J.E., et al.: Toward understanding the impact of artificial intelligence on labor. Proc. Natl. Acad. Sci. U.S.A. **116**, 6531–6539 (2019). https://doi.org/10.1073/pnas.1900949116
17. Dörr, S.: Corporate Digital Responsibility. Springer, Heidelberg (2021). https://doi.org/10.1007/978-3-662-63853-8
18. Shneiderman, B.: Human-centered artificial intelligence: three fresh ideas. THCI **12**, 109–124 (2020). https://doi.org/10.17705/1thci.00131
19. Shneiderman, B.: Human-centered artificial intelligence: reliable, safe & trustworthy. Int. J. Hum.-Comput. Interact. **36**, 495–504 (2020). https://doi.org/10.1080/10447318.2020.1741118
20. Floridi, L., Cowls, J.: A unified framework of five principles for AI in society. In: Floridi, L. (ed.) Ethics, Governance, and Policies in Artificial Intelligence. PSS, vol. 144, pp. 5–17. Springer, Cham (2021). https://doi.org/10.1007/978-3-030-81907-1_2
21. ISO ISO/IEC DIS 23894: Information technology - Artificial intelligence - Guidance on risk management (1). https://www.iso.org/standard/77304.html. Accessed 17 Jun 2022
22. Paulsen, H., Zorn, V., Inkermann, D., et al.: Soziotechnische Analyse und Gestaltung von Virtualisierungsprozessen. Gr. Interakt. Org. **51**, 81–93 (2020). https://doi.org/10.1007/s11612-020-00507-z

23. Seeber, I., Bittner, E., Briggs, R.O., et al.: Machines as teammates: a research agenda on AI in team collaboration. Inf. Manag. **57**, 103174 (2020). https://doi.org/10.1016/j.im.2019. 103174

24. Mancini, L., Vidal Legaz, B., Vizzarri, M., et al.: Mapping the role of raw materials in sustainable development goals: a preliminary analysis of links, monitoring indicators and related policy initiatives. EUR, Scientific and technical research series, vol. 29595. Publications Office of the European Union, Luxembourg (2019)

25. EC: The European Green Deal (2019). https://ec.europa.eu/info/sites/default/files/european-green-deal-communication_en.pdf. Accessed 05 May 2022

26. EU: Annual Sustainable Growth Strategy (2019). https://eur-lex.europa.eu/legal-content/EN/TXT/PDF/?uri=CELEX:52020DC0575&from=en. Accessed 05 May 2022

27. AI H: High-level expert group on artificial intelligence. Ethics guidelines for trustworthy AI (2019)

28. eurostats: Indikatoren: Indikatoren für nachhaltige Entwicklung (2020). https://ec.europa.eu/eurostat/de/web/sdi/indicators. Accessed 05 May 2022

29. Hacker, W.: Arbeitsgestaltung bei Digitalisierung. Z. Arb. Wiss. **76**, 90–98 (2022). https://doi.org/10.1007/s41449-022-00302-0

30. Bocken, N., Short, S., Rana, P., et al.: A value mapping tool for sustainable business modelling. Corp. Gov. **13**, 482–497 (2013). https://doi.org/10.1108/CG-06-2013-0078

31. Hunkeler, D., Lichtenvort, K., Rebitzer, G.: Environmental Life Cycle Costing. CRC Press, Boca Raton (2008)

32. Aliabadi, M.M., Huang, Y.: Vector-based sustainability analytics: a methodological study on system transition toward sustainability. Ind. Eng. Chem. Res. **55**, 3239–3252 (2016). https://doi.org/10.1021/acs.iecr.5b03391

33. Winans, K., Dlott, F., Harris, E., et al.: Sustainable value mapping and analysis methodology: enabling stakeholder participation to develop localized indicators mapped to broader sustainable development goals. J. Clean. Prod. **291**, 125797 (2021). https://doi.org/10.1016/j.jclepro.2021.125797

34. Terzi, S., Bouras, A., Dutta, D., et al.: Product lifecycle management – from its history to its new role. IJPLM **4**, 360 (2010). https://doi.org/10.1504/IJPLM.2010.036489

Value Driven Transformation of Care Work – A Use Case

Vanita Römer[1]([⊠]), Julia Friedrich[1], Christian Zinke-Wehlmann[1], and Robert Wolf[2]

[1] University Computer Center, Research and Development Department, University of Leipzig, Augustusplatz 10, 04109 Leipzig, Germany
{vanita.roemer,julia.friedrich,
christian.zinke-wehlmann}@uni-leipzig.de
[2] Bosold Pflege GmbH, Bornaische Straße 109, 04279 Leipzig, Germany
rwolf@pflege-in-leipzig.de

Abstract. A holistic design of person-related services, like care work, requires a combined vision, that takes into consideration the customer's, as well as the caregiver's, and the organizational perspective. This is especially important when agile and collaborative work-systems are being implemented in person-related service systems, as different perspectives - and therefore beliefs, needs and values of the people involved - are to be considered. This paper presents a new perspective on values that need to be mapped and shaped when agile work systems in caregiving services are being designed. As a result, it describes a transformational process that has, at its center, concrete collaboration and service values out of which practical implications and an organization (re-)design process is deduced. This leads to a value-driven transformational process that takes into account all aspects of an organization to sustainably develop person-related service systems and that challenges existing service management and design approaches.

Keywords: Value mapping · Care-giving service · Person-related service · Agile work systems

1 Introduction

Providers of home care services in Germany face a variety of challenges these days. The aging society, economic pressure and a fading of social welfare systems are impacting health-care providers at a large scale. The Covid-19 pandemic represented an extraordinary challenge to the current health care system. As a result, work place satisfaction among health care professionals is comparably low [1] and the lack of specialized workers in the health care sector [2] is a pressing issue that calls for action on various levels of society. At the same time, the aging society is bringing about a steady increase in the number of clients [3], which makes the question of how to improve elderly and health care services in terms of both quality and efficiency more and more urgent.

© IFIP International Federation for Information Processing 2022
Published by Springer Nature Switzerland AG 2022
L. M. Camarinha-Matos et al. (Eds.): PRO-VE 2022, IFIP AICT 662, pp. 555–563, 2022.
https://doi.org/10.1007/978-3-031-14844-6_44

In practice, these questions were very often answered by focusing on documentation and monitoring as well as efficient process design in the health care provision. The creation of Collaborative Networks (CN) between e.g. hospitals and other care providers can be seen as an example for that [4]. Yet, such structures often focus on the care provider's and the service provision perspective and do not consider the employee's perspective nor the perspective of the local community or neighborhood. The reform of home care, which started in Germany in the mid-1990s, and the associated economization of care, led to staff reductions, an increase in time pressure, reduced scope for decision-making in care, and an increased volume of work [5]. The focus on efficiency criteria in a strongly body- and activity-related understanding of care (which neglects the social components of care) led to the interaction component, i.e. the importance of personal attention and the consideration of individual values and needs, being pushed into the background (ibid.). As a result, neither employees' nor clients' needs and values are fully addressed.

Only recently, new approaches try to develop a holistic collaborative structure that involves efficient service delivery as well as humane values for both employees and clients. Also, in CN literature, elderly care became more and more present and strategic development and research plans were presented [6]. One concrete example of an elderly care institution that follows the new collaborative paradigm is the Buurtzorg ("Neighborhood Care") home care concept that was originally developed in 2006 in the Netherlands [7]. Its idea is to challenge the ruling system of healthcare, where rigid structures and hierarchies were an obstacle to delivering optimal and personalized home-care (ibid.). Out of three central principles, Buurtzorg created a CN by developing and designing organizational structures for person-related services. Similar to the *Values of Agile* as stated in the Agile Manifesto for software development [8], which also take the customer and the service into the center of business development, Buurtzorg started to organize around a set of values that guides their organization's development strategy.

While (predominantly) technology-driven transformation processes in production and tech organization have been studied intensively in the past, we see a lack of research on processes of innovation in CNs in person-related services. Therefore, the main objective of this paper is to answer the following research questions:

- What values are relevant for CNs in person-related service systems in the use case?
- What are the practical implications of these values for the organization itself and the different stakeholders of person-related services in the use case?

To provide an answer, we are going to examine the transformation process of a service supplier from a conventional home care service approach towards Buurtzorg with a focus on the concept of value that is implied and its practical realization. Before the transformational process the care provider offered a conventional home care as well as a day care service for elderly persons. Networking with local hospitals were close, as often former hospital patients required homecare for the following phase of recovery. The work organization was top-down and centrally organized through the central office, therefore documentation processes were a daily chore.

The analyzed Buurtzorg team is attached to this conventional care provider and was created by employees of this outpatient care provider who were enthusiastic about the care concept of Buurtzorg. At the beginning of the research process, the Buurtzorg team consisted of 6 professionals forming one team in a local neighborhood. The challenge for this team was to create an organizational structure under the given circumstances that allowed care work in accordance to the leading values of Buurtzorg.

2 Methodology

While the concept of care work in accordance to the Buurtzorg concept is well established in the Netherlands after it started in 2006, the approach is relatively new in Germany. This paper is based on the findings of an empirical analysis of a Buurtzorg team, which was founded in 2019 and is based in a German city. Therefore, qualitative data were collected through semi-structured interviews in 2020 with two representatives of the service organization. These initial interviews marked the second step of the research process of Social Service Engineering (SSE) approach, which built the basis of our approach [9]. The aim of the SSE approach is the creation of a design process for humane person-related services which focuses on the interaction between people as the core of the service by combining methods of work science [10] with those of service engineering and design and supports value creation within the service network.

Starting with the (1) preparation and selection as well as planning of use of analytical methods, the (2) analysis of the actual state of the service, with regard to processes, work conditions and service environment or framework conditions, itself states the second step of SSE. This is followed by (3) an assessment, (4) a concrete objective and (5) the development of solutions (technical or methodological), which are finally (6) implemented and (7) evaluated. At this point of the research process all steps are ongoing, with the evaluation process still to be carried out. For the analysis and assessment, various workshops have been carried out, involving different members of the Buurtzorg team and management. These workshops focused on the analysis and description of roles within the service providing organization as well as on the identification of crucial values, their implications of the organization and requirements for the organization itself. The evaluation will include qualitative semi-structured interviews as well as an analysis that focus on the defined values and their deployment regarding the organization. Here, we will focus on the outcome of steps (3) to (5), which are described in Sects. 3.2 and 4 of this paper. Yet, also the other steps form part of the transformational process and therefore need to be mentioned here, although they do not show in the presented results.

The fact that the analyzed Buurtzorg team is part of an organization that employs conventional home care teams in parallel to the collaborative structure also allowed us to compare the different understandings of care and their impact on the understanding of values as well as their implications for the organization. It also has an implication on the organizational structures and the transformation process, as i.e. finances and administrative support are shared among the different sectors of the home care provider. Yet, it is only to be mentioned here and cannot be examined deeper in the context of the presented results.

3 Understanding Values of Buurtzorg

3.1 Values of Buurtzorg Netherlands Put in Practice

In the development of the Buurtzorg model, the central motivation was to improve elderly home-care, with humane values at the center of transformation [11]. With the aim of changing radically the way home care is provided in the Netherlands, Jos de Blok created a business model around central values and principles on which self-managing clients and self-managing teams can recur. The central principles of Buurtzorg can be stated as follows [12]:

1. humane values above the bureaucratic administration
2. simplicity above complexity
3. practical above hypothetical

In practice, these principles lead to a fundamentally different work system that allows professionals to act more flexible, creative and autonomous on the job, creating space for appreciation of the individual needs of clients and, thus, lead to a high quality in personal interaction. In addition, the high efficiency of administration that is created on basis of these principles states an economic advantage of the model. This is achieved by creating network structures around the patients that are based on the individual needs of the patient. Other than in different home care settings, where the goal is to keep patients as patients, the Buurtzorg model aims to empower patients to be or become as autonomous as possible with the support of their care networks. This implies also a collaboration between the formal (i.e. physicians, therapists, etc.) and informal (neighbors, family, partner, friends, etc.) care networks that surround the patients, which is facilitated by the Buurtzorg team. All in all, a holistic and practical care-giving approach is fundamental to the Buurtzorg care concept.

Apart from patients' autonomy, also the caregivers' autonomy within teams of 6 to 12 professionals plays a central role in the management concept. This is based on the idea, that a top-down management of professionals is hindering for efficient and practical solutions. The teams themselves have a better insight and concrete knowledge of the situation as well as of the environment and, thus, must have the autonomy to make crucial as well as on non-critical decisions. This also means a valuation and exploitation of the specific and local knowledge that is provided by the active professionals, in the Buurtzorg care concept.

The caregivers' autonomy comes along with a minimal administrative effort: Currently in Buurtzorg Netherlands, for more than 10,000 care workers and assistants, there are only 15 regional coaches and 45 back-office staff members who assist them. This means a percentage of 8% of the whole staff is administrative, in a comparison to the usual percentage in the Netherlands of 25% [13]. This is also possible due to an evaluation system, in which the administration provides key business indicators to the teams as a clear and practically applicable overview on their current performance.

This approach is supported by a web-based IT structure that is embedded in the above described processes and supports communication and knowledge management as well as administrative processes of the everyday care work.

As outlined here, Buurtzorg can be considered a self-organized and digitally enabled collaborative system that consists of autonomous teams, supported by a lean and effective administration. Its success and growth are extraordinary and need to be analyzed on various levels [14], but would be beyond the scope of this paper. The presented values can be seen as guiding lines, that allow a basic understanding of what the Buurtzorg model is built on. Yet, practical implications of these values can differ from organization to organization, adapting to the different starting points, ecosystems and framework conditions, especially, when the system is transferred to other countries, as in our use case.

3.2 Values of Buurtzorg in the Use Case

The German health care and elderly care system is different to the Dutch, which is why a separate description for our use case and the system in which it is embedded is necessary. Generally, it has to be stated that the German care system is based on the mostly public health care and long-term care insurance system, which determines the reimbursement of costs for each of the three care levels. Quality in the sector is subdivided in structure, process and outcome quality and measured with preliminarily set professional standards [14]. Section 71 (1) of the social security statute book ("Sozialgesetzbuch", abbr. SGB) prescribes that each home care providing organization is under the permanent responsibility of a certified nursing professional. In practice, this responsibility is assumed by a nursing service manager ("Pflegedienstleitung"), who takes over all administrative and organizational tasks, such as personnel planning, organization of care tours and monitoring of compliance with legal quality standards. In addition, the accounting of services is highly complex due to the separation of medical and nursing activities, which may not be carried out by all nursing team members but depends on the individual qualification. The associated meticulous planning and invoicing of services generates framework conditions that come with a high administrative effort. In this use case, the Buurtzorg team was therefore faced with the challenge of examining the extent to which this new understanding of care is also valid under the German conditions and which transformation processes are necessary with regard to the organizational and cultural structure.

In the conducted interviews, the team stated, that it previously defined core values that can be understood as guidelines for their collaboration. In addition to the understanding of care, these values also focus on the understanding of their work and also include sustainability aspects.

Value in Service(s) (client perspective): At the heart of Buurtzorg's understanding of care is the premise that care should empower the client to achieve the highest possible level of autonomy or, if possible, ultimately help them out of their need for care. Following the Dutch model, it is therefore necessary, to exploit the social network of the client (communities are strengthened). In contrast to conventional health care providers, the Buurtzorg team aims to improve the client's health condition and wellbeing in order to achieve independence from the care provider. The CN in Buurtzorg is not only understood as a network of caring and medical professionals, but also includes relatives, neighbors, and other relevant stakeholders such as the hairdresser. Social embedment and value creation for all stakeholders within the CN is understood as an integral part of the service.

Value in Collaboration (care worker perspective): Self-organization of care work is another core value for the team. The Buurtzorg team decides together on the admission of new clients, plans all processes with regard to care of their patients themselves, communicates with doctors and client's relatives and sets its own roster without the support of a nursing service manager. In accordance with the Dutch model, two external roles support the team. One is the coach, who mediates, reflects and coaches in terms of team-building measures and advises on conflicts, reflects on communication structures. The second is the team facilitator, who provides professional support and guidance, in setting up, and ensuring billability of services. The Buurtzorg premise of minimum documentation in favor of strengthening the interaction between client and care worker and, thus, taking into consideration humane values and the social dimension of care work, is also one of the guidelines of work. The culture of trust and empowerment enables the care workers to work in a highly self-determined way.

Community Value (sustainability perspective): The team values the approach of neighborhood care. This means that the care team shows presence in the local district and is an active part of the community. As the distances between the clients and the office are short, this approach also allows car-free home care service. The team members visit their clients by bike which supports ecological sustainability as well as increases the neighborhood's attractiveness. At the same time, it is a stress reducing factor because it eliminates the need to search for parking spaces at every client visit and keep of logbooks for company cars.

4   Practical Implications for Value-Centered Care Work

In the use case, the Buurtzorg approach was implemented into already existing infrastructures of a day care provider. This implied a secure and established network of suppliers and clients in which it was introduced, on the one hand, but also existing organizational structures and therefore a preconditioning on the other hand. In addition to the different country-specific legal and bureaucratic framework, this also required an adapted and specific model and transformation process. In various workshops and interviews, the case-specific requirements were collected and framed into principles and values for the local Buurtzorg model, as described above At first semi-structured interviews were conducted in order to frame the existing values that underly the current status of the organization as well as their employees. On this basis, moderated workshops were carried out that included a collective idea collection and a moderated prioritizing in order to form a of the organizational values as well as a perspective on the development of the organization. Then, practical implications for the transformation were deduced out of the central values and principles.

As a theoretical base, the MTO ("Mensch-Technik-Organisation") concept [15] was introduced. The MTO concept is a socio-technical approach for transformational processes in organizations to facilitate a holistic design approach that includes three aspects of an organization: human, technology and organization. The three aspects, as well as their interdependencies, must be considered equally for a holistic transformational process. For the use case the practical implications as shown in Fig. 1 have been defined:

Central fields of action can be defined for each of the three aspects. In the organizational aspect, areas of responsibility as well as concrete role definitions have to be

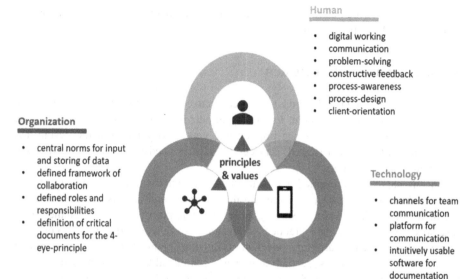

Fig. 1. Practical implications of central Buurtzorg values in the use case

developed. Also, central norms of digital collaboration have to be defined and established. This addresses the Value in Collaboration in the organization by facilitating and clarifying the communicative and collaborative processes for all persons involved. Additionally, the Community Value is represented in the way, the organization delivers the service to the individual and therefore needs to be represented in the collaboration and service framework. In the human aspect, capacity building for employees and managers is a field of action, that means, that new skills and knowledge have to be gained in order to put into practice a different working system. This is especially crucial when, as it was partly the case, the same persons had been working beforehand in a different constellation and/or collaboration model. The previous experiences and patterns have to be considered and worked on respectively, in order to not unconsciously recreate the underlying patterns and values. Apart from that, the internal organization's culture has to be considered. A base of trust and feedback-culture is essential not only for the transformation, but also for the ongoing work of autonomous and self-organized teams. Apart from that, the client orientation needs to be a fundamental part to be considered. In this way, an inclusion of the Value in Service can be assured in the transformation process. Finally, also the implemented technology and software need to fulfill the specific requirements of the defined values as well as of the organization and the persons who will work with them. In the use case, the managers had very specific ideas and requirements of the software that should be implemented in the new teams. This was also due to the, above described, German care system that demands for specific documentation and control instances. Apart from that, a not yet implemented knowledge and communication platform is considered to be introduced to support the collaboration within the care network and growing number of Buurtzorg teams. Of course, all of the implemented software needs to be aligned with the standards of the European Union's General Data Protection Regulation.

5 Discussion and Conclusion

The value of a service is subjective to the perspective of each person/entity involved in the service system or ecosystem. Especially in person-related service it is a complex operation to frame and define the implied and generated value. Yet, the design and development of a (person-related) service also always needs to consider the values it (re-)creates and represents.

In this paper, we presented a way to include humane values in a transformation of a collaboration and service system and the practical implications that derived from the inclusion of those values. Starting from the example of Buurtzorg Netherlands, case specific values and their practical implications were assessed in order to create a framework for a local Buurtzorg model that fits into the organization's legal environment as well as the organization's preconditions. Three central value concepts were defined on this basis, that were Value in Service (client perspective), Value in Collaboration (care worker perspective) and Community Value (sustainability perspective), which then set the basis for the development of the practical transformational approach.

Finally, practical implications and areas of action were defined, which were put in practice in the use case. It can be seen, that a thorough use case analysis is fundamental for the transformation process and service development. The interlinking organization's aspects as well as the underlying values form a complex figure, which could be used for developing further methodological approaches. Too long, value has been only regarded on a business level, which was rather damaging especially when applied to person-related service systems. The here presented approach does not only clearly state and concretize the system's underlying values, but also considers them as a central starting point for organizational transformation. This is a new and innovative way that can fundamentally change work and collaboration systems.

Of course, the here presented results have limitations. On one hand, the critics of a possible self-exploitation of the care workers has to be taken into consideration when a self-organized collaborative system is to be applied in care work. Although this was not an issue that occurred in this use case, competencies might need to be developed also on this matter. On the other hand, the qualitative approach has not been validated or scaled up yet and, thus, has a limited generalizability. The validation and theoretical enhancement are ongoing processes. However, the results are mainly empirically driven principles that have the potential to enrich exploratively the approaches of agile and human-oriented transformation of organizations.

Acknowledgments. This research and development project are funded by the German Federal Ministry of Education and Research (BMBF) within the "Innovations for Tomorrow's Production, Services, and Work" Program (funding number 02L18A182) and implemented by the Project Management Agency Karlsruhe (PTKA). The authors are responsible for the content of this publication.

References

1. Janson, P., Rathmann, K.: Prävention und Gesundheitsförderung **16**(4), 344–353 (2021). https://doi.org/10.1007/s11553-020-00826-5
2. Ehrentraut, O., Huschik, G., Moog, S., Sulzer, L.: Langzeitpflege im Wandel (2019)
3. OECD: Elderly population (indicator) (2022). https://data.oecd.org/pop/elderly-population. htm. Accessed 14 Apr 2022
4. Baldissera, T.A., Camarinha-Matos, L.M.: Designing elderly care ecosystem in collaborative networks environment. In: 2017 International Conference on Computing Networking and Informatics (ICCNI), Lagos, 29.10.2017–31.10.2017, pp. 1–9. IEEE (2017)
5. Auth, D.: Ökonomisierung der Pflege – Formalisierung und Prekarisierung von Pflegearbeit. WSI (2013). https://doi.org/10.5771/0342-300X-2013-6-412
6. Camarinha-Matos, L.M., Afsarmanesh, H., Ferrada, F., Oliveria, A.I., Rodas, J.: A Comprehensive Research Roadmap for ICT and Ageing. SIC (2013). https://doi.org/10.24846/v22 i3y201301
7. Kreitzer, M.J., Monsen, K.A., Nandram, S., de Blok, J.: Buurtzorg nederland: a global model of social innovation, change, and whole-systems healing. Global Adv. Health Med. (2015). https://doi.org/10.7453/gahmj.2014.030
8. Beck, K., et al.: Manifesto for Agile Software Development (2001). https://agilemanifesto. org/. Accessed 14 Apr 2022
9. Friedrich, J., Römer, V., Gilbert, K., Zinke-Wehlmann, C., Steputat-Rätze, A., Pietrzyk, U.: Collaborative Networks in person-related services – designing humane and efficient interaction processes in childcare. In: Camarinha-Matos, L.M., Boucher, X., Afsarmanesh, H. (eds.) PRO-VE 2021. IAICT, vol. 629, pp. 374–381. Springer, Cham (2021). https://doi.org/ 10.1007/978-3-030-85969-5_34
10. Friedrich, J., Gilbert, G., Pietrzyk, U., Römer, V., Steputat-Rätze, A., Zinke-Wehlmann, C.: Perspektiven auf die Gestaltung von Interaktionsarbeit. Whitepaper (2021). https://doi.org/ 10.25368/2021.4
11. Nandram, S., Koster, N.: Organizational innovation and integrated care: lessons from Buurtzorg. J. Integr. Care (2014). https://doi.org/10.1108/JICA-06-2014-0024
12. Nandram, S.S.: Organizational Innovation by Integrating Simplification. Springer, Cham (2015). https://doi.org/10.1007/978-3-319-11725-6
13. Buurtzorg. https://www.buurtzorg.com/about-us/our-organisation/. Accessed 14 Apr 2022
14. Johansen, F., van den Bosch, S.: The scaling-up of Neighbourhood Care: from experiment towards a transformative movement in healthcare. Futures (2017). https://doi.org/10.1016/j. futures.2017.04.004
15. Strohm, O., Ulrich, E.: Unternehmen arbeitspsychologisch bewerten. vdf, Hochschulverl. an der ETH Zürich, Zürich (1997)

Exploring the Barriers and Mitigation Strategies in Collaborative Network Development: A Case Study from Equipment Manufacturing Company

Yan Zhang, Juanqiong Gou$^{(\boxtimes)}$, and Shuyao He

School of Economic and Management, Beijing Jiaotong University, Beijing, China
{20120626,jqgou}@bjtu.edu.cn

Abstract. Recently, more and more manufacturing companies build collaborative platforms to improve collaboration ability, so as to cope with the the high complexity and uncertainty of the industrial market environment. As a new paradigm of cooperation, collaborative networks have attracted more and more attention. The development and evolution of CN is a long process, and there are some obstacles in practical application. Current research on CN is theoretical and there is a lack of exploration in practice in terms of organizational construction and operation of manufacturing companies. Therefore, this paper uses a case study to analyze four levels: value mechanism, structural mechanism, sharing mechanism and technology mechanism, taking an actual assembly and manufacturing company as an example. The purpose of this study is to analyze and summarize the key barriers in the practice of the company through empirical investigation. And based on the mitigation measures of the case company and relevant literature studies, we have made some relevant recommendations and research ideas to address the barriers.

Keywords: Collaborative network organization · Development barriers · Mitigation measures

1 Introduction

In the face of the world's new technological revolution, dynamic changes in demand and the rapid explosion of innovation, how to continue to gain competitive advantages to cope with market uncertainty and complexity is a problem that enterprises are concerned about. The strength and height of enterprise growth depend on dynamic competitiveness, and synergy is the main dynamic competitiveness [1]. As a new cooperation paradigm, Collaborative Network (CN) has been applied in many fields and has certain development potential. CN members are autonomous and independent of each other in the cooperative relationship and share resources to achieve common promotion and optimization.

Whether the organization has truly achieved synergistic development is reflected in whether it has the characteristics of mutual benefit and symbiosis. These characteristics are embodied in the value mechanism, structural mechanism, sharing mechanism

L. M. Camarinha-Matos et al. (Eds.): PRO-VE 2022, IFIP AICT 662, pp. 564–576, 2022.
https://doi.org/10.1007/978-3-031-14844-6_45

and technical mechanism [2]. The value mechanism is reflected in the collaboration between partners based on the concept of mutuality and consistent values, which is the basis of the cooperative relationship. The structural mechanism includes the power and responsibility structure of network members, communication mechanism, governance principles, etc., which provide operational guarantees for the sustainable development of CN. Sharing is the driving force behind CN's continuous innovation. The generation of synergies primarily depends on the sharing mechanism, including the sharing of information, resources and knowledge. The continuous development of digital technology has enhanced the collaborative efficiency of CN, reduced the cost of information exchange, and improved organizational performance [3].

At present, some scholars have carried out research on various details of collaborative network theory, such as the classification of CNs and the basic elements of value creation [4], the consistency analysis of value systems in Collaborative Network Organization (CNO) and management [5], the business of strengthening cooperative relationships and process analysis [6], trust analysis and evaluation in CNs [7], etc. The establishment of collaborative relationship is based on an effective collaborative response mechanism, reasonable performance management and willingness of members to actively contribute knowledge. However, there are still some barriers in the practice of transforming enterprises from individual to collaborative network operation. Barriers such as partner individualism, lack of consistent values and interests, lack of autonomy and flexible response mechanisms can hinder synergy [8]. In order to deeply analyze the causes of these barriers, this paper uses the actual assembly manufacturing enterprise as an example to analyze and summarize the barriers and solutions.

The following two research questions will be the core of the paper:

A: What are the key barriers for companies in CN development?

B: What measures has the company taken to mitigate barriers during the development of CN?

The paper is structured as follows: after introducing and contextualizing the research question in Sect. 1, Sect. 2 presents the theoretical development of CNO and the main barriers. Section 3 provides a case and introduces the process of data collection and analysis. Section 4 then describes the CNO development barriers and mitigation measures of the case company from four aspects. Finally, Sect. 5 presents the conclusion.

2 Related Works

2.1 Collaborative Network Organizations

CN is a knowledge-driven paradigm of collaboration. In the past few years, CNs have been organized in various forms, such as virtual enterprises, virtual communities, virtual laboratories, value units, supply chain collaboration, etc., which have created opportunities for enterprises to seek heterogeneous resources to respond to dynamic markets agilely. With the emergence of collaborative value, various fields have begun to pay attention to and strive to promote the construction of CN, such as: the establishment of special courses for university alliances, the construction of information sharing platforms for government departments, and the sharing of medical resources. The above cooperation models inevitably revolve around the activities among members, including the determination of organizational structure and governance principles, which are collectively referred to as the construction of Collaborative Network Organizations (CNOs).

The main driver of CNO is the dynamic alignment of resources in response to goals. CNOs have two organizational models, Virtual Organization (VO) and Virtual organizations Breeding Environment (VBE), which complement each other. VO has strong flexibility and can be established in a short period of time to respond to dynamic changes in the market. VO can be driven by continuous production or service provision activities, or by goals of seizing a single collaborative opportunity [9]. But generally, people decide to participate in CN based on a certain premise of trust. VO dissolves immediately after the end of cooperation, so it is difficult to build a trust relationship. VBE is a long-term strategic alliance, which is more conducive to establishing a good trust mechanism and governance principles between organizations.

In order to combine the advantages of the two organizations, Afsarmanesh, H [10] proposed a new paradigm of virtual network organization VBE-VO. VBE provides the resources and environment to support VO. When a business opportunity is identified by members of the VBE, a subset of the organization is selected to form a VO that responds positively to the opportunity. In this process, Afsarmanesh, H [11] emphasized the necessity of the establishment of VBE, which provided a nurturing environment for the dynamic and agile formation of VO driven by opportunity. On this basis, Liu Q [12] further proposed a three-layer collaboration framework for agile operation of small teams, that is, an operation layer is added between VBE and VO. The operation layer can rapidly schedule resources, track progress, and provide timely feedback. At the same time, it further strengthens the trust between organizations.

At present, how to promote the development of collaborative technology innovation is a major challenge facing manufacturing enterprises. The CNO theory emphasizes the dynamic response of the organization and the reallocation of resources, which gives manufacturing enterprises a new power to promote the development of collaborative innovation.

2.2 Developmental Barriers to CNO

The value-added logic of CNO symbiosis is mainly reflected in four aspects: value mechanism, structural mechanism, sharing mechanism and technical mechanism [2]. Its ultimate goal is to recognize that the overall value of the collaborative network is greater than the sum of the individuals. Nevertheless, the actual enterprise implementation process confronts challenges in these four areas because there are many obstacles in the complex transformation of enterprises from individual operations to CN operations. The value mechanism is when partners establish the same values and common goals. However, when the goals of the individual enterprise conflict with the goals of the collaborative network, it is difficult to achieve collaborative innovation [13]. CN is a network formed by various entities (people, organizations, devices, etc.), which are largely autonomous and heterogeneous in geographic location, culture, values, and social capital [12].The differences in various aspects lead to conflicts in collaboration, which ultimately fails to achieve the goal of synergy. In essence, conflicts are caused by members' different values and different views on cooperation results [5].

The structural mechanism refers to the power responsibility structure, communication structure and contractual relationship established between VBE enterprises for the stable development of collaborative relationship [2]. In order to promote the development of CN, it is necessary to decentralize the management of manufacturing enterprises. However, the redistribution of power is based on the improvement of the quality of managers, and blind decentralization will only lead to more serious accidents [14]. In addition, the inter-organizational communication system is inconsistent, resulting in a general atmosphere of communication, sharing, and collaboration [2]. At the same time, due to the instability of VO and the increase in the number of VBE alliance enterprises, high communication and coordination costs are also one of the difficulties faced by CNOs.

The sharing mechanism refers to the sharing of information, resources and knowledge among cooperative members. The barriers to sharing across organizations are mainly reflected in the perspectives of organizations and individuals. Research at the organizational level focuses on management, system, economy, technology, etc. Furthermore, the centralized hierarchy has a negative impact on knowledge sharing [15]. Individual barriers focus on incentive systems, individual trust, risk assessment, cultural factors, etc. [16]. For example, the innovation performance of VO members is affected by partners [17], and unfair behavior among CN members will increase distrust, resulting in reduced willingness and efficiency of information sharing [18].

The technical mechanism refers to the interactive platform provided for CN operations through various digital technologies. The abstract representation of attributes within a CNO is currently a challenge because of the large number of entities, roles, resources, governance principles, etc. within a CNO. Also members have barriers to resource sharing, instant access to resources and permission access [11]. Data sharing between organizations is also difficult due to the lack of standards for data sets and barriers to data processing [16].

In summary, the current theoretical research on CNO is comparatively mature, but there are still some barriers to the actual operation of the enterprise. The next section analyses and summarizes the barriers and solutions measures, taking the equipment manufacturing company as an example.

3   A Case Study

3.1   Company Background

The data for our study comes from a Chinese equipment manufacturing general assembly company (hereinafter referred to as CompanyE), which is responsible for the integrated assembly business. Integrated assembly plays an important role in the equipment manufacturing process and is a key and core technology for assembly manufacturing. CompanyE was established in 1983 as a wholly owned subsidiary of a group. The group's business can be split into two parts: drawing design and R&D production. The drawing design is done by the internal design institute of the group, while the R&D production is carried out by the research institutes under the group. In the past few years, the research institutes within the Group have all focused on the research and development of their respective core technologies, and there is business overlap in processing and trial production and material selection services.

On the one hand, however, the importance of collaborative innovation among institutions is becoming more and more evident. This is because product performance targets become higher and higher, traditional technologies are no longer able to meet functional requirements, and the solution of technical problems is increasingly shifting towards integrated functional solutions. On the other hand, collaboration between all parties is required at the requirements analysis stage to optimize and refine the entire design solution. This is because the supply side needs to constantly adapt the design, develop the production and improve the component models as the customer's customization requirements increase. CompanyE acts as a connector between all parties, connecting design institutes and research institutes upstream and component suppliers downstream, forming a large pool of resources. CompanyE takes advantage of the connection and actively builds a collaborative platform to connect all parties in order to respond to customized needs in an agile manner, forming integrated and innovative design solutions and ultimately realizing R&D and production.

In December 2020, CompanyE began to focus on technology synergy and requested authorization and resources from the Group's headquarters to build a synergy platform. Under the authority of the head office, CompanyE began to build the synergy network organization, design its operational framework and related governance principles, and decided to focus its synergy business on technical advisory services and technical research services. On the one hand, the technical consulting service is to form a technical team to interact with the designers immediately when the institutes are faced with the demand from the design institutes, and eventually form a professional group to prepare technical solutions according to the demand. On the other hand, the technical support service is a collaborative effort between the technical staff of each institute to determine the solution to a difficult part of the equipment development and production. In short, both business types are driven by organizational synergy, but there are a number of obstacles in E's practice of building a collaborative network organizational structure as well as in the operation process.

3.2   Data Collection

Exploring the barriers in the development of CNO requires an understanding of the group's organizational structure and strategic objectives, which leads to further analysis of the barriers to development and solutions in driving the operation of CNO's collaborative framework in CompanyE. This paper uses in-depth interviews as the main way to obtain data and conducts a follow-up study and several interviews to obtain valid information on the development of CNO in CompanyE. We selected managers and technical staff from different institutes to ask questions about various aspects such as the technology collaboration model, elements of collaborative innovation, factors influencing collaborative innovation performance, indicators and methods of performance evaluation, and the sharing and utilization of innovation resource elements, the specific information of which is shown in Table 1. At the same time, we also collected a large number of textual reports from CompanyE to better understand the development context and strategic planning of the company.

Table 1. Key information and descriptions of the interview

Key information for the interview	Descriptions
Identity of the interviewer	Manager of the Strategic Planning Department, Director of the Process Research Institute, Director of the branch plant, three operational staffs and two technically competent staffs
Examples of interview questions	(1) A brief introduction to the CompanyE's key businesses, culture and strengths in driving technological synergy and innovation (2) Is there currently a platform for information sharing or transfer between the CompanyE and other Group companies? (3) What are the reasons, objectives and dilemmas for the company's technological co-innovation?
Key responses from respondents	(1) Connect to many resources (2) On the technical side, there is currently product data management system, mainly for sharing design drawings. On the business side, for the time being, contact is made via an internal company email address as well as by telephone (3) Difficulties in transcending traditional organizational structures, building collaborative platforms, evaluating collaborative performance etc

During the interview, we adopted a flexible and responsive approach, respecting the wishes of the interviewees to express themselves. No questions were guided when the interviewees did not deviate from the questions, leaving them free to fully express their views and ideas [19]. The interviews were conducted using a semi-structured scheme, with questions asked of the interviewer based on questions prepared in advance, and questions asked flexibly during the interview based on the key points of the interviewer's answers [20], to obtain as complete information as possible (Table 2).

Table 2. Types of data collected and descriptions

Type of data	Descriptions
Onsite semi-structured interviews	15 h of recorded audio interviews with people from different departments and positions, including technical staff, branch directors and the head of development planning
Organizational documentation	(1) Approximately 330 pages of the Synergy Network Organizational Design Planning Report, Risk Assessment Report, Performance Assessment Methodology, Program Report on Operational Mechanisms, etc (2) Approximately 845 pages of the Technology Innovation Capacity Assessment Methodology, Business Management Methodology, Risk Handling Regulations, etc (3) Approximately 105 pages of PPT report on the project of building a technological innovation collaborative network organization, including background description, problem analysis, principles of collaborative operation, financial analysis, etc
WeChat chat records	The research process included interviews with the company's internal management and technical staff via WeChat, and the information was collated together as a basis for analysis

Table 3. Barriers and measures in DBE development

CNO's four mechanisms	Barriers	Corresponding measures
The value mechanism	Inter-organizational objectives cannot be aligned and their competitive and cooperative relationships are influenced by the extent of overlap between organizations in terms of resources as well as knowledge	Measure 1
The structural mechanism	Group molecules do not have enough voice and control to drive CNO operations	Measure 2
The sharing mechanism	1. Inequitable access to knowledge 2. Single channel of reward and insufficient reward 3. Enhanced awareness of property rights and increased risk perception	Measure 3
The technical mechanism	1.Data interoperability and data fusion between different systems is not achieved 2.Communication between institutes is mainly by telephone, resulting in a lot of valuable information not being recorded and reused	Measure 4

3.3 Data Analysis

In interviewing activities, data analysis begins during data collection, and analysis while collecting improves the quality of the data [20]. The raw data obtained from the interviews are descriptive transcripts such as text or audio recordings, translated or collated into text-based data that needs to be filtered and interpreted to make sense of them. We used a selective coding technique to code the text data. When a class of data could be interpreted in terms of thematically consistent literature, we combined them under a core class concept. When new themes emerged that were not explained by sufficient literature, we conducted secondary targeted interviews. This is done until the final coded core genus concept is reviewed by experts and companies and found to be logical and correct [21].

To answer our research question: What are the barriers companies face in promoting CN? We collected interview transcripts from respondents and extracted key messages that were important in driving the research.

The CompanyE has gone through a total of four stages of thinking and design in promoting CN construction. First, in terms of the value mechanism, the basis of collaborative innovation is to have a unified philosophy and goal between collaborators. Therefore, a common value must be established among collaborators to ensure the sustainable growth of CN. The second is the structural mechanism. The CompanyE is bound by the power of the group head office, and the promotion of CN must be approved and decentralized by the group head office. The third is the sharing mechanism. If the willingness to share is not obvious among organizations, it will lead to inefficient resource allocation. Fourthly, in terms of technology, digital technology provides the "predictability" of risk for empowering organizations to work together in symbiotic networks, allowing them to achieve greater synergy. Therefore, it is necessary to build a synergistic platform.

4 Barriers and Mitigation Measures in CNO Development

This section presents the obstacles in the process of CNO promotion for companies, and summarizes the corresponding mitigation measures with relevant theoretical analysis and suggests solutions that can be referred to.

4.1 Barriers and Mitigation Measures in the Value Mechanism

If goals are not aligned between organizations, this can create many obstacles to the development of collaborative networks. The competing relationship between organizations depends on the degree of overlap between different organizations in terms of resources and knowledge. Although some of the research institutes under the group have different core technology research, they have overlapping business in some processing and trial production and material selection services, and there is a greater possibility of competition between the institutes in the overlapping business during the promotion of CNO, which makes it difficult to achieve efficient synergy.

In the process of collaborative network operation, it is important to promote continuous cooperation between organizations. Daming You [22] suggests that the high interconnectedness of technical resources is reflected in the fact that different organizations have heterogeneous resources that are interdependent on each other. Each branch and each institute has its own core technology, so it is easier to achieve synergy in technological innovation. However, because CNO theory emphasizes that VO is a goal-driven organization, goals cannot be achieved without the processing and piloting and validation of technological innovation solutions by some organizations, and some organizations have overlapping resources and competitive relationships in these operations. More serious conflicts can lead to different organizations not being able to cooperate in technological innovation. To address this issue, CompanyE has attempted to account for the performance of technology innovation research and processing and pilot production separately, with organizations' processing and pilot production operations being competitively bid for. This formed a win-win, competitive technology innovation alliance between different organizations.

Measure 1: When there is competition between organizations in the associated side business of the synergistic main business, the associated side business is abstracted to account for performance separately. Construct a goal-focused cooperation system that drives organizational behavior and business activities with goals.

4.2 Barriers and Mitigation Measures in the Structural Mechanism

In terms of power structure, CompanyE belongs to the general assembly company of the group enterprise, with insufficient voice and control, and it is difficult to drive synergy development through itself due to the limitations of the section-based organizational structure. Therefore, establishing a person responsible for technical synergy operations is the first key obstacle.

At present, there is a lot of interactive information between assembly companies and institutes and design houses, so synergy is essential. However, who is responsible for the construction and operation of the synergy network is the company's first problem. Generally speaking, the more innovation resources a company possesses, the more quickly it can absorb and use external resources [23]. The CompanyE has set up four R&D studios and a process research institute, bringing together senior technical engineers from within the company who have developed several projects. Not only have they won several awards in the group's technology innovation competitions, but they have also published a number of technical breakthrough articles in the industry's best journals. In addition, E actively builds innovation platforms and carries out R&D capacity building by establishing several laboratories in conjunction with universities; It actively promotes its external achievements. E accumulates the advantages of technology and talent and therefore applies for authorization from the group, which gives E the corresponding authority to promote the development of CNO.

Measure 2: In the Group's section hierarchy management model, companies with the appropriate qualifications and capabilities are authorized to actively promote the operation of CN, and the Group increases its financial, equipment and personnel support.

4.3 Barriers and Mitigation Measures in the Sharing Mechanism

Knowledge transfer in VO organizations is a key link for VO members to absorb external technological resources, and it is also an important way to improve the organization's innovation capability to gain sustainable competitive advantage [24]. Knowledge sharing among VO members is conducive to identifying market opportunities and conducting innovative R&D to quickly capture the market, as many opportunities lurk in the uncertainty of the dynamic environment [25]. However, the data from the E interviews show that alliance members are not strongly willing to share resources for three reasons. First, some members felt that the willingness of some members to contribute knowledge was not evident when partners were more of a soliciting type of member, which was not considered to be a fair way of acquiring knowledge. Secondly, the willingness of technical staff to contribute knowledge is not strong due to the single reward channel and insufficient reward. Thirdly, the increasing awareness of intellectual property rights and the enhanced risk perception of enterprises in the era of big data have caused difficulties in knowledge sharing [25].

In CNs, enterprises optimize and improve their knowledge reserves through knowledge contribution and knowledge acquisition, thus enhancing their own innovation capabilities [27]. The company has established a set of feedback mechanisms to promote information sharing among VO members and to avoid the negative cooperative attitude of soliciting members. On the one hand, mutual evaluation data between members is returned to the operating platform after VO cooperation is completed; On the other hand, the AI assistant of the operation platform analyzes the activity of members according to the discussion of each meeting initiated by VO. By combining the two feedback evaluations, if a member is recorded as not actively participating in the knowledge contribution process three times, he or she is restricted from applying to join the VO organization. This reduces the resistance to knowledge contribution to a certain extent, advances information sharing among VO members, and improves the expression of each subject's knowledge.

In terms of reward channels, currently organizations only have one form of reward, namely increased production value, which is a performance indicator used by the Group to account for the amount of value of employees' work at the end of the year. In order to motivate members to participate in knowledge contributions in technological innovation, E Company has tried to increase incentives at the request of its members, and has developed a method for evaluating the innovation capability of technical staff, taking into account feedback from members and the operating platform. e Company has conducted a comprehensive evaluation of the innovation capability of technical staff through financial and non-financial indicators to encourage and guide all staff to take the initiative in technological innovation [24]. In addition, CompanyE has established incentive allowances for its core cadre, which are paid by the group headquarters, to increase incentives for process technicians.

Alliance members cannot avoid focusing on individual interests when implementing their tasks, and the ownership of intellectual property rights is a key concern for members. To address this issue, E has attempted to establish a third-party monitoring and evaluation body, consisting of industry experts, to determine the attribution of intellectual property rights based on the degree of contribution made by each institute in the innovation project and the members. This creates a level playing field for alliance members and allows them to maximize their own interests while collaborating on technological innovation.

Measure 3: Focus on the influencing factors of VO members' willingness to contribute knowledge, include non-financial indicators in the assessment, and seek feedback from members on a regular basis.

4.4   Barriers and Mitigation Measures in the Technical Mechanism

The process of promoting technological synergy involves many participants who often need to transfer and exchange information, so an operational platform for information sharing needs to be built. Through analysis of interview data, we found that CompanyE faced two main obstacles in building the operation platform. On the one hand, there are many independent systems in the group companies, such as the product data management system, the metering apparatus management system and the Skylark mail system. There was no data interoperability and data integration between different systems, so the duplication of data entry and authenticity made the operational staff work less efficiently, while bringing a lot of uncertainty to the business. On the other hand, the communication and coordination between the institutes of the group is based on telephone interviews, which leads to a lack of valuable information being recorded and reused. In addition to the formal corporate information system, technical communication between organizations takes place by telephone or through tools such as WeChat, which contains a great deal of corporate data and knowledge and the wisdom of a large number of technical staff.

Afsarmanesh, H. [13] proposed the concept of VBE management system (VMS), which provides the mechanisms and tools required to meet the operational and evolutionary needs of VBE, and this provides an idea for the construction of an operational platform. According to the analysis of the interviews, CompanyE has been working to eliminate obstacles to data sharing and system integration. In terms of system integration, the information technology team of CompanyE has attempted to define data interfaces to enable data sharing and information transfer, and has sorted out the data resources required for several collaborative scenarios such as electronic drawing sharing, design sign-off, document preparation and technical seminars, and has first broken through the data interoperability function for important scenarios on the operation platform.

Information interaction between organizations in the group usually takes place through a combination of email and telephone. On the one hand, the timeliness of email delivery is poor, and on the other hand, when there are too many design participants, it is necessary to send multiple copies of the same email and dock multiple participants at the same time, which increases the workload of the contact person and causes duplication of information in the system. In order to provide a fair and secure cooperation environment, CompanyE advocates transferring all information resources delivered through informal channels to the operation platform and actively developing relevant functional modules on the operation platform to achieve openness of data and information and structure of communication data. At the same time, based on the principle of confidentiality of technological collaboration and innovation, the platform only provides keys to the collaborators involved in the project to participate in seminars and view documents. All documents are approved, copied and printed by specific personnel, and the system leaves a trace.

Measure 4: Focus on the factors that hinder the construction of the enterprise operation platform and the informal channels of information transfer, and solve the problems through the professional information technology team targeted.

Based on the results of the interviews, this section dissects and proposes mitigation measures for the barriers that exist in four areas: value mechanisms, structural mechanisms, sharing mechanisms, and technology mechanisms, preparing the groundwork for the development of CNO-based technological innovation synergies in CompanyE. Table 3 summarizes the main discussions in Sect. 4.

5 Conclusion

This study analyzed the barriers to CNO development and the corresponding mitigation strategies. The conclusions are presented in three main areas. First, this paper utilizes a case study approach to interview employees and managers of CompanyE in different capacities. The analysis of the interview data summarizes The barriers and mitigation measures faced by CompanyE in the process of developing CNO in four aspects: value, structure, sharing and technology.

Second, in the field of practice, CNO rollout is a complex system project that requires companies to go through a long process of change. CompanyE in this case connects designers who design based on customers' needs upstream and parts suppliers downstream, connecting many resources, and tries to build CNO and build a collaborative platform to achieve agile response to demand and collaborate to obtain new value, which provides a reference for manufacturing companies that play the role of "connector" to develop CNO.

Thirdly, existing CNO research mainly focuses on theoretical level, and more case studies are needed to bring new research questions to the academic community. This paper focuses on the main obstacles and mitigation measures faced by enterprises in the process of CNO development, which complements the literature in the field of CNO development and provides new ideas and methods for CNO-related research.

Acknowledgements. The presented research works have been supported by "the National Nature Science Foundation of China" (6172029). The presented research works have been supported by "China National Railway Group Limited Science and Technology Research and Development Program Key Subjects" (N2021S009).

References

1. Huang, J., Zhang, G., Xie, Y.: Research on the innovation and path of networked cooperative development mechanism of small and medium-sized enterprises under growth orientation. Sci. Technol. Prog. Countermeasures **34**(23), 106–113 (2017)
2. Chen, Ch., Zhu, L., Liu, C., Xu, S.: The theory of synergy and symbiosis. School of Bus. (11), 120 (2021)
3. Sanders, N.R., Premus, R.: Modeling the relationship between firm IT capability, collaboration, and performance. J. Bus. Logistics **26**(1), 1–23 (2011)
4. Camarinha-Matos, L.M., Afsarmanesh, H.: Collaborative networks. In: Wang, K., Kovacs, G.L., Wozny, M., Fang, M. (eds.) PROLAMAT 2006. IFIP, vol. 207, pp. 26–40. Springer, Boston, MA (2006). https://doi.org/10.1007/0-387-34403-9_4
5. Macedo, P., Camarinha-Matos, L.M.: Value systems alignment analysis in collaborative networked organizations management. Appl. Sci. **7**, 1231 (2017). https://doi.org/10.3390/app7121231
6. Heil Cancian, M., Rabelo, R., Gresse von Wangenheim, C.: Collaborative business processes for enhancing partnerships among software services providers. J. Enterprise Inf. Syst. (5/6), 1–26 (2015). https://doi.org/10.1080/17517575.2014.985617
7. Msanjila, S.S., Afsarmanesh, H.: Trust analysis and assessment in virtual organization breeding environments. Int. J. Prod. Res. **46**(5), 1253–1295 (2008). https://doi.org/10.1080/00207540701224350
8. Shadi, M., Afsarmanesh, H.: Addressing behavior in collaborative networks. In: Camarinha-Matos, L.M., Pereira-Klen, A., Afsarmanesh, H. (eds.) PRO-VE 2011. IFIP, vol. 362, pp. 263–270. Springer, Heidelberg (2011). https://doi.org/10.1007/978-3-642-23330-2_29
9. Camarinha-Matos, L.M.: Collaborative networked organizations: Status and trends in manufacturing. Comput. Ind. Eng. **33**(2), 199–208 (2009). https://doi.org/10.1016/j.arcontrol.2009.05.006
10. Camarinha-Matos, L.M., Afsarmanesh, H.: Collaborative networks: a new scientific discipline. J. Intell. Manuf. **16**, 439–452 (2005). https://doi.org/10.1007/s10845-005-1656-3

11. Afsarmanesh, H., Camarinha-Matos, L.M.: A framework for management of virtual organization breeding environments. In: Camarinha-Matos, L.M., Afsarmanesh, H., Ortiz, A. (eds.) PRO-VE 2005. IFIP, vol. 186, pp. 35–48. Springer, Boston (2005). https://doi.org/10.1007/0-387-29360-4_4

12. Liu, Q., Gou, J., Camarinha-Matos, L.M.: Towards agile operation for small teams in knowledge intensive organizations: a collaboration framework. In: Camarinha-Matos, L.M., Afsarmanesh, H., Ortiz, A. (eds.) PRO-VE 2020. IFIP, vol. 598, pp. 263–272. Springer, Cham (2020). https://doi.org/10.1007/978-3-030-62412-5_22

13. Afsarmanesh, H., Camarinha-Matos, L.M., Msanjila, S.S.: Models, methodologies, and tools supporting establishment and management of second-generation VBEs. IEEE Trans. Syst. Man Cybern. Part C (Appli. Rev.) 41(5), 692–710 (2011). https://doi.org/10.1109/TSMCC.2010.2076326

14. Ji, P., Deng, C.: A brief discussion on the dilemma of flat management. Small Medium-Sized Enterp. Manag. Sci. Technol. (in Chinese) 11, 31–32 (2015)

15. Tsai, W.P.: Social structure of "coopetition" within a multiunit organization: coordination, competition, and intraorganizational knowledge sharing. Organ. Sci. 13(2), 179–190 (2002)

16. Sheng, S., Wu, H., Hu, B.J.: An empirical study of barriers to open sharing of scientific data. Libr. Intell. Work 63(17), 23–30 (2019). https://doi.org/10.13266/j.issn.0252-3116.2019.17.003

17. Xie, X., Zuo, L., Liu, S.: The impact of SME collaborative innovation model on the effect of collaborative innovation–a dual moderating effect model of synergistic mechanism and synergistic environment. Sci. Technol. Manag. 35(05), 72–81 (2014)

18. Chen, Y., Wu, C.W.: The impact of relationship fairness between alliance firms on cooperation performance - the mediating role of relationship commitment and the moderating role of goal congruence. Forecasting 33(06), 15–19 (2014)

19. Myers, M.D., Newman, M.: The qualitative interview in IS research: examining the craft. Inf. Organ. 17(1), 2–26 (2007)

20. Alex, B.: Using qualitative interviews in CAM research: a guide to study design, data collection and data analysis. Complement. Ther. Med. 13(1), 65–73 (2005)

21. Klein H K, MD Myers. A Set of Principles for Conducting and Evaluating Interpretive Field Studies in Information Systems[J]. Mis Quarterly, 1999, 23(1):67–93

22. You, D., Huang, H.Z.: Research on the evaluation index system of breakthrough technology innovation alliance partner selection. Seeking 12, 121–126 (2016). https://doi.org/10.16059/j.cnki.cn43-1008/c.2016.12.023

23. He, Y., Wu, J.: Research on the influence of corporate ecological position on cross-organizational technological collaborative innovation. Sci. Res. 38(06), 1108–1120 (2020). https://doi.org/10.16192/j.cnki.1003-2053.2020.06.016

24. Jiang, Z.S., Hu, L.Y., Chen, K.K.: Decisions of knowledge transfer in technology innovation alliance: a stackelberg leader-followers model. Oper. Res. Int. Journal 10(2), 231–242 (2010)

25. Zhang, H.: A study on the sources of variation in the effectiveness of knowledge transfer in technology alliances - a perspective of inter-organizational learning and strategic flexibility. Sci. Res. 31(11), 1687–1696, 1707 (2013). https://doi.org/10.3969/j.issn.1003-2053.2013.11.012

26. Zhou, H., Wu, T.: Evolutionary game analysis of knowledge sharing behavior among members of technology innovation alliances. Value Eng. 38(29), 119–121 (2019). https://doi.org/10.14018/j.cnki.cn13-1085/n.2019.29.054

27. Liang, F., Zhang, Z.: A study on the innovation effect of external knowledge search and its duality. J. Intell. 38(01), 171–179+86 (2019)

Value Co-creation in Ecosystems

Towards a Catalogue of Strategy Elements for Specifying a Digital Platform Business Strategy

Frank Berkers[1,2(✉)], Oktay Turetken[2], Baris Ozkan[2], and Paul Grefen[2]

[1] Netherlands Organisation for Applied Scientific Research (TNO), PO Box 96800,
2509 JE The Hague, The Netherlands
frank.berkers@tno.nl
[2] School of Industrial Engineering, Eindhoven University of Technology, PO Box 513,
5600 MB Eindhoven, The Netherlands

Abstract. Digital platforms have become essential in modern society. However, despite their appeal and potential, digital platforms have proven to fail often due to diverse strategic reasons including pricing, timing, competition, trust, openness, critical mass, and network effects. Despite the reported risk of failures, there is a lack of guidelines that support organizations in defining business strategies for digital platforms. In this paper, we address part of this problem. In the study we identify strategic considerations from digital business strategy, platform and multi-sided business strategy literature, and the Balanced Scorecard, and integrate them into a catalogue of nineteen strategy elements. This supports the specification of a coherent set of strategic objectives for a digital platform business strategy. A digital platform business strategy transforms an organization into a collaborative networked organization as four out of five strategy perspectives clearly reflect the need and of interaction with the ecosystem of the organization.

Keywords: Digital platform · Business strategy · Strategic objectives

1 Introduction

Digital platforms are essential in the fabric of the modern society [1]. Renowned digital platforms, like Amazon, Uber, AirBnB and many others have shown strong growth and gained significant attention. Their growth can be attributed to increased scale, speed, scope of business, having multiple sources of value creation and capture [2] and their capability to establish network effects between supply and demand sides interacting on the platform [3]. Due to this intriguing development, many organizations, including digital natives, start-ups, as well as incumbents, have been considering engaging in a digital business strategy based on a digital platform. Despite its attractiveness, digital platform business strategies have proven to fail very often. For each aspiring story like Spotify, there are tragic failures like Rdio, Milk, Guvera, Beats Music or Grooveshark. Studies on platform failure indicate that platforms fail often due to strategic reasons related to

L. M. Camarinha-Matos et al. (Eds.): PRO-VE 2022, IFIP AICT 662, pp. 579–591, 2022.
https://doi.org/10.1007/978-3-031-14844-6_46

pricing, timing, competition, trust, openness, sharing, critical mass, and network effects [4–7].

Digital platform business requires organizations to shift from linear value chain thinking to collaborative network thinking to establish seamless customer-centric services for both supply and demand sides and thereby leveraging network effects [8, 9]. An effective digital platform business strategy should exploit the specific characteristics of digitalization and platforms, while addressing the common aspects any business strategy should have [2]. Despite the reported risk of failure of platforms [4, 5], the extant literature lacks a structured guidance that supports specifying a business strategy for a digital platform. Digital strategy literature predominantly focusses on the strategy making process [10–12], whereas the emergent platform literature focuses predominantly on identifying the numerous business specific platform variables [9, 13, 14]. Both streams show limited overlap with the conventional business strategy frameworks, such as the Balanced Scorecard (BSC) [15]. Hence, our study is driven by the following research question: *"Which aspects should be considered in the specification of strategic objectives that form a digital platform business strategy?"*.

Accordingly, we studied the strategic considerations in the fields of digital business strategy [2, 10–12], platform and multi-sided business strategy [3, 8, 9, 13, 14, 16, 17] and the Balanced Scorecard [15], and followed a clustering approach [18] to develop a *catalogue* of strategy elements. The resulting catalogue features 19 strategy elements organized along 5 perspectives: finance, value proposition, ecosystem, processes, and learning and growth. The proposed catalogue supports the specification of strategic objectives for a digital platform business strategy.

We observed that several strategy elements, e.g., network effects, and composition of the strategy perspectives explicitly reflect that a digital platform business strategy requires the rearrangement of the focal organization and its ecosystem partners into a collaborative networked organization [19].

With this study, we aim to contribute to research on platform strategy and collaborative networks by integrating the concepts around platform strategy, digital strategy and overarching business strategy to support the specification of digital platform business strategies. Furthermore, our approach aims to contribute to practice by providing a catalogue that supports organizations in deriving strategic objectives for a digital platform business strategy, leveraging specific aspects of digitalization and platforms, while also addressing the common aspects of business strategy, such as skills, internal processes, organizational culture and leadership. Practical support is necessary, as digital platform business strategies are key in modern society to balance efficient, flexible, agile and sustainable systems [1].

In the next section, we introduce the theoretical background and related work. In Sect. 3, we describe the research approach. In Sect. 4, we present the developed catalogue and illustrate a selection of its underpinnings. Finally, we conclude this paper by discussing our contributions, limitations and future research directions.

2 Background and Related Work

Hagiu & Wright [20] define a platform as '*an organization that creates value primarily by enabling direct interactions between two (or more) distinct types of affiliated customers'*. Interactions can refer to exchange of goods and services between multiple parties. Enabling interaction between two parties makes this strategy to a large extent different from more conventional models in which transformation of inputs into outputs is central. One of the key characteristics of a platform is the possibility to obtain and leverage network effects [20]. Network effects occur if the presence of a certain type or number of customers attracts new customers. Several synonyms are used for the term platform business model, e.g., two- or multi-sided business model or marketplace. Eisenmann et al. [3] distinguish the following four key elements of a platform strategy: (1) Supply side users ensure supply of goods or services. (2) Demand side users are in demand for the supplied goods and services. (3) The platform provider is the point of contact for the transaction and provides components (hardware, software, and service modules in an architecture) in most user transactions and rules (including standards, protocols, policies, and contracts) to coordinate participants. Finally, (4) the platform sponsor designs the components and rules and determines who may participate in the network as the platform providers and users. Often, this role coincides with the platform provider. A key strategic consideration is the extent to which these four elements are open to participation by other parties [3]. Pagani [21] refers to this as control points. A well-known example to illustrate this is the control that Apple store exerts to the offered apps, versus the relative lack of control in the Android store. Although not always acknowledged explicitly, many platform businesses are relying on digital systems [22].

Consequently, we define a digital platform business strategy as a business strategy enabled by a digital system that enables direct interactions between two (or more) distinct types of affiliated customers [20]. A digital business strategy is generally seen as 'a business strategy, inspired by digital technologies, digital capabilities, and digital resources, to provide revenue and value-producing opportunities' [2, 10].

Business strategy is often viewed in terms of the achievement and maintenance of competitive advantage in specific product-market domains [23]. Key strategic issues, typically identified at the business unit level of an organization, focus on maintaining and achieving competitive advantage, and the integration and coordination of 'arena, advantage, access and activities' [23]. One of the business strategy tools popular in industry and the scientific literature is the Balanced Scorecard (BSC) [24]. These foundations and processes of business strategy making are still in use after decades. The digital aspect has, however, made important complications to the strategy making process, as digitization does not only affect business propositions, but also the rate of proposition renewal by the incorporation of new technologies. This continuously generates new opportunities and threats for organizations. Bharadway et al. [2] contend that digital strategy differs from general business strategy in scope, scale, speed and sources of value creation and capture. They explicitly identify multisided and networked business models as relevant sources of value creation in a digital strategy.

Business strategies are often expressed as a coherent set of strategic objectives [25]. Strategy frameworks, such as the BSC, provide commonly recognized aspects of a business strategy (which we defined as the *strategy elements*), that can be used to define strategic objectives. Various works that aim to build an integral view on platform strategy center on the platform in business strategy and identify a wealth of strategic elements [9, 13, 14,

26–28]. For example, Floetgen et al. [28] find no less than 51 recurring constructs. Yet, these works do not include or refer to the conventional elements of business strategy, e.g., internal processes or human capital, as represented in the BSC. Furthermore, these works hardly address the themes in which *digital* business strategy differs from business strategy [2]. In the field of digital strategy, the focus is predominantly on the strategy making processes [10, 11], rather than the identification of strategy elements. Business models are also seen as concretizations of business strategy [29]. Consequently we see strategy elements as sources for requirements for business models that implement a business strategy.

In response to the growing interest in platforms Rietveld & Schilling [27] identify four key themes in platform competition: (a) network effects and their implications; (b) platform ecosystems and corporate scope; (c) heterogeneity in platforms, complements and users; and (d) platform governance and ecosystem orchestration. Floetgen et al. [28] organize their 51 recurring constructs in ecosystem and market, complements, complementors, owner, platform and user. Ardolino et al. [14] describe a digital multi-sided platform using a framework consisting of 19 variables with multiple options along the dimensions of platform sides, revenue, control, competition and architecture. Yablonsky [30] proposes a multidimensional framework integrating business and technological innovations and management, allowing executives to examine the interrelationships across a platform business model portfolio on a regular basis. Tura et al. [26] present a framework for platform design, involving four elements: 1) platform architecture, 2) value creation logic, 3) governance, and 4) platform competition. Eisape [13] introduces a platform business model canvas, based on literature, to help capture platform business models in a comprehensive way.

In summary, a digital platform business strategy is seen as a special type of business strategy enabled by a digital system that allows for direct interactions between two (or more) distinct types of affiliated customers. Business strategies are specified by strategic objectives. Strategy frameworks like the BSC provide strategy elements for which such objectives can be specified.

Although the studies that aim to build an integral view on platform strategy provide a wealth of platform specific strategic elements, aspects of conventional business strategy, such as human and organizational capital and internal processes, are merely neglected. Furthermore, in digital strategy, the focus is on the strategy making processes rather than on indicating what strategic elements should be addressed. This leads to lack of a strategic framework that incorporates strategy elements related to platform business strategy, digital business strategy and business strategy.

3   Research Design

To identify the aspects that should be considered in the specification of strategic objectives forming a digital platform business strategy, we need to refer to works from the fields of platform, digital and business strategy. This requires the identification and clustering of potential strategy elements. As indicated in the previous section, the literature already provides several, yet dispersed and disconnected, strategy frameworks consisting of strategy elements or clusters of strategy elements. The task at hand thus predominantly consists of locating, mapping and clustering these elements. This task closely resembles the core of the Constant Comparison Method (CCM) [18]. The CCM includes an iterative process of (i) identifying and comparing expressions (e.g., in pieces of text) that are linked to emerging categories; (ii) integrating categories and their properties followed by (iii) delimiting and writing theory. In the iterative process, the categories can be integrated into overarching categories and newly identified expressions can be appended into a category, by constantly comparing incidents with categories and categories with categories. The process ends when new incidents do not lead to creation or revision of categories.

In our case, we base our resulting 5 categories and 19 strategy elements on the categories of the existing strategy frameworks and their underlying strategy elements (e.g., [2, 15, 26]) and the strategy elements identified in the literature that do not refer to an overarching framework (e.g., [3, 9]). We start our CCM variant by mapping and clustering both categories and strategy elements of key frameworks representing platform business strategy, digital business strategy, and business strategy [2, 15, 26]. Next, we iteratively incorporate the literature from the fields of platform strategy and digital business strategy that provides strategy elements and relevant frameworks, also by referring to extensive literature reviews on these topics (e.g., [3, 14, 16, 27]). Given our objective to develop a framework that can be *deployed and used in practice* [31], we aim to incorporate a limited set of strategy elements (instead of developing an framework with an exhaustive list of strategy elements). Hence, we take the representation and the four perspectives of the BSC as a reference basis. We end the application of the constant comparison method when newly identified articles do not alter the existing categories.

4 The Catalogue

We have executed the research design described in the previous section and consequently constructed the catalogue consisting of 19 strategy elements organized along 5 perspectives (i.e., cluster of strategy elements), namely finance, value proposition, ecosystem, processes, and learning and growth. Figure 1 presents the structure of the final version and below we elaborate these perspectives.

The *Finance* (I) perspective describes how the focal organization should appear to its shareholders to succeed financially [15]. It describes the tangible outcomes of the (digital platform business) strategy in traditional financial terms, such as ROI, shareholder value, profitability, revenue growth, and lower unit costs [15].

The *Value Proposition* (II) perspective describes the strategy how the key value proposition offered to customers will achieve the organization's vision. It defines the clear, measurable and demonstrable benefits [15], as well as the intangible values [15] and the experience [32] consumers of all sides of the platform get when interacting with the platform, e.g., by buying a particular product or service. The organization intends to use this to generate sales and loyalty from targeted customers. This value proposition forms the context in which tangible and intangible assets create value for the focal firm and society [1, 15].

The *Ecosystem* (III) perspective describes the position and relationships the focal organization should have with other ecosystem members to achieve its vision. It defines how the focal organization builds its position in the ecosystem.

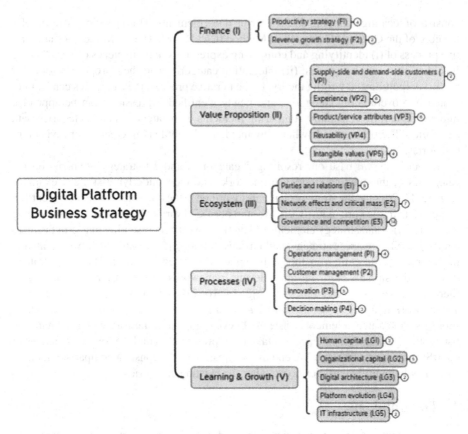

Fig. 1. The catalogue of strategy elements for a digital platform business strategy.

The *Processes* (IV) perspective defines the strategic considerations regarding the cross-organizational business processes the organization must excel at to satisfy its shareholders and customers [33]. This perspective identifies the few critical processes that create and deliver the differentiating customer value proposition.

The *(Digital) Learning and Growth* (V) perspective defines how the organization will sustain its ability to change and improve to achieve its vision. It identifies the intangible assets that are most important to strategy. The objective is to identify the jobs (human capital), systems (the information capital), and climate (the organization capital) that are required to support the value-creating processes. These intangible assets must be integrated and aligned with the critical internal processes.

Table 1 presents the 19 strategy elements that are aligned with the 5 perspectives.

Table 1. Catalogue of Strategy Elements for Digital Platform Business Strategy

---

Finance (I)

Productivity strategy (F1) describes how the organization will create greater value at the same costs or the same value at lower costs. The cost structure defines how the costs for delivering value are composed. Asset utilization is the degree to which (tangible and intangible) assets are used to their full potential.

Revenue growth strategy (F2) describes how the organization will grow its sources of income. Enhanced customer value defines how an enhanced customer value leads to increased revenues. Expanding revenue sources identifies new or increased sources of income.

Value Proposition (II)

Supply-side and demand-side customers (VP1) define both sides, or segments, of the two-sided value proposition. These segments interact via the platform.

Experience (VP2) illustrates the customer's process and context in which s/he is using the value proposition, i.e., in which value is co-created. It defines the parts of the customer journey that are addressed in the value proposition. It specifies the desired type of relationship the organization will have with the customers of both sides and the processes, interfaces, and interactions the customers of both sides will use when using the value proposition.

Product/service attributes (VP3) specify specific product and service attributes that are necessary for delivering the experience defined in the customer journey. It also specifies how data and digital technology is used in the delivery of the experience.

Reusability (VP4) specifies how the value proposition can be used and reconfigured or extended for other supply and demand combinations.

Intangible values (VP5) define how the value proposition confirms the image and brand of the organization, how it meets the regulatory standards and wider stakeholder expectations.

Ecosystem (III)

Parties and relations (E1) specify the parties that the organization will have relations with. This includes the following roles: the *focal company*; who serves as users' *primary point of contact* with the platform; who exercises *property rights*; who *determines* who may participate in a platform-mediated network and for developing its technology. It also specifies the *partners that are critical* to delivering the value proposition and *those that extend* the value proposition, including complementing parties.

Network effects and critical mass (E2) identifies if and how each of the four potential network effects are applicable. The different types of network effects are same-side (supply) (how existing offerings on the supply side attract additional offerings), same-side (demand), cross-side from supply to demand, cross-side from demand to supply. It also identifies how the organization achieves critical masses for any of these network effects.

Governance and competition (E3) specify how governance is arranged between platform providers, sponsors, core, and enriching partners, as well as if multi-homing is allowed for supply and demand. It also specifies the governance processes that guide the control and decision making. It identifies the components of the platform whose design or availability to other parties has effects on the value proposition and specifies their level of openness. It identifies the (five forces of) competition: competitors, new entrants, alternatives, users and core and enriching partners.

(*continued*)

Table 1. (*continued*)

Processes (IV)

Operations management (P1) identifies the key planning, organizing, and supervising processes that manage the operation of the platform. It identifies the key partner (interfacing) services that affect the value proposition.

Customer management (P2) identifies the key processes that guide the monitoring of the level of performance of the value proposition as well as identification of new opportunities.

Innovation (P3) specifies the key innovation processes required to improve the value proposition and their underlying processes and assets. It specifies how increases in the responsiveness of renewal of products and services are achieved.

Decision making (P4) identifies the key processes that constitute the decision making with respect to the value proposition and its underlying processes and assets. It specifies how increases in the responsiveness of decision making can be achieved by utilizing data and digital technologies.

(Digital) Learning and Growth (V)

Human capital (LG1) specifies the necessary improvements of human capital, e.g., new or improved skills, trainings, how-to knowledge for delivering the value proposition.

Organization capital (LG2) specifies the necessary change in organizational capital, e.g., change in culture (digitalization), leadership, alignment, and teamwork.

Digital architecture (LG3) identifies the digital industry architecture (technology) in which the platform is embedded and identifies the elements that constitute the dependencies and those that are depending on the platform.

Platform evolution (LG4) identifies the potential future evolutions of the platform in terms of value propositions, markets, segments, and functionalities.

IT infrastructure (LG5) identifies the requirements with respect to the information systems that constitute the platform technology, with respect to speed, scope, and scalability (up/down).

Due to the space limitations, we only illustrate the underpinnings of the three strategy elements of the ecosystem perspective of the catalogue. A full account of all strategy elements with their underpinnings can be found at https://bit.ly/cdpbsse2.

Parties and Relations (E1). This strategy element identifies the parties the platform needs to interact with directly and the relations necessary to achieve the envisioned position in the ecosystem. Scholars indicate that for digital business, platform business and service-dominant business interaction with ecosystem partners is critical (*value creation network, value chain, service eco-system,* or simply *key actors* and *actor roles*) [11, 26, 32, 34]. Bharadway et al. [2] contend that digital business strategy solicits for exploitation of the extended business ecosystem; that effectiveness of scaling can be achieved through alliances and partnerships; and that speed or agility can be obtained through formation of new business networks that provide complementary capabilities. More specific roles that need to be identified are *focal company* [3, 32] *platform provider* (users' primary point of contact) [30], *owners* (exercise property rights, determine who may participate in a platform-mediated network and for developing its technology) [13, 28, 30]. The partners critical to delivering the value proposition are referred to as *core partners* [32], *complementors* [27], *key partnerships, partner, contributor* [13] *sponsors* [3, 30] and the partners that extend the value proposition, including *complementing* or *enriching parties* ([27, 28, 32]) and *collaboration management: core relationships, enriching relationships* [32, 35].

Network Effects and Critical Mass (E2). This strategy element specifies which network effects should be established and how critical mass can be achieved. Network effects, or externalities, are an essential part of the attraction and thus the value proposition to users, as e.g., a platform with a wider and more qualitative range of offerings will attract more demand side users and vice versa. Although Tura et al. [26] and Ardolino et al. [14] see network effects and network externalities as part of the value creation logic, it is positioned as a separate element under the perspective of Ecosystems (III), as establishing network effects requires interplay between the different sides and the different parties and relations with the platform. Bharadway et al. [2] contend that leveraging network effects of multisided platforms is critical for scaling. Four types of network effects can be distinguished: *same-side* (supply), *same-side* (demand), *cross-side* (supply to demand), *cross-side* (demand to supply) [16]. Underlying elements that may contribute to network externalities and their implications are, among others, *installed base and number*; *heterogeneity* and *quality of complementary goods* and its *providers*; and *heterogeneity* and *quality of demand users* [27].

Strategies to consider to establish the *critical masses* that are needed for network effects to take place, are *platform launch* [26]; *subsidies; seeding; marquee users; micro-market launch*; and *piggybacking* [16], *presence of "blockbuster" complements;* and *complement exclusivity* [27], *bundling; exploit irregular topologies; attracting users en masse; harnessing virality; balancing consumers and producers;* and *platform disintermediation* [30].

Governance and Competition (E3). This strategy element defines the key parameters of the platform and the party that controls these. Eisenmann et al. [3], Floetgen et al. [28] and Tura et al. [26] explain which decisions related to openness and 'conditions to access' can be made, and how these affect the attraction to both sides of users, their platform service providers and sponsors, and digital platform ecosystem performance in general. Digital platforms and architectures have many of such control points [2, 14, 20, 26, 36]. Strategies like business models on platforms (*envelopment*) [17, 34] and *multi-homing* [8, 14] also affect the competitive position of a platform. Due to the digital nature, many of these control points (e.g., access or pricing) could theoretically be changed overnight. Governance defines the *control, decision making and 'creation and enforcement of rules'* [27], and *rules and standards, protocols, policies* and *contracts* [34]. It specifies how governance is arranged between platform providers, sponsors, core, and enriching partners, as well as if multi-homing is allowed for supply and demand. It is relevant for participation in the strategy as it identifies the components of the platform whose design or availability to other parties has effects on the value proposition and specifies their level of *openness*. The determination of these should be considered in light of the competition. Parker et al. [9] distinguish *platform-platform*, *platform-partner* and *partner-partner* types of competition that may come from new entrants, alternatives, users, and core and enriching partners [8, 13, 14, 26].

The catalogue reflects the observations that a digital platform business strategy requires collaboration and positioning of the focal organization in an ecosystem. For example, the strategy element *'network effects'* requires the platform to establish a seamless experience of transaction execution from both supply and demand sides. This implies, among other things, that the complementors on the supply side are identified, well-balanced in their offerings, and engaged with the platform. Vice versa, a large and accessible set of customers is valuable and extremely costly to build up and maintain for individual supply side actors. As another example, the *governance strategy* element specifies how and by whom decisions are made with respect to rules, access, etc. Clearly, for the decision to participate in a platform by supply-side and demand-side customers, it makes a difference if conditions for access are changed overnight or if they can have influence on that, e.g., via standardization bodies. For many of the other strategy elements collaborative and ecosystem influences are much more emphasized as compared to the original BSC. Three other differences can be observed. Firstly, the ecosystem perspective and its underlying strategy elements thus explicitly draw attention of the focal firm on how to participate in and serve collaborative networks. Secondly, the perspective value proposition replaces the customer perspective, which emphasizes the focus on the experience for customers on supply and demand sides. Thirdly, the process perspective is not internal anymore, as processes are necessarily cross organizational boundaries. Consequently, this perspective and the underlying strategy element 'Operations Management (P1)', force the focal firm to specify its integration and interoperability policies through which it will interact with the partners in its collaborative network.

We argue that, in order avoid strategic failures, as mentioned in [4, 5], a framework that integrates the strategy elements from the domains of platform strategy, digital business strategy, and business strategy, and thereby addressing known risks, is indispensable. Even more so in an Society 5.0 context [1], where cyberspace and physical space are highly integrated to balance economic advancement and resolution of societal challenges, e.g., environmental sustainability, multi-sided digital platform approaches are expected to gain increased attention. Platforms can help to reduce emissions from mobility [37], and optimize material usage in the circular economy [38].

5   Conclusions

In this paper, we present a catalogue of strategy elements along 5 strategic perspectives as an answer to our inquiry of the aspects that should be considered in the specification of strategic objectives forming a digital platform business strategy. A digital platform business strategy is considered a special type of digital and business strategy enabled by a digital system. Although it is widely acknowledged that platform strategy and digital business strategy are subtypes of business strategy, thus far, no strategic framework has incorporated strategy elements related to platform business strategy, digital business strategy, and business strategy. Following an approach inspired by the constant comparison method, we developed a catalogue of strategy elements that aims to bridge the fields of platform strategy, digital business strategy, and business strategy.

With this work, we contribute to research on platform strategy and collaborative networks by integrating the concepts of platform strategy and digital strategy into the overarching concept of business strategy. Given the frequent platform failures and expected increasing demand for platforms in context of modern society, and given the increasing need for balancing productivity, sustainability, and resilience [1], the importance of guiding organizations in addressing known risks related to platforms, digitization and business in general, is evident.

The aspired practical relevance of this contribution is that it supports business organizations in detailing a digital platform business strategy by identifying and specifying coherent and complete set of strategic objectives that together form a complete business strategy. The presented catalogue is developed as an integral artifact of a method [31]. This method supports first the derivation of strategic objectives by answering for the strategy elements in the catalogue *"What must be achieved in light of this strategy element and its underlying concepts, to reach the digital platform business strategy?"*. In practice, the focal firm should start with deriving strategic objectives for the prioritized strategy elements of each of the perspectives. Secondly, these specified objectives are transformed into business model design requirements, to support the organization in designing business models in line with strategy. The proposed method, including the catalogue, has been applied in the two real-life business cases in the mobility and manufacturing domains for evaluation with practitioners. However, these applications are kept outside the scope of this paper due to space limitations.

This study has several limitations which have to be considered when interpreting its results. For practical reasons the number of strategy elements to consider in a strategy specification process should be limited to arrive at a structured, concise design. We targeted on defining a limited set of elements as demonstrated in the BSC. This restriction may, however, conceal the richness of elements identified in the original frameworks, as exemplified by the 51 recurring constructs for platform strategy reported in [28]. Thus, in using this catalogue, it would be helpful for practitioners guiding the process to be familiar with the underlying models. For this purpose, readers are referred to https://bit.ly/cdpbsse2.

Although application in a real-life business case in the manufacturing industry has positively confirmed the practicality and value of our approach, further research should further operationalize the catalogue and propose a process that guides users in how to deal with the resulting strategic objectives, e.g., by turning them into investment plans or business model designs. Following this, further research includes formal evaluation and application of the approach in different practical contexts, and following design science guidelines [39].

Furthermore, this work targets at generic digital platform business strategies, building on platform literature that is developed and applied in different settings. However, in more specific application contexts of digital platforms (such as finance, or health), the development process used for the proposed catalogue could be further carefully specialized accordingly, leading to domain-specific catalogues.

References

1. European Commission, Industry 5.0, (2021). https://ec.europa.eu/info/res earch-and-innovation/research-area/industrial-research-and-innovation/industry-50_en (Accessed 08 Feb 2022)
2. Bharadway, A., El Sawy, O.A., Pavlou, P.A.: Digital business strategy: toward a next generation of Insights. MIS Q. 37(2), 471–482 (2013)
3. Eisenmann, T.R., Parker, G., Van Alstyne, M.W.: Opening platforms: how, when and why? SSRN Electron. J. (2008). https://doi.org/10.2139/ssrn.1264012
4. Yoffie, D.B., Gawer, A., Cusumano, M.: A study of more than 250 platforms a reveal why most fail, University of Surrey (2019)
5. Evans, D.S., Schmalensee, R.: Failure to launch: critical mass in platform businesses. Rev. Netw. Econ. 9(4), 1 (2010)
6. Van Alstyne, M.W., Parker, G.G., Choudary, S.P.: 6 Reasons Platforms Fail. HbR (2016). https://hbr.org/2016/03/6-reasons-platforms-fail (Accessed Feb 08 2022)
7. Zhu, F., Iansiti, M.: Why some platforms thrive and others don't. HbR (2019). https://hbr.org/2019/01/why-some-platforms-thrive-and-others-dont (Accessed Feb 08 2022)
8. Reillier, L.C., Reillier, B.: Platform Strategy: How to Unlock the Power of Communities and Networks to Grow Your Business. Taylor & Francis (2017)
9. Parker, G.G., Van Alstyne, M.W., Choudary, S.P.: Platform revolution: How networked markets are transforming the economy and how to make them work for you. WW Norton & Company (2016)
10. Dang, D., Vartiainen, T.: Digital strategy patterns in information systems research. In: PACIS 2019, May 2019
11. Lipsmeier, A, Kühn, A., Joppen, R., Dumitrescu, R.: Process for the development of a digital strategy. In: Procedia CIRP, vol. 88 (2020)
12. Schallmo, D., Williams, C.A., Lohse, J.: Digital strategy - Integrated approach and generic options. Int. J. Innov. Manag. 23(8) (2019)
13. Eisape, D.A.: The platform business model canvas - designing and visualizing platform business models. Int. J. Innov. Stud. Sci. Eng. Technol. 6(2), 60–72 (2020)
14. Ardolino, M., Saccani, N., Adrodegari, F., Perona, M.: A business model framework to characterize digital multisided platforms. J. Open Innov. Technol. Mark. Complex. 6(1) (2020). https://doi.org/10.3390/joitmc6010010
15. Kaplan, R.S., Norton, D.P.: Harvard Bus. Rev. 70(1), 71 (1992)
16. Eisenmann, T., Parker, G., Van Alstyne, M.W.: Strategies for two-sided markets. Harv. Bus. Rev. 84(10) (2006)
17. Eisenmann, T., Parker, G., Van Alstyne, M.: Platform envelopment. Strateg. Manag. J. 32(12), 1270–1285 (2011). https://doi.org/10.1002/smj.935
18. Lincoln, Y.S., Guba, E.G.: Naturalistic Inquiry. SagePublications Inc, Newbury Park, California (1985)
19. Camarinha-Matos, L.M., Afsarmanesh, H.: Collaborative networked organizations. A Res. agenda Emerg. Bus. Model. (2004). https://doi.org/10.1007/b116613
20. Hagiu, A., Wright, J.: Multi-Sided Platforms. Int. J. Ind. Organ. 43 (2015)
21. Pagani, M.: Digital business strategy and value creation: framing the dynamic cycle of control points. MIS Q. 37(2), 617–632 (2013)
22. Adali, O.E, Ozkan, B., Turetken, O., Grefen, P.: Identification of service platform requirements from value propositions: a service systems engineering method. In: Working Conference on Virtual Enterprises, pp. 311–322 (2021)
23. Varadarajan, P.R., Clark, T.: Delineating the scope of corporate, busines and marketing strategy. J. Bus. Res. 31, 93–105 (1994)

24. Madsen, D.Ø., Stenheim, T.: The balanced scorecard: a review of five research areas. Am. J. Manag. **15**(2), 24–41 (2015)
25. Quezada, L.E., Cordova, F.M., Palominos, P., Godoy, K., Ross, J.: Method for identifying strategic objectives in strategy maps. Int. J. Prod. Econ. **122**(1), 492–500 (2009)
26. Tura, N., Kutvonen, A., Ritala, P.: Platform design framework: conceptualisation and application. Technol. Anal. Strateg. Manag. **30**(8), 881–894 (2018). https://doi.org/10.1080/095 37325.2017.1390220
27. Rietveld, J., Schilling, M.A.: Platform competition: a systematic and interdisciplinary review of the literature. J. Manage. **47**(6), 1528–1563 (2021). https://doi.org/10.1177/014920632096 9791
28. Floetgen, R., Novotny, M., Urmetzer, F., Böhm, M.: Connecting the dots of digital Platform ecosystem research: constructs, causal links and future research. In: ECIS (2021)
29. Casadesus-Masanell, R., Ricart, J.E.: From strategy to business models and onto tactics. Long Range Plann. **43**(2–3), 195–215 (2010). https://doi.org/10.1016/j.lrp.2010.01.004
30. Yablonsky, S.: Multidimensional framework for digital platform innovation and management: from business to technological platforms. Syst. Res. Behav. Sci. **35**(4), 485–501 (2018)
31. Berkers, F., et al.: Deriving collaborative business model design requirements from a digital platform business strategy. In: Camarinha-Matos, L.M., Afsarmanesh, H., Ortiz, A. (eds.) PRO-VE 2020. IFIP, vol. 598, pp. 47–60. Springer, Cham (2020). https://doi.org/10.1007/ 978-3-030-62412-5_4
32. Lüftenegger, E., Comuzzi, M., Grefen, P.W.P.J.: Designing a tool for service-dominant strategies using action design research. Serv. Bus. **11**(1), 161–189 (2015). https://doi.org/10.1007/ s11628-015-0297-7
33. Turetken, O., Grefen, P., Gilsing, R., Adali, O.E.: Service-dominant business model design for digital innovation in smart mobility. Bus. Inf. Syst. Eng. **61**(1), 9–29 (2019)
34. Yablonsky, S.: A Multidimensional framework for digital platform innovation and management: from business to technological platforms. Syst. Res. Behav. Sci. **35**(4), 485–501 (2018). https://doi.org/10.1002/sres.2544
35. Andres, B., Poler, R.: A decision support system for the collaborative selection of strategies in enterprise networks. Decis. Support Syst. **91**, 113–123 (2016)
36. Dattee, B., Alexy, O., Autio, E.: Maneuvering in poor visibility: how firms play the ecosystem game when uncertainty is high. Acad. Manag. J. **61**(2), 466–498 (2018). https://doi.org/10. 5465/amj.2015.0869
37. Scandelius, C., Cohen, G.: Sustainability program brands: platforms for collaboration and co-creation. Ind. Mark. Manag. **57**, 166–176 (2016)
38. Konietzko, J., Bocken, N., Hultink, E.J.: Online platforms and the circular economy. In: Bocken, N., Ritala, P., Albareda, L., Verburg, R. (eds.) Innovation for sustainability. PSS-BIAFE, pp. 435–450. Springer, Cham (2019). https://doi.org/10.1007/978-3-319-97385-2_23
39. Peffers, K., Rothenberger, M., Tuunanen, T., Vaezi, R.: Design science research evaluation. Des. Sci. Res. Inf. Syst. Adv. theory Pract. (2012)

Boosting Value Co-creation in Design Through the Product-Service System Digital Twin: Questions to Be Answered

Marco Bertoni[(✉)]

Department of Mechanical Engineering, Blekinge Institute of Technology, Karlskrona, Sweden
marco.bertoni@bth.se

Abstract. Digital Twins (DTs) are among the most hyped technologies of the 2020 s. Yet, the research dealing with the use of DTs in early Product-Service Systems design remains insufficiently systematized. Based on the findings of multiple-case studies in the Swedish manufacturing industry, the objective of this paper is to collect and present a set of 'questions that need to be answered' to foster the development and utilization of DTs in the PSS realm. The results highlight how the DTs should be composed of several layers to boost value co-creation in design, in a way to incorporate the digital 'counterpart' for more abstract entities, from processes to human behaviors to more intangible assets.

Keywords: Product-Service Systems · Digital Twins · Servitization · Circularity

1 Introduction

The use of exact duplicates to manage complex systems dates back to NASA's moon missions of the 1960 s and 1970 s [1]. NASA used mirrored systems, the precursor of Digital Twins (DTs), to rescue the Apollo 13 crew when it ran into trouble. Nearly 50 years later, DTs have long left NASA's labs, and are on the verge of a widespread adoption across a wide range of businesses. Intuitively, when manufacturers can see real-time data on how their products are operating, they can make dramatic improvements in design, innovation, efficiency, and production [2]. Twinning physical products in the digital realm enables them to run different scenarios to assess the long-term consequences of their decisions [3], to avoid costly and time-consuming situations ahead, such as potentially costly breakdowns.

In the realm of Product-Service Systems (PSS), DTs are regarded as one of the most relevant digital technologies for designing, operating, and supporting servitized solutions. Pirola and colleagues [4] describe how they can be used to raise decision makers' awareness about the interplay between hardware and services in operations, to know more about the behavior of customers and their latent needs, to map failures and plan interventions accordingly. They can also be used to support the construction of decision-making models based on the outcome of several virtual test-drives (i.e.,

© IFIP International Federation for Information Processing 2022
Published by Springer Nature Switzerland AG 2022
L. M. Camarinha-Matos et al. (Eds.): PRO-VE 2022, IFIP AICT 662, pp. 592–602, 2022.
https://doi.org/10.1007/978-3-031-14844-6_47

simulations) of various circular strategies in ultra-realistic scenarios [5]. Much before the new hardware and services are launched, engineers can know more about the value generated by their innovative solution concepts and business models, assessing if they are able to fulfil availability, quality, and risks mitigation requirements [6].

Yet, even though several real and theorized examples of DTs are discussed in academia and industry, a gap remains between their expected vs. realized potential of DTs when it comes to support engineers in 'intentionally designing' PSS solutions. Current research is often not able to describe how DTs can lead to a more informed, expedited, and innovative design process, one that benefits from the coevolution between physical and digital objects since an early stage. The objective of this paper is to present a list of 'questions that need to be answered' by future research aimed at fostering the development and utilization of DTs in PSS design. The remainder or this paper presents and discusses 14 questions - across 4 different layers - that are believed to be relevant for the PSS community to further elaborate upon 'in what areas' and 'in which ways' are DTs able to support the early-stage design activities of innovative circular and servitized solutions.

2 Towards the PSS DT: A Review of Main Efforts and Themes

In recent years, the manufacturing industry has invested heavily in the development of service-based business models. Pay-for-performance and pay-per-use are some of the schemes that have been proposed in literature to fulfil increasingly sophisticated customer needs for availability, quality, and reduced risks [7]. Yet, many real-life implementations of have been observed to be commercially unsuccessful [8], often due to the lack of transparency of the customers' behavior and to the difficulties in tracking the current state of the PSS hardware during the use phase [9].

In servitization studies, digitalization is advocated as a major strategy to overcome these issues, and to leverage the way value is captured and co-created in service-based business models [10]. The adoption of emerging digital technologies and Industry 4.0 - namely, smart sensors, internet of things (IoT), cloud computing, data analytics, blockchain, AI, 5G, cyber-physical systems, or augmented reality – is seen as a major opportunity for the product manufactures to take a step forward in their servitization journey [11]. With the adoption of digital technologies, companies can develop smart and connected products with highly software-enabled systems, which enable capabilities such as monitoring, control, optimization, and autonomy [12] as well as ecosystem collaboration [10]. Among the digital technologies discussed today, DTs are among the most hyped ones [13], due to their ability of providing a consolidated access point to various lifecycle information, in a way that enables better real-time remote monitoring and control, enhanced intra- and inter-team synergy and collaborations, more efficient and informed decision support system, increased personalization of products and services, as well as predictive and remote services through new value propositions and business models [14].

2.1 Major Initiatives at the PSS, Digitalization, and Circularity Intersection

The increasing interest on PSS to break today's linear 'take-make-use-dispose' pattern of consumption can be tracked down to the Circular Economy Action Plan (CEAP) [15], which is a main planning document synced with the European Green Deal [16], Europe's new agenda for sustainable growth. While stressing how 80% of products' environmental impacts are determined at the design phase, the CEAP spotlights the need to incentivize manufacturers in adopting product-as-a-service models - where producers keep the ownership and responsibility of the product throughout its lifecycle. Several projects in the EU FP7 framework programme have already explored the role of servitization to cope with the needs of the new generation of consumers, such as SERVICEGAP (id: 244552), T-REX (id: 609005), USE-IT-WISELY (id: 609027) and FLEXINET (id: 608627). The CEAP further stresses the important role played by digitalization in this transformative journey. The PROSECO project (id: 609143) and the ProSSaLiC exchange program (id: 269322) have been among the first European initiatives elaborating on the role played by ICT solution to support the adoption of a product-as-a-service model. In Horizon 2020, more projects have explored the opportunity offered by digital technologies to support the servitization transformation, such as DIVERSITY (id: 636692), ICP4Life project (id: 636862), FALCON (id: 636868) and PSYMBIOSYS (id: 636804). Innovation actions such a ReCiPSS (id: 776577) and CIRCUSOL (id: 776680) have been exploring with more detail how to decouple resource consumption through PSS, yet without a distinctive focus on how the information generated by digital models can enable this transformation.

Both the quantity and heterogeneity of the research efforts at European level can be seen as a proxy for the increased interest in servitised business models and circularity. Yet, the landscape of applications and demonstrators is not only scattered but also mostly oriented towards considering digitalization as an 'end product' of the act of design (i.e., when a physical resource is replaced by a digital service) rather than a means to an end (i.e., that of helping the team in 'intentionally designing' the PSS). The great deal of research focused on the development of technology enablers is not counterbalanced by the development of practices on how to use digitalization for generating PSS concepts and evaluating them. Little is said about how to facilitate an 'effective and efficient' design process for circular and servitized solutions using digital technologies, and a gap is seen when it comes to propose 'design guidelines' that can be reused across industrial sectors and specific applications.

2.2 Value Co-creation in Design with the PSS DT

DTs are often discussed as one of the most promising tools in the engineering toolbox to cope with the ambiguities that characterize early-stage development activities of circular business solutions and PSS [17]. Yet, while most of the current efforts are concentrated on manufacturing and maintenance issues, much less is known about the use of DTs for innovation and development purposes [18, 19]. In 2019, only 2 studies were deemed relevant by Zhang et al. [20] with regards to how the DT can enhance service offerings. Most of the literature being analyzed was found to be out-of-scope from a design standpoint, mainly because it largely focused on some forms of maintenance services for production equipment and large assets. A later review from Bertoni and Bertoni [21] showed how this stream of research often concentrates on the development of standalone applications that match with the requirements of a specific case study. The development of 'frameworks' and 'methods' - rather than of models, tools, and algorithms – was also found to be a major matter of concern, particularly when addressing early-stage decision making. Existing contributions were also seen to address the 'realization' and 'support functionality' life cycle stages of the PSS without discussing the benefit vs. cost of using the DT during early design.

From a value co-creation viewpoint, the DT is seen as a major tool to support cross-functional collaboration and knowledge sharing, and to integrate insights from the various actors taking part to the PSS design process. The main 'value' of the PSS DT, as discussed by West et al. [22], is that of making possible to translate the raw data into information and knowledge, and ultimately into wisdom, so to facilitate joint decision-making activities across all the actors within the PSS ecosystem. In practice, DTs facilitate a process where technical considerations are translated into a business context to help identify the consequences of different options, hence highlighting the opportunity around a design decision - and the value co-creation process itself - rather than focusing on the technology per se.

3 Research Methodology

The questions presented in Sect. 4 are based on the findings from a multiple-case study approach [23] involving 4 manufacturing companies headquartered in Sweden, in 3 separate industrial sectors (Fig. 2). The research effort is framed by the Design Research Methodology (DRM) framework [24]. The DRM consists of four stages: Research Clarification (RC), Descriptive Study I (DS-I), Prescriptive Study (PS) and Descriptive Study II (DS-II). The work presented in this paper covers a review-based RC, a comprehensive DS-I and PS, and an initial DS-II. The 4 case companies were selected through a logic of literal replication to find similar results in different contexts, with the intention to provide compelling arguments for the themes and questions proposed in the following sections.

Common to the different cases is an interest on the use of DTs to support the servitization transformation in manufacturing, creating new opportunities for services, platforms, intelligent products, and novel business models. As stated by Company A, a major Swedish construction equipment manufacturer, the adoption of DT technologies is foreseen to accelerate the development of smart and connected products with highly software-enabled systems, The latter are expected to unlock value-adding capabilities for the systems being designed, such as monitoring, control, optimization, and autonomy, as well as ecosystem collaboration, offering for instance diagnostic, predictive and remote services through new value propositions and business models. In the aerospace sector, as stated by Company D, real-time connected digital models are of great interest for the development of decision environments where alternative solutions concepts (that mix hardware, software, and service aspects) can be evaluated considering more than just performances and cost, but rather sustainability and value co-creation at system and super-system level.

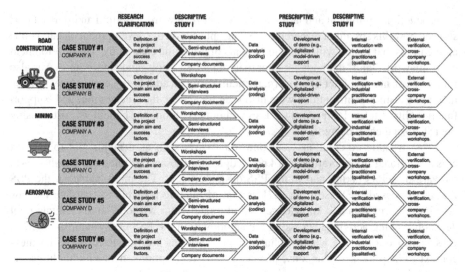

Fig. 1. Research methodology.

The list of questions proposed in Sect. 4 has emerged from the analysis of field data gathered through multiple channels (interviews, workshops, analysis of working documents, model demonstrations and more) in a way to ensure triangulation of the research results. The data collected from these different means were coded and analyzed to identify suitable topics for the development of suitable proof-of-concepts to be used in the PS phase to elicit even more requirements for the different components of the PSS DT. External verification activities (e.g., multi-day dissemination events) have been conducted in the frame of an ongoing 'research profile' initiative at the author home institution to verify and ensure the generalizability of the presented findings. These have involved a total of 8 manufacturing companies with different industrial backgrounds.

4   Questions to Be Answered

The findings from the DS-I phase show how the case companies forecast DTs to soon become a commodity in engineering design decision making. DTs are seen as a precious instrument to obtain richer information about customers' affordances, as well as to detail functional requirements and constraints. DS-I also highlighted how companies are still far from fully realizing the vision of a digital-driven PSS design process. This requires a coordinated research effort to catalyze best practices from several domains along the whole digital PSS lifecycle, such as product design, sustainable business development, service engineering, enterprise modelling, signal processing, telecommunication, big data analytics, IoT technologies, interoperability, and more. For this reason, the PSS DT is envisioned to expand from the seminal vision of Grieves and Vickers [25], to incorporate the digital 'counterpart' for more abstract entities, such as human behaviors to more intangible assets [26]. Four main research themes and related questions are then seen to frame future research on the PSS Digital Twin (Fig. 1).

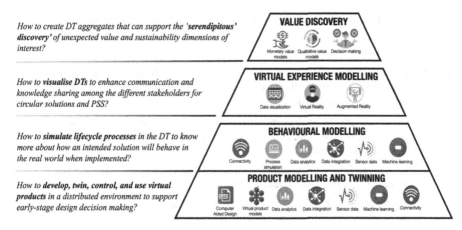

How to create DT aggregates that can support the 'serendipitous' discovery' of unexpected value and sustainability dimensions of interest?

How to visualise DTs to enhance communication and knowledge sharing among the different stakeholders for circular solutions and PSS?

How to simulate lifecycle processes in the DT to know more about how an intended solution will behave in the real world when implemented?

How to develop, twin, control, and use virtual products in a distributed environment to support early-stage design decision making?

Fig. 2. Research themes for the PSS Digital Twin

4.1 Product/Hardware Modelling and Twinning

DTs hold much promise when it comes to simulate a PSS under varying conditions, to predict the availability of the hardware, to inform about the features needed to make a solution more circular, and to forecast the expected performances of new designs in operation. Yet, questions remain concerning (1) the cost-benefit trade-off of developing, twinning, controlling, and using virtual products in a distributed design environment, and (2) how to make practical use of the DTs in a cross-functional decision-making - communicating the results from alternative scenarios across heterogeneous disciplines and knowledge domains. In the words of Company A, the different DT model components quickly become highly 'complicated' and difficult to be used in real-time simulation. Hence, a major aspect of interest for PSS DT research is related to the development reduced-order models or more manageable data-driven models that sacrifice 'resolution' to foster cross-functional collaboration.

Another important issue is 'scalability'. While most of the examples presented in literature target the development of a single-object DT, the descriptive study points to the need of demonstrating the ability of scaling up DT instances into DT aggregates, going from capturing the behavior of a small set of objects to simulating thousands of context-aware and integrated twins. Two more questions of interest deal with (1) the application of machine learning algorithms to extract relevant knowledge from the data collected by the DT, and (2) the use of artificial intelligence applications to reduce the computational time needed to verify all the scenarios generated by the twin.

Table 1. Research questions – product modelling and twinning.

RQ ID	Description	Timeframe
RQ1.1	How should virtual product models be developed, and twinning be realized between the physical and virtual world, to support early-stage design decision making?	Short-term
RQ1.2	How should product data be pre-processed, and algorithms customized, to predict the behavior of products in a circular business model and PSS?	Short-term
RQ1.3	How should DTs become context-aware, and able to consider the situation of the entities surrounding it?	Short term
RQ1.4	How should the virtual product be represented, communicated, and shared across the distributed cross-functional team?	Short-medium term

4.2 Behavioral Modelling

Having synchronized digital replicas of the various PSS lifecycle processes is believed to be critical to know more about how products and services can be improved, how interventions can be planned and how reactive and agile quality improvement processes can be implemented. Future research will need to push the PSS DT beyond the State-of-the-Art for pure products, enabling the representation of a wide range of lifecycle processes that influence value provision for customers and stakeholders. The goal should be that of (1) developing a systematic approach for determining the level of granularity and precision needed by the DT to be able to simulate (and hence benchmark) alternative PSS embryos during early design, and (2) understanding how behavioral models should be used to increase the awareness of the design team of critical system performances of the PSS. The possibility of accessing data from already existing related products - together with the deployment of data analysis approaches to populate upfront simulations - are seen as a critical aspect to be investigated in this domain.

Table 2. Research questions – behavioral modelling.

RQ ID	Description	Timeframe
RQ2.1	How should data collection strategies be designed to create relevant behavioral models for circular PSS processes (including manufacturing, delivery, maintenance, decommissioning and more?)	Short-term
RQ2.2	How should behavioral models be continuously updated to allow the simulation of engineering trade-offs in the PSS DT considering the uncertainty of future PSS operating contexts?	Short term
RQ2.3	How should the results from the behavioral models be communicated to the cross-functional design team to enhance decision making awareness in a globally distributed environment?	Short-medium term

4.3 Virtual Experience Modelling

The case study companies have expressed a growing interest towards the use of Augmented Reality (AR) and Virtual Reality (VR) applications to enable the design team to 'immerse' itself in the solutions being designed. Literally, AR and VR have been discussed as means to plunge 'into the shoes' of the customers to know more about the tangible and intangible value creation aspects of alternative PSS concepts. The value of these technologies is found both in their ability to support distributed design verification sessions, and in the opportunity to exploit multisensorial stimuli to know more about the intangible aspects related to the PSS service experience. AR and VR are discussed as an opportunity for designers to 'virtually experience' the benefits and drawbacks of a PSS concept early in the process. AR and VR can are seen as a key technology in the process of gamifying the design work, so that a PSS embryo can be embodied and tested without delay in different scenarios – e.g., probing its ability to trigger a sustainable behavior among customers and consumers - much like what can be done today in computer games.

Table 3. Research questions – Virtual experience modelling.

RQ ID	Description	Timeframe
RQ3.1	How should AR and VR be used to create 'virtual experiences' able to communicate both tangible and intangible values of a PSS concept?	Medium term
RQ3.2	How should AR and VR be used to support distributed collaborative work in PSS design?	Medium term
RQ3.3	How can the gamification of the PSS design process be supported using AR and VR applications?	Medium-long term

4.4 Value Discovery

The study further points to the need of developing of an additional layer of simulation capabilities for the DT to tackle so called 'unknown unknowns'. These are generally defined as unexpected or unforeseeable phenomena (e.g., risks, but even value creation opportunities) that cannot be foreseen simply because they cannot be anticipated based on experience or investigation. This is a main limiting factor of virtual testing (and Digital Twins) compared to physical-based investigations and prototypes [27], whose main added value is that of revealing such phenomena. Facilitating the discovery of such 'unknown unknowns' (e.g., at super-system level) through DT aggregates has been often underscored as a major topic for future research. How to setup the DT (including visualization) to support such a 'serendipitous' discovery of unexpected value and sustainability dimensions of interest is a major aspect to be tackled by future initiatives.

Table 4. Research questions – Value discovery.

RQ ID	Description	Timeframe
RQ4.1	How should DT instances be aggregated and connected to be able to measure value creation for a solution at super-system level?	Short-medium term
RQ4.2	How should DTs be designed to facilitate the discovery of new value and sustainability dimensions of interest for circular and servitized solutions?	Medium term
RQ4.3	How should qualitative and quantitative data be gathered from the physical world to discover new and unknown dimensions of value for circular solutions and PSS?	Medium term
RQ4.4	How should value-related dimensions for circular/servitized solutions be modelled in the DT to support decision making?	Medium term

5 Discussion

The four-layer framework and related research questions presented in Fig. 2 aim to provide a snapshot of the main issues raised across industries and cases about the role of the PSS DT in design. The opportunity to boost value co-creation in the PSS design process using DTs is widely acknowledges by the industrial partners involved in this research. Yet, it is works noticing that 14 questions proposed in Sect. 4 originate from case studies dealing with the development of 'complex' systems (i.e., following the classical Systems Engineering V-model [28]) and within companies mainly active in the Business-to-Business (B2B) market, meaning that Business-to-Consumers (B2C) aspects have not been strongly emphasized by the partner companies during the study.

The development of the PSS DT along the proposed themes is expected to positively impact industrial value chains by creating an understanding of how to link customer value - moving from experienced-based data management to real-time data management to support new services and to contribute to new digitalized business model knowledge.

DTs are seen not only as a tool to optimize procedures and act at the right time, but also to avoid making unwitting assumptions when the problem domain is dominated by a high degree of uncertainty and ambiguity. This is typical when working with the design of solutions (PSS) rather than products, which is when having value as main driver for design decision making instead of requirements (such as when comparing traditional one-sale offers against circular and servitized solutions). The ability to use simulation and digital technologies to mitigate uncertainty/ambiguity - and to take a first step when coping with such wicked problems - is of great interest for the business partners when it comes to plan for the design and implementation of the DT concept.

6 Conclusions

The results of this work point to the need of understanding, crafting, and verifying DT-enabled design processes, 'connecting the dots' and making clear how current processes for PSS design should make the best out of the DT opportunity. Future work will look at the development of decision support systems that are able to exploit the data-driven updating mechanisms of the DTs to explore the value generated by alternative digitalized services and new business models already in early design. In doing so, the interoperability and applicability issues will be in the spotlight to realize the integration of different modules in a single decision-making platform.

At the same time, more evidence is needed from the application of the PSS DT in a range of case studies with regards to the real benefit of replacing more qualitative approaches with data-intensive methods and tools (or just to complement them). A major aspect to consider is how the DT can be used in a cross-functional team setting where not everybody is a simulation expert. The role of data visualization and representation should not be underestimated in this respect.

Acknowledgements. This research has received financial support from the Swedish Knowledge and Competence Development Foundation (Stiftelsen för kunskaps- och kompetensutveckling), Sweden, through the Model Driven Development and Decision Support research profile at Blekinge Institute of Technology, Sweden.

References

1. Barricelli, B.R., Casiraghi, E., Fogli, D.: A survey on digital twin: definitions, characteristics, applications, and design implications. IEEE Access. **7**, 167653–167671 (2019)
2. Uhlemann, T.H.J., Schock, C., Lehmann, C., Freiberger, S., Steinhilper, R.: The digital twin: demonstrating the potential of real time data acquisition in production systems. Proc. Manuf. **9**, 113–120 (2017)
3. Macchi, M., Roda, I., Negri, E., Fumagalli, L.: Exploring the role of digital twin for asset lifecycle management. IFAC PapersOnLine. **51**(11), 790–795 (2018)
4. Pirola, F., Boucher, X., Wiesner, S., Pezzotta, G.: Digital technologies in product-service systems: a literature review and a research agenda. Comput. Ind. **123**, 103301 (2020)
5. Rocca, R., Rosa, P., Sassanelli, C., Fumagalli, L., Terzi, S.: Integrating virtual reality and digital twin in circular economy practices: a laboratory application case. Sustainability-Basel. **12**(6), 2286 (2020)
6. Machchhar, R.J., Toller, C.N.K., Bertoni, A., Bertoni, M.: Data-driven value creation in Smart Product-Service System design: state-of-the-art and research directions. Comput. Ind. **137**, 103606 (2022)
7. Mert, G., Herder, C.F., Menck, N., Aurich, J.C.: Innovative services for customized, availability-oriented business models for the capital goods industry. Proc. CIRP **47**, 501–506 (2016)
8. Apostolov, H., Fischer, M., Olivotti, D., Dreyer, S., Breitner, M.H., Eigner, M.: Modeling framework for integrated, model-based development of product-service systems. Proc. CIRP **73**, 9–14 (2018)
9. Malakuti, S., Schlake, J., Ganz, C., Harper, K.E., Petersen, H.: Digital twin: an enabler for new business models. In: Proceedings of the Automation Congress (2019)
10. Kohtamäki, M., Parida, V., Oghazi, P., Gebauer, H., Baines, T.: Digital servitization business models in ecosystems: a theory of the firm. J. Bus. Res. **104**, 380–392 (2019)
11. Paschou, T., Rapaccini, M., Adrodegari, F., Saccani, N.: Digital servitization in manufacturing: a systematic literature review and research agenda. Ind. Market Manag. **89**, 278–292 (2020)

12. Porter, M.E., Heppelmann, J.E.: How smart, connected products are transforming companies. Harvard Bus. Rev. **93**(10), 96–114 (2015)
13. Emerging Technologies and Trends Impact Radar (2021). https://www.gartner.com/en/doc uments/4006010
14. Rasheed, A., San, O., Kvamsdal, T.: Digital twin: values, challenges and enablers from a modeling perspective. IEEE Access **8**, 21980–22012 (2020)
15. European Union: A new Circular Economy Action Plan for a cleaner and more competitive Europé. https://eur-lex.europa.eu/resource.html?uri=cellar:9903b325-6388-11ea-b735-01aa75ed71a1.0017.02/DOC_1&format=PDF
16. European Green Deal. https://ec.europa.eu/info/strategy/priorities-2019-2024/european-green-deal_en
17. Barni, A., Fontana, A., Menato, S., Sorlini, M., Canetta, L.: Exploiting the digital twin in the assessment and optimization of sustainability performances. In: 2018 International Conference on Intelligent Systems, pp. 706–713. IEEE (2018)
18. Tao, F., Zhang, H., Liu, A., Nee, A.Y.: Digital twin in industry: state-of-the-art. IEEE T. Ind. Inform. **15**(4), 2405–2415 (2018)
19. Melesse, T.Y., Di Pasquale, V., Riemma, S.: Digital Twin models in industrial operations: state-of-the-art and future research directions. IET Coll. Intell. Manuf. **3**(1), 37–47 (2021)
20. Zhang, H., Ma, L., Sun, J., Lin, H., Thürer, M.: Digital twin in services and industrial product service systems: review and analysis. Proc. CIRP. **83**, 57–60 (2019)
21. Bertoni, M., Bertoni, A.: Designing solutions with the product-service system digital twin. what is now and what is next. Comput. Ind. **138**, 103629 (2022)
22. West, S., Stoll, O., Meierhofer, J., Züst, S.: Digital twin providing new opportunities for value co-creation through supporting decision-making. Appl. Sci. **11**(9), 3750 (2021)
23. Yin, R.K.: Case study research: design and methods. Sage publications, Thousand Oaks (2013)
24. Blessing, L.T., Chakrabarti, A.: DRM: A design research methodology. Springer, London (2009)
25. Grieves, M., Vickers, J.: Digital twin: mitigating unpredictable, undesirable emergent behavior in complex systems. In: Kahlen, F.-J., Flumerfelt, S., Alves, A. (eds.) Transdisciplinary Perspectives on Complex Systems, pp. 85–113. Springer, Cham (2017). https://doi.org/10.1007/978-3-319-38756-7_4
26. Dietz, M., Pernul, G.: Digital twin: Empowering enterprises towards a system-of-systems approach. Bus. Inf. Syst. Eng. **62**(2), 179–184 (2020)
27. Glaessgen, E., Stargel, D.: The digital twin paradigm for future NASA and US Air Force vehicles. In: 53rd AIAA/ASME/ASCE/AHS/ASC Structures, Structural Dynamics and Materials Conference: Special Session on the Digital Twin, p. 1818 (2012)
28. Walden, D.D., Roedler, G.J., Forsberg, K.: INCOSE systems engineering handbook version 4: updating the reference for practitioners. In: INCOSE International Symposium, pp. 678–686 (2015)

Value Co-creation in Data-Driven Product-Service Systems: An Industrial Perspective

Carl Nils Konrad Toller$^{(\boxtimes)}$ ⓘ and Marco Bertoni ⓘ

Blekinge Institute of Technology, Karlskrona, Sweden
carl.toller@bth.se

Abstract. Value co-creation is an important aspect for servitized companies operating a Product-Service System business. However, their relation to value co-creation might depend on where they are on the servitization journey. This paper described the result of a multiple-case study with three industrial partners and their perspectives on the challenges and opportunities with value co-creation for data-driven Product-Service Systems.

Keywords: Value co-creation · Data-driven design · Product-service systems

1 Introduction and Research Approach

Nowadays, the notion of PSS is often discussed in relation to the so-called Fourth Industrial Revolution (FIR) [1] and to the transition towards cyber-physical production systems [2], where systems of collaborating computational entities, connected with the surrounding physical world and its ongoing processes, provide and use data-accessing and processing services available on the internet. The relationship between Information and Communication Technologies (ICT) and PSS is seen by many researchers and practitioners as interdependent or symbiotic [3]. The data collected by intelligent devices are used in PSS design to develop and populate decision-making models [4, 5].

Yet, many companies have been observed to struggle when it comes to capitalizing on such a 'data opportunity' for value co-creation. A survey from Valencia Cardona et al. [6] shows how one of the most significant challenges for manufacturing firms is to clearly define the value proposition of the Smart PSS. While consumers may perceive the load of data and information generated as irrelevant, the design team may also struggle to derive useful information and knowledge from the data being collected.

The discussion on value co-creation in PSS design is mostly focused today on the development of service-centric design methods that focus on customer value co-creation [7, 8], the design of the underlying value creation proposition and architecture [9, 10], and frameworks to support the collaboration process between the customer and the provider during the entire PSS development [11].

L. M. Camarinha-Matos et al. (Eds.): PRO-VE 2022, IFIP AICT 662, pp. 603–612, 2022.
https://doi.org/10.1007/978-3-031-14844-6_48

The purpose of this paper is to shift the focus of the ongoing academic discussion to highlight which opportunities and challenges are perceived by industrial companies when boosting value co-creation in PSS design through data-driven approaches. The research question at the center of this work is described as:

What challenges and opportunities are differently servitized companies seeing in value co-creation and operational data utilization?

The findings presented in this paper emerge from a multiple-case study conducted in collaboration with three industrial partners in Sweden that feature different levels of maturity in their servitization journey. These case companies were selected through a logic of literal replication, to find similar results in different contexts and provide compelling arguments for the findings presented in the following sections. Semi-structured interviews were conducted at the case companies to gather information and perspectives on value co-creation. The questions were prepared beforehand and focused mainly on value co-creation, servitization, and data utilization. The findings from the studies presented in this contribution have the goal to spotlight common themes among the firms when it comes to value co-creation and data utilization in design. Additionally, reflections on how to meet and solve these are concluding this paper.

2 Theoretical Framework

2.1 About Value and Value Co-creation

A common definition for 'value' is hard to agree upon. An early attempt to capture its meaning can be found in Miles [12], who describes it simply as the ratio between performance and cost. Later definitions have had the objective to pinpoint with more granularity the nature of the 'value' concept. Among them, the European Committee for Standardization defined it as 'satisfaction of needs in comparison to expenses' [13].

In turn, a need describes 'what' a solution shall do to solve a problem or fulfill a wish of a customer [14]. The latter is often referred to as Voice of the Customer (VoC). To add more complexity, a need is not necessarily one-dimensional, rather its degree of fulfillment and satisfaction can have multiple characteristics and change depending on the market, as in the Kano model [15]. However, evaluating and verifying something expressed naturally and informally is challenging. Hence, the needs must be translated to requirements which are the formal and verifiable statements expressed in an abstract and technologically neutral way [16].

What is value co-creation then? This paper borrows the definition by Ranjan and Read [17] which states that value is co-created when a customer actively collaborates with the provider, directly or indirectly, through one or more stages of production and consumption, referred to as co-production and value-in-use. From a co-production standpoint, value co-creation can practically take part as a co-joint effort between provider and customer in eliciting requirements and ensuring that the design can interpret and fulfill these. On the other hand, value-in-use reflects the more servitized aspect of a PSS and mitigates collaboration during the service deployment. Ultimately, value co-creation can be seen as a natural part for servitized firms and a good path for enhancing value delivery throughout the life cycle.

2.2 Value Co-creation in PSS Design

PSS stresses the importance of designing products and services that manage to fulfill customers' needs beyond the functional perspective and thus can value co-creation serve as a good approach for achieving this. From a conceptual standpoint, the need for value co-creation throughout the operational phase means that the requirements of the system will change during the life cycle, and thus there is an inherent need for including changeability in the design of a PSS. Recent research highlights how value co-creation is one of the major challenges which PSS faces, e.g. in the words of West et al. [18]:

> *"The smartness of a product-service offering is not linked to how many new technologies are exploited. Instead, it depends on the extent it actively enables new forms of value co-creation."*

While in traditional one-sale models the customers are passively involved in the process of value creation, the servitized solution leverages the importance of co-creative value by emphasizing aspects such as interaction and personalized customer experience [18]. Liu et al. [19] provide a good example and framework of the value co-creation process for Smart PSS.

Bertoni et al. [20] bring forward Value-Driven Design (VDD) for PSS as a modeling methodology to keep track of the co-creation of value during the design process. Instead of a strategy that aims at fulfilling and maximizing each requirement individually, VDD adopts a higher-level optimization strategy where the requirements are combined to a unified conformity. A major issue with value modeling today is related to the need to incorporate data streams from the operational stages of the product/service to enable better decisions that are more grounded on the actual behavior of a solution along its life cycle.

3 The Case Companies

As previously mentioned, this paper is a result of interviews made at three different case companies and their perspectives on PSS value co-creation and operational data. Following is a short description of each of them.

Company A is a traditional manufacturing firm that has a clear focus on delivering products to its customers. They operate in the infrastructure equipment sector and have a worldwide market base where they provide vehicles for road construction. Onward, the firm offers services directly connected to the reliability and maintenance of the machines. However, in recent years they have started a servitization journey and have investigated the opportunities of offering more PSS solutions by expanding the service portfolio. The value is mainly oriented around the functional aspects and non-functional properties are mostly limited to a "must-have"-basis. At the same time, telemetry is implemented to allow real-time data collection and the ability to track their machines in their operational context. Today, a plethora of data is continuously collected and stored but the utilization is still rather low. The collected information is almost exclusively used during the operational phase and connected to maintenance and management by the customers. So far, the data is not used during the design phase and conceptual development to any significant extent.

Company B is active in the facility sector and supplies solutions for a variety of contexts related to the movement of people. They are, in comparison to the first case company, more invested in services and see it as a vital part of their business portfolio, which accounts for a substantial part of their revenues. They are a well-established enterprise with customers spread across the world. On the other hand, they are not so far ahead in the operational data domain. Using data collection strategies during the operational phase is not a common practice in their sector and market niche, despite their products and solutions being complex and involving a plethora of components.

The final case company, Company C, is a start-up in the logistics and transportation market. The firm is only a few years old and has a high focus on technology and data utilization in its PSS solutions. The business strategy is here more result-oriented PSS where the physical hardware is not necessary as important as the services and the connected technologies. Company C is more mature than A and B when it comes to utilizing operational data in design. The operational data is a natural part of the design process, their system architecture, and the life cycle. They have additionally seen the potential and to a large extent deployed data capitalization as a part of their result-oriented PSS business.

Concluding, the case companies' characteristics and positioning on value co-creation and data utilization are summarized in Table 1. Firstly, the degree of servitization can be viewed using the stages of PSS business models defined by [21]. Secondly, the degree of value co-creation and data utilization is qualitatively estimated from low to high where low refers to no or insignificant relation to value co-creation or data utilization and high refers to a well-established process and culture of value co-creation or leveraging data. The data utilization is further divided in a customer and provider perspective.

Table 1. The case companies

	PSS orientation	Data utilization Customer	Data utilization Provider
Company A	Product-oriented	Medium	Low
Company B	Use-oriented	Low	Low
Company C	Result-oriented	High	High

4 Descriptive Study Findings

The multiple case study and interview series resulted in five interviews lasting for about one hour each. The transcripts were refined, and valuable information was extracted from a case database. Despite that the three case companies are rather different, they are to a large extent sharing the same set of challenges and opportunities when it comes to value co-creation and data utilization which can be summarized as follows.

4.1 Educating the Customer

Understanding the customers' behavior is fundamental for delivering a 'good design', and a data-driven design process is seen to provide exactly the context-specific customer information that designers need for decision-making. Company C showed a good example of this when describing how it managed to fully incorporate field data in the design process to faster build knowledge about the operational scenario while reducing shrinking the lead time for prototyping. Even if not all companies were found to be as mature on this matter, they shared the same view with regard to the potential of data-driven design.

Data helps us better understand how the products are actually used. It gives us room for more evidence-based decision-making.

Product Owner, Company B

At the same time, all the companies were aware of how a data-driven approach can reduce biases in the definition of needs and requirements for design solutions.

Quantitative methods are important for validating qualitative input. Without it, there is a risk of only hearing the loudest customer.

Product Owner, Company B

However, they also concluded that the market in general – and their customers in particular - have not yet fully grasped the potential of data-driven design to boost value co-creation. This issue was found not to depend on the degree of servitization reached by each company. On the contrary, they all expressed difficulties when it comes to educating the customers in recognizing the potential of data utilization, and they all provided examples of 'hesitant' customers, not yet ready to jump on board.

It is hard for the customer to understand, and it requires that they rethink how they run their operations.

Vice President Product, Company C

A closer look shows that sometimes the PSS providers themselves do not fully understand how to capitalize on the data being shared, thus struggling to develop a convincing selling point and convey the message onward. What is lacking is a pot of good examples that can be used to convey the benefits linked to data sharing.

The customers are not ready and do not fully understand the benefits of collecting and leveraging operational data for servitization. But neither do we fully grasp it.

Product Owner, Company B

Moreover, value co-creation can sometimes be difficult to argue for in general. The infrastructure company experienced difficulties in moving the discussion away from performance and cost. They felt that they did not know how to raise more holistic aspects toward a total cost of ownership and life-cycle view.

It is very hard to get the customer to move away from purchasing costs, they tend to focus on performance and price solely.

Product Family Owner, Company A

Company B and C, which both have a more service-balanced portfolio, found it easier to address these holistic perspectives and to argue for value co-creation.

4.2 Filtering Out the Noise

In PSS design, data can be generated by several sources along the entire solution life cycle. While some literature emphasizes the topics of data 'democratization' and accessibility as the main hurdle for PSS providers, companies A and B have pointed to a different issue. A major concern for them is that of motivating internally why certain types of data are even worth being collected, which is that of providing arguments and evidence on how different data types can generate value in the design process.

We collect a lot of data today, but we do not know how to use it and why these specific data sets are actually collected.

Product Manager, Company A

Several interviews pointed to the need of defining a consistent data collection strategy, battling with the issue of how to filter out the 'noise' from the available data sets. Even if Company A and C were found to have the most established operational data collection procedures, they showed concerns when it comes to having the full picture of what 'data' are needed to create value-adding solutions.

There are many asking for data, but few can go further in-depth and say exactly what kind of data they want.

Product Owner, Company B

The companies in the study further highlighted the main value-added of a data-driven approach being that of providing evidence about how PSS solutions are de-facto operated in the field depending on the context, as opposed to relying on anecdotal or personal evidence.

We do not fully understand how our products are operating in different contexts in comparison to how they were developed.

R&D Manager, Company A

This issue is emphasized when operating in global markets, mainly because the application of more classical need finding methods (interviews, observations, and more) becomes a behemoth task for PSS providers. In practice, only a data-driven approach is seen to affordably provide information on how PSS are working in different contexts in the global arena.

4.3 Thinking Ahead

Noticeably, the implementation of (late) changes in the PSS hardware is acknowledged to be a labor-intensive process. The deadline for completing the physical design is often quite long before the start of production as the tools, supply chain, and production requires long lead times.

Most of the design is fixed up to a year before the start of production.

Project Manager, Company A

The study shows that it is significantly more time- and resource-consuming to implement a design change on the product component of the PSS compared to its software side. Furthermore, a design iteration normally takes longer for the physical hardware, and this makes engineers scratch their heads when trying to balance the two development processes.

A software change can be done in a night but any change to the hardware requires coordination between multiple stakeholders and take much longer.

Vice President Product, Company C

The need to develop (and test) one or more physical prototypes is a clear example of the misalignment between the hardware and software design cycles. A way-out strategy for engineering designers is often to emphasize the changeability and upgradeability of the physical product, to make room for later changes without requiring significant rework. In practice, while the service component of a solution might change during the PSS life cycle, the product is designed from day one to be able to accommodate such changes.

5   Concluding Remarks

Regardless of the industry, degree of servitization, and size of the company, there are challenges and hurdles when working with value co-creation and data utilization. There is a difficulty in collecting the "right" data as well as knowing how to leverage this for both direct value co-creation in terms of service offerings but also indirect through design improvements.

A first acknowledgment from the study is that there is a correlation between the degree of servitization and the extent of value co-creation, value-in-use. Hence, aiming for higher servitization and a more service-dense business model can be a natural strategy for increasing value co-creation. Both Company A and B expressed that they see servitization as an opportunity to increase the value of their system by offering a higher value-in-use. Company C shared this view but has come further in the implementation and actively operated with a strong value-in-use focus. However, it is important to ensure competencies in service development if it is desired to grow in this domain. This could be achieved by either accumulating the competencies or by setting up partnerships with service providers.

Looking at the co-production perspective, Company C exhibited a large maturity for co-production stemming from a strategic decision to maximize the customer's input throughout the design process. Company A found it challenging to navigate among the customers' voices and saw a risk of sub-optimization when only listening to a few. Company B had similar worries that the more diverse the product portfolio and market becomes the harder it gets to find the "sweet spots" of customer input. All companies experienced challenges with getting the customers on board in co-production and getting them involved actively in the design process. Identifying customers that represent most of the market for co-production partnerships could be a good initial step to start exploring this domain more systematically. Value co-creation requires a commitment from both the customer and the provider.

All companies expressed an opportunity in how operational data can be used as leverage for value co-creation. From a co-production perspective the operational data, which is a combination of user-generated and context-dependent, enables the provider to tap directly into the customer's interaction with the system. However, collecting and extracting insight from operational data only provides a part of the picture. For this to be useful, it needs to be connected to the customer experience. Kim and Hong [22] elaborate on this when they derived a method for developing personalized services based on customer experience and contextual data. This shows that value co-creation requires collaboration between ethnographic and data-driven approaches. Simply connecting the requirements' metrics to sensory data is one example.

One way to utilize data for value co-creation in the design process is by quantifying the system value and deriving measurements based on available data. The companies will then be able to assess the value delivery of a system and evaluate how different concepts perform more objectively, as is the aim of VDD. By better understanding how different parameters influence value, it is possible to perform value optimizations and concept evaluations in more detail or even assess the value delivery in real-time. Therefore, it is recommended that the companies investigate how the requirement fulfillment can be expressed using available data.

The operational data can further be used directly for creating value-in-use concluding that data utilization has the potential to increase the value co-creation in both dimensions. However, the challenge experienced was identifying which data is valuable to collect and share. None of the companies had an explicit data collection strategy, even though Company C had one implicitly, and a clear understanding of how to use data for creating value co-creation. A workshop or discussion about identifying good data collection strategies could add great value for achieving a higher utilization of data and increasing the value of the data itself. In general, the emergence of data provides good potential for value co-creation, if the company can understand the "what" and "how".

6   Future Directions

Based on the multiple-case study, a few wishes for future research could be found. Firstly, there is a need to develop support for how a servitized company can work with value co-creation and more efficiently transfer it into the PSS design. Secondly, operational data has a great potential for supporting value co-creation, but their inter-relationship is still unclear and how it can be implemented in Smart PSS. Support for navigating between value and data is required. Finally, the result in this study remains at a holistic level and more in-depth case studies would be useful to go further in the challenges and opportunities for PSS-oriented businesses when it comes to value co-creation and data utilization.

Acknowledgments. The research leading to these results has received financial support from the Swedish Knowledge and Competence Development Foundation (Stiftelsen för kunskaps- och kompetensutveckling) through the Model-Driven Development and Decision Support research profile at Blekinge Institute of Technology.

References

1. Gaiardelli, P., et al.: Product-service systems evolution in the era of Industry 4.0. Serv. Bus. **15**(1), 177–207 (2021). https://doi.org/10.1007/s11628-021-00438-9
2. Wiesner, S., Marilungo, E., Thoben, K.-D.: Cyber-physical product-service systems – challenges for requirements engineering. Int. J. Autom. Technol. **11**(1), 17–28 (2017). https://doi.org/10.20965/ijat.2017.p0017
3. Zheng, P., Wang, Z., Chen, C.-H., Pheng Khoo, L.: A survey of smart product-service systems: key aspects, challenges and future perspectives. Adv. Eng. Inform. **42**, 100973 (2019). https://doi.org/10.1016/j.aei.2019.100973
4. Sala, R., Bertoni, A., Pirola, F., Pezzotta, G.: The data-driven product-service systems design and delivery (4DPSS) methodology. In: Lalic, B., Majstorovic, V., Marjanovic, U., von Cieminski, G., Romero, D. (eds.) APMS 2020. IAICT, vol. 592, pp. 314–321. Springer, Cham (2020). https://doi.org/10.1007/978-3-030-57997-5_37
5. Machchhar, R.J., Bertoni, A.: Data-driven design automation for product-service systems design: framework and lessons learned from empirical studies. Proc. Des. Soc. **1**, 841–850 (2021). https://doi.org/10.1017/pds.2021.84
6. Valencia Cardona, A., Mugge, R., Schoormans, J.P., Schifferstein, H.N.: Challenges in the design of smart product-service systems (PSSs): experiences from practitioners. In: Proceedings of the 19th DMI: Academic Design Management Conference on Design Management in an Era of Disruption, London, UK, 2–4 September 2014. Design Management Institute (2014)
7. Rizvi, M.A.K., Yip, M.H., Chew, E.K., Carnemolla, P.K.: Designing through value co-creation: a study of actors, practices and possibilities. In: 2019 IEEE International Conference on Industrial Engineering and Engineering Management (IEEM), Macao, Macao, pp. 571–575. IEEE (2019). https://doi.org/10.1109/IEEM44572.2019.8978902
8. Yip, M.H., Rizvi, M.A.K., Chew, E.: Managing value co-creation: an integrated design framework for service-centric product-service systems. In: 2019 Portland International Conference on Management of Engineering and Technology (PICMET), Portland, OR, USA, pp. 1–13. IEEE (2019). https://doi.org/10.23919/PICMET.2019.8893876
9. Scholtysik, M., Reinhold, J., Koldewey, C., Dumitrescu, R.: Sustainability through the digitalization: exploring potentials and designing value co-creation architectures for product-service-systems. Proc. Des. Soc. **1**, 2871–2880 (2021). https://doi.org/10.1017/pds.2021.548
10. West, S., Zou, W., Rodel, E., Stoll, O.: Value co-creation in digitally-enabled product-service systems. In: Kohtamäki, M., et al. (eds.) The Palgrave Handbook of Servitization, pp. 403–417. Springer, Cham (2021). https://doi.org/10.1007/978-3-030-75771-7_26

11. Orellano, M., Boucher, X., Neubert, G., Coulon, A.: A framework to support value co-creation in PSS development. In: Lalic, B., Majstorovic, V., Marjanovic, U., von Cieminski, G., Romero, D. (eds.) APMS 2020. IAICT, vol. 592, pp. 361–368. Springer, Cham (2020). https://doi.org/10.1007/978-3-030-57997-5_42

12. Miles, L.D.: Techniques of Value Analysis and Engineering. McGraw-Hill, New York (1972)

13. EN12973: EN12973:2020: Value Management, European Committee for Standardization, Brussels (2020)

14. Griffin, A., Hauser, J.R.: The voice of the customer. Mark. Sci. 12, 1–27 (1993)

15. Matzler, K., Hinterhuber, H.H.: How to make product development projects more successful by integrating Kano's model of customer satisfaction into quality function deployment. Technovation 18, 25–38 (1998). https://doi.org/10.1016/S0166-4972(97)00072-2

16. Ryan, M.J., Wheatcraft, L.S., Dick, J., Zinni, R.: On the definition of terms in a requirements expression. INCOSE Int. Symp. 25, 169–181 (2015). https://doi.org/10.1002/j.2334-5837.2015.00055.x

17. Ranjan, K.R., Read, S.: Value co-creation: concept and measurement. J. Acad. Mark. Sci. 44(3), 290–315 (2014). https://doi.org/10.1007/s11747-014-0397-2

18. West, S., Gaiardelli, P., Rapaccini, M.: Exploring technology-driven service innovation in manufacturing firms through the lens of Service Dominant logic. IFAC-PapersOnLine 51, 1317–1322 (2018). https://doi.org/10.1016/j.ifacol.2018.08.350

19. Liu, Z., Ming, X., Song, W., Qiu, S., Qu, Y.: A perspective on value co-creation-oriented framework for smart product-service system. Procedia CIRP 73, 155–160 (2018). https://doi.org/10.1016/j.procir.2018.04.021

20. Bertoni, A., Bertoni, M., Panarotto, M., Johansson, C., Larsson, T.C.: Value-driven product service systems development: methods and industrial applications. CIRP J. Manuf. Sci. Technol. 15, 42–55 (2016). https://doi.org/10.1016/j.cirpj.2016.04.008

21. Tukker, A., Tischner, U. (eds.): New Business for Old Europe: Product-Service Development, Competitiveness and Sustainability. Greenleaf, Sheffield (2006)

22. Kim, Y.S., Hong, Y.: A systematic method to design product-service systems using personalisation services based on experience evaluations. IJPD. 23, 353 (2019). https://doi.org/10.1504/IJPD.2019.105491

Boosting Value Co-creation in the Road Construction Industry Through Virtual Prototyping

Giulia Wally Scurati[(✉)], Alessandro Bertoni, and Marco Bertoni

Blekinge Tekniska Högskola, Karlskrona, Sweden
{giulia.wally.scurati,alessandro.bertoni,marco.bertoni}@bth.se

Abstract. When construction companies move forward in their servitization journey, there is an increasing need to exploit digital tools and models to facilitate the complex and dynamic interactions between entrepreneurs, customers, equipment manufacturers, energy providers and more during the early stages of the construction project design. This paper presents the application Augmented Reality (AR) and Virtual Reality (VR) applications to create distributed 'experience environments' for value co-creation in the road construction industry, where to foster participation of all the stakeholders in the needs identification process and the trade-off of the value drivers of the project. After presenting the modelling approach pursued in the work, the lessons learned gathered from preliminary verification activities are presented, pointing to future work in the field.

Keywords: Virtual Reality · Augmented Reality · Virtual prototyping · Road construction · Servitization · Product-service systems

1 Introduction

Over the last decade, plenty of companies across heterogeneous industrial sectors have started to reconsider how they conduct their business, typically by increasing customer orientation and evolving the way in which the offer of products and services is developed, integrated, and delivered [1]. The construction industry is no exception to this phenomenon. Technological developments and the need to adopt more efficient and sustainable production processes are leading to changes in traditional business models [2].

When construction companies move forward in their servitization journey, they are increasingly relying on developing digitalization capabilities to interact and co-create value with their customers. Yet, despite the common view of the industry is that digital tools can be applied both at the 'front-end' and 'back-end' of the development process - to boost and improve the extent of servitization and deliver more value to customers – their application in the earliest stages of the process is still limited. Digitalization is seen mostly as an 'end product' of the servitization journey – i.e., the creation of digitally-enabled services to enhance productivity and sustainability [3] – rather than a tool in

© IFIP International Federation for Information Processing 2022
Published by Springer Nature Switzerland AG 2022
L. M. Camarinha-Matos et al. (Eds.): PRO-VE 2022, IFIP AICT 662, pp. 613–622, 2022.
https://doi.org/10.1007/978-3-031-14844-6_49

the hands of the engineer to 'intentionally design' value-adding solutions and Product-Service Systems. One major aspect of interest is the use of digital tools and models to facilitate the complex and dynamic interactions between the different actors taking part in the early planning and design stages of construction projects. Entrepreneurs, customers, equipment manufacturers, energy providers and more are required to be active in the discussion and share their knowledge when alternative construction strategies are generated, evaluated and benchmarked, so as to identify the solution concepts that can deliver the highest possible value for all parties. Of particular interest to foster value co-creation during the front-end of a construction project is the use of digital means for the creation of 'experience environments' (see: [4]). Augmented Reality (AR) and Virtual Reality (VR) applications are of interest to enhance the participation of stakeholders to support multi-disciplinary needs identification, and to prioritize among heterogeneous value drivers during trade-off studies and concept selection [5].

The main aim of this paper is to present the results from the development of a prototype of such an experience environment in a case study involving a major road construction equipment manufacturer. Its objective is first to present the design of such an environment for value co-creation in relation to the need expressed by the company's stakeholders. The paper describes the modelling approach pursued in the research work, presenting its application in the selected case study. Finally, this work presents lessons learned from preliminary verification activities with the partner company, pointing to future work for this case study and in the field.

2   Theoretical Framework: The Role of AR and VR for Value Co-creation

Digitalization is acknowledged as a viable path toward addressing increasingly complex and dynamic customer interactions [6]. More in detail, Lenka et al. [7] spotlight how digitalization can leverage the analytic capability of manufacturing firms. This is described as the ability to transform the data available at hand into predictive insights and actionable directives that have operational value for the organization.

The constant inflow of data from intelligent and connected products can be exploited in a customer-centric simulation environment to assess and visualize the value of different design options. These simulated scenarios help in experiencing critical interdependencies before a solution is realised 'in the field', hence testing the levers that firms can use to optimize customers' key performance indicators.

Together with other Industry 4.0 technologies, AR and VR have shown to be effective tools to support value co-creation through inter-firm collaboration, creation of new services, customization of services and products, and long-term relationships with customers [8]. VR and AR applications have been successfully applied, for instance for training and remote maintenance as part of a Product-Service System [9, 10].

VR and AR have been extensively used to facilitate cooperation and value co-creation among practitioners, overcoming physical distances and improving creative expression [11]. They can also empower customers in co-creation activities by providing platforms enriched with participatory elements [12]. Mixed reality technologies (combining AR and VR) are acknowledged to be transformative means to actively engage clients, strategically affecting their brand perception and satisfaction [13]. These opportunities could be exploited in design, purchase, factory planning, and more in general, in any decision-making context, especially in collaborative situations [11, 13, 14].

In fact, there is a growing interest in using VR in Computer Supported Cooperative Work (CSCW) systems, especially in design processes, due to the possibility to share information and knowledge, make decisions and review results [15]. The use of VR environments for CSCW appears to be more mature for remote and synchronous collaboration. However, different devices and AR/VR technologies have shown potential for different types of collaboration modalities in the CSCW framework.

Digitalization in general – and AR/VR in particular - are of great interest to cope with the complexity of co-creation processes, decreasing the risk of interpretative ambiguity associated with the different stakeholders' knowledge and expectations. AR/VR applications make it possible to visualize phenomena in a way that different perspectives can be easily integrated, mainly thanks to their interactivity, editability, associability and distributed nature [14]. Users can share and actively manipulate virtual models, simulating the outcomes of proposed changes in real-time. Hence, VR and AR tools can enable companies and customers to identify possible problems and solutions together at an early stage, improving efficiency, success rate, and profitability of co-creation activities.

One of the industries for which VR and AR collaborative environments can be beneficial is the construction sector. They can be exploited to deliver new and better services, improving collaboration, projects understanding and performance. Moreover, their use can be strategic also to improve the company's image, boosting its reputation as a smart solutions provider [16]. In particular, one of the major identified trends in this area regards construction project management, while an emerging one concerns construction equipment [17]. The former stresses collaborative aspects, while the latter includes the design, planning, selection and monitoring of equipment (e.g., excavators and trucks). The intention of this work is to integrate common aspects in both topics.

3   An Experience Environment Using Visualization and Interactive Scenario-Based Analysis for Value Co-creation

3.1   Case Study

The case study company is a world-leading total-solution provider of articulated haulers, wheel loaders, excavation equipment, road development machines, and compact construction equipment. The company business is facing rapid transformations, largely driven by several macro trends, including electrification, digitalization, connectivity, artificial intelligence and sustainability.

The major need highlighted by the company's stakeholders concerned the potential to present and discuss design choices and their impact on the context of use (i.e., construction sites). This includes, for instance, how a machine or system design choice can affect the possibilities for site optimization. At the same time, desired changes in a site layout and operations could be enabled or hindered by design decisions. Having an overview and understanding of possible advantages and disadvantages in the integration of different product development and site planning strategies requires merging and visualizing multiple stakeholder perspectives.

In particular, the case study has investigated the conditions for carrying out a major emission- and fossil-free infrastructure project in south-western Sweden. The overall goal was to develop a decision support environment that could operate throughout the entire value chain of the project to evaluate alternative construction strategies and boost value co-creation, by fostering the active involvement of customers, contractors and machine/system suppliers in decision making. The proposed VR application is part of such an environment, its main goal being that of supporting the visualization of the results of the underlying scenario modelling work, hence facilitating the interaction between the stakeholders in the project while making decisions.

3.2   Integrating VR with Simulation Models

The proposal is to use a virtual experience environment as a platform for output results and visualization, as well as a model interface. Objects and events in the environment are editable in two ways. First, models features' and behaviours, as well as contextual factors (e.g., site, material flows) and requirements (e.g., productivity, sustainability) derive from updatable external data platforms, secondly, they can be further modified by choices made by users interacting with the application interface, displaying the output result in a VR environment.

A draft of the VR application was developed together with practitioners from the company. The aim is to support the company practitioners' and customers' decision-making, displaying the value of innovative solutions in the transition towards fossil-free and autonomous systems. In order to achieve such an aim, the VR application works both as an input and output interface between the simulation platform and the users and as a visualization solution for output results in the virtual environment.

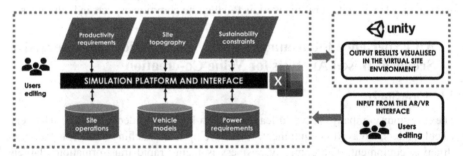

Fig. 1. Requirements and simulation/models can be edited by the users through the simulation platform and interface and the VR environment's interface. Output results are displayed in the visualization environment.

The interaction between the VR application and the simulation models is visualized in Fig. 1. Here the users' interaction in the VR application can serve as input for three types of simulation models, namely the vehicle simulation model, the site operation simulation model and the power simulation model.

The vehicle simulation model represents the mechanical feature and behaviour of a single machine and it encompasses various configurations and control strategies via mathematical optimization such as linear, quadratic, stochastic, and/or dynamic programming, and/or heuristics. The site operation simulation models evolve over time via discrete event simulation representing vehicles and material flows in a construction site for a predefined time window using the system configuration and control strategies. The power simulation models assess the needs for power delivery and distribution to the construction site in predefined time windows (e.g. the stress on the electrical network while charging multiple vehicles simultaneously). The simulation platform integrates contextual variables such as site topography, productivity and sustainability constraints, all variables that impact simulation results and that can be negotiated or traded off when planning for alternative construction site design. The VR application is linked to the simulation environment to facilitate such multi-dimensional trade-off decisions by both providing an effective way of communicating results to multiple decision-makers and by enabling scenario-based analysis of the results by allowing an interactive interface for modifying contextual variables and site operations variables.

4   Prototype Implementation

4.1   Generation of the 3D Virtual Environment

The first step in the development of the application was the selection of a real physical environment as a case study. In this case, the case study was based on a road construction site located in south-western Sweden, starting from available video material captured through camera drones. We isolated a stretch of about 16 km and individuated this specific stretch on Google Maps. Data from the map and video were integrated to design the 3D environment using Unity 3D (https://unity.com/). The environment was hence developed starting from terrain based on the 2D map (Fig. 2) and edited as required by the images captured by the camera drone perspective (Fig. 3).

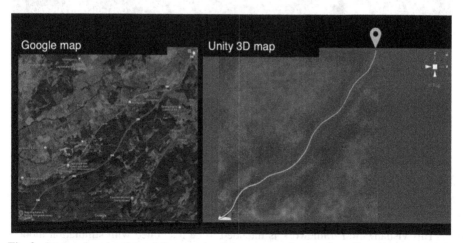

Fig. 2. Start and end points of the stretch of the construction road on Google maps and the corresponding path on the Unity 3D terrain.

Fig. 3. Screenshot from the camera drone video used to generate the virtual scene and the corresponding 3D virtual environment.

4.2   Visualization Hypotheses and Interface Mock-Up

The application will allow visualizing possible construction strategies integrating different system configurations merging products and site design. Relevant visualization data in the 3D environment and 2D map can include vehicles models, numbers, and paths, material and energy flows, the position and number of charging points and charging timing. Stakeholders could visualize the current system elements and layout, edit them, and generate a new scenario. A hypothesis of interface and settings was also integrated showing a possible input component can be seen in Fig. 4.

Fig. 4. Application interface. On the right, is an example of a 3D view of vehicle paths. On the right, are possible factors to manipulate and simulate in the virtual environment.

This visualization framework is intended to be integrated with simulation models and external data platforms related to the various scenario, displaying system requirements, resources demand, operators needed, consumption data, financial, and overall sustainability impact of different alternatives. Finally, users would be able to set system constraints in terms of resource demand and consumption, individuating the optimal solution matching their overall needs and expectations. Specifically, they would decide the parameters to set as independent variables and see how they affect the whole system.

4.3 Industrial Feedback

The approach of integrating the simulation platform and the experience environment has been tested in an industrial pre-study featuring the design of a fully electrical construction site. The tool leverages visualization and interactive scenario-based analysis for collaborative generation, evaluation and comparison of new designs. This includes different aspects of product-service systems designs, construction sites and activities planning, to merge the stakeholders' perspectives.

The current 3D environment was presented to stakeholders from the industrial partner. The environment was explored as an output component through a camera view moving through the site and showing different perspectives. The user could visualize the top view showing possible material flows following machines (Fig. 4) as well as close-up views of vehicles and construction areas following an operator through the site (Fig. 5).

Fig. 5. The user can explore the site following a virtual operator showing the construction equipment and operations.

The study was developed as a proof-of-concept featuring a realistic setting and showed the potential to quickly forecast, in an early stage of development, the economic and environmental impacts of new machines and systems configurations. This capability is expected to consistently reduce the development time and the time to market for cost-efficient autonomous solutions based on electromobility in the construction equipment, speeding up the shift to a fossil-free industry, while, at the same time, lowering the environmental impact and delivering a safer workspace by moving away workers from the risky environment.

The next steps discussed with the company's stakeholders consist of the implementation of more specific case studies, starting from the identification of constraints and variables in decision-making processes. Some of the possible factors can be observed in the current interface (Fig. 4).

5 Discussion and Conclusions

In this work, we presented the concept of a virtual experience environment value co-creation in decision making through the simulation, editing and comparison of possible system configurations for the construction industry.

The presented application is based on shared visualization of a simulated real environment, real-time manipulation and updates by integrating products and context requirements. This concept merges the advantages of VR in value co-creation, considering interactivity, editability, interoperability, and associability. The successful implementation of the application will require the integration of simulation models and external data. Interoperability aspects will be boosted by the implementation and integration of digital twins.

Moreover, there will be further investigation of visual information and interaction aspects. This includes experimenting with a variety of visual representations, graphic quality, and simulation realism and details. It can also include multisensory stimuli, different devices, input and feedback technologies, and user configurations. For instance, the design might vary considering in-presence and remote setups, haptic displays, immersive devices as well as AR versions.

Results from this activity will constitute a first proposal and testing platform for the company, as a means to improve communication with stakeholders and find converging objectives, shaping solutions in a collaborative and more efficient way. The current results highlight the potential and expectations for the system's concept for the case study. This positive outcome emerged throughout the collaboration with our industrial partner and from the feedback to the initial prototype. However, the effectiveness of the experience environment for specific decisions compared to traditional supports will be assessed in future works. The next steps will require additional discussion with the company stakeholders, to further develop the prototype according to the decision processes to investigate and compare. Moreover, further studies should consider situational factors like the number of decision-makers involved, their expertise, as well as time constraints and collaboration modalities in the CSCW framework.

Future development will also include more efficient modelling and generation of the 3D environment, directly from data acquired by camera drones, since the current method is not suitable to support large infrastructure models.

An experience environment can work as a 'boundary object' for value drivers trade-off in complex system planning and design, adding to value models [18] visualization and interactivity levels, allowing a more effective representation and understanding of value and activity flow in collaborative contexts.

Importantly, there are several aspects to be considered beyond the technology and design ones. The development and integration of similar tools with the company's business and practices will require further reflection on the new emerging roles and interactions for customers and service providers, to fully enable the potential of mixed reality tools for value co-creation.

Finally, the problem identification, the requirements definition, and the investigation of the rationale and logic of the presented approach have been performed in collaboration with a single company, thus those can be subjected to the traditional biases of single case analysis. Future case studies on the use of integrated VR environments and simulation models to support value co-creation will be extended to other companies and businesses to gain more insight into the potential of these tools according to various contexts and emerging needs.

Acknowledgments. The research leading to these results has received financial support from the Swedish Knowledge and Competence Development Foundation (Stiftelsen för kunskapsoch kompetensutveckling), Sweden, through the Model Driven Development and Decision Support research profile, and from the Swedish Transport Administration through the Elektrifierad Infrastrukturbyggnation project at Blekinge Institute of Technology, Sweden.

References

1. Kamp, B., Parry, G.: Servitization and advanced business services as levers for competitiveness. Ind. Market. Manage. **60** (2017)
2. Goulding, J.S., Pour Rahimian, F., Arif, M., Sharp, M.D.: New offsite production and business models in construction: priorities for the future research agenda. Archit. Eng. Des. Manage. **11**(3), 163–184 (2015)
3. Galera-Zarco, C., Campos, J.A.: Exploring servitization in industrial construction: a sustainable approach. Sustainability **13**(14), 8002 (2021)
4. Bu, L., Chen, C.H., Ng, K.K., Zheng, P., Dong, G., Liu, H.: A user-centric design approach for smart product-service systems using virtual reality: a case study. J. Clean. Prod. **280**, 124413 (2021)
5. Bertoni, M., Bertoni, A., Isaksson, O.: Evoke: a value-driven concept selection method for early system design. J. Syst. Sci. Syst. Eng. **27**(1), 46–77 (2018)
6. Lerch, C., Gotsch, M.: Digitalized product-service systems in manufacturing firms: a case study analysis. Res. Technol. Manag. **58**(5), 45–52 (2015)
7. Lenka, S., Parida, V., Wincent, J.: Digitalization capabilities as enablers of value co-creation in servitizing firms. Psychol. Mark. **34**, 92–100 (2017)
8. Bonamigo, A., Frech, C.G.: Industry 4.0 in services: challenges and opportunities for value co-creation. J. Serv. Market. (2020)
9. Scurati, G.W., Gattullo, M., Fiorentino, M., Ferrise, F., Bordegoni, M., Uva, A.E.: Converting maintenance actions into standard symbols for Augmented Reality applications in Industry 4.0. Comput. Ind. **98**, 68–79 (2018)
10. Riboldi, N., Scurati, G.W., Ferrise, F., Bordegoni, M., Pedrini, S.: Improving maintenance services through virtual reality. In: Manufacturing in the Era of 4th Industrial Revolution: A World Scientific Reference Volume 3: Augmented, Virtual and Mixed Reality Applications in Advanced Manufacturing, pp. 49–72 (2020)
11. El-Jarn, H., Southern G.: Can co-creation in extended reality technologies facilitate the design process?. J. Work-Appl. Manage. (2020)

12. Zhang, T., Lu, C., Torres, E., Cobanoglu, C.: Value co-creation and technological progression: a critical review. Eur. Bus. Rev. **32**, 687–707 (2020)

13. Cuomo, M.T., Tortora, D., Festa, G., Ceruti, F., Metallo, G.: Managing omni-customer brand experience via augmented reality: a qualitative investigation in the Italian fashion retailing system. Qual. Market Res. Int. J. (2020)

14. Kostis, A., Ritala, P.: Digital artifacts in industrial co-creation: how to use VR technology to bridge the provider-customer boundary. Calif. Manage. Rev. **62**(4), 125–147 (2020)

15. Pedersen, G., Koumaditis, K.: Virtual Reality (VR) in the Computer Supported Cooperative Work (CSCW) domain: a mapping and a pre-study on functionality and immersion. In: Chen, J.Y.C., Fragomeni, G. (eds.) HCII 2020. LNCS, vol. 12191, pp. 136–153. Springer, Cham (2020). https://doi.org/10.1007/978-3-030-49698-2_10

16. Delgado, J.M.D., Oyedele, L., Beach, T., Demian, P.: Augmented and virtual reality in construction: drivers and limitations for industry adoption. J. Constr. Eng. Manage. **146**(7) (2020)

17. Zhang, Y., Liu, H., Kang, S.C., Al-Hussein, M.: Virtual reality applications for the built environment: research trends and opportunities. Autom. Constr. **118**, 103311 (2020)

18. Panarotto, M., Bertoni, M., Johansson, C.: Using models as boundary objects in early design negotiations: analysis and implications for decision support systems. J. Des. Res. **17**(2–4), 214–237 (2019)

Designing Value-Robust Product-Service Systems by Incorporating Changeability: A Reference Framework

Raj Jiten Machchhar$^{(\boxtimes)}$ and Alessandro Bertoni

Department of Mechanical Engineering, Blekinge Institute of Technology, 37179 Karlskrona, Sweden

{raj.jiten.machchhar,alessandro.bertoni}@bth.se

Abstract. When a Product-Service System (PSS) has a longer lifecycle, it is subjected to several internal and external changes along its path that may deteriorate its value. A PSS capable of delivering value despite the circumstances is called a value robust PSS, and one way of achieving value robustness is by incorporating changeability. A lot of uncertainties prevail in decision-making concerning changeability as change is a phenomenon not clearly understood in PSS design. To bridge this gap, this paper presents a reference framework to support the definition and quantification of changeability in PSS design to enable the delivery of a value robust PSS. The paper is mainly focused mainly on the realization of the concept of changeability in PSS design, crossing the boundary between rich literature in the field of PSS and Systems Engineering.

Keywords: Product-Service Systems · Uncertainty · Risk · Changeability · Value robustness · Value-driven design

1 Introduction

It is nowadays widely acknowledged that manufacturing industries are transitioning to a servitized business model, where the perspective changes from a pure product-based offering to a Product-Service Systems offering (PSS). These systems have the potential to generate consistent revenue over time and foster a stronger customer relationship [1]. Such a business model accentuates the need to capture, measure, and enhance value throughout the lifecycle as the value expectation must be measured at various instances along time as against one-time during delivery [2]. Thus, inculcating capabilities for value sustainment of the PSS along the lifecycle becomes one of the key decision-making aspects of PSS design [3]. Along similar lines, Systems engineering (SE) literature stresses that complex systems with a longer lifecycle go through a lot of internal and external changes along the path, namely, change in the requirements, change in the system itself, and change in the context [4, 5]. In such a case, a system capable of achieving a higher value despite the circumstances is called a value robust system [5]. One way of achieving value robustness is by developing a *"changeable"* system that can

© IFIP International Federation for Information Processing 2022
Published by Springer Nature Switzerland AG 2022
L. M. Camarinha-Matos et al. (Eds.): PRO-VE 2022, IFIP AICT 662, pp. 623–630, 2022.
https://doi.org/10.1007/978-3-031-14844-6_50

be suitably modified to counter value deteriorating events [5, 6]. A lot of uncertainty exists in decision-making during the design phase as the internal and external changes that may arise during the lifecycle of the system are not clearly understood [7]. This viewpoint is shared in PSS literature, where uncertainties are seen as one of the major barriers to forecasting a phenomenon [8].

The theme of changeable PSS and how to deal with the multiple uncertainties, already since the beginning of the engineering design of PSS, is still poorly discussed in the literature. To bridge this knowledge gap, the paper aims to provide a comprehensive outlook on various levels of complexities, and thus uncertainties, framing the theoretical discussion into a reference framework highlighting what are the aspects and drivers that shall be considered in the efforts of quantifying the changeability of a PSS to support the development of value robust PSS. To achieve such an aim, the paper presents the results of a research effort based on the combination of literature review in the field of PSS and SE combined with the analysis of qualitative empirical data mainly collected in collaboration with company partners, following a diagnosis, invention, and reflective learning cycle (as elaborated by [9]), that has finally led to the formulation of the proposed reference framework for the designing value-robust PSS by incorporating changeability.

2 Product-Service System Value and Changeability

The value-driven paradigm can provide methodological guidance for making PSS design decisions [10]. Thus, value and its assessment have a vital role in the PSS development process, although a consistent understanding of what value means is missing [11]. For the scope of this paper, the definition adopted is the one proposed by [12], where value is measured in terms of benefits for multiple concerning stakeholders under the applicable constraints such as cost. [11] argue that a distinction is necessary to clarify the roles of each actor in the value creation process. Such a perspective remains beyond the scope of this paper. In the realm of PSS, the perspective of value shall abandon the one-time delivery perspective typical of traditional products, to embrace the through-life creation perspective [13]. As highlighted by [2], several value creation opportunities exist in the operational stage of the PSS by accordant support from the provider in the form of maintenance, exchange services, updates, etc. Assuming that the purpose of any system is to maximize the value for the associated stakeholders, these systems need to withstand the adverse effects of all the internal and external changes that might occur along their lifecycle. To ensure sustained value delivery, *"functional"* and *"non-functional"* requirements are often defined during the design of a system, where functional requirements govern *"what"* the system must achieve and non-functional requirements govern *"how"* the system should achieve the functional requirements [14]. The non-functional requirements are usually the properties of the system that determine how successful the system will be in delivering the intended value, and are typically bundled together as *"ilities"* [5].

One such *"ility"* is changeability, which is a property of a system that enables the system to reach various conceivable states under the implied constraints, allowing the system to meet the value expectation during the operational stage [5]. Some researchers propose changeability as an over-arching property, comprising many change-related properties such as adaptability, flexibility, scalability, etc., however, at a fundamental level, changeability is the ability of the system to either change the "*form*" or "*function*", thus bring about a change in its operation as a response change in the requirement, system or context [5]. Concerning PSS, many researchers have acknowledged that a PSS comprises three elements: 1) product, 2) service and 3) infrastructure [15, 16]. In this respect, changeability is not limited to the tangible counterpart, but rather to the entire domain of components within each PSS element, respectively. Such a perspective is also acknowledged in PSS, where changeability is attributed to the system's ability to respond to unexpected perturbations cumulatively [3].

3   The Need for Quantifying Changeability in PSS Design

Changeability is seen as a potential approach for achieving value robustness, and thus, there is an evident need to develop more changeable PSS solutions. However, to what extent must the PSS be changeable is a difficult question as changeability comes at an additional penalty in the form of investment cost, change cost, and change time [5, 6]. Thus, from an engineering design perspective, the need is to rather quantify changeability that can enable the tradeoffs between changeability and cost for value robustness. Some of the known issues of changeability quantification and perspectives on the implication of those on PSS are as follows. To quantify change, one must quantify system states, and the issue concerning complex systems is that discretely quantifying the states is a challenging task [6]. This challenge aggravates as a PSS is an amalgam of products, services, and infrastructure, and all three elements are acknowledged to be changeable concerning the form and function. The next issue is particularly regarding the function or operation of the PSS. A complex system is subjected to a higher degree of unbounded control variables [4]. This may require an educated guess bounding the conceivable states of the PSS for confining the design space. The final issue is concerning digitalization, where changes in the form of software and digital services are relatively easier and quicker compared to traditional hardware changes, [16]. Thus, design decisions must now consider the impact of small and incremental changes in the expected value of the PSS. To summarize, concerning PSS, the problem first transcends to comprehending what are the possibilities of change within each PSS element and then finding the right balance of change to maximize value dynamically. Thus, the tradeoffs become more complex and multi-dimensional. Towards this end, while researchers have argued the need for a better support system for defining and managing uncertain variables [17], changeability quantification is not widely exploited for value robustness in PSS. If the changeability of a PSS plays a relevant role to assure its value robustness along the lifecycle, then it emerges as an intrinsic requirement to be able to define and quantify such changeability since the early stage of PSS design.

As per [18], to rationalize a changeable PSS, one must understand the complexities that are a potential source of uncertainties in the PSS lifecycle. In such a case, five essential aspects for engineering a complex system were proposed by [19], namely, "*structural*", "*behavioral*", "*contextual*", "*temporal*", and "*perceptual*". Referred to as complexity aspects in this work, they can be described as follows. Structural complexity relates to the physical manifestation of the system components and their relationships.

Behavioral complexity relates to the operation of the system to deliver the intended value. Contextual complexity relates to the external factors that can influence the behavioral aspects of the system. Temporal complexity relates to understanding the impact of contextual factors as a function of time. And, perceptual complexity relates to the value perceived by each stakeholder along with their cognitive biases. [20] state that these aspects of complexity are directly associated with a certain level of uncertainty, arguing that from structural to perceptual, the uncertainty grows exponentially. As the uncertainty in decision-making increases, so does the risk, emphasizing the need to build systems capable of withstanding the associated risks [18].

However, the dynamics of the PSS in a changing context are often difficult to capture, rendering sub-optimal solutions driven by the challenges is incorporating uncertainty in the requirement definition for PSS design [17]. Additionally, literature shows how the PSS value proposition hinges on through-life value creation for both the provider and the customer [2, 12]. Thus, a time perspective is inherently entangled with PSS, yet temporal aspects seem to be largely neglected in the early PSS design. Some approaches to estimating the cost implications of changes in product and service configurations have been proposed (e.g. [21]). However, a systematic evaluation of how time-dependent changes in the context can lead to value deterioration of the PSS is still missing. Additionally incorporating contextual awareness is being largely discussed for PSS from an operational perspective, but a majority of demonstrative adaptive changes in the PSS are focused on digital services [22]. Uncertainty is ubiquitous in the engineering design of such solutions from a time perspective, and a reliable decision comes by the consideration of system-context interactions to be stochastic and not deterministic. As [8] argues, completely removing the uncertainties can lead to higher risk as various possibilities were not thoroughly evaluated. However, if the uncertainties are balanced, risks can be negotiated to be within acceptable limits.

4   A Reference Framework for Changeability Quantification in PSS Design

To achieve a viable solution to these uncertainties, this paper outlines a reference framework for changeability quantification in PSS design (refer to Fig. 1). The framework positions the five complexity aspects (structural, behavioral, contextual, temporal, and perceptual) from a PSS perspective, where each aspect imposes inherent uncertainties in decision-making. It is assumed that perceptual uncertainty does not have an independent stance, but rather is a function of all the previously accumulated uncertainties. To address perceptual uncertainty, all the former uncertainties need to be addressed systematically. In a broad sense, a system is subjected to three types of changes [4, 5, 7]: 1) change in the requirement, where stakeholders' expectation of the system changes with time. For example, the system is subjected to capability change, inclusion in SoS, etc. 2) change in the system with time, meaning a system experiences capability degradation, physical damage, or similar value deterioration avenues. 3) change in the context, where the externalities change with time such as the price of fuel, the operational environment, the users' preferences, the cost of electricity, technological advancement, etc. These are regarded as change drivers in Fig. 1 as they enforce the PSS to change for resisting value deterioration.

Also, Fig. 1 details three essential facets for a system to change [5]: 1) the change "*agent*", 2) the change "*mechanism*", and 3) the change "*effect*". The agent is the enabler of a change in the system. An emphasis on external enablers makes the system flexible while an emphasis on internal enablers makes the system adaptable. However, both cater to making the system more changeable. The mechanism is the path that the system takes to reach the desired state under the applicable constraints. These paths have been indicated by dashed lines in Fig. 1. The effect is the change in the initial and final state of the system. The effect can be a change in the form, function, or both of a system and it is indicated by fluctuating blue and yellow bars in Fig. 1, respectively. The accumulation of underlying structural, behavioral, contextual, and temporal uncertainties leads to a risk that the PSS might fail in achieving the desired value. Thus, the perceived value is subjected to an ever-expanding variation concerning time due to the cumulative effect of uncertainties (grey triangle in Fig. 1).

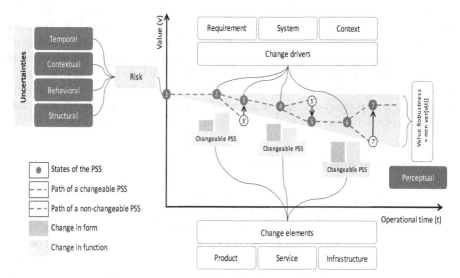

Fig. 1. A reference framework for quantifying changeability in PSS design (Color figure online)

To operationalize the framework and provide an example of application, Fig. 1 depicts the value of the PSS along with the operational phase, and some crucial states of the PSS that depict the value of the PSS as a function of time have been indicated numerically. State 1 indicates the original value of the PSS, i.e., the expected value of the PSS at the commencement of operation as agreed upon by various stakeholders. The PSS will continue delivering the desired value if no change drivers are acting as shown from states 1 to 2. Essentially, these are the same states of the PSS because no change has been incurred, although depicted via different numbers for illustrative purposes. The dashed black line shows the path taken by the changeable PSS. At state 2, it is assumed that one of the change drivers is acting that deteriorates the value of the PSS. For example, the PSS may have encountered a change in context enforcing a change in atleast one of the PSS elements to recover part of its value. The dashed red line shows the path taken by the non-changeable PSS to reach a hypothetical new state 3'. But since the PSS is changeable, it can be suitably modified to achieve the best possible value in the circumstances. Thus, state 3 represented by the changeable PSS has a value in this case and the arrow connecting the changeable PSS state and the non-changeable PSS state is the value appreciated. A PSS may change its state regardless of a change in any of the PSS elements, and thus there may be a change in its value. For example, the value deterioration from states 3 to 4 can be due to system degradation. Here, the change driver is the system itself, but none of the elements of the PSS have changed. A value recovery may happen via actions such as maintenance, replacement, etc. Notably, the y-axis is not a utility function but rather a value function that is adopted as a ratio of benefits and costs. Thus, there could be instances where the value of the non-changeable PSS is higher than the changeable PSS. As an example, consider the requirement of taking scenery photographs as well as portraits. Artificial intelligence and software advancements have enabled smartphone cameras to generate reasonable bokeh effects on photographs. A digital camera capable of swapping lenses may not be a viable option from an economic stance for many customers. State 5 indicates that the value of the changeable PSS is rather lower in this case. The arrow connecting state 5 and state 5' is the value depreciated. As the PSS operates, these cycles of value appreciation and depreciation are repeated along its path as shown in Fig. 1. Also, while the transition from one state to another is depicted to be linear, these transitions can be instantaneous or highly non-linear as well. Value robustness is then the minimization of the variance of value as a function of time, where variance is the measure of the dispersion of value from the expectation.

5   Conclusion and Delimitations

The paper has presented a reference framework to support the definition and quantification of changeability in PSS design to enable the delivery of value robust PSS. The contribution of the paper is focused mainly on the realization of the concept of changeability in PSS design, crossing the boundary between rich literature in the field of PSS and SE. Additionally, it shall be regarded as an effort toward nurturing the academic discussion about changeability quantification in PSS design. Such work is part of a broader research initiative aiming to develop a simulation-based support framework that will enable decision-making about value robustness for a PSS. Ultimately the goal is to mitigate the risks rather than eliminate the uncertainties when designing PSS [8]. One way to mitigate the risks is to shorten the period of the operational phase [23]. But complex systems are typically associated with a longer lifecycle, leading to a higher probability of encountering unfavorable circumstances. In such a case, a changeable PSS is proposed as a measure for countering these circumstances, thus achieving value robustness. PSS elements consist of the product, service, and infrastructure. In this light, changeability is implied to the entire domain of PSS components which makes changeability quantification a crucial aspect of PSS design.

As a delimitation, it must be said that a typical lifecycle of a PSS consists of various stages, right from design and manufacturing to the retirement of the system. Along this path, there are several opportunities for value creation that inherit many challenges from economic, environmental, and social stances [22]. To delimit the area of contribution, this paper primarily focused on the operational stage of the PSS. Based on [15], the operational stage of a PSS is proposed to comprise the following three stages: 1) the *"use"* and *"reuse"* stage where the PSS is operational to achieve the desired value, 2) the *"maintenance"* of the PSS, consisting of all activities to ensure that the desired level of value is nurtured, and 3) *"reconfiguration"* of the PSS, consisting of all activities to ensure value sustainment of the PSS within the operational stage. This viewpoint enables the authors to exclude change-related ilities outside the operational stage and delimit the scope for this paper. For example, reproducibility in the form of *"remanufacturing"* or *"recycling"* [22] can be an ability of a system to enhance the value in the next cycle but falls beyond the scope of this paper.

Acknowledgments. The work was performed in the frame of the Strategic Innovation Program Swedish Mining Innovation, concurrently funded by the Swedish Innovation Agency (VINNOVA), the Swedish Research Council for Sustainable Development, (FORMAS) & the Swedish Energy Agency (Energimyndigheten). The research also received financial support from the Swedish Knowledge & Competence Development Foundation through the MD3S research profile at Blekinge Institute of Technology.

References

1. Zheng, P., Wang, Z., Chen, C.-H., Pheng Khoo, L.: A survey of smart product-service systems: key aspects, challenges and future perspectives. Adv. Eng. Inform. **42**, 100973 (2019). https://doi.org/10.1016/j.aei.2019.100973
2. Matschewsky, J., Lindahl, M., Sakao, T.: Capturing and enhancing provider value in product-service systems throughout the lifecycle: a systematic approach. CIRP J. Manuf. Sci. Technol. **29**, 191–204 (2020). https://doi.org/10.1016/j.cirpj.2018.08.006
3. Bertoni, A., Bertoni, M.: Modeling 'ilities' in early product-service systems design. Procedia CIRP **83**, 230–235 (2019). https://doi.org/10.1016/j.procir.2019.03.091
4. Mekdeci, B., Ross, A.M., Rhodes, D.H., Hastings, D.E.: A taxonomy of perturbations: determining the ways that systems lose value. In: 2012 IEEE International Systems Conference, SysCon 2012, pp. 1–6 (2012). https://doi.org/10.1109/SysCon.2012.6189487
5. Ross, A.M., Rhodes, D.H., Hastings, D.E.: Defining changeability: reconciling flexibility, adaptability, scalability, modifiability, and robustness for maintaining system lifecycle value. Syst. Eng. **11**, 246–262 (2008). https://doi.org/10.1002/sys.20098
6. Rehn, C.F., et al.: Quantification of changeability level for engineering systems. Syst. Eng. **22**, 80–94 (2019). https://doi.org/10.1002/sys.21472
7. Mekdeci, B., Ross, A.M., Rhodes, D.H., Hastings, D.E.: Pliability and viable systems: maintaining value under changing conditions. IEEE Syst. J. **9**, 1173–1184 (2015). https://doi.org/10.1109/JSYST.2014.2314316
8. Erkoyuncu, J.A., Roy, R., Shehab, E., Cheruvu, K.: Understanding service uncertainties in industrial product–service system cost estimation. Int. J. Adv. Manuf. Technol. **52**, 1223–1238 (2011). https://doi.org/10.1007/s00170-010-2767-3
9. Avison, D.E., Lau, F., Myers, M.D., Nielsen, P.A.: Action research. Commun. ACM. **42**, 94–97 (1999). https://doi.org/10.1145/291469.291479

10. Bertoni, A., Bertoni, M., Panarotto, M., Johansson, C., Larsson, T.C.: Value-driven product service systems development: methods and industrial applications. CIRP J. Manuf. Sci. Technol. **15**, 42–55 (2016). https://doi.org/10.1016/j.cirpj.2016.04.008

11. Grönroos, C., Voima, P.: Critical service logic: making sense of value creation and co-creation. J. Acad. Mark. Sci. **41**, 133–150 (2013). https://doi.org/10.1007/s11747-012-0308-3

12. Rondini, A., Bertoni, M., Pezzotta, G.: At the origins of product service systems: supporting the concept assessment with the engineering value assessment method. CIRP J. Manuf. Sci. Technol. **29**, 157–175 (2020). https://doi.org/10.1016/j.cirpj.2018.08.002

13. Isaksson, O., Larsson, T.C., Rönnbäck, A.Ö.: Development of product-service systems: challenges and opportunities for the manufacturing firm. J. Eng. Des. **20**, 329–348 (2009). https://doi.org/10.1080/09544820903152663

14. Cysneiros, L.M., Yu, E.: Non-functional requirements elicitation. In: do Prado Leite, J.C.S., Doorn, J.H. (eds.) Perspectives on Software Requirements, vol. 735, pp. 115–138. Springer, Boston, MA (2004). https://doi.org/10.1007/978-1-4615-0465-8_6

15. Machchhar, R.J., Toller, C.N.K., Bertoni, A., Bertoni, M.: Data-driven value creation in smart product-service system design: state-of-the-art and research directions. Comput. Ind. **137**, 103606 (2022). https://doi.org/10.1016/j.compind.2022.103606

16. Pirola, F., Boucher, X., Wiesner, S., Pezzotta, G.: Digital technologies in product-service systems: a literature review and a research agenda. Comput. Ind. **123**, 103301 (2020). https://doi.org/10.1016/j.compind.2020.103301

17. Vasantha, G.V.A., Roy, R., Corney, J.R.: Advances in designing product-service systems. J. Indian Inst. Sci. **95**, 429–448 (2016)

18. McManus, H., Hastings, D.: A framework for understanding uncertainty and its mitigation and exploitation in complex systems. Presented at the INCOSE International Symposium (2005)

19. Rhodes, D.H., Ross, A.M.: Five aspects of engineering complex systems emerging constructs and methods. In: 2010 IEEE International Systems Conference, pp. 190–195 (2010). https://doi.org/10.1109/SYSTEMS.2010.5482431

20. Gaspar, H.M., Hagen, A., Erikstad, S.O.: On designing a ship for complex value robustness. Ship Technol. Res. **63**, 14–25 (2016). https://doi.org/10.1080/09377255.2015.1119923

21. Bertoni, A., Bertoni, M.: PSS cost engineering: a model-based approach for concept design. CIRP J. Manuf. Sci. Technol. **29**, 176–190 (2020). https://doi.org/10.1016/j.cirpj.2018.08.001

22. Li, X., Wang, Z., Chen, C.-H., Zheng, P.: A data-driven reversible framework for achieving Sustainable Smart product-service systems. J. Clean. Prod. **279**, 123618 (2021). https://doi.org/10.1016/j.jclepro.2020.123618

23. Richter, A., Sadek, T., Steven, M.: Flexibility in industrial product-service systems and use-oriented business models. CIRP J. Manuf. Sci. Technol. **3**, 128–134 (2010). https://doi.org/10.1016/j.cirpj.2010.06.003

Assessing Digital Platform Requirements from Value Co-creation Perspective

Noor Jungerius, Baris Ozkan[(✉)], Onat Ege Adali, and Oktay Turetken

School of Industrial Engineering, Eindhoven University of Technology, PO Box 513,
5600 MB Eindhoven, The Netherlands
l.e.jungerius@student.tue.nl,
{b.ozkan,o.e.adali,o.turetken}@tue.nl

Abstract. Digital platforms are transforming industries enabling value co-creation whereby actors exchange and recombine resources in the platform's service system. The digital platform requirements constantly change as the service system value propositions and the resource configurations improve and resource misconfigurations leading to negative value experiences are identified. Therefore, it is imperative for the platform designers to assess the extent to which their platform facilitates platform actors' desired value co-creation at a given time. This paper proposes a value proposition-driven platform requirements assessment method to address this need. More specifically, the method supports the elicitation of requirements based on the value propositions of the desired value co-creation of the digital platform. Subsequently, it supports the assessment of the platform based on these requirements. The method is developed following the design science research methodology, demonstrated in assessing a digital healthcare platform and evaluated by conducting a focus group study.

Keywords: Service systems engineering · Value cocreation · Digital platform · Requirements engineering

1 Introduction

Digital platforms have become more prominent over the past decade. They are increasingly conceptualized as the enablers of value co-creation, whereby a collaborative network of actors exchange and recombine heterogeneous resources in their service ecosystems [1]. Value propositions—the invitations to engage with the platform for the co-creation of value—are central to value co-creation and thus to the success of a digital platform [1, 2]. Many successful digital platform and value proposition examples can be given from the mobility (e.g., Uber), healthcare (e.g., PatientsLikeMe), and online marketplace (e.g., eBay) business domains, which reflect the multi-actor and the collaborative characteristics of value co-creation.

Despite its attractiveness, the digital platform as a complex and emerging technological artefact involves many design challenges, including identifying and managing

Published by Springer Nature Switzerland AG 2022
L. M. Camarinha-Matos et al. (Eds.): PRO-VE 2022, IFIP AICT 662, pp. 631–644, 2022.
https://doi.org/10.1007/978-3-031-14844-6_51

platform requirements [2, 3]. These challenges are often related to multi-actor and value co-creative perspectives on requirements [4], as well as the need to manage the constant evolution of the platform service system for its survival [5]. Thus, platfom requirements that emerge due to changes in value propositions, resource reconfigurations, and actors should be identified in the ongoing platform design process. In parallel, resource misintegrations (e.g., system errors, missing information), which cause value co-destruction, should be eliminated to prevent negative value experiences [6]. Therefore, it is imperative for the platform designers to understand at a given time the extent to which the platform can satisfy the needs of the actors of the value co-creation. The traditional IS approaches and requirements evaluation criteria, such as the user acceptance or system quality, fall short of addressing the digital platform's multi-actor, value co-creative and dynamic nature [3, 7]. This paper proposes *a method to guide the elicitation of platform requirements based on the desired value co-creation and the assessment of a deployed digital platform on these requirements.*

To develop our method, we adopt a service systems engineering view [8] and consider the digital platform as a technology and a complex resource to enable one or more service systems [1, 5]. We follow the design science research paradigm [9] and follow the methodological guidelines and process proposed by Peffers et al. [10]. We demonstrate our method by applying it through a real digital health platform business case and evaluate it by conducting a focus group study.

The remainder of the paper is structured as follows. Section 2 presents the related work. Section 3 elaborates on the research design followed. Section 4 introduces the proposed method and demonstrates its application in a real business case. In Sect. 5, we present the evaluation of the method. Finally, Sect. 6 concludes the paper with the limitations of our study and the opportunities for future work.

2 Related Work

Identifying and assessing software requirements in a multi-actor socio-technical system context has been an interesting field of research for decades [11]. A significant number of studies followed the conventional goal-oriented approaches and proposed requirement identification methods to bridge the business-level and software-level understandings of what a software system should do [12]. However, only a few studies explicitly account for the value propositions in the requirements identification and assessment process. Lessard et al. [4] adopt a service system view on value proposition design and propose a service systems metamodel and a goal-oriented requirements language for modelling service systems. In addition, they propose a heuristic to guide the elicitation of requirements for the service systems based on their metamodel. Immonen et al. [13] identify the digital services, ecosystem members, infrastructure, and capabilities as the core digital service ecosystem elements and propose a service requirement engineering method to support the development of a digital service. Adali et al. [2] proposed a method to identify platform requirements from value propositions by extending the VP-BSIM method such that requirements are generated the form of UML use cases. To our best knowledge, none of these proposals guides the assessment of deployed platforms based on the requirements derived from the desired value co-creation, which is manifest in the actors' value propositions. The present study addresses this gap.

3   Research Design

To perform our research, we adopted the design science research (DSR) paradigm [9] and followed the guidelines and process proposed by Peffers et al. [10]. Accordingly, this research is problem-initiated and involves the following DSR activities:

Problem Identification and Motivation: We provide our research motivation and problem in the introduction section of this paper.

Identification of Solution Objectives: In line with our research aim, we identify three objectives for our method: the method should support the elicitation of requirements of a digital platform based on the desired value co-creation (DO1), the method should support the assessment of a deployed digital platform on the elicited requirements (DO2), and the method should be satisfactory regarding the three criteria of the Technology Acceptance Model [14] namely, usefulness, ease of use, and the use intention of the method's target users (DO3).

Design and Development: We followed a Situational Method Engineering (SME) approach [15] and applied the extension-based strategy to design and develop our method. Accordingly, the base method, the VP-BSIM, guides the transformation of a set of value propositions into modular, standardized, and contextualized actor resource reconfigurations by repurposing the business services paradigm in the context of service systems engineering [16]. The business services that the VP-BSIM generates describe the functionality of the overall service system; however, not in the form and detail of system requirements (i.e., platform requirements). Therefore, we extended the VP-BSIM with method chunks selected from Dubois et al. [17] to guide the translation of business services into platform requirements and to assess a deployed platform according to the requirements afterwards. To assess the identified platform goals (i.e. platform requirements) (design objective DO2) we adopted the assessment procedure proposed by Horkoff and Yu [18] that allows the qualitative and interactive evaluation of requirements represented in goal models.

Demonstration, Evaluation and Communication: A design artefact should be demonstrated and evaluated according to selected evaluation criteria [9, 10]. The method was demonstrated through its application for a real digital healthcare data exchange platform business case. Subsequently, the method was evaluated in a focus group with practitioners using the guidelines proposed by Tremblay et al. [19] and according to the evaluation criteria set by DO3. The present paper communicates our DSR research as the last research activity of a complete DSR cycle.

4   Method Description and Demonstration

In this section, we describe the Extended VP-BSIM platform assessment method (Fig. 1) and demonstrate it in a business case. In Sect. 4.1, we briefly introduce the business case. In Sect. 4.2, we present the method steps and illustrate how we applied these steps to the business case.

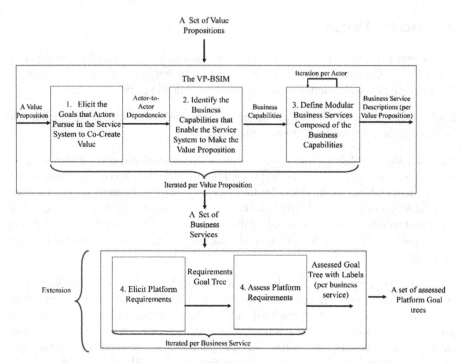

Fig. 1. The Steps of the Extended VP-BSIM (with the original and extended steps)

4.1 Business Case: Digital Platform for the Sharing of Digital Health Data

The Dutch government aims to integrate the citizens into health data exchange. They enacted a new law stating that citizens have the right to freely access and control their health records and are entitled to an electronic copy. To collect all citizen health records and provide them with efficient and integrated mechanisms for health data access and control, the concept of "personal healthcare environment" (PGO in Dutch) platform was developed. We demonstrate our method in the PGO platform developed by a Dutch platform development company. We chose this business case as the company was already in need of assessing and improving the PGO platform according to the expectations of its stakeholders (i.e., platform actors). In the demonstration, the paper's authors applied the method in consultation with employees from the company and other stakeholders, including the citizen users. During the demonstration, we focused on the *"Control of own health data"*, which was identified as the core service system value proposition by the platform development company.

4.2 The Assessment Method Steps and Demonstration

The first three steps of our method comprise the original VP-BSIM steps, and Steps 4 and 5 represent the extension steps. In the following, we only the summarise the VP-BSIM method steps. For a detailed description of these steps, we refer the reader to the original VP-BSIM paper [16].

Step 1-Elicit Goals that Actors Pursue in the Service System to Co-create Value: The first step of the Extended VP-BSIM constitutes a value proposition-driven analysis to ensure that the business services to be identified enable the co-creation of value outlined by the system service value propositions. This step comprises two sub-steps: In the first sub-step, the service system value proposition is structured by defining the actors' value contributions/propositions, co-production activities, and costs and benefits in the service system. For this, the service-dominant business model radar (SDBM/R) is employed [20]. In the second sub-step, each actor's value proposition and co-production activities are decomposed into strategic and intentional dependencies using Strategic Dependency (SD) and Strategic Rationale (SR) models from the i* framework [11]. An SD model provides an intentional description of a process (i.e., value co-creation) in terms of a network of dependency relationships among actors. SR models describe the intentional relationships internal to actors, such as means-ends relationships. As such, the outputs of this step are SD and SR Models that define the strategic and intentional relationships between the actors of the service system.

Application of Step 1: The service system value proposition "Control of own health data" was transformed into an SDBM/R blueprint (Fig. 2). Next, SD and SR diagrams were created based on the service system proposition and the individual actors' value propositions (Fig. 3 and Fig. 4).

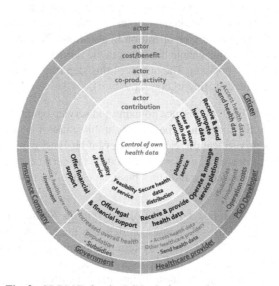

Fig. 2. SDBM/R for the PGO platform under assessment.

Step 2-Identify the Business Capabilities that Enable the Service System to Make the Value Proposition: The second step of the Extended VP-BSIM focuses on identifying the business capabilities actors need to apply and integrate within their service system to co-create value. This step uses Capability-Business Service Domain Mapping

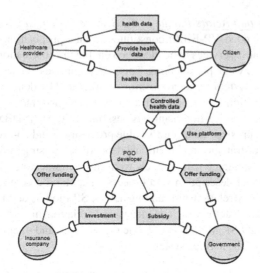

Fig. 3. Strategic dependency model for the PGO platform under assessment.

technique [21] to identify the business capabilities that fulfil the intentional and strategic interdependencies defined in Step 1. To identify the business capabilities, first, service domains—collections of tasks called service operations under an actor's control—are defined. Then, each service operation under a service domain is matched with a business capability that facilitates the service operation in question. The output of this step is a set of business capabilities that enable the actors in the service system to co-create value as outlined by a value proposition. The output of this step is a service domain-business capability matrix provided at (tinyurl.com/2pt62vuf).

Application of Step 2: First, the service domains and service operations were identified by analyzing SR and SD diagrams. The process architecture of the PGO company was also analyzed for their verification. Next, the relevant business capabilities of the PGO platform stakeholders were defined and matched to the service operations. This step application resulted in the service domain - business capability matrix in Fig. 5.

Step 3-Define Modular Business Services Composed of the Business Capabilities: The third and final step of VP-BSIM focuses on defining modular business services that describe the functionality of the service system. Furthermore, it formalizes each identified service with a description. This step uses Service Analysis with Feature Binding Technique [22] to compose the business capabilities identified in Step 2 into modular business services. The composition of the business capabilities into business services is guided by the three design properties such that business services are stateless, self-contained, and represent a domain-specific service. The business services are specified using a template provided at (tinyurl.com/2pt62vuf). It should be noted while the scope of the method in Steps 1 and 2 is the whole service system, in Step 3 the scope changes to a single actor (i.e., the actor utilizing the extended VP-BSIM to identify its business services), and this step should be repeated for every actor.

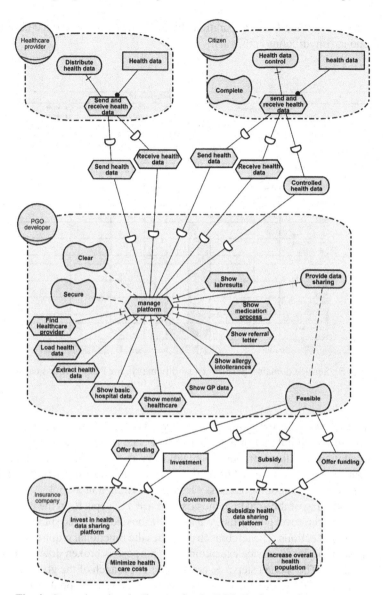

Fig. 4. Strategic rationale diagram for the PGO platform under assessment.

Application of Step 3: In the demonstration, we applied this step for the actor PGO developer company. In Step 2, Data retrieval, Data transformation, Data viewing, and Data sharing were identified as the PGO developer's business capabilities. The capabilities were evaluated on the three criteria for modularity, i.e., whether they rely on features or information that reside in another business service and represent a domain-specific service. After this evaluation, Data viewing and Data sharing were identified as modular business services, whereas Data transformation and Data retrieval were merged into one modular business service Data Preparation (Fig. 5). The business service descriptions can be found at (tinyurl.com/2pt62vuf).

Service Domains	Service Operations	Business capabilities							
		PGO developer				Citizen	Healthcare provider	Government	Insurance company
		Data retrieval	Data transformation	Data viewing	Data sharing	Data control	Data providing	Data sharing initiative support	Data sharing initiative support
Financial support	Offer funding							X	X
Data management	Load health data	X							
	Find healthcare provider	X							
	Extract health data		X						
	Transform health data		X						
	Show basic hospital data			X		X	X		
	Show mental health data			X		X	X		
	Show GP data			X		X	X		
	Show allergy intolerances			X		X	X		
	Show referral letter			X		X	X		
	Show medication process			X		X	X		
	Show lab results			X		X	X		
	Export health data				X	X	X		

▬▬▬ - Data preparation   ▬▬▬ - Data viewing   ▬▬▬ - Data sharing

Fig. 5. Service domain - business capability matrix for PGO business case.

Step 4: Elicit Requirements Per Business Service: The goal of this step is to elicit the requirements of the digital platform per business service in the form of a goal tree. For this, the elicitation technique proposed by Dubois et al. [17] is adapted. The goal tree for each business service is created using the template and the procedure in Fig. 6. The input of this step is the modular business services determined in Step 3.

For the modelling of the goal tree, the goal and task concepts from the i* framework are used [11]. The top-level goal in the goal tree is the business service split into purposes and the subsequent actions. The left branch describes the functional requirements related to the purpose of business service execution. This purpose is broken down into *actions*, modelled as tasks. The second step is to create the right branch of the goal tree. For this branch, *the non-functional requirements* are elicited. The starting point for this branch is the management of the business service. The outcomes associated with this purpose are aligned with the *quality dependencies* as given in the SR model from Step 1. These outcomes in turn, are decomposed into actions. The output of this step is a goal model for each business service.

Application of Step 4: The PGO platform requirements per business service were identified by creating a goal tree for all three PGO-developed business services. The goal tree of the business service "Data preparation" is given in Fig. 7. Step-4 was developed to meet the first solution objective (DO1). Using the VP-BSIM outputs as inputs to this step ensured the desired value co-creation was considered throughout the process. Actions at the bottom of the goal tree can be traced back to the business services they support, and subsequently, the business services can be traced back to the desired co-created value. Therefore, traceability to the overall co-created value is established for every action. The template of the goal tree gave appropriate handles to elicit the requirements effectively. Moreover, eliciting the requirements per business service scoped the task of defining the requirements for a digital platform.

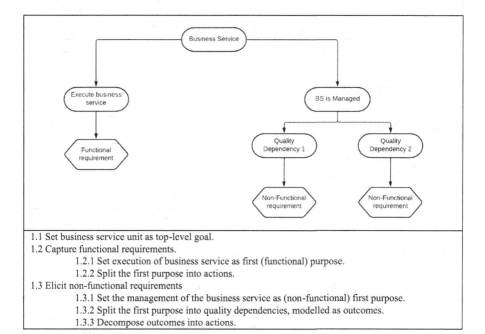

Fig. 6. Goal tree template adapted from [17].

Step 5: Assess Requirements with Current Digital Platform Based on Goal Achievement:
The goal of the fifth and last step is to assess the extent of fulfilment of the requirements by the deployed digital platform. For this, the qualitative and interactive evaluation method for goal-oriented models by Horkoff and Yu [18] is adapted. This step is executed as a workshop involving representatives of the actors of the service system (i.e., platform actors). Accordingly, the platform requirements modelled in a goal tree per business service (Step 4) are labelled by assessing the level of achievement of the goal by the current platform. The labels are provided in.

Table 1. This step is to be iterated for each goal tree. First, the participants label the tasks representing the requirements at the bottom of the goal tree. Next, the labels are propagated through the links to their corresponding actions, outcomes, or purposes. When one action, outcome, or purpose receives multiple labels (i.e., label bag), the rules in.

Table 1 are used to determine the final label. Some items may require further assessment per the rules (i.e., human judgement).

Table 1. Assessment labels and the propagation rules adapted from [18]

Assessment Labels					
Satisfied (Full)	Partially satisfied	Conflict	Unknown	Partially denied	Denied (Full)
✓	✓.	⌐	?	X.	X

Rules for Label Propagation	
Input	*Resulting label*
1. There is only one incoming label. Example: Only ✓.	The label Example: ✓.
2. incoming labels are full and of the same polarity. Example: { ✓ , ✓ }	The full label Example: ✓
3. All incoming labels are of the same polarity and a full label is present. Example: { X, X and X }	The full label Example: X
4. Labels are not all full or not of the same polarity. Example: { X. , ✓ , ⌐ }	Human judgement

With the completion of this step, all actions, outcomes, and purposes have a label indicating the degree to which they are fulfilled. The output of the method's final step is a goal tree with labels indicating the assessment result of the goal tree.

Application of Step 5: In this final step, the deployed digital platform was assessed with the newly elicited requirements represented in goal trees (provided at (tinyurl.com/2pt 62vuf). For this, a workshop was held with representatives from the three most important PGO platform actors. All actions were discussed, assessed and labelled one by one. Finally, the action labels in the model were propagated, resulting in labels for the entire goal tree. The labels that needed a human judgment were reassessed. During the discussions, the participants also discussed the possible improvements to the platform, i.e., how the platform can fully satisfy the requirements derived from this business service. Figure 7 shows the final goal tree, in which the top-level goal for the business service 'Data Preparation' was found to be partly satisfied by the current platform implementation. This step was incorporated to meet the second solution objective (DO2). Comparing the deployed digital framework with every action in the goal tree side by side enables the assessment of how the digital framework performs on every business service. The labels with their colours gave an efficient and logical overview of the performance of a digital platform on a certain business service.

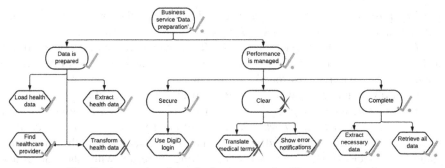

Fig. 7. Assessed goal tree for business service 'Data preparation'.

5   Method Evaluation

In this section, we present the evaluation findings according to our third solution objective (DO3). A focus group of four participants (Table 2) was organized to evaluate the method, following the guidelines in [19]. The method was evaluated according to the three criteria: usefulness, ease of use and the intention to use. The focus group was moderated by the first author of this paper and guided by open-ended questions that reflect the three evaluation criteria.

Table 2. Participants of the focus group

Participant	Stakeholder type	Function
1	Citizen	Intended platform user, the primary platform beneficiary
2	Healthcare provider	IT consultant, responsible for implementing PGOs at several mental health institutes in The Netherlands
3	PGO developer	Managing director, actively involved in the implementation of the Gezondheidsmeter
4	PGO developer	Project manager, responsible for communication with citizens using PGOs

Usefulness: Overall, the participants considered the method effective in reaching the goal of eliciting the requirements and assessing a deployed digital platform. The participants agree that the method would be useful to arrive at a consensus when not all stakeholders agree on certain decisions concerning a digital platform. A strength of the method is the clear visualization of the goal tree. The participants deemed the template of the goal tree easy to follow, meaning it gives appropriate handles to elicit the requirements per category. Moreover, it was found successful in capturing problems within the deployed digital platform. However, as the actors are not modelled in the goal trees, the participants found it difficult to trace who was responsible for assessing an action in Step 5.

Perceived Ease of Use: All participants agreed that the method was easy to use and understandable. Participant-3 stated: *"It took me a minute to fully understand it, but once I got the gist, it was very easy to use"*. They mentioned that the colours of the labels gave a good overview of the overall assessment of the goal trees. Moreover, the template of the goal tree was found easy to understand. The definition of the labels was not always found completely clear. Participant-3 mentioned this as a weakness: *"Sometimes we used an orange conflict label when we could also use a green partially satisfied label. The criteria for when to use what label was not completely clear to me."*. This issue was not considered a problem during the assessment, as the participants discussed the decision, but afterwards, when sharing the results with other parties that were not present at the assessment.

Intention to Use: Overall, the participants evaluated the method less positively with respect to this criterion than the other two. The participants found the method more suitable for the use of requirement engineers, who would use an elicitation and assessment tool in their work. However, participant-2 acknowledged the added value of the method by stating: *"I am charmed by the simplicity of the method."*

Based on the evaluation findings, two directions were identified for the improvement of the method: (1) *Establishing traceability between requirements by visualizing actor dependencies:* The lack of visualization of the actor dependencies in the goal trees resulting from Step-4 of the method was considered a limitation of the method. To improve the method, further extensions that allow visual traceability could be investigated, such as creating additional SD and SR diagrams or incorporating goal tree actions into specification models such as UML activity diagrams [17]. However, when considering this, the ease of use for users who are not experts in requirements engineering should not be forgotten, and method complexity should be avoided. (2) *Improvement of assessment labelling:* An evaluation finding was that some labels could be used interchangeably and cause communication issues when not documented. An additional documentation substep in Step 5.1 could improve the method on this aspect.

6   Conclusion and Future Work

In this paper, we proposed a method for the assessment of a digital platform based on the requirements identified from the desired value co-creation to be enabled by the platform. To develop the method, we adopted design science research and extended the VP-BSIM method by applying situational method engineering. We demonstrated the method by applying it for the assessment of a personal healthcare environment platform and evaluated the method in a focus group study.

The scientific implication of our study is establishing links between high level value co-creation concerns and low-level platform requirements by adopting a service system engineering approach. Our method encompasses the entire process for the assessment of a digital platform on the desired value co-creation. The practical implication of our research is the methodological guidelines provided for the practice of the platform development in which multi-actor design and value co-creation are central concerns.

Our research is subject to several limitations. In the evaluation, the focus group was limited to four attendees of three actor types. Another limitation is that our evaluation was based on a single instantiation of the method. Applying the method to multiple and different contexts and having more participants will provide more findings and evidence concerning the validity and utility of our method. Additionally, the intention to use could be evaluated more precisely when more requirements engineers are involved in the focus groups.

Future research would ideally investigate the improvement directions as stated above. Additionally, the method is intended for the assessment of a deployed digital platform. However, the method might also prove to be useful when a platform is yet to be designed, for example, in greenfield development, when one starts a business from scratch. The method might assist business developers in creating a platform that adheres to the intended value co-creation and involves all stakeholders in the development process. The method can also be applied to "from the scratch" platform development projects to evaluate if the method is indeed useful for these situations. Finally, future research can investigate incorporating the aspects of participatory and human-centred design methods [23] into the method for the enhancement of collaborative decision making.

References

1. Lusch, R.F., Nambisan, S.: Service innovation: a service-dominant logic perspective. MIS Q. **39**(1), 155–175 (2015). https://doi.org/10.25300/MISQ/2015/39.1.07
2. Adali, O.E., Ozkan, B., Turetken, O., Grefen, P.: Identification of service platform requirements from value propositions: a service systems engineering method. Presented at the PRO-VE, France (2021)
3. de Reuver, M., Sørensen, C., Basole, R.C.: The digital platform: a research agenda. J. Inf. Technol. **33**(2), 124–135 (2018). https://doi.org/10.1057/s41265-016-0033-3
4. Lessard, L., Amyot, D., Aswad, O., Mouttham, A.: Expanding the nature and scope of requirements for service systems through Service-Dominant Logic: the case of a telemonitoring service. Requirements Eng. **25**(3), 273–293 (2020). https://doi.org/10.1007/s00766-019-003 22-z
5. Blaschke, M., Haki, K., Aier, S., Winter, R.: Capabilities for digital platform survival: insights from a business-to-business digital platform, p. 17 (2018)
6. Laud, G., Bove, L., Ranaweera, C., Leo, W.W.C., Sweeney, J., Smith, S.: Value co-destruction: a typology of resource misintegration manifestations. J. Serv. Mark. **33**(7), 866–889 (2019). https://doi.org/10.1108/JSM-01-2019-0022
7. Haki, K., Blaschke, M., Aier, S., Winter, R.: A value co-creation perspective on information systems analysis and design. Bus. Inf. Syst. Eng. **61**(4), 487–502 (2019). https://doi.org/10. 1007/s12599-018-0557-x
8. Böhmann, T., Leimeister, J.M., Möslein, K.: Service systems engineering. Bus. Inf. Syst. Eng. **6**(2), 73–79 (2014). https://doi.org/10.1007/s12599-014-0314-8
9. Hevner, A.R., March, S.T., Park, J., Ram, S.: Design science in information systems research. MIS Q.**28**(1), 75 (2004). https://www.doi.org/10.2307/25148625
10. Peffers, K., Tuunanen, T., Rothenberger, M.A., Chatterjee, S.: A design science research methodology for information systems research. J. Manag. Inf. Syst. **24**(3), 45–77 (2007). https://doi.org/10.2753/MIS0742-1222240302
11. Yu, E.S.K. (ed.): Social Modeling for Requirements Engineering. MIT Press, Cambridge (2011)

12. Horkoff, J., et al.: Goal-oriented requirements engineering: an extended systematic mapping study. Requirements Eng **24**(2), 133–160 (2019). https://doi.org/10.1007/s00766-017-0280-z

13. Immonen, A., Ovaska, E., Kalaoja, J., Pakkala, D.: A service requirements engineering method for a digital service ecosystem. Serv. Oriented Comput. Appl. **10**(2), 151–172 (2016)

14. Davis, F.D.: Perceived usefulness, perceived ease of use, and user acceptance of information technology. MIS Q. **13**(3), 319 (1989). https://doi.org/10.2307/249008

15. Ralyté, J., Deneckère, R., Rolland, C.: Towards a generic model for situational method engineering. In: Eder, J., Missikoff, M. (eds.) Advanced Information Systems Engineering. CAiSE 2003. LNCS, vol. 2681, pp. 95–110. Springer, Heidelberg (2003). https://doi.org/10.1007/3-540-45017-3_9

16. Adali, O.E., Ozkan, B., Türetken, O., Gilsing, R.A., Grefen, P.: A method to transform value propositions of a service system into business services. Presented at the ECIS 2021, 2021.

17. Dubois, E., Kubicki, S., Ramel, S., Rifaut, A.: Capturing and aligning assurance requirements for business services systems. In: Ardagna, C.A., Damiani, E., Maciaszek, L.A., Missikoff, M., Parkin, M. (eds.) Business System Management and Engineering. LNCS, vol. 7350, pp. 71–92. Springer, Heidelberg (2012). https://doi.org/10.1007/978-3-642-32439-0_5

18. Horkoff, J., Yu, E.: Evaluating goal achievement in enterprise modeling–an interactive procedure and experiences. In: IFIP Working Conference on The Practice of Enterprise Modeling, pp. 145–160 (2009).

19. Tremblay, M.C., Hevner, A.R., Berndt, D.J.: The use of focus groups in design science research. In: Design Research in Information Systems, vol. 22, pp. 121–143. Springer, Boston (2010). https://doi.org/10.1007/978-1-4419-5653-8_10.

20. Turetken, O., Grefen, P., Gilsing, R., Adali, O.E.: Service-dominant business model design for digital innovation in smart mobility. Bus. Inf. Syst. Eng. **61**(1), 9–29 (2019). https://doi.org/10.1007/s12599-018-0565-x

21. Kohlborn, T., Korthaus, A., Chan, T., Rosemann, M.: Identification and analysis of business and software services—a consolidated approach. IEEE Trans. Serv. Comput. **2**(1), 50–64 (2009). https://doi.org/10.1109/TSC.2009.6

22. Lee, J., Muthig, D., Naab, M.: An approach for developing service oriented product lines. Limerick, Ireland, pp. 275–284, September 2008. https://doi.org/10.1109/SPLC.2008.34.

23. Freire, K., Sangiorgi, D., et al.: Service design and healthcare innovation: From consumption to co-production to co-creation. In: Service Design and Service Innovation Conference, pp. 39–50 (2010)

Assessing the Readiness of the Emerging Ecosystem (Actor) for the Pay-per-Outcome Business Model

Prasanna Kumar Kukkamalla[✉], Veli-Matti Uski, Olli Kuismanen, Hannu Kärkkäinen, and Karan Menon

Tampere University, Tampere, Finland
{prasanna.kukkamalla,veli-matti.uski,olli.kuismanen,
hannu.karkkainen,karan.menon}@tuni.fi

Abstract. This study analyses the readiness of an emerging ecosystem for Pay-per-Outcome (PPO) business model. We adopted a qualitative exploratory research approach to assess the readiness of firms (as an individual firm) and the emerging ecosystem in the Indoor Environment Quality (IEQ) industry. The maturity model was used to assess the readiness of emerging ecosystem and individual companies. The study identifies 11 critical dimensions in readiness from an emerging ecosystem perspective. We follow a 4-step process 1) Individual companies' current readiness level, 2) Individual companies' target level, 3) Emerging ecosystem's current readiness level, and 4) Emerging ecosystem's target level. This is the first of its kind to the best of our knowledge that studied the emerging ecosystem readiness for the PPO business model.

Keywords: Readiness assessment · Pay-per-Outcome · PPO · Business model · Emerging ecosystem · Indoor Environment Quality · Manufacturing · Maturity model

1 Introduction

Pay-per-Outcome (PPO) (customer pay for the achieved outcome or result) business models are gaining substantial attention from manufacturing industries and the academic community. Studies, for example [1–4] have discussed the economic and competitive advantages of these models. Due to the complexity (a collaboration between actors, activities and resources associated with the business portfolio) of these business models, any firm alone, cannot operationalise the service offering [5]. Operationalizing these business models involves key plans and activities which lead to a collaboration with other partners, possibly creating an alliance or network (Emerging ecosystem). The evolution and success of the ecosystem depend on the effective integration of actors based on their capabilities and skills. Prior to establishing an ecosystem firms need to assess their current level of readiness for a specific product or service offering.

© IFIP International Federation for Information Processing 2022
Published by Springer Nature Switzerland AG 2022
L. M. Camarinha-Matos et al. (Eds.): PRO-VE 2022, IFIP AICT 662, pp. 645–660, 2022.
https://doi.org/10.1007/978-3-031-14844-6_52

Several readiness assessment tools have been developed to assess the readiness of firms for a particular phase of transformation [6–8]. Even though studies [8, 10, 11] have discussed firms' readiness for Industry 4.0, digital transformation, circular economy, service design and business model emerging, the readiness of the emerging ecosystem (actors) to implement the PPO business model is not yet explored. To fill this gap, this study focused on four companies that have joined a firm ecosystem to offer Indoor Environment Quality (IEQ) as a service. IEQ [12] is defined as:

'A holistic concept, encompassing elements such as indoor lighting quality, acoustic comfort, and thermal comfort (temperature and relative humidity)'.

The indoor environment influences the health, well-being, and performance of the occupants [13]. A slight change in occupants' performance can produce a great impact on the operational cost of the company [14]. Studies [15, 16] have provided evidence on the impact of the indoor environment on an organisation's operational expenses. The rise in operational cost of building especially for good indoor environment quality maintenance pushes building maintenance companies to seek an alternative solution to keep the cost low. This situation has created an opportunity for IEQ companies to create a good indoor environment as a service than IEQ equipment sales without compromising indoor environment quality.

For this reason, the present study specifically focused IEQ industry to assess whether these companies are ready to adopt the PPO business model. We framed the following research question to solve above stated research gap:

RQ: How to assess the emerging ecosystem's readiness (through participant companies' readiness) to implement a Pay-per-outcome business model?

2   Theoretical Background

2.1   Readiness of Emerging Ecosystem

In recent years ecosystems have gained interest from the scientific community. The success of the company is not any more dependent on its internal capabilities but also on how well the company can acknowledge and utilize other actors within the ecosystem [9]. Even though all companies collaborate with other actors, a strategic ecosystem requires deeper collaboration with two or more companies [17]. Studies have discussed how well the ecosystem performs and how it should be developed [9].

Prior to establishing an ecosystem, firms need to assess partners' current level of readiness. The readiness of the ecosystem can be assessed through various models, e.g. a study [9] developed a readiness model with five main dimensions, Culture, Ecosystem, Operations, Governance and Strategy, which each is divided into 5–6 sub-dimensions, such as Digital Culture and Business and IT synergy. Other readiness assessment models for ecosystems have been developed for industries such as the software industry [9], construction industry [9] and logistics [18].

However, all these studies are focusing on the assessment of established ecosystem readiness rather than an emerging ecosystem. Moreover, the knowledge about the emerging ecosystem readiness and its actors' readiness assessment has not yet been revealed.

2.2 Pay-per-Outcome Business Model Readiness Analysis

Pay-per-X (PPX) business models, such as pay-per-use (PPU) and Pay-per-Outcome (PPO) business models have changed the logic of the equipment manufacturing companies' operations. PPO business model defined [1] as:

"a new business model of outcome-based contracts where the firm is tasked to achieve outcomes of equipment as a service contract instead of the traditional maintenance, repair and overhaul activities"

In the PPO business model, the customers don't own the equipment but pay for the value received from the usage of the equipment [19]. The change in ownership and responsibilities from the customer to the product/service provider creates extra responsibilities for the provider, which requires the development of new capabilities and partaking in new activities [20]. In this kind of situation, the self-diagnosing capabilities and skills of firms would minimise the risk of failure of these business models. Few readiness models have been developed to understand the development of complex systems such as business model transformation [21], product-service systems [6], Industry 4.0 [22] and smart manufacturing [23, 24].

3 Methodology

Our study implemented an embedded single case study [25] of the emerging ecosystem comprising four individual companies, engaged in the IEQ industry, to understand their current level of readiness to implement a PPO business model. Yin [25] indicates the use of case studies when the goal is to analyse contemporary events. Therefore, a case-based approach was conducted with a series of workshops to collect data for assessing a set of conditions for PPO business model readiness. Case selection followed a meticulous process where an emerging ecosystem targeting to implement and roll out a PPO business was selected. The case ecosystem used in this study operates in the construction and building operation industry, providing an Indoor Environment Quality as-a-Service. Four companies that have already acquired some of the required competencies for the business model transformation were analysed. A short description of the case companies is presented in Table 1.

Table 1. Case companies and participants' profile

Company	Description	Interviewee profile
C1	HVAC maintenance service provider	Chairman
C2	A technology company specializing in smart building automation	Chief operating officer
C3	An equipment manufacturing company specialising in intelligent and energy-efficient HVAC technology, air management solutions and fans for industrial processes	President and Business Director
C4	A consulting company specialising in construction, construction design, and community and environment design	Senior specialist

* HVAC: Heating, ventilation, and air conditioning

The research process was carried out in semi-structured interviews with the help of the PPX maturity model[1] which consists of 7 dimensions, 19 sub-dimensions, 5 maturity levels, and relevant boundary conditions (See Appendix). Each of the interviews was conducted using MS Teams and lasted 90 min. The interviewees were asked to analyse 1) the current PPO readiness of their company in the readiness model subdimensions and 2) the emerging ecosystem, and then 3) define target readiness levels for the ecosystem as well as 4) a target for their own company, as a part of the ecosystem. First, we explained the dimension of the readiness model and readiness levels. Then we asked participants to select appropriate statements that represent their current level (As an individual company) and emerging ecosystem. A set of the question was prepared to get participants' responses, for example, the question related to the business strategy dimension was framed like this:

Question:
Business strategy: Considering the business strategy for PPO business models, which of the following sentence best describes your company?

- *We have not defined any PPO business model strategy*
- *Business strategy for PPX business model(s) is experimented on, but strategic objectives are unclear, and decisions are reactive and ad hoc.*
- *Business strategy for PPO business model(s) is defined and documented*
- *PPO strategy is defined and continuously developed through denied key performance indicators*
- *PPO business strategy is fully integrated and vital part of the corporate strategy.*

---

[1] The maturity model (See Appendix) was adopted from the research paper *Pay-Per-X Business Models for Equipment Manufacturing Companies: A Maturity Model*. This paper is under review process. We will provide full citation details before the Pro-ve-2022 conference.

We also asked participants for their target level for each dimension as an individual company and an emerging ecosystem. Then these results were transferred into Excel sheets for analysis.

4   Results

The summary of the case companies' current and target readiness levels and emerging ecosystem current and target readiness levels for the PPO business model is presented in Table 2.

In the three subdimensions dealing with risk management, the majority of companies (C1, C2 and C3) were ranked between 3–4 for business risks, operational risks and cyber security risks. However, they ranked ecosystem readiness between 1–2. C4 ranked itself at level 5 for the cybersecurity risks dimension but ranked 1 for the ecosystem. The reason for the low level is explained by C4 as:

'…we don't have cyber security risk management because there are no protocols. On how we manage the data.'.

Company C2 ranked themselves as level 4 and C4 ranked themselves as level 2 in the business strategy dimension. Even though individually the companies ranked themselves high they believed that the ecosystem level was at 1.5 (Mean level). One manager from C4 expressed:

'….at least I haven't seen any documents or files that would tell how we work, how we work together, and how we will go on from this point.'

The majority of companies (C1, C2 and C3) ranked themselves between 3–4 levels in data analytics dimension but ranked lower level between 1–3 for the ecosystem. Company C1 ranked itself level 4 in data analysis and data utilization dimensions but ranked level 1 for the ecosystem. C1 expressed as:

'….we haven't done as an ecosystem. We haven't done any data analysis. We have buildings, but we haven't done it yet. There's no and then the data channel…, we haven't talked about it at all.'

For smart products and factory dimensions, C1 ranked 1 but 3 for ecosystem readiness.

C1 explained the reason for level 1 as:

'We don't produce machines. We produce services,…since we are not producing technology products..'

Concerning companies' readiness for connectivity, the majority of companies (C2, C3 and C4) ranked 3. Company C1 and C4 assessed the ecosystem at level 3. Regarding the companies' readiness for competence management, C1 and C3 ranked 3. C2, C3 and C4 ranked ecosystem at level 2. For smart product & factory dimensions, the majority

Table 2. Readiness assessment of companies and emerging ecosystem

Dimension	Subdimension	Case companies current level				Mean	Case companies target level				Mean	Emerging ecosystem current level (rating from case companies)				Mean	Emerging ecosystem target level (rating from case companies)				Mean
		C1	C2	C3	C4		C1	C2	C3	C4		C1	C2	C3	C4		C1	C2	C3	C4	
OG	Operational governance	2	2	3	2	2.25	4	3	4	3	3.5	3	1	1	1	1.5	4	3	5	3	3.75
	People governance	3	3	2	1	2.25	4	3	4	3	3.5	3	2	1	1	1.75	4	3	5	3	3.75
	Data & information governance	2	3	2	1	2	4	3	5	3	3.75	3	1	1	1	1.5	4	3	5	3	3.75
ST	Business strategy	3	4	3	2	3	4	5	5	4	4.5	1	2	2	1	1.5	4	5	5	3	4.25
	Resource allocation	3	3	2	2	2.5	4	3	4	4	3.75	2	2	1	2	1.75	4	3	4	4	3.75
	Strategic alignment	4	3	3	2	3	4	4	3	4	3.75	2	3	2	2	2.25	4	4	4	4	4
RM	Business risks	3	4	4	2	3.25	4	3	5	3	3.75	1	2	1	1	1.25	3	3	5	3	3.5
	Operational risks	3	3	4	2	3	4	3	4	3	3.5	1	2	1	1	1.25	3	3	4	3	3.25
	Cybersecurity risks	3	3	4	5	3.75	3	4	5	5	4.25	1	2	1	1	1.25	3	3	5	5	4
CC	Competences	3	2	3	2	2.5	4	4	4	3	3.75	3	2	2	2	2.25	4	4	4	3	3.75
	Culture	3	3	4	3	3.25	3	4	4	4	3.75	2	3	2	2	2.25	3	4	5	3	3.75
PLP	Beginning of life processes	3	3	3	2	2.75	4	4	5	4	4.25	2	2	1	2	1.75	4	4	5	3	4
	Middle of life processes	4	3	3	2	3	4	4	4	3	3.75	3	1	1	1	1.5	4	4	4	3	3.75
	End of life processes	2	3	1	2	2	3	3	3	4	3.25	2	1	1	2	1.5	3	3	3	4	3.25

(continued)

Table 2. (*continued*)

Dimension	Subdimension	Case companies current level				Mean	Case companies target level				Mean	Emerging ecosystem current level (rating from case companies)				Mean	Emerging ecosystem target level (rating from case companies)				Mean
		C1	C2	C3	C4		C1	C2	C3	C4		C1	C2	C3	C4		C1	C2	C3	C4	
PPT	Smart product & factory	1	3	3	3	2.5	1	4	5	4	3.5	3	2	3	3	2.75	4	4	5	4	4.25
	Connectivity	2	3	3	3	2.75	3	5	5	3	4	3	2	2	3	2.5	4	5	5	3	4.25
DA	Data access	4	3	3	2	3	4	3	5	3	3.75	3	2	1	2	2	4	3	5	3	3.75
	Data analysis	4	3	3	3	3.25	4	4	5	3	4	1	3	2	2	2	4	4	5	3	4
	Data utilization	4	2	3	2	2.75	4	3	5	3	3.75	1	2	1	2	1.5	3	3	5	3	3.5
Mean level						2.77					3.78					1.78					3.80

Dimensions: OG (Organizational Governance), ST (Strategy), RM (Risk Management), CC (Competences & Culture), PLP (Product Lifecycle processes), PPT (Product & Production Technology), DA (Data Analytics).

Levels: 1. Initial, 2. Experimenting, 3. Defined, 4. Advanced, 5. Optimized of companies (C2, C3 and C4) agreed that they were at level 3, whereas the majority of companies (C1, C3 and C4) ranked the ecosystem's current at level 3.

Regarding the mean level of readiness, 11 out of 19 readiness dimensions, such as Operational Governance, People Governance, Data & Information Governance, Business Strategy, Resource Allocation, Business Risks Operational Risks, Cybersecurity Risks, Middle Life Processes, End of Life Processes, and Data Utilization ranked below 2 (Table 2) for the emerging ecosystem.

Finally, it was observed from Table 2, the mean current level of readiness of individual companies was 2.77, and the ecosystem was 1.78. The mean level of companies' target was 3.78 and the emerging ecosystem target level was 3.80.

5 Discussion and Conclusions

Our study answered the research question *How to assess the emerging ecosystem's readiness (through participant companies' readiness) to implement a Pay-per-outcome business model?* by assessing the current level and target level of readiness of companies and ecosystem through the readiness assessment model.

The contribution of this study is three-fold. First, as per our knowledge, individual companies (within the ecosystem) readiness for PPO business model adaptation was not discussed in earlier studies. A study [26] focused on ecosystem readiness for blockchain technology adaptation. Another study [27] focused on industrial ecosystem readiness in the circular economy. A study [28] discussed readiness and maturity assessment for the industry 4.0 ecosystem was studied. However, the emerging ecosystem's readiness to adopt the PPO business model has not yet been addressed. Our study fulfils the research gap by assessing emerging ecosystem and individual companies' readiness for PPO business model adaptation in the IEQ industry. This is first of its kind study, in our knowledge that assesses the readiness of individual companies (within the ecosystem).

Second, few studies have discussed the readiness assessment process, for example, in a study [22] simulation models were employed to assess the readiness of manufacturing firms before and after Industry 4.0 implementation. In another study [29] Industry 4.0 readiness online self-check was used to assess the readiness of companies. The results were validated with companies in a workshop. But in our study, we followed 4 steps process to assess the readiness of the ecosystem. In the first step, we assess individual companies' current readiness levels. Then we assess individual companies' target levels. In the third step we assess the ecosystem's current readiness level, and then the ecosystem target level. By following this 4-step process we identify differences between the readiness level of induvial companies and their view on the current level of the emerging ecosystem. We identify the least and high ranked readiness levels from both individual companies and the ecosystem. These findings showed that the emerging ecosystem readiness is not the sum of individual companies' readiness for the PPO business model. For example, C3 ranked level 1 for an ecosystem for business risks, but they ranked themselves at level 4. A contradictory pattern was found in the smart product & factory subdimension. C1 ranked level 3 for the ecosystem but ranked level 1 for themselves. This kind of variation in levels indicates that even though individual companies' readiness is high, they believe that other partners in the emerging ecosystem's readiness is not high. One company expressed that they haven't seen any document or files that guides all partners on how to work together as an ecosystem. So, based on this study findings, it is reasonable to say that ecosystem PPO readiness is not the sum of individual companies' readiness for the PPO business model.

The 4-steps process helps companies to assess capabilities first from their perspective and then from the ecosystem perspective, which creates buy-in for their role in the ecosystem – that it's not "the others" who create the readiness of the emerging ecosystem.

Third, we identify dimensions that ranked low level and high level from emerging ecosystems and individual companies' perspectives. Eleven out of 19 readiness dimensions, such as Operational Governance, People Governance, Data & Information Governance, Business Strategy, Resource Allocation, Business Risks Operational Risks, Cybersecurity Risks, Middle Life Processes, End of Life Processes, and Data Utilization ranked below 2 levels (Table 2) from an emerging ecosystem perspective. No dimension was ranked at level 3 or above 3. This finding suggests that the emerging ecosystem is away from being ready for PPO business model adaptation. However, individual companies were ranked high in these 11 dimensions. The overall readiness for emerging ecosystem readiness can be levelled up by transferring the knowledge and skills across the ecosystem from an actor who is dominant in a specific dimension.

In the next step, we will use this study's findings to identify needed resources and skills and actors to establish an ecosystem to implement the PPO business model.

This study specifically focused on companies engaged in the IEQ industry, so this study's findings cannot be generalized to all types of industries. Another limitation is the phase of the emerging ecosystem. The ecosystem is not fully established, and the roles of actors are not defined. The research setting was another limitation, as we have assessed ecosystem readiness first from each case firm's perspective.

Appendix

Dimension	Subdimension	Maturity level				
		1. Initial	2. Experimenting	3. Defined	4. Advanced	5. Optimized
Organizational governance	Operational governance	No PPX-specific operational governance	Operational PPX architecture requirements identified with ad hoc implementation and development	Necessary operational PPX architecture requirements are documented and related governance measures are standardized	Operational PPX architecture requirements are defined and compliance is systematically monitored through related key performance indicators	Operational PPX governance is integrated across company with best practices in place
	People governance	No PPX-specific roles or responsibilities related to PPX business model(s) defined	Responsibilities related to PPX are identified with ad hoc implementation and development	Necessary roles and responsibilities for PPX business model(s) are documented, defined and systematically governed	PPX-related roles and responsibilities are defined with systematic performance monitoring through defined standards and key performance indicators	Roles and responsibilities related to PPX are optimized and defined with respect to all company activities
	Data & information governance	No set rules for PPX data & information governance	PPX data & information governance requirements are identified with ad hoc implementation and development	Necessary data governance requirements are documented and standardized, with data storage infrastructure defined in production	Data & information governance requirements are defined, with compliance systematically monitored and developed through defined key performance indicators	Data & information governance measures are optimized and integrated across company
Strategy	Business strategy	No defined business strategy for PPX business model(s)	Strategy for PPX business model(s) is experimental with ad hoc implementation and development	Strategy for PPX business model(s) is defined and documented	PPX is strategy is defined and continuously developed through defined key performance indicators	PPX business strategy is fully developed and integral part of the corporate strategy

(continued)

(continued)

Dimension	Subdimension	Maturity level				
		1. Initial	2. Experimenting	3. Defined	4. Advanced	5. Optimized
	Resource allocation	No plan for allocating resources towards PPX business model(s)	Basic PPX resource requirements are identified with ad hoc assignment	Procedures for allocating resources towards PPX business model(s) are standardized, allowing systematic resource allocation for specific PPX activities	PPX resource requirements are identified and documented across company, allowing systematic resource management and prioritization at an organizational level	PPX resource allocation follows best practices and is optimized across company
	Strategic alignment	No strategic alignment between PPX and other strategic objectives	Limited understanding of PPX and its relationship to other strategic objectives with ad hoc alignment practices	Strategic understanding and objectives are shared between relevant business	Strategic objectives are shared across company with compliance and performance monitored through common key performance indicators	Full strategic alignment allowing optimization and development of common strategic goals across company
Risk management	Business risks	No PPX-related business risk management	PPX-related business risks are acknowledged with ad hoc management practices	PPX-related business risk are documented, with systematic and defined risk management practices in place	PPX-related business risk management is systematic and monitored, allowing predictive risk management	PPX-related business risk management is proactive, with continuous improvement and optimization of risk management practices
	Operational risks	No PPX-related operational risk management	PPX-related operational risks are acknowledged with ad hoc management practices	PPX-related operational risk are documented, with systematic and defined risk management practices in place	PPX-related operational risk management is systematic and monitored, allowing predictive risk management	PPX-related operational risk management is proactive, with continuous improvement and optimization of risk management practices

(continued)

(continued)

Dimension	Subdimension	Maturity level				
		1. Initial	2. Experimenting	3. Defined	4. Advanced	5. Optimized
	Cybersecurity risks	No PPX-related cybersecurity risk management	PPX-related cybersecurity risks are acknowledged, with ad hoc management practices	PPX-related cybersecurity risk are documented, with systematic and defined risk management practices in place	PPX-related cybersecurity risk management is systematic and monitored, allowing predictive risk management	PPX-related cybersecurity risk management is proactive, with continuous improvement and optimization of risk management practices
Competences & culture	Competences	No identified any PPX-related competences	PPX-related competences are acknowledged with ad hoc acquisition	Basic PPX-related competence requirements are defined and documented, allowing systematic competence acquisition	PPX-related competences are acquired as well as developed systematically	All PPX-related competences can be acquired and managed proactively
	Culture	Culture is product-oriented, with no cooperation between different business units	Organizational culture supports experimentation with limited & ad hoc cooperation between some business units	Organizational culture supports innovation and is open towards PPX, with frequent collaboration between some business units	Organizational culture is committed to PPX business model(s) with common incentives, with frequent collaboration across all related business units	Organizational culture fully supports PPX, with complete trust and open communication at all organizational levels and relevant business units
Product lifecycle processes	Beginning of life processes	No identified beginning of life processes for PPX business model(s)	PPX-related beginning of life processes are identified with ad hoc implementation	PPX-related beginning of life processes are defined and systematically implemented for specific project(s)	PPX-related beginning of life processes are defined and implemented across company with systematic management through defined metrics	PPX-related beginning of life processes are optimized and continuously improved across company

(continued)

(continued)

Dimension	Subdimension	Maturity level				
		1. Initial	2. Experimenting	3. Defined	4. Advanced	5. Optimized
	Middle of life processes	No identified middle of life processes for PPX business model(s)	PPX-related middle of life processes are identified with ad hoc implementation	PPX-related middle of life processes are defined and systematically implemented for specific project(s)	PPX-related middle of life processes are defined and implemented across company with systematic management through defined metrics	PPX-related middle of life processes are optimized and continuously improved across company
	End of life processes	No identified end of life processes for PPX business model(s)	PPX-related end of life processes are identified with ad hoc implementation	PPX-related end of life processes are defined and systematically implemented for specific project(s)	PPX-related end of life processes are defined and implemented across company, with systematic management through defined metrics	PPX-related end of life processes are optimized and continuously improved across company
Product & production technology	Smart product & factory	No machine data collection capabilities for PPX business model(s)	PPX data collection capabilities are tested in machine(s), allowing contract-specific, ad hoc data collection from customer(s)	PPX data collection technologies are standardized, with systematic data collection from customer machine	PPX data collection capabilities is integrated in all machines, with performance monitored through defined key performance indicators	Production technology fully supports data-based products for PPX, with performance optimized through cost minimization and efficiency
	Connectivity	No connectivity between machines or production processes for PPX business model(s)	PPX product- and production-related connectivity technologies are experimental and non-standardized	PPX product- and production-related connectivity technologies are standardized and we have access to customer(s)' machine	PPX product- and production-related connectivity technologies are standardized and monitored through defined quality control measurements for development needs	PPX product- and production-related connectivity technologies are optimized and continuously improved, allowing 2-way/remote connection and control of machines

(continued)

(continued)

Dimension	Subdimension	Maturity level				
		1. Initial	2. Experimenting	3. Defined	4. Advanced	5. Optimized
Data analytics	Data access	No access to PPX data	PPX data is identified, but siloed and accessed manually & ad hoc	PPX data is defined, enabling continous data flow and basic automation with online access	PPX data is systematically accessed, with related key performance indicators defined and utilized in quality control	All PPX data can be accessed, with cost-efficient, high-performing and optimized best practices in place
	Data analysis	No PPX data analysis	PPX data analysis is unstructured, allowing descriptive analysis and basic monitoring	PPX data analysis capabilities are defined, enabling diagnostic analysis & recommendations and manual machine tuning	PPX data analysis is systematic and predictive, with performance monitored through defined key performance indicators	PPX data analysis is prescriptive/self-learning, with automation and self-adjusting capabilities
	Data utilization	PPX data not utilized in decision-making	PPX data utilized for awareness purposes in basic reporting with ad hoc utilization in decision-making	PPX data established as an asset and utilized to support decision-making	PPX data utilzied broadly in the development of overall company strategy, with performance monitored through defined key performance indicators	PPX data is considered as central to company strategy and operations development

References

1. Ng, I.C.L., Ding, D.X., Yip, N.: Outcome-based contracts as new business model: the role of partnership and value-driven relational assets. Ind. Mark. Manag. **42**, 730–743 (2013). https://doi.org/10.1016/j.indmarman.2013.05.009
2. Visnjic, I., Jovanovic, M., Neely, A., Engwall, M.: What brings the value to outcome-based contract providers? Value drivers in outcome business models. Int. J. Prod. Econ. **192**, 169–181 (2017). https://doi.org/10.1016/j.ijpe.2016.12.008
3. Grubic, T., Jennions, I.: Do outcome-based contracts exist? The investigation of power-by-the-hour and similar result-oriented cases. Int. J. Prod. Econ. **206**, 209–219 (2018). https://doi.org/10.1016/j.ijpe.2018.10.004
4. Sjödin, D., Parida, V., Jovanovic, M., Visnjic, I.: Value creation and value capture alignment in business model innovation: a process view on outcome-based business models. J. Prod. Innov. Manag. **37**, 158–183 (2020). https://doi.org/10.1111/jpim.12516
5. Snihur, Y., Tarzijan, J.: Managing complexity in a multi-business-model organization. Long Range Plann. **51**, 50–63 (2018). https://doi.org/10.1016/j.lrp.2017.06.010
6. Neff, A.A., Hamel, F., Herz, T.P., Uebernickel, F., Brenner, W., vom Brocke, J.: Developing a maturity model for service systems in heavy equipment manufacturing enterprises. Inf. Manag. **51**, 895–911 (2014). https://doi.org/10.1016/j.im.2014.05.001
7. Balasubramanian, S., Shukla, V., Sethi, J.S., Islam, N., Saloum, R.: A readiness assessment framework for Blockchain adoption: a healthcare case study. Technol. Forecast. Soc. Change. **165**, 120536 (2021). https://doi.org/10.1016/j.techfore.2020.120536
8. Schroderus, J., Lasrado, L.A., Menon, K., Kärkkäinen, H.: Towards a pay-per-X maturity model for equipment manufacturing companies. Procedia Comput. Sci. **196**, 226–234 (2022). https://doi.org/10.1016/j.procs.2021.12.009
9. Gökalp, E., Martinez, V.: Digital transformation maturity assessment: development of the digital transformation capability maturity model. Int. J. Prod. Res., 1–21 (2021). https://doi.org/10.1080/00207543.2021.1991020
10. Aboelmaged, M.G.: Predicting e-readiness at firm-level: an analysis of technological, organizational and environmental (TOE) effects on e-maintenance readiness in manufacturing firms. Int. J. Inf. Manage. **34**, 639–651 (2014). https://doi.org/10.1016/j.ijinfomgt.2014.05.002
11. Teso, G., Walters, A.: Assessing manufacturing SMEs' readiness to implement service design. Procedia CIRP **47**, 90–95 (2016). https://doi.org/10.1016/j.procir.2016.03.063
12. Tiele, A., Esfahani, S., Covington, J.: Design and development of a low-cost, portable monitoring device for indoor environment quality. J. Sens. **2018**, 1–14 (2018). https://doi.org/10.1155/2018/5353816
13. Mendell, M.J., et al.: Improving the health of workers in indoor environments: priority research needs for a national occupational research agenda. Am. J. Public Health **92**, 1430–1440 (2002). https://doi.org/10.2105/AJPH.92.9.1430
14. Al Horr, Y., Arif, M., Kaushik, A., Mazroei, A., Katafygiotou, M., Elsarrag, E.: Occupant productivity and office indoor environment quality: a review of the literature. Build. Environ. **105**, 369–389 (2016). https://doi.org/10.1016/j.buildenv.2016.06.001
15. Feige, A., Wallbaum, H., Janser, M., Windlinger, L.: Impact of sustainable office buildings on occupant's comfort and productivity. J. Corp. Real Estate **15**, 7–34 (2013). https://doi.org/10.1108/JCRE-01-2013-0004
16. Heerwagen, J.: Green buildings, organizational success and occupant productivity. Build. Res. Inf. **28**, 353–367 (2000). https://doi.org/10.1080/096132100418500
17. Paulus-Rohmer, D., Schatton, H., Bauernhansl, T.: Ecosystems, strategy and business models in the age of digitization - how the manufacturing industry is going to change its logic. Procedia CIRP **57**, 8–13 (2016). https://doi.org/10.1016/j.procir.2016.11.003

18. Leal, A.G., dos Santos, A.S., Miyake, M.Y., Marte, C.L.: Assessment of maturity and efficacy of Toll Collection Ecosystems. In: 16th International IEEE Conference on Intelligent Transportation Systems (ITSC 2013), pp. 523–528. IEEE (2013). https://doi.org/10.1109/ITSC.2013.6728284

19. Uski, V.-M., et al.: Review of PPX business models: adaptability and feasibility of PPX models in the equipment manufacturing industry. In: IFIP Advances in Information and Communication Technology, pp. 358–372. Springer, Cham (2022). https://doi.org/10.1007/978-3-030-94335-6_26

20. Uuskoski, M., Menon, K., Kärkkäinen, H., Koskinen, K.: Perceived risks and benefits of advanced pay-per-use type of business models based on Industry 4.0 enabled technologies in manufacturing companies. In: Chiabert, P., Bouras, A., Noël, F., Ríos, J. (eds.) PLM 2018. IAICT, vol. 540, pp. 498–507. Springer, Cham (2018). https://doi.org/10.1007/978-3-030-01614-2_46

21. Poandl, E.M., Vorbach, S., Müller, C.: A maturity assessment for the business model of startups. In: The International Society for Professional Innovation Management (ISPIM), pp. 1–9 (2019)

22. Mohammad, E., Albarakah, L., Kudair, S., Karaman, A.S.: Evaluating the Industry 4.0 readiness of manufacturing companies: a case study in Kuwait. In: Proceedings of the 11th International Conference on Industrial Engineering and Operations Management, pp. 6625–6636 (2021)

23. Jayasekara, D., Pawar, K., Ratchev, S.: A framework to assess readiness of firms for cloud manufacturing. In: Proceedings - 2019 IEEE International Conference on Engineering, Technology and Innovation ICE/ITMC 2019 (2019). https://doi.org/10.1109/ICE.2019.879 2648

24. Sheen, D.P., Yang, Y.: Assessment of readiness for smart manufacturing and innovation in Korea. In: 2018 IEEE Technology and Engineering Management Conference TEMSCON 2018, pp. 11–15 (2018). https://doi.org/10.1109/TEMSCON.2018.8488424

25. Yin, R.K.: Case Study Research: Design and Methods. SAGE, Thousand Oaks (2014)

26. Lustenberger, M., Malešević, S., Spychiger, F.: Ecosystem readiness: blockchain adoption is driven externally. Front. Blockchain **4** (2021). https://doi.org/10.3389/fbloc.2021.720454

27. Parida, V., Burström, T., Visnjic, I., Wincent, J.: Orchestrating industrial ecosystem in circular economy: a two-stage transformation model for large manufacturing companies. J. Bus. Res. **101**, 715–725 (2019). https://doi.org/10.1016/j.jbusres.2019.01.006

28. Govindasamy, A., Arularasan, A.: Readiness and maturity assessment model to measure the Industry 4.0 ecosystem. In: Kannan, R.J., Geetha, S., Sashikumar, S., Diver, C. (eds.) International Virtual Conference on Industry 4.0. LNEE, vol. 355, pp. 57–67. Springer, Singapore (2021). https://doi.org/10.1007/978-981-16-1244-2_5

29. Machado, C.G., Winroth, M., Almström, P., Ericson Öberg, A., Kurdve, M., AlMashalah, S.: Digital organisational readiness: experiences from manufacturing companies. J. Manuf. Technol. Manag. **32**, 167–182 (2021). https://doi.org/10.1108/JMTM-05-2019-0188

Sociotechnical Strategies
in Collaborative Systems

Collaborative Networks and Sustainability in Education 4.0: An Approach to Achieve Complex Thinking Competencies in Higher Education

Jhonattan Miranda[1][(✉)], María Soledad Ramírez-Montoya[2],
Edgar O. López-Caudana[2], Yesica Escalera-Matamoros[3], and Arturo Molina[1]

[1] School of Engineering and Sciences, Tecnologico de Monterrey, Mexico City, Mexico
{jhonattan.miranda,armolina}@tec.mx
[2] Institute for the Future of Education, Tecnologico de Monterrey, Monterrey, N.L., Mexico
{solramirez,edlopez}@tec.mx
[3] Facultad de Arquitectura, Centro de Investigaciones de Diseño Industrial, Universidad Nacional Autonoma de Mexico, Mexico City, Mexico
yesica.escalera@cidi.unam.mx

Abstract. Today, collaborative networks are considered one of the critical elements that shape Education 4.0 in higher education. They are necessary to connect, cooperate, and collaborate with key external stakeholders during training and co-creation processes. Students use them to be immersed in real-world scenarios with complex environments. Consequently, Higher Education Institutions are relevant and critical in promoting and designing these collaborations where students can train and acquire desirable competencies. In this work, the competencies for complex thinking have been adopted in students' training to include specific transversal and disciplinary competencies and encourage the development of sustainable systems. Therefore, key stakeholders must foster sustainability in design processes through collaborative networks. We present two case studies involving collaborative networks and sustainability in this work.

Keywords: Collaborative networks · Sustainability · Education 4.0 · Complex thinking · Higher education · Educational innovation

1 Introduction

Collaborative Networks (CNs) are a strategic driver for confronting current challenges in higher education because they stimulate collective actions to leverage operational advantages, sharing or using complementary human, technological, and knowledge resources. Currently, collaborative activities between internal and external actors are critical to performing training and co-creations that are necessary within the framework of Education 4.0, which seeks to implement Industry 4.0 technologies to improve or create systems in education [1]. Therefore, through new active teaching-learning methods, cutting-edge

© IFIP International Federation for Information Processing 2022
Published by Springer Nature Switzerland AG 2022
L. M. Camarinha-Matos et al. (Eds.): PRO-VE 2022, IFIP AICT 662, pp. 663–674, 2022.
https://doi.org/10.1007/978-3-031-14844-6_53

infrastructure incorporating physical, virtual, and cyber-physical systems, and the participation of key internal and external stakeholders, the students can be trained in the current-profile competencies required for the 21st-century student [1].

In this sense, Higher Education Institutions (HEIs) are challenged to play a relevant role in preparing the new generation of professionals to be highly competitive in their professional lives. Therefore, in this work, complex thinking has been adopted as a meta-competency for students. Complex thinking comprises a set of transversal and disciplinary competencies such as critical, systemic, creative, innovative, and scientific thinking that improve students' decision-making processes and competitive performance in their professions [2]. Also, these competencies allow students to carry out research, design, and creation activities and develop sustainable solutions.

Consequently, new teaching-learning activities, resources, and dynamics have emerged to guide teachers and academicians in resolving current challenges in higher education. Then, students must get involved in real-world problems to train desirable competencies. In this context, there is evidence that universities are one of the main promoters of the development of sustainable solutions and through active teaching-learning techniques, it is possible to integrate external stakeholders to strengthen co-creation processes through CNs [3].

In this work, we seek to provide a new reference framework for the design of teaching-learning systems that is based on the components of Education 4.0, with a special emphasis on the components of sustainability and stakeholders. With this reference framework, it is sought to answer if with the resulted education systems (product, process, and infrastructure) it is possible to scale in the training of the complex thinking competencies. For this reason, this work presents CNs and sustainability as critical elements to consider in emerging teaching-learning systems designed within the Framework of Education 4.0.

The rest of this paper is structured as follows: In Sect. 2, the current challenges in higher education and the core components of Education 4.0 are presented. Section 3 shows the relevance of CNs and sustainability in the framework of Education 4.0 today. Section 4 presents the conceptual framework of this work applied in higher education. In Sect. 5, two case studies illustrate how the presented concepts can be practiced. Finally, conclusions are presented in Sect. 6.

2 Education 4.0: Challenges and Core Components

Challenges in higher education continuously emerge in various ways at different moments because educational processes are dynamic and multidimensional (cognitive, emotional, technological, and social) [4]. Thus, social phenomena, technological advances, and megatrends affect current processes and set the agenda for a specific and crucial discussion in the next few years. However, significant challenges have been identified as higher education priorities, highlighting the need to provide quality and accessible education for all. Several authors have presented education challenges on the agenda of many institutions and organisations worldwide today [5, 6].

Additionally, the disruption caused by the COVID-19 pandemic has led to considerable adverse effects that have caused the gap to become even more prominent in several dimensions. Consequently, the challenges are more complex due to the immediate attention they demand [7].

The pandemic triggered the urgency to improve processes, models, infrastructure, and accessibility to carry out the desired operations to achieve quality education for all. The challenges described in this work are framed within Education 4.0. According to Miranda et al. (2021), *"Education 4.0 is the current period in which higher education institutions apply new learning methods, innovative didactic, management tools innovative didactic and sustainable infrastructures complemented mainly by new and emerging ICT, to enhance the processes of knowledge generation and information transfer. The combination of these resources during the teaching-learning processes will support the formation and development of critical competencies desirable in today's students."* [8].

2.1 Challenges in Higher Education

In this work, six critical challenges are linked to the concept of Education 4.0. It is sought through Education 4.0 to reduce and mitigate challenges and provide pending solutions to them. Below are these six challenges:

(i)   **Train the new generation of professionals to acquire complex thinking competencies.** Complex thinking has been identified as a core competency because it comprises desired transversal and disciplinary competencies to be trained in today's students [2]. These competencies encourage students to react highly competitively to complex events, make better decisions, and participate in collaborative environments.

(ii) **Engage students through active teaching-learning methods.** The lack of students' attention during their training sessions and intrinsic motivation to participate actively in the teaching-learning processes of formal courses has been a challenging issue that institutions seek to mitigate.

(iii) **Strengthen the digital transformation in higher education.** The step towards digital transformation in the era of Technologies 4.0 entails significant challenges requiring the attention and collaboration of various actors. These include participants from government, companies, academia and society because solving digital education challenges demands incorporating technological infrastructure, trained personnel, and appropriate dynamics to efficiently carry out the teaching-learning processes. But digital transformation is not only an issue at the institutional level but also at the level where individuals, teachers, students, and collaborators closely connect due to the need to have, operate, and implement technologies.

(iv) **Provide access to adequate infrastructure and initiatives that reduce or eliminate the digital divide.** Access to good infrastructure during teaching-learning processes is a significant challenge addressed in different dimensions, by different actors, and in various social and demographic contexts. However, It is reported today that many institutions lack adequate facilities and have limited services. Also, facilities that promote collaborative work must have innovative furniture, connected tools, and other educational and didactic resources. The pandemic led to remote activities in asynchronous and synchronous formats and included technologies such as hologram-teacher, remote laboratories, virtual classrooms, cyber-physical classrooms, and hybrid classrooms. However, access to infrastructure must also be considered at the individual level because remote work tools are necessary to access essential services that allow computer and mobile device connectivity. Many problems involve families' low income, geographical areas, and digital lag.

(v) **Encourage collaborative networking and partnership.** CNs with leading stakeholders are strategic for cooperation and collaboration on projects. Also, they are excellent platforms to immerse the students into real-life problems in teaching-learning and co-creation processes. Strategies such as Open Innovation and Triple/Quadruple Helix have been widely used to promote and facilitate co-design and co-creation processes [9]. In addition, thanks to the incorporation of 4.0 Technologies, it has been possible to improve communication and remote collaborative work. The external actors specialising in specific themes complement the most active teaching-learning processes and are more immersive to real-world environments.

(vi) **Promote sustainable development to achieve quality education, equity, inclusion, and attention.** The path toward a sustainable society is part of the 2030 plan of various institutions, organisations, and governments. They look to the UN Sustainable Development Goals (SDGs) to achieve this [10]. In addition, the dynamic world in which we live demands incorporating creative and innovative solutions and immediate reactions. Therefore, the new generation of professionals trained in HEIs must promote affordable, replicable, and sustainable solutions that positively impact society. For this, HEIs are challenged to provide a universal education of quality, equity, and inclusion. Efforts must be focused here.

2.2 Core Components of Education 4.0

To provide creative, innovative, and sustainable solutions that help close the digital gap and address the priority challenges outlined in this work, it is propose using the Education Framework 4.0 to provide a plurality of solutions [1]. It will allow us to evaluate that the designed and implemented programs contain desirable components in current training programs. Miranda et al. (2021) determined four core components to consider in implementing and designing teaching-learning systems within Education 4.0 [8]. In this work, six core components are considered, and they are described below:

(i) Competencies: train critical competencies for the 21st-century challenges, (ii) Teaching-learning processes: apply active teaching-learning methods and formats in different delivery modalities, (iii) 4.0 Technologies: Use emerging technologies to enable teaching-learning processes (iv) Infrastructure: provide adequate infrastructures such as innovative facilities, services, and systems to improve training processes, (v) Stakeholders: due to the relevance of using CN within the student training processes and the participation of leading actors from government, companies, academia, and society, and (vi) Sustainability: one of the purposes of Education 4.0 is to provide access to quality, affordable, sustainable education with high social impact. To achieve this, collaborators must design ad-hoc teaching-learning systems characterised by social, economic, and environmental sustainability (Fig. 1).

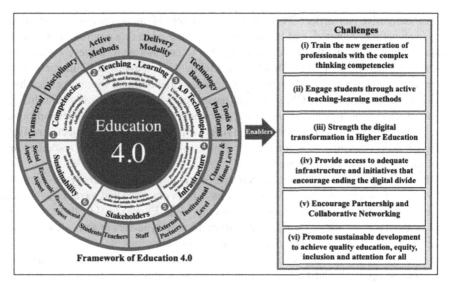

Fig. 1. Education 4.0 as enablers to provide solutions to the challenges facing Higher Education today

3 Collaborative Networks and Sustainability in Education 4.0

Since the participation of key stakeholders is considered a core component of Education 4.0, CNs are necessary today in the training processes of students since they stimulate the co-creation of solutions with strategies and actors and promote the students' immersion in real-world settings. These interactions, complemented with tools and teaching-learning processes, are necessary for training the competencies that shape complex thinking. These dynamics will be positively reflected in the analysis, research, and design techniques and the development of solutions for societal demands. Therefore, this section addresses the CN as a strategy to be implemented in today's higher education and the ad hoc designs for sustainable solutions.

3.1 Collaborative Networks in Education 4.0

Because Education 4.0 relies on the strategic participation of internal and external stakeholders, training programs and projects must be designed that stimulate their collaboration, resulting in collaborative projects that resolve real-world problems. Various partnerships and CNs can be accommodated as part of the teaching-learning dynamics in the student's training that involves them in complex environments. These also place them in scenarios to apply their learning in practice, using emerging technology tools to participate in co-creation activities. That is why today's CNs are considered a strategy in emerging teaching-learning programs.

Collaborative Networks (CNs) "consist of a variety of entities that are autonomous, geographically distributed, and heterogeneous in their operating environment, culture, social capital and goals that have come together to collaborate to achieve better, common, or compatible goals" [9]. Thanks to 4.0 Technologies, today's CN interactions are supported mainly by ICTs, allowing close, flexible collaborations without geographical restrictions. Consequently, CN strategies have high potential as drivers of value co-creation, sharing resources and knowledge, combining complementary skills and capacities, and even sharing responsibilities and risks [11]. Thus, academic projects involving CNs generate disruptive teaching-learning processes and leverage the resources and infrastructure of strategic stakeholders.

Historically, collaborations between university-university, university-government, university-company, and university-society have been practices that have brought great benefits and results to the academic community. With Education 4.0, these practices take on even greater relevance and benefit from the new dynamics in active learning and technologies as all these collaborators participate in joint projects.

It is necessary to promote complex thinking competencies so that students can make decisions to apply the best physical/digital resources and create innovative and sustainable solutions to current and future problems. Therefore, higher education has the challenge of enabling spaces where students have direct contact with complex scenarios of the real world, either through emulating those scenarios or becoming involved in real situations where the participation of external stakeholders is relevant to achieving solutions.

That is why CNs have been considered a pivotal strategy to accompany the core processes in Higher Education: (i) knowledge generation, (ii) information and knowledge transfer, and (iii) managerial processes.

Therefore, the different types of CNs have been considered and are in force today in the teaching-learning processes. They should be used within the framework of Education 4.0: (i) Goal-Oriented CNs, (ii) CN Breeding Environments, (iii) Interplay of multiple CNs, and (iv) Hybridisation of cognition and resilience.

Today, some activities are powered by 4.0 Technologies, allowing collaborations to be increasingly close, accessible, and without geographical restrictions. In addition, other approaches include citizen science, which encourages society's participation in academic programs and projects. Another trending example is CNs with Open Education strategies. All of which are excellent instruments in university programs and lifelong learning programs.

3.2 Sustainability in Education 4.0

The literature has documented that the teaching-learning systems based on Education 4.0 have provided significant benefits to society and allow us to obtain systems that are increasingly efficient, agile, personalised, and affordable [12]. Moreover, sustainability is a relevant domain in educational systems design. Sustainability in education seeks not only to generate a positive social effect but also to improve profitability and be eco-friendly. This has allowed sustainability's impact to be positive and scalable to reach larger audiences and produce even more positive effects. For this, Technologies 4.0 in education have played a critical role in developing new products, services, and platforms. Therefore it is a desirable component with two primary purposes (i) to promote collaboration through online real-time cloud platforms and (ii) to promote the co-creation of new products and services. Therefore, today, 4.0 Technologies in education can be considered enablers of sustainability.

Sustainability is closely related to new product development processes that are ethical as well as operationally robust. It is conceived multidimensionally in environmental, social and economic aspects, also known as the triple bottom line of sustainability [13].

In this context arises the term "sustainable development." It can be understood under the umbrella of the three aspects (social, economic, and environmental). In 1987, sustainable development was defined for the first time as "development that meets the needs of the present without compromising the ability of future generations to meet their own needs" [14]. In this sense, there are initiatives promulgated by the UN as Sustainable Development Goals (SDGs).

4   Conceptual Framework Applied in Higher Education

In the context presented, the concepts and components are then integrated into a conceptual framework that incorporates sustainability and value that seeks new solutions with positive social, economic, and environmental effects. The conceptual framework proposed in this document is oriented around research in the design of new products and the known concepts of Education 4.0, so the constructions that support the development of this framework are identified from the existing literature. The proposed framework has the purpose of guiding designers during the design and development of new didactic products, teaching-learning processes, and educational infrastructure through the generation of generic, partial, and particular models. The framework is further developed in iterations based on known tools and techniques that foster sustainability and collaborative networks.

Therefore, it is desirable to consider practices that stimulate the development of sustainable products-services in co-creation processes. This signifies ad-hoc designs for sustainability and applied tools such as DfX (Sustainability and Environment), Life Cycle Assessment, eco-design, and sustainability taxonomy.

Once the contextual problem/challenge/opportunity has been identified and addressed, it is necessary to build a teaching-learning process using CNs with the components of Education 4.0 as the primary enablers.

Finally, the expected result is to yield (i) knowledge generation and information transfer, (ii) co-design and co-creation, (iii) new products and services, (iv) technology transfer, and (v) entrepreneurship and enterprise creation. Figure 2 shows the Conceptual Framework of CNs and Sustainability applied in higher education (See Fig. 2).

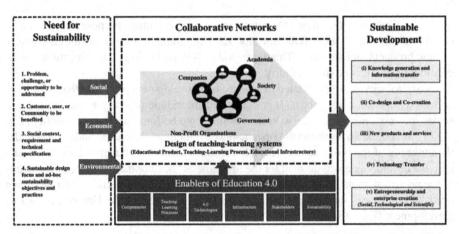

Fig. 2. Conceptual Framework of Collaborative Networks and Sustainability applied in Higher Education

5   Two Case Studies

Historically, the collaboration among academicians from different universities has led to the development of internships and exchanges in academic and industrial fields. However, today relevant efforts to promote shared value, risk, and responsibility, co-creation through multi-disciplinary and interdisciplinary projects, and shared goals and purposes. These are powered by current technologies that make communication, relationship, and process control even closer; they are considered different from before. In this work, two cases are presented where CNs and Sustainability are implemented in the framework of complex thinking. This section offers one case for sharing knowledge and product design and a second for designing training programs, both considering Education 4.0.

5.1   Didactic Product Development: Multifunctional Machine-Tool

This case study presents the co-design and co-creation of a didactic product developed between researchers and students from various disciplines of Tecnologico de Monterrey and UNAM. In addition, key stakeholders such as technological partners and primary and secondary users of various public and private institutions participated in the co-creation dynamics. The main objective of this CN was to scale the level of maturity of a new product and bring it to market through technology transfer or a venture. This project was within the framework of a collaboration called a "research, technology transfer, and entrepreneurship consortium," through which both institutions shared responsibilities and commitments. Figure 3 summarises the process carried out among the actors involved (See Fig. 3).

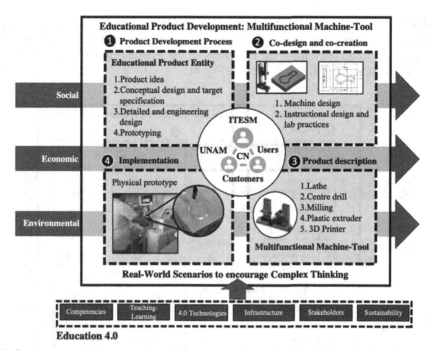

Fig. 3. Summary of the process carried out among the actors involved in the didactic product development: Multifunctional Machine-Tool

The developed product was didactic and aimed to pursue the desirable dynamics of Education 4.0 and include training complex thinking competencies in Industry 4.0. The system designed was a numerical control multifunctional machine tool with three main characteristics: (i) it is *small*; its dimensions were reduced for easy transport, and it did not require secondary installations; (ii) it is *reconfigurable*; its physical and software parts can be reconfigured to offer different manufacturing processes (milling, turning, 3D-printing, and laser cutting); (iii) it is *low-cost*; it was designed ad-hoc for sustainability and pursuing best practices for its manufacturing and assembly; and (iv) its design was based on *user experience*, which allows incorporating active dynamics in the teaching-learning processes. In this case, the complex thinking competencies are included in two moments, the first during the design process of the machine, and the second through the training of the competencies in the implementation of the machine. To achieve the latter, a laboratory practice book was designed.

5.2 Teaching-Learning Process Development: The Scientific and Technological Entrepreneurship Bootcamp

This second case study presents the co-design and co-creation of a teaching-learning process developed by researchers from Tecnologico de Monterrey and partners from the government of Mexico City and Durango State. This teaching-learning process sought to train researchers in transversal competencies (complex thinking) and disciplinary competencies (entrepreneurship, marketing, and business models, emphasising technological and scientific developments). The program was taught in a remote-modality-bootcamp format with synchronous sessions. This type of program seeks to stimulate development and promote technology from the laboratory to the market. Figure 4 summaries the design process and resulting content (See Fig. 4).

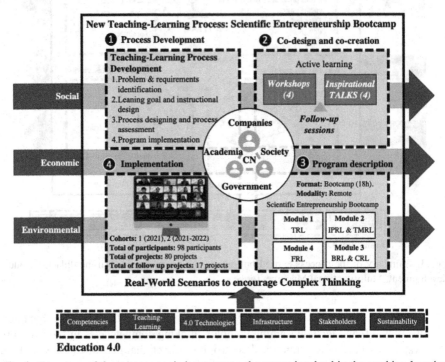

Fig. 4. Summary of the process carried out among the actors involved in the teaching-learning processes development: Entrepreneurship Bootcamp

Thirty-eight scientific projects in Mexico City were involved in public and private HEIs; 5 projects had special follow-up sessions during the 2021 cohort. Sixty projects were in public and private HEIs in Durango state; 12 of these projects had special follow-up sessions during the 2022 cohort. A general result shows that 85% of the projects will pursue a technology transfer strategy, and the other 15% will pursue the creation of an enterprise. Also, it was observed that the most relevant pain was the decision-making process of choosing the pathway to the different alternatives for bringing the product to the market. Finally, it was observed that the topics of creating technology packages, intellectual property strategy, and funding and finance around entrepreneurship processes must be strengthened and fostered.

6   Conclusions

In this work, we presented an approach to CNs and Sustainability within the framework of Education 4.0, showing the relevance of strategic participation by various actors during the co-design, co-creation, and teaching-learning processes. Since this type of collaboration involves design and development processes, the concept of sustainability was pursued to focus efforts on obtaining new products and services with positive social, economic and environmental effects. These topics are relevant for learners' responsiveness and engagement in real-world scenarios. This project promoted complex thinking competencies, and two case studies were analysed.

We sustain that through Education 4.0, it is possible to reduce, mitigate, or provide adequate solutions to current challenges in Higher Education. In addition, we observed that in the design processes of either products or functions within the framework of Education 4.0, it is possible to achieve didactic systems that develop desirable competencies in the current student profile. It can also be mentioned that by following the Reference Framework for Education 4.0, it is possible to be guided throughout the design and creation processes to have the desirable components.

With the dynamics carried out in the case studies, it was possible to verify that the design of new systems in education can have two main effects (i) it encourages the co-creation of sustainable solutions among the members of the CN, (ii) in Within the framework of Education 4.0, it is possible to design teaching-learning dynamics that allow stimulating complex thinking competencies.

Acknowledgments. The authors acknowledge the financial and technical support of Writing Lab, Institute for the Future of Education, Tecnologico de Monterrey, Mexico, in the production of this work. Also, the authors would like to acknowledge the participation of our partners from UNAM for their contributions in developing Case Study 5.1 and COCYTED from the Government of Durango, Mexico, and SECTEI from the Government of Mexico City for their contributions in developing Case Study 5.2.

References

1. Miranda, J., Ramírez-Montoya, M.S., Molina, A.: Education 4.0 reference framework for the design of teaching-learning systems: two case studies involving collaborative networks and open innovation. In: Camarinha-Matos, L.M., Boucher, X., Afsarmanesh, H. (eds.) PRO-VE 2021. IAICT, vol. 629, pp. 692–701. Springer, Cham (2021). https://doi.org/10.1007/978-3-030-85969-5_65
2. Ramírez-Montoya, M.S., Castillo-Martínez, I.M., Sanabria-Z, J., Miranda, J.: Complex thinking in the framework of Education 4.0 and open innovation—a systematic literature review. J. Open Innov. Technol. Market Complex. **8**(1), 4 (2022)
3. Sukiennik, M., Zybała, K., Fuksa, D., Kęsek, M.: The role of universities in sustainable development and circular economy strategies. Energies **14**(17), 5365 (2021)
4. Illeris, K.: The three dimensions of learning (2002)
5. Terziev, V., Lyubcheva, M., Georgiev, M.: Domestic and international challenges in higher education (2021). Available at SSRN 3840258
6. Núñez-Canal, M., de Obesso, M.D.L.M., Pérez-Rivero, C.A.: New challenges in higher education: a study of the digital competence of educators in Covid times. Technol. Forecast. Soc. Chang. **174**, 121270 (2022)
7. Zarei, S., Mohammadi, S.: Challenges of higher education related to e-learning in developing countries during COVID-19 spread: a review of the perspectives of students, instructors, policymakers, and ICT experts. Environ. Sci. Pollut. Res., 1–7 (2021)

8. Miranda, J., et al.: The core components of education 4.0 in higher education: three case studies in engineering education. Comput. Electr. Eng. **93**, 107278 (2021)
9. Miranda, J., Rosas-Fernández, J.B., Molina, A.: Collaborative networking to enable innovation and entrepreneurship through open innovation hubs: the entrepreneurship learning centre of Mexico City. In: Camarinha-Matos, L.M., Afsarmanesh, H., Ortiz, A. (eds.) PRO-VE 2020. IAICT, vol. 598, pp. 311–323. Springer, Cham (2020). https://doi.org/10.1007/978-3-030-62412-5_26
10. United States Sustainable Development Goals: Sustainable development goals. The energy progress report. Tracking SDG, 7 (2019)
11. Camarinha-Matos, L.M., Afsarmanesh, H.: Collaborative networks: a new scientific discipline. J. Intell. Manuf. **16**(4–5), 439–452 (2005)
12. Molina, A., Ponce, P., Miranda, J., Cortés, D.: Sensing, smart and sustainable products (S^3 products). In: Enabling Systems for Intelligent Manufacturing in Industry 4.0, pp. 71–139. Springer, Cham (2021). https://doi.org/10.1007/978-3-030-65547-1_3
13. Haapala, K.R., Zhao, F., Camelio, J., Sutherland, J.W., Skerlos, S.J., Dornfeld, D.A., et al.: A review of engineering research in sustainable manufacturing. J. Manuf. Sci. Eng. **135**(4), 041013 (2013)
14. World Commission on Environment and Development. Our Common Future. Oxford University Press, Oxford, UK (1987)

Responsible Research and Innovation Through Gender-Responsive Collaborative Virtual Hubs

Ana Inês Oliveira[1,2(✉)], Sanaz Nikghadam-Hojjati[1,2], and Filipa Ferrada[1,2,3]

[1] UNINOVA Institute, Centre of Technology and Systems (CTS), Caparica, Portugal
{aio,sanaznik,faf}@uninova.pt
[2] NOVA School of Science and Technology, FCT-NOVA, Caparica, Portugal
[3] Sustain.RD Center, ESTSetúbal, Instituto Politécnico de Setúbal, Campus do IPS, Setúbal, Portugal

Abstract. Responsible Research and Innovation (RRI) through science and technology has a great potential to transform the future and advance society in social, environmental, economic, ethical, and legal aspects. Advancing RRI keys, like gender-responsiveness and gender equality, science literacy and science education, public engagement, open access, ethics, governance, is essential for its development. The present exploratory research paper aims to investigate the role of Collaborative Networks (CN) and gender-responsive collaborative virtual hubs in developing RRI actions. To achieve this goal, authors studied, developed, and synthesized several related concepts. The main contribution of this research work is presenting the theoretical concept based on CNs applied to distinct virtual hubs aiming to promote gender responsive innovation.

Keywords: Responsible Research and Innovation · Gender responsiveness · Hub entities · Collaborative hub · Virtual Meta Hub · Collaborative Networks

1 Introduction

In recent years, as a result of the progress in scientific research and innovation (R&I), attention has been paid to leverage legal, ethical, environmental, economic, and social aspects in terms of the relationship between science and society. This trend is conceptualized by the European Commission through with the introduction of the concept of Responsible Research and Innovation (RRI) [1]. In this context, RRI intends to bridge societal values, needs and expectations about R&I with technological innovation through the engagement of public and responsible multi-actors like citizens, researchers, business, policy makers, governmental and non-governmental organizations, between others. More recently, under the Horizon 2020 work programme "Science with and for Society" (SwafS), six keys constitute the RRI practices they are: Ethics, Science Education, Gender Equality, Open Access, Governance and Public Engagement. This paper, focuses on the gender key by proposing an approach that implies that R&I processes are gender responsive, reflecting the encouragement of equal participation and equal and fair

L. M. Camarinha-Matos et al. (Eds.): PRO-VE 2022, IFIP AICT 662, pp. 675–686, 2022.
https://doi.org/10.1007/978-3-031-14844-6_54

distribution of benefits. In this way, this work aims to investigate the role Collaborative Networks (CN) and innovations hubs moved by the following research question: How can CNs contribute to gender responsive and inclusive innovation? The proposed work, is an exploratory work that settles on establishing a sustainable and resilient approach on collaboration innovation hubs, supported by the contributions from the CN and gender research areas aligned with the knowledge from established innovation hubs.

In this regard, an analysis on collaboration and gender responsiveness concepts in research and innovation activities and systems is performed followed by the proposal of a theoretical model addressing collaborative virtual hubs.

2 Background

Research and Innovation. Research and Innovation (R&I) is a vital lever to ensure sustainable, scientific, and inclusive development. It boosts the production sector's resilience, improves economic competitiveness, and causes socio-economic transformation. R&I is strongly involved in producing new knowledge, developing innovative products, processes, services, and methodologies for emerging real-life problems, enables higher productivity, efficiency, competitiveness, and prosperity [2]. To consider effects and potential environmental, social, and economic impacts of the R&I activities outcomes, European Union suggested the new term of Responsible Research and Innovation (RRI) which raised from predecessors including Ethical, Legal and Social Aspects studies (ELSA) [3–7]. There are various definitions for RRI, however, all of them are prioritizing finding solutions for societal problems and challenges as the main focus of the R&I activities as well as the responsibility to avoid harmful effects, developing innovation-affected communities' engagement, and providing enough knowledge for targeted communities to implement the innovative solutions [8]. One important aspect of RRI is advancing diversity and gender equality in the R&I system [9] that could not be achieved without multi-actor based collaboration in R&I activities which is defined as research involving coordination between the researchers, institutions, organizations, and/or communities [10]. In this context, Collaborative Networks (CN) can play an important role in RRI, acting as key enabler to collaborative work among such heterogeneous stakeholders, by providing common infrastructure, governance principles, business processes and integrated services, fostering inclusiveness and sustainability in the R&I actions.

Gender Responsiveness Research and Innovation. According to United Nations Development Programme (UNDP), Gender Responsiveness (GRs) refers to the activities and outcomes that reflect optimized perception and understanding of gender roles and gender inequalities and activities aimed to encourage equal and inclusive participation and equal and fair distribution of benefits [11]. GRs by accepting biological difference aim to change mindsets and attitude by creating and fostering an environment in which everyone gets equal opportunities and benefits. Lack of Gender Responsive (GR) in research, innovation, product and service production, process, methodology which mostly is result of "default male bias" currently strongly impacts women life and impose negative consequences on society. For example, female drivers which involve in car crashes have a 47% greater chance of serious injury than their male counterparts, and a 71% higher chance of a moderate injury because car safety features are designed for men [12] and most of crash-test dummies are designed based on the "average" male [13]. We can find a lot of other facts related to "default male bias" and gender irresponsiveness in different aspect of our lives such as medical and health care [14], medicine production [15], dealing with traumas [16], research funding [17], digitalization [18], decision making [19], research and innovation activities [20]. "Default male bias" facts shows that our world was not built for women and still has a huge gap to be adequate for them. According to World Bank reports, closing gender gaps can enhance economic productivity and improve development outcomes [21]. To close this gap, Gender-Responsive Research, and Innovation (GR R&I) is vital, since gender responsive research and innovation implies both inclusion of women and men in the innovation process and that the innovation content caters to the needs of both women and men with their interesting diversities in e.g., race, religion, (dis) ability, age. GR R&I have the potential to save lives, resources, and time [6]. Also, Gender Equality (GE, referring to gender-equal participation and representation in R&I) is integral to innovation, and in most R&I fields, improving GE is the key element for achieving technological innovation and innovative sustainable solutions, and its socio-economic ramifications [22].

Hub Entities. Collaboration is increasingly recognized to be important for research and innovation [23] and "Hub Entities" which are community-based, non-profit corporations with offices in a determined geographical location [24] which are responsible to achieve certain goals, could contribute to R&I capacity and productivity by focusing on the collaboration and coordination between autonomous but linked research and innovation ecosystem´s stakeholders. Hub entities are applying hub organizational structure, which is not a hierarchically controlled one, but neither is it a pure network structure in which all control is delegated to the nodes. A hub could be defined as a "modified network" in which a significant amount of the power and decision making are distributed to the teams [25–27]. They are different from those organizational models that provide business support without a traditional incubator. Hubs have strong contribution and participation in the innovation ecosystem by combining structured organizational models with incubators support programmes [28]. While a precise definition of hubs remains elusive, we can note that they are more than just a shared workspace, and they can be distinguished from accelerators and incubators, and Labs. They furthermore have diverse origins and can vary significantly in their focuses, for example they may target technology, innovation, research, science, business, or entrepreneurship. Some of Hubs are founded by different sectors such academic institution, civil society actors, private sectors, government, or a combination of all of them. They gain their funding from a variety of resources and operate using diverse business modes [29, 30]. The most common hubs based on their focuses area are innovation hubs, research hub, collaboration hub, learning hub.

Innovation Hub: It refers to an area with two main characteristics: i) innovative activities which predominates within the region in compared with neighboring regions; ii) a strong linkages and knowledge flow via the main region into neighboring region. The idea and principles of Innovation hubs comes from trade, financial and transportation hubs [31]. This type of hubs is central point for the innovation communities' activities within these areas of focus. They are built on the top of innovations communities' main stakeholders' labs, offices and mainly focus on innovative products, services, and training programmes development in a specific area of their innovation community [32]. They play as the backbone of innovation ecosystem and community.

Research Hub: This type of hubs' mission is to accelerate the pace of scientific research. They are mostly a technology enabled agent, which bring together academic, industrial, and research and innovation sectors stakeholders to develop new scientific and innovative solutions for specific issues in their targeted communities. Research Hubs by brining valuable expertise and experience together to conduct research on subjects that are important for the local, national, and international communities [33, 34].

Collaboration Hub: It refers to a type of physical or virtual workspace which designed to promote collaboration, communication, interaction, community building teamwork, and productivity. It includes plenty of flexible physical and virtual activity-based work environment for knowledge sharing, collaborating, socializing, brainstorming, meetings, matchmaking, and networking.

Learning Hub: It refers to a technology-rich physical or virtual (or both) environment that provide a variety of opportunities (formal, informal, long term, short term, etc.) for learners to come together with peers, educators, and other stakeholders and have access to the relevant knowledge, guidance from educators and peers, and develop new opportunities [35].

Digital Innovation Hubs: Also, known as DIHs, is a concept formally launched by the European Commission (EC) and defined as an entity which is helping "...companies in the region become more competitive by improving their business/production processes as well as products (and services) by means of digital technology" [36]. They are considered as actors or initiatives that support digitalization and the development of the surrounding innovation ecosystem [37].

This paper addresses these topics by proposing a model supported by CNs, Gender Responsive principles and innovation hubs, as described below.

3   Gender-Responsive Collaborative Virtual Hubs

One step towards a gender-responsive research and innovation ecosystem to the co-developing of knowledge and innovation, is aiming a suitable environment where concrete models, methodologies, and tools for advancing gender-responsive, human-centered, and inclusive can be considered. In this line, areas such as Collaborative Networks, Gender-Responsive, and Research and Innovation Hubs are taken into consideration as the foundation for a gender-responsive collaborative virtual hub, as illustrated in Fig. 1.

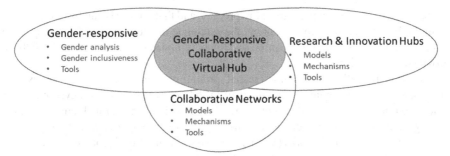

Fig. 1. Key areas for gender-responsive collaborative virtual hub

In this regard, it becomes appropriated a baseline aligned with the concepts provided by Collaborative Networks (CN) scientific discipline [38]. As such, these can have different typologies and be classified into two major groups: the long-term strategic networks and the goal-oriented networks [39].

On this specific context, for giving the required support for gender-responsive collaboration, it is envisaged the conception of a long-term alliance for the provision of the necessary supporting environment that encapsulates the governing of the different types of supporting entities that must collaborate to support the creation of innovation local living-hubs. This type of collaboration is called Virtual Meta Hub (VMH) and includes a catalog comprising the tools and the methods that can be used to instantiate Virtual Local Hubs (VLH) that are gender responsive compliant. For the creation of a new Virtual Local Hub, two situations can occur: to adapt an existing hub with these virtualization methodologies and tools, or the creation of a new hub that is compliant from the beginning with such methodologies and tools.

During the creation of such VMH, relevant stakeholders shall consider the necessary environment in which a set of models, mechanisms and tools shall be made available and prepared to be updated according to new generated knowledge.

In its turn, the VLHs are goal-oriented networks that involves different types of supporting entities in a defined region, that must collaborate to provide the required support for the promotion of co-creation and/or co-development teams that are gender responsive, making the local innovation ecosystem actors more prepared in the scope of real-life action research.

For the creation of a VLHs, the catalogue of the VMH can be adapted according to the exactly local requirements. For such instantiation, some context-awareness guidelines must exist, enabling an AI-based suggestion system to provide the most suitable environment for a specific VLH being instantiated.

Moreover, as way to enrich the entire process, and that all VLHs can benefit the most from the VMH according to its context, the catalogue included in the VMH, should be a self-organized catalogue that can be dynamically updated according to the feedback provided by the existing VLHs.

Additionally, all teams being created promoting gender responsive innovation are dynamic virtual organizations involved in the co-creation and co-development of innovation in the context of their hubs, called co-Creation Innovation Teams (co-CIT).

Figure 2 illustrates the gender-responsive collaborative approach that includes the three different types of networks (Virtual Meta Hub, Virtual Local Hub, and co-Creation Innovation Team) together with their bidirectional interaction for suggestion and for updating.

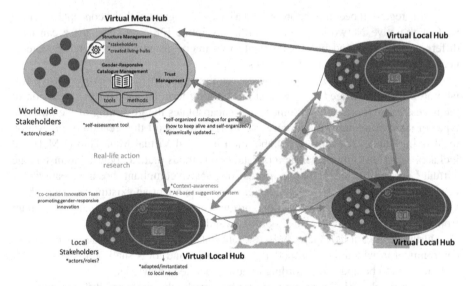

Fig. 2. Gender-responsive collaborative virtual hubs approach

4 Virtual Meta Hub

The main purpose of the Virtual Meta Hub is to promote collaboration between innovation hubs, social sciences researchers and institutions, gender experts at a large scale, aiming to generate new and disruptive plans, methodologies, and tools to promote inclusion and women innovators and develop gender-responsive innovation. In the context of this network, several Virtual Local Hubs might be instantiated aiming at promoting inclusion and gender equal participation in local innovation ecosystems.

A system to support the management of this environment needs to provide services to manage the meta hub stakeholders' profiles and competences, to support gender-responsive innovation management, to facilitate trust building and resilience among all and promote sustainability by means of a suitable incentives and expectations management.

The main strategic goal is to offer gender-responsive best practices, methodologies, and tools (like a catalogue), training and learning services towards their instantiation/uptake in VLHs.

To capture, synthetize and organize the base concepts, principles, and recommended practices of the previous mention networks, it is used the ARCON modeling framework [40]. Through this framework, it is possible to identify the main elements of the networks, namely the endogenous and exogenous. Considering the focus of this paper, only the *endogenous* elements of the VMH are here considered, once it is the foundation for the entire ecosystem.

Thus, the endogenous elements for the VMH represent essentially the *structural*, *componential*, *functional*, and *behavioral* and all the four elements are classified according to *activity entity*, *passive entity*, *action,* and *concept*, as depicted in Table 1.

Table 1. Main endogenous elements for the virtual meta hub

Structural	*Active entity*
	▪ **Actor**
	 • Primary-entity
	 • Support-entity
	
	Passive entity
	N/A
	Action
	N/A
		Concept
		▪ **Role**
		 • VMH member
		  – Administrator
		  – Adviser
		  – Support provider
		 • Spot member
			▪ **Relationship**
			 • Exchanging
			 • Sharing
			 • Trusting
			 • Socializing
			▪ **Network**
			 • VMH-self
			  network
			 • subnetwork

Componential	*Active entity*
	--- 	
	Passive entity
	▪ **Domain Specific Device**
	 • Manufacturing
	  Machinery
	▪ **ICT Resource**
	 • Hardware
	 • Software
	  – Management
	   system
	  – Catalogue
		▪ **Human Resources**
		 • Contact person for VMH
		 Contact person for a stakeholder
		▪ **Info/knowledge/asset/resources**
		 • Profile/competence data
		  – Stakeholders profile data
		  – Catalogue
		 • Inheritance information
		 Update knowledge from
		 virtual local hubs
		 • Ontologies
		  – Common ontologies
		  – Domain ontologies
			• Catalogue
			  – Resources
			  – Methods
			  – tools
			 • Bag of assets
			  – Governance
			   information
			  – Value
			   system
			  – Templates
			▪ **Network result**
			 Virtual local
			 hub instantiation
			Action
			N/A
			Concept
			N/A

(*continued*)

Table 1. (*continued*)

Functional	*Active entity*
	N/A
	Passive entity
	N/A
	Action
	▪ **Fundamental Processes**
	• VMH management process
	  – Membership management
	  – Trust management
	  – Value system info management
	  – Support institution management
	• Participants operational processes
	  – Participants Trust assessment
	  – VLH instantiation
	  – VLH creation
	  – VLH registration
		▪ **Background Processes**
		• VMH management process
		  – Creation of new items for catalogue
		  – Catalogue evolution
		  – VLH inheritance management
		  – IP management
		• Gender-responsive policies creation
		Concept
		▪ **Methodology and approach**
		• VMH creation and setup
		  – Co-creation of VMH
		  – Governance rules
		  – Value system definition
		  – VMH set up
			• VMH operation handling
			  – Members information quality assurance
			  – Ontology management
			  – Social processes
			  – Governance rules updating
			  – IP Management
			  – Catalogue evolution
			Gender-responsive policies updating

Behavioral	*Active entity*
	N/A
	Passive entity
	N/A
	Action
	N/A
	Concept
	▪ **Prescriptive behavior**
	• Cultural principles
	  – Tradition
	  – Culture
	• Governance principles
	  – General principles
	  – Domain specific principles
		– Gender-responsive principles
		• Incentive policies and reward
		▪ **Contract and Agreement**
		• VMH adhesion agreement
		Agreement amendments
		▪ **Obligatory behavior**
		• VMH Bylaws
		  – Conflict resolution policies
		  – Membership policy
		  – Contact enforcement
		  – Financial policies
		• Internal regulations
		  – Gende-responsive guidelines
		  – Sanctions principles
			▪ **Constraint and condition**
			• Confidentiality constraints
			• Legal constraints
			• Internal normative constraints
			• Standard constraints
			Physical constraints

To properly model the VMH, it is also important to consider the exogenous elements that are related to the interactions between the network as whole or in relation to others. Therefore, although out of the scope of this paper, dimensions such as *market*, *support*, *societal* and *constituency* should be also defined.

The VMH life cycle follows the ARCON reference model and represents all stages that the VMH passes during its lifetime, namely creation, operation and evolution, and dissolution as depicted in Fig. 3.

The creation of the VMH requires two main steps: *(i)* initiation and mobilization and *(ii)* start-up. The VMH is created by a group of founding stakeholders being one of them, the initiator (an organization), assigned to conduct the creation actions. The initiation and mobilization require the setup of a common base infrastructure, the establishment of a base ontology, the establishment of the VMH profile, namely name, legal identity, vision, goal, etc., and the engaging of potential stakeholders (e.g., local hubs) to join the VMH. In its turn, the start-up requires the parametrization of the necessary systems, creation, and population of information repositories.

The operation and evolution of the VMH requires support to stakeholders' profiles and competences management, new stakeholders' registration, gender-responsive innovation catalogue management, collaboration & knowledge creation and sharing, assisting the instantiation of VLH, portfolio management (catalogue with all instantiated VLHs and experiments) and facilitate trust building and resilience among all and promote sustainability by means of a suitable incentives and expectations management.

Finally, the dissolution of the VMH requires a detailed plan to properly deal with the accumulated knowledge, stakeholder's information, gender-responsive catalogues, and other, based on established agreements covering rights and responsibilities.

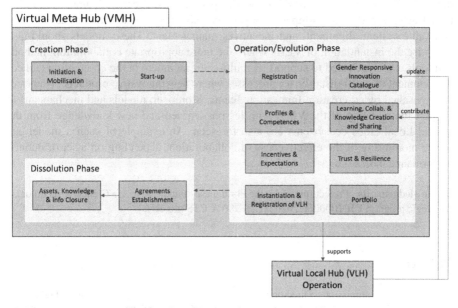

Fig. 3. Virtual Meta Hub Base Functionality

5   Conclusion and Future Work

Following the trends for leveraging Responsible Research and Innovation, it is important to consider structures that enable collaboration that is gender-responsive and inclusive. For such, this paper presents exploratory research with the aim at investigating how Collaborative Networks can contribute to gender-responsive and inclusive innovation. As the background, several concepts were studied, and synthesized in Sect. 2, namely research and innovation, gender-responsiveness research and innovation, and hub entities, that despite being commonly used, their exact definitions are sometimes unclear. In the following Sect. 3, it was perceived the definition of gender-responsive collaborative virtual hub, that is nurtured by models, methodologies, and tools coming from areas such as Collaborative Networks, Gender-Responsive, and Research and Innovation Hub. Therefore, considering the great contribution from CNs, three different types of networks were defined: the Virtual Meta Hub, the Virtual Local Hub, and the co-Creation Innovation Team. With the main purpose of promoting collaboration between innovation hubs, the focus of Sect. 4 was in the definition of the main endogenous elements of the Virtual Meta Hub following the ARCON reference framework. Also, the description of its main functionalities considering its life cycle was included.

For further developments, besides the definition of the other elements of the VMH and VLH, it is necessary to design and develop models and mechanisms to support the management and governance principles of the learning and collaborative VMH, that includes stakeholders profiling and competence management (namely regarding their R&I competences), competences gap analysis, innovation readiness assessment, and value system alignment, and incentives management. These models should also comprise the instantiation of VLHs where the more appropriate collaboration methods and tools can be selected to support its multi-actor members in the co-creation and co-development of multi-disciplinary processes where new innovative products or services are envisaged by co-creation Innovation Teams. Moreover, models and mechanisms to support the updating of the VMH with lessons learned and new knowledge from the Virtual Local Hubs ecosystems are also foreseen. An example of such a model can be the monitoring of the effectiveness of collaboration, depending on a set of defined performance indicators.

Acknowledgements. Project funded by the Portuguese "Fundação para a Ciência e Tecnologia" "Strategic program UIDB/00066/2020" (UNINOVA-CTS project).

References

1. European Commission, Directorate-General for Research and Innovation, Iagher, R., Monachello, R., Warin, C.: Science with and for Society in Horizon 2020 : Achievements and Recommendations for Horizon Europe. Publications Office (2020). https://doi.org/10.2777/32018
2. European Commission. European Semester Thematic Factsheet Research and Innovation (2017)

3. Von Schomberg, R.: A vision of responsible research and innovation. Respons. Innovat. Manag. Respons. Emerg. Sci. Innov. Soc. (2013). https://doi.org/10.1002/978111855142 4.ch3

4. van den Hoven, J., Jacob, K.: Options for Strengthening Responsible Research and Innovation (2013)

5. Zwart, H., Landeweerd, L., van Rooij, A.: Adapt or perish? Assessing the recent shift in the European research funding arena from 'ELSA' to 'RRI.' Life Sci. Soc. Policy **10**(1), 1–19 (2014). https://doi.org/10.1186/s40504-014-0011-x

6. Buitendijk, S., Maes, K.: Gendered research and innovation: integrating sex and gender analysis into the research process. League Eur. Res. Univ. **18** (2015)

7. Burget, M., Bardone, E., Pedaste, M.: Definitions and conceptual dimensions of responsible research and innovation: a literature review. Sci. Eng. Ethics **23**(1), 1–19 (2016). https://doi. org/10.1007/s11948-016-9782-1

8. Peckham, J.: What is responsible innovation, and why should tech giants take it seriously? Future US Inc. (2018). https://www.techradar.com/news/what-is-responsible-innovation-and-why-should-tech-giants-take-it-seriously

9. Responsible Research and Innovation. How to Put Gender Equality into Practice? Zarządzanie Publiczne **2** (2017). https://doi.org/10.4467/20843968zp.16.014.7229

10. Bansal, S., Mahendiratta, S., Kumar, S., Sarma, P., Prakash, A., Medhi, B.: Collaborative research in modern era: need and challenges. Ind. J. Pharmacol. **51**(3) (2019). https://doi.org/10.4103/ijp.IJP_394_19

11. Nelson, G.: Gender Responsive National Communications Toolkit (2015)

12. Bose, D., Segui-Gomez, M., Crandall, J.R.: Vulnerability of female drivers involved in motor vehicle crashes: an analysis of US population at risk. Am. J. Publ. Health **101**(12) (2011). https://doi.org/10.2105/AJPH.2011.300275

13. Linder, A., Svedberg, W.: Review of average sized male and female occupant models in European regulatory safety assessment tests and European laws: gaps and bridging suggestions. Accid. Anal. Prevent. **127** (2019). https://doi.org/10.1016/j.aap.2019.02.030

14. Thompson, J., Blake, D.: Women's experiences of medical miss -diagnosis: how does gender matter in healthcare settings? Women's Stud. J. **34**(1) (2020)

15. Zucker, I., Prendergast, B.J.: Sex differences in pharmacokinetics predict adverse drug reactions in women. Biol. Sex Diff. **11**(1) (2020). https://doi.org/10.1186/s13293-020-003 08-5

16. Perman, S.M., et al.: Public perceptions on why women receive less bystander CPR than men in out of hospital cardiac arrest. Circulation **138** (Supplement 2) (2018)

17. Norström, T.: Men are more likely than women to receive research funding from FAS. One explanation is that male applicants are more senior than female applicants. Lakartidningen **109**, 43–44 (2012)

18. Pulgarín, A.M.R., Woodhouse, T.: The Costs of Exclusion: Economic Consequences of the Digital Gender Gap (2021)

19. Watch, U.W.: Facts & figures: rural women and the millennium development goals (2012)

20. UNESCO. Women in Science: Fact Sheet No. 55 June 2019 FS/2019/SCI/55 (2019)

21. Wong, Y.N.: World Development Report 2012: Gender equality and development. Forum Develop. Stud. **39**(3) (2012). https://doi.org/10.1080/08039410.2012.722769

22. Nielsen, M.W., Bloch, C.W., Schiebinger, L.: Making gender diversity work for scientific discovery and innovation. Nat. Hum. Behav. **2**(10) (2018). https://doi.org/10.1038/s41562-018-0433-1

23. Huang, J.S.: Building research collaboration networks - an interpersonal perspective for research capacity building. J. Res. Admin. **45**(2) (2014)

24. Law Insider Inc. Hub Entity Definition (2022). https://www.lawinsider.com/dictionary/hub-entity

25. Battaglia, D., Landoni, P., Rizzitelli, F.: Organizational structures for external growth of University Technology Transfer Offices: an explorative analysis. Technol. Forecast. Soc. Change **123** (2017). https://doi.org/10.1016/j.techfore.2017.06.017
26. Pankowska, M.: Organizational analytics in enterprise architecture development. WSEAS Trans. Inf. Sci. Appl. **14** (2017)
27. Highsmith, J.: Agile Project Management: Creating Innovative Products (2009)
28. JO Education. Technology Innovation Hub: What do you Need to Know? (2021). https://www.joeducation.eu/technology-innovation-hub-what-do-you-need-to-know/
29. Littlewood, D.C., Kiyumbu, W.L.: 'Hub' organisations in Kenya: what are they? What do they do? And what is their potential? Technol. Forecast. Soc. Change **131** (2018). https://doi.org/10.1016/j.techfore.2017.09.031
30. World Bank. The Business Models of mLabs and mHubs-An Evaluation of info Dev's Mobile Innovation Support Pilots (2014)
31. Baark, E., Sharif, N.: From trade hub to innovation hub: the role of Hong Kong's innovation system in linking China to global markets. Innov. Manag. Policy Pract. **8**(1) (2006). https://doi.org/10.5172/impp.2006.8.1.193
32. The European Institute of Innovation & Technology (EIT). EIT Innovation Hubs (2022). https://eit.europa.eu/our-communities/eit-innovation-communities/innovation-hubs
33. Policies for Action (P4A). Research Hubs (2022). https://www.policiesforaction.org/research-hubs
34. O. H. and S. University. Research Hubs (2021). https://www.ohsu.edu/school-of-medicine/biomedical-sciences-graduate-program/research-hubs
35. Selinger, M.: Learning Hubs: Where Learning Takes Place in a Digital World (2013)
36. Rabarijaona, L.P., Andriamaroson, B.J., Ravaoalimalala, V.E., Ravoniarimbinina, P., Migliani, R.: Digital Innovation Hubs in Smart Specialisation Strategies, vol. 67 (2001)
37. Goetheer, J.D., Butter, M.: Digital Innovation Hubs Catalogue (2017)
38. Camarinha-Matos, L.M., Afsarmanesh, H.: Collaborative networks: a new scientific discipline. J. Intell. Manuf. **16**(4–5), 439–452 (2005)
39. Camarinha-Matos, L.M., Afsarmanesh, H.: Towards a reference model for collaborative networked organizations. In: BASYS 2006. IIFIP, vol. 220, pp. 193–202. Springer, Boston (2006). https://doi.org/10.1007/978-0-387-36594-7_21
40. Camarinha-Matos, L.M., Afsarmanesh, H. (eds.): Collaborative Networks: Reference Modeling. Springer, Boston (2008). https://doi.org/10.1007/978-0-387-79426-6

Roadmapping Towards Mature Collaborative Reconfigurable Manufacturing System

Ehsan Yadegari$^{(\boxtimes)}$ (ID) and Xavier Delorme (ID)

Mines Saint-Etienne, Univ Clermont Auvergne, INP Clermont Auvergne, CNRS,
UMR 6158 LIMOS, 42023 Saint-Etienne, France
ehsan.yadegari@emse.fr

Abstract. Reconfigurable Manufacturing System (RMS) has received a great deal of attention among researchers and industrial activists after being promoted by new manufacturing paradigms like Industry 4.0. Consequently, researchers are working on introducing a comprehensive, mature and collaborative framework of RMS. Still, there are several practical obstacles in the way of introducing collaborative RMS into corporates. Among these obstacles is a lack of knowledge about the status quo and strategic guides to realize new frameworks, especially when it is considering strategic decisions in a collaborative decision making (CDM) system. Thus, the main novelty of the present study is to gather and introduce 194 key performance indicators (KPIs) to give a general picture of the way of implementing newly developed collaborative RMSs. This framework covers four key axes in the RMS framework at the same time, including Servitization, Sustainability, Uncertainty, and Digitalization. Each axis is featured with several dimensions and for each dimension there are from two to 19 KPIs to monitor the implementation level. The KPIs have their own description and example of the formula. In addition, based on the PCDA cycle, the relationships between strategic objectives, KPIs, targets, and initiatives are given to connect the various parts of changing strategy.

Keywords: KPI · Reconfigurable Manufacturing System · Collaborative decision making · Sustainability · Uncertainty · Servitization · Digitalization

1 Introduction

Manufacturing firms in the current industrial environment have to deal with several deep changes that require increasing standard in products and designs and management of processes. The main factors that force the change from traditional manufacturing system to the Next Generation Manufacturing System (NGMSs) are dynamic market demand, high flexibility, CDM between different parts of the value network, quality products, growing customization, flexible batches, and short life cycle of products [1]. Over the years, the limitation of dedicated manufacturing systems (DMSs), cellular manufacturing systems (CMSs), and flexible manufacturing systems (FMSs) have become clear with adaptation to the newly emerged market features. For instance, DMSs make sure of

L. M. Camarinha-Matos et al. (Eds.): PRO-VE 2022, IFIP AICT 662, pp. 687–697, 2022.
https://doi.org/10.1007/978-3-031-14844-6_55

production of the core products with a high production rate but with low flexibility. The features of products should remain unchanged during the lifetime of system and making changes is highly expensive and hard to make [2, 3]. Using FMSs, automated numerically controlled workstations can be connected using a suitable handling system from a central control unit. The key benefit of FMSs is higher flexibility for managing resources and produce a wide range of parts. Still, in many cases, the output of these system is less than DMSs and the equipment increase the final price of the parts [3]. Some of the drawbacks of these two systems were covered by CMSs, which are featured with using several independent working cells assigned to families of products that have identical processing requirements [4]. In spite of this advantage, CMSs are made to manufacture a specific number of products with a reliable demand level and adequately long life-cycle [5]. To overcome the limitation of the available systems, NGMSs combined high flexibility, reconfigurability, and artificial intelligence properties to meet the dynamic market demands [6]. Koren was the first one to introduce RMS in 1999. The NGMS are designed to make fast changes in structure, hardware, and software components possible and change production capacity and functionality rapidly within a part family to deal with rapid market changes or regulation changes [2].

The expected features of DMSs, FMS, RMs, CMSs and matured RMS are listed in Table 1. Clearly, RMSs is designed to contain the advantages of traditional manufacturing system along with flexibility and high throughput and matured RMS try to develop new aspects in the traditional RMSs.

Table 1. Comparison among the features of the existing manufacturing systems, based on [2, 7].

	DMS	FMS	CMS	RMS	Matured RMS
Cost per part	Low	Reasonable	Medium	Medium	Customised
Demand	Stable	Variable	Stable	Variable	Variable
Flexibility	No	General	General	Customised	Customised
Machine structure	Fixed	Fixed	Fixed	Changeable	Changeable
Product family formation	No	No	Yes	Yes	Yes
Productivity	Very high	Low	High	High	Productivity
System structure	Fixed	Changeable	Fixed	Changeable	Changeable
Variety	No	Wide	Wide	High	High
Uncertainty	No	No	No	somehow	Yes
Digitalization	No	No	No	No	Yes
Servitization	No	No	No	No	Yes
Sustainability	No	No	No	No	Yes

The RMSs are a new group of manufacturing systems with adjustable structure both in terms of hardware and software architecture [2, 8] and combine the following six main features [9, 10]: *Modularity, Integrability, Diagnosibility, Diagnosibility, Convertibility, Customisation* and *Scalability*.

There has been a growing trend of studies on RMS that cover a wide range of research questions [11]. Many of papers published in this filed are featured with introducing new methods to add some of the new features to available manufacturing systems [12], while providing methodologies for designing new RMS have not received the attention it merits.

Boucher et al. [7] introduced a matured collaborative RMS system and indicated that the technology is pretty mature on solutions to implement RMS; however, there is a relatively low level of adoption in the industry and for SMEs and CDM aspects in particular. To deal with these important points, the authors tried to take the main development in industry of the future into account along the recent years as a way to push the scientific production on RMS one the path forward. From this viewpoint, the latest gap analysis method is based on the main complementary issues of industry of the future and collaborative decision making between different decision makers in the network which are listed below:

- **Uncertainty management:** Managing different types of uncertainty can be the taken into account as the core of RMS. However, the industrial transition is pushing the limits of challenges and solutions to deal with uncertainty of production processes.
- **Digitalization:** Refers to using digital technologies to achieve new business models, revenues, and value-producing opportunities; it is the process toward a digital business.
- **Servitization:** By servitized organizations we refer to manufacturing/technology firms that provide services to their clients. Over the past decade, servitization has become a key strategy to keep competitive advantages for manufacturing organizations [13]
- **Sustainability:** To deal with the increasing concerns about sustainability, produces have been forced to introduce measures for examining sustainable manufacturing performance. These measures are aimed at integrating sustainability aspects.

In addition, creating tangible changes and potentials is a great challenge today. As to production system, we have to deal with several figures known as indicators [14]. These numbers reflect a general and compact picture of the process as a tool for assessment that provide the chance for a faster analysis [15]. For instance, current indicators are generally and only concentrated on the quality of product in time or may give the general effectiveness. Still, given the implementation of a fresh framework for a company, here we look for a comprehensive indicator bank that gives the strategic manager a chance to examine the current potential and determine diverse dimensions of the framework. In addition, it should enable them to examine the progress along with introducing changes. This paper is an attempt to give an introduction to the collaborative RMS indicator bank and the way these data are gathered. In addition, it showed the way such indicators connect the various elements in the change strategy.

Table 2. Keywords and investigated concepts to create the indicator bank.

No	Axis	Keywords	No. of indicators	No. of papers	important references
1	Uncertainty	Green, Sustainability, Sustainable, Environmental, Waste, Resource utilization, Emissions, Social, welfare +indicator or criteria or KPI	99	65	[19, 20]
2	Digitalization	Uncertain, Indeterminacy, prediction, Scalability, Diagnosability +indicator or criteria or KPI	60	41	[21, 22]
3	Servitization	Servitization, Tangible, Intangible, Customer Service, Customization +indicator or criteria or KPI	44	57	[8, 21, 23]
4	Sustainability (Environmental, Social. Cost factors)	Modularity, integrability, Convertibility, Technology, Products, Data, digitalization, digital +indicator or criteria or KPI	47	31	[24, 25]

2 Research Methodology

The criteria are key elements for planning and controlling a manufacturing process. They are more important for management and the main elements for selecting indicators. Through these evaluation, coordination, and control functions, purposes are used as a key instrument for management [16].

Given the fact that these indicators function as a tool for managers, general indicator structure is usually concentrated on financial or strategic matters. The ZVEI KPI system, the Profitability-Liquidity KPI system, and the DuPont System of Financial control are among the most common financial indicator systems [17]. In addition, the Balanced Score card relies on a framework to create key indicators about vision and strategy of a firm [18]. The Balanced Score Card is under consideration in this study as it implies that developing indicator systems is the same as creating an indicator bank through examining the related products.

It is important in the search approach phase to have a proper choice of the database to make sure the literature is of high quality and covers a large volume of documents found in the field of a required change in a firm. Afterwards, the phrases used to search and the information found in the publications are searched and filtered. For instance, as shown in the Sect. 3, the framework used in this study covers some key elements based on which we can achieve key concepts. Using the keywords in the definition for each challenge, the keywords that we can use in our search were extracted. For instance, in terms of sustainability, a search is performed in WoS using keywords such as "Emissions + indicator." The categories chosen to search based on the concepts and challenges explained in the Sect. 3 are listed in Table 2. In addition, the number of articles and the key references to create the indicators bank are listed. Figure 1 illustrates the strategy of gathering and selecting the bank of indicators. The PRISMA statement recommendations were used for information search including identifying papers for screening, eligibility, and included papers. The inclusion criteria were keywords on the title, abstract or keyword sections; published by scientific peer-reviewed journals, and published in WoS or Scopus. Papers published over the past seven years were more in focus (2015–2022).

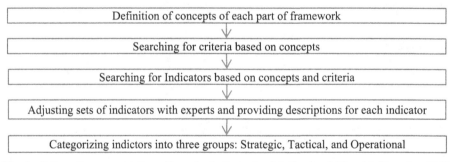

Fig. 1. Schematic representation of how the indicator bank is Prepared (Provided based on [26])

3 Resulting Monitoring System for Collaborative RMS

The obtained indicator bank is designed to monitor mature RMS framework implementation in manfacturing companies that produce physical goods or offer services and products at the same time. It gives us four axes based on the framework, including sustainability, uncertainty, servitization, and digitalization, each with many dimensions.

Each dimension contains 2–19 KPIs to monitor the implementation status. One example of KPI and the pertinent operation KPI measure for each dimension in the axis 3 (Servitization) are listed in Table 3. All KPIs rely on quantitative scales that measure the implementation status of a collaborative RMS-concept in terms of percentage or degree. In general, 194 KPIs were introduced so that each had the same structure (Table 3). Each KPI contains a title, a description, detailing of the collaborative RMS-concept, an example to improve understanding, and the measurement-scale to examine levels of implementation.

4   Roadmap Toward Collaborative RMS

The relationship between the proposed framework and a performance measuring system is shown in Fig. 2 namely indicators, targets, and initiatives. As mentioned in the Sect. 1, the proposed framework can be used in various organizations depending on the case and the level of their potentials. In addition, a company might need to alter its one or more framework dimensions depending on their challenges for making decision (see [7]). Thus, in the case of a systematic change inside an organization, we need a change strategy with clear dimensions and cause-and-effect relationship. Acceptable performance level is measured based on "targets" for the defined indicators. In addition, initiatives are developed to cover the gap of current and ideal states based on total budget, manpower, and other constraints.

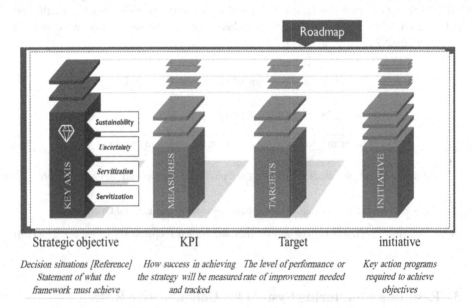

Fig. 2. Roadmap toward collaborative RMS.

Table 3. Maturity dimensions and assessment items for Axis 3 (Servitization).

Axis 3, Dimension 1: Customization (7 items)

Tool customization, Controller customization, Operation customization, System customization, Size customization, Colour customization, Design customization
Example KPI: Tool customization
Operational KPI measure: [binary] Possibility to use same tools to assemble different variants

---

Axis 3, Dimension 2: Tangible/Intangible Services (2 items)

Number of Service Types, Number of Services
Example KPI: Number of Services
Operational KPI measure: [number] of the of services offered by the company. The more services a company offers, the higher is the degree of servitization

---

Axis 3, Dimension 3 – Revenue of Servitization (13 items)

Share of Direct revenue from Services, Share of Indirect revenue from Services, Share of Direct Costs from Services, Share of Indirect Costs from Services, Growth in sales, Growth in revenue, Growth in profit, Return on investment, Market share growth, Profit as a percentage of sales, Return on investment, Cost saving, Market share growth
Example KPI: Share of Direct revenue from Services
Operational KPI measure: [%] of annual revenue from directly selling services/total revenue from selling products and services

---

Axis 3, Dimension 4 – Customer Service (11 items)

Number of Customers Serviced, Product-Service (P-S) Continuum, Value Basis of Activity, Services Reputation, Alignment with customer's requirements, Bringing service to market quickly, Number of service evaluation, Service as the main reason customers selecting us, Customer retention rate, Customer satisfaction, Degree of loyalty
Example KPI: Number of Customers Serviced
Operational KPI measure: [number] of customers reached by the firm's services

---

Axis 3, Dimension 5 – Service orientation of the company (8 items)

Service orientation of corporate values, Service orientation of management behavior, Service orientation of employees behavior, Service orientation of employee recruitment, Service orientation of employee compensation, Service orientation of employee training
Example KPI: Service orientation of employee training
Operational KPI measure: [Degree] which refers to the extent to which service-related performance is evaluated and rewarded within the organization (Musser based on Likert scale)

Axis 3, Dimension 6 – Strategic intent for future service offering (6 items)

Strategic intent to develop a service breadth, Strategic intent to develop a service depth, Developing brand identification, Additional services to loyal customers, Constant learning from supplier/customer/competitors, Ability of service customization Supplement two new services in the next year
Example KPI: Strategic intent to develop a service breadth
Operational KPI measure: [%] number of supplement of new services in a year / the number of target

---

Axis 3, Dimension 7 – Logistics of Service (10 items)

Infrastructure for service delivery, Info Sys applied in service delivery, Inter-organisational info sharing, Number of services not finally delivered, On-time contract delivery, Time of service delivery, Number of errors in service delivery, Time between service order and service delivery, Percentage of use of service delivery capability, Delivered On time
Example KPI: Delivered On time
Operational KPI measure: [%] of orders delivered on time

Figure 3 illustrates the introduced performance measurement system. Incrementing the chance of independence between the component and process (workstation modularity)" is considered as a criterion in RMS dimension. Therefore, to track progress to achieve the target (i.e. the level of workstation modularity), it is covered as an indicator. As a result, to fill the gap between the current and preferred performance, an initiative is developed named "to change the workstation through redesigning the layout."

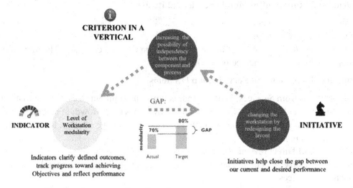

Fig. 3. An example of performance measurement system.

To have a complete description of how the roadmap will be practically applying the indicator bank, here we provide an example of developing servitization on HeiQ Materials AG, an international textile chemical company that produces advanced technologies for its customers. The senior managers of a company have to have a meticulous understanding of the service offerings in that specific industry benchmark companies and their competitors. Then they are able to assess if the number of offering services and their depth is sufficient or if there is a need to ameliorate. Moreover, the organization can make an assessment of the types of services in its current situation and rank them as basic, intermediate, or advanced. As an example, the HeiQ Materials Company has applied many services to develop value by collaborating with the clients. As a result of this, they have fitted service offerings to customers' specific demands and prolonged the depth of each service to fulfill customer needs. The organization's service portfolio shows a combination of base (technical support, troubleshooting, legal compliance services), intermediary (customer training, mill recommendations, environmental health safety, and sustainability support), and advanced services (usually internal to a customer, e.g. testing customers product, marketing support, ingredient branding). By going throw the depth in service approach, HeiQ extends the value in collaboration with its customers through its business offerings. Finally, in five years, this company has gained about a thirty percent compound annual growth rate in its sale [27].

To complete the above description, four key scenarios are taken into account to have a comprehensive measure of progress for each goal.

- **Scenario A:** Objective measured using indicator Progress of Initiative A and other indicators that are not measurable currently.
- **Scenario B:** Objective measured using indicators of Progress of Initiative B.

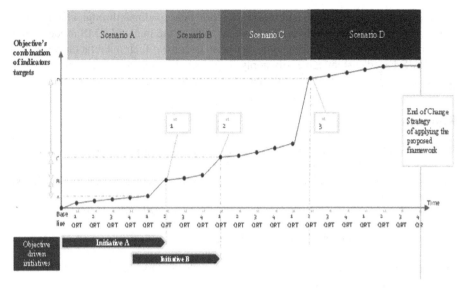

Fig. 4. Scenarios in measuring the performance of each concept

- **Scenario C:** Objective measured through indicators not covered by the drive initiatives progress.
- **Scenario D:** Objectives measured using indicators, improving one or more indicators, targeting ambitious because of the effect of other driven objectives initiatives accomplishment.

These four scenarios in measuring the performance of each indicator of each concept of the proposed framework are illustrated in Fig. 4.

5 Conclusion and Further Research

Industry 4.0 has created many manufacturing opportunities. One of the most important of these axes is RMS. Although most RMS models were focused on operational and production-level models in a factory, recently the attention of the researchers has been drawn to axis such as digitalization, Uncertainty, Servitization, Sustainability. Moreover, despite research on participatory RMS models, there is still a great need for progress measurement tools to control changes in organizations, machines, and value networks. One of the important measurement tools, which simultaneously causes the compatibility of different components of the value chain, is indicators. In this study, for the first time, based on components of mature collaborative RMSs, 194 indicators were collected, classified, and defined by a systematic search in the literature. With this indicator bank, the organization that wants to become a mature organization in the field of collaborative RMS can firstly measure its current status compared to the optimal state, and secondly, during the continuous improvement, it can measure its percentage of progress by dashboards prepared based on this indicator bank. Moreover, the paper tried to explain how to implement these indicators and introduce a practical roadmap through change management. Concisely, by this indicator bank, as well as the matured RMS model which was introduced in the paper, companies that wish to convert their manufacturing system to an RMS-based system can easily apply the selected indicators. Moreover, the paper subject that which roadmap to implement this system is efficient and user-friendly.

References

1. Mehrabi, M.G., Ulsoy, A.G., Koren, Y.: Reconfigurable manufacturing systems: key to future manufacturing. J. Intell. Manuf. **11**(4), 403–419 (2000)
2. Koren, Y., Shpitalni, M.: Design of reconfigurable manufacturing systems. J. Manuf. Syst. **29**(4), 130–141 (2010)
3. Xing, B., et al.: Reconfigurable manufacturing system for agile mass customization manufacturing (2006)
4. Heragu, S.S.: Group technology and cellular manufacturing. IEEE Trans. Syst. Man Cybern. **24**(2), 203–215 (1994)
5. Benjaafar, S., Heragu, S.S., Irani, S.A.: Next generation factory layouts: research challenges and recent progress. Interfaces **32**(6), 58–76 (2002)
6. Molina, A., et al.: Next-generation manufacturing systems: key research issues in developing and integrating reconfigurable and intelligent machines. Int. J. Comput. Integr. Manuf. **18**(7), 525–536 (2005)
7. Boucher, X., et al.: Towards reconfigurable digitalized and servitized manufacturing systems: conceptual framework. In: Ameri, F., Stecke, K.E., von Cieminski, G., Kiritsis, D. (eds.) APMS 2019. IAICT, vol. 566, pp. 214–222. Springer, Cham (2019). https://doi.org/10.1007/978-3-030-30000-5_28
8. Bortolini, M., Galizia, F.G., Mora, C.: Reconfigurable manufacturing systems: literature review and research trend. J. Manuf. Syst. **49**, 93–106 (2018)
9. Bi, Z.M., et al.: Reconfigurable manufacturing systems: the state of the art. Int. J. Prod. Res. **46**(4), 967–992 (2008)
10. Setchi, R.M., Lagos, N.: Reconfigurability and reconfigurable manufacturing systems: state-of-the-art review. In: 2nd IEEE International Conference on Industrial Informatics, INDIN 2004. IEEE (2004)
11. Cerqueus, A., Delorme, X.: A bi-objective based measure for the scalability of reconfigurable manufacturing systems. In: Dolgui, A., Bernard, A., Lemoine, D., von Cieminski, G., Romero, D. (eds.) APMS 2021. IAICT, vol. 631, pp. 544–552. Springer, Cham (2021). https://doi.org/10.1007/978-3-030-85902-2_58
12. Andersen, A.-L., Nielsen, K., Brunoe, T.D.: Prerequisites and barriers for the development of reconfigurable manufacturing systems for high speed ramp-up. Procedia CIRP **51**, 7–12 (2016)
13. Johnson, M., et al.: Reconciling and reconceptualising servitization research: drawing on modularity, platforms, ecosystems, risk and governance to develop mid-range theory. Int. J. Oper. Prod. Manage. **41**, 465–493 (2021)
14. Lieberoth-Leden, C., et al.: Logistik 4.0. Handbuch Industrie **4**, 451–606 (2017)
15. Schuh, G., Kampker, A., Ziskoven, H.: Rechtsformen, Rechnungswesen und Controlling. In: Schuh, G., Kampker, A. (eds.) Strategie und Management produziernder Unternehmen, pp. 383–461. Springer, Heidelberg (2011). https://doi.org/10.1007/978-3-642-14502-5_6
16. Schuh, G., Kampker, A.: Strategie und Management produzierender Unternehmen: Handbuch Produktion und Management 1. Springer, Heidelberg (2010). https://doi.org/10.1007/978-3-642-14502-5

17. Kornas, T., et al.: A multivariate KPI-based method for quality assurance in lithium-ion-battery production. Procedia CIRP **81**, 75–80 (2019)
18. Samir, K., et al.: Key performance indicators in cyber-physical production systems. Procedia CIRP **72**, 498–502 (2018)
19. Pfaffel, S., Faulstich, S., Rohrig, K.: Considering uncertainties of key performance indicators in wind turbine operation. Appl. Sci. **10**(3), 898 (2020)
20. Delgado, L., et al.: A multi-layer model for long-term KPI alignment forecasts for the air transportation system. J. Air Transp. Manag. **89**, 101905 (2020)
21. Djödin, D., et al.: An agile co-creation process for digital servitization. J. Bus. Res. **112**, 478–491 (2020)
22. Schumacher, A., Sihn, W.: Development of a Monitoring system for implementation of industrial digitalization and automation using 143 key performance indicators. Procedia CIRP **93**, 1310–1315 (2020)
23. Wilkinson, A., et al.: Towards an operations strategy for product-centric servitization. Int. J. Oper. Prod. Manage. (2009)
24. Mickovski, S., Thomson, C.: Developing a framework for the sustainability assessment of eco-engineering measures. Ecol. Eng. **109**, 145–160 (2017)
25. Maurya, S.P., et al.: Identification of indicators for sustainable urban water development planning. Ecol. Ind. **108**, 105691 (2020)
26. Rademaekers, K., et al.: Selecting Indicators to Measure Energy Poverty. Final report. Trinomics, Rotterdam (2016)
27. Maheepala, S., Warnakulasooriya, B., Weerakoon Banda, Y.: Measuring servitization. In: Kohtamäki, M., Baines, T., Rabetino, R., Bigdeli, A. (eds.) Practices and Tools for Servitization, pp. 41–58. Springer, Cham (2018). https://doi.org/10.1007/978-3-319-765 17-4_3

Author Index